ORGANIZATIONAL BEHAVIOR:

A Reader

Edited by

H. Kirk Downey
Assistant Professor of Organizational Behavior
Oklahoma State University

Don Hellriegel
Professor of Organizational Behavior
Texas A&M University

John W. Slocum, Jr.
Professor of Organizational Behavior
The Pennsylvania State University

West Publishing Co.
St. Paul • New York • Boston
Los Angeles • San Francisco

The West Series In Management

Consulting Editors:

 Don Hellriegel
 and
 John W. Slocum, Jr.

Burack-Smith	Personnel Management: A Human Resource Systems Approach
Downey-Hellriegel-Slocum	Organizational Behavior: A Reader
Hellriegel-Slocum	Organizational Behavior: Contingency Views
Huse	Organization Development and Change
Mathis-Jackson	Personnel: Contemporary Perspectives and Application
Morris-Sashkin	Organization Behavior in Action: Skill Building Experiences
Newport	Supervisory Management: Tools and Techniques
Ritchie-Thompson	Organization and People: Readings, Cases and Exercises in Organizational Behavior
Whatley-Kelley	Personnel Management In Action: Skill Building Experiences

COPYRIGHT © 1977 By WEST PUBLISHING CO.

All rights reserved

Printed in the United States of America

Library of Congress Cataloging in Publication Data

Main entry under title:

Organizational behavior.

 Bibliography: p.
 1. Organizational behavior—Addresses, essays, lectures. I. Downey, H. Kirk. II. Hellriegel, Don. III. Slocum, John W.
HD58.7.07 301.18'32'08   77-1435
ISBN 0-8299-0137-x

PREFACE

As you opened this book, you may have been asking yourself "Why should I be concerned with learning about organizational behavior?" Our response is simple and straightforward. If you are interested in becoming a manager, the field of organizational behavior and this reader in particular should contribute to the development of the human skills and conceptual skills needed for your effective performance as a manager. *Human skills* refer to abilities needed to lead, motivate, manage conflict, build group effort—in other words, all of those skills needed to work with and through other people. To effectively apply your human skills, you must also be a good diagnostician. *Conceptual skills* emphasize improving your abilities for: (1) diagnosing the human problems in management; (2) recognizing your situation and how it relates to the organization as a whole as well as to the external environment; (3) understanding how your actions and actions in other parts of the organization are interdependent and how changes in one part can impact other parts; and (4) knowing how and when to use models or frameworks for managing organizational problems, especially those problems concerned with the people part of organization.

OBJECTIVES

The primary objective of this book of readings is to assist you in the development of the human and conceptual skills you will need to be an effective manager. To move you toward this primary objective, several sub-objectives were considered in the selection of readings. First, there was the selection of readings most likely to be important to the present and future human and conceptual skills needed by managers. This means there is very little focus on historical developments in the organizational behavior field. A second sub-objective was to favor readings that provide conceptual frameworks, reviews of our present state of knowledge, and the implications of all of this for managerial behavior and practice. Thus, we play down the inclusion of readings that primarily report on isolated and specific research studies. A third sub-objective was to select readings that portray the real-world complexity of behavior within organizations, but do so in a manner that can be grasped with a reasonable degree of study and concentration. This is because we assume you have previously had an introductory management course and/or have had prior organizational experience. The fourth sub-objective was to include readings that are representative of the major topical areas normally covered in an advanced undergraduate or introductory graduate level course in organizational behavior. As a result, there is a broad rather than narrow scope to the included readings. However, the readings included within each topical area were chosen partly because of their richness and depth of content. Finally, the fifth sub-objective was to include compatible with organiz.

could be used to illustrate the contingency view of organizational behavior which is discussed in the following section.

CONTINGENCY VIEW

The field of organizational behavior has developed rapidly over the past ten years. The first stage seemed to focus on a *pure* research and theoretical orientations designed to understand the "whats" and "whys" of behavior in organizations. The second stage, which built upon the first, sought universal "truths" and practices for the improvement of organizations. Through continuing research and theorizing, it became apparent that research findings and practices which seemed valid under one set of circumstances didn't hold up under other conditions. The third and present stage of organizational behavior, which builds upon the preceding two stages, emphasizes the *contingency view* for understanding the "whys" of behavior and the "hows" for increasing effectiveness.

The contingency view identifies various types of "if-then" relationships and may make different recommendations for managerial practices given different contingencies. For example, several of the readings in the leadership section will suggest there is no one best style of leadership and that leadership style should probably change under different contingencies. The contingency view of organizational behavior places considerable emphasis on developing your conceptual skills in terms of knowing how to diagnose and understand the types of situations you are likely to experience as a manager. We do not want to suggest that the contingency view offers detailed guidelines like the "four easy steps" to solve a specific problem under a particular set of contingencies. The spirit of the contingency view emphasizes diagnosis and general approaches that are likely to be more effective than others, given certain contingencies. For example, the amount of participation in decision-making by lower level members should generally be consistent with the tasks (routine versus nonroutine) being performed by these individuals, the external environment (stable versus changing) impacting on them, and the relative needs of these individuals (physiological and security needs versus esteem and self-actualization needs). This means that the contingency view seeks to understand the interrelationships within and among the various parts of an organization as well as its external environment. Each part can be considered separately (such as considering the personality characteristics of specific individuals) or as units interacting with other parts (such as the impact of a work group on the performance of one or more of its members).

In sum, the contingency view contends there is no one best way of managing for all situations. It also means that managers are *not* free to manage in random ways that might fit their personal biases. Given certain combinations of contingencies (such as a stable external environment and routine tasks), it is possible to specify general approaches and practices in organizational behavior that are likely to be more effective than others.

ORGANIZATION

This book is organized in five major parts which are each divided into sections. The major parts are identified in the Table of Contents as: Foundations, Individual Processes, Group Processes, Individual/Group/Organizational Interfaces, and Change Processes. The sections within each part provide additional focus to the range of topics that are central to organizational behavior. For example, Part IV, which considers Individual/Group/Organization Interfaces, is further organized into sections on motivation, leadership, and organization structure and climate. This approach permits a flexible use of the book by enabling you to cover the topical areas in a variety of sequences.

USES

The major market for this book is undergraduate and graduate courses in organizational behavior. When used at the undergraduate level, the students should have previously completed a basic course in management.

The book is designed for use in two basic modes. In one mode, it can be the core book in the organizational behavior course, possibly supplemented with other materials. In the second mode, this book can be a supplement to an organizational behavior textbook or experimental learning book. For those desiring to use this book as a supplement to an organizational behavior text, a cross-reference matrix is presented at the back of this book. This matrix keys the readings to appropriate chapters in organizational behavior texts.

A second major market for this book is professional managers and specialists in human resource management within organizations. For these individuals, the book might be a useful means of "refreshing" their conceptual and human skills in the organizational behavior area.

APPRECIATION

We owe our deep appreciation to the many publishers and authors who have granted us permission to use their articles and materials. A full acknowledgement to the contributors and publishers is provided at the beginning of each article or paper. We are ever grateful for the institutional support and professional secretarial assistance provided at each of our universities.

October, 1976

H. Kirk Downey
Don Hellriegel
John W. Slocum, Jr.

CONTENTS

PART ONE: FOUNDATIONS   1

"Adaptive Experiments: An Approach to Organizational Behavior Research" Edward E. Lawler, III 3

"Uncertainty: Measures, Research and Sources of Variation" H. Kirk Downey and John W. Slocum, Jr. 13

"Managerial Perceptions and Strategic Behavior" Carl R. Anderson and Frank T. Paine 26

PART TWO: INDIVIDUAL PROCESSES   37

Individuals in Organizations   37

"Reinforcement Theory and Contingency Management in Organizational Settings" W. Clay Hamner 39

"On the Folly of Rewarding A, While Hoping for B" Steven Kerr 55

"Personality vs. Organization" Chris Argyris 67

Problem Solving   79

"The Manager's Job: Folklore and Fact" Henry Mintzberg 80

"Stories Managers Tell: A New Tool for Organizational Problem Solving" Ian I. Mitroff and Ralph H. Kilmann 96

PART THREE: GROUP PROCESSES   105

"Group Dynamics and the Individual" Dorwin Cartwright and Ronald Lippitt 107

"Socially Relevant Science: Reflections on Some Studies of Interpersonal Conflict" Morton Deutsch 119

"The Effectiveness of Nominal, Delphi, and Interacting Group Decision Making Processes" Andrew H. Van De Ven and Andre L. Delbecq 141

"A Strategic Contingencies' Theory of Intraorganizational Power" D. J. Hickson, C. R. Hinings, C. A. Lee, R. E. Schneck and J. M. Pennings 156

vii

PART FOUR: INDIVIDUAL/GROUP/ORGANIZATIONAL INTERFACES — 171

Motivation — 171

"Hypothesis of Work Behavior Revisited and an Extension"
Abraham K. Korman 173

"The Satisfaction-Performance Controversy—Revisited"
Charles N. Greene and Robert E. Craft, Jr. 187

Leadership Processes — 201

"A Normative Model of Leadership Styles"
Victor H. Vroom and Philip W. Yetton 203

"Path-Goal Theory of Leadership" Robert House and
Terence Mitchell 224

"Participative Management: Quality vs. Quantity"
Raymond E. Miles and J. B. Ritchie 234

Organization Structure and Climate — 245

"Bureaucracy and Beyond" Fred E. Emery 246

"Organizational Climates: An Essay" Benjamim Schneider 255

PART FIVE: CHANGE PROCESSES — 267

Nature of Planned Change — 269

"Towards a Typology of Organizational Change Models"
Don Hellriegel and John W. Slocum, Jr. 270

"OD Reaches Adolescence: An Exploration of Its Underlying Values"
Frank Friedlander 279

Some Approaches to Planned Change — 289

"Management by Objectives: The Team Approach"
Wendell L. French and Robert W. Hollmann 291

"Survey-Guided Development Using Human Resources Measurement in
Organizational Change" David G. Bowers and Jerome L. Franklin . . . 303

"A New Strategy of Job Enrichment" J. Richard Hackman,
Greg Oldham, Robert Janson, and Kenneth Purdy 314

"A Structural Approach to Organizational Change" Robert A. Luke, Jr.,
Peter Block, Jack M. Davey, and Vernon R. Averch 333

ORGANIZATIONAL BEHAVIOR:
A Reader

†

PART ONE

FOUNDATIONS

In order to understand organizational behavior and gain insights from the articles presented in this book, it is necessary to be aware of and have a keen appreciation for the methods which guide research in this area. Additionally, before behavior within organizations can be understood we must be aware of the organization as a whole and the manner in which its environment influences the organization. In this first part, the selections have been chosen to provide the reader with such a background or foundation for studying organizational behavior. These foundations focus on: (1) the methods utilized in the study of organizational behavior; and (2) the manner in which the organization's environment provides the context for behavior in organizations.

The methods that are used to develop knowledge about organizational behavior stem from the so-called scientific method and thus are not totally unique to the field of organizational behavior. These methods should be viewed as both descriptive and prescriptive. They are prescriptive in that the community of scholars who are the most concerned with the development of organizational behavior knowledge are expected and expect others to conform to these methods. They are descriptive to the extent that most research in organizational behavior knowledge is in fact developed utilizing, albeit imperfectly, these methodologies.

In the first selection, Lawler, in "Adaptive Experiments: An Approach to Organizational Behavior Research," points out problems which occur when traditional experimental methods are used in organizational behavior. Lawler states that traditional designs for field experiments are difficult to use in organizations because the methodological requirements tend to run counter to the realities of life in organizations. Similarly, Lawler states that knowledge gained from laboratory experiments tends to be difficult to generalize for application to real organizational settings. Having pointed out these problems with traditional experimental forms for organizational behavior, Lawler suggests and describes an alternative experimental form which he labels "adaptive experiments."

While the primary emphasis in organizational behavior is on the behavior of individuals within organizational settings, the contexts or settings which surround organizations obviously can and do affect their internal operations. The study of the contextual settings of organizations involves classifying and understanding the impact of environments on organizations. Environments, as used here, is a concept which includes much more than simply the physical characteristics which are usually associated with the term environment in everyday language. An organization's environment includes attributes or characteristics of the social system which supports and surrounds the organization as well as physical characteristics.

In the second selection, Downey and Slocum, "Uncertainty: Measures, Research, and Sources of Variation," examine past uses of the concept of uncertainty to capture the essence of an environment's influence. After reviewing these past uses, the authors present a model for understanding the manner in which environments influence organizations. The model suggests an interpretative process in which an environment's impact is a function of both the environment's characteristics and the perceptual processes of the organizational members.

Anderson and Paine, in the third selection, "Managerial Perceptions and Strategic Behavior," assume a model of uncertainty similar to that presented by Downey and Slocum and proceed to build a model of the manner in which the environment influences the type of strategies that the organization is likely to adapt. In the Anderson and Paine model, the uncertainty perceived in the organization's environment interacts with the organization's perceived need for internal change to produce differences in the strategies that organizations utilize. Additionally, the authors provide examples from real organizations which provide insight into their model.

ADAPTIVE EXPERIMENTS: AN APPROACH TO ORGANIZATIONAL BEHAVIOR RESEARCH

Edward E. Lawler, III

The behavioral science and management literature suggests many ways in which organizations can be changed to increase their effectiveness and to provide a better quality of work life for employees. Job enrichment, autonomous work groups, the Scanlon Plan and participative management are but a few of the frequently suggested approaches. Unfortunately there is little systematic evidence to indicate the effectiveness of any of these approaches to organization design and management. The available research consists primarily of poorly documented case studies and a number of correlational studies which show the relationships between certain practices and a limited number of measures of organizational effectiveness (12). In the absence of evidence on their effectiveness, it is hard to make a convincing case for the adoptions of these practices. In addition, improvement and further development of these new approaches is retarded because feedback on the effectiveness is lacking. Thus, it is imperative that information about the effects of a wide variety of managerial practices and organization designs be developed. How can this be done? What kinds of research designs are appropriate?

EXPERIMENTS

Questions about the effects of organization designs and practices are questions of causality: we need to learn what causes what. The need for causal information has important implications for the kinds of research which need to be done. Since case studies and correlational studies do not provide convincing causal evidence, some other research design is needed. At first glance, carefully controlled experimental designs which follow the physical science model and that include control groups and random assignment seem called for since they can produce convincing causal evidence and can be utilized in field settings (2). Those field experiments which have been done enjoy wide visibility (4, 17) and provide graphic testimony of the value of field experiments. Despite the obvious advantages of doing field experiments in organizations, however, very few have been done.

Given the obvious value of field experiments it is worth considering why there have been so few. A number of explanations are frequently given: organizations are not willing to allow field experiments to be done, they are too expensive, organizational researchers are not willing to do the hard work which is necessary to perform them, and organizational researchers are not aware of these designs. Although all of these explanations have some validity, they fail to highlight the basic reason why so few experiments are done in organizations: the methodological requirements of traditional experiments fail to mesh with the realities of life in organizations.

Preparation of this paper was supported by a grant from the Ford Foundation and the Economic Development Administration of the Department of Commerce. Reprinted by permission of the publisher from *Academy of Management Review,* in press (1977).

Stated another way, the demands of all experimental designs are unrealistic in light of the realities of how organizations actually operate. All designs require, among other things, random assignment of subjects to conditions, a control group, a limited carefully defined experimental treatment, and control over variables which might confound the experiment. These are all conditions which are difficult, if not impossible, to obtain in ongoing organizations.

Random assignment is difficult to obtain because people and organizational units want to have a say in how they are treated and indeed some psychologists argue they should have a say (1). This is both an ethical issue of informed consent and a practical issue of what people are willing to accept simply because someone says it will be so. It is also not clear in many cases whether it is individual or organizational units that should be randomly assigned. In many cases, it probably should be organizational units that are randomly assigned since the changes affect whole units in a similar manner, but there often are too few of them. In addition, management for its own reasons frequently favors doing experiments in particular parts of the organization and as a result is not willing to accept random assignment.

Control groups are often difficult to set up in organizations because very few have units that are comparable in the relevant ways. Different parts of organizations and different organizations always seem to differ in important ways even though they exist in the same environment and have the same purpose. It is, of course, virtually impossible to impose comparability just for the purpose of having a control group and an experimental group which differ in only one respect. This represents an intrusion into an organization that is difficult to justify in terms of either an improved quality of work life or increased organizational effectiveness. Finally, even if a control group can be established, it is often difficult to maintain it as a control group. Often it is contaminated by what is going on in the experimental group because of the kind of intra-organization communication which exists. Campbell (2) has suggested several strategies for justifying the establishment and maintenance of a control group and they can work under some conditions in organizations but the basic point remains that the establishment and maintenance of a control group in an organization is a precarious undertaking.

It is often difficult to introduce a limited, carefully defined, experimental treatment. The introduction of any change into an on-going organizational setting is a very complex process—so complex that it is often difficult to define in advance just how and when the change will be introduced. To a substantial degree, the introduction process has to be modified as it evolves which means that it can be described only after it has occurred. Similarly, the actual change may have to be modified as the introduction process evolves in order to gain acceptance. Thus, the idea of a carefully predefined intervention with a defined introduction process is usually unrealistic in organizational change research.

The situation is further complicated by the fact that the environments organizations face are always changing and organizations must change in order to cope with them. Thus, unlike the laboratory where other factors can be controlled, it is difficult in a field setting to study the effects of a single change in isolation. In most situations, organizations simply cannot stop introducing change and in addition, the environment is often changing in ways that interfere with the experiment. Thus, the researcher is faced with a series of changes some of which he or she has planned and others which haven't been planned.

Given the difficulty of doing traditional experiments in organizations, it seems unlikely that enough of them can ever be done to fill the large need which exists for information on the effectiveness of different organizational designs and practices. One possible approach is to do laboratory experiments since the requirements of a traditional experiment can be met in the laboratory. There are, however, real questions of external validity that center on the difficulty of capturing the essence of a complex organization in a laboratory setting. Simply stated, organizations are very difficult to simulate. This is not to say that laboratory experiments shouldn't be done, rather it is to say that there are enough questions about their external validity that we cannot depend on them. Thus, we need to develop alternatives to traditional laboratory and field experiments.

ADAPTIVE EXPERIMENTS

One approach which seems to make sense is to do research which recognizes the realities of the field situation yet incorporates some of the key attributes of traditional experimental designs. By taking the right approach to evaluating the changes which take place in organizations, researchers can often do just this. These changes may be naturally occurring or ones that are introduced as part of the experiment. The crucial research issues do not involve the source of the change, they involve which measures are taken and how they are analyzed. If a broad measurement net is used and a control or comparison group or groups can be established, a great deal can be learned.

Perhaps the best term to use in describing the type of experiments being suggested here is adaptive: they are adaptive in the sense that the final form is likely to be known only after the change has been completed and all the data have been collected. Adaptive experiments are not substitutes for traditional experiments as far as assessing causality is concerned. However, they are a definite improvement over static one time correlational studies. They typically allow us to rule out certain spurious causes for the existence of a relationship that cannot be ruled out with a correlational study. Adaptive experiments would seem to fit what Campbell and Stanley (3) call the nonequivalent control group design which they classify as quasi experimental. This involves before and after measures, a control group and non-random assignment of subjects.

Campbell and Stanley (3) make the point that this is a preferred design in many ways and one that in many field situations is superior to the pure experimental designs because of greater external validity. It does a good job of controlling for the effects of history, maturation, testing, instrumentation regression (one of the groups picked because it is extreme) and mortality. All of these can be dismissed as causes of any changes in the experimental group because of the existence of the comparison or control group. This is an important point because organizational researchers often are apologetic for their inability to do traditional experiments. They needn't be, adaptive experiments can do many of the same things and they fit better with the realities of organizational life.

Because they lack random assignment, adaptive experiments cannot do everything a true experiment can. It is difficult to rule out the possibility that the change had the effects it did because of some characteristic of the particular population or situation where it was put into place. This problem can be dealt with to some extent if it can be demonstrated that the experimental and control groups are comparable on such things as age, education, production, etc., even though they were not randomly selected. It is also difficult to rule out the possibility that a third variable caused the change. However, if a good job is done of monitoring changes in possible third variables (e.g., changes in pay during a job design experiment) it is sometimes possible to rule out many potential third variables and thus increase the possibility that the intervention is responsible for the change. In effect, all third variables that change in ways that don't fit the change in the dependent variable can be ruled out as can all those that don't change at all (20).

The key to any adaptive experiment lies in the skillful application of the measurement package. An ideal measurement package should have five characteristics: it should be longitudinal, usually covering several years; it should cover all parts of the organization where the change will be implemented as well as some other roughly comparable areas where it is expected the change will not be introduced; it should involve a broad range of economic and behavioral measures; it should be performed by an individual who is not actively involved in the change process; and finally, it should incorporate measures which will specify the nature of the change as it evolves and suggest hypotheses about the effects of the change. Because of the crucial importance of measurement, the remainder of this paper will consider each of these five elements which need to be built into measurement packages for adaptive experiments.

LONGITUDINAL

Little of the research in the field of organizational behavior has been longitudinal in nature. The longitudinal research which has been done suggests that a number of the outcomes from organizational change efforts appear considerably after the introduction of the change as Likert (15) has pointed out. Apparently, changes directed toward improving the quality of work life first impact on organizational process, employee satisfaction, and motivation. These in turn affect such things as absenteeism, turnover, quality of decision making, employee skill levels, and product quality. These factors in turn influence costs, but often the influence is not immediate or direct and thus, the impact on costs and therefore profit is delayed. For example, changes in job design seem almost immediately to affect job satisfaction and absenteeism. However, their impact on turnover often doesn't appear for six or more months, and their impact on operating costs may not appear for a year or even longer. This delay occurs since savings from absenteeism come from being able to reduce the number of extra employees who are hired to fill in for absentees and this cannot be done until it is clear that absenteeism has been reduced permanently. The situation is further complicated because the time lag between the actual change and changes in the measures of organizational effectiveness may not be the same for all measures.

CONTROL OR COMPARISON GROUPS

It is always desirable to compare changes in the experimental situation with those in a similar situation where no such change has been attempted, so as to determine what improvements or problems in the experimental situation may have been due to factors other than the change effort. However, this is often difficult to do because similar situations are not available. Like random assignment, it is highly desirable but often difficult to obtain in field settings. Still it can often be approximated if data are collected on a variety of sites, some of which are not expected to be changed. If this turns out to be true, then they can be treated as comparison sites. Where no obvious comparable sites exist, all that can be done is to collect data everywhere that the change is expected to impact and wait to see if it does impact everywhere. If it doesn't impact everywhere, then a *post hoc* comparison group can be established. If it does impact everywhere, then an effort should be made to find an area where no change has occurred or a group that has been less affected by the change. Lawler, Hackman, and Kaufman (13) successfully used one approach to establishing a *post hoc* control group. In their job redesign study, the employees changed their jobs only half time so the researchers compared the subjects' attitudes during the two different time periods

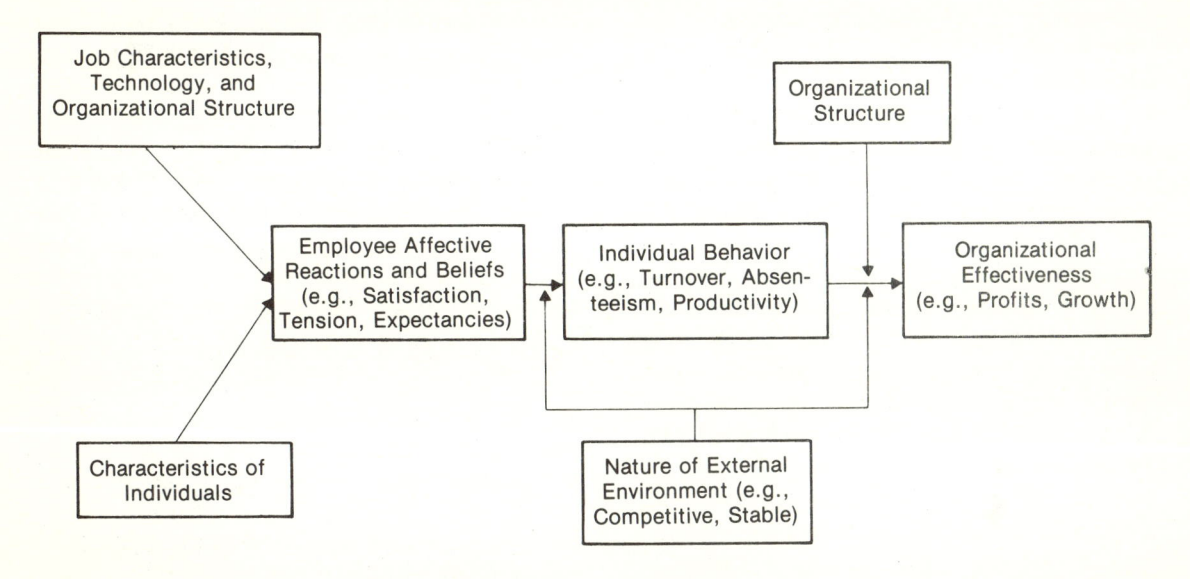

Figure 1. Model of Determinants of Organizational Effectiveness

so that the subjects served as their own control. If it turns out no *post hoc* control group can be established, the study must be interpreted as an interrupted time series design. As Campbell and Stanley point out, even though this design is inferior to the noncomparable control group design, it can yield useful data.

TYPES OF MEASURES

The comparisons which adaptive experiments require can only be done if comprehensive standardized measures are used in all situations. Without standardization, valid comparisons cannot be made among groups. Without comprehensive measures, the crucial change areas may be missed. Figure 1 shows one view of the causes of organizational effectiveness and quality of work life and illustrates some areas that need to be measured. It shows that the characteristics of individuals combine with the characteristics of the work environment to produce attitudes and beliefs. Job, technology, and organizational structure are the crucial aspects of the environment. In turn, organizational effectiveness is a function of the combined behavior of the individuals as modified by the kind of organization structure and control system that is used to coordinate their behaviors. Figure 1 also shows that the external environment is an important influence on both the kind of behavior which results from attitudes and the effectiveness of organizations. This model argues that six different kinds of variables need to be measured. A lot is known about how to measure some of these variables, but in other areas little is known. A brief review of the state of measurement in each of these areas will illustrate this point and introduce the reader to the kind of measures which are available in each area.

1. *Characteristics of Individuals.* Relatively speaking, a great deal is known about measuring the characteristics of individuals, particularly with respect to the measurement of what individuals can do. A number of standardized tests have been developed, and they have been shown to predict behavior. Not as much is known about how to measure aspects of individuals' willingness to perform a job once they take it (7). Such things as

motivation and personality have proven to be difficult things to measure, but useful measures of need strength do exist (9). The Human Resource Accounting approach represents one attempt to quantify the characteristics of individuals: this is a promising approach, but at this point it is not of proven utility (6, 19). At this time, the most sensible thing to do is to measure those things which have been shown by previous research to affect the reactions of employees to different management practices and organization designs. Essentially this means measuring the demographic characteristics of individuals, some personality characteristics (e.g., self-esteem), and the strength of employees' desires for such things as pay, autonomy, and interesting work.

2. *Job, Technology, and Organization Structure*. Some work has been done on measuring the characteristics of the work situation with which an individual is presented. An adequate assessment of the work situations needs to include an examination of the nature of the technology, the design of jobs, and the structure of the organization. An adequate measure of technology needs to look at issues of work flow, adequacy of standards, type of technology, degree of technological development and appropriateness of technology. So far little work has been done in the field of organizational behavior on how to measure technology so the researcher who wishes to measure it must do a considerable amount of developmental work.

Significant advance has been made in looking at the characteristics of jobs from the point of view of their potential impact on the person (9, 10, 11). A great deal of effort in the field of sociology has gone into measuring the structural characteristics of organizations. Reasonably good measures presently exist for such things as degree of bureaucracy and how the organization is shaped (18). It is particularly important that good measures of job and organization structure as well as technology be used in adaptive experiments, because they are often the major things that are altered as part of planned change programs. Unless they are measured accurately, it is difficult to identify exactly how the functioning of the organization has changed as a result of a change effort.

3. *Attitudes and Beliefs*. Thousands of questionnaire and interview forms have been used to try to measure employee attitudes and beliefs. A virtual infinity of questionnaire items are available for use in assessing attitudinal change. However, none of the widely used questionnaires is comprehensive in the sense that it measures all attitudes and beliefs likely to be affected by membership in an organization. Attitudes concerned with individual, group, intergroup, and organization level factors need to be treated. We need to know how individuals feel about things such as their pay and jobs as well as how they feel about their work group and how the organization as a whole functions and deals with them. Measures which look at all of these and which can be used in a number of sites are needed.

4. *Individual Behavior*. Performance is difficult to measure at the individual level because frequently objective indicators are not present. This is an area where it is particularly difficult (if not impossible) to develop standardized measures that can be used in all sites. On the other hand, standardized measures of accidents, absenteeism, turnover, and tardiness can be developed and need to be. It is surprising to go through the research literature and find out that there is little agreement on what these terms mean. There is no commonly accepted operational definition of when a person is absent, turnover, or tardy. In the literature, one person's tardiness is another's absenteeism. As a recent paper points out, it is possible to move toward

greater agreement, and indeed such an approach is needed (16).

Also missing are well developed methods to evaluate the costs of individual behavior. Some interesting work has been done in this field recently and the results are encouraging (16). It appears to be possible through cost accounting techniques to measure the costs of such counter-productive behaviors as absenteeism, turnover, and tardiness in dollar terms. Further developments here are important if we are to assess the impact of different job designs and management styles, since these are factors that they impact upon directly.

5. *Organizational Effectiveness*. Organizational performance is normally measured quite well with respect to financial indicators. Such data provide a readily available but incomplete criterion against which to assess organizational performance. They are incomplete in the sense that they fail to measure the total effect of organizations on the communities in which they operate, and they fail to measure the impact of the organization on the people who work there. Some have suggested that organizations do social accounting (5) in order to measure the full impact that they have. The development of a generally applied social accounting system would help in efforts to evaluate different organizational designs and management practices. Unfortunately, at this time, it is not developed well enough so that it can be used. Thus, research must focus on the traditional measures of organizational effectiveness and on a broad array of measures which tap the impact of the organization on the individual (e.g., satisfaction, turnover, accidents).

6. *External Environment*. A number of aspects of the external environment need to be measured. There is a considerable amount of evidence which shows that the nature of the external environment influences how effective different organization structures are

and how individuals will react to new organization designs. For example, the labor market has a strong influence on how employees react to feelings of job dissatisfaction and it needs to be measured. When jobs are plentiful, employees are much more likely to quit than when they aren't. The cultural environment has been shown to influence employee reaction to participative decision making practices and enriched jobs. Other studies have shown that market factors such as stability and competitiveness influence how effective different organization structures are (14). Finally, the existence of a union and collective bargaining influence what changes can be initiated and how successful they will be. This means that in measuring organizations, it is important to measure the character of the union-management relationship. It is also quite possible the certain kinds of changes in management practices and organization design will affect the nature of the union and the union-management relationship. Thus, it is important that they be viewed as factors which may be altered just like profits, individual behavior, and individuals' attitudes.

In summary, the nature of the external business environment, the cultural environment, the union-management relationship, and the external labor market all need to be measured. In some areas, there are readily available measures (e.g., labor market), but in others such as the nature of the union and the union-management relationship, work needs to be done to develop appropriate measures.

Overview: Types of Measures

No discipline or set of disciplines has all the measures that are needed to assess organizational change. The measures suggested by Figure 1 draw upon engineering, accounting, economics, sociology, and psychology. This means that the measures of organizations which are used by adaptive experiments need to be done by interdisciplinary teams or at least to draw upon the products of such teams. It also means that a rather extensive measurement program is needed. It is not practical in most studies to collect all the measures suggested by Figure 1; the cost is simply too great. Nevertheless, it represents an ideal to be aspired to and a list that can be used to test the breadth of measurement in future studies.

Even planned change efforts often involve multiple changes and almost all changes affect multiple outcomes. In the end only part of the data which has been collected may need to be analyzed. In some ways, this is inefficient since it involves collecting more data than is "needed." The problem, of course, is that at the beginning of the study is is often impossible to specify what data are needed. Thus, the only safe approach is to collect sufficient data such that the design of the study can be adapted to the intervention as it actually unfolds. To do less is to risk missing the effect of the intervention. As the study progresses, certain measures may be dropped but at the beginning a broad data collection approach is in fact not inefficient; quite to the contrary, it is the only efficient thing to do. This point highlights an important difference between lab experiments where a careful, limited and defined change can be introduced and the results captured by a few measures and a field situation where this is almost impossible.

THIRD PARTY RESEARCH ROLE

The study of an organization change by a group which is not an active part of the change program offers a number of advantages over a study done by the person(s) doing the change. There is always a credibility problem when the person doing the change reports on the effectiveness of the change effort. Particularly in the case of a large success, people are suspicious of reports of an organization change effort, and there are data which suggest that this suspicion has a basis in reality. A recent review of evaluation research projects not concerned with organizational problems found that significantly more successes are reported when affiliated researchers (the change agent or a colleague at the same institution) do evaluations than when they are done by a third party who had a vested interest in doing the research well and not in the success of the change effort (8). On the other hand, a problem with third party evaluators is that they may be too motivated to find fault.

When a person is engaged in both change and measurement, there is often a conflict between what is good for research and what is good for the change. This can take the form of competing demands for time and energy, or it can take the form of problems about whether particular measures should be collected. Thus, it would seem that having a separate assessor should improve the quality of evaluation research, because it reduces these role conflicts. Gordon and Morse (8) in their review of evaluation research present data which support this point. They found that evaluations done by third parties are typically better methodologically than those done by affiliated researchers.

The research on new organization practices and designs is often criticized because failures are never reported. The reason for this is obvious. The change agent has little reason to report a failure even though others might learn from it. Having a third party involved might help to stimulate the reporting of more failures. Presumably, the assessor would be interested in reporting failures because professional credit would come to him or her as long as the assessment was done well. Finally, having a third party involved means that a different, perhaps more objective, description of what has gone on will be present. Organization change efforts are often correctly criticized because they are not described in a way that allows an outsider to understand and replicate what has gone on. One reason for this is that the effort is usually reported by the person doing the change. As an involved party to the change, he or she often is in a poor position to assess what a naive outsider needs to know about the effort and to describe it. Further, as a result of the change agent's involvement, he or she often sees the situation in a quite different light than does the outsider. It is possible to argue about who has the more accurate view of the actual change program—the outsider or the person doing the change—but it seems hard to argue that it would be very informative to have *both* their views.

MEASUREMENT OF THE CHANGE

One of the realities of organizational change is that most interventions or changes tend to change as they are implemented. In essence, although they start out to be one thing, they often end up being another when they are actually put into place. This means that any adaptive experiment must concentrate on measuring the intervention as it evolves. To some extent this can be captured by questionnaires and more traditional methodologies but there is a risk that these will miss the essence of the intervention. For one thing they are poor at recording the day-to-day events which surround the implementation of the change and they often are not broad enough to capture all aspects of the change. This suggests that it is important to utilize the change agent (if one exists) and to build into the experimental design someone who will act as an observer of the change. Both the change agent and the observer should be charged with writing a history of the change. They should not, however, be limited to simply recording the events around the change. They both should be an important source of insight about what the impact of the change actually is. They can be invaluable in suggesting how the data should be analyzed in order to best capture the effects of the change and they can suggest changes as the measurement program develops. The observer and the change agent probably will have somewhat different views of what has gone on and as to what changes have occurred. Thus, they are more likely to be complementary data sources rather than overlapping ones. The role of the observer would seem to be particularly important since change agents are notorious for not adequately describing their efforts (21).

In traditional experiments, describing the change usually isn't a problem but in the kind of experiments we are discussing here it can be. For one thing, they involve the collection of a tremendous amount of data; this is necessary because it usually is not clear where a change will occur, but help is needed in terms of hypothesis generating when the data are analyzed. In addition, they involve changes which often cannot be specified until after the change has occurred. Thus, the expected impact can only be specified after the experiment is over. It is crucial that this be done, however, even if it is done post hoc, otherwise the experiment will end up as a massive data processing exercise. Finally, many of the changes which may occur probably will be unexpected and thus will go undetected if a sensitive observer is not present to record them and to suggest how they may impact on other measures.

SUMMARY AND CONCLUSIONS

A strong case can be made for the vital importance of assessing the relative effectiveness of different management practices and organization designs by studying what happens when they are introduced into organizations. Failure to do this dooms us to repeating the use of ineffective methods and to the slow development of better approaches to organizational design and theory. Unfortunately, this kind of research does not allow the frequent use of traditional experimental designs. Still research can be done which allows for assessing causality if adaptive research designs are used. Doing adaptive research requires a comprehensive set of standardized measures, a number of sites so that meaningful comparisons can be made, a long time period, a third party, and a careful assessment of the nature of the change. Research that meets these requirements is feasible and can come to conclusions about causation, but it takes a large investment of time and effort. This investment seems small, however, in comparison to the importance of the questions which are being addressed.

REFERENCES

1. Argyris, C., *Intervention Theory and Method* (Reading, Mass.: Addison-Wesley, 1971).

2. Campbell, D. T., "Reforms as Experiments," *American Psychologist,* Vol. 24 (1969), 409-429.

3. Campbell, D. T. and J. C. Stanley, *Experimental and Quasi-Experimental Designs for Research* (Chicago: Rand McNally, 1966).

4. Coch, L. and J. P. R. French, "Overcoming Resistance to Change," *Human Relations,* Vol. 1 (1948), 512-532.

5. Dierkes, M. and R. A. Bauer, (Eds.), *Corporate Social Accounting* (New York: Praeger, 1973).

6. Flamholtz, E., *Human Resource Accounting* (Encino, Calif.: Dickenson, 1974).

7. Ghiselli, E. E., *The Validity of Occupational Aptitude Tests* (New York: John Wiley & Sons, Inc., 1966).

8. Gordon, G. and E. U. Morse, "Evaluation Research: A Critical Review," Chapter in *The Annual Review of Sociology,* Vol. 1 (1975), 339-361.

9. Hackman, J. R. and E. E. Lawler, "Employee Reactions to Job Characteristics." *Journal of Applied Psychology,* Vol. 60 (1971), 259-286.

10. Hackman, J. R. and G. R. Oldham, "Development of the Job Diagnostic Survey," *Journal of Applied Psychology,* Vol. 60 (1975), 159-170.

11. Jenkins, G. D., D. A. Nadler, E. E. Lawler, and C. Cammann, "Standardized Observations: An Approach to Measuring the Nature of Jobs," *Journal of Applied Psychology,* Vol. 60 (1975), 171-180.

12. Katzell, R. A. and D. Yankelovich, *Work, Productivity, and Job Satisfaction* (New York: Psychological Corporation, 1975).

13. Lawler, E. E., J. R. Hackman, and S. Kaufman, "Effects of Job Redesign: A Field Experiment," *Journal of Applied Social Psychology,* Vol. 3 (1973), 49-62.

14. Lawrence, P. R. and J. W. Lorsch, *Organization and Environment* (Boston: Division of Research, Graduate School of Business Administration, Harvard University, 1967).

15. Likert, R., *New Patterns of Management* (New York: McGraw-Hill, 1961).

16. Macy, B. A., and P. H. Mirvis, "A Methodology for Assessment of Quality of Work Life and Organizational Effectiveness in Behavioral-Economic Terms," *Administrative Science Quarterly,* Vol. 21 (1976), 212-226.

17. Morse, N. and E. Reimer, "The Experimental Change of a Major Organizational Variable," *Journal of Abnormal and Social Psychology,* Vol. 52 (1956), 120-129.

18. Price, J. L., *Handbook of Organizational Measurement* (Lexington, Mass.: Heath, 1972).

19. Rhode, J. G. and E. E. Lawler, "Human Resource Accounting: Accounting Systems of the Future?" Chapter in M. Dunnette (Ed.), *Work and Nonwork in the Year 2001* (Belmont, Calif.: Wadsworth, 1973).

20. Vroom V. H. "A Comparison of Static and Dynamic Correlation Methods in the Study of Organizations" *Organizational Behavior and Human Performance,* Vol. 1 (1966), 55-70.

21. Weiss, C. H. *Evaluating Action Programs* (Boston, Mass.: Allyn and Bacon, 1972).

UNCERTAINTY: MEASURES, RESEARCH, AND SOURCES OF VARIATION

H. Kirk Downey
John W. Slocum

Contingency approaches, in a relatively short span of time, have had such a strong impact on organization theory that they have come to be considered "in vogue" (32). Pioneering contingency work (3, 19, 31, 34) provides the basic foundation on which much of present organizational research is built. Current research aimed at an examination of the roots of contingency approaches has focused increasingly upon the conceptual and methodological adequacy of its central concept—uncertainty. Given the central role of uncertainty in modern organization theory, it is imperative that organizational research become more introspective regarding this concept.

Uncertainty is a term which is used daily in a variety of ways. This everyday acquaintance with uncertainty can be seductive in that it is all too easy to *assume* that one knows what he is talking about. This problem is not new to organization research. Uncertainty is in danger of becoming in the 1970's the "communication" or "motivation" of the early 1960's. Accordingly, the objectives of this paper are to: (a) briefly review past research on uncertainty; (b) outline a suggested formulation of uncertainty useful in contingency centered research and in the examination of conceptualizations and instrumentations of uncertainty; and (c) suggest sources of uncertainty variation which are implied by the formulation outlined here.

PREVIOUS RESEARCH

Previous research relating to uncertainty concepts as applied to organizational research can be grouped into two basic categories: (a) studies utilizing uncertainty as an independent variable in the analysis of contingency theory propositions, and (b) studies directly concerning dimensions and/or instrumentations of uncertainty.

Analysis of Contingency Theory Propositions

Burns and Stalker (3) were among the first to explicitly and systematically utilize the concept of uncertainty in the interpretation of contingency theory propositions. They operationalized the concept of uncertainty by describing the environments of 20 British firms. The descriptions were gleaned from unstructured interviews, observations, and anecdotal impressions of both the researchers and firm members. No attempts were made to systematically isolate dimensions utilized in describing or measuring uncertainty. This technique was adequate given the exploratory nature of Burns and Stalker's propositions. The study, however, did not produce a systematic means for viewing environments useful to future studies.

Lawrence and Lorsch (19, 20) extended the earlier work of Burns and Stalker in an examination of 10 U.S. industrial firms.

Portions of this paper were presented at the 34th Annual Meeting, Academy of Management, 1974. This research was supported by grants from the Center for Research, College of Business administration, The Pennsylvania State University. Reprinted by permission of the publisher from *Academy of Management Journal,* Vol. 18 (1975), pp. 562-578.

Using level of information to tap environmental characteristics without resorting to descriptive lists of environmental elements, they state that uncertainty concerning subenvironments (sales, production, and research and development) is composed of three elements: (a) lack of clarity of information, (b) general uncertainty of causal relationships, and (c) time span of feedback about results.

A single questionnaire item was used to measure top managements' perceptions of these uncertainty elements for each of the three subenvironments. Summative operations were performed on the items to produce three subenvironment uncertainty scores and one total firm uncertainty score. Firms studied in the Lawrence and Lorsch research were selected in order to maximize the researchers' expectations of environmental differences between industries. The researchers accept their operationalizations of uncertainty based upon the face validity of the concept and the instrument. The results of the measures tended to agree with the researchers' prior expectations, which were based upon interviews and clinical knowledge. These observations by themselves, however, do not establish the validity of these measures. Thus, the general reliability and validity of the instrument remain open to examination.

Lorsch and Allen (23) extended the earlier research of Lawrence and Lorsch in a study of four divisions and the corporate headquarters of six multidivisional firms. As in the Lawrence and Lorsch study, firms and divisions studied were selected to accentuate differences in environments and performance. The uncertainty measure employed was the same as that used in the earlier study of Lawrence and Lorsch. Lorsch and Allen's analysis was designed to test contingency positions, and not to build scales for use in other projects. Lorsch and Allen, however, did report the statistically significant differences in perceived uncertainty which were found among the four divisions of each of the four conglomerate firms. The conglomerates were selected because of the diversity of product-market environments which could be expected within the total firm. Additionally, the four divisions within each firm were selected to represent the product-market environment diversity in each firm. Given these sample selection procedures, it is reasonable to expect that the market subenvironments for the divisions within each conglomerate firm would show significant differences in the three uncertainty elements. Although one firm's four divisions were reported as statistically different ($p < .05$) on all three uncertainty dimensions in the market subenvironment, the other three firms' divisions were reported as statistically different, respectively, on only two, one, and zero of the three market dimensions.

Analysis of Environmental Uncertainty Concepts

Tosi et al. (32) undertook a direct analysis of Lawrence and Lorsch's (19) operationalization of uncertainty in an effort to replicate their work. Their analysis involved 122 managers (top and middle levels) in 22 firms representing 12 industries. Lawrence and Lorsch's questionnaire was used to measure perceived uncertainty. Early in the replication attempt, it became apparent that internal scale reliability results were less than those desired. Consequently, Tosi et al. attempted to examine Lawrence and Lorsch's uncertainty measure by correlating questionnaire scales and subscales with criterion measures of uncertainty, and by employing factor analysis to determine major groupings.

Tosi et al. constructed three volatility indices for each firm and industry as criterion measures of uncertainty. These volatility indices were correlated with the subenvironment and total uncertainty scores obtained from Lawrence and Lorsch's instrument. The results of the correlations were "low and inconsistent, ranging from -0.294 to 0.036" (32, p. 24). Those correlations which were statistically significant were in a negative direction.

Tose et al. performed a factor analysis on the results of the Lawrence and Lorsch questionnaire. Their expectations were that three factors would be extracted and these would fit Lawrence and Lorsch's subenvironment conceptualizations. Four factors were extracted (eigenvalues and communalities were not reported), however, which according to Tosi et al. "are not interpretable in a manner similar to that proposed by Lawrence and Lorsch (32, p. 24). Explicit questions raised by Tosi et al. concerning Lawrence and Lorsch's measure of uncertainty include: (a) If the logic of the contingency approach is accepted (the degree of perceived uncertainty is a function of environmental characteristics), should not there be at least some correlation between volatility measures of the environment and perceived uncertainty? and (b) Is the intuitively appealing logic of the contingency approach of Lawrence and Lorsch a result of inferences whose accuracy "are due to clinical, intuitive assessment skills as opposed to measurement with a simple nine-item questionnaire" (32, p. 24)?

While the importance of the above questions to contingency approaches cannot be dismissed easily, Tosi et al.'s analysis falls short of providing answers. Several problems with their analysis obscure potential interpretation. First, the use of coefficients of variation to measure volatility seems questionable unless time related effects (autocorrelation, etc.) are removed from the original data, a problem noted by Lawrence and Lorsch (21). No indication was given that this was done. Second, Tosi et al. failed to report central tendencies and dispersions for the variables correlated, and did not report the techniques used in their correlational analysis. Because of the failure to report these data, at least two additional interpretations of the low and inconsistent correlations cannot be ruled out: (a) the correlations are based upon restricted ranges of the correlated variables and thus must be considered spurious; and (b) the relationships between the correlated variables are nonlinear and thus were not tapped by Pearson's correlation techniques. Third, the subjects involved in the Tosi et al. research included "middle" level managers in an unreported and potentially highproportion, a problem noted also by Lawrence and Lorsch (21). These subjects may not be an adequate source of information regarding uncertainties faced by the total firm. Fourth, the volatility indices used by Tosi et al. implicitly assume uncertainty to be an environmental trait that can be "objectively" measured. If uncertainty were defined as a perceptual quality, as will be suggested in this paper, the volatility of an organization's activities would not adequately provide a criterion measure of uncertainty. High coefficients of variation do not necessarily indicate that the firm cannot predict its future performance. For example, long run trends, regardless of changes inherent within them, may be highly predictable. Also, cycles, regardless of their deviation heights, may be highly predictable and well known. It is the deviation from the expected which is important in regard to uncertainty, and not the size of the trend or cycle itself.

Duncan (8) sought to facilitate contingency research through clarifying uncertainty concepts by relating two dimensions of organization environments, complexity and dynamism, to a manager's perception of uncertainty. Duncan's measure of perceived uncertainty was developed from a semantic analysis of individuals' verbalizations of the concept of uncertainty. The validity of this instrument is based primarily on the ability of individuals to verbalize their views concerning the relevant dimensions of uncertainty.

The three dimensions included in Duncan's measure of uncertainty include: (a) lack of information regarding the environmental factors associated with a given decision making situation, (b) lack of knowledge about the outcome of a specific decision in terms of how much the organization would lose if the decision were incorrect, and (c) the ability or inability to assign probabilities as to the effect of a given factor on the success or failure of a decision unit in performing its function (8, p. 24). Both uncertainty and environmental dimensions were defined in terms of organizational members' perceptions. Relating perceived environmental dimensions to perceived uncertainty, Duncan reported that decision units in simple-static environments experienced the least amount of perceived uncertainty. The highest degree of perceived uncertainty was reported in decision units in dynamic-complex environments. Additionally, the dynamic dimension appeared to be more important than the complexity dimension in terms of understanding perceived uncertainty.

Duncan also emphasized that environmental characteristics should not be considered as constant features in an organization. Duncan suggests that environmental characteristics are:

> dependent on the perceptions of organizational members and thus can vary in their incidence to the extent that individuals differ in their perceptions (8, p. 24).

Because of this view of the importance of individual perception in defining environmental characteristics, Duncan states that future research should begin to identify individual differences affecting perceptions of environmental characteristics.

Integrating the Research

The bulk of the research reviewed here regarding the concept of uncertainty primarily has concerned the empirical testing of contingency theory propositions. In application of uncertainty concepts, agreement with researcher expectations and face validity of instruments are the primary means for analysis of the concept.

Duncan (8) and Tosi et al. (32) represent two of the relatively few direct attempts which have been made to analyze the key contingency theory concept of uncertainty. Tosi et al. have raised serious questions regarding the methodological soundness of Lawrence and Lorsch's measure of uncertainty and at a more general level have raised, but failed to provide insight into, the question of objectively defined criterion measures of uncertainty. Duncan has raised the question and demonstrated the importance of individual characteristics in perceptions of uncertainty and environmental properties.

While differing subjects (Organization levels, etc.), different instruments, and a lack of total data reporting make integrative interpretation of past research difficult, ambiguity about the nature of uncertainty itself tends to obscure examination of this central concept. Is uncertainty perceived or objective?

This ambiguity would be reduced if uncertainty were restricted to a perceptual concept. Lawrence and Lorsch's and Duncan's operationalizations of uncertainty clearly are perceptual. Further, Duncan's review of past uses of uncertainty explicitly rejected information and decision theory uses of uncertainty because of their lack of consideration for the human actor.

Dill (6) originally suggested that information, and thus uncertainty, be used to specify the environment's effects on an organization. He did not suggest that information be used to specify the environment itself. Koffka (17) suggests that behavior best can be understood by reference to the behavioral environment (the environment as perceived and reacted to by individuals) rather than by reference to the physical environment (the objective physical environment). This view presents the environment as a set of stimuli which lack meaning or information value until perceived by an individual. Perception refers to the process by which individuals organize and evaluate stimuli (27). Thus uncertainty, as a counterpart to information, should be considered as perceptually based.

Restriction of uncertainty to a perceptual concept does contain the inherent problem that variations in uncertainty are related to characteristics of the individual. It does now, however, preclude the expectation that uncertainty also is related to environmental attributes. Specific attributes of physical environments tend to elicit similar perceptions of uncertainty by individuals. These similar perceptions of uncertainty by individuals, however, stem from similarities in individual perceptual processes rather than from the existence of uncertainty as an attribute of the physical environment. For example, Woodward (34), Harvey (12), Zwerman (36), and Litschert (22) used technological factors; Keller et al. (18) used number of product changes; and Blandin et al. (1) used R & D expenditures per net sales dollar as indices of uncertainty. The use of these measures to predict responses to uncertainty, however, is dependent on an assumed similarity of individual reactions to these stimuli.

This perceptual view of uncertainty raises the issue of how total organizations relate to uncertainty. Zaltman et al. (35), while discussing innovation, suggests that all those factors which influence individual perceptions directly or indirectly influence the organization's perceptions. The present authors would tentatively take this one step further and suggest that an organization's perceptions (as some type of summative concept) are subject to these same individual influences because the organization's perceptions are a result of the perceptions of individual organization members. Also, the perceptions of individual organization members in part result from organization perceptions. For example, the founders of organizations tend to define the domains of organizations based on their perceptions of environmental attributes. Once these domain decisions are made, the organization tasks implied by these domains define a set of relevant environmental attributes which can be expected to elicit a set of uncertainties by the organization as a whole. This treatment of uncertainty is similar to that Galbraith (11) called task uncertainty. The perception of uncertainty by individuals charged with organization design decisions is elicited by the environmental attributes in the task environment which have been created by the organization. While it is not suggested that domain decisions are never altered, it does appear that they tend to take on a functional autonomy of their own. The manner in which domain decisions are altered is not well understood. It is beyond the scope of this analysis and will be ignored for the purpose of this paper. Based on their responses to the task environment's elicitation of uncertainty, according to Galbraith (11), organizational designers use combinations of slack resources, the creation of self-contained tasks, investments in vertical information systems, and the creation of lateral relations to create environments in which individual organization members are expected to operate. In turn, these enacted environments can be expected to elicit perceptions of uncertainty by individual organization members. Thus, uncertainty is based upon the attributes of the environments that have been created for those individuals by the organization and the characteristics of those individuals' conceptual processes.

This view of individual members' perceptions of uncertainty does not imply that the uncertainty of the organization is an arithmetic summation of the individuals' perceptions of uncertainty. Individual perceptions of uncertainty can be expected to affect their task performance. To the extent that task performance meets the expectation inherent in the domain and organizational design decisions, the organization's individual members' perceptions of uncertainty are considered as functional. If these perceptions of uncertainty negatively affect task performance, they are considered as dysfunctional.

A perceptual view of uncertainty and its relationship to created environments, as well as to total organization environments, is capable of explaining certain apparent contradictions in the literature. For example, Perrow (26) has suggested that environments are neither certain nor uncertain but are simply perceived differently by different organizations. At the same time, Galbraith (11) implies that if an organization unjustifiably perceives its environment with certainty and in fact it is uncertain, it most likely will consume slack resources in the performance of its tasks. For example, Perrow (26) suggests that if a prison perceives its task to be a custodial one, the environment is not uncertain. If, however, it views the goal as rehabilitation, it will tend to perceive its environment as uncertain. In this case, every individual is unique and the therapy must be custom designed. In both the custodial and the rehabilitation prison, the environment is the same but the perception of the organization is different. The perception of low uncertainty in the custodial prison may or may not reflect the organization's perception of its total environment. This low perception of uncertainty is relevant only after a domain decision has been made. This domain decision has now resulted in a task environment. Thus, Perrow is describing a low level of uncertainty elicited by a task environment, not the level of uncertainty elicited by the total organization environment as perceived by individuals who make the domain decision. It is suggested that the perceptions of uncertainty elicited by the prison's total environment may have determined, in part, the domain decision maker(s)' domain definitions.

Galbraith (11), on the other hand, suggests that the production scheduler does not perceive his environment with uncertainty because the organization uses slack resources to buffer the production system from uncertainty. The present authors' view of uncertainty would agree with Galbraith's description, but would point out that the domain decisions which have been made for an organization include expectations of task performance levels, and thus the task environment in which the production scheduler is operating does not elicit perceptions of uncertainty for that individual. The resources used in this buffering can be considered as slack only in the organization's total environment, not as slack within the task environment which is presented to the production scheduler. Thus, Galbraith's unjustifiable perception of uncertainty is more clearly thought of as an unjustifiable domain decision.

While the mechanisms which serve to alter domain decisions, task environment, etc., extend beyond the purposes of this paper, this discussion has attempted to establish the importance of uncertainty perceptions in organization theory and the importance of restricting the concept of uncertainty to a perceptual one.

It is not argued that environments, organizational or individual, do not exist. Organizational environments, before or after the making of domain decisions, and individual environments, after the making of organization design decisions, do exist and have real attributes. It is argued, however, that individual responses to environments in general, and uncertainty in particular, are or should be treated as perceptual qualities. Further, if uncertainty is to be a useful concept in contingency theory, operationalizations must reflect this notion. Operationalization here is meant to include attempts to construct instrumentations of uncertainty, attempts to validate those instrumentations, and the use of the instrumentations in the testing of contingency theory propositions.

Before the exact role of uncertainty can be examined empirically in organizational research, the mechanisms by which individuals perceive uncertainty must be explored. The remainder of this paper offers suggestions for future research which would examine these sources of uncertainty. These suggestions are offered to guide the researcher in his selection or development of operationalizations, but to do so tentatively; they do not pretend to provide more than a basic framework for analysis.

THE NATURE OF UNCERTAINTY

Reviewing the manner in which uncertainty has been employed, Duncan (8) identified three basic definitions in the literature, all of which are explicitly or implicitly grounded in the concept of information as a counterpart of uncertainty. Information theorists define uncertainty, or more precisely its counterpart, "information," in terms which are at least two levels of abstraction from the full richness of human actors. This level of abstraction results from what Cherry (4) has identified as the essential concern of information theory—signs and the statistical relations between signs. Definitions of information and uncertainty found in information theory, although suited to the needs of information theorists, tend to be too narrowly defined for use in contingency theory formulations. Stated somewhat differently, information theorists' definitions of information and uncertainty are not concerned with users of information.

Decisions theorists, on the other hand, have moved one level of abstraction closer to the human actor in their treatment of information and uncertainty through the inclusion of users in their analyses. The restriction here does not stem from the decision theorists' unwillingness to consider individual inputs into a decision situation. The restriction does stem, however, from their "focus on the more mathematical aspects of uncertainty such as the individual's ability or inability to assign probabilities to events" (8, p. 24).

At a broader level of analysis, Duncan found definitions such as those of Lawrence and Lorsch to be vague and not based on theoretical considerations. He attempted to counter this problem by use of respondents' verbalizations of uncertainty. While this approach was empirically grounded and insured a conceptualization rich in terms of the human actor, it does not necessarily ensure a useful concept for research because of two basic problems: (a) the role of individual characteristics; and (b) objectively defined criterion measures of uncertainty. These questions involve the nature of man's relationship to his environment.

Sommerhoff (29) suggests that the distinctive feature of living systems is the "goal-directedness" of their activities. While Sommerhoff's analysis of goal directed behavior and "directive correlation" goes far beyond the purposes of this discussion, his analysis provides direction for a man-environment model of uncertainty. The goal directed model of man implies man's behavior, conscious and/or unconscious, is based upon his present relationship to his environment relative to future potential relationships which take the form of goal-events. Man is not seen as responding to his environment in order to reach some goal in the traditional sense of the term. Rather, man is viewed as interacting with his environment in order to form or develop new relationships with hish environment. Additionally, this interaction is seen as based on the existence of conditional functional relationships between factors in man's behavior and factors in his environment.

Uncertainty Defined

Uncertainty can be defined as a state that exists when an individual defines himself as engaging in directed behavior based upon less than complete knowledge of (a) his existing relationship with his environment, (b) the existence of and knowledge of conditional, functional relationships between his behavior and environmental variables to the occurrence of a future (t_1) self-environment relation and (c) the place of future (t_1) self-environment relations within the longer time frame ($t_2...t_n$) of a self-environment relations hierarchy.

This definition of uncertainty can be thought of more clearly as a psychological state similar to that proposed by Michael (25) and Downey (7). According to Michael, the state of psychological uncertainty arises from the individual losing control, not only of the situation, but also of one's self. Michael sees this need for control as culturally intensified, but basically grounded in the nature of man which depends upon learning rather than on instinct for survival. This need for a sense of control over the self is, in turn, a function of the development of self as an internalization of the "generalized other" (24). Thus, although the definition of uncertainty offered above tends to be behavioralistic, it is theoretically grounded in the view of man as seeking meaning for himself as a result of goal directed behavior.

The perception of environmental stimuli is an interpretive process (28). This interpretive process is a function of the lack of inherent meaning of signals associated with environmental characteristics (4) and the less than infinite data processing capacity of the human organism. Man cannot interact directly with his environment; instead, he must map it.

Given that reality is infinite in terms of its elements (16), it also can be postulated that an individual's mapping always must be less than complete. This lack of completeness of cognitive mappings provides a constant potential for less than complete perceived knowledge.

The Environment

This paper does not consider the perception of uncertainty to be a direct result of an individual's environment. At the same time, the environment does provide basic inputs into the individual's mapping processes. Additionally, the environment is seen as a moderator of sources of perceived uncertainty variability. Consequently, an explicit formulation of environments is necessary. This formulation, however, must be free from either perceptual or man-environment relations oriented concepts.

Emery (9) and Emery and Trist (10) have postulated a view of environments in terms of their causal texture, which is defined as "the extent and manner in which the variables relevant to the constituent organization (organism) are independent of a particular part, causally related, or interwoven with each other." This dimension is compatible with the view of uncertainty stated here.

Using this dimension, Emery developed four ideal types of environments and, more important for this analysis, postulated types of behavioral responses which are necessary for survival in each environmental type. These ideal types and their respective behavior requirements are as follows:

1. *Placid-randomized*—goals and noxiants are relatively stable and are randomly distributed through the environment.
Behavioral requirements—tactics-strategy . . . "attempting to do one's best on a purely local basis."

2. *Placid-clustered*—goals and noxiants remain stable but they tend to hang together in "lawful" ways. This structuring enables parts of the environment to potentially serve as signs of other parts.
Behavioral requirements—tactical response to each sign in the environment becomes dysfunctional. Thus, strategies become necessary in order to subordinate tactical responses to higher order goals.

3. *Disturbed-reactive*—the basic type-two environment remains relatively unchanged but more than one system (organization or organism) of the same "kind" is present. Thus, responses or movements within the environment by a system will likely be accompanied by responses (potentially competitive and hostile) from other like systems.
Behavioral requirements—strategies utilized in a type-two environment must be broadened to include competitive strategies and tactics.

4. *Turbulent fields*—significant variance arises from the environmental field itself in addition to that which arises from the simple interaction of like systems (organizations or organisms) in the environment. Reactions precede action.
Behavioral requirements—given "present" adaptive processes, time of adaption increases "beyond all bounds of what is practical."

Sources of Uncertainty Variation

Given this view of man, environments, and the definition of uncertainty, it can be postu-

```
ENVIRONMENT ———/\/\/\——→ MAPPING ———/\/\/\——→ PERCEIVED UNCERTAINTY
                          PROCESSES
                              ↑
                  1. Perceived Environmental Characteristics
                  2. Individual Cognitive Processes
                  3. Behavioral Response Repertoire
                  4. Social Expectations
```

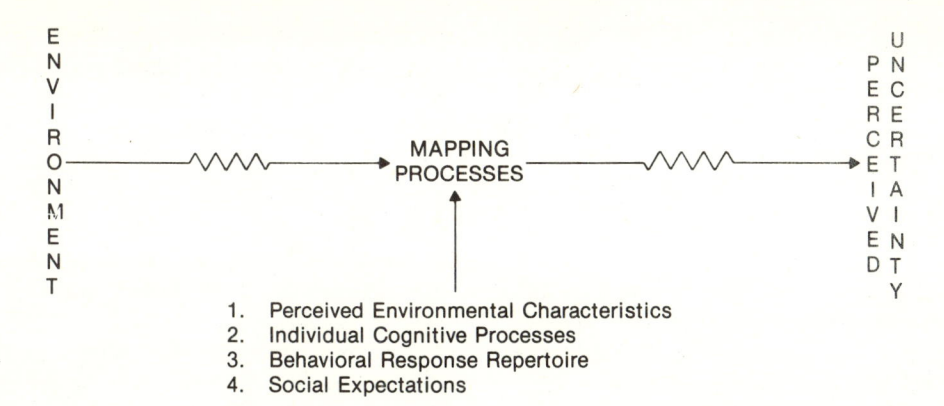

Figure 1. A Basic Model for Uncertainty Perception

lated that perceived uncertainty can be expected to vary with (a) perceived characteristics of the environment, (b) individual differences in cognitive processes, (c) individual behavioral responses repertoires, and (d) social expectations for the perception of uncertainty. Each of these sources of variability is indicated in Figure 1.

Environmental Characteristics—Duncan (8) demonstrated that the perception of uncertainty is associated with the perception of environmental characteristics. Based on the work of Emery and Trist (10), Thompson (31), and Terreberry (30), he characterized environments along two dimensions—complexity and dynamism.

A dynamic environment is one in which the relevant factors for decision making are in a constant state of change. This dynamic quality can be expected to preclude the testing and reuse of conceptual maps by the individual over time. This constant state of map obsolescence can be expected to increase the perception of uncertainty.

A complex environment is one in which the number of interactive relationships relevant for decision making require a high degree of abstraction in order to produce manageable mappings. This increased abstract quality of mappings can be expected to increase the individual's lack of knowledge concerning his own abstract mappings. Thus, the perception of complexity and/or dynamism in the environment can be expected to be positively related to the perception of uncertainty.

Individual Cognitive Processes—Duncan (8) suggests that individuals with a tolerance for ambiguity may perceive situations as less uncertain than do individuals with lower tolerances. While this basic proposition tends to be supported by empirical research (2, 15), it tends to view cognitive processes unidimensionally.

Studies concerning the multiple dimensionality of individual perception and evaluation processes have been labeled studies of "cognitive complexity". The usefulness of these studies for this discussion has been reduced by two important considerations. First, the majority of these studies focus upon the perception of *and* the ability to cope effectively with complexity. Second, the vast majority of these studies have focused upon the development and testing of single instruments (33).

Vannoy (33) attempted empirically to establish and isolate dimensions of cognitive complexity through a factor analysis of 20 different measures of cognitive style which had been developed with relatively similar goals. It is important to remember, however, that these goals included more than the perception of uncertainty. Vannoy's study resulted in the extraction of eight factors, of which six were considered interpretable. This study led him to conclude that three broad classes of behavior tendencies underlie cognitive complexity. First, there appears to be a tendency to emphasize one or a very few judgmental variables to the exclusion of others. Second, there appears to be a dimension related to the coarseness of distinctions which are utilized on any one variable. Third, there appears to be a dimension related to the tendency to view the world as ordered or unordered (33).

Similarly, Emery (9) suggested four potential responses to environments which are "overly complex"—(a) trivialization; (b) fragmentation; (c) dissociation, and (d) reliance on values as behavioral guides. Three of the above responses (a, b, and c) are passive individual responses based upon a unilateral redefinition of one's environment. The fourth (d) response assumes a suprasystem of superordinate values capable of guiding the individual's bahavior. This concept of perceived uncertainty suggests that an individual's redefinition can be expected whenever an individual feels unable to perform the behaviors required by his environment, regardless of the environmental perceptions of others, to reach his goal.

The three individual attempts (a, b, and c) to downgrade complex types of environments are based essentially on defense mechanisms. The first of these individual responses, trivialization, is the tendency to downgrade the complexity of an environment by forcing environmental factors into a single or a few dimensions. The second individual response, fragmentation, is the tendency to divide or disintegrate the total environment into parts which are then treated without regard to toal environmental results. The third dimension, dissociation, is the tendency to downplay the relevance of the behavior of other actors in the environment. A fourth individual response is Emery's reliance on values as behavioral guides. This response is the tendency to rely upon abstract, supraordinate value systems as behavioral guides, thus negating the need for consideration of the effects of specific behaviors.

Although Emery's interests, relative to those of Vannoy, are more closely aligned with the present researchers' purposes, the factor analytic work of Vannoy nonetheless is supportive of the multidimensional view of individual cognitive processes. Additionally, the researcher wishing to operationalize these dimensions will find guidance in the work of Vannoy.

Behavioral Response Repertoire—The third source of perceived uncertainty variability posited in the literature concerns the availability of and the individual's capacity to display appropriate behavioral responses to given environmental characteristics. The capacities considered here do not include an individual's innate qualities such as those which might influence individual cognitive processes but, rather, capacities stemming from the individual's experience. The basic proposition might be that a greater variety (not necessarily duration) of individual experience will increase the behavioral repertoire of the individual. This increased repertoire is assumed to be a function of both primary and vicarious learning situations. This proposition is supported by Dalton (5), Dill et al. (6), and Thompson (31) through their analysis of "early" career patterns of successful organizational members, which are seen as providing the opportunity to interact with others in order to learn skills, data, and attitudes appropriate for later positions. This increased repertoire could be assumed to increase the probability of an individual's eliciting an appropriate behavioral response when faced with a specific environment.

Social Expectations—Given the incompleteness of conceptual mapping processes, it can be posited that regardless of the individual and the environmental setting, the potential for perceived uncertainty is present. At the same time, causal observation of behavior supports the existence of certain individuals displaying few or no signs of uncertainty. This observation leads to an expectation that organizational socialization processes include the "proper" display of perceptions of uncertainty. To the extent that these processes result in reflexive expectations, a socially learned component in the individual's tendency to perceive uncertainty can be postulated.

These social expectations are related to all relevant others, as defined by the individual. At the same time, the organizational researcher might be able to justify the assumption that at least a major portion of the relevant others for an individual performing an organization role can be organizationally defined. To the extent that this assumption is valid, the researcher may be able to utilize structural variables as measures of these expectations. For example, the degree of discretion defined for a position might be considered as an indicator of the organizational expectations of that position regarding uncertainty. Stated differently, if an organization expects a position incumbent to display little discretion, it can be assumed that the organization also expects the occupant to perceive little uncertainty. Thompson (31) and Jacques (13, 14) give a thorough discussion of the discretionary content of jobs.

CONCLUSIONS

At least three suggestions have been given for future research concerning uncertainty. First, the definition of uncertainty offered here suggests that environmental uncertainty can be considered as a contradiction in terms and thus misleading. At the same time, however, a perceptual definition of uncertainty suggests a need to explore the manner in which both individual characteristics and environmental attributes affect the perception of uncertainty. This work has been begun by Duncan (8) and should now be extended by consideration of alternative sources of perceived uncertainty variability. Further, the need for research directed toward the relationship between environmental attributes, individual characteristics, and the perception of uncertainty will continue to be obscured until uncertainty ceases to be considered as an environmental attribute.

Second, this paper's view of uncertainty suggests that if organizational uncertainty is to be used in research, it is necessary to specify the basis for this uncertainty. Organizational uncertainty is not well represented by a simple summation of individuals' perceptions of uncertainty. While the potential role of individual characteristics in the perception of uncertainty might be reason enough to prohibit such a treatment, the ultimate inadequacy of this summation process lies elsewhere. Individuals within an organization do not work within a single environment. If the researcher's unit of analysis is the "total" organization, he needs to direct his analysis at those individuals who are concerned with domain decisions. Further, his use of these individuals as data sources should guard explicitly against the multiple roles which organization members may occupy. If the researcher is concerned with intraorganization factors, he is well advised to seek consideration of task environment characteristics. This does not assume that uncertainties perceived by individuals within task environments are not related to uncertainties perceived by individuals involved with the organization's total environment. They most likely are related and/or moderated by domain and organizational design decisions. The manner in which these elicited uncertainties are related is not well known and deserves immediate attention by researchers.

Finally, past research can be better integrated and interpreted by using uncertainty as a perceptual concept and through more explicit specification of the enacted environment which can be considered as having elicited uncertainty by individual organizational members.

REFERENCES

1. Blandin, J., W. Brown, and J. Koch. "Uncertainty and Information Gathering Behavior: An Empirical Investigation" (Thirty-Fourth Annual Academy of Management Meetings, 1974).

2. Budner, S. "Intolerance of Ambiguity as a Personality Variable," *Journal of Personality,* Vol. 30 (1962), 20-50.

3. Burns, T., and G. Stalker. *The Management of Innovation* (Chicago: Quadrangle Books, 1961).

4. Cherry, C. *On Human Communication* (Cambridge, Mass.: The MIT Press, 1966).

5. Dalton, M. *Men Who Manage* (New York: Wiley, 1959).

6. Dill, W., T. Hilton, and W. Reitman. *The New Managers* (Englewood Cliffs, N.J.: Prentice-Hall, 1962).

7. Downey, K. "Perceived Uncertainty: Conceptual Frameworks and Research Instruments" (Thirty-Fourth Annual Academy of Management Meetings, 1974).

8. Duncan, R. "Characteristics of Organizational Environments and Perceived Environmental Uncertainty," *Administrative Science Quarterly,* Vol. 17 (1972), 313-327.

9. Emery, F. "The Next Thirty Years: Concepts, Methods, and Anticipation," *Human Relations,* Vol. 20 (1967), 199-237.

10. Emery F., and E. Trist. "The Causal Texture of Organizational Environments," *Human Relations,* Vol. 18 (1965), 21-32.

11. Galbraith, J. *Designing Complex Organizations* (Reading, Mass.: Addison-Wesley, 1973).

12. Harvey, E. "Technology and the Structure of Organizations," *American Sociological Review,* Vol. 33 (1968), 247-259.

13. Jacques, E. *Measurement of Responsibility* (London: Tavistock Publications, 1956).

14. Jacques, E. *Equitable Payment* (London: Heinemann, 1961).

15. Kahn, R., D. Wolfe, R. Quinn, and J. Snoek. *Organizational Stress: Studies in Role Conflict* (New York: Wiley, 1964).

16. Kaplan, A. *The Conduct of Inquiry* (Scranton, Pa.: Chandler, 1964).

17. Keller, R., J. Slocum, and G. Susman. "Uncertainty and Type of Management Systems in Continuous Process Organizations," *Academy of Management Journal,* Vol. 17 (1974), 56-68.

18. Koffka, K. *Principles of Gestalt Psychology* (New York: Harcourt and Brace, 1935).

19. Lawrence, P., and J. Lorsch. "Differentiation and Integration in Complex Organizations," *Administrative Science Quarterly,* Vol. 12 (1967), 1-47.

20. Lawrence, P., and J. Lorsch. *Organization and Environment* (Homewood, Ill.: Irwin, 1967).

21. Lawrence, P., and J. Lorsch. "A Reply to Tosi, Aldag, and Storey," *Administrative Science Quarterly,* Vol. 18 (1973), 397-398.

22. Litschert, R. "The Structure of Long Range Planning Groups," *Academy of Management Journal,* Vol. 14 (1971), 33-43.

23. Lorsch, J., and S. Allen. *Managing Diversity and Interdependence: An Organizational Study of Multidivisional Firms* (Boston: Harvard University Graduate School of Business Administration, Division of Research, 1973).

24. Mead, G. H. *Mind, Self, and Society,* Charles W. Morris (Ed.) (Chicago: University of Chicago Press, 1934).

25. Michael, D., *Learning to Plan and Planning to Learn* (San Francisco: Josey Bass, 1973).

26. Perrow, C. *Organizational Analysis: A Sociological View* (Belmont, Calif.: Wadsworth, 1970).

27. Secord, P., and C. Backman. *Social Psychology* (New York: McGraw-Hill, 1964).

28. Shaw, M., and P. Costanzo. *Theories of Social Psychology* (New York: McGraw-Hill, 1970).

29. Sommerhoff, G. "The Abstract Characteristics of Living Systems," in F. E. Emery (Ed.), *Systems Thinking* (Baltimore: Penguin, 1969).

30. Terreberry, S. "The Evolution of Organizational Environments," *Administrative Science Quarterly,* Vol. 12 (1968), 590-613.

31. Thompson, J. *Organizations in Action* (New York: McGraw-Hill, 1967).

32. Tosi, H., R. Aldag, and R. Storey. "On the Measurement of the Environment: An Assessment of the Lawrence and Lorsch Environmental Uncertainty Scale," *Administrative Science Quarterly,* Vol. 18 (1973), 27-36.

33. Vannoy, J. "Generality of Cognitive Complexity—Simplicity as a Personality Construct," *Journal of Personality and Social Psychology,* Vol. 2 (1965), 385-396.

34. Woodward, J. *Industrial Organization: Theory and Practice* (London: Oxford University Press, 1965).

35. Zaltman, G., R. Duncan, and J. Holbek. *Innovations and Organizations* (New York: Wiley, 1973).

36. Zwermen, W. *New Perspecives on Organization Theory* (Westport, Conn.: Greenwood, 1970).

MANAGERIAL PERCEPTIONS AND STRATEGIC BEHAVIOR

Carl R. Anderson
Frank T. Paine

Organization theorists have been concerned for several years with the relationship between environmental properties and internal characteristics of the firm. Only recently, however, have they taken into account this relationship as mediated by the strategy formulation processes of boundary personnel either for the institutional level of the organization or for particular subunits in that organization (6, 13). On the other hand, specialists in policy have long considered the role of the strategy formulation process as the crucial step in "matching" internal and external characteristics of the firm. It has been the present authors' experience, however, that the policy area has not substantially utilized or extended the systematic research dealing with environmental characteristics and their effects, either behavioral or physical.

Depending on perceptions of both environmental and internal properties, managers have considerable leeway in making strategic choices to meet various contingencies. It may be inappropriate, therefore, for the researcher simply to examine the relationship between certain absolute properties of the environment and the internal characteristics of the firm without examining in detail the strategy choices made by the boundary person(s). The premise here is that these strategies are strongly influenced by two sets of forces or perceptions: first, the perception of environmental uncertainty and, second, the perception of the need for change in strategic properties of the organization (such as mission, objectives, strategies, and structure) in order to meet environmental demands. The key point in the discussion is the perceptual process of the boundary-spanning manager(s) at each point at which a strategy decision occurs.

Saunders (17), in discussing the need for increased understanding of the strategy formulation process, expressed many of these authors' concerns in the following comments:

1. Assumptions about policy formulation are not consistent with the facts as noted by those in other fields who observe the process.

2. Since the policy formulation process is not well understood, the revision of strategy presents difficult issues.

3. A difficult point occurs in achieving a complete discussion of strategy implementation, since formulation is not well understood.

4. A conceptual problem exists in treating the product (strategy) of a process (formulation) without some fairly good knowledge of that process. The position is often taken that the strategy formulation process is not subject to any constraints.

Although it is not contended that the model developed here is a complete model of the strategy formulation process, it does incorporate essential variables, especially

Reprinted by permission of the publisher from *Academy of Management Journal,* Vol. 18 (1975), pp. 811-823.

those constraints which occur before or during the process. Strategy formulation is subject to many subjective (behavioral, political, emotional) forces which influence its ultimate form. It is contended that these various forces can best be dealt with in a perceptual framework. Two major outcomes from this perceptual analysis are expected: first, a means of analyzing the formulation process itself rather than characteristics which precede or follow the process and, second, a means of prescribing corrective action in the implementation of the formulation process.

The major thrust of the article will be a normative discussion of the strategy process. Although a large body of descriptive literature exists, especially in the form of case studies, it is felt that it is more important to construct a strategy formulation model on the basis of previous research and theoretical constructs from two areas which have not previously been integrated to any great extent: first, the relatively large body of literature dealing with the influence of the environment on the organization, labeled organization theory, and, second, the literature dealing with the strategy formulation process. Once such a model has been constructed, it then would be desirable to apply descriptive literature in order to test its various propositions.

MANAGERIAL PERCEPTIONS

Following the arguments of Weick (23), it is generally accepted that the perception of environmental and internal characteristics (rather than the "objective" characteristics of the environment) are the important properties to consider in the strategy formulation process (6). Given this perceptual base, it is easy to understand why objective measurement of the environment with the intention of predicting strategic properties of the firm has yielded few, if any, concrete results (13). In other words, all managers operating in highly uncertain (or certain) environments do not necessarily perceive the same degree of uncertainty (or certainty). This perceptual difference in turn affects the formulation of policy decisions.

A large body of evidence exists which supports this position. Child (4) found that managerial perceptions and actions strongly influence responses by the organization to its particular environment. Snow and Miles (20), in a study of responses to environmental conditions, report that actions taken by the organization in responding to its environment are consistent with managerial perception rather than with the objective characteristics of the environment. Downey (6) suggests that the managerial perceptual process is independent of the environment but that the environment does provide inputs into the manager's strategy making process. Duncan (7) emphasizes that organizational response is strongly influenced by the perceptual process, which, in turn, is affected by managerial characteristics such as tolerance for ambiguity.

It is the contention here that the perception of factors external to the boundary manager is a key factor in accounting for different decision frameworks and resulting strategies in the same objective environment. The fact that similar types of environments have been noted to elicit similar organization responses (such as in the Woodward studies) from organizations in these environments can be attributed to the fact that members of these organizations have similar perceptual processes (6). However, as pointed out above, a growing body of evidence exists which documents different response patterns in similar environments. An interesting situation occurs when different response patterns in the same environment are equally successful. Current frameworks appear to be inadequate to handle this case.

In an operative sense, the interpretation of objective information is biased by the perceptual process. For example, Dearborn and Simon (5) give evidence supporting the contention that executives perceive problems from the perspective of their own functional area (departmental bias). Richards (16) supports this proposition in a study of strategic failure. He reported that a state of "benign optimism" existed among the companies that eventually experienced severe failure in part or all of their operations. In addition, instances of contrary information (contrary to accepted strategies) tended to be suppressed.

Harrison (10, p. 35) suggests three elements of the perceptual process which summarize other perceptual frameworks (24).

1. *Selectivity:* Separation of information for further consideration.

2. *Closure:* Compilation of pieces of information into a meaningful whole.

3. *Interpretation:* Use of previous experience as an aid in judging the information previously collected.

It is clear that these authors have identified several sources of bias which influence strategy decisions. Bias in selectivity occurs in the Dearborn example, and Richards reports bias in both selectivity and interpretation. In the opinion of the present authors, the nature of these sources is crucial to the successful understanding of the strategy formulation process.

PERCEIVED ENVIRONMENTAL UNCERTAINTY

Perception of environmental uncertainty will be defined according to Duncan's (7) and Galbraith's (9) formulation. Duncan has described uncertainty along two dimensions, both of which are based on objective characteristics. These dimensions are complexity and dynamism. In dynamic environments the factors relevant to strategy making are constantly changing; complex environments include a number of relationships interacting in such a way that they require a high level of abstraction on the part of the policy maker.

Researchers have shown market heterogeneity and technology as two important properties of these types of environments. Duncan described three aspects of complex and dynamic environments which appear to be highly useful in indicating uncertainty. These include: (a) a shortage of information about environmental factors which influence a given decision making situation, (b) a lack of knowledge about the effects of an incorrect decision (how much would the organization lose?), and (c) the ability (or inability) of managers to determine the probability that a given environmental factor will affect the success or failure of a decision unit in performing its function.

Galbraith's definition of uncertainty as "the difference between the amount of information required to perform the task and the amount already possessed by the organization" (9, p. 35), however, seems to be a more useful concept for the strategy formulation process. In strategy formulation the critical area is not uncertainty per se but the processing of accurate information to deal with uncertainty. Uncertainty in strategy formulation therefore is dependent on the amount of information required in formulation, its reliability, and the amount of information which the organization currently has available. In this application of uncertainty, then, the perception of the need for information as an indicator of uncertainty becomes important to understanding the formulation process.

PERCEIVED NEED FOR CHANGE

Traditionally, experts in policy have considered such factors as distinctive competence, internal resources, and unique capabilities of prime importance. These concepts all refer to strategic properties (or capabilities) of the firm. However, it rarely has been suggested that perceptions rather than absolute characteristics of these strategic properties are the important variables. Perceived need for change is defined as the perception by the strategy formulator (boundary spanner) of a distinct lack of competence, capabilities, or internal resources to carry out a planned program of action.

Two authors, in particular, have dealt with the perceptual variable. Child (4) suggests that perceptions are responsible for the choices which managers make in fitting the organization and its environment. Andrews (2) deals indirectly with the perception of strategic characteristics by pointing out that the potential capabilities of a company tend to be underestimated or misperceived. Andrews emphasizes that the problems of perception of strategic properties are equally as important as the problem of forecasting the effects of the environment in the face of uncertainty. Andrews notes four general strengths of a company which influence perception: (a) experience in making and marketing a product line, (b) developing strenghts and weaknesses of the individuals in the organization, (c) the degree to which individual capabilites are applied to the task, and (d) the quality of coordination of individual and group effort. In the present authors' experience, Andrews' framework is typical of the traditional policy formulation theory which has not systematically examined the nature of the perceptual process.

It is argued here, then, that the internal adjustment process is not a random one, but can be explained in terms of two perceptual processes: the perceived uncertainty in the environment and the perceived need to alter strategic properties. The strategic choices (or moves) are affected by these two different kinds of perceptual factors. The following model is an attempt to combine the two perceptual processes into a meaningful framework for explanatory and predictive uses.

ASSUMPTIONS

The following constitute the assumptions which have been made in the design of the strategy formulation model:

1. The model is applicable to the situation in which a single individual formulates strategy or to the situation in which a single individual dominates a coalition of strategy formulators. It is also applicable where there is a nondominated coalition, but moderator variables such as the risk propensity of the group and conflicting perceptions (decision making by compromise) add complexity to the problem of making predictions about strategic behavior.

2. The environment (especially environmental uncertainty) is a relatively constant factor in the formulation process which cannot be substantially influenced by the decision maker. This assumption does not preclude the organization from taking action to influence the environment as a result of selected strategies. It is assumed that during the formulation process, environmental factors comprise a series of conditions over which the decision maker has no control. This appears to be a realistic assumption in light of the definition of uncertainty as the need for reliable information.

3. It is assumed that there is a set of strategy related behaviors which are relevant for each of the four model quadrants. The above literature review provides support for this assumption. The model discussion expands this data base.

4. Every environment contains a certain degree of uncertainty or uncontrollable elements. However, the degree of environmental uncertainty is extremely variable and depends on both absolute characteristics and, more importantly, managerial perceptions. Similarly, organizations only rarely face conditions when there is no need for internal change. Need for change is assumed to be a function of absolute characteristics and, more importantly, managerial perceptions.

5. The important assumption is made that strategy formulation must be consistent, for behavioral (implementation) reasons, with perceptual rather than with absolute characteristics of the environment. It is the contention of this paper that maximum effort toward implementation of strategy will be achieved only when strategy is consistent with perceptions of the environment and internal characteristics.

6. It is also assumed, following the arguments of Cyert, March, and Simon, that individuals will be motivated to reduce uncertainty if uncertainty is perceived. Behaviors therefore are predictable in several of the quadrants. Similarly, predictable behaviors are expected to occur with regard to the "Perceived Need for Change" dimension, since individuals are motivated to reduce "gaps" between existing and desired states (12).

THE MODEL

Figure 1 presents the model which was derived from the previous discussion. In order to enhance understanding, each perceptual variable has been reduced to two dimensions: perceptions of environmental certainty and uncertainty, and low and high perceived need for change. The resulting four quadrants present different kinds of strategy formulation problems which require different strategies for effective solution. The model is intended as a framework for analysis of the strategy formulation process. With a few notable exceptions (11), such a framework has not been available to the strategy analyst. It is important to begin concentrating on the characteristics of the strategy situation and the policy maker in order to better explain this important area.

The response patterns of policy makers may be viewed as affecting several strategic properties: (a) mission or domain, (b) objectives, (c) strategies and policies, (d) organizational form, and (e) the role performance of policy makers themselves (15). The mission or domain may be described as the scope of operations in terms of product and market or of service and client. The objective may be described as hoped for results, goals, or targets. Policies may be described as broad guides for the achievement of objectives; strategies may be viewed as specific major actions or patterns of action for attainment of objectives. The strategies may be planned ahead of time (standing plans) or emerge over time based on *ad hoc* decisions (adaptive planning or contingency planning). The organization form relates to the compiling of roles and programs (generalized procedures) for various members of the organization and the resulting flow of information and authority. The role performance of a policy maker is the actual pattern of behavior that is followed and the actual functions and duties performed. The analysis of characteristics of these strategic properties provides a pattern for each quadrant which is significantly different from that of each other quadrant.

Hypotheses about these descriptive relationships have not been proved through substantial empirical research dealing with managerial perceptions. Only tentative patterns of perceptual relationships can be identified from earlier research efforts. Therefore, the following discussion of the model quadrants does not rely on an empirical perceptual data base but imputes managerial perceptions to their "most likely" situations.

The discussion can be viewed as suggesting several areas of research need in the perceptual/strategy framework. This initial step of identifying tentative patterns can be of major importance in understanding strategic behavior. The model can be applied to the study of policy making in organizations in various stages of development. For example, the significant differences in characteristics between the small, young growth-oriented organization and the stable, mature organization could be better understood by the use of some of the quadrants in the model. Those institutions which are trying to become established are characterized by an active

Perceived Need for Internal Change

	Low	High
Certain (Perceived Environmental Uncertainty)	**Cell 1** 1. Fixed and well defined 2. Optimization; maintenance; efficiency 3. Process planning; maintain competence 4. Closed/stable/mechanistic 5. Commitment to existing power structure; less active search for environmental information	**Cell 2** 1. Need for identification and readjustment 2. Optimization; improve economies of operation; planned change 3. Process planning; integration; improve distinctive competence 4. Closed/stable/mechanistic 5. Commitment to existing power structure; systematic; conservative; less active search for environmental information; "integrative," entrepreneur
Uncertain	**Cell 3** 1. Continually adjusted to feedback 2. Satisficing; maintain capacity to cope with uncertainty 3. Adaptive or contingency planning; search of advance information; penetration 4. Open/adaptive/organic 5. Adaptive planner; information gathering	**Cell 4** 1. Varied and flexible 2. Satisficing; survival; develop effective problem solving 3. Adaptive or contingency planning; divestiture; merger; diversification 4. Open/adaptive/organic 5. Search for external information; adaptive; "sharp departure" entrepreneur

Key: 1. Mission or domain   4. Organization form
2. Objectives   5. Role performance of policy maker
3. Strategies and policies

Figure 1. The Perceptually Based Strategy Model

flexible search for environment related information about appropriate changes to reduce the perceived uncertainty. A larger, more mature organization has built up commitments to the status quo; it may carry out its environment boundary relationships in a more routine, standardized way reflecting a measure of perceived certainty.

In addition, the characteristics of organizations (or divisions of organizations) may be predicted to vary in at least three dimensions depending on their quadrant location. The three dimensions are: (a) strategic mode: planning, adaptive planning, or entrepreneurial (14); (b) search behavior for environment related information; and (c) internal stability vs. internal change motivation.

The planning mode (process planning) is characterized by reliance on the planning analyst, reliance on cost—benefit analyses of competing proposals, and the integration of decisions and strategies. The planning mode tends to be useful when the organization can afford the costs of planning, when the objectives are operationally definable, and when the environment is reasonably predictable and stable. The adaptive (adaptive planning, contingency planning, "muddling through") mode is characterized by a diffusion of power among many members of a complex coalition, the formation of reactive solutions to existing problems, decision making in incremental steps, and disjointed, uncoordinated decisions. Use of the adaptive mode means frequent replanning or readjusting and implies the perception of a complex, changing environment. Many large established organizations such as government agencies, corporations, and universities, even though they may have some sort of formal planning system, tend to be adaptive.

The entrepreneurial mode is characterized by a pro-active search for new opportunities in a yielding environment, centralized power, bold actions in changing strategic properties of the organization, and growth as a dominant goal. The entrepreneurial mode is typified by the young organization or new venture division of a larger organization. It also may be seen in organizations in crisis.

Systematic variations are expected in the information search behavior of policy makers operating in environments characterized by varying levels of uncertainty or scarcity of strategy related information. Those policy makers who perceive high uncertainty are expected to use all information sources more frequently, to rely more on external information sources, to allocate more time to information gathering activities, and to make more use of informal sources than are those policy makers who perceive low uncertainty (3). Furthermore, organizations with a stability orientation have built more commitments to existing power structures, processes, and traditions than have those organizations with an internal change motivation.

STRATEGIC MOVES IN EACH QUADRANT

While there is (depending on the stage of development, share of market, and forecasted market growth rate) an opportunity to exercise a great deal of discretion in each quadrant, each of the four quadrants seems to be associated with a set of possible strategic moves (or outputs) for the organization or division, based on the appropriate perceptions. A sample of suggested, or hypothesized, moves will be discussed here. Again, a perceptual data base is not currently available for application, and perceptions have been imputed to "most likely" situations. The model predicts that firms, or divisions, operating in Quadrant I have a process planning orientation, have a less active search for environment related information, and are stability motivated. The descriptive literature has depicted this type of firm as fitting a mature, relatively stable situation with the organization using allocation plans to defend its domain.

The model predicts that firms operating in Quadrant II have a planning or entrepreneurial orientation, resort to less active search for environment related information, and have a high motivation to change. Firms which have been described in these terms are in situations in which they can take advantage of the environment (if a yielding one) by substantial reallocation of resources toward improving internal strengths and reducing weaknesses.

Model Quadrant III is described as implying a more active search for environment related information, an adaptation orientation (more frequent replanning) and stability (internal) motivation. This quadrant has been described as fitting a coalition of anxious analyzers (20), making modest market and technological adjustments to keep pace.

Firms operating in Quadrant IV would engage in more active search for environment related information, have an adaptation or entrepreneurial orientation, and be characterized by internal change motivation. The literature has described these firms as fitting a situation where a divided coalition of influencer forces may be taken over by enthusiastic prospectors searching for innovation, new domains, expansion, and perhaps divestiture possibilities. It is not proposed that every organization or division will fit exactly into one of the quadrants described. It is proposed, however, that the perceived uncertainty—perceived gap condition provides one basis for describing possible outcomes from the organization-environment interaction.

In Quadrant I the mission or domain would tend to be fixed and well defined; the objectives would be operational and would emphasize optimizing, efficient performance and maintenance. Strategies and policies would tend to stress defending the domain with stability but with allocations for maintaining distinctive competence. Some expansion may take place in "sure bet" areas. There might be some attempts to reduce whatever uncertainty is perceived by integration to protect supplies and/or markets. Resources would be allocated to maintain an efficient technological process and to maintain market share. The organization form would incline toward being closed/stable/mechanistic. The main policy makers may rely on standing plans and specific policies, especially if the organization is large and established.

The Quadrant I type is found in many lines of endeavor—the retirement division of Civil Service, a paper mill, an established beer distributor. The Volkswagenwerk situation from 1949-1965 (after it integrated, before it diversified) also illustrates Quadrant I, as do the strategic moves used by those who took over Hamm's beer from Heublein in 1974.

In Quadrant II the current mission or domain of the organization or division might need some identification and readjustment. However, the objectives are likely to be planned change in internal properties to improve economies of operation. The strategies and policies tend to include integration for synergistic effects, improving distinctive competence in technological process, market segmentation, and concentration on a few product types for economy. The organization form is likely to be closed/stable/mechanistic. Again the policy maker(s) may rely on standing plans, or alternatively may follow an entrepreneurial mode. The entrepreneur would perceive he had advance information and a potential competitive advantage; he may take the bold move of extensive integration to reduce the gap. The planner would be more systematic, methodical, and conservative in actions even though he perceived a relatively certain environment.

Nordhoff, when he integrated the Volkswagenwerk in 1948, exemplifies the integrative entrepreneur. And in the mature field of aerosol packaging, Barr-Stolfort planned several allocations to improve its technology and to concentrate on a limited number of product types for economy. Both of these firms appear to illustrate Quadrant II.

In Quadrant III the domain of the organization is somewhat more varied than in Quadrants I and II and is continually adjusted to feedback. The objectives include maintaining sufficient capacity to cope with perceived uncertainty in a satisficing manner. The strategies and policies include market penetration with allocations to continue active search for advance environment related information (21), and some diversification into related products (if the firm is mature). Product differentation and market segmentation may be relied on to reduce uncertainty. Also, imitation may be used sometimes to serve the same purpose. The organization form is likely to be open/adaptive/organic. Divisionalization may occur (19). A matrix structure may be introduced. The main role of the policy maker(s) is that of an adaptive planner (or an anxious analyzer) with frequent readjustments.

Quadrant III is illustrated by IBM and Xerox with their market penetration and by American car manufacturers with their divisionalization and imitation of European small cars and luxury cars.

In Quadrant IV, with perceived uncertainty and a high gap, the mission is varied and flexible. The objectives would be to develop (or acquire) effective problem solving with satisficing models and to survive. Some rather bold strategies and policies appear to be associated with this quadrant. Taking action to reduce the gap and reduce uncertainty may require some tough divestiture decisions. Acquisition and/or merger may bring strength, or disaster. The organization may act like an enthusiastic prospector searching for new ventures or a new domain. Diversification into related or even unrelated products is another way of coping with the environment. On the other hand, a conservative organization may follow a more modest course of product imitation rather than allocating resources to an R & D search (18). The organization seems to need an open/adaptive/organic form with perhaps matrix, project, or new venture components. An entrepreneurial role for the policy maker may be followed in which he dominates the coalition and takes action to reduce uncertainty; a sharp departure from the status quo is made. Or sometimes an adaptor role for the policy maker(s) may be used where there is a divided coalition of influencer forces. Changes may be slower and perhaps even too late in some cases with the adaptor role.

The Quadrant IV situation can be seen in many organizations—the young organization trying to get established, the mature organization in crisis, organizations suddenly faced with a changed environment. Franklin National Bank, Penn Central, and Head Ski are examples. In fact, many organizations find themselves in Quadrant IV today.

SUMMARY AND CONCLUSIONS

For some time the proposition has been accepted that organizations are not environmentally independent. The process by which the organization and the environment interact, however, has not been firmly established. Certainly, the strategy formulation process is a crucial part of that interaction. This paper has attempted to provide some insights concerning the environment/strategy formulation/internal properties interaction.

An important question to ask is, how useful is the proposed perceptual model? It appears that the model provides a means of integrating the contributions from the organization theory and strategy areas. Positing the formulation process as the boundary position between external characteristics as they relate to the firm and its strategic properties is not a novel way of viewing the strategy process. However, through incorporation of the perceptual framework advanced by organization theorists, significant insights can be gained with regard to the strategy process.

Will the model significantly advance the state of knowledge in the strategy area? The authors believe so. Organization theorists and strategy experts have gone their separate ways for too long. It is apparent that the two areas have a great deal in common and should be exchanging theoretical frameworks to the benefit of both. It is difficult, if not impossible, to consider environmental effects and organization responses without considering or examining the perceptual processes of those people who are responsible for altering internal states of the firm. We see the following as a logical sequence of research steps to test the hypothesized model. First, organizations must be classified according to the two perceptual variables. This requires operationalization of uncertainty and need for change. The literature review suggests several criteria which can be applied. Classification according to this scheme would place a firm in one of the four cells.

Second, the common characteristics (if any) of the organizations in each cell must be identified. Essentially, this step would involve a testing of the propositions as set forth in Figure 1. This could be accomplished in at least two ways: through analysis of comprehensive cases and through collection of empirical data and systematic comparison of a large number of organizations, such as the Aston or Woodward Studies.

Third, the model should be tested as a means for analyzing and correcting "errors" in the strategy formulation process. Through examination of perceptions of key boundary personnel, insights can be gained concerning the interpretation and operationalization of the environment. Application of the model in this manner should determine its ultimate usefulness. These insights become quite obvious in cases of mismatch between the organization and its environments, but they suggest the need for a systematic approach to the analysis.

Fourth, individual differences which account for differences in the perceptual processes should be documented. At least two important variables appear to contribute to these individual differences: tolerance for ambiguity, as suggested by Duncan (7), and internal-external control (1).

A final step, which is seen as the ultimate goal of this line of research, is the construction of a decision tree to aid in strategy formulation similar to that developed by Vroom (22) for general managerial decision making. Such a decision tree probably would not lead the strategy formulation to an ultimately correct decision, but it should lead the manager to consider the proper variables as developed in the model. In the past the strategic choice variable has been difficult to incorporate into a systematic comparative research design. The use of this perceptual framework provides sufficient structure for such an attempt.

NOTES

For background, see *Heublein, Inc. (B)* (ICH 13G126).

See *Aerosol Techniques, Inc.* (ICH 13G155).

REFERENCES

1. Anderson, C., D. Hellriegel, and J. W. Slocum. "Managerial Response to Environmental Hazard" (Paper presented at the National Academy of Management Meeting, 1974).

2. Andrews, K. R. *The Concept of Corporate Strategy* (Homewood, Ill.: Dow Jones-Irwin, 1971).

3. Blandin, J. S., W. B. Brown, and J. L. Koch. "Uncertainty and Information Gathering Behavior: An Empirical Investigation" (Paper presented at the National Academy of Management Meeting, 1974).

4. Child, J. "Organization Structure, Environment, and Performance—The Role of Strategic Choice," *Sociology*, Vol. 6, (1972), 1-22.

5. Dearborn, D. C., and H. A. Simon. "Selective Perception, A Note on the Departmental Identifications of Executives," in T. C. Costello and S. S. Zalkind (Eds.), *Psychology in Administration* (Englewood Cliffs, N. J.: Prentice Hall, 1963).

6. Downey, H. K. "Perceived Uncertainty: Conceptual Frameworks and Research Instruments" (Paper presented at the National Academy of Management Meeting, 1974).

7. Duncan, R. "Characteristics of Organizational Environments and Perceived Environmental Uncertainty," *Administrative Science Quarterly*, Vol. 17 (1972), 313-327.

8. Emery, F. E., and E. L. Trist. "The Causal Texture of Organizational Environments," in W. A. Hill and D. Egan (Eds.), *Readings in Organization Theory* (Boston: Allyn and Bacon, 1966).

9. Galbraith, J. *Designing Complex Organizations* (Reading, Mass.: Addison-Wesley, 1973).

10. Harrison, E. F. *The Managerial Decision Making Process* (Boston: Houghton Mifflin, 1975).

11. Hofer, C. W. "Toward a Contingency Theory of Strategic Behavior" (Paper presented at the National Academy of Management Meeting, 1974).

12. MacCrimmon, K. R. "Managerial Decision-Making," in J. W. McGuire (Ed.), *Contemporary Management: Issues and Viewpoints* (Englewood Cliffs, N. J.: Prentice-Hall, 1974).

13. Miles, R. E., C. C. Snow, and J. Pfeffer. "Organization-Environment: Concepts and Issues," *Industrial Relations*, Vol. 13 (1974), 244-264.

14. Mintzberg, H. "Strategy Making in Three Modes," *California Management Review*, Vol. 16, No. 2 (1973), 44-53.

15. Paine, F., and W. Naumes. *Organizational Strategy and Policy: Text, Cases and Incidents* (Philadelphia, Pa.: W. B. Saunders, 1975).

16. Richards, M. D. "An Exploratory Study of Strategic Failure," *Academy of Management Proceedings*, 1973, pp. 40-46.

17. Saunders, C. B. "What Should We Know About Strategy Formulation," *Academy of Management Proceedings*, 1973, pp. 29-35.

18. Schoeffler, S., R. Buzzell, and D. Heany. "Input of Strategic Planning on Profit Performance," *Harvard Business Review*, Vol. 52, No. 2 (1974), 137-145.

19. Scott, B. R. *Stages in Corporate Development, Part II*. Harvard Business School, 4—371—295 BP999, 1971.

20. Snow, C. C., and R. E. Miles. "Managerial Perceptions and Organizational Adjustment Processes" (Unpublished paper; see 13, p. 256).

21. Terreberry, S. "The Evaluation of Organizational Environments," *Administrative Science Quarterly*, Vol. 12 (1968), 590-613.

22. Vroom, V. "A New Look at Managerial Decision Making," *Organizational Dynamics,* Vol. 1, No. 4 (1973), 66-80.

23. Weick, K. E. *The Social Psychology of Organizing* (Reading, Mass.: Addison-Wesley, 1969).

24. Zalkind, S. S., and T. W. Costello. "Perception: Some Recent Research and Implications for Administration," *Administrative Science Quarterly*, Vol. 7 (1962), 219-220.

PART TWO

INDIVIDUAL PROCESSES

In the preceding part, the emphasis was on the manner in which environmental contingencies affect the structure of organizations. In Part II, the focus is on how individuals adapt to the organization in which they must function. Organizations learn to survive by developing different patterns of structure, goals, etc., relative to the environment in which they function. In this part, the basic emphasis on adaptation is still the same, but the focus shifts from the organization to the individual. The readings in this Part illustrate how individuals develop different patterns of adaptation to the realities or organizational life. These patterns represent responses to circumstances within their organizations.

Individuals In Organizations

In the first section, the underlying framework is learning theory. Learning theory helps us to understand how relatively stable patterns of individual behavior develop in organizations. In the first selection, "Reinforcement Theory and Contingency Management in Organizational Settings," Hamner deals with two basic approaches to understanding behavior. He describes the difference between classical and operant conditioning. For most organizations, operant conditioning is a more useful model for understanding and influencing employee behavior. Reinforcement is the critical construct in operant conditioning. If a behavior is positively reinforced, the probability of that behavior occurring again increases, but if a behavior is negatively reinforced, the likelihood of that behavior occurring again decreases. Hamner also provides guidelines by which the manager can apply these concepts.

Kerr, in "On the Folly of Rewarding A, While Hoping for B," presents some general examples of where organizational reward systems go wrong. Organizations often unintentionally reward behaviors that they want to discourage, while failing to reinforce desired behaviors. An organization's reward system should positively reinforce desired behaviors. Too often the reward system constitutes an obstacle to be overcome. Managers who complain that their workers are not motivated might do well to consider the possibility that their reward systems are not consistent with the desired behaviors. Kerr offers examples of this misuse in politics, war, medicine, universities, and manufacturing organizations. Kerr provides some useful guidelines for managers to follow if they want to avoid rewarding the "wrong" behavior.

Argyris, in "Personality vs. Organization," presents some general stereotypes of individuals in organizations. He defines behavioral patterns between the individual and organization that are in direct conflict. Argyris contends that organizations demand adherence to rules and regulations to increase effectiveness. These demands make the individual a servant to the organization. Individuals, on the other hand, are looking for jobs in which they can demonstrate their creativity, abilities, and relative independence. Because of these different goals, the clash between the individual's desires and those of the organization are inevitable. He concludes that there are four interdependent forces working in an organizaion—structure and technology, leadership and interpersonal relations, administrative controls and regulations, and human controls—and unless management recognizes all these forces, it is doomed to failure.

REINFORCEMENT THEORY AND CONTINGENCY MANAGEMENT IN ORGANIZATIONAL SETTINGS

W. Clay Hamner

Traditionally management has been defined as the process of getting things done through other people. The succinctness of this definition is misleading in that, while it may be easy to say *what* a manager does, it is difficult to describe the determinants of behavior, i.e. to tell *how* the behavior of the manager influences the behavior of the employee toward accomplishment of a task. Human behavior in organizational settings has always been a phenomenon of interest and concern. However, it has only been in recent years that a concerted effort has been made by social scientists to describe the principles of reinforcement and their implications for describing the determinants of behavior as they relate to the theory and practice of management (e.g. see Nord, 1969; Wiard, 1972; Whyte, 1972; Jablonsky and DeVries, 1972; Hersey and Blanchard, 1972; and Behling, Schriesheim, and Tolliver, in press).[1]

Organizational leaders must resort to environmental changes as a means of influencing behavior. Reinforcement principles are the most useful method for this purpose because they indicate to the leader how he might proceed in designing or modifying the work environment in order to effect specific changes in behavior (Scott and Cummings, 1973). A reinforcement approach to management does not consist of a bag of tricks to be applied indiscriminately for the purpose of coercing unwilling people (Michael & Meyerson, 1962). Unfortunately, many people who think of Skinnerian applications (Skinner, 1969) in the field of management and personnel think of manipulation and adverse control over employees. Increased knowledge available today of the positive aspects of conditioning as applied to worker performance should help to dispel these notions.

The purpose of this paper is to describe the determinants of behavior as seen from a reinforcement theory point of view, and to describe how the management of the contingencies of reinforcement in organizational settings is a key to successful management. Hopefully, this paper will enable the manager to understand how his behavior affects the behavior of his subordinates and to see that in most cases the failure or success of the worker at the performance of a task is a direct function of the manager's own behavior. Since a large portion of the manager's time is spent in the process of modifying behavior patterns and shaping them so that they will be more goal oriented, it is appropriate that this paper begin by describing the processes and principles that govern behavior.

LEARNING AS A PREREQUISITE FOR BEHAVIOR

Learning is such a common phenomenon that we tend to fail to recognize its occurrence.

Reprinted by permission of the publisher from *Organizational Behavior and Management: A Contingency Approach,* Henry L. Tosi and W. Clay Hamner (eds.) Chicago, Ill.: St. Clair Publishing, Inc., 1974, Abridged.

Nevertheless, one of the major premises of reinforcement theory is that all behavior is learned—a worker's skill, a supervisor's attitude and a secretary's manners. The importance of learning in organizational settings is asserted by Costello and Zalkind when they conclude:

> Every aspect of human behavior is responsive to learning experiences. Knowledge, language, and skills, of course; but also attitudes, value systems, and personality characteristics. All the individual's activities in the organization—his loyalties, awareness of organizational goals, job performance, even his safety record have been learned in the largest sense of that term (1963, p. 205).

There seems to be general agreement among social scientists that learning can be defined as *a relatively permanent change in behavior potentiality that results from reinforced practice or experience.* Note that this definition states that there is change in behavior potentiality and not necessarily in behavior itself. The reason for this distinction rests on the fact that we can observe other people responding to their environments, see the consequences which accrue to them, and be vicariously conditioned. For example, a boy can watch his older sister burn her hand on a hot stove and "learn" that pain is the result of touching a hot stove. This definition therefore allows us to account for "no-trial" learning. Bandura (1969) describes this as imitative learning and says that while behavior can be *acquired* by observing, reading, or other vicarious methods, "*performance* of observationally learned responses will depend to a great extent upon the nature of the reinforcing consequences to the model or to the observer" (p. 128).

Luthans (1973, p. 362) says that we need to consider the following points when we define the learning process:

1. Learning involves a change, though not necessarily an improvement, in behavior. Learning generally has the connotation of improved performance, but under this definition bad habits, prejudices, stereotypes, and work restrictions are learned.

2. The change in behavior must be relatively permanent in order to be considered learning. This qualification rules out behavioral changes resulting from fatigue or temporary adaptations as learning.

3. Some form of practice or experience is necessary for learning to occur.

4. Finally, practice or experience must be reinforced in order for learning to occur. If reinforcement does not accompany the practice or experience, the behavior will eventually disappear.

From this discussion, we can conclude that learning is the acquisition of knowledge, and performance is the translation of knowledge into practice. The primary effect of reinforcement is to strengthen and intensify certain aspects of ensuing behavior. Behavior that has become highly differentiated (shaped) can be understood and accounted for only in terms of the history of reinforcement of that behavior (Morse, 1966). Reinforcement generates a reproducible behavior process in time. A response occurs and is followed by a reinforcer, and further responses occur with a characteristic temporal patterning. When a response is reinforced it subsequently occurs more frequently than before it was reinforced. Reinforcement may be assumed to have a characteristic and reproducible effect on a particular behavior, and usually it will enhance and intensify that behavior (Skinner, 1938; 1953).

TWO BASIC LEARNING PROCESSES

Before discussing in any detail exactly how the general laws or principles of reinforcement can be used to predict and influence behavior, we must differentiate between two types of behavior. One kind is known as *voluntary* or *operant* behavior, and the other is known as *reflex* or *respondent* behavior. Respondent behavior takes in all responses of human beings that are *elicited* by special stimulus changes in the environment. An example would be when a person turns a light on in a dark room (stimulus change), his eyes contract (respondent behavior).

Operant behavior includes an even greater amount of human activity. It takes in all the responses of a person that may at some time be said to have an effect upon or do something to the person's outside world (Keller, 1969). Operant behavior *operates* on this world either directly or indirectly. For example, when a person presses the up button at the elevator entrance to "call" the elevator, he is operating on his environment.

The process of learning or acquiring reflex behavior is *different* from the processes of learning or acquiring voluntary behavior. The two basic and distinct learning processes are known as *classical conditioning* and *operant conditioning*. It is from studying these two learning processes that much of our knowledge of individual behavior has emerged.

Classical Conditioning [2]

Pavlov (1902) noticed, while studying the automatic reflexes associated with digestion, that his laboratory dog salivated (unconditioned response) not only when food (unconditioned stimulus) was placed in the dog's mouth, but also when other stimuli were presented before food was placed in the dog's mouth. In other words, by presenting a neutral stimulus (ringing of a bell) every time food was presented to the dog, Pavlov was able to get the dog to salivate to the bell alone.

A stimulus which is not a part of a reflex relationship (the bell in Pavlov's experiment) becomes a *conditioned stimulus* for the response by repeated, temporal pairing with an *unconditioned* stimulus (food) which already elicits the response. This new relationship is known as a conditioned reflex, and the pairing procedure is known as classical conditioning.

While it is important to understand that reflex behavior is conditioned by a different process than is voluntary behavior, classical conditioning principles are of little use to the practicing manager. Most of the behavior that is of interest to society does not fit in the paradigm of reflex behavior (Michael and Meyerson, 1962). Nevertheless, the ability to generalize from one stimulus setting to another is very important in human learning and problem solving, and for this reason, knowledge of the classical conditioning process is important.

Operant Conditioning [3]

The basic distinction between classical and operant conditioning procedures is in terms of the *consequences* of the conditioned response. In classical conditioning, the sequence of events is independent of the subject's behavior. In operant conditioning, consequences (rewards and punishments) are made to occur as a consequence of the subject's response or failure to respond. The distinction between these two methods is shown in Figure 1.

In Figure 1, we see that classical conditioning involves a three stage process. In the diagram, let S refer to *stimulus* and R to *response*. We see that in stage 1, the unconditioned stimulus (food) elicits an unconditioned response (salivation). In stage 2, a neutral stimulus (bell) elicits no known response. However, in stage 3, after the ringing of the bell is repeatedly paired with the presence of food, the bell alone becomes a conditioned stimulus and elicits a conditioned response (salivation). The subject has no control over the unconditioned or conditioned response, but is "at the mercy" of his environment and his past conditioning history.

Note however, that for voluntary behavior, the consequence is dependent on the behavior of the individual in a given stimulus setting. Such behavior can be said to "op-

```
           S (food)    ─────────────────────→  R (salivation)
                                         ↗
           S (bell)    ─────────────────────→  R (none)
```

Classical Conditioning Process

– – – – – – – – (S = stimulus, R = responses, arrow = leads to) – – – – – – – –

(a)

```
           S  ────→  R (voluntary behavior)  ────→  Consequences
```

Operant Conditioning Process

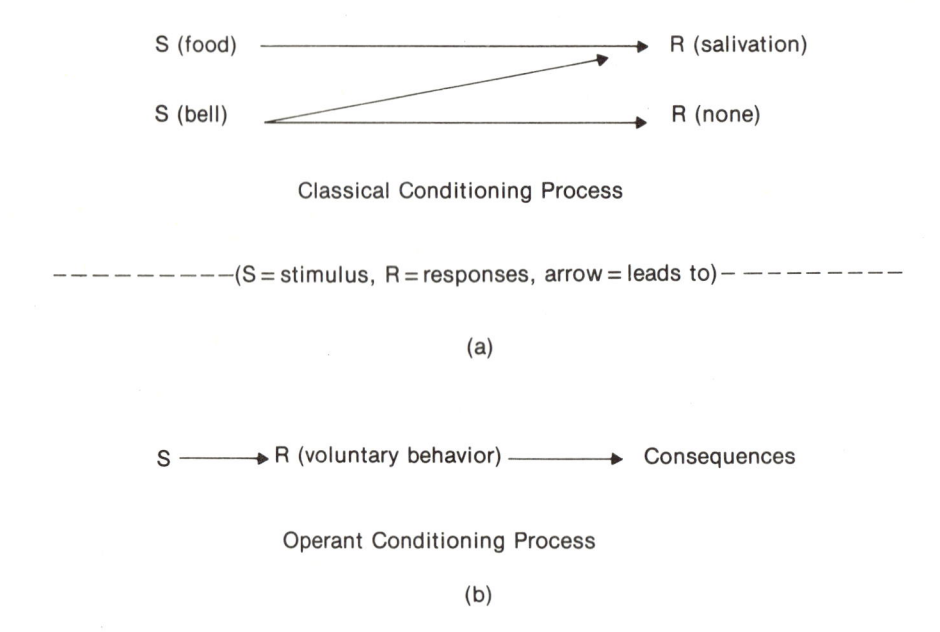

(b)

Figure 1. Classical vs. Operant Conditioning

erate" (Skinner, 1969) on the environment, in contrast to behavior which is "respondent" to prior eliciting stimuli (Michael and Meyerson, 1962). Reinforcement is not given every time the stimulus is presented, but is *only* given when the correct response is made. For example, if an employee taking a work break, puts a penny (R) in the soft drink machine (S), nothing happens (consequence). However, if he puts a quarter (R) in the machine (S), he gets the soft drink (consequence). In other words, the employee's behavior is *instrumental* in determining the consequences which accrue to him.

The interrelationships between the three components of (1) *stimulus* or environment, (2) *response* or performance, and (3) consequences or *reinforcements* are known as the *contingencies* of reinforcement. Skinner (1969) says "The class of responses upon which a reinforcer is *contingent* is called an operant, to suggest the action on the environment followed by reinforcements (p. 7)." Operant conditioning presupposes that human beings explore their environment and act upon it. This behavior, randomly emitted at first, can be constructed as an operant by making a reinforcement contingent on a response. Any stimulus present when an operant is reinforced acquires control in the sense that the rate of response for that individual will be higher when it is present. "Such a stimulus does not act as a *goad;* it does not elicit the response (as was the case in classical conditioning of reflex behavior)[4] in the sense of forcing it to occur. It is simply an essential aspect of the occasion upon which response is made and reinforced (Skinner, 1969: p. 7)."

Therefore, an adequate formulation of the interaction between an individual and his environment must always specify three thing: (1) the occasion upon which a response occurs, (2) the response itself and (3) the reinforcing consequences. Skinner holds that the consequences determine the likelihood that a given operant will be performed in the future. Thus to change behavior, the consequences of the behavior must be changed, i.e. the contingencies must be rearranged (the ways in which the consequences are related to the behavior) (Behling, *et al,* in press). For Skinner, this behavior generated by a given set of contingencies can be accounted for without appealing to hypothetical inner states (e.g. awareness or expectancies). "If a conspicuous stimulus does not have an effect, it is not because the organism has not attended to it or because some central gatekeeper has screened it out, but because the stimulus plays no important role in the prevailing contingencies (Skinner 1969, p. 8)."

Arrangement of the Contingencies or Reinforcement

In order to *understand* and *interpret* behavior, we must look at the interrelationship among the components of the contingencies of behavior. If one expects to influence behavior, he must also be able to manipulate the consequences of the behavior (Skinner, 1969). Haire (1964) reports the importance of being able to manipulate the consequences when he says,

> Indeed, whether he is conscious of it or not, the superior is bound to constantly shaping the behavior of his subordinates by the way in which he utilizes the rewards that are at his disposal, and he will inevitably modify the behavior patterns of his work group thereby. For this reason, it is important to see as clearly as possible what is going on, so that the changes can be planned and chosen in advance, rather than simply accepted after the fact.

After appropriate reinforcers that have sufficient incentive value to maintain stable responsiveness have been chosen, the contingencies between specific performances and reinforcing stimuli must be arranged (Bandura, 1969). Employers intuitively use rewards in their attempt to modify and influence behavior, but their efforts often produce limited results because the methods are used improperly, inconsistently, or inefficiently. In many instances considerable rewards are bestowed upon the workers, but they are not made conditional or contingent on the behavior the manager wishes to promote. Also, "long delays often intervene between the occurrence of the desired behavior and its intended consequences; special privileges, activites, and rewards are generally furnished according to fixed time schedules rather than performance requirements; and in many cases, positive reinforcers are inadvertently made contingent upon the wrong type of behavior (Bandura, 1969, pp. 229-230)."

One of the primary reasons that managers fail to "motivate" workers to perform in the desired manner is due to a lack of understanding of the power of the contingencies of reinforcement over the employee and of the manager's role in arranging these contingencies. The laws or principles for arranging the contingencies are not hard to understand, and if students of behavior grasp them firmly, they are powerful managerial tools which can be used to increase supervisory effectiveness.

As we have said, operant conditioing is the process by which behavior is modified by manipulation of the contingencies of the behavior. To understand how this works, we will first look at various *types* (arrangements) of contingencies, and then at various *schedules* of the contingencies available. Rachlin (1970) described the four basic ways available to the manager of arranging the contingencies—*positive reinforcement, avoidance learning, extinction, and punishment*. The difference among these types of contingencies depends on the consequence which results from the behavioral act. Positive reinforcement and avoidance learning are methods of strengthening *desired* behavior, and extinction and punishment are methods of weakening *undesired* behavior.

Positive reinforcement. "A positive reinforcer is a stimulus which, when added to a situation, strengthens the probability of an operant response (Skinner, 1953, p.73)." The reason it strenghtens the response is explained by Thorndike's (1911) Law of Effect. This law states simply that behavior which appears to lead to a positive consequence tends to be repeated, while behavior which appears to lead to a negative consequence tends not to be repeated. A positive consequence is called a reward.

Reinforcers, either positive or negative, are classified as either; (1) unconditioned or primary reinforcers, or (2) conditioned or secondary reinforcers. Primary reinforcers such as food, water, and sex are of biological importance in that they are innately rewarding and have effects which are independent of past experiences. Secondary reinforcers such as job advancement, praise, recognition, and money derive their effects from a consistent pairing with other reinforcers (i.e., they are conditioned). Secondary reinforcement, therefore, depends on the individual and his past reinforcement history. What is rewarding to one person may not be rewarding to another. Managers should look for a reward system which has maximal reinforcing consequences to the group he is supervising.

Regardless of whether the positive reinforcer is primary or secondary in nature, once it has been determined that the consequence has reward value to the worker, it can be used to increase the worker's performance. So the *first step* in the successful application of reinforcement procedures is to select reinforcers that are sufficiently powerful and durable to "maintain responsiveness while complex patterns of behavior are being established and strengthened" (Bandura, 1969, p. 225).

The *second step* is to design the contingencies in such a way that the reinforcing events are made contingent upon the desired behavior. This is the rule of reinforcement which is most often violated. Rewards must result from performance, and the greater the degree of performance by an employee, the greater should be his reward. Money as a reinforcer will be discussed later, but it should be noted that money is not the only reward available. In fact, for unionized employees, the supervisor has virtually no way to tie money to performance. Nevertheless, other forms of rewards, such as recognition, promotion and job assignments, can be made contingent on good performance. Unless a manager is willing to discriminate between employees based on their level of performance, the effectiveness of his power over the employee is nil.

The arrangement of positive reinforcement contingencies can be pictured as follows:

Stimulus ⟶ Desires Response ⟶ Positive Consequences

$$(S \rightarrow R \rightarrow R^+)$$

The stimulus is the work environment which leads to a response (some level of performance). If this response leads to positive consequences, then the probability of that response being emitted again increases (Law of Effect). Now, if the behavior is undesired, then the supervisor is conditioning or teaching the employee that undesired behavior will lead to a desired reward. It is important therefore that the reward administered be equal to the performance input of the employee. Homans (1950) labels this as the rule of distributive justice and stated that this reciprocal norm applies in both formal (work) and informal (friendship) relationships. In other words, the employee *exchanges* his services for the rewards of the organization. In order to maintain desired performance, it is important that the manager design the reward system so that the level of reward administered is proportionately contingent on the level of performance emitted.

The *third step* is to design the contingencies in such a way that a reliable procedure for eliciting or inducing the desired response patterns is established; otherwise, if they never occur there will be few opportunities to influence the desired behavior through contingent management. If the behavior that a manager wishes to strengthen is already present, and occurs with some frequency, then contingent applications of incentives can, from the outset, increase and maintain the desired performance patterns at a high level.

However, as Bandura (1969) states, "When the initial level of the desired behavior is extremely low, if the criterion for reinforcement is initially set too high, most, if not all, of the person's responses go unrewarded, so that his efforts are gradually extinguished and his motivation diminished (p. 232)."

The nature of the learning process is such that acquiring the new response patterns can be easily established. The principle of operant conditioning says that an operant followed by a positive reinforcement is more likely to occur under similar conditions in the future. Through the process of *generalization,* the more nearly alike the new situation of stimulus is to the original one, the more the old behavior is likely to be emitted in the new environment. For example, if you contract with an electrician to rewire your house, he is able to bring with him enough old behavioral patterns which he generalized to this unfamiliar, but similar, stimulus setting (the house) in order to accomplish the task. He has learned through his past reinforcement history that, when in a new environment, one way to speed up the correct behavior needed to obtain reward is to generalize from similar settings with which he has had experience. Perhaps one reason an employer wants a person with work experience is because the probability of that person emitting the correct behavior is greater and thus the job of managing that person simplified.

Just as generalization is the ability to react to similarities in the environment, *discrimination* is the ability to react to differences in a new environmental setting. Usually when an employee moves from one environment (a job, a city, an office) to another he finds that only certain dimensions of the stimulus conditions change. While all of the responses of the employee in this new setting will not be correct, by skilled use of the procedures of reinforcement currently being discussed, we can bring about the more precise type of stimulus control called discrimination. When we purchase a new car, we do not have to relearn how to drive a car (generalizable stimulus). Instead we need only to learn the difference in the new car and the old car so that we can respond to these differences in order to get reinforced. This procedure is called *discrimination training.* "If in the presence of a stimulus a response is reinforced, and in the absence of this stimulus it is extinguished, the stimulus will control the probability of the response in high degree. Such a stimulus is called a *discriminative stimulus* (Michael and Meyerson, 1962)."

The development of effective discriminative repertoires is important for dealing with many different people on an interpersonal basis. Effective training techniques will allow the supervisor to develop the necessary discriminative repertoires in his new employees (e.g. see Bass and Vaughan, 1966 *Training in Industry: The Management of Learning*).

Using the principles of generalization and discrimination in a well-designed training program allows the manager to accomplish the third goal of eliciting or inducing the desired response patterns. Training is a method of *shaping* desired behavior so that it can be conditioned to come under the control of the reinforcement stimuli. Shaping behavior is necessary when the response to be learned is not currently in the individual's repertoire and when it is a fairly complex behavior. In shaping, we teach a desired response by reinforcing the series of successive steps which lead to the final response. This method is essentially the one your parents used when they first taught you to drive. You were first taught how to adjust the seat and mirror, fasten the seat belt, turn on the lights and windshield wipers, and then how to start the engine. Each time you succesfully completed each stage you were positively reinforced by some comment. You then were allowed to practice driving on back roads and in empty lots. By focusing on one of these aspects at a time and reinforcing proper responses, your parents were able to shape your driving behavior until you reached the final stage of being able to drive. After your behavior was shaped, driving other cars or driving in new territories was accomplished successfully by the process of generalization and discrimination. This same process is used with a management trainee who is rotated from department to department for a period of time until he has "learned the ropes." After his magagerial behavior has been minimally shaped, he is transferred to a managerial position where, using the principles of generalization and discrimination, he is able to adjust to the contingencies of the work environment.

Avoidance Learning. The second type of contingency arrangement available to the manager is called escape, or avoidance learning. Just as with positive reinforcement, this is a method of strengthening desired behavior. A contingency arrangement in which an individual's performance can terminate an already noxious stimulus is called *escape* learning. When behavior can prevent the onset of a noxious stimulus the procedure is called *avoidance learning*. In both cases, the results is the development and maintenance of the desired operant behavior (Michael and Meyerson, 1962).

An example of this kind of control can be easily found in a work environment. Punctuality of employees is often maintained by avoidance learning. The noxious stimulus is criticism by the shop steward or office manager for being late. In order to avoid criticism other employees make a special effort to come to work on time. A supervisor begins criticizing a worker for "goofing off." Other workers may intensify their efforts to escape the criticism of the supervisor.

The arrangement of an escape reinforcement contingency can be diagrammed as follows:

Noxious Stimulus → Desired Response → Removal of Noxious Stimulus
$(S^- \rightarrow R \nrightarrow S^=)$

The distinction between the process of strengthening behavior by means of positive reinforcement techniques and avoidance learning techniques should be noted carefully. In one case, the individual works hard to gain the consequences from the environment which results from good work, and in the second case, the individual works hard to avoid the noxious aspects of the environment itself. In both cases the same behavior is strengthened.

While Skinner (1953) recognizes that avoidance learning techniques can be used to condition desired behavior, he does not advocate their use. Instead a Skinnerian approach to operant conditioning is primarily based on the principles of positive reinforcement.

Extinction. While positive reinforcement and avoidance learning techniques can be used by managers to strenghten desired behavior, extinction and punishment techniques are methods available to managers for reducing undesired behavior. When positive reinforcement for a learned or previously conditioned response is withheld, individuals will continue to exhibit that behavior for an extended period of time. Under repeated nonreinforcement, the behavior decreases and eventually disappears. This decline in response rate as a result of nonrewarded repetition of a task is defined as *extinction*.

The diagram of the arrangement of the contingency of extinction can be shown as follows:

(1) Stimulus → Response → Positive Consequence
$(S \rightarrow R \rightarrow R^+)$
(2) Stimulus → Response → Withholding of Positive Consequences
$(S \rightarrow R \nrightarrow R^+)$
(3) Stimulus → Withholding of Response
$(S \nrightarrow R)$

The behavior which was previously reinforced because (a) it was desired or (b) by poor reinforcement practices is no longer desired. To extinguish this behavior in a naturally recurring situation, response patterns substained by positive reinforcement (Stage 1) are frequently eliminated (Stage 3) by discontinuing the rewards (Stage 2) that ordinarily produce the behavior. This method when combined with a positive reinforcement method is the procedure of behavior modification recommended by Skinner (1953). It leads to the least negative side effects and when the two methods are used together, it allows the employee to get the rewards he desires and allows the organization to eliminate the undesired behavior.

Punishment. A second method of reducing the frequency of undesired behavior is through the use of punishment. Punishment is the most controversial method of behavior modification, and most of the ethical questions about operant methods of control center around this technique. "One of the principal objections to aversive control stems from the widespread belief that internal, and often unconscious, forces are the major determinant of behavior. From this perspective, punishment may temporarily suppress certain expressions, but the underlying impulses retain their strength and press continuously for discharge through alternative actions (Bandura, 1969, p. 292)." While Skinner (1953) discounts the internal state hypothesis, he recommends that extinction rather than punishment be used to decrease the probability of the occurrence of a particular behavior.

Punishment is defined as presenting an aversive or noxious consequence contingent upon a response, or removing a positive consequence contingent upon a response. Based on the Law of Effect, as rewards strengthen behavior, punishment weakens it. This process can be shown as follows:

(1) Stimulus→Undesired→Noxious Consequences
                Behavior   Withholding of Positive
    ($S \rightarrow R \rightarrow R^-$)   Consequence
    ($\rightarrow$ or $\nrightarrow R^+$)

(2) Stimulus $\nrightarrow$ Undesired Behavior
    ($S \nrightarrow R$)

Notice carefully the difference in the withholding of rewards in the punishment process and the withholding of rewards in the extinction process. In the extinction process, we withhold rewards for behavior that has previously been administered the rewards because the behavior was desired. In punishment, we withhold a reward because the behavior is undesired, has never been associated with the reward before, and is in fact a noxious consequence. For example, if your young son began imitating an older neighborhood boy's use of profanity and you thought it was "cute," you might reinforce the behavior by laughing or by calling public attention to it. Soon, the son learns one way to get the recognition he craves is to use profanity—even though he may have no concept of its meaning. As the child reaches an accountable age, you decide that his use of profanity is no longer as cute as it once was. To stop the behavior you can do one of three things: (1) You can withhold the previous recognition you gave the child by ignoring him (extinction), (2) You can give the child a spanking (punishment by noxious consequence), or (3) You can withhold his allowance or refuse to let him watch television (punishment by withholding of positive consequences not previously connected with the act).

It should be noted that method 2 and perhaps method 3 would be considered cruel because of the parent's own inconsistencies. Punishment should rarely be used to extinguish behavior that has previously been reinforced if the person administering the punishment is the same person who previously reinforced the behavior. However, had the parent failed to extinguish the use of profanity prior to sending the child out in society (e.g. school, church), it is possible that the society may punish the child for behavior that the parent is reinforcing or at least tolerating. It is often argued therefore that the failure to use punishment early in the life of a child for socially unacceptable behavior (e.g. stealing, driving at excessive speeds, poor table manners) is more cruel than the punishment itself, simply because the society will withhold rewards or administer adversive consequences for the behavior which the parents should have extinguished.

The use of aversive control is frequently questioned on the assumption that is produces undesirable by-products. In many cases this concern is warranted. Bandura (1969) states that it depends on the circumstances and on the past reinforcement history of the reinforcement agent and the reinforcement target as to whether punishment or extinction should be used. He says:

> Many of the unfavorable effects, however, that are sometimes associated with punishment are not necessarily inherent in the methods themselves but result from the faulty manner in which they are applied. A great deal of human behavior is, in fact, modified and closely regulated by natural aversive contingencies without any ill effects. On the basis of negative consequences people learn to avoid or to protect themselves against hazardous falls, flaming or scalding objects, deafening sounds, and other hurtful stimuli.... In instances where certain activities can have injurious effects, aversive contingencies *must* be socially arranged to ensure survival. Punishment is rarely indicted for ineffectiveness or deleterious side effects when used, for example, to teach young children not to insert metal objects into electrical outlets, not to cross busy thoroughfares.... Certain types of negative sanctions, if applied considerately, can likewise aid in eliminating self-defeating and socially detrimental behaviour without creating any special problems (p. 294).

Rules for Using Operant Conditioning Techniques

Several rules concerning the arrangement of the contingencies of reinforcement should be discussed. While these rules have common sense appeal, the research findings indicate that these rules are often violated by managers when they design control systems.

Rule 1. Don't reward all people the same. In other words, differentiate the rewards based on performance as compared to some defined objective or standard. We know that people compare their own performance to that of their peers to determine how well they are doing ("Social Comparison Theory", Festinger, 1954) and they compare their rewards to the rewards of their peers ("Equity Theory", Adams, 1965) in order to determine how to evaluate their rewards. While some managers seem to think that the fairest system of compensation is one where everyone in the same job classification gets the same pay, employees want differentiation so that they know their importance to the organization. Based on social comparison and equity theory assumptions, it can be argued that managers who reward all people the same are encouraging, at best, only average performance. Behavior of high performance workers is being extinguished (ignored) while the behavior of average performance and poor performance workers is being strengthened by positive reinforcement.

Rule 2. Failure to respond has reinforcing consequences. Managers who find the job of differentiating between workers so unpleasant that they fail to respond must recognize that failure to respond modifies behavior. "Indeed, whether he is conscious of it or not, the superior is bound to be constantly shaping the behavior of his subordinates by the way in which he utilizes the rewards that are at his disposal, and he will inevitably modify the behavior of his work group (Haire, 1964)." Managers must be careful that they examine the performance consequence of their nonaction as well as their action.

Rule 3. Be sure to tell a person what he can do to get reinforced. By making clear the contingencies of reinforcement to the worker, a manager may be actually increasing the individual freedom of the worker. The employee who has a standard against which to measure his job will have a built-in feedback system which allows him to make judgments about his own work. The awarding of the reinforcement in an organization where the worker's goal is specified will be associated with the performance of the worker and not based on the biases of the supervisor. The assumption is that the supervisor rates the employee accurately (see Scott and Hamner, 1973a) and that he then reinforces the employee based on his ratings (see Scott and Hamner, 1973b). If the supervisor fails to rate accurately or administer rewards based on performance, then the stated goals for the worker will lose stimulus control, and the worker will be forced to search for the "true" contingencies, i.e. what behavior should he perform in order to get rewarded (e.g. ingratiation? loyalty? positive attitude?).

Rule 4. Be sure to tell a person what he is doing wrong. As a general rule, very few people find the act of failing rewarding. One assumption of behavior therefore is that a worker wants to be rewarded in a positive manner. A supervisor should never use extinction or punishment as a sole method for modifying behavior, but if used judiciously in conjunction with other techniques designed to promote more effective response options (Rule 3) such combined procedures can hasten the change process. If the supervisor fails to specify why a reward is being withheld, the employee may associate it with past desired behavior instead of the undesired behavior that the supervisor is trying to extinguish. The supervisor then extinguishes good performance while having no affect on the undesired behavior.

Rules 3 and 4, when used in combination, should allow the manager to control behavior in the best interest of reaching organizational goals. At the same time they should give the employee the clarity he needs to see that his own behavior and not the behavior of the supervisor controls his outcomes.

Rule 5. Don't punish in front of others. The reason for this rule is quite simple. The punishment (e.g. reprimand) should be enough to extinguish the undesired behavior. By administering the punishment in front of the work group, the worker is doubly punished in the sense that he is also put out of face (Goffman, 1959). This additional punishment may lead to negative side-effects in three ways. First, the worker whose self-image is damaged may feel that he must retaliate in order to protect himself. Therefore, the supervisor has actually increased undesired responses. Secondly, the work group may misunderstand the reason for the punishment and through "avoidance learning" may modify their own behavior in ways not intended by the supervisor. Third, the work group is also being punished in the sense that observing a member of their team being reprimanded has noxious or aversive properties for most people. This may result in a decrease in the performance of the total work group.

Rule 6. Make the consequences equal to the behavior. In other words be fair. Don't cheat the worker out of his just rewards. If he is a good worker, tell him. Many supervisors find it very difficult to praise an employee. Others find it very difficult to counsel an employee about what he is doing wrong. When a manager fails to use these reinforcement tools, he is actually reducing his effectiveness. When a worker is overrewarded he may feel guilty (Adams, 1965) and based on the principles of reinforcement, the worker's current level of performance is being conditioned. If his performance level is less than others who get the same reward, he has no reason to increase his output. When a worker is underrewarded, he becomes angry with the system (Adams, 1965). His behavior is being extinguished and the company may be forcing the good employee (underrewarded) to seek employment elsewhere while encouraging the poor employee (overrewarded) to stay.

An Argument for Positive Reinforcement

Most workers enter the work place willingly if not eagerly. They have a sense of right and wrong and have been thoroughly conditioned by their parents and by society. By the time they reach adulthood, it can be assumed that they are mature. For these reasons, it is argued here as well as by others (Skinner, 1953; Wiard, 1972), that the only tool needed for worker motivation is the presence or absence of positive reinforcement. In other words, managers do not, as a general rule, need to use avoidance learning or punishment techniques in order to control behavior.

Whyte (1972) says "positive reinforcers generally are more effective than negative reinforcers in the production and maintenance of behavior" (p. 67). Wiard (1972) points out, "There may be cases where the use of punishment has resulted in improved performance, but they are few and far between. The pitfalls of punishment can be encountered with any indirect approach" (p. 16). However, a positive reinforcement program is geared toward the desired results. It emphasizes what needs to be done, rather than what should not be done. A positive reinforcement program is result oriented, rather than process oriented. A well designed program encourages individual growth and freedom, whereas negative approach (avoidance learning and punishment) encourages immaturity in the individual and therefore eventually in the organization itself.

The reason organizations are ineffective according to Skinner (1969) is because they insist on using avoidance learning or punishment techniques, and because they fail to use a positive reinforcement program in an effective manner. He says:

> The contingencies of positive reinforcement arranged by governmental and religious agencies are primitive, and the agencies continue to lean heavily on the puritanical solution. Economic reinforcement might seem to represent an environmental solution, but it is badly programmed and the results are unsatisfactory for both the employer (since not much is done) and the employee (since work is still work). Education and the management of retardates and psychotics are still largely aversive. In short, as we have seen, the most powerful forces bearing on human behavior are not being effectively used. . . . Men are happy in an environment in which active, productive, and creative behavior is reinforced in effective ways (pp. 63-64).

Schedules of Positive Reinforcement

The previous discussion was primarily concerned with methods of arranging the contingencies of reinforcement in order to modify behavior. Two major points were discussed. First, some type of reinforcement is necessary in order to produce a change in behavior. Second, a combined program of positive reinforcement and extinction are more effective for use in organizations than are programs using punishment and/or avoidance learning techniques. The previous discussion thus tells what causes behavior and why it is important information for the manager, but it does not discuss the several important issues dealing with the scheduling or administering of positive reinforcement.

According to Costello and Zalkind (1963), "The speed with which learning takes place and also how lasting its effects will be is determined by the timing of reinforcement" (p. 193). In other words, the effectiveness of reinforcement varies as a function of the schedule of its administration. A reinforcement schedule is a more-or-less formal specification of the occurrence of a reinforcer in relation to the behavioral sequence to be conditioned, and effectiveness of the reinforcer depends as much upon its scheduling as upon any of its other features (magnitude, quality and degree of association with the behavioral act) (Adam and Scott, 1971).

There are many conceivable arrangements of a positive reinforcement schedule which managers can use to reward his workers (Fester and Skinner, 1957). Aldis (1961) identifies two basic types of schedules which have the most promise concerning possible worker motivation. These schedules are *continuous* and *partial reinforcement* schedules.

Continuous reinforcement schedule. Under this schedule, every time the correct operant is emitted by the worker, it is followed by a reinforcer. With this schedule, behavior increases very rapidly but when the reinforcer is removed (extinction) performance decreases rapidly. For this reason it is not recommended for use by the manager over a long period of time. It is also difficult or impossible for a manager to reward the employee continuously for emitting desired behavior. Therefore a manager should generally consider using one or more of the partial reinforcement schedules when he administers both financial and non-financial rewards.

Partial reinforcement schedules. Partial reinforcement, where reinforcement does not occur after every correct operant, leads to slower learning but stronger retention of a response than total or continuous reinforcement. "In other words, *learning is more permanent when we reward correct behavior only part of the time*" (Bass and Vaughan, 1966, p. 20). This factor is extremely relevant to the observed strong resistance to changes in attitudes, values, norms, and the like.

Ferster and Skinner (1957) have described four basic types of partial reinforcement schedules for operant learning situations. They are:

1. *Fixed interval schedule.* Under this schedule a reinforcer is administered only when the desired response occurs after the passage of a specified period of time since the previous reinforcement. Thus a worker paid on a weekly basis would receive a full pay check every Friday, assuming that the worker was performing minimally acceptable behavior. This method offers the least motivation for hard work among employees (Aldis, 1961). The kind of behavior often observed with fixed-interval schedules is a pause after reinforcement and then an increase in rate of responding until a high rate of performance occurs just as the interval is about to end. Suppose the plant manager visits the shipping department each day a approximately 10:00 A.M. This fixed schedule of supervisory recognition will probably cause performance to be at its highest just prior to the plant manager's visit and then performance will probably steadily decline thereafter and not reach its peak again until the next morning's visit.

2. *Variable internal schedule.* Under this schedule, reinforcement is administered at some variable interval of time around some average. This schedule is not recommended for use with a pay plan (Aldis, 1961), but it is an ideal method to use for administering praise, promotions, and supervisory visits. Since the reinforcers are dispensed unpredictably, variable schedules generate higher rates of response and more stable and consistent performance (Bandura, 1969). Suppose our plant manager visits the shipping department on an *average* of once a day but at randomly selected time intervals, i.e., twice on Monday, once on Tuesday, not on Wednesday, not on Thursday, and twice on Friday, all at different times during the day. Performance will be higher and have less fluctuation than under the fixed interval schedule.

3. *Fixed ratio schedule.* Here a reward is delivered only when a fixed number of desired responses take place. This is essentially the piece-work schedule for pay. The response level here is significantly higher than that obtained under any of the interval (or time-based) schedules.

4. *Variable ratio schedule.* Under this schedule, a reward is delivered only after a number of desired responses with the number of desired responses changing from the occurrence of one reinforcer to the next, around an average. Thus a person working on a 15 to 1 vari-

able ratio schedule might receive reinforcement after ten responses, then twenty responses, then fifteen responses, etc., to an average of one reinforcer per fifteen responses. Gambling is an example of a variable ratio reward schedule. Research evidence reveals that of all the variations in scheduling procedures available, this is the most powerful in sustaining behavior (Jablonsky and DeVries, 1972). In industry, this plan would be impossible to use as the only plan for scheduling reinforcement. However, Aldis (1961) suggests how this method could be used to supplement other monetary reward schedules:

Take the annual Christmas bonus as an example. In many instances, this "surprise" gift has become nothing more than a ritualized annual salary supplement which everybody expects. Therefore, its incentive-building value is largely lost. Now suppose that the total bonus were distributed at irregular intervals throughout the year and in small sums dependent upon the amount of work done. Wouldn't the workers find their urge to work increased? (p. 63).

An important point to remember is that to be effective a schedule should always include the specification of a contingency

TABLE 1. Operant Conditioning Summary*

Arrangement of Reinforcement Contingencies	Schedule of Reinforcement Contingencies	Effect on Behavior When Applied to the Individual	Effect on Behavior When Removed from the Individual
	Continuous Reinforcement	Fastest method to establish new behavior.	Fastest method to extinguish a new behavior.
	Partial Reinforcement	Slowest method to establish a new behavior.	Slowest method to extinguish a new behavior.
	Variable Partial Reinforcement	More consistent response frequencies.	Slower extinction rate.
	Fixed Partial Reinforcement	Less consistent response frequencies.	Faster extinction rate.
Positive Reinforcement		Increased frequency over pre-conditioning level.	Return to pre-conditioning level.
Avoidance Reinforcement			
Punishment		Decreased frequency over pre-conditioning level.	Return to pre-conditioning level.
Extinction			

*Adapted from Behling et al., reprinted with permission of the author from "Present Theories and New Directions in Theories of Work Effort," *Journal Supplement and Abstract Service* of the American Psychological Corporation.

between the behavior desired and the occurrence of a reinforcer. In many cases it may be necessary to use each of the various schedules for administering rewards—for example, base pay on a fixed interval schedule, promotions and raises on a variable interval schedule, recognition of above average performance with a piece-rate plan (fixed ratio) and supplementary bonuses on a variable ratio schedule. The effect of each of the types of reinforcement schedules and the various methods of arranging reinforcement contingencies on worker performance is summarized in Table 1.

The necessity for arranging appropriate reinforcement contingencies is dramatically illustrated by several studies in which rewards were shifted from a response-contingent (ratio) to a time-contingent basis (interval). During the period in which rewards were made conditional upon occurrence of the desired behavior, the appropriate response patterns were exhibited at a consistently high level. When the same rewards were given based on time and independent of the worker's behavior, there was a marked drop in the desired behavior. The reinstatement of the performance-contingent reward schedule promptly restored the high level of responsiveness (Lovaas, Berberich, Perloff, and Schaeffer, 1966; Baer, Peterson, and Sherman, 1967). Similar declines in performance were obtained when workers were provided rewards in advance without performance requirements (Ayllen and Azrin, 1965; Bandura and Perloff, 1967).

Aldis (1961) encourages businessmen to recognize the importance of a positive reinforcement program. He also says that experimentation with various schedules of positive reinforcement is the key to reducing job boredom and increasing worker satisfaction. He concludes:

> Most of us fully realize that a large proportion of all workers hold jobs that are boring and repetitive and that these employees are motivated to work not by positive rewards but by various oblique forms of threat. . . . The challenge is to motivate men by positive rewards rather than by negative punishments or threats of punishments. . . Businessmen should recognize how much their conventional wage and salary systems essentially rely on negative reinforcement.
>
> Thus the promise of newer methods of wage payments which rely on more immediate rewards, on piece-rate pay, and greater randomization does not lie only in the increase in productivity that might follow. The greater promise is that such experiments may lead to happier workers as well (p. 63).

NOTES

1. The author is indebted to Professor William E. Scott, Jr., Graduate School of Business, Indiana University for sharing with him his Skinnerian philosophy.

2. Classical conditioning is also known as respondent conditioning and Pavlovian conditioning.

3. Operant conditioning is also known as instrumental conditioning and Skinnerian conditioning.

4. Parentheses added.

5. This is true because the criterion variable is some measure of performance, and performance is directly tied to the reinforcement consequences for the current employees used to derive the selection model.

REFERENCES

Adam, E. E., and W. E. Scott, "The application of behavioral conditioning procedures to the problems of quality control." *Academy of Management Journal*, 1971, 14, 175-193.

Adams, J. S., "Inequity in social exchange," in L. Berkowitz (ed.), *Advances in Experimental Psychology* (Academic Press, 1965) 157-189.

Aldis, O., "Of pigeons and men," *Harvard Business Review*, 1961, Vol. 39, 59-63.

Ayllon, T. and N. H. Azrin, "The measurement and reinforcement of behavior of psychotics," *Journal of the Experimental Analysis of Behavior*, 1965, Vol. 8, 357-383.

Baer, D. M., R. F. Peterson, and J. A. Sherman, "The development of imitation by reinforcing behavioral similarity to a model," *Journal of the Experimental Analysis of Behavior*, 1967, Vol. 10, 405-416.

Bandura, A. and B. Perloff, "The efficacy of self-monitoring reinforcement systems," *Journal of Personality and Social Psychology*, 1967, Vol. 7, 111-116.

Bandura, A., *Principles of Behavior Modification* (New York: Holt, Rinehart and Winston, Inc., 1969).

Bass, B. M. and J. M. Vaughan, *Training in Industry: The Management of Learning* (Belmont, Calif.: Wadsworth Publishing Company, 1966).

Behling, O., C. Schriesheim, and J. Tolliver, "Present theories and new directions in theories of work effort," *Journal Supplement Abstract Service of the American Psychological Corporation*, in press.

Costello, T. W. and S. S. Zalkind, *Psychology in Administration* (Englewood Cliffs, N. J.: Prentice-Hall, Inc., 1963).

Festinger, L., "A theory of social comparison processes," *Human Relations*, 1954, Vol. 7, 117-140.

Ferster, C. B., and B. F. Skinner, *Schedules of Reinforcement* (New York: Appleton-Century-Crofts, 1957).

Goffman, E., *The Presentation of Self in Everyday Life* (New York: Doubleday, 1959).

Haire, Mason, *Psychology in Management*, 2nd ed., (New York: McGraw-Hill, 1964).

Hersey, P. and K. H. Blanchard, "The management of change: Part 2," *Training and Development Journal*, February, 1972, 20-24.

Jablonsky, S. and D. DeVries, "Operant conditioning principles extrapolated to the theory of management," *Organizational Behavior and Human Performance*, 1972, Vol. 7, 340-358.

Keller, F. S., *Learning: Reinforcement Theory* (New York: Random House, 1969).

Lovaas, O. I., J. P. Berberich, B. F. Perloff, and B. Schaeffer, "Acquisition of imitative speech for schizophrenic children," *Science*, 1966, Vol. 151, 705-707.

Luthans, F., *Organizational Behavior* (New York: McGraw-Hill, 1973).

Michael, J. and L. Meyerson, "A behavioral approach to counseling and guidance," *Harvard Educational Review*, 1962, Vol. 32, 382-402.

Morse, W. H., "Intermittent reinforcement," in W. K. Honig, (ed.), *Operant Behavior* (New York: Appleton-Century-Crofts, 1966).

Nord, W. R., "Beyond the teaching machine: The neglected area of operant conditioning in the theory and practice of management," *Organizational Behavior and Human Performance*, 1969, 375-401.

Pavlov, I. P., *The Work of the Digestive Glands*, (Translated by W. H. Thompson), (London: Charles Griffin, 1902).

Rachlin, H., *Modern Behaviorism* (New York: W. H. Freeman and Co., 1970).

Scott, W. E. and L. L. Cummings, *Readings in Organizational Behavior and Human Performance*, Revised Edition (Homewood, Ill.: Irwin, 1973).

Scott, W. E., and W. Clay Hamner, "The effects of order and variance in performance on supervisory ratings of workers," Paper presented at the *45th Annual Meeting*, Midwestern Psychological Association, Chicago, 1973.

Scott, W. E., and W. Clay Hamner, "The effect of order and variance in performance on the rewards given workers by supervisory personnel," mimeo, Indiana University, 1973.

Skinner, B. F., *The Behavior of Organisms* (New York: Appleton-Century, 1938).

Skinner, B. F., *Science and Human Behavior* (New York: The Macmillan Company, 1953).

Skinner, B. F., *Contingencies of Reinforcement* (New York: Appleton-Century-Crofts, 1969).

Thorndike, E. L., *Animal Intelligence* (New York: Macmillan, 1911).

Wiard, H., "Why manage behavior? A case for positive reinforcement," *Human Resource Management*, Summer, 1972, 15-20.

Whyte, W. F., "Skinnerian theory in organizations," *Psychology Today*, April, 1972, 67-68, 96, 98, 100.

ON THE FOLLY OF REWARDING A, WHILE HOPING FOR B

Steven Kerr

Whether dealing with monkeys, rats, or human beings, it is hardly controversial to state that most organisms seek information concerning what activities are rewarded, and then seek to do (or at least pretend to do) those things, often to the virtual exclusion of activities not rewarded. The extent to which this occurs of course will depend on the perceived attractiveness of the rewards offered, but neither operant nor expectancy theorists would quarrel with the essence of this notion.

Nevertheless, numerous examples exist of reward systems that are fouled up in that behaviors which are rewarded are those which the rewarder is trying to *discourage*, while the behavior he desires is not being rewarded at all.

In an effort to understand and explain this phenomenon, this paper presents examples from society, from organizations in general, and from profit making firms in particular. Data from a manufacturing company and information from an insurance firm are examined to demonstrate the consequences of such reward systems for the organizations involved, and possible reasons why such reward systems continue to exist are considered.

SOCIETAL EXAMPLES

Politics

Official goals are "purposely vague and general and do not indicate . . . the host of decisions that must be made among alternative ways of achieving official goals and the priority of multiple goals . . ." (8, p. 66). They usually may be relied on to offend absolutely no one, and in this sense can be considered high acceptance, low quality goals. An example might be "build better schools." Operative goals are higher in quality but lower in acceptance, since they specify where the money will come from, what alternative goals will be ignored, etc.

The American citizenry supposedly wants its candidates for public office to set forth operative goals, making their proposed programs "perfectly clear," specifying sources and uses of funds, etc. However, since operative goals are lower in acceptance, and since aspirants to public office need acceptance (from at least 50.1 percent of the people), most politicians prefer to speak only of official goals, at least until after the election. They of course would agree to speak at the operative level if "punished" for not doing so. The electorate could do this by refusing to support candidates who do not speak at the operative level.

Instead, however, the American voter typically punishes (withholds support from) candidates who frankly discuss where the money will come from, rewards politicians who speak only of official goals, but hopes that candidates (despite the reward system) will discuss the issues operatively. It is

Reprinted by permission of the publisher from *Academy of Management Journal,* Vol. 18 (1975), pp. 769-783.

academic whether it was moral for Nixon, for example, to refuse to discuss his 1968 "secret plan" to end the Vietnam war, his 1972 operative goals concerning the lifting of price controls, the reshuffling of his cabinet, etc. The point is that the reward system made such refusal rational.

It seems worth mentioning that no manuscript can adequately define what is "moral" and what is not. However, examination of costs and benefits, combined with knowledge of what motivates a particular individual, often will suffice to determine what for him is "rational."[1] If the reward system is so designed that it is irrational to be moral, this does not necessarily mean that immorality will result. But is this not asking for trouble?

War

If some oversimplification may be permitted, let it be assumed that the primary goal of the organization (Pentagon, Luftwaffe, or whatever) is to win. Let it be assumed further that the primary goal of most individuals on the front lines is to get home alive. Then there appears to be an important conflict in goals—personally rational behavior by those at the bottom will endanger goal attainment by those at the top.

But not necessarily! It depends on how the reward system is set up. The Vietnam war was indeed a study of disobedience and rebellion, with terms such as "fragging" (killing one's own commanding officer) and "search and evade" becoming part of the military vocabulary. The difference in subordinates' acceptance of authority between World War II and Vietnam is reported to be considerable, and veterans of the Second World War often have been quoted as being outraged at the mutinous actions of many American soldiers in Vietnam.

Consider, however, some critical differences in the reward system in use during the two conflicts. What did the GI in World War II want? To go home. And when did he get to go home? When the war was won! If he disobeyed the orders to clean out the trenches and take the hills, the war would not be won and he would not go home. Furthermore, what were his chances of attaining his goal (getting home alive) if he obeyed the orders compared to his chances if he did not? What is being suggested is that the rational soldier in World War II, *whether patriotic or not*, probably found it expedient to obey.

Consider the reward system in use in Vietnam. What did the man at the bottom want? To go home. And when did he get to go home? When his tour of duty was over! This was the case *whether or not* the war was won. Furthermore, concerning the relative chance of getting home alive by obeying orders compared to the chance if they were disobeyed, it is worth noting that a mutineer in Vietnam was far more likely to be assigned rest and rehabilitation (on the assumption that fatigue was the cause) than he was to suffer any negative consequence.

In his description of the "zone of indifference," Barnard stated that "a person can and will accept a communication as authoritative only when . . . at the time of his decision, he believes it to be compatible with his personal interests as a whole" (1, p. 165). In light of the reward system used in Vietnam, would it not have been personally irrational for some orders to have been obeyed? Was not the military implementing a system which *rewarded* disobedience, while *hoping* that soldiers (despite the reward system) would obey orders?

Medicine

Theoretically, a physician can make either of two types of error, and intuitively one seems as bad as the other. A doctor can pronounce a patient sick when he is actually well, thus causing him needless anxiety and expense, curtailment of enjoyable foods and activities, and even physical danger by subjecting him to needless medication and surgery. Alternately, a doctor can label a sick person well, and thus avoid treating what may be a serious, even fatal ailment. It might be natural to conclude that physicians seek to minimize both types of error.

Such a conclusion would be wrong.[2] It is estimated that numerous Americans are presently afflicted with iatrogenic (physician *caused*) illnesses (9). This occurs when the doctor is approached by someone complaining of a few stray symptoms. The doctor classifies and organizes these symptoms, gives them a name, and obligingly tells the patient what further symptoms may be expected. This information often acts as a self-fulfilling prophecy, with the result that from that day on the patient for all practical purposes is sick.

Why does this happen? Why are physicians so reluctant to sustain a type 2 error (pronouncing a sick person well) that they will tolerate many type 1 errors? Again, a look at the reward system is needed. The punishments for a type 2 error are real: guilt, embarrassment, and the threat of lawsuit and scandal. On the other hand, a type 1 error (labeling a well person sick) "is sometimes seen as sound clinical practice, indicating a healthy conservative approach to medicine" (9, p. 69). Type 1 errors also are likely to generate increased income and a stream of steady customers who, being well in a limited physiological sense, will not embarrass the doctor by dying abruptly.

Fellow physicians and the general public therefore are really *rewarding* type 1 errors and at the same time *hoping* fervently that doctors will try not to make them.

GENERAL ORGANIZATIONAL EXAMPLES

Rehabilitation Centers and Orphanages

In terms of the prime beneficiary classification (2, p. 42) organizations such as these are supposed to exist for the "public-in-contact," that is, clients. The orphanage therefore theoretically is interested in placing as many children as possible in good homes. However, often orphanages surround themselves with so many rules concerning adoption that it is nearly impossible to pry a child out of the place. Orphanages may deny adoption unless the applicants are a married couple, both of the same religion as the child, without history of emotional or vocational instability, with a specified minimum income and a private room for the child, etc.

If the primary goal is to place children in good homes, then the rules ought to constitute means toward that goal. Goal displacement results when these "means become ends-in-themselves that displace the original goals" (2, p. 229).

To some extent these rules are required by law. But the influence of the reward system on the orphanage's management should not be ignored. Consider, for example, that the:

1. Number of children enrolled often is the most important determinant of the size of the allocated budget.

2. Number of children under the director's care also will affect the size of his staff.

3. Total organizational size will determine largely the director's prestige at the annual conventions, in the community, etc.

Therefore, to the extent that staff size, total budget, and personal prestige are valued by the orphanage's executive personnel, it becomes rational for them to make it difficult for children to be adopted. After all, who wants to be the director of the smallest orphanage in the state?

If the reward system errs in the opposite direction, paying off only for placements, extensive goal displacement again is likely to result. A common example of vocational rehabilitation in many states, for example, consists of placing someone in a job for which he has little interest and few qualifications, for two months or so, and then "rehabilitating" him again in another position. Such behavior is quite consistent with the prevailing reward system, which pays off for the number of individuals placed in any position for 60 days or more. Rehabilitation counselors also confess to competing with one another to place relatively skilled clients, sometimes ignoring persons with few skills who would be harder to place. Extensively disabled clients find that counselors often prefer to work with those whose disabilities are less severe.[3]

Universities

Society *hopes* that teachers will not neglect their teaching responsibilities but *rewards* them almost entirely for research and publications. This is most true at the large and prestigious universities. Cliches such as "good research and good teaching go together" notwithstanding, professors often find that they must choose between teaching and research oriented activities when allocating their time. Rewards for good teaching usually are limited to outstanding teacher awards, which are given to only a small percentage of good teachers and which usually bestow little money and fleeting prestige. Punishments for poor teaching also are rare.

Rewards for research and publications, on the other hand, and punishments for failure to accomplish these, are commonly administered by universities at which teachers are employed. Furthermore, publication oriented resumés usually will be well received at other universities, whereas teaching credentials, harder to document and quantify, are much less transferable. Consequently it is rational for university teachers to concentrate on research, even if to the detriment of teaching and at the expense of their students.

By the same token, it is rational for students to act based upon the goal displacement which has occurred within universities concerning what they are rewarded for. If it is assumed that a primary goal of a university is to transfer knowledge from teacher to student, then grades become identifiable as a means toward that goal, serving as motivational, control, and feedback devices to expedite the knowledge transfer. Instead, however, the grades themselves have become much more important for entrance to graduate school, successful employment, tuition refunds, parental respect, etc., than the knowledge or lack of knowledge they are supposed to signify.

It therefore should come as no surprise that information has surfaced in recent years concerning fraternity files for examinations, term paper writing services, organized cheating at the service academies, and the like. Such activities constitute a personally rational response to a reward system which pays off for grades rather than knowledge.

BUSINESS RELATED EXAMPLES

Ecology

Assume that the president of XYZ Corporation is confronted with the following alternatives:

1. Spend $11 million for antipollution equipment to keep from poisoning fish in the river adjacent to the plant; or
2. Do nothing, in violation of the law, and assume a one in ten chance of being caught, with a resultant $1 million fine plus the necessity of buying the equipment.

Under this not unrealistic set of choices it requires no linear program to determine that XYZ Corporation can maximize its probabilities by flouting the law. Add the fact that XYZ's president is probably being rewarded (by creditors, stockholders, and other salient parts of his task environment) according to criteria totally unrelated to the number of fish poisoned, and his probable course of action becomes clear.

Evaluation of Training

It is axiomatic that those who care about a firm's well-being should insist that the organization get fair value for its expenditures. Yet it is commonly known that firms seldom bother to evaluate a new GRID, MBO, job enrichment program, or whatever, to see if the company is getting its money's worth. Why? Certainly it is not because people have not pointed out that this situation exists; numerous practitioner oriented articles are written each year to just this point.

The individuals (whether in personnel, manpower planning, or wherever) who normally would be responsible for conducting such evaluations are the same ones often charged with introducing the change effort in the first place. Having convinced top management to spend the money, they usually are quite animated afterwards in collecting arigorous vignettes and anecdotes about how successful the program was. The last thing many desire is a formal, systematic, and revealing evaluation. Although members of top management may actually *hope* for such systematic evaluation, their reward systems continue to *reward* ignorance in this area. And if the personnel department abdicates its responsibility, who is to step into the breach? The change agent himself? Hardly! He is likely to be too busy collecting anecdotal "evidence" of his own, for use with his next client.

Miscellaneous

Many additional examples could be cited of systems which in fact are rewarding behaviors other than those supposedly desired by the rewarder. A few of these are described briefly below.

Most coaches disdain to discuss individual accomplishments, preferring to speak of teamwork, proper attitude, and a one-for-all spirit. Usually, however, rewards are distributed according to individual performance. The college basketball player who feeds his teammates instead of shooting will not compile impressive scoring statistics and is less likely to be drafted by the pros. The ballplayer who hits to right field to advance the runners will win neither the batting nor home run titles, and will be offered smaller raises. It therefore is rational for players to think of themselves first, and the team second.

In business organizations where rewards are dispensed for unit performance or for individual goals achieved, without regard for overall effectiveness, similar attitudes often are observed. Under most Management by Objectives (MBO) systems, goals in areas where quantification is difficult often go unspecified. The organization therefore often is in a position where it *hopes* for employee effort in the areas of team building, interpersonal relations, creativity, etc., but it formally *rewards* none of these. In cases where promotions and raises are formally tied to MBO, the system itself contains a paradox in that it "asks employees to set challenging, risky goals, only to face smaller paychecks and possibly damaged careers if these goals are not accomplished" (5, p. 40).

It is *hoped* that administrators will pay attention to long run costs and opportunities and will institute programs which will bear fruit later on. However, many organizational reward systems pay off for short run sales and earnings only. Under such circumstances it is personally rational for officials to sacrifice long term growth and profit (by selling off equipment and property, or by stifling research and development) for short term advantages. This probably is most pertinent in the public sector, with the result that many public officials are unwilling to implement programs which will not show benefits by election time.

As a final, clear-cut example of a fouled-up reward system, consider the cost-plus contract or its next of kin, the allocation of next year's budget as a direct function of this year's expenditures. It probably is conceivable that those who award such budgets and contracts really hope for economy and prudence in spending. It is obvious, however, that adopting the proverb "to him who spends shall more be given," rewards not economy, but spending itself.

TWO COMPANIES' EXPERIENCES

A Manufacturing Organization

A midwest manufacturer of industrial goods had been troubled for some time by aspects of its organizational climate it believed dysfunctional. For research purposes, interviews were conducted with many employees and a questionnaire was administered on a companywide basis, including plants and offices in several American and Canadian locations. The company strongly encouraged employee participation in the survey, and made available time and space during the workday for completion of the instrument. All employees in attendance during the day of the survey completed the questionnaire. All instruments were collected directly by the researcher, who personally administered each session. Since no one employed by the firm handled the questionnaires, and since respondent names were not asked for, it seems likely that the pledge of anonymity given was believed.

A modified version of the Expect Approval scale (7) was included as part of the questionnaire. The instrument asked respondents to indicate the degree of approval or disapproval they could expect if they performed each of the described actions. A seven point Likert scale was used, with one indicating that the action would probably bring strong disapproval and seven signifying likely strong approval.

Although normative data for this scale from studies of other organizations are unavailable, it is possible to examine fruitfully the data obtained from this survey in several ways. First, it may be worth noting that the questionnaire data corresponded closely to information gathered through interviews. Furthermore, as can be seen from the results summarized in Table 1, sizable differences between various work units, and between employees at different job levels within the same work unit, were obtained. This suggests that response bias effects (social desirability in particular loomed as a potential concern) are not likely to be severe.

Most importantly, comparisons between scores obtained on the Expect Approval scale and a statement of problems which were the reason for the survey revealed that the same behaviors which managers in each division thought dysfunctional were those which lower level employees claimed were rewarded. As compared to job levels 1 to 8 in Division B (see Table 1), those in Division A claimed a much higher acceptance by management of "conforming" activities. Between 31 and 37 percent of Division A employees at levels 1-8 stated that going along with the majority, agreeing with the boss, and staying on everyone's good side brought approval; only once (level 5-8 responses to one of the three items) did a majority suggest that such actions would generate disapproval.

Furthermore, responses from Division A workers at levels 1-4 indicate that behaviors geared toward risk avoidance were as likely to be rewarded as to be punished. Only at job levels 9 and above was it apparent that the reward system was positively reinforcing behaviors desired by top management. Overall, the same "tendencies toward conservatism and apple-polishing at the lower levels" which divisional management had complained about during the interviews were those claimed by subordinates to be the most rational course of action in light of the existing reward system. Management apparently was not getting the behaviors it was *hoping* for, but it certainly was getting the behaviors it was perceived by subordinates to be *rewarding*.

An Insurance Firm

The Group Health Claims Division of a large eastern insurance company provides another rich illustration of a reward system which reinforces behaviors not desired by top management.

Attempting to measure and reward accuracy in paying surgical claims, the firm systematically keeps track of the number of returned checks and letters of complaint received from policyholders. However, underpayments are likely to provoke cries of outrage from the insured, while overpayments often are accepted in courteous silence. Since it often is impossible to tell from the physician's statement which of two surgical procedures, with different allowable benefits, was performed, and since writing for clarifications will interfere with other standards used by the firm concerning "percentage of claims paid within two days of receipt," the new hire in more than one claims section is soon acquainted with the informal norm: "When in doubt, pay it out!"

TABLE 1
Summary of Two Divisions' Data Relevant to
Conforming and Risk-Avoidance Behaviors
(Extent to Which Subjects Expect Approval)

Dimension	Item	Division and Sample	Total Responses	1, 2, or 3 Disapproval	4	5, 6, or 7 Approval
Risk Avoidance	Making a risky decision based on the best information available at the time, but which turns out wrong.	A, levels 1-4 (lowest)	127	61	25	14
		A, levels 5-8	172	46	31	23
		A, levels 9 and above	17	41	30	30
		B, levels 1-4 (lowest)	31	58	26	16
		B, levels 5-8	19	42	42	16
		B, levels 9 and above	10	50	20	30
	Setting extremely high and challenging standards and goals, and then narrowly failing to make them.	A, levels 1-4	122	47	28	25
		A, levels 5-8	168	33	26	41
		A, levels 9+	17	24	6	70
		B, levels 1-4	31	48	23	29
		B, levels 5-8	18	17	33	50
		B, levels 9+	10	30	0	70

TABLE 1 (Continued)

				Percentage of Workers Responding		
Dimension	Item	Division and Sample	Total Responses	1, 2, or 3 Disapproval	4	5, 6, or 7 Approval
Risk Avoidance (Cont.)	Setting goals which are extremely easy to make and then making them.	A, levels 1-4	124	35	30	35
		A, levels 5-8	171	47	27	26
		A, levels 9+	17	70	24	6
		B, levels 1-4	31	58	26	16
		B, levels 5-8	19	63	16	21
		B, levels 9+	10	80	0	20
Conformity	Being a "yes man" and always agreeing with the boss.	A, levels 1-4	126	46	17	37
		A, levels 5-8	180	54	14	31
		A, levels 9+	17	88	12	0
		B, levels 1-4	32	53	28	19
		B, levels 5-8	19	68	21	11
		B, levels 9+	10	80	10	10
	Always going along with the majority.	A, levels 1-4	125	40	25	35
		A, levels 5-8	173	47	21	32
		A, levels 9+	17	70	12	18
		B, levels 1-4	31	61	23	16
		B, levels 5-8	19	68	11	21
		B, levels 9+	10	80	10	10
	Being careful to stay on the good side of everyone, so that everyone agrees that you are a great guy.	A, levels 1-4	124	45	18	37
		A, levels 5-8	173	45	22	33
		A, levels 9+	17	64	6	30
		B, levels 1-4	31	54	23	23
		B, levels 5-8	19	73	11	16
		B, levels 9+	10	80	10	10

The situation would be even worse were it not for the fact that other features of the firm's reward system tend to neutralize those described. For example, annual "merit" increases are given to all employees, in one of the following three amounts:

1. If the worker is "outstanding" (a select category, into which no more than two employees per section may be placed): 5 percent

2. If the worker is "above average" (normally all workers not "outstanding" are so rated): 4 percent

3. If the worker commits gross acts of negligence and irresponsibility for which he might be discharged in many other companies: 3 percent.

Now, since (a) the difference between the 5 percent theoretically attainable through hard work and the 4 percent attainable merely by living until the review date is small and (b) since insurance firms seldom dispense much of a salary increase in cash (rather, the worker's insurance benefits increase, causing him to be further overinsured), many employees are rather indifferent to the possibility of obtaining the extra one percent reward and therefore tend to ignore the norm concerning indiscriminant payments.

However, most employees are not indifferent to the rule which states that, should absences or latenesses total three or more in any six-month period, the entire 4 or 5 percent due at the next "merit" review must be forfeited. In this sense the firm may be described as *hoping* for performance, while *rewarding* attendance. What it gets, of course, is attendance. (If the absence-lateness rule appears to the reader to be stringent, it really is not. The company counts "times" rather than "days" absent, and a ten-day absence therefore counts the same as one lasting two days. A worker in danger of accumulating a third absence within six months merely has to remain ill (away from work) during his second absence until his first absence is more than six months old. The limiting factor is that at some point his salary ceases, and his sickness benefits take over. This usually is sufficient to get the younger workers to return, but for those with 20 or more years' service, the company provides sickness benefits of 90 percent of normal salary, tax-free! Therefore . . . .)

CAUSES

Extremely diverse instances of systems which reward behavior A although the rewarder apparently hopes for behavior B have been given. These are useful to illustrate the breadth and magnitude of the phenomenon, but the diversity increases the difficulty of determining commonalities and establishing causes. However, four general factors may be pertinent to an explanation of why fouled up reward systems seem to be so prevalent.

Fascination with an "Objective" Criterion

It has been mentioned elsewhere that:

> Most "objective" measures of productivity are objective only in that their subjective elements are a) determined in advance, rather than coming into play at the time of the formal evaluation, and b) well concealed on the rating instrument itself. Thus industrial firms seeking to devise objective rating systems first decide, in an arbitrary manner, what dimensions are to be rated, . . . usually including some items having little to do with organizational effectiveness while excluding others that do. Only then does Personnel Division churn out official-looking documents on which all dimensions chosen to be rated are assigned point values, categories, or whatever (6, p. 92).

Nonetheless, many individuals seek to establish simple, quantifiable standards against which to measure and reward performance. Such efforts may be successful in highly predictable areas within an organization, but are likely to cause goal displacement when applied anywhere else. Overconcern with attendance and lateness in the insurance firm and with number of people placed in the vocational rehabilitation division may have been largely responsible for the problems described in those organizations.

Overemphasis on Highly Visible Behaviors

Difficulties often stem from the fact that some parts of the task are highly visible while other parts are not. For example, publications are easier to demonstrate than teaching, and scoring baskets and hitting home runs are more readily observable than feeding teammates and advancing base runners. Similarly, the adverse consequences of pronouncing a sick person well are more visible than those sustained by labeling a well person sick. Team-building and creativity are other examples of behaviors which may not be rewarded simply because they are hard to observe.

Hypocrisy

In some of the instances described the rewarder may have been getting the desired behavior, notwithstanding claims that the behavior was not desired. This may be true, for example, of management's attitude toward apple-polishing in the manufacturing firm (a behavior which subordinates felt was rewarded, despite management's avowed dislike of the practice). This also may explain politicians' unwillingness to revise the penalties for disobedience of ecology laws, and the failure of top management to devise reward systems which would cause systematic evaluation of training and development programs.

Emphasis on Morality or Equity Rather than Efficiency

Sometimes consideration of other factors prevents the establishment of a system which rewards behaviors desired by the rewarder. The felt obligation of many Americans to vote for one candidate or another, for example, may impair their ability to withhold support from politicians who refuse to discuss the issues. Similarly, the concern for spreading the risks and costs of wartime military service may outweigh the advantage to be obtained by committing personnel to combat until the war is over.

It should be noted that only with respect to the first two causes are reward systems really paying off for other than desired behaviors. In the case of the third and fourth causes the system *is* rewarding behaviors desired by the rewarder, and the systems are fouled up only from the standpoints of those who believe the rewarder's public statements (cause 3), or those who seek to maximize efficiency rather than other outcomes (cause 4).

CONCLUSIONS

Modern organization theory requires a recognition that the members of organizations and society possess divergent goals and motives. It therefore is unlikely that managers and their subordinates will seek the same outcomes. Three possible remedies for this potential problem are suggested.

Selection

It is theoretically possible for organizations to employ only those individuals whose goals and motives are wholly consonant with those of management. In such cases the same behaviors judged by subordinates to be rational would be perceived by management as desirable. State-of-the-art reviews of selection techniques, however, provide scant grounds for hope that such an approach would be successful (for example, see 12).

Training

Another theoretical alternative is for the organization to admit those employees whose goals are not consonant with those of management and then, through training, socialization, or whatever, alter employee goals to make them consonant. However, research on the effectiveness of such training programs, though limited, provides further grounds for pessimism (for example, see 3).

Altering the Reward System

What would have been the result if:

1. Nixon had been assured by his advisors that he could not win reelection except by discussing the issues in detail?

2. Physicians' conduct was subjected to regular examination by review boards for type 1 errors (calling healthy people ill) and to penalties (fines, censure, etc.) for errors of either type?

3. The President of XYZ Corporation had to choose between (a) spending $11 million dollars for antipollution equipment, and (b) incurring a fifty-fifty chance of going to jail for five years?

Managers who complain that their workers are not motivated might do well to consider the possibility that they have installed reward systems which are paying off for behaviors other than those they are seeking. This, in part, is what happened in Vietnam, and this is what regularly frustrates societal efforts to bring about honest politicians, civic-minded managers, etc. This certainly is what happened in both the manufacturing and the insurance companies.

A first step for such managers might be to find out what behaviors currently are being rewarded. Perhaps an instrument similar to that used in the manufacturing firm could be useful for this purpose. Chances are excellent that these managers will be surprised by what they find—that their firms are not rewarding what they assume they are. In fact, such undesirable behavior by organizational members as they have observed may be explained largely by the reward systems in use.

This is not to say that all organizational behavior is determined by formal rewards and punishments. Certainly it is true that in the absence of formal reinforcement some soldiers will be patriotic, some presidents will be ecology minded, and some orphanage directors will care about children. The point, however, is that in such cases the rewarder is not *causing* the behaviors desired but is only a fortunate bystander. For an organization to *act* upon its members, the formal reward system should positively reinforce desired behaviors, not constitute an obstacle to be overcome.

It might be wise to underscore the obvious fact that there is nothing really new in what has been said. In both theory and practice these matters have been mentioned before. Thus in many states Good Samaritan laws have been installed to protect doctors who stop to assist a stricken motorist. In states without such laws it is commonplace for doctors to refuse to stop, for fear of involvement in a subsequent lawsuit. In college basketball additional penalties have been instituted against players who foul their opponents deliberately. It has long been argued by Milton Friedman and others that penalties should be altered so as to make it irrational to disobey the ecology laws, and so on.

By altering the reward system the organization escapes the necessity of selecting only desirable people or of trying to alter undesirable ones. In Skinnerian terms (as described in 11, p. 704), "As for responsibility and goodness—as commonly defined—no one . . . would want or need them. They refer to a man's behaving well despite the absence of positive reinforcement that is obviously sufficient to explain it. Where such reinforcement exists, 'no one needs goodness.' "

NOTES

1. In Simon's (10, pp. 76-77) terms, a decision is "subjectively rational" if it maximizes an individ-

ual's valued outcomes so far as his knowledge permits. A decision is "personally rational" if it is oriented toward the individual's goals.

2. In one study (4) of 14,867 films of tuberculosis, 1,216 positive readings turned out to be clinically negative; only 24 negative readings proved clinically active, a ratio of 50 to 1.

3. Personal interviews conducted during 1972-1973.

REFERENCES

1. Barnard, Chester I. *The Functions of the Executive* (Cambridge, Mass.: Harvard University Press, 1964).

2. Blau, Peter M., and W. Richard Scott. *Formal Organizations* (San Francisco: Chandler, 1962).

3. Fiedler, Fred E. "Predicting the Effects of Leadership Training and Experience from the Contingency Model," *Journal of Applied Psychology,* Vol. 56 (1972), 114-119.

4. Garland, L. H. "Studies of the Accuracy of Diagnostic Procedures," *American Journal Roentgenological, Radium Therapy Nuclear Medicine,* Vol. 82 (1959), 25-38.

5. Kerr, Steven. "Some Modifications in MBO as an OD Strategy," *Academy of Management Proceedings*, 1973, pp. 39-42.

6. Kerr, Steven. "What Price Objectivity?" *American Sociologist,* Vol. 8 (1973), 92-93.

7. Litwin, G. H., and R. A. Stringer, Jr. *Motivation and Organizational Climate* (Boston: Harvard University Press, 1968).

8. Perrow, Charles. "The Analysis of Goals in Complex Organizations," in A. Etzioni (Ed.), *Readings on Modern Organizations* (Englewood Cliffs, N. J.: Prentice-Hall, 1969).

9. Scheff, Thomas J. "Decision Rules, Types of Error, and Their Consequences in Medical Diagnosis," in F. Massarik and P. Ratoosh (Eds.), *Mathematical Explorations in Behavioral Science* (Homewood, Ill.: Irwin, 1965).

10. Simon, Herbert A. *Administrative Behavior* (New York: Free Press, 1957).

11. Swanson, G. E. "Review Symposium: Beyond Freedom and Dignity," *American Journal of Sociology,* Vol. 78 (1972), 702-705.

12. Webster, E. *Decision Making in the Employment Interview* (Montreal: Industrial Relations Center, McGill University, 1964).

PERSONALITY VS. ORGANIZATION

Chris Argyris

Approximately every seven years we develop the itch to review the relevant literature and research in personality and organization theory, to compare our own evolving theory and research with those of our peers—an exercise salutary, we trust, in confirmation and also confrontation. We're particularly concerned to measure our own explicit model of man with the complementary or conflicting models advanced by other thinkers. Without an explicit normative model, personality and organization theory (P. and O. theory) tends to settle for a generalized description of behavior as it is observed in existing institutions—at best, a process that embalms the status quo; at worst, a process that exalts it. Current behavior becomes the prescription for future action.

By contrast, I contend that behavioral science research should be normative, that it is the mission of the behavioral scientist to intervene selectively in the organization whenever there seems a reasonable chance of improving the quality of life within the organization without imperiling its viability. Before surveying the P. and O. landscape, however, let's review the basic models of man and formal organization.

FUNDAMENTALS OF MAN AND ORGANIZATION

The following steps indicate how the worlds of man and formal organization have developed:

1. Organizations emerge when the goals they seek to achieve are too complex for any one man. The actions necessary to achieve the goals are divided into units manageable by individuals—the more complex the goals, other things being equal, the more people are required to meet them.

2. Individuals themselves are complex organizations with diverse needs. They contribute constructively to the organization only if, *on balance*, the organization fulfills these needs and their sense of what is just.

3. What are the needs that individuals seek to fulfill? Each expert has his own list and no two lists duplicate priorities. We have tried to bypass this intellectual morass by focusing on some relatively reliable predispositions that remain valid irrespective of the situation. Under any circumstances individuals seek to fulfill these predispositions; at the same time, their exact nature, potency, and the degree to which they must be fulfilled are influenced by the organizational context—for example, the nature of the job. In their attempt to live, to grow in competence, and to achieve self-acceptance, men and women tend to program themselves along the lines of the continua depicted in Figure 1.

Together, these continua represent a developmental logic that people ignore or suppress with difficulty, the degree of difficulty depending on the culture and the context, as well as the individual's interac-

Reprinted by permission of the publisher from *Organizational Dynamics,* Vol. 3, No. 2: Autumn/ 1974, © 1974 by AMACOM, a division of American Management Associations.

tions with the key figures in his or her life. The model assumes that the thrust of this developmental program is from left to right, but nothing is assumed about the location of any given individuals along these continua.

A central theme of P. and O. theory has been the range of differences between individuals and how it is both necessary and possible to arrange a match between the particular set of needs an individual brings to the job situation and the requirements—technical and psychological—of the job itself, as well as the overall organizational climate.

We have written four studies that highlighted an individual's interrelationship with the work context. In each study, a separate analysis was made of each participant that included (1) the predispositions that he or she desired to express, (2) the potency of each predisposition, (3) the inferred probability that each would be expressed, and (4) a final score that indicated the degree to which the individual was able to express his or her predispositions.

A personal expression score enabled us to make specific predictions as to how individuals would react to the organization. We had expected individuals with low scores, for example, to state that they were frustrated and to have poorer attendance records and a higher quit rate—expectations that also showed how individual differences in predispositions were differentially rewarded in different types of departments. Bank employees with a need to distrust and control others, for example, instinctively opted for positions in the internal audit department of the bank.

So much for the model of man. Now to organizations, which have a life of their own, in the sense that they have goals that unfortunately may be independent of or antagonistic to individual needs. The next step was to determine if there was a genetic logic according to which organizations were programmed.

Observation and reading combined to suggest that most organizations had pyramided structures of different sizes. The logic behind each of these pyramids—great or small—was first, to centralize information and power at the upper levels of the structure; second, to specialize work. According to this logic, enunciated most clearly by Frederick Winslow Taylor and Max Weber, management should be high on the six organizational activities summarized in Figure 2.

This model assumed that the closer an organization approached the right ends of the continua, the closer it approached the ideal of formal organization. The model assumed nothing, however, about where any given organization would be pinpointed along these continua.

PERSONALITY VS. ORGANIZATION

Given the dimensions of the two models, the possibilities of interaction are inevitable and varied; so is the likelihood of conflict between the needs of individuals and the structured configuration of the formal organization. The nature of the interaction between the individual and the organization and the probability of conflict vary according to the conditions depicted in Figure 3.

From this model, we can hypothesize that the more the organization approaches the model of the formal organization, the more individuals will be forced to behave at the infant ends of the continua. What if—still operating at the level of an intellectual exercise—the individuals aspired toward the adult end of the continua? What would the consequences be? Wherever there is an incongruence between the needs of individuals and the requirements of a formal organization, individuals will tend to experience frustration, psychological failure, short-time perspective, and conflict.

What factors determine the extent of the incongruence? The chief factors are: first, the lower the employee is positioned in the hierarchy, the less control he has over his

Infants begin as	Adults strive toward
(1) being dependent and submissive to parents (or other significant adult)	(1) relative independence, autonomy, relative control over their immediate world
(2) having few abilities	(2) developing many abilities
(3) having skin-surfaced or shallow abilities	(3) developing a few abilities in depth
(4) having a short time perspective	(4) developing a longer time perspective

Figure 1. Developmental Continua

	Designing specialized and fractionalized work	
low	Designing production rates and controlling speed of work	high
low	Giving orders	high
low	Evaluating performance	high
low	Rewarding and punishing	high
low	Perpetuating membership	high
low		high

Figure 2. Continua of Organizational Activities

working conditions and the less he is able to employ his abilities; second, the more directive the leadership, the more dependent the employee; and last, the more unilateral the managerial controls, the more dependent the employee will feel.

We have said that individuals find these needs difficult to ignore or suppress, and if they are suppressed, frustration and conflict result. These feelings, in turn, are experienced in several ways:

The employee fights the organization and tries to gain more control—for example, he may join a union.

The employee leaves the organization, temporarily or permanently.

The employee leaves it psychologically, becoming a half-worker, uninvolved, apathetic, indifferent.

The employee downgrades the intrinsic importance of work and substitutes higher pay as the reward for meaningless work. Barnard observed almost 40 years ago that organizations emphasized financial satisfactions because they were the easiest to provide. He had a point—then and now.

We want to emphasize several aspects about these propositions. The personality model provides the base for predictions as to the impact of any organizational variable upon the individual, such as organizational structure, job content, leadership style, group norms, and so on. The literature has concentrated on employee frustration expressed in fighting the organization, because it's the commonest form of response, but we shouldn't ignore the other three responses.

In a study of two organizations in which technology, job content, leadership, and managerial controls confined lower-skilled employees to the infancy end of the continua, their response was condition three—no union, almost no turnover or absenteeism, but also apathy and indifference.

Last, we believe that the model holds regardless of differences in culture and political

If the individual aspired toward	And the organization (through its jobs, technology, controls, leadership, and so forth) required that the individual aspire toward
(1) adulthood dimensions (2) infacy dimension (3) adulthood dimension (4) infancy dimension	(1) infancy dimensions (2) adulthood dimensions (3) adulthood dimensions (4) Infancy dimensions

Figure 3. Conditions of Interaction

ideology. The fundamental relationships between individuals and organizations are the same in the United States, England, Sweden, Yugoslavia, Russia, or Cuba, a drastic statement but, we think, a true one.

RESEARCH THAT TESTS THE MODEL

Several studies in the past six years designed specifically to test the validity of the model all bore it out, to a greater or lesser extent. One study involved a questionnaire that measured self-expression as defined by our model. In a random sample of 332 U.S. salaried managers, hourly-paid workers, and self-employed businessmen, it was found that the lower the self-actualization, the more likely employees were to exhibit the following behavior: To day-dream, to have aggressive feelings toward their superiors, to have aggressive feelings toward their co-workers, to restrict output or make avoidable errors, to postpone difficult tasks or decisions, to emphasize money as the reward for service, and to be dissatisfied with their current jobs and think about another job.

A study in a different culture—Brazil—dealt with 189 employees in 13 banks. It revealed that 86 percent of the employees registered a discrepancy between their own felt needs and the formal goals of the organization. All agreed that the organizational goals were important, but only the top managers felt an absence of conflict between their own needs and the goals of the organization.

A second U.S. study involving 329 respondents—104 businessmen, 105 managers, and 120 workers—confirmed the model, but not in most cases to a degree that was statistically significant. On balance, however, the respondents supported the proposition that employees who perceive their work situations as highly bureaucratic feel more isolated, alienated, and powerless.

RESEARCH THAT SUPPORTS THE MODEL

Additional studies with no formal relationship to the model nevertheless tend to underwrite it. A national sample of 1,533 employees in 1972, for example, showed that among all age groups interesting work was more important than money in providing job satisfaction.

Bertil Gardell, a Swedish psychologist, examined four plants in mass production and process industries, seeking to relate production technology to alienation and mental health. Among his findings were these:

The more skilled the task and the more control the individual feels over how he performs it, the more independence and the less stress he experiences.

There is a big discrepancy between people as to which jobs they deem interesting; some employees, for example, describe jobs with low discretion as interesting—this is a contradiction of our model, but they account for only 8 percent of the employees surveyed.

Income is not a factor in determining alienation. A high-income employee with little control over his job feels just as alienated as the man laboring for a pittance.

Gardell concluded:

> Severe restrictions in worker freedom and control and in skill level required are found to be related to increased work alienation and lowered level of mental health even after control is made for age, sex, income, type of leadership, and satisfaction with pay. The relation between task organization and mental health is valid, however, only after allowance is made for work alienation. In both industries certain people regard jobs of low discretion and skill level as interesting and free from constraint, but these groups amount to only 8 percent in each industry and are strongly overrepresented as to workers about 50 years of age.
>
> Within the mass-production industry, restrictions in discretion and skill level are found to go together with increased feelings of psychological stress and social isolation. People working under piece rate systems—compared with hourly paid workers—find their work more monotonous, constrained, and socially isolating, as well as having lower social status. . . .
>
> High self-determination and job involvement are found to be related to high demands for increased worker influence on work and company decisions in the process industries, while in the mass production industries demand for increased worker influence is greatest among those who feel their work to be monotonous and constrained. Perceptions of strong worker influence by collective arrangements are accompanied by increased demands for individual decision-power as well as increased job satisfaction and decreased alienation.

A batch of studies reaffirmed the relationship between job specialization and feelings of powerlessness on the job and of frustration and alienation. One that compared craftsmen, monitors, and assemblers found that job satisfaction varied dramatically according to the degree of specialization: Job satisfaction was lowest among the assemblers—14 percent; next were the monitors—52 percent; and last were the craftsmen—87 percent. The same study found a strong relationship between job specialization and powerlessness on the job. Thus, 93 percent of the assemblers and 57 percent of the monitors, but only 19 percent of the craftsmen, experienced a lack of freedom and control.

Still other studies related job levels to the degree of dissatisfaction with the jobs. A comparison of 15 managers with 26 supervisors and 44 workers showed that the degree of satisfaction paralleled their position in the hierarchy, with managers the most satisfied and workers the least satisfied.

Frederick Herzberg reported a study of 2,665 Leningrad workers under 30 that again correlated job level with job satisfaction. Researchers who have concentrated on the higher levels of the organization typically have found a systematic tendency—the higher the positions held by the individuals in the organization, the more positive their attitudes tended to be.

An unusual study by Allan Wicker compared undermanned situations in which participants assumed more responsibility and performed larger tasks with overmanned situations in which the tasks were small and the responsibilities minute. Not surprisingly, in the overmanned situations employees reported less meaningful tasks and less sense of responsibility.

Can we reduce powerlessness at work, a factor closely linked to job alienation? One suggestive article points up three possibilities: Employees should allocate their own tasks; crews should be allowed to select themselves through sociometric procedures; the members of the group should select the group leaders.

Finally, research throws light on the question of whether time is the great reconciler. How long do dissatisfaction and frustration with the job persist? The answer appears to be—indefinitely. An interesting comparison of an old and a new assembly plant found that after 14 years the presumably acclimated employees were more dissatisfied and less involved with the product and the company than the new employees. Familiarity breeds frustration, alienation, and contempt.

RESEARCH RESULTS EXPLAINED BY THE MODEL

If employees are predisposed toward greater autonomy and formal organizations are designed to minimize autonomy, at least at the lower levels, we would expect to find a significant correlation between job status and job satisfaction—the lower the job, the less the job satisfaction. This has been found in a number of studies. Harold Wilensky, for example, reported in one of his studies the proportion of satisfied employees ranged from 90 percent for professors and mathematicians to 16 percent for unskilled auto workers. Furthermore, he found that the percentage of people who would go into similar work if they could start over again varied systematically with the degree of autonomy, control, and the chance to use their abilities that they experienced in their current jobs.

Several studies focused on the relationship between control and job satisfaction. An analysis of 200 geographically separate systems that were parts of larger organizations—for example, automotive dealers, clerical operations, manufacturing plants, and power plants in the same company—revealed that the greatest discrepancy between actual and ideal control occurred at the level of the rank-and-file employee. Ninety-nine percent of the work groups wanted more control over their immediate work area. Still another study found that employees became more dissatisfied after moving to a new, more efficient plant because of the reduction of their control over work. These studies were in the United States. Similar research in Yugoslavia and Norway further buttressed the point that employees want to enlarge the degree of their control over their immediate work world.

What about the impact of control upon turnover? The logic of the model leads us to predict that employees would be more likely to quit an organization when they experienced too much control by the organization or its representatives. Once again, research supports the hypothesis. One study found that the authoritarian foreman was a major factor in labor turnover; a second showed that there was a close relationship between the supervisor's inequitable treatment—he could not be influenced, did not support his subordinates, and did not attempt to redress employee grievances—and the turnover rate. Employees, in short, fled from unfair treatment.

One assemblage of studies would appear at first glance to contradict the model. We refer to those studies that show that lower-skilled workers appear to be more interested in how much money they make than they are in how interesting their jobs are. As John Goldthorpe and others demonstrate, however, they are merely being realists. Goldthorpe, in particular, points out repeatedly and documents in detail the fact that workers do desire intrinsically satisfying jobs, but find such aspirations to be unrealistic. In the long run, however great the reluctance and the pain, they adapt.

His research dealt with British workers but a number of studies in the United States replicate his findings. As you move up the job hierarchy, employees consistently assign a higher value to job characteristics that potentially fulfill growth needs. Medium- and high-status white-collar workers, for example, placed primary emphasis on work-content factors as a source of job satisfaction, while low-status white-collar workers and blue-collar workers tended to play them down. As our model would predict, employees seek out job satisfactions they feel are second rate, because higher-level satisfactions are unattainable—certainly in their current jobs.

In summary, this research demonstrates first, that the overall impact of the formal organization on the individual is to decrease his control over his immediate work area, decrease his chance to use his abilities, and increase his dependence and submissiveness; second, that to the extent to which the individual seeks to be autonomous and function as an adult he adapts by reactions ranging from withdrawal and noninterest, to aggression, or perhaps to the substitution of instrumental money rewards for intrinsic rewards. The weight of the deprivations and the degree of adaptation increase as we descend the hierarchy. Formal organizations, alas, are unintentionally designed to discourage the autonomous and involved worker.

JOB ENLARGEMENT OR ENRICHMENT

Job enlargement in the true sense, not the multiplication of meaningless tasks, but quite literally the enrichment of the job either by adding tasks that provide intrinsic satisfactions or increasing the worker's control over the tasks he already performs, obviously conforms to our models. And we would expect that employees whose jobs were enriched would be more satisfied with their jobs and less likely to manifest their dissatisfaction in ways that undermine the organization. Looking at the other side of the coin, we also would expect that more positive attitudes would be accompanied by increased productivity.

And we would not be disappointed. No fewer than eight studies testify that designing jobs that permit more self-regulation, self-evaluation, self-adjustment, and participation in goal-setting both improved attitudes and increased productivity.

Of particular importance is a study by Hackman and Lawler that correlated the core dimensions of jobs—variety, autonomy, task identity, and feedback—with motivation, satisfaction, performance, and attendance. The principal findings of their study are these:

The higher the jobs are on core dimensions, the higher the employees are rated by their supervisors as doing better quality work and being more effective performers.

When jobs rank high on the core dimensions, employees report feeling more intrinsically motivated to perform well.

Core dimensions are strongly and positively related to job satisfaction and involvement.

The job satisfaction items that strongly correlate with the job core dimension are related to control over one's own work, feeling of worthwhile accomplishment, and self-esteem.

The strength of the relationships described above increases with those employees who seek to meet higher-order needs. This finding is significant because research seldom examines individual differences in this way.

Hackman and Lawler differentiate between horizontal enlargement—increasing the number of things an employee does—and vertical enlargement—increasing the degree to which an employee is responsible for making most major decisions about his work. They would argue and we would concur that a combination of both types of enlargement—what we have earlier called role enlargement—is optimal.

What about practice? The concept of job enrichment isn't new. A study of IBM published in 1948 included an assessment of job enrichment and its benefits.

We would expect a concept so fulfilling, so helpful in meeting the goals of both the employee and the organization to be widely adopted. And we would be disappointed. A recent survey of 300 of the top 1,000 *Fortune* industrials showed that only 4 percent had made any formal, systematic attempt to enrich jobs. And even they had enriched only a very small percentage of their total jobs.

What accounts for the lag in adopting job enrichment? Two factors seem to be at work and to reinforce each other. First, most managements are convinced that job enrichment doesn't pay off economically. This belief, in turn, leads them to exhibit signs of the ostrich syndrome—they ignore the accumulating body of evidence as to the substantial psychic dividends that employees derive from job enrichment.

Let me quote from just two of the voluminious research studies that demonstrate the efficiency of job enrichment. The first is the ambitious and significant attempt by the Gaines dog food division of General Foods to design an entire plant using horizontal and vertical enlargement of work. The key features of the design are the following:

1. Autonomous work groups that develop their own production schedules, manage production problems, screen and select new members, maintain self-policing activities, and decide questions such as who gets time off and who fills which work station.

2. Integrated support functions. Each work team performs its own maintenance, quality control, and industrial engineering functions—plus challenging job assignments.

3. Job mobility and rewards for learning. People are paid not on the basis of the job they are doing, but of the basis of the number of jobs that they are prepared to do.

4. Self-government for the plant community.

The transition from a work environment on the infant ends of our continua to the adult ends was not easy for the people involved. Drastic change never is, even when the participants benefit from the change. The results to date, however, are impressive. A similar plant, organized along traditional lines, would require 110 employees; this one was manned by 70. The plant has met or exceeded production goals. Employees reported greater opportunities for learning and self-actualization. And team leaders and plant managers were more involved in community affairs than foremen and managers of comparable plants.

A second significant experiment in job enlargement is taking place at Volvo's new auto assembly plant in Kalmar, Sweden. Volvo faced serious problems—wildcat strikes, absenteeism, and turnover that were getting out of hand. Turnover in the old car assembly plant was over 40 percent annually. Absenteeism was running 20 to 25 percent. Now, assembly has been divided among teams of 15 to 25 workers, who will decide how to distribute the job of car assembly among themselves. Each team determines its own work pace, subject to meeting production standards that are set for them. Each team selects its own boss, and deselects him if it's unhappy with him.

The new plant cost approximately 10 percent more than it would have if it had been constructed along traditional lines. Will the benefits justify the extra expense? Time alone will tell—the plant has been on stream for only a matter of months—but Pehr Gyllenhammar, the managing director of Volvo, hopes that it will realize both his economic and social objectives: "A way must be found to create a workplace that meets the needs of the modern working man for a sense of purpose and satisfaction in his daily work. A way must be found of attaining this goal without an adverse effect on productivity."

THE MODEL OF MAN AND THE DESIGN OF ORGANIZATION

Organizations depend on people. Thus, many organizational variables are designed around an explicit or implicit model of man. Taylor's molecularized jobs, for example, took a one-dimensional view of man and assumed that one could hire a hand; by contrast, the champions of vertical and horizontal job enrichment assume that one hires a whole human being.

Then there are the theorists who take the sociological viewpoint and impoverish their theories by ignoring the psychological element and treating man as a black box.

In each case the complexity of organizational reality leads them into contradictions, the significance of which they either play down or ignore altogether. Crozier, for example, although lacking an explicit model of man, also concluded that his data did not confirm the inhumanity of organizations toward individuals—but how can one define inhumanity without a concept of man? Nevertheless, in the same work he stated that monotonous and repetitive work produces nervous tension in workers, that apathy and social isolation are great, and that work loads produce pressure.

Charles Perrow is a technological determinist who argues that the structure of organization depends on the requirements of the technology. An electronics plant making components should have a different structure from one making inertial guidance system components because of differences in the kind of research required by their technology, unanalyzable versus analyzable, or the number of exceptions it requires—few or many. Perrow's insight, valid but partial, is an inadequate concept to explain the total relationship between man and organization, an inadequacy that Perrow himself is coming to recognize. He concedes that "personality factors can have a great deal of influence upon the relations between coordination and subordinate power," that Robert McNamara, for example, was the key factor in changes in the Defense Department.

To elevate any one as *the* defining characteristic of organizations as Perrow did with technology and make all other characteristics dependent variables only leads to poor theory and inadequate and incomplete explanations of behavior in organizations. An error of equal magnitude is to ignore either the sociological or the psychological view in studying organizations.

We need a synthesis of the sociological and psychological views in studying man and a recognition that there are no fewer than four sets of independent but interacting characteristics that determine the behavior of any organization—structure and technology, leadership and interpersonal relations, administrative controls and regulations, and human controls. The strength of each of the four will vary from organization to organization, vary within different parts of the same organization, and vary over time within the same parts of each organization. However, any major change in an organization's structure is doomed to failure unless major changes take place in all four characteristics.

RATIONAL MAN DECISION THEORISTS

In addition to those with no explicit model of man we have the rational man decision theorists such as Simon, Cyert, and March, whose partial view of man focuses on the concept of man as a finite information processing system striving to be rational and to "satisfice" in his decision making. What this model neglects are the issues stressed by P. and O. theory, such as dependence, submissiveness, the need for psychological success, confirmation, and feelings of essentiality. As we have written elsewhere, "Simon saw management's task as designing organizational structures and mechanisms of organization influence which ingrained into the nervous system of every member what the organization required him to do. Intendedly, rational man was expected to follow authority, but he was also given appropriate and indirect inducements to produce."

Cyert and March retain the basic perspectives of the pyramidal structure—specialization of tasks and centralization of power and information—but they add elements of reality and sophistication. By cranking into their models the concepts of people as members of coalitions politicking against each other for scarce resources and settling for the quasi-reduction of conflicts between them, they were able to predict more accurately how the organization was going to behave, for example, in setting prices.

That the rational man thinkers have indeed helped managers to make more effective decisions in some situations—those in which factors involved corresponded to their model—shouldn't lead us to ignore the more frequent situations in which the rational man theories were either a poor predictive tool or acted themselves to exacerbate the situation. Recent research suggests that managers may resist the management information systems designed by the rational man theorists precisely because they work well—for example, accomplish the desired objective of reducing uncertainty. What accounts for the apparent paradox? Man is not primarily rational, or rather he reacts in response to what we like to call the rationality of feelings. He dislikes being dependent and submissive toward others; he recognizes the increased probability that when management information systems work best he will tend to experience psychological failure. The organization's goals are being met at the expense of his own. Management information systems, in consequence, have become to managers at many levels what time-study people were to the rank and file years ago—an object of fear commingled with hatred and aggression.

Another trend that totally escapes the rational man theorists is the increasing hostility of an increasing number of young people toward the idea that organizations should be able to buy off people to be primarily rational, to submit to the mechanisms of organizational influence, and to suppress their feelings.

A third trend flows from the combined impact of the first two. Given the inability to predict the relationship of emotionality versus rationality in any particular context, and the reaction against rational man and organizational mechanisms of influence, add to these elements the largely unintended support of the status quo, and the use of "satisficing" to rationalize incompetence, and we end up with an interaction of forces that makes change in organizations seem almost impossible.

Hard to follow or accept? The line of argument is as follows:

1. To the degree that man accepts inducements to behave rationally, he acts passively in relation to the way power, information, and work are designed in the organization.

2. Over time, such individuals sterilize their self-actualizing tendencies by any one or a combination of approaches: They suppress them, deny them, or distort them. Eventually, they come to see their legitimate role in the organization—at least, as it bears on the design of power, information, and tasks—as pawns rather than as initiators.

3. A little further down the road, individuals come to view being passive and controlled as good, natural, and necessary. Eventually, they may define responsibility and maturity in these terms.

4. Individuals soon create managerial cultures—some have already done so—in which the discussion of self-actualizing possibilities is viewed as inappropriate.

5. The youth who because of the very success of the system are able to focus more on the self-actualizing needs will attempt to change things. They will come up, however, against facts one to four and end up terribly frustrated.

6. The frustration will tend to lead to regression, with two probable polarized consequences—withdrawal into communes or militancy.

7. Because we know very little about how to integrate self-actualizing activities with rational activities, older people will resent the hostility of youth or look upon their withdrawal as a cop-out.

The last and most important point is that the rational man theory, unlike P. and O. theory, could not predict the single most important trend about public and private organizations—their increasing internal deterioration and lack of effectiveness in producing services or products. As citizen, consumer, and presumably an organization man, you either feel it or you don't. We do feel strongly on this score. And we cite that while 25 years ago 75 percent of the respondents in a national survey felt that public and private organizations performed well, only 25 percent had the same opinion in 1972. How many believe that the percentage would be higher today?

THE CASE FOR NORMATIVE RESEARCH

Most of the research that we have reviewed has been descriptive research that contents itself with describing, understanding, and predicting human behavior within organizations. In our research the emphasis is normative and based upon the potentialities of man. We're interested in studying man in terms of what he is capable of, not merely how he currently behaves with organizations.

Looked at from this normative viewpoint, the most striking fact about most organizations is the limited opportunities they afford most employees to fulfill their potential. We can show empirically that the interpersonal world of most people in ongoing organizations is characterized by much more distrust, conformity, and closedness than trust, individuality, and openness. This world —we call it Pattern A—fits with, if indeed it isn't derived from, the values about effective human behavior endemic in the pyramidal structure or in what Simon calls the mechanisms of organizational influence. Thus, findings based on descriptive research will tend to opt for the status quo.

Moreover, unless we conduct research on new worlds, scholars will tend to use data obtained in the present world as evidence that people do not want to change. Many of them are doing so already. What they forget is how human beings can desire or even contemplate worlds that they have learned from experience to view as unrealistic.

Take a recent publication by Ernest Gross in which he suggests that concepts like individual dignity and self-development probably reflect academic values instead of employee desires, because employees rarely report the need to express such values. The question still remains whether this state of affairs implies that people should accept them and should be trained to adapt to them. Gross appears to think so. He stated that there is little one can do by way of providing opportunities for self-actualization and, if it were possible, providing them would frighten some people. Furthermore, he noted that assembly-line jobs didn't require a worker to demonstrate initiative or to desire variety. "One wants him (the worker) simply to work according to an established pace. Creativity, then, is not always desirable."

Note the logic. Gross starts by asserting that the P. and O. theorists cannot state that one *should* (his italics) provide workers with more challenge or autonomy in accordance with their values because to do so would be to rest their case not on a scientific theory, but on a program for organizations. Then he suggests that no one has proved how harmful dissatisfaction, anxiety, dependency, and conformity are to the individual—which is probably correct. He goes on to argue that these conditions are, to a degree, both unavoidable and helpful, although offering no empirical data to support his assertion. Then he concludes that employees should be educated to live within this world:

Perhaps the most general conclusion we can draw is that since organizations appear to be inevitable. . . a major type of socialization of the young ought to include methods for dealing with the organization. . . . (For example) and important consideration in the preparation of individuals for work should include training for the handling of or adjustment to authority.

At this point Gross has taken a normative position, but one with which I vigorously dissent.

I am very concerned about those who hold that job enrichment may not be necessary because workers in an automobile factory have about the same attitude toward their jobs as do workers in jobs with greater freedom and job variety. But what is the meaning of the response to a question such as "How satisfied would you say you are with your present job?" if the man is working under conditions of relative deprivation? We think that what it means is that workers recognize that they are boxed in, that few opportunities are available to them for better-paid or more interesting work; in consequence, they become satisfied with the jobs they have because the jobs they want are unobtainable. It is frequently observed that the greatest dissatisfaction on a routine job occurs during the first years. After three to five years, the individual adapts to the job and feels satisfied. On the other hand, Neil Herrick in a recent book with the catchy title *Where Have All the Robots Gone?* reported that for the first time, there was a major drop in the number of Americans expressing job satisfaction.

That most jobs as currently designed are routine and provide few opportunities for self-actualization, that the social norms and the political actions that support these norms tend to produce mostly individuals who simultaneously value and fear growth and who strive for security and safety, tell only part of the unfortunate tale of the present industrial conditions. Employees perceive—and the perception is accurate—that few men at the top want to increase their opportunities for self-actualization; even fewer men at the top are competent to do the job.

Make no mistake—employees are conservative on this issue. They have no interest in seeing their physiological and security needs frustrated or denied because their organization collapsed while trying to increase their chances for self-actualization. And the possibility of such a collapse is a real one. Our own experience and the published research combine to suggest that there now does not exist a top-management group so competent in meeting the requirements of the new ethic that they do not lose their competence under stress. With expert help and heavy emphasis on top-management education, one such group was still encountering great difficulties after five years of attempting to raise the quality of life within its organization.

If the ethic, as employees themselves recognize, is so difficult to realize in practice, is the effort worthwhile? Is a game with so many incompetent players worth the playing?

On two counts we feel strongly that it is: First, on normative grounds we feel that social science research has an obligation to help design a better world. Second, we feel that the game is worth the playing because eventually some people and some organizations can be helped to play it effectively. Take the case of job enrichment. Let us assume that all jobs can be enriched. The assumption is probably unrealistic; many jobs in fact, can never be enriched. If we opt for the world that is psychologically richer, however, we will induce employees at every level into developing whatever opportunities for enrichment exist in each job situation.

I believe with Maslow in taking the behavior that characterizes rare peak experiences and making it the behavior toward which all employees should aspire. The skeptic argues that such behavior is so rare that it is useless to try to achieve it. I agree that the behavior is rare, but go on to plead for systematic research that will tell us how the behavior may be made more frequent. Twenty years ago no one had pole-vaulted higher than 16 feet. Yet no one took this as a given. Today the 16-foot mark is broken continually because people refused to view the status quo as the last word and focused on enhancing the potentiality of man. Over time, a similar focus on enhancing the potentiality of man-on-the-job should produce similar breakthroughs.

Problem Solving

In the second section, our interest is in describing the nature of managerial work and how managers solve problems. The earliest attempts to describe managerial work were those associated with Fayol, who proposed that managerial work consisted of various interrelated functions, such as planning, organizing, coordinating, controlling, and commanding. Managers in organizations are concerned with effective performance. Indeed, one can readily appreciate that the functions proposed by Fayol are important concepts. Planning establishes the expectations, organizing implements expectations, and controlling evaluates the performance in terms of the established and implemented expectations.

In the first selection, "The Manager's Job: Folklore and Fact," Mintzberg argues that the notions of Fayol are not meaningful in modern organizations. He bases his arguments on his observations of the chief executives of large consulting firms. He states that managerial work should be described in terms of three role behaviors: interpersonal, informational, and decisional. The interpersonal roles require that the manager act as a figurehead, leader, and liaison. Duties that involve interpersonal roles may sometimes be routine, involving little serious communication and no important decision-making. Nevertheless, they are important to the smooth functioning of an organization. By virtue of his or her interpersonal contacts, the manager is a nerve center of the organizational unit. In order to disseminate this information to his or her subordinates, the manager plays three roles: monitor, disseminator, and spokesman. Information, of course, is not an end in itself; it is a basic input to decision-making. Mintzberg comments that the manager plays a major role in the decision-making system of his or her department. As a decision-maker, the managerial roles include being an entrepreneur, disturbance handler, resource allocator, and negotiator. According to this view, the manager would be described as a facilitator of organizational processes performing numerous roles and activities as part of his work.

In the second article, "Stories Managers Tell: A New Tool for Organization Problem Solving," Mitroff and Kilmann describe the psychological processes that managers use to solve problems. These authors discuss the process of information gathering and decision-making, and conclude that how a manager gathers data about his or her environment and how a decision is reached affects not only the type of decision reached, but the type of organization in which the individual would like to work. Individuals who use their senses to gather information and then apply logical rules and regulations to reach a decision prefer different roles and organizations than do individuals who gather information by intuition and then reach decisions based on their "gut" feelings. The latter type of manager prefers working on fuzzy or ill-defined problems that revolve around the human purposes of organizations. On the other hand, the former tends to be matter-of-fact, works on defined problems and in organizations with rules and regulations, and is concerned with realistic and short-term goals.

THE MANAGER'S JOB: FOLKLORE AND FACT

Henry Mintzberg

If you ask a manager what he does, he will most likely tell you that he plans, organizes, coordinates, and controls. Then watch what he does. Don't be surprised if you can't relate what you see to these four words.

When he is called and told that one of his factories has just burned down, and he advises the caller to see whether temporary arrangements can be made to supply customers through a foreign subsidiary, is he planning, organizing, coordinating, or controlling? How about when he presents a gold watch to a retiring employee? Or when he attends a conference to meet people in the trade? Or on returning from that conference, when he tells one of his employees about an interesting product idea he picked up there?

The fact is that these four words, which have dominated management vocabulary since the French industrialist Henri Fayol first introduced them in 1916, tell us little about what managers actually do. At best, they indicate some vague objectives managers have when they work.

The field of management, so devoted to progress and change, has for more than half a century not seriously addressed *the* basic question: What do managers do? Without a proper answer, how can we teach management? How can we design planning or information systems for managers? How can we improve the practice of management at all?

Our ignorance of the nature of managerial work shows up in various ways in the modern organization—in the boast by the successful manager that he never spent a single day in a management training program; in the turnover of corporate planners who never quite understood what it was the manager wanted; in the computer consoles gathering dust in the back room because the managers never used the fancy on-line MIS some analyst thought they needed. Perhaps most important, our ignorance shows up in the inability of our large public organizations to come to grips with some of their most serious policy problems.

Somehow, in the rush to automate production, to use management science in the functional areas of marketing and finance, and to apply the skills of the behavioral scientist to the problem of worker motivation, the manager—that person in charge of the organization or one of its subunits—has been forgotten.

My intention in this article is simple: to break the reader away from Fayol's words and introduce him to a more supportable, and what I believe to be a more useful, description of managerial work. This description derives from my review and synthesis of the available research on how various managers have spent their time.

In some studies, managers were observed intensively ("shadowed" is the term some of

---

Reprinted by permission of the publishers from *Harvard Business Review,* Vol. 53. (July-August, 1975) pp. 49-61. Copyright © 1975 by the President and Fellows of Harvard College; all rights reserved.

them used); in a number of others, they kept detailed diaries of their activities; in a few studies, their records were analyzed. All kinds of managers were studied—foremen, factory supervisors, staff managers, field sales managers, hospital administrators, presidents of companies and nations, and even street gang leaders. These "managers" worked in the United States, Canada, Sweden, and Great Britain. In the ruled insert on page 86 is a brief review of the major studies that I found most useful in developing this description, including my own study of five American chief executive officers.

A synthesis of these findings paints an interesting picture, one as different from Fayol's classical view as a cubist abstract is from a Renaissance painting. In a sense, this picture will be obvious to anyone who has ever spent a day in a manager's office, either in front of the desk or behind it. Yet, at the same time, this picture may turn out to be revolutionary, in that it throws into doubt so much of the folklore that we have accepted about the manager's work.

I first discuss some of this folklore and contrast it with some of the discoveries of systematic research—the hard facts about how managers spend their time. Then I synthesize these research findings in a description of ten roles that seem to describe the essential content of all managers' jobs. In a concluding section, I discuss a number of implications of this synthesis for those trying to achieve more effective management, both in classrooms and in the business world.

SOME FOLKLORE AND FACTS ABOUT MANAGERIAL WORK

There are four myths about the manager's job that do not bear up under careful scrutiny of the facts.

One

Folklore: The manager is a reflective, systematic planner. The evidence on this issue is overwhelming, but not a shred of it supports this statement.

Fact: Study after study has shown that managers work at an unrelenting pace, that their activities are characterized by brevity, variety, and discontinuity, and that they are strongly oriented to action and dislike reflective activities. Consider this evidence:

Half the activities engaged in by the five chief executives of my study lasted less than nine minutes and only 10% exceeded one hour.[1] A study of 56 U.S. foremen found that they averaged 583 activities per eight-hour shift, an average of 1 every 48 seconds.[2] The work pace for both chief executives and foremen was unrelenting. The chief executives met a steady stream of callers and mail from the moment they arrived in the morning until they left in the evening. Coffee breaks and lunches were inevitably work related, and ever-present subordinates seemed to usurp any free moment.

A diary study of 160 British middle and top managers found that they worked for a half hour or more without interruption only about once every two days.[3]

Of the verbal contacts of the chief executives in my study, 93% were arranged on an ad hoc basis. Only 1% of the executives' time was spent in open-ended observational tours. Only 1 out of 368 verbal contacts was unrelated to a specific issue and could be called general planning. Another researcher finds that "in *not one single case* did a manager report the obtaining of important external information from a general conversation or other undirected personal communication."[4]

No study has found important patterns in the way managers schedule their time. They seem to jump from issue to issue, continually responding to the needs of the moment.

Is this the planner that the classical view describes? Hardly. How, then, can we explain this behavior? The manager is simply responding to the pressures of his job. I found that my chief executives terminated many of their own activities, often leaving meetings before the end, and interrupted their desk work to call in subordinates. One president not only placed his desk so that he could look down a long hallway but also left his door open when he was alone—an invitation for subordinates to come in and interrupt him.

Clearly, these managers wanted to encourage the flow of current information. But more significantly, they seemed to be conditioned by their own work loads. They appreciated the opportunity cost of their own time, and they were continually aware of their ever-present obligations—mail to be answered, callers to attend to, and so on. It seems that no matter what he is doing, the manager is plagued by the possibilities of what he might do and what he must do.

When the manager must plan, he seems to do so implicitly in the context of daily actions, not in some abstract process reserved for two weeks in the organization's mountain retreat. The plans of the chief executives I studied seemed to exist only in their heads—as flexible, but often specific, intentions. The traditional literature notwithstanding, the job of managing does not breed reflective planners; the manager is a real-time responder to stimuli, an individual who is conditioned by his job to prefer live to delayed action.

Two

Folklore: The effective manager has no regular duties to perform. Managers are constantly being told to spend more time planning and delegating, and less time seeing customers and engaging in negotiations. These are not, after all, the true tasks of the manager. To use the popular analogy, the good manager, like the good conductor, carefully orchestrates everything in advance, then sits back to enjoy the fruits of his labor, responding occasionally to an unforeseeable exception.

But here again the pleasant abstraction just does not seem to hold up. We had better take a closer look at those activities managers feel compelled to engage in before we arbitrarily define them away.

Fact: In addition to handling exceptions, managerial work involves performing a number of regular duties, including ritual and ceremony, negotiations, and processing of soft information that links the organization with its environment. Consider some evidence from the research studies:

A study of the work of the presidents of small companies found that they engaged in routine activities because their companies could not afford staff specialists and were so thin on operating personnel that a single absence often required the president to substitute.[5]

One study of field sales managers and another of chief executives suggest that it is a natural part of both jobs to see important customers, assuming the managers wish to keep those customers.[6]

Someone, only half in jest, once described the manager as that person who sees visitors so that everyone else can get his work done. In my study, I found that certain ceremonial duties—meeting visiting dignitaries, giving out gold watches, presiding at Christmas dinners—were an intrinsic part of the chief executive's job.

Studies of managers' information flow suggest that managers play a key role in securing "soft" external information (much of it available only to them because of their status) and in passing it along to their subordinates.

Three

Folklore: The senior manager needs aggregated information, which a formal management information system best provides. Not too long ago, the words *total information system* were everywhere in the management literature. In keeping with the classical view of the manager as that individual perched on the apex of a regulated, hierarchical system, the literature's manager was to receive all his important information from a giant, comprehensive MIS.

But lately, as it has become increasingly evident that these giant MIS systems are not working—that managers are simply not using them—the enthusiasm has waned. A look at how managers actually process information makes the reason quite clear. Managers have five media at their command—documents, telephone calls, scheduled and unscheduled meetings, and observational tours.

Fact: Managers strongly favor the verbal media—namely, telephone calls and meetings. The evidence comes from every single study of managerial work. Consider the following:

In two British studies, managers spent an average of 66% and 80% of their time in verbal (oral) communication.[7] In my study of five American chief executives, the figure was 78%.

These five chief executives treated mail processing as a burden to be dispensed with. One came in Saturday morning to process 142 pieces of mail in just over three hours, to "get rid of all the stuff." This same manager looked at the first piece of "hard" mail he had received all week, a standard cost report, and put it aside with the comment, "I never look at this."

These same five chief executives responded immediately to 2 of the 40 routine reports they received during the five weeks of my study and to four items in the 104 periodicals. They skimmed most of these periodicals in seconds, almost ritualistically. In all, these chief executives of good-sized organizations initiated on their own—that is, not in response to something else—a grand total of 25 pieces of mail during the 25 days I observed them.

An analysis of the mail the executives received reveals an interesting picture—only 13% was of specific and immediate use. So now we have another piece in the puzzle: not much of the mail provides live, current information—the action of a competitor, the mood of a government legislator, or the rating of last night's television show. Yet this is the information that drove the managers, interrupting their meetings and rescheduling their workdays.

Consider another interesting finding. Managers seem to cherish "soft" information, especially gossip, hearsay, and speculation. Why? The reason is its timeliness; today's gossip may be tomorrow's fact. The manager who is not accessible for the telephone call informing him that his biggest customer was seen golfing with his main competitor may read about a dramatic drop in sales in the next quarterly report. But then it's too late.

To assess the value of historical, aggregated, "hard" MIS information, consider two of the manager's prime uses for his information—to identify problems and opportunities[8] and to build his own mental models of the things around him (e.g., how his organization's budget system works, how his customers buy his product, how changes in the economy affect his organization, and so on). Every bit of evidence suggests that the manager identifies decision situations and builds models not with the aggregated abstractions an MIS provides, but with specific tidbits of data.

Consider the words of Richard Neustadt, who studied the information-collecting habits of Presidents Roosevelt, Truman, and Eisenhower:

"It is not information of a general sort that helps a President see personal stakes; not summaries, not surveys, not the *bland amal-*

gams. Rather... it is the odds and ends of *tangible detail* that pieced together in his mind illuminate the underside of issues put before him. To help himself he must reach out as widely as he can for every scrap of fact, opinion, gossip, bearing on his interests and relationships as President. He must become his own director of his own central intelligence."[9]

The manager's emphasis on the verbal media raises two important points:

First, verbal information is stored in the brains of people. Only when people write this information down can it be stored in the files of the organization—whether in metal cabinets or on magnetic tape—and managers apparently do not write down much of what they hear. Thus the strategic data bank of the organization is not in the memory of its computers but in the minds of its managers.

Second, the manager's extensive use of verbal media helps to explain why he is reluctant to delegate tasks. When we note that most of the manager's important information comes in verbal form and is stored in his head, we can well appreciate his reluctance. It is not as if he can hand a dossier over to someone; he must take the time to "dump memory"—to tell that someone all he knows about the subject. But this could take so long that the manager may find it easier to do the task himself. Thus the manager is damned by his own information system to a "dilemma of delegation"—to do too much himself or to delegate to his subordinates with inadequate briefing.

Four

Folklore: Management is, or at least is quickly becoming, a science and a profession. By almost any definitions of *science* and *profession*, this statement is false. Brief observation of any manager will quickly lay to rest the notion that managers practice a science. A science involves the enaction of systematic, analytically determined procedures or programs. If we do not even know what procedures managers use, how can we prescribe them by scientific analysis? And how can we call management a profession if we cannot specify what managers are to learn? For after all, a profession involves "knowledge of some department of learning or science" (*Random House Dictionary*).[10]

Fact: The managers' programs—to schedule time, process information, make decisions, and so on—remain locked deep inside their brains. Thus, to describe these programs, we rely on words like *judgment* and *intuition*, seldom stopping to realize that they are merely labels for our ignorance.

I was struck during my study by the fact that the executives I was observing—all very competent by any standard—are fundamentally indistinguishable from their counterparts of a hundred years ago (or a thousand years ago, for that matter). The information they need differs, but they seek it in the same way—by word of mouth. Their decisions concern modern technology, but the procedures they use to make them are the same as the procedures of the nineteenth-century manager. Even the computer, so important for the specialized work of the organization, has apparently had no influence on the work procedures of general managers. In fact, the manager is in a kind of loop, with increasingly heavy work pressures but no aid forthcoming from management science.

Considering the facts about managerial work, we can see that the manager's job is enormously complicated and difficult. The manager is overburdened with obligations; yet he cannot easily delegate his tasks. As a result, he is driven to overwork and is forced to do many tasks superficially. Brevity, fragmentation, and verbal communication characterize his work. Yet these are the very characteristics of managerial work that have impeded scientific attempts to improve it. As

RESEARCH ON MANAGERIAL WORK

Considering its central importance to every aspect of management, there has been surprisingly little research on the manager's work, and virtually no systematic building of knowledge from one group of studies to another. In seeking to describe managerial work, I conducted my own research and also scanned the literature widely to integrate the findings of studies from many diverse sources with my own. These studies focused on two very different aspects of managerial work. Some were concerned with the characteristics of the work—how long managers work, where, at what pace and with what interruptions, with whom they work, and through what media they communicate. Other studies were more concerned with the essential content of the work—what activities the managers actually carry out and why. Thus, after a meeting, one researcher might note that the manager spent 45 minutes with three government officials in their Washington office, while another might record that he presented his company's stand on some proposed legislation in order to change a regulation.

A few of the studies of managerial work are widely known, but most have remained buried as single journal articles or isolated books. Among the more important ones I cite (with full references in the footnotes) are the following:

Sune Carlson developed the diary method to study the work characteristics of nine Swedish managing directors. Each kept a detailed log of his activities. Carlson's results are reported in his book *Executive Behavior*. A number of British researchers, notably Rosemary Stewart, have subsequently used Carlson's method. In *Managers and Their Jobs,* she describes the study of 160 top and middle managers of British companies during four weeks, with particular attention to the differences in their work.

Leonard Sayles's book *Managerial Behavior* is another important reference. Using a method he refers to as "anthropological," Sayles studied the work content of middle- and lower-level managers in a large U.S. corporation. Sayles moved freely in the company, collecting whatever information struck him as important.

Perhaps the best-known source is *Presidential Power,* in which Richard Neustadt analyzes the power and managerial behavior of Presidents Roosevelt, Truman, and Eisenhower. Neustadt used secondary sources—documents and interviews with other parties—to generate his data.

Robert H. Guest, in *Personnel,* reports on a study of the foreman's working day. Fifty-six U.S. foremen were observed and each of their activities recorded during one eight-hour shift.

Richard C. Hodgson, Daniel J. Levinson, and Abraham Zaleznik studied a team of three top executives of a U.S. hospital. From that study they wrote *The Executive Role Constellation*. These researchers addressed in particular the way in which work and socioemotional roles were divided among the three managers.

William F. Whyte, from his study of a street gang during the Depression, wrote *Street Corner Society*. His findings about the gang's leadership, which George C. Homans analyzed in *The Human Group,* suggest some interesting similarities of job content between street gang leaders and corporate managers.

My own study involved five American CEOs of middle- to large-sized organizations—a consulting firm, a technology company, a hospital, a consumer goods company, and a school system. Using a method called "structural observation," during one intensive week of observation for each executive I recorded various aspects of every piece of mail and every verbal contact. My method was designed to capture data on both work characteristics and job content. In all, I analyzed 890 pieces of incoming and outgoing mail and 368 verbal contacts.

a result, the management scientist has concentrated his efforts on the specialized functions of the organization, where he could more easily analyze the procedures and quantify the relevant information.[11]

But the pressures of the manager's job are becoming worse. Where before he needed only to respond to owners and directors, now he finds that subordinates with democratic norms continually reduce his freedom to issue unexplained orders, and a growing number of outside influences (consumer groups, government agencies, and so on) expect his attention. And the manager has had nowhere to turn for help. The first step in providing the manager with some help is to find out what his job really is.

BACK TO A BASIC DESCRIPTION OF MANAGERIAL WORK

Now let us try to put some of the pieces of this puzzle together. Earlier, I defined the manager as that person in charge of an organization or one of its subunits. Besides chief executive officers, this definition would include vice presidents, bishops, foremen, hockey coaches, and prime ministers. Can all of these people have anything in common? Indeed they can. For an important starting point, all are vested with formal authority over an organizational unit. From formal authority comes status, which leads to various interpersonal relations, and from these comes access to information. Information, in turn, enables the manager to make decisions and strategies for his unit.

The manager's job can be described in terms of various "roles," or organized sets of behaviors identified with a position. My description, shown in Figure 1, comprises ten roles. As we shall see, formal authority gives rise to the three interpersonal roles, which in turn give rise to the three informational roles; these two sets of roles enable the manager to play the four decisional roles.

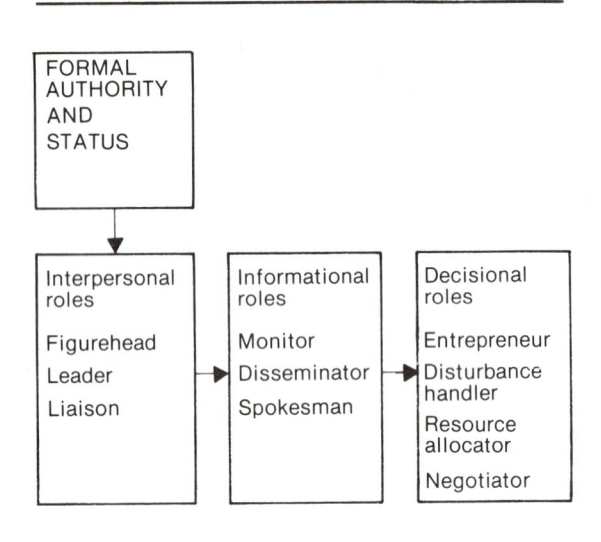

Figure 1. The Manager's Roles

Interpersonal Roles

Three of the manager's roles arise directly from his formal authority and involve basic interpersonal relationships.

1. First is the *figurehead* role. By virtue of his position as head of an organizational unit, every manager must perform some duties of a ceremonial nature. The president greets the touring dignitaries, the foreman attends the wedding of a lathe operator, and the sales manager takes an important customer to lunch.

The chief executives of my study spent 12% of their contact time on ceremonial duties; 17% of their incoming mail dealt with acknowledgments and requests related to their status. For example, a letter to a company president requested free merchandise for a crippled schoolchild; diplomas were put on the desk of the school superintendent for his signature.

Duties that involve interpersonal roles may sometimes be routine, involving little serious communication and no important decision making. Nevertheless, they are important to the smooth functioning of an organization and cannot be ignored by the manager.

2. Because he is in charge of an organizational unit, the manager is responsible for the work of the people of that unit. His actions in this regard constitute the *leader* role. Some of these actions involve leadership directly—for example, in most organizations the manager is normally responsible for hiring and training his own staff.

In addition, there is the indirect exercise of the leader role. Every manager must motivate and encourage his employees, somehow reconciling their individual needs with the goals of the organization. In virtually every contact the manager has with his employees, subordinates seeking leadership clues probe his actions: "Does he approve?" "How would he like the report to turn out?" "Is he more interested in market share than high profits?"

The influence of the manager is most clearly seen in the leader role. Formal authority vests him with great potential power; leadership determines in large part how much of it he will realize.

3. The literature of management has always recognized the leader role, particularly those aspects of it related to motivation. In comparison, until recently it has hardly mentioned the *liaison* role, in which the manager makes contacts outside his vertical chain of command. This is remarkable in light of the finding of virtually every study of managerial work that managers spend as much time with peers and other people outside their units as they do with their own subordinates—and, surprisingly, very little time with their own superiors.

In Rosemary Stewart's diary study, the 160 British middle and top managers spent 47% of their time with peers, 41% of their time with people outside their unit, and only 12% of their time with their superiors. For Robert H. Guest's study of U.S. foremen, the figures were 44%, 46%, and 10%. The chief executives of my study averaged 44% of their contact time with people outside their organizations, 48% with subordinates, and 7% with directors and trustees.

The contacts the five CEOs made were with an incredibly wide range of people: subordinates; clients, business associates, and suppliers; and peers—managers of similar organizations, government and trade organization officials, fellow directors on outside boards, and independents with no relevant organizational affiliations. The chief executives' time with and mail from these groups is shown in Figure 2. Guest's study of foremen shows, likewise, that their contacts were numerous and wide ranging, seldom involving fewer than 25 individuals, and often more than 50.

As we shall see shortly, the manager cultivates such contacts largely to find informa-

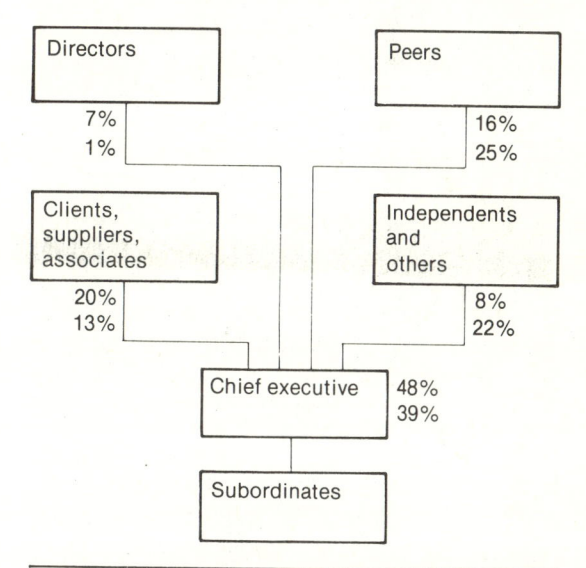

```
   Directors                    Peers
       |                          |
      7%                        16%
      1%                        25%
       |                          |
  Clients,                  Independents
  suppliers,                and
  associates                others
       |                          |
     20%                         8%
     13%                        22%
       \                        /
        _____Chief executive_/
                    |   48%
                    |   39%
              Subordinates
```

Note: The top figure indicates the proportion of total contact time spent with each group and the bottom figure, the proportion of mail from each group.

Figure 2. The Chief Executives' Contacts

tion. In effect, the liaison role is devoted to building up the manager's own external information system—informal, private, verbal, but, nevertheless, effective.

Informational Roles

By virtue of his interpersonal contacts, both with his subordinates and with his network of contacts, the manager emerges as the nerve center of his organizational unit. He may not know everything, but he typically knows more than any member of his staff.

Studies have shown this relationship to hold for all managers, from street gang leaders to U.S. presidents. In *The Human Group,* George C. Homans explains how, because they were at the center of the information flow in their own gangs and were also in close touch with other gang leaders, street gang leaders were better informed than any of their followers.[12] And Richard Neustadt describes the following account from his study of Franklin D. Roosevelt:

"The essence of Roosevelt's technique for information-gathering was competition. 'He would call you in,' one of his aides once told me, 'and he'd ask you to get the story on some complicated business, and you'd come back after a couple of days of hard labor and present the juicy morsel you'd uncovered under a stone somewhere, and *then* you'd find out he knew all about it, along with something else you *didn't* know. Where he got this information from he wouldn't mention, usually, but after he had done this to you once or twice you got damn careful about *your* information.' "[13]

We can see where Roosevelt "got this information" when we consider the relationship between the interpersonal and informational roles. As leader, the manager has formal and easy access to every member of his staff. Hence, as noted earlier, he tends to know more about his own unit than anyone else does. In addition, his liaison contacts expose the manager to external information to which his subordinates often lack access. Many of these contacts are with other managers of equal status, who are themselves nerve centers in their own organization. In this way, the manager develops a powerful data base of information.

The processing of information is a key part of the manager's job. In my study, the chief executives spent 40% of their contact time on activities devoted exclusively to the transmission of information; 70% of their incoming mail was purely informational (as opposed to requests for action). The manager does not leave meetings or hang up the telephone in order to get back to work. In large part, communication *is* his work. Three roles describe these informational aspects of managerial work.

1. As *monitor,* the manager perpetually scans his environment for information, interrogates his liaison contacts and his subordinates, and receives unsolicited information, much of it as a result of the network of personal contacts he has developed. Remember that a good part of the information the manager collects in his monitor role arrives in verbal form, often as gossip, hearsay, and speculation. By virtue of his contacts, the manager has a natural advantage in collecting this soft information for his organization.

2. He must share and distribute much of this information. Information he gleans from outside personal contacts may be needed within his organization. In his *disseminator* role, the manager passes some of his privileged information directly to his subordinates, who would otherwise have no access to it. When his subordinates lack easy contact with one another, the manager will sometimes pass information from one to another.

3. In his *spokesman* role, the manager sends some of his information to people outside his unit—a president makes a speech to lobby for an organization cause, or a foreman suggests

a product modification to a supplier. In addition, as part of his role as spokesman, every manager must inform and satisfy the influential people who control his organizational unit. For the foreman, this may simply involve keeping the plant manager informed about the flow of work through the shop.

The president of a large corporation, however, may spend a great amount of his time dealing with a host of influences. Directors and shareholders must be advised about financial performance; consumer groups must be assured that the organization is fulfilling its social responsibilities; and government officials must be satisfied that the organization is abiding by the law.

Decisional Roles

Information is not, of course, an end in itself; it is the basic input to decision making. One thing is clear in the study of managerial work: the manager plays the major role in his unit's decision-making system. As its formal authority, only he can commit the unit to important new courses of action; and as its nerve center, only he has full and current information to make the set of decisions that determines the unit's strategy. Four roles describe the manager as decision-maker.

1. As *entrepreneur,* the manager seeks to improve his unit, to adapt it to changing conditions in the environment. In his monitor role, the president is constantly on the lookout for new ideas. When a good one appears, he initiates a development project that he may supervise himself or delegate to an employee (perhaps with the stipulation that he must approve the final proposal).

There are two interesting features about these development projects at the chief executive level.

First, these projects do not involve single decisions or even unified clusters of decisions. Rather, they emerge as a series of small decisions and actions sequenced over time. Apparently, the chief executive prolongs each project so that he can fit it bit by bit into his busy, disjointed schedule and so that he can gradually come to comprehend the issue, if it is a complex one.

Second, the chief executives I studied supervised as many as 50 of these projects at the same time. Some projects entailed new products or processes; others involved public relations campaigns, improvement of the cash position, reorganization of a weak department, resolution of a morale problem in a foreign division, integration of computer operations, various acquisitions at different stages of development, and so on.

The chief executive appears to maintain a kind of inventory of the development projects that he himself supervises—projects that are at various stages of development, some active and some in limbo. Like a juggler, he keeps a number of projects in the air; periodically, one comes down, is given a new burst of energy, and is sent back into orbit. At various intervals, he puts new projects on-stream and discards old ones.

2. While the entrepreneur role describes the manager as the voluntary initiator of change, the *disturbance handler* role depicts the manager involuntarily responding to pressures. Here change is beyond the manager's control. He must act because the pressures of the situation are too severe to be ignored: strike looms, a major customer has gone bankrupt, or a supplier reneges on his contract.

It has been fashionable, I noted earlier, to compare the manager to an orchestra conductor, just as Peter F. Drucker wrote in *The Practice of Management:*

"The manager has the task of creating a true whole that is larger than the sum of its parts, a productive entity that turns out more than the sum of the resources put into it. One analogy is the conductor of a symphony orchestra, through whose effort, vision and leadership individual instrumental parts that are so much noise by themselves become the living whole of music. But the conductor has the composer's score; he is only interpreter. The manager is both composer and conductor."[14]

Now consider the words of Leonard R. Sayles, who has carried out systematic research on the manager's job:

"(The manager) is like a symphony orchestra conductor, endeavouring to maintain a melodious performance in which the contributions of the various instruments are coordinated and sequenced, patterned and paced, while the orchestra members are having various personal difficulties, stage hands are moving music stands, alternating excessive heat and cold are creating audience and instrument problems, and the sponsor of the concert is insisting on irrational changes in the program."[15]

In effect, every manager must spend a good part of his time responding to high-pressure disturbances. No organization can be so well run, so standardized, that it has considered every contingency in the uncertain environment in advance. Disturbances arise not only because poor managers ignore situations until they reach crisis proportions, but also because good managers cannot possibly anticipate all the consequences of the actions they take.

3. The third decisional role is that of *resource allocator*. To the manager falls the responsibility of deciding who will get what in his organizational unit. Perhaps the most important resource the manager allocates is his own time. Access to the manager constitutes exposure to the unit's nerve center and decision-maker. The manager is also charged with designing his unit's structure, that pattern of formal relationships that determines how work is to be divided and coordinated.

Also, in his role as resource allocator, the manager authorizes the important decisions of his unit before they are implemented. By retaining this power, the manager can ensure that decisions are interrelated; all must pass through a single brain. To fragment this power is to encourage discontinuous decision-making and a disjointed strategy.

There are a number of interesting features about the manager's authorizing others' decisions. First, despite the widespread use of capital budgeting procedures—a means of authorizing various capital expenditures at one time—executives in my study made a great many authorization decisions on an ad hoc basis. Apparently, many projects cannot wait or simply do not have the quantifiable costs and benefits that capital budgeting requires.

Second, I found that the chief executives faced incredibly complex choices. They had to consider the impact of each decision on other decisions and on the organization's strategy. They had to ensure that the decision would be acceptable to those who influence the organization, as well as ensure that resources would not be overextended. They had to understand the various costs and benefits as well as the feasibility of the proposal. They also had to consider questions of timing. All this was necessary for the simple approval of someone else's proposal. At the same time, however, delay could lose time, while quick approval could be ill considered and quick rejection might discourage the subordinate who had spent months developing a pet project.

One common solution to approving projects is to pick the man instead of the proposal. That is, the manager authorizes those projects presented to him by people whose judgment he trusts. But he cannot always use this simple dodge.

4. The final decisional role is that of *negotiator*. Studies of managerial work at all levels indicate that managers spend considerable time in negotiations: the president of the football team is called in to work out a contract with the holdout superstar; the corporation president leads his company's contingent to negotiate a new strike issue; the

foreman argues a grievance problem to its conclusion with the shop steward. As Leonard Sayles puts it, negotiations are a "way of life" for the sophisticated manager.

These negotiations are duties of the manager's job; perhaps routine, they are not to be shirked. They are an integral part of his job, for only he has the authority to commit organizational resources in "real time," and only he has the nerve center information that important negotiations require.

The Integrated Job

It should be clear by now that the ten roles I have been describing are not easily separable. In the terminology of the psychologist, they form a gestalt, an integrated whole. No role can be pulled out of the framework and the job be left intact. For example, a manager without liaison contacts lacks external information. As a result, he can neither disseminate the information his employees need nor make decisions that adequately reflect external conditions. (In fact, this is a problem for the new person in a managerial position, since he cannot make effective decisions until he has built up his network of contacts.)

Here lies a clue to the problems of team management.[16] Two of three people cannot share a single managerial position unless they can act as one entity. This means that they cannot divide up the ten roles unless they can very carefully reintegrate them. The real difficulty lies with the informational roles. Unless there can be full sharing of managerial information—and, as I pointed out earlier, it is primarily verbal—team management breaks down. A single managerial job cannot be arbitrarily split, for example, into internal and external roles, for information from both sources must be brought to bear on the same decisions.

To say that the ten roles form a gestalt is not to say that all managers give equal attention to each role. In fact, I found in my review of the various research studies that

sales managers seem to spend relatively more of their time in the interpersonal roles, presumably a reflection of the extrovert nature of the marketing activity;

production managers give relatively more attention to the decisional roles, presumably a reflection of their concern with efficient work flow;

staff managers spend the most time in the informational roles, since they are experts who manage departments that advise other parts of the organization.

Nevertheless, in all cases the interpersonal, informational, and decisional roles remain inseparable.

TOWARD MORE EFFECTIVE MANAGEMENT

What are the messages for management in this description? I believe, first and foremost, that this description of managerial work should prove more important to managers than any prescription they might derive from it. That is to say, *the manager's effectiveness is significantly influenced by his insight into his own work.* His performance depends on how well he understands and responds to the pressures and dilemmas of the job. Thus managers who can be introspective about their work are likely to be effective at their jobs. The ruled insert on pages 94-95 offers 14 groups of self-study questions for managers. Some may sound rhetorical; none is meant to be. Even though the questions cannot be answered simply, the manager should address them.

Let us take a look at three specific areas of concern. For the most part, the managerial logjams—the dilemma of delegation, the data base centralized in one brain, the problems of working with the management scientist—revolve around the verbal nature of the manager's information. There are great dangers in centralizing the organization's data bank in the minds of its managers. When they leave, they take their memory with them. And when subordinates are out of convenient verbal reach of the manager, they are at an informational disadvantage.

1. *The manager is challenged to find systematic ways to share his privileged information.* A regular debriefing session with key subordinates, a weekly memory dump on the dictating machine, the maintaining of a diary of important information for limited circulation, or other similar methods may ease the logjam of work considerably. Time spent disseminating this information will be more than regained when decisions must be made. Of course, some will raise the question of confidentiality. But managers would do well to weigh the risks of exposing privileged information against having subordinates who can make effective decisions.

If there is a single theme that runs through this article, it is that the pressures of his job drive the manager to be superficial in his actions—to overload himself with work, encourage interruption, respond quickly to every stimulus, seek the tangible and avoid the abstract, make decisions in small increments, and do everything abruptly.

2. *Here again, the manager is challenged to deal consciously with the pressures of superficiality by giving serious attention to the issues that require it, by stepping back from his tangible bits of information in order to see a broad picture, and by making use of analytical inputs.* Although effective managers have to be adept at responding quickly to numerous and varying problems, the danger in managerial work is that they will respond to every issue equally (and that means abruptly) and that they will never work the tangible bits and pieces of informational input into a comprehensive picture of their world.

As I noted earlier, the manager uses these bits of information to build models of his world. But the manager can also avail himself of the models of the specialists. Economists describe the functioning of markets, operations researchers simulate financial flow processes, and behavioral scientists explain the needs and goals of people. The best of these models can be searched out and learned.

In dealing with complex issues, the senior manager has much to gain from a close relationship with the management scientists of his own organization. They have something important that he lacks—time to probe complex issues. An effective working relationship hinges on the resolution of what a colleague and I have called "the planning dilemma."[17] Managers have the information and the authority; analysts have the time and the technology. A successful working relationship between the two will be effected when the manager learns to share his information and the analyst learns to adapt to the manager's needs. For the analyst, adaptation means worrying less about the elegance of the method and more about its speed and flexibility.

It seems to me that analysts can help the top manager especially to schedule his time, feed in analytical information, monitor projects under his supervision, develop models to aid in making choices, design contingency plans for disturbances that can be anticipated, and conduct "quick-and-dirty" analysis for those that cannot. But there can be no cooperation if the analysts are out of the mainstream of the manager's information flow.

3. *The manager is challenged to gain control of his own time by turning obligations to his advantage and by turning those things he wishes to do into obligations.* The chief executives of my study initiated only 32% of their own contacts (and another 5% by mutual agreement). And yet to a considerable extent they seemed to control their time. There were two key factors that enabled them to do so.

First, the manager has to spend so much time discharging obligations that if he were to

SELF-STUDY QUESTIONS FOR MANAGERS

1
Where do I get my information, and how? Can I make greater use of my contacts to get information? Can other people do some of my scanning for me? In what areas is my knowledge weakest, and how can I get others to provide me with the information I need? Do I have powerful enough mental models of those things I must understand within the organization and in its environment?

2
What information do I disseminate in my organization? How important is it that my subordinates get my information? Do I keep too much information to myself because dissemination of it is time-consuming or inconvenient? How can I get more information to others so they can make better decisions?

3
Do I balance information collecting with action taking? Do I tend to act before information is in? Or do I wait so long for all the information that opportunities pass me by and I become a bottleneck in my organization?

4
What pace of change am I asking my organization to tolerate? Is this change balanced so that our operations are neither excessively static nor overly disrupted? Have we sufficiently analyzed the impact of this change on the future of our organization?

5
Am I sufficiently well informed to pass judgment on the proposals that my subordinates make? Is it possible to leave final authorization for more of the proposals with subordinates? Do we have problems of coordination because subordinates in fact now make too many of these decisions independently?

6
What is my vision of direction for this organization? Are these plans primarily in my own mind in loose form? Should I make them explicit in order to guide the decisions of others in the organization better? Or do I need flexibility to change them at will?

7
How do my subordinates react to my managerial style? Am I sufficiently sensitive to the powerful influence my actions have on them? Do I fully understand their reactions to my actions? Do I find an appropriate balance between encouragement and pressure? Do I stifle their initiative?

8
What kind of external relationships do I maintain, and how? Do I spend too much of my time maintaining these relationships? Are there certain types of people whom I should get to know better?

9
Is there any system to my scheduling, or am I just reacting to the pressures of the moment? Do I find the appropriate mix of activities, or do I tend to concentrate on one particular function or one type of problem just because I find it interesting? Am I more efficient with particular kinds of work at special times of the day or week? Does my schedule reflect this? Can someone else (in addition to my secretary) take responsibility for much of my scheduling and do it more systematically?

10
Do I overwork? What effect does my work load have on my efficiency? Should I force myself to take breaks or to reduce the pace of my activity?

11
Am I too superficial in what I do? Can I really shift moods as quickly and frequently as my work patterns require? Should I attempt to decrease the amount of fragmentation and interruption in my work?

12
Do I orient myself too much toward current, tangible activities? Am I a slave to the action and excitement of my work, so that I am no longer able to concentrate on issues? Do key problems receive the attention they deserve? Should I spend more time reading and probing deeply into certain issues? Could I be more reflective? Should I be?

13
Do I use the different media appropriately? Do I know how to make the most of written communication? Do I rely excessively on face-to-face communication, thereby putting all but a few of my subordinates at an information disadvantage? Do I schedule enough of my meetings on a regular basis? Do I spend enough time touring my organization to observe activity at first hand? Am I too detached from the heart of my organization's activities, seeing things only in an abstract way?

14
How do I blend my personal rights and duties? Do my obligations consume all my time? How can I free myself sufficiently from obligations to ensure that I am taking this organization where I want it to go? How can I turn my obligations to my advantage?

---

view them as just that, he would leave no mark on his organization. The unsuccessful manager blames failure on the obligations; the effective manager turns his obligations to his own advantage. A speech is a chance to lobby for a cause; a meeting is a chance to reorganize a weak department; a visit to an important customer is a chance to extract trade information.

Second, the manager frees some of his time to do those things that he—perhaps no one else—thinks important by turning them into obligations. Free time is made, not found, in the manager's job; it is forced into the schedule. Hoping to leave some time open for contemplation or general planning is tantamount to hoping that the pressures of the job will go away. The manager who wants to innovate initiates a project and obligates others to report back to him; the manager who needs certain environmental information establishes channels that will automatically keep him informed; the manager who has to tour facilities commits himself publicly.

The Educator's Job

Finally, a word about the training of managers. Our management schools have done an admirable job of training the organization's specialists—management scientists, marketing researchers, accountants, and organizational development specialists. But for the most part they have not trained managers.[18]

Management schools will begin the serious training of managers when skill training takes a serious place next to cognitive learning. Cognitive learning is detached and informational, like reading a book or listening to a lecture. No doubt much important cognitive material must be assimilated by the manager-to-be. But cognitive learning no more makes a manager than it does a swimmer. The latter will drown the first time he jumps into the water if his coach never takes him out of the lecture hall, gets him wet, and gives him feedback on his performance.

In other words, we are taught a skill through practice plus feedback, whether in a real or a simulated situation. Our management schools need to identify the skills managers use, select students who show potential in these skills, put the students into situations where these skills can be practiced, and then give them systematic feedback on their performance.

My description of managerial work suggests a number of important managerial skills—developing peer relationships, carrying out negotiations, motivating subordinates, resolving conflicts, establishing information networks and subsequently disseminating information, making decisions in conditions of extreme ambiguity, and allocating resources. Above all, the manager needs to be introspective about his work so that he may continue to learn on the job.

Many of the manager's skills can, in fact, be practiced, using techniques that range from role playing to videotaping real meetings. And our management schools can enhance the entrepreneurial skills by designing programs that encourage sensible risk taking and innovation.

No job is more vital to our society than that of the manager. It is the manager who determines whether our social institutions serve us well or whether they squander our talents and resources. It is time to strip away the folklore about managerial work, and time to study it realistically so that we can begin the difficult task of making significant improvements in its performance.

NOTES

1. All the data from my study can be found in Henry Mintzberg, *The Nature of Managerial Work* (New York: Harper & Row, 1973).

2. Robert H. Guest, "Of Time and the Foreman," *Personnel*, May 1956, p. 478.

3. Rosemary Stewart, *Managers and Their Jobs* (London: Macmillan, 1967); see also Sune Carlson, *Executive Behaviour* (Stockholm: Strömbergs, 1951), the first of the diary studies.

4. Francis J. Aguilar, *Scanning the Business Environment* (New York: Macmillan, 1967), p. 102.

5. Unpublished study be Irving Choran, reported in Mintzberg, *The Nature of Managerial Work*.

6. Robert T. Davis, *Performance and Development of Field Sales Managers* (Boston: Division of Research, Harvard Business School, 1957); George H. Copeman, *The Role of the Managing Director* (London: Business Publications, 1963).

7. Stewart, *Managers and Their Jobs;* Tom Burns, "The Directions of Activity and Communication in a Departmental Executive Group," *Human Relations* 7, no. 1 (1954): 73.

8. H. Edward Wrapp, "Good Managers Don't Make Policy Decisions," HBR September-October 1967, p. 91; Wrapp refers to this as spotting opportunities and relationships in the stream of operating problems and decisions; in his article Wrapp raises a number of excellent points related to this analysis.

9. Richard E. Neustadt, *Presidential Power* (New York: John Wiley, 1960), pp. 153-154; italics added.

10. For a more thorough, though rather different, discussion of this issue, see Kenneth R. Andrews, "Toward Professionalism in Business Management," HBR March-April 1969, p. 49.

11. C. Jackson Grayson, Jr., in "Management Science and Business Practice," HBR July-August 1973, p. 41, explains in similar terms why, as chairman of the Price Commission, he did not use those very techniques that he himself promoted in his earlier career as a management scientist.

12. George C. Homans, *The Human Group* (New York: Harcourt, Brace & World, 1950), based on the study by William F. Whyte entitled *Street Corner Society*, rev. ed. (Chicago: University of Chicago Press, 1955).

13. Neustadt, *Presidential Power*, p. 157.

14. Peter F. Drucker, *The Practice of Management* (New York: Harper & Row, 1954), pp. 341-342.

15. Leonard R. Sayles, *Managerial Behavior* (New York: McGraw-Hill, 1964), p. 162.

16. See Richard C. Hodgson, Daniel J. Levinson, and Abraham Zaleznik, *The Executive Role Constellation* (Boston: Division of Research, Harvard Business School, 1965), for a discussion of the sharing of roles.

17. James S. Hekimian and Henry Mintzberg, "The Planning Dilemma," *The Management Review*, May 1968, p. 4.

18. See J. Sterling Livingston, "Myth of the Well-Educated Manager," HBR January-February 1971, p. 79.

Ian I. Mitroff
Ralph H. Kilmann

STORIES MANAGERS TELL: A NEW TOOL FOR ORGANIZATIONAL PROBLEM SOLVING

If accounting and finance are the backbone of organizations, then the stories which permeate all organizations of any size are their lifeblood. Stories are so central to organizations that not only do organizations depend on them, but stronger still, they couldn't function without them. Big or small, every organization is dependent upon countless stories for its functioning.

While organizations typically generate stories of all kinds, there is one type that is of special interest, what we call "epic myths of the organization." While the purposes such myths serve are many and varied, if there is a central purpose, it is to define the unique quality of a particular organization.

Countless biographies and autobiographies attest to the power that stories play within modern corporations. These autobiographies retell, in a form strikingly similar to the great epic myths of the past, the life of the organization and that of the individual within it. They describe in heroic terms, more dramatic than life itself, the difficult circumstances under which the organization was born, the tremendous struggle that was necessary to keep it alive in the early perilous years of its existence, how those involved made great personal sacrifices born out of intense dedication, how the organization slowly began to grow, and finally, how in later years it achieved a success far greater than anyone had ever dared dream. The story becomes the corporate myth, the basic transcript that establishes and perpetuates corporate traditions. In short, it gives basic meaning to the corporation. It is recalled and recounted at formal occasions and at coffee break bull sessions. It is used to indoctrinate new employees. It helps to define "what this place is really like, what makes it tick, and finally, what's so special about it." The corporate myth is the "spirit of the organization," and as such, it is infused into all levels of policy and decision making.

Through the systematic study of managerial autobiographies, countless interviews, and behavioral exercises with managers, we have evolved a technique for eliciting organizational myths or stories. More to the point, we have developed a technique for showing the practical implications of such stories for day-to-day corporate decision making. The outcome is a new approach to problem solving and planning.

THE IDEAL ORGANIZATION— DIFFERENT STORIES FROM DIFFERENT MANAGERS

One reason why organizational stories have been so little studied is that most managers are only dimly aware of their existence, let alone their importance. Stories are like dreams. Most of us have to be trained not

Reprinted by permission of the publisher from *Management Review,* Vol. 64, No. 7: July, 1975, © 1975 by AMACOM, a division of American Management Associations.

only to recognize them, but also to appreciate their significance. For this reason, it is almost impossible to get at the stories that govern organizations directly. Like dreams they have to be gotten at indirectly. Direct approaches only drive them further underground. Asking a manager to sit down and talk about his organization's "story" makes as much sense as asking someone to sit down and talk about his unconscious. Little wonder, then, why insightful organizational autobiographies are so rare. Only the most reflective managers can perceive the stories that guide their organizations and make them run.

We have found that it is much easier for managers to talk or write a story about their *ideal* organization than about their current (or real) organization. In fact, we have found that managers can more readily make up or recall a characteristic story about their real organization *after* they have first described their ideal. The reason is that ideal stories or images are not constrained by the countless number of complex details that go into the history of any real organization.

In comparison to real stories, stories about an ideal organization are relatively unconstrained. The tellers of stories about ideal situations are not obliged to stick to reality or to account for it. Their images of the ideal are purer and simpler than their images of the real could ever be. In addition, images of the ideal are often easier to get at than are images of the real because everyone has some notion of an ideal. It is often easier to describe what one would like to have than it is to say precisely what's wrong with one's current environment. Finally, asking managers to write a story about their ideal organization has the effect of opening them up and freeing their creative talents whereas asking them to write about their real organization often has the effect of constraining their creative potential. And if ideals more readily reveal the hopes, dreams, and aspirations of people, then they also more readily reveal their fears and anxieties. For these reasons, we have asked managers to write about their ideal organization, and we have studied their stories in detail.

One of the most striking findings of our investigations is that different managers tend to have very different concepts of an ideal organization. Different managers produce very different kinds of organizational stories. To gain understanding of the basis for these differences, we have studied the personalities of different managers. We have found that:

Managers of the same personality type tend to tell the same kind of story, that is, they have the same concept of an ideal organization.

Managers of opposing personalities have drastically different concepts of an ideal organization. The ideal organization of one type is literally the living hell of an opposing type.

To get at these personality differences, we have administered a relatively short test to hundreds of managers. After the managers have taken the personality test, they are asked to write a short story on the concept of their ideal organization. They are instructed that the content and structure of the story is completely up to them. The stories need not be of any particular length or form. After this is done, the managers are put into various groups, and each group is then asked to come up with a story that best expresses the group's concept of an ideal organization. The groups are formed on the basis of the personality test: All the managers of the same personality type are put into the same group. We do this because we have generally found that such homogeneous groups tend to strengthen the effect of personality differences. That is, the groups—different from each other in the personality characteristics of their members, but each composed of managers with similar personalities—accentuate the differences in the concepts of an ideal organization held by managers with different personalities.

A PERSONALITY FRAMEWORK FOR CLASSIFYING MANAGERS

The personality framework that we have used to classify managers is that of C. G. Jung. The Jungian structure was chosen for two main reasons: (1) the dimensions of the framework are directly related to different managerial and organizational styles, and hence the classifications are of direct relevance to management; (2) the Jungian framework does not prescribe any one of its four major personality types as being superior to or better than any of the others. Instead, each type is seen as having major strengths and weaknesses. The framework can help managers to see that their personal style has certain costs or limitations as well as benefits, and that as a result, they need their managerial counterparts, with markedly different personal styles, to compensate for their weaknesses—and vice versa.

Two particular dimensions of the Jungian framework are of particular importance. The first dimension corresponds to the way in which a manager typically takes in data from the outside world. This is the *input-data dimension*. The second dimension corresponds to the way in which a manager typically makes a decision based on the data. This is the *decision-making dimension*.

According to Jung, individuals can take in data from the outside world by either *sensation* or *intuition*; most individuals tend to use one kind of data-input process rather than the other. Sensing, or sensation, types typically take in information via their senses. Sensing types are most comfortable when attending to the details, the specifics, of any situation. That is, sensing types tend to break every situation down into isolated bits and pieces; further, they feel most comfortable when they have gathered some "hard facts" that pertain to the situation. In contrast, intuitive types typically take in information by looking at the whole of a situation. They concentrate their attention on the hypothetical possibilities in a situation rather than getting bogged down and constrained by details and an endless array of hard facts. All individuals perceive the world with both of these functions at different times. But as Jung repeatedly argued, individuals tend to develop a habitual way of perceiving a situation and, in fact, cannot apply both types of perceiving or data input at the same time.

Also, Jung posited that there are two basic ways of reaching a decision with regard to any situation: *thinking* and *feeling*. Thinking types base their decisions on impersonal, logical modes of reasoning. That is, thinking types don't feel comfortable unless they have a logical or an analytical (for example, mathematical) basis for making a decision. Feeling types on the other hand make their decisions based on extremely personal considerations, for example, how they feel about the particular person or situation, whether they like the person, value the situation, and so forth. Thinking types want to depersonalize every situation, object, and person by "explaining" them. Feeling types on the other hand want to personalize every situation, object, and person by stressing their individual uniqueness.

Thinking is the psychological function that generalizes; feeling, the function that individuates. Thinking takes two objects that are inherently dissimilar and seeks to find what they have in common. Feeling on the other hand takes two objects, or people, or situations, that are inherently alike and emphasizes or seeks to find what is distinctly dissimilar about them. In short, thinking emphasizes sameness; feeling, characteristic differences or uniqueness—for example, that no two people are exactly alike, that each person is unique.

In summary, however an individual takes in data, by intuition or sensation, he may come to some conclusion about the data by either a logical, impersonal analysis—thinking—or by a subjective, personal process—feeling.

Combining the two data-input modes—sensation and intuition—with the two decision-making modes—feeling and thinking—in all possible ways allows us to talk about the following four Jungian personality types:

Sensing-thinking types (STs)
Sensing-feeling types (SFs)
Intuition-thinking types (NTs)
Intuition-feeling types (NFs)

The stories these four types tell are, in general, very different.

Sensing-Thinking Managers

The stories of STs typically contain an extreme emphasis and concentration on specifics, on factual details. STs are extremely sensitive to the physical features of their work environment. For example, the stories of STs display an extreme preoccupation with environments that are neither "too hot" nor "too cold" but "just right." The ideal organization of STs is characterized by complete control, certainty, and specificity. In their ideal organization, everybody knows exactly what his or her job is. There is no uncertainty as to what is expected in any circumstance. Further, ST organizations are impersonal: The emphasis is on work, and work roles, not on the particular individuals who fill the roles. The ideal organization of STs is authoritarian, if not the epitome of bureaucracy. There is a single leader at the top and a well-defined hierarchical line of authority that extends from the very top down to all of the lower rungs of the organization. In an ST organization, the individuals exist to serve the goals of the organization, not the organization to serve the goals of the individuals. The goals of an ST organization are realistic, down-to-earth, limited, and more often than not, narrowly economic. Finally—and it should come as no surprise—the heroes of STs are tough-minded individuals who know how "to step on people to get the job done." The greatest achievement of the heroes of STs is that they were available when the firm needed what they had to offer most: They brought "order and stability out of extreme chaos; they gave the firm a specific, well-defined sense of direction."

Intuition-Thinking Managers

The stories of NTs are marked by an extreme emphasis on broad, global issues. In describing their ideal organization, NTs do not specify the detailed work rules, roles, or lines of authority but focus instead on general concepts and issues. To put it somewhat differently, if the organizational goals of STs are concerned with well-defined, precise *micro*economic issues—"We need to make X dollars by September to stay solvent"—then the goals of NTs are concerned with fuzzy, ill-defined, *macro*economic issues—"There ought to be an equitable wage for all workers." NT organizations are also impersonal like ST organizations. However, where STs focus on the details of a specific impersonal organization, NTs focus on impersonal concepts and global theories of organization. For example, they are concerned with concepts of efficiency in the abstract. Likewise, whereas in an ST organization individuals exist to serve the present and specific needs of their particular organization, in an NT organization individuals exist to serve the intellectual and theoretical concepts of organizations in general. In a word, if ST organizations are impersonally realistic, then NT organizations are impersonally idealistic.

The heroes of NTs are broad conceptualizers. If the heroes of STs are problem solvers, then the heroes of NTs are problem formulators, that is, the finders, if not the creators, of new problems. The heroes of NTs take an organization designed to accomplish a very specific, limited set of goals (for example, turn out a specific product) and create new goals. They envision new products, horizons, and businesses in their firm.

Intuition-Feeling Managers

The stories of NFs are also marked by an extreme preoccupation with broad, global themes and issues. NFs also show an extreme disdain towards getting down to specifics. NFs are similar to NTs in that both take a broad view of organizations. However, NFs differ from NTs in that where the emphasis of NTs is on the general *theory* or *theoretical* aspects of organizations, the emphasis of NFs is on the most general *personal* and *human* goals of organizations. Thus NF organizations are concerned with "serving humanity," with "making a contribution to mankind." NFs differ from both STs and NTs in that for both STs and NTs the individual exists to serve the organization, where for NFs the organization exists to serve the personal and social needs of people. Since in Jungian personality theory the NF type is the extreme opposite of the ST type—as the SF type is the extreme opposite of the NT—it is not surprising to find that the ideal organization of NFs is the exact opposite of STs. Thus, if an ST organization is authoritarian and bureaucratic with well-defined rules of behavior, then an NF organization is completely decentralized with no clear lines of authority, no central leader, and with no fixed, prescribed rules of behavior. The stories of NFs incessantly talk about "flexibility" and "decentralization." As a matter of fact, many of the stories of NFs contain diagrams of their ideal organization that show them to be circular or wheel-like in structure rather than hierarchical. NF organizations are also idealistic as opposed to realistic. In essence, NF organizations are the epitome of organic, adaptive institutions.

The heroes of NFs are not only able to envision new lines of direction, that is, new goals, objectives, and so forth, for their organization—in this sense they are like the heroes of NTs—but they are also able to give the organization a new sense of direction in the human or personal sense.

Sensing-Feeling Managers

If the ideal organizations of STs and NFs are extreme opposites, then the organizations of NTs and SFs are also extreme opposites. If NTs are concerned with the general theory of all organizations but not with the details of any particular organization, then SFs don't care about theory or issues in general at all. SFs are instead concerned with the detailed human relations in their particular organization. SFs are like STs in that both are concerned with details and facts. However, SFs differ from STs in that the latter are concerned with detailed *work rules* and *roles* whereas the former are concerned with the *human qualities of the specific people* who fill the roles. SFs are in this sense similar to NFs. Both SFs and NFs are concerned with the people in the organization. SFs differ from NFs in the sense that where NFs are concerned with people in general, SFs are concerned with individuals in particular. SF organizations are also realistic as opposed to idealistic. Like STs, SFs are also concerned with the detailed work environment although, where for STs the environment of concern is physical, for SFs it is the interpersonal environment that is of concern. The heroes of SFs are those very special people who are able to create a highly personal, very warm human climate in their organization. They make you want to come to work. Indeed, the organization becomes just like home, like being one of the family.

Unfortunately, it would take too much space to give an illustration of every one of these four kinds of stories. However, the following typical example of an SF story may help to convey the spirit of what we've been talking about:

Utopia in the Business World

The day had been a particularly harrowing one at the office with more than the normal amount of frustrations with the administration, the workers, and even the public. I went home and fell exhausted into bed.

Suddenly I awoke and looked around. Where was I? What was this strange place? Who were these people? At that moment I was approached by a smiling person with hand extended who said, "Welcome to our organization. We are glad to have you with us. My name is _____. I will take you around to meet the rest of the staff."

Everyone I met was friendly and in the days to come proved to be most helpful. My duties were explained to me quite clearly and thoroughly. The procedure with which I had to work was written in such a way that there was very little chance of misinterpretation.

All of the staff worked quite well with each other with a minimum of disagreements. The separate department heads would meet once a week with the Administrator who would keep them informed of new developments. The department heads would then keep the workers informed. Once a month the Administrator would address the entire staff. There was a free and easy exchange of ideas. There was no CIA atmosphere nor was there always a lot of rumors floating around. No one ever said, "I hear by the grapevine." Everyone was fully informed as to the opportunities available to them.

A door slammed and suddenly I was transported from the ideal organization back to the world from which I came.

IMPLICATIONS FOR ORGANIZATIONAL PROBLEM SOLVING

It has been our experience that the phenomenon of storytelling has a tremendous impact on managers. This is especially the case where managers of different psychological type are able to share their stories in an atmosphere of freedom and trust, that is, without fear of ridicule. The biggest value of such experiences is that they make managers aware, as perhaps never before, of basic differences that have always existed but that are obscured in everyday life. One rarely has the chance to witness in as explicit and systematic a way the operation of fundamental psychological differences.

The greatest value in sharing organizational stories lies in the fact that it sensitizes managers to other realities—to the fact that there are other ways of perceiving and analyzing organizational disturbances and problems. In this sense, the value of such an experience extends far beyond the seemingly trivial exercise of storytelling.

We would contend that the kinds of real problems that organizations face have aspects of every one of the psychological viewpoints we have been discussing. Almost by definition, *real* problems do not fit neatly into one and only one slice of psychological space. Rather, real problems, as opposed to idealized problems, change drastically in character—they look vastly different—as we view them from different perspectives. If we associate (1) the ST viewpoint, with its emphasis on day-to-day specifics and details, with the operational phase of organizational problem solving, (2) the NT view with long-range strategic planning, (3) the NF orientation with the setting of long-range human goals, and (4) the SF view with day-by-day human relations, then all problems of any importance not only have features that involve every one of these aspects, but organizational problems ought to be conceptualized as such. We would argue that the failure to view problems as involving all four viewpoints can be disastrous to an organization. By ignoring one or more of these viewpoints an organization can fail to recognize and hence to treat an important side of its problems.

METHOD OF APPLICATION

The implications of the approach we have been describing can be summarized as follows: We start by assuming that one or more subunits in an organization are identified as experiencing some conflict or problem. Our first step is to bring together all of the individuals concerned with the problem or their representatives if there is a large number of individuals. Each individual is asked to write out his view of the problem—what he sees as the objectives of the problem, the issues involved, the value assumptions made, and so forth. Alternatively, we ask each individual to write a story describing how the problem arose, the individuals who were involved, what got them to see the problem in a particular way, how they approached the problem, and what an ideal resolution of the problem would look like. The individuals are then formed into a Jungian group, that is, an ST, NT, SF, and NF group, and are asked to develop a group statement by combining or integrating their individual statements or stories. When the group statements have been prepared, each group shares with the others their view of the problem as indicated by their group discussions. This typically results in four very different perspectives.

The next stage in the process explicitly examines the four differentiated group products and attempts to integrate them into some new form or synthesis. The process involves having two or more individuals from each of the four Jungian groups meet as an integrated group. This group then is asked to discuss their different perspectives, their assumptions, values, stories, and so forth. A lively debate usually develops in which the different perspectives are exaggerated, challenged, examined, denied, projected, and so forth. During this process, each individual is encouraged and pushed as much as possible to critically question and address the strengths and weaknesses of his own perspective. Once each individual in the integrated group has achieved this objective, the process moves toward a synthesis stage. The atmosphere changes, and each member of the group attempts to provide innovative solutions, capitalizing on the strengths of each position while minimizing or subduing the weaknesses. Finally, this group proposes some integrated solution that addresses the issues developed by the different perspectives.

The essential point to be emphasized is that this problem-solving process can be designed and applied to any organizational problem, whether the problem is one of macroorganization design—that is, how to organize to address the variety of task environments that the organization faces—or arises within a given organization design—for example, how to integrate two already existing subunits. This conclusion springs from the consistently favorable results we have achieved in applying the Jungian framework to a broad range of concepts and issues in a number of organizations. It seems to us that a wide variety of organizational phenomena have their roots in the basic differences between Jungian personality types, that is, in the fact that different types see things differently. Consequently, regardless of the substantive issue at hand, the methodology is useful in addressing itself to the underlying dimensions of the issue.

This kind of problem-solving process needs to be a recurring component of any management system, it needs to be institutionalized in a form similar to the one we have described. We are suggesting that a major issue for organization design is that *organizations need to design a problem-solving system* in order to adapt successfully to different problems and different task environments. Such a system has to have the objective of *continually* addressing itself to the different sources of conflicts and value issues in the organization—that is, different people, different problems, different designs—and of providing a design mechanism to coordinate and integrate the different perspectives that are so necessary if innovative solutions are to arise. In fact, we see that the ability of an organization to confront needed changes and different problems is heavily based on the organization's ability to design itself for the possibility of taking advantage of such confrontations—organizations must ensure that these various confrontations do not occur by chance, by the dictates of a few individuals, or via a reactive as opposed to a proactive stance. Rather, how to realize the stimulus to growth that is implicit in confrontations is an organization design problem that must be approached explicitly—one that requires the organization to allocate resources to implement a system for using confrontations.

We do not mean to suggest, however, that organizations have not instituted problem-solving systems, but rather that within present problem-solving systems, organizations have not made use of the unique information and perspectives that result from storytelling—whether these are stories about ideal or real organizations. Most efforts at problem solving and decision making rely on typical accounting data. And while contemporary management information systems have begun to include broader and more varied sources of information, this information is still consciously derived and highly quantitative. The use of organizational stories, however, taps the unconscious, qualitative phenomena that pervades organizations. From our research and consulting experience we have found that for appreciating and analyzing complex problems, this latter type of information is as important or even more important than rigorous accounting data. Storytelling, when applied in a problem-solving framework as we have described, can thus be an extremely important source of data for the organization—data that would otherwise be ignored or overlooked. As such, storytelling procedures do become a new tool for organizational problem solving.

*

PART THREE

GROUP PROCESSES

This part is primarily concerned with groups and relations between groups within formal organizations. While the individual group members can have an important impact on group processes, the primary unit for discussion in this part is the "group," rather than the individual. Thus, the focus is in terms of the impact of groups on individuals and the impacts of groups on each other.

The first reading in this section by Cartwright and Lippitt, "Group Dynamics and the Individual," serves to answer a number of fundamental questions about the nature of groups, the relation between individuals and groups, and the need for a contingency view to assess whether a particular group is likely to have desirable or undesirable impacts. The authors develop their contingency view by presenting a diagnostic framework for assessing the possible conformity pressures in groups as well as the possible forces which encourage differences or heterogeneity within groups. In sum, they address a number of questions that are fundamental to the nature, impact, and desired role of groups, such as the following: What are the properties of groups? Under what circumstances are groups good or bad? How should you react to groups? How should groups treat their individual members?

In the second selection in the part, Deutsch, "Socially Relevant Science: Reflections on Some Studies of Interpersonal Conflict," presents the results of three experimental studies in interpersonal conflict. The experiments were designed to detect the effects of a variety of factors on outcomes of individuals in conflict. Some of the factors considered were: the use of threats, the use of irrevocable commitments, the size of the conflict, and the degree of competitive elements in the conflict situation. In addition to reporting these experimental results, Deutsch discusses the need for research to involve socially relevant science. The author points out that all too often research is considered either socially relevant or scientific. Finally, Deutsch describes how interpersonal conflict research can have implications for and can be generalized to group, organization, and even international levels.

Whereas, the previous two articles focused on interacting groups in organizations, the third article in this section, "The Effectiveness of Nominal, Delphi, and Interacting Group Decision Making Processes," considers two alternative group processes that can be successfully used under certain conditions. *Interacting* groups are conventional unstructured (or structured by the leader) face-to-face group meetings. Van De Ven and Delbecq carefully compare the nature of interacting, nominal, and delphi group processes in terms of ten different dimensions. They also review and report on their own research data which points out the relative effectiveness of these processes for certain types of applied group decision problems. Their findings suggest that these two group processes, particularly the nominal group technique, are far superior to the common interacting group approach for certain types of group problems. The nominal group technique and the delphi process represent important social technologies for improving the effectiveness of problem solving groups within organizations. In particular, the nominal group technique or a version of it can be readily used by managers at all levels and areas of an organization.

The last reading in this part by Hinnings, et al., "A Strategic Contingencies' Theory of Organizational Power," is different in scope. It considers intergroup relations with respect to the relations between formal units (such as sections, departments, and divisions) in the organization. The authors present the key contingencies that are likely to influence the relative power of one formal unit compared to another in the organization. The three contingency variables considered to influence, in combination, the relative power of a formal unit are: (1) the degree to which one unit copes with uncertainty for other units; (2) the degree to which a unit's coping activities are substitutable by other units; and (3) the degree of centrality of a unit in linking the units of the organization together. The components of these contingency variables and their linkages to influence the power of a unit are outlined in Figure 1, which provides an overall framework for understanding the flow of the entire article.

Dorwin Cartwright
Ronald Lippitt

GROUP DYNAMICS AND THE INDIVIDUAL

How should we think of the relation between individuals and groups? Few questions have stirred up so many issues of metaphysics, epistemology, and ethics. Do groups have the same reality as individuals? If so, what are the properties of groups? Can groups learn, have goals, be frustrated, develop, regress, begin and end? Or are these characteristics strictly attributable only to individuals? If groups exist, are they good or bad? How *should* an individual behave with respect to groups? How *should* groups treat their individual members? Such questions have puzzled man from the earliest days of recorded history.

In our present era of "behavioral science" we like to think that we can be "scientific" and proceed to study human behavior without having to take sides on these problems of speculative philosophy. Invariably, however, we are guided by certain assumptions, stated explicitly or not, about the reality or irreality of groups, about their observability, and about their good or bad value.

Usually these preconceptions are integral parts of one's personal and scientific philosophy, and it is often hard to tell how much they derive from emotionally toned personal experiences with other people and how much from coldly rational and "scientific" considerations. In view of the fervor with which they are usually defended, one might suspect that most have a small basis at least in personally significant experiences. These preconceptions, moreover, have a tendency to assume a homogeneous polarization—either positive or negative.

Consider first the completely negative view. It consists of two major assertions: first, groups don't really exist. They are a product of distorted thought processes (often called "abstractions"). In fact, social prejudice consists precisely in acting as if groups, rather than individuals, were real. Second, groups are bad. They demand blind loyalty, they make individuals regress, they reduce man to the lowest common denominator, and they produce what *Fortune* magazine has immortalized as "group-think."

In contrast to this completely negative conception of groups, there is the completely positive one. This syndrome, too, consists of two major assertions: first, groups really do exist. Their reality is demonstrated by the difference it makes to an individual whether he is accepted or rejected by a group and whether he is part of a healthy or sick group. Second, groups are good. They satisfy deep-seated needs of individuals for affiliation, affection, recognition, and self-esteem; they stimulate individuals to moral heights of altruism, loyalty, and self-sacrifice; they provide a means, through cooperative interaction, by which man can accomplish things unattainable through individual enterprise.

Reprinted by permission of the publisher from *International Journal of Group Psychotherapy*, Vol. 7, No. 1, January 1957, pp. 86-102.

This completely positive preconception is the one attributed most commonly, it seems, to the so-called "group dynamics movement." Group dynamicists, it is said, have not only *reified* the group but also *idealized* it. They believe that everything should be done by and in groups—individual responsibility is bad, man-to-man supervision is bad, individual problem-solving is bad, and even individual therapy is bad. The only good things are committee meetings, group decisions, group problem-solving, and group therapy. "If you don't hold the group in such high affection," we were once asked, "why do you call your research organization the Research Center For Group Dynamics? And, if you are for groups and group dynamics, mustn't you therefore be *against* individuality, individual responsibility, and self-determination?"

FIVE PROPOSITIONS ABOUT GROUPS

This assumption that individuals and groups must necessarily have incompatible interests is made so frequently in one guise or another that it requires closer examination. Toward this end we propose five related assertions about individuals, groups, and group dynamics, which are intended to challenge the belief that individuals and groups must necessarily have incompatible, or for that matter, compatible interests.

1. *Groups do exist; they must be dealt with by any man of practical affairs, or indeed by any child, and they must enter into any adequate account of human behavior.* Most infants are born into a specific group. Little Johnny may be a welcome or unwelcome addition to the group. His presence may produce profound changes in the structure of the group and consequently in the feelings, attitudes, and behavior of various group members. He may create a triangle where none existed before or he may break up one which has existed. His development and adjustment for years to come may be deeply influenced by the nature of the group he enters and by his particular position in it—whether, for example, he is a first or second child (a personal property which has no meaning apart from its reference to a specific group).

There is a wealth of research whose findings can be satisfactorily interpreted only by assuming the reality of groups. Recall the experiment of Lewin, Lippitt, and White in which the level of aggression of an individual was shown to depend upon the social atmosphere and structure of the group he is in and not merely upon such personal traits as aggressiveness.[1] By now there can be little question about the kinds of results reported from the Western Electric study which make it clear that groups develop norms for the behavior of their members with the result that "good" group members adopt these norms as their *personal* values.[2] Nor can one ignore the dramatic evidence of Lewin, Bavelas, and others which shows that group decisions may produce changes in individual behavior much larger than those customarily found to result from attempts to modify the behavior of individuals *as* isolated individuals.[3]

2. *Groups are inevitable and ubiquitous.* The biological nature of man, his capacity to use language, and the nature of his environment which has been built into its present form over thousands of years require that man exist in groups. This is not to say that groups must maintain the properties they now display, but we cannot conceive of a collection of human beings living in geographical proximity under conditions where it would be correct to assert that no groups exist and that there is no such thing as group membership.

3. *Groups mobilize powerful forces which produce effects of the utmost importance to*

individuals. Consider two examples from rather different research settings. Seashore has recently published an analysis of data from 5,871 employees of a large manufacturing company.[4] An index of group cohesiveness, developed for each of 228 work groups, permitted a comparison of members working in high and in low cohesive groups. Here is one of his major findings: "Members of high cohesive groups exhibit less anxiety than members of low cohesive groups, using as measures of anxiety: (a) feeling 'jumpy' or 'nervous,' (b) feeling under pressure to achieve higher productivity (with actual productivity held constant), and (c) feeling a lack of support from the company."[5] Seashore suggests two reasons for the relation between group cohesiveness and individual anxiety: "(1) that the cohesive group provides effective support for the individual in his encounters with anxiety-provoking aspects of his environment, thus allaying anxiety, and (2) that group membership offers direct satisfaction, and this satisfaction in membership has a generalized effect of anxiety-reduction."[6]

Perhaps a more dramatic account of the powerful forces generated in groups can be derived from the publication by Stanton and Schwartz of their studies of a mental hospital.[7] They report, for example, how a patient may be thrown into an extreme state of excitement by disagreements between two staff members over the patient's care. Thus, two doctors may disagree about whether a female patient should be moved to another ward. As the disagreement progresses, the doctors may stop communicating relevant information to one another and start lining up allies in the medical and nursing staff. The patient, meanwhile, becomes increasingly restless until, at the height of the doctors' disagreement, she is in an acute state of excitement and must be secluded, put under sedation, and given special supervision. Presumably, successful efforts to improve the interpersonal relations and communications among members of the staff would improve the mental condition of such a patient.

In general, it is clear that events occurring in a group may have repercussions on members who are not directly involved in these events. A person's position in a group, moreover, may affect the way others behave toward him and such personal qualities as his levels of aspiration and self-esteem. Group membership itself may be a prized possession or an oppressive burden; tragedies of major proportions have resulted from the exclusion of individuals from groups, and equally profound consequences have stemmed from enforced membership in groups.

4. *Groups may produce both good and bad consequences.* The view that groups are completely good and the view that they are completely bad are both based on convincing evidence. *The only fault with either is its one-sidedness.* Research motivated by one or the other is likely to focus on different phenomena. As an antidote to such one-sidedness it is a good practice to ask research questions in pairs, one stressing positive aspects and one negative: What are the factors producing conformity? *and* what are the factors producing nonconformity? What brings about a breakdown in communications? *and* what stimulates or maintains effective communications? An exclusive focus on pathologies or upon positive criteria leads to a seriously incomplete picture.

5. *A correct understanding of group dynamics permits the possibility that desirable consequences from groups can be deliberately enhanced.* Through a knowledge of group dynamics, groups can be made to serve better ends, for knowledge gives power to modify human beings and human behavior. At the same time, recognition of this fact produces some of the deepest conflicts within the behavioral scientists, for it raises the whole problem of social manipulation. Society must not close its eyes to Orwell's horrible picture

of life in 1984, but it cannot accept the alternative that in ignorance there is safety.

To recapitulate our argument: groups exist; they are inevitable and ubiquitous; they mobilize powerful forces having profound effects upon individuals; these effects may be good or bad; and through a knowledge of group dynamics there lies the possibility of maximizing their good value.

A DILEMMA

Many thoughtful people today are alarmed over one feature of groups: the pressure toward conformity experienced by group members. Indeed, this single "bad" aspect is often taken as evidence that groups are bad in general. Let us examine the specific problem of conformity, then, in order to attain a better understanding of the general issue. Although contemporary concern is great, it is not new. More than one hundred years ago Alexis de Tocqueville wrote: "I know of no country in which there is so little independence of mind and real freedom of discussion as in America. . . . In America the majority raises formidable barriers around the liberty of opinion. . . . The master (majority) no longer says: 'You shall think as I do or you shall die'; but he says: 'You are free to think differently from me and to retain your life, your property, and all that you possess, but they will be useless to you, for you will never be chosen by your fellow citizens if you solicit their votes; and they will affect to scorn you if you ask for their esteem. You will remain among men, but you will be deprived of the rights of mankind. Your fellow creatures will shun you like an impure being; and even those who believe in your innocence will abandon you, lest they should be shunned in their turn.' "[8]

Before too readily accepting such a view of groups as the whole story, let us invoke our dictum that research questions should be asked in pairs. Nearly everyone is convinced that individuals should not be blind conformers to group norms, that each group member should not be a carbon copy of every other member, but what is the other side of the coin? In considering why members of groups conform, perhaps we should also think of the consequences of the removal of individuals from group membership or the plight of the person who really does not belong to any group with clear-cut norms and values. The state of anomie, described by Durkheim, is also common today. It seems as if people who have no effective participation in groups with clear and strong value systems either crack up (as in alcoholism or suicide) or they seek out groups which will demand conformity. In discussing this process, Talcott Parsons writes: "In such a situation it is not surprising that large numbers of people should . . . be attracted to movements which can offer them membership in a group with a vigorous esprit de corps with submission to some strong authority and rigid system of belief, the individual thus finding a measure of escape from painful perplexities or from a situation of anomie."[9]

The British anthropologist, Adam Curle, has stressed the same problem when he suggested that in our society we need not four, but five freedoms, the fifth being freedom from that neurotic anxiety which springs from a man's isolation from his fellows, and which, in turn, isolates him still further from them.

We seem, then, to face a dilemma: the individual needs social support for his values and social beliefs; he needs to be accepted as a valued member of some group which *he* values; failure to maintain such group membership produces anxiety and personal disorganization. But, on the other hand, group membership and group participation tend to cost the individual his individuality. If he is to receive support from others and, in turn, give support to others, he and they must hold in common some values and beliefs. Deviation from these undermines any possibility of group support and acceptance.

Is there an avenue of escape from this dilemma? Certainly, the issue is not as simple as we have described it. The need for social support for some values does not require conformity with respect to all values, beliefs, and behavior. Any individual is a member of several groups, and he may be a successful deviate in one while conforming to another (think of the visitor in a foreign country or of the psychologist at a convention of psychiatrists). Nor should the time dimension be ignored; a person may sustain his deviancy through a conviction that his fate is only temporary. These refinements of the issue are important and should be examined in great detail, but before we turn our attention to them, we must assert that we do *not* believe that the basic dilemma can be escaped. To avoid complete personal disorganization man must conform to at least a minimal set of values required for participation in the groups to which he belongs.

PRESSURES TO UNIFORMITY

Some better light may be cast on this problem if we refer to the findings of research on conformity. What do we know about the way it operates?

Cognitive Processes

Modern psychological research on conformity reflects the many different currents of contemporary psychology, but the major direction has been largely determined by the classic experiment of Sherif on the development of social norms in perceiving autokinetic movement[10] and by the more recent study of Asch of pressures to conformity in perceiving unambiguous visual stimuli.[11]

What does this line of investigation tell us about conformity? What has it revealed, for instance, about the conditions that set up pressures to conformity? Answers to this question have taken several forms, but nearly all point out that social interaction would be impossible if some beliefs and perceptions were not commonly shared by the participants. Speaking of the origin of such cognitive pressures to uniformity among group members, Asch says: "The individual comes to experience a world that he shares with others. He perceives that the surroundings include him, as well as others, and that he is in the same relation to the surroundings as others. He notes that he, as well as others, is converging upon the same object and responding to its identical properties. Joint action and mutual understanding require this relation of intelligibility and structural simplicity. In these terms the 'pull' toward the group becomes understandable."[12]

Consistent with this interpretation of the origin of pressures to uniformity in a perceptual or judgmental situation are the findings that the major variables influencing tendencies to uniformity are (a) the quality of the social evidence (particularly the degree of unanimity of announced perceptions and the subject's evaluation of the trustworthiness of the other's judgments), (b) the quality of the direct perceptual evidence (particularly the clarity or ambiguity of the stimuli), (c) the magnitude of the discrepancy between the social and the perceptual evidence, and (d) the individual's self-confidence in the situation (as indicated either by experimental manipulations designed to affect self-confidence or by personality measurements).

The research in this tradition has been productive, but it has emphasized the individual and his cognitive problems and has considered the individual apart from any concrete and meaningful group membership. Presumably any trustworthy people adequately equipped with eyes and ears could serve to generate pressures to conformity in the subject, regardless of his specific relations to them. The result of this emphasis has been to ignore certain essential aspects of the conformity problem. Let us document this assertion with two examples.

First, the origin of pressures to uniformity has been made to reside in the person whose conformity is being studied. Through eliminating experimentally any possibility that pressures might be exerted by others, it has been possible to study the conformity of people as if they existed in a world where they can see or hear others but not be reacted to by others. It is significant, indeed, that conformity does arise in the absence of direct attempts to bring it about. But this approach does not raise certain questions about the conditions which lead to *social* pressures to conformity. What makes some people try to get others to conform? What conditions lead to what forms of pressure on others to get them to conform? The concentration of attention on the conformer has diverted attention away from the others in the situation who may insist on conformity and make vigorous efforts to bring it about or who may not exert any pressure at all on deviates.

A second consequence of this emphasis has been to ignore the broader social meaning of conformity. Is the individual's personal need for a social validation of his beliefs the only reason for conforming? What does deviation do to a person's acceptance by others? What does it do to his ability to influence others? Or from the group's point of view, are there reasons to insist on certain common values, beliefs, and behavior? These questions are not asked or answered by an approach which limits itself to the cognitive problems of the individual.

Group Processes

The group dynamics orientation toward conformity emphasizes a broader range of determinants. Not denying the importance of the cognitive situation, we want to look more closely at the nature of the individual's relation to particular groups with particular properties. In formulating hypotheses about the origin of pressures to uniformity, two basic sources have been stressed. These have been stated most clearly by Festinger and his co-workers, who propose that when differences of opinion arise within a group, pressures to uniformity will arise (a) if the validity or "reality" of the opinion depends upon agreement with the group (essentially the same point as Asch's), or (b) if locomotion toward a group goal will be facilitated by uniformity within the group.[13]

This emphasis upon the group, rather than simply upon the individual, leads one to expect a broader set of consequences from pressures to uniformity. Pressures to uniformity are seen as establishing: (a) a tendency on the part of each group member to change his own opinion to conform to that of the other group members, (b) a tendency to try to change the opinions of others, and (c) a tendency to redefine the boundaries of the group so as to exclude those holding deviate opinions. The relative magnitudes of these tendencies will depend on other conditions which need to be specified.

This general conception of the nature of the processes that produce conformity emerged from two early field studies conducted at the Research Center for Group Dynamics. It was also influenced to a considerable extent by the previous work of Newcomb in which he studied the formation and change of social attitudes in a college community.[14] The first field study, reported by Festinger, Schachter, and Back, traced the formation of social groups in a new student housing project. As each group developed, it displayed its own standards for its members. The extent of conformity to the standards of a particular group was found to be related directly to the degree of cohesiveness of that group as measured by sociometric choices. Moreover, those individuals who deviated from their own group's norms received fewer sociometric choices than those who conformed. A process of rejection for nonconformity had apparently set in.[15] The second field study, reported by Coch and French, observed similar processes. This study was conducted in a textile factory and was concerned with conformity to production standards set by groups of workers. Here an individual worker's reaction to new work methods was found to depend upon the standards of his group and, here too, rejection for deviation was observed.[16]

The next phase of this research consisted of a series of experiments with groups created in the laboratory. It was hoped thereby to be able to disentangle the complexity of variables that might exist in any field setting in order to understand better the operation of each. These experiments have been reported in various publications by Festinger, Back, Gerard, Hymovitch, Kelley, Raven, Schachter, and Thibaut.[17,18,19,20,21,22] We shall not attempt to describe these studies in detail, but draw upon them and other research in an effort to summarize the major conclusions.

First, a great deal of evidence has been accumulated to support the hypothesis that pressures to uniformity will be greater the more members want to remain in the group. In more attractive or cohesive groups, members attempt more to influence others and are more willing to accept influence from others. Note that here pressures to conformity are high in the very conditions where satisfaction from group membership is also high.

Second, there is a close relation between attempts to change the deviate and tendencies to reject him. If persistent attempts to change the deviate fail to produce conformity, then communication appears to cease between the majority and the deviate, and the rejection of the deviate sets in. These two processes, moreover, are more intense the more cohesive the group. One of the early studies which documented the process of rejection was conducted by Schachter on college students.[23] It has recently been replicated by Emerson on high school students who found essentially the same process at work, but he discovered that among his high school students efforts to influence others continued longer, there was a greater readiness on the part of the majority to change, and there was a lower level of rejection within a limited period of time.[24] Yet another study, conducted in Holland, Sweden, France, Norway, Belgium, Germany, and England, found the same tendency to reject deviates in all of these countries. This study, reported by Schachter, et al., is a landmark in cross-cultural research.[25]

Third, there is the question of what determines whether or not pressures to uniformity will arise with respect to any particular opinion, attitude, and behavior. In most groups there are no pressures to uniformity concerning the color of necktie worn by the members. Differences of opinion about the age of the earth probably would not lead to rejection in a poker club, but they might do so in certain fundamentalist church groups. The concept of *relevance* seems to be required to account for such variations in pressures to uniformity. And, if we ask, "relevance for what?" we are forced again to look at the group and especially at the goals of the group.

Schachter has demonstrated, for example, that deviation on a given issue will result much more readily in rejection when that issue is relevant to the group's goals than when it is irrelevant.[26] And the principle of relevance seems to be necessary to account for the findings of a field study reported by Ross.[27] Here attitudes of fraternity men toward restrictive admission policies were studied. Despite the fact that there was a consistent policy of exclusion in these fraternities, there was, surprisingly, little evidence for the existence of pressures toward uniformity of attitudes. When, however, a field experiment was conducted in which the distribution of actual opinions for each fraternity house was reported to a meeting of house members together with a discussion of the relevance of these opinions for fraternity policy, attitudes then tended to change to conform to the particular modal position of each house. Presumably the experimental treatment made uniformity of attitude instrumental to group locomotion where it had not been so before.

SOURCES OF HETEROGENEITY

We have seen that pressures to uniformity are stronger the more cohesive the group. Shall we conclude from this that strong, need-satisfying, cohesive groups must always produce uniformity on matters that are important to the group? We believe not. We cannot, however, cite much convincing evidence since research has focused to date primarily upon the sources of pressures to uniformity and has ignored the conditions which produce heterogeneity.

Group Standards about Uniformity

It is important, first, to make a distinction between conformity and uniformity. A group might have a value that everyone should be as different from everyone else as possible. Conformity to this value, then, would result not in uniformity of behavior but in nonuniformity. Such a situation often arises in therapy groups or training groups where it is possible to establish norms which place a high value upon "being different" and upon tolerating deviant behavior. Conformity to this value is presumably greater the more cohesive the group and the more it is seen as relevant to the group's objectives. Unfortunately, very little is known about the origin and operation of group standards about conformity itself. We doubt that the pressure to uniformity which arises from the need for "social reality" and for group locomotion can simply be obliterated by invoking a group standard of tolerance, but a closer look at such processes as those of group decision-making will be required before a deep understanding of this problem can be achieved.

Freedom to Deviate

A rather different source of heterogeneity has been suggested by Kelley and Shapiro.[28] They reason that the more an individual feels accepted by the other members of the group, the more ready he should be to deviate from the beliefs of the majority under conditions where objectively correct deviation would be in the group's best interest. They designed an experiment to test this hypothesis. The results, while not entirely clear because acceptance led to greater cohesiveness, tend to support this line of reasoning.

It has been suggested by some that those in positions of leadership are freer to deviate from group standards than are those of lesser status. Just the opposite conclusion has been drawn by others. Clearly, further research into group properties which generate freedom to deviate from majority pressures is needed.

Subgroup Formation

Festinger and Thibault have shown that lower group wide pressures to uniformity of opinion result when members of a group perceive that the group is composed of persons differing in interest and knowledge. Under these conditions subgroups may easily develop with a resulting heterogeneity within the group as a whole though with uniformity within each subgroup.[29] This conclusion is consistent with Asch's finding that the presence of a partner for a deviate greatly strengthens his tendency to be independent.[30] One might suspect that such processes, though achieving temporarily a greater heterogeneity, would result in a schismatic subgroup conflict.

Positions and Roles

A more integrative achievement of heterogeneity seems to arise through the process of role differentiation. Established groups are usually differentiated according to "positions" with special function attached to each. The occupant of the position has certain behaviors prescribed for him by the others in the group. These role prescriptions differ, moreover, from one position to another, with the result that conformity to them produces heterogeneity within the group. A group function, which might otherwise be suppressed by pressures to uniformity, may be preserved by the establishment of a position whose responsibility is to perform the function.

Hall has recently shown that social roles can be profitably conceived in the context of conformity to group pressures. He reasoned that pressures to uniformity of prescriptions concerning the behavior of the occupant of a position and pressures on the occupant to conform to these prescriptions should be greater the more cohesive the group.[31] A study of the role of aircraft commander in bomber crews lends strong support to this conception.

In summary, it should be noted that in all but one of these suggested sources of heterogeneity we have assumed the process of conformity—to the norms of a subgroup, to a role, or to a group standard favoring heterogeneity. Even if the price of membership in a strong group be conformity, it need not follow that strong groups will suppress differences.

MORE THAN ONE GROUP

Thus far our analysis has proceeded as though the individual were a member of only one group. Actually we recognize that he is, and has been, a member of many groups. In one of our current research projects we are finding that older adolescents can name from twenty to forty "important groups and persons that influence my opinions and behavior in decision situations." Indeed, some personality theorists hold that personality should be viewed as an "internal society" made up of representations of the diverse group relationships which the individual now has and has had. According to this view, each individual has a unique internal society and makes his own personal synthesis of the values and behavior preferences generated by those affiliations.

The various memberships of an individual may relate to one another in various ways and produce various consequences for the individual. A past group may exert internal pressures toward conformity which are in conflict with a present group. Two contemporaneous groups may have expectations for the person which are incompatible. Or an individual may hold a temporary membership (the situation of a foreign student, for example) and be faced with current conformity pressures which if accepted will make it difficult to readjust when returning to his more permanent memberships.

This constant source of influence from other memberships toward deviancy of every member of every group requires that each group take measures to preserve its integrity. It should be noted, however, that particular deviancy pressures associated with a given member may be creative or destructive when evaluated in terms of the integrity and productivity of the group, and conformity pressures from the group may be supportive or disruptive of the integrity of the individual.

Unfortunately there has been little systematic research on these aspects of multiple group membership. We can only indicate two sets of observations concerning (a) the intrapersonal processes resulting from multiple membership demands, and (b) the effects on group processes of the deviancy pressures which arise from the multiple membership status of individual members.

Marginal Membership

Lewin, in his discussion of adolescence and of minority group membership, has analyzed some of the psychological effects on the person of being "between two groups" without a firm anchorage in either one.[32] He says: "The transition from childhood to adulthood may be a rather sudden shift (for instance, in some of the primitive societies), or it may occur gradually in a setting where children and adults are not sharply separated groups. In the case of the so-called 'adolescent difficulties,' however, a third state of affairs is often prevalent: children and adults constitute two clearly defined groups; the adolescent does not wish any longer to belong to the children's group and, at the same time, knows that he is not really accepted in the adult group. He has a position similar to what is called in sociology the 'marginal man' . . . a person who stands on the boundary between two groups. He does not belong to either of them, or at least he is not sure of his belongingness in either of them.[33] Lewin goes on to point out that there are characteristic maladjustive behavior patterns resulting from this unstable membership situation: high tension, shifts between extremes of behavior, high sensitivity, and rejection of low status members of both groups. This situation rather than fostering strong individuality, makes belonging to closely knit, loyalty-demanding groups very attractive. Dependency and acceptance are a welcome relief. Probably most therapy groups have a number of members who are seeking relief from marginality.

Overlapping Membership

There is quite a different type of situation where the person does have a firm anchorage in two or more groups but where the group standards are not fully compatible. Usually the actual conflict arises when the person is physically present in one group but realizes that he also belongs to other groups to which he will return in the near or distant future. In this sense, the child moves between his family group and his school group every day. The member of a therapy group has some sort of time perspective of "going back" to a variety of other groups between each meeting of the therapy group.

In their study of the adjustment of foreign students both in this country and after returning home, Watson and Lippitt observed four different ways in which individuals cope with this problem of overlapping membership.

1. Some students solved the problem by "living in the present" at all times. When they were in the American culture all of their energy and attention was directed to being an acceptable member of this group. They avoided conflict within themselves by minimizing thought about and contact with the other group "back home." When they returned to the other group they used the same type of solution, quickly shifting behavior and ideas to fit back into the new present group. Their behavior appeared quite inconsistent, but it was a consistent approach to solving their problem of multiple membership.

2. Other individuals chose to keep their other membership the dominant one while in this country. They were defensive and rejective every time the present group seemed to promote values and to expect behavior which they felt might not be acceptable to the other group "back home." The strain of maintaining this orientation was relieved by turning every situation into a "black and white" comparison and adopting a consistently rejective posture toward the present, inferior group. This way of adjusting required a considerable amount of distorting of present and past realities, but the return to the other group was relatively easy.

3. Others reacted in a sharply contrasting way by identifying wholeheartedly with the present group and by rejecting the standards of the other group as incorrect or inferior at the points of conflict. They were, of course accepted by the present group, but when they returned home they met rejection or felt alienated from the standards of the group (even when they felt accepted).

4. Some few individuals seemed to achieve a more difficult but also more creative solution. They attempted to regard membership in both groups as desirable. In order to succeeed in this effort, they had to be more realistic about perceiving the inconsistencies between the group expectations and to struggle to make balanced judgments about the strong and weak points of each group. Besides taking this more objective approach to evaluation, these persons worked on problems of how the strengths of one group might be interpreted and utilized by the other group. They were taking roles of creative deviancy in both groups but attempting to make their contributions in such a way as to be accepted as loyal and productive members. They found ways of using each group membership as a resource for contributing to the welfare of the other group. Some members of each group were of course threatened by this readiness and ability to question the present modal ways of doing things in the group.[34]

Thus it seems that the existence of multiple group memberships creates difficult problems both for the person and for the group. But there are also potentialities and supports for the development of creative individuality in this situation, and there are potentialities for group growth and achievement in the fact that the members of any group are also members of other groups with different standards.

SOME CONCLUSIONS

Let us return now to the question raised at the beginning of this paper. How should we think of the relation between individuals and groups? If we accept the assumption that individuals and groups are both important social realities, we can then ask a pair of important questions. What kinds of effects do groups have on the emotional security and creative productivity of the individual? What kinds of effects do individuals have on the morale and creative productivity of the group? In answering these questions it is important to be alerted to both good and bad effects. Although the systematic evidence from research does not begin to provide full answers to these questions, we have found evidence which tends to support the following general statements.

Strong groups do exert strong influences on members toward conformity. These conformity pressures, however, may be directed toward uniformity of thinking and behavior, or they may foster heterogeneity.

Acceptance of these conformity pressures, toward uniformity or heterogeneity, may satisfy the emotional needs of some members and frustrate others. Similarly, it may support the potential creativity of some members and inhibit that of others.

From their experiences of multiple membership and their personal synthesis of these experiences, individuals do have opportunities to achieve significant bases of individuality.

Because each group is made up of members who are loyal members of other groups and who have unique individual interests, each group must continuously cope with deviancy tendencies of the members. These tendencies may represent a source of creative improvement in the life of the group or a source of destructive disruption.

The resolution of these conflicting interests does not seem to be the strengthening of individuals and the weakening of groups, or the strengthening of groups and the weakening of individuals, but rather a strengthening of both by qualitative improvements in the nature of interdependence between integrated individuals and cohesive groups.

NOTES

1. K. Lewin, R. Lippitt, and R. White, "Patterns of Aggressive Behavior in Experimentally Created 'Social Climates.'" *Journal of Social Psychology*, Vol. 10 (1939), pp. 271-299.
2. F. J. Roethlisberger and W. J. Dickson, *Management and the Worker* (Cambridge: Harvard University Press, 1939).

3. K. Lewin, "Studies in Group Decision," in *Group Dynamics: Research and Theory*. D. Cartwright and A. Zander, ed. (Evanston: Harper & Row, Publishers, 1953).

4. S. E. Seashore, *Group Cohesiveness in the Industrial Group* (Ann Arbor: Institute for Social Research, 1954).

5. *Ibid.*, p. 98.

6. *Ibid.*, p. 13.

7. A. H. Stanton and M. S. Schwartz, *The Mental Hospital* (New York: Basic Books, Inc., Publishers, 1954).

8. A. Tocqueville, *Democracy in America,* Vol. 1 (New York: Alfred A. Knopf, Inc., 1945 (original publication, 1835), pp. 273-275.

9. T. Parsons, *Essays in Sociological Theory,* rev. ed. (New York: Free Press of Glencoe, Inc. 1954), pp. 128-129.

10. M. Sherif, *The Psychology of Social Norms* (New York: Harper & Row, Publishers, 1936).

11. S. E. Asch. *Social Psychology* (New York: Prentice-Hall, Inc., 1952).

12. *Ibid.*, p. 484.

13. L. Festinger, "Informal Social Communication," *Psychology Review,* Vol. 57 (1950), pp. 271-292.

14. T. M. Newcomb, *Personality and Social Change* (New York: Holt, Rinehart & Winston, Inc., 1943).

15. L. Festinger, S. Schachter, and K. Back, *Social Pressures in Informal Groups* (New York: Harper & Row, Publishers, 1950).

16. L. Coch and J. R. P. French, "Overcoming Resistance to Change," *Human Relations,* Vol. 1 (1948), pp. 512-532.

17. K. W. Back, "Influence Through Social Communication," *Journal of Abnormal and Social Psychology,* Vol. 46 (1951), pp. 9-23.

18. L. Festinger, H. B. Gerard, B. Humovitch, H. H. Kelley, and B. Raven, "The Influence Process in the Presence of Extreme Deviates," *Human Relations,* Vol. 5 (1952), pp. 327-346.

19. L. Festinger and J. Thibaut, "Interpersonal Communication in Small Groups," *Journal of Abnormal and Social Psychology,* Vol. 46 (1951) pp. 92-99.

20. H. B. Gerard, "The Effect of Different Dimensions of Disagreement on the Communication Process in Small Groups," *Human Relations,* Vol. 6 (1953) pp. 249-271.

21. H. H. Kelley, "Communication in Experimentally Created Hierarchies," *Human Relations,* Vol. 4 (1951), pp. 39-56.

22. S. Schachter, "Deviation, Rejection, and Communication," *Journal of Abnormal and Social Psychology,* Vol. 46 (1951), pp. 190-207.

23. *Ibid*.

24. F. M. Emerson, "Deviation and Rejection: An Experimental Replication," *American Sociological Review,* Vol. 19 (1954), pp. 688-693.

25. S. Schachter, *et al.,* "Cross-cultural Experiments on Threat and Rejection," *Human Relations,* Vol. 7 (1954), pp. 403-439.

26. Schachter.

27. I. Ross, "Group Standards Concerning the Admission of Jews," *Social Problems,* Vol. 2 (1955), pp. 133-140.

28. H. H. Kelley and M. M. Shapiro, "An Experiment on Conformity to Group Norms Where Conformity Is Detrimental to Group Achievement," *American Sociological Review,* Vol. 19 (1954), pp. 667-677.

29. Festinger and Thibault.

30. Asch.

31. R. L. Hall, "Social Influence on the Aircraft Commander's Role," *American Sociological Review,* Vol. 20 (1955), pp. 292-299.

32. K. Lewin, *Field Theory in Social Science* (New York: Harper & Row, Publishers, 1951).

33. *Ibid.*, p. 143.

34. J. Watson and R. Lippitt, *Learning Across Cultures* (Ann Arbor: Institute for Social Research, 1955).

SOCIALLY RELEVANT SCIENCE: REFLECTIONS ON SOME STUDIES OF INTERPERSONAL CONFLICT

Morton Deutsch

From the onset of my career in social psychology, I have been continuously concerned with the interrelations among experimental research, theory, and social policy. I started my graduate study not long after Hiroshima and Nagasaki and my work in social psychology has been shadowed by the atomic cloud ever since. I have taken this occasion as an opportunity to force myself to reflect on several of my research studies and how they have been affected by images that have arisen out of my concern about the possibilities of nuclear war. In so doing, I seek to explore a few of the issues in the phrase "socially relevant science."

Before turning to a discussion of some recent research, let me consider two early studies of mine, "An Experimental Study of the Effects of Cooperation and Competition upon Group Process" (1949a) and *Interracial Housing* (Deutsch & Collins, 1951). The study of cooperation and competition was initiated under two major influences, one of which shaped its substantive focus and the other of which determined its form and its scientific goals. The substantive focus grew out of my concern about nuclear war. Like many others at the time, I thought that mankind would not long survive unless the nations of the world cooperated with one another. This thought got focused on the United Nations Security Council and was crystallized in two contrasting images: the members of the council working together cooperatively with a problem-solving attitude or the members competing with one another to obtain a relative advantage for their own nations. I suspect that my initial concern crystallized this way because the United Nations Security Council was in the public spotlight and also because I was then a student at the Research Center for Group Dynamics at M.I.T. There it was natural to think of group process and group productivity and of factors influencing them.

As my attention shifted from the relations among nations to relations within a group, the problem took on a more generalized form. The problem was now transformed into an attempt to understand the fundamental features of cooperative and competitive relations and the consequences of these different types of interdependencies in a way that would be generally applicable to the relations between individuals, groups, or nations. The problem had become a theoretical one with the broad scientific goal of attempting to interrelate and give insight into a variety of phenomena through several funda-

American Psychologist, Vol. 24, No. 12 (December, 1969) pp. 1076-1092. Copyright 1969 by the American Psychological Association. Reprinted by Permission.
Presidential Address before the Eastern Psychological Association on April 11, 1969, in Philadelphia, Pennsylvania. Preparation of this paper was supported by a contract with the Office of Naval Research, NONR-4294(00), and a grant from the National Science Foundation, GS-302.

mental concepts and several basic propositions. The intellectual atmosphere of Kurt Lewin's Research Center for Group Dynamics was such as to push its students to theory building. The favorite slogan at the Center was "there is nothing so practical as a good theory."

Thus, I turned my social concern about the possibilities of nuclear war into a theoretically oriented investigation of cooperation and competition. In so doing, did I lose contact with my original concern? Is there any relevance, at all, of a theory of cooperation and competition and an experimental study of small groups to the prevention of a nuclear holocaust? Before answering this question, let me state that my tendencies to grandiosity, although not insignificant, are under control. I have never thought that any efforts of mine, whether as a scientist pursuing systematic knowledge or as a citizen engaging in political action, would be a crucial factor in influencing the likelihood of such large-scale events. Nevertheless, I have maintained the hope that the cumulative efforts of many individuals pushing in the same direction may have significant effects. In addition, I have assumed that the acquisition and dissemination of systematic knowledge is inherently of social value: Misjudgment, evil, corruption, and the abuse of power are abetted by ignorance, but are reduced by the dissemination of knowledge.

Thus, I have hoped that my intellectual work on cooperation and competition combined with the work of other social scientists on related problems might significantly affect ways of thinking about these types of social relations and that, as a consequence, systematic, and possibly new, ideas about preventing destructive conflicts among nations might emerge. If anyone wishes to accuse me of being optimistic, of course, he would be right. After all, my initial theoretical and empirical work in the area of cooperation-competition centered on the differential *effects* of these types of relationships. Only later did I work on the factors influencing whether a cooperative or competitive relationship would develop. This later work (which has been described under such labels as "interpersonal conflict," "bargaining," "conflict resolution") is much more directly related to the question of preventing destructive conflicts. Yet, it turns out that one of the major simplifying ideas about factors affecting conflict resolution arising out of my more recent work complements my earlier theoretical analysis of the effects of cooperation and competition. Namely, the characteristic processes and effects elicited by a given type of social relationship (cooperative or competitive) tend also to elicit that type of social relationship. Thus, the strategy of power and the tactics of coercion, threat, and deception result from and also result in a competitive relationship. Similarly, the strategy of mutual problem solving and the tactics of persuasion, openness, and mutual enhancement elicit and also are elicited by a cooperative orientation.

Table 1 presents in condensed, outline form some of the basic ideas involved in my analysis of the effect of cooperation and competition. In essence, the theory states that the effects of one person's actions upon another will be a function of the nature of their interdependence and the nature of the action that takes place. Skillfully executed actions of an antagonist will elicit rather different responses than skillful actions from an ally, but a bumbling collaborator may evoke as much negative reaction as an adroit opponent. The theory links type of interdependence and type of action with three basic social-psychological processes—which I have labeled "substitutability," "cathexis," and "inducibility"—and it then proliferates a variety of social-psychological consequences from these processes as they are affected by the variables with which the theory is concerned. I shall not attempt here to spell out how this is done. The theory has been published (Deutsch, 1949b, 1962a), and my interest in this presentation is on the conditions determining the initiation of cooperation and competition rather than upon their effects.

The point I wish to make is that if you take a situation in which there is a mixture of cooperative and competitive elements (most bargaining and "conflict" situations are of this nature), you can move it in one direction or the other by creating as initial states the typical consequences of effective cooperation and competition. In such indeterminate situations, the tendency to relate cooperatively will be increased by anything that will "highlight mutual interests," "enhance mutual power," lead to "trusting, friendly attitudes, and a positive responsiveness to the other's needs," "minimize the salience of opposed interest," lead to "open, honest communications," etc. On the other hand, the likelihood of a competitive relation will be increased by attempts to "reduce the other's power," "suspicious, hostile, exploitative attitudes," "the magnification of the opposed interests," the use of tactics of "threat, intimidation, or coercion," "devious communication and espionage," etc.

I have attempted to express an idea that is still in a rudimentary stage of intellectual development. If it is nurtured carefully, it may have considerable sweep and may help us to deal with social conflict productively rather than destructively. However, the theoretical and empirical work being done on the resolution of conflict reflects the intellectual efforts of many social scientists from a variety of disciplines, and by my emphasis on my own work I do not wish to give a misleading picture of the unique significance of my contributions. My own work is only a small part of the total scientific activity in this area, and it is the cumulative results of these diverse efforts that are beginning to have social utility.

Initially, the major utility of these cumulating efforts has been in the emergence of a mode of thinking with an array of concepts that highlight some of the central processes involved in conflicts and that provide a coherent basis of organizing the details of such processes. This has served to reduce the mystical aura of the inevitability of destructiveness often associated with conflict, it has provided new insights to many people engaged in the handling of conflict, and it has occasionally been reflected in important public statements. Thus, the historically significant speech of President Kennedy at American University on June 10, 1963, in which he outlined "A Strategy of Peace," and which signaled the start of a thaw in American Soviet relations, was clearly very much influenced by the newly emerging social science mode of thinking about resolving conflict. More recently, the Kerner Commission Report on riots also was enlightened by this new perspective. Under the leadership of such applied behavioral science groups as the National Training Laboratory Institute for Applied Behavioral Science, there has been a widespread application of social-psychological approaches to conflict resolution in industrial and school settings.

Let me now turn to a rather different type of study, our study of interracial housing. Like the work on cooperation-competition, it was stimulated by the belief that "the social scientist has a responsibility, not merely to further his own esthetic and intellectual pleasures in the course of research but also to contibute to the solution of important social problems (Deutsch & Collins, 1951, xi)." However, the interracial housing study, unlike the earlier one, was guided throughout by a continuous concern with social usefulness. We selected interracial relations in housing for investigation because we felt that residential segregation was of central importance to intergroup relations in general. Residential segregation by its very nature leads to a de facto segregation in many other areas such as schools, churches, banks, playgrounds, and shopping and community centers. It also usually leads to major economic disadvantages for the ghetto resident. Another

TABLE 1
Basic Concepts in the Analysis of the Effects of Cooperation and Competition

Type of perceived interdependence between P and O	Type of action by O	Effect of O's actions on P	Some theoretically expected consequences of an exchange of effective actions between P and O in cooperative and competitive relationships
Cooperative: P's and O's goals are linked in such a way that their probabilities of goal attainment are positively correlated; as one's chances increase or decrease so does the other's chances.	Effective: (O's action increases O's chances of goal attainment and, thus, also P's.)	Positive substitutability: P will not need to act to accomplish what O has accomplished. Positive cathexis: P will value O's actions and will be attracted to O in similar, future situations (i.e., as a fellow cooperator). Positive inducibility: P will facilitate O's actions and be open to positive influence from O.	Task orientation: highlighting of mutual interests; coordinated effort with division of labor and specialization of function; substitutability of effort rather than duplication; the enhancement of mutual power becomes an objective. Attitudes: trusting, friendly attitudes with a positive interest in the other's welfare and a readiness to respond helpfully to the other's needs and requests. Perception: increased sensitivity to common interests; a sense of convergence of beliefs and values. Communication: open, honest communication of relevant information; each is interested in accurately informing as well as being informed; communication is persuasive rather than coercive in intent.
	Ineffective: (O's action decreases O's chances of goal attainment and, thus, also P's.)	Negative substitutability: P will need to act to accomplish what O has failed to accomplish. Negative cathexis: P will reject O's actions and will reject O in similar, future situations (i.e., as a fellow coorperator). Negative inducibility: P will hinder O's actions and be negatively influenced by O.	
Competitive: P's and O's goals are linked in such a way that their probabilities of goal attainment are negatively correlated; as one's chances increase, the other's decreases.	Effective: (O's action increases O's chances of goal attainment and, thus, decreases P's chances.)	Negative substitutability: P will need to act to accomplish what O has accomplished. Negative cathexis: P will dislike the occurrence of O's successes and will reject O as a future competitor. Negative inducibility: P will hinder or block O's actions and react negatively to O's influence attempts.	Task orientation: emphasis on antagonistic interests; the minimization of the other's power becomes an objective. Attitudes: suspicious, hostile attitudes with a readiness to exploit the other's needs and weakness and a negative responsiveness to the other's requests. Perception: increases sensitivity to opposed interests, to threats, and to power differences while minimizing the awareness of similarities. Communication: little communication or misleading communication; espionage or other techniques to obtain information the other is unwilling to give; each seeks to obtain accurate information about the other but to mislead, discourage, or intimidate the other; coercive tactics are employed.
	Ineffective: (O's action decreases O's chances of goal attainment and, thus, increases P's chances.)	Positive substitutability: P will not need to repeat O's mistakes. Positive cathexis: P will value the occurrence of O's failures and will prefer O as a future competitor. Positive inducibility: P will facilitate O's blunders and be ready to help O make mistakes.	

reason for the focus on housing, with a particular emphasis on a comparison of integrated and segregated occupancy patterns, was the realization that the Federal Housing Act of 1949 would soon give rise to many public housing developments. Public officials in localities throughout the country would be making decisions in the near future about whether these developments would be racially integrated or segregated. (The usual practice in the past had been some form of segregation.) It was our hope that our research might have some influence on these decisions.

Our study compared integrated interracial housing developments in New York City with segregated biracial developments in Newark in an ex post facto experimental design. The developments were selected to be as comparable as possible except for their occupancy patterns. We studied behavior and attitudes of blacks as well as whites, of adults as well as children. As in all such ex post facto field studies the design was not as tight as one would like, but we did a reasonably careful job of seeking a variety of evidence to test the various alternative explanations for our findings. Our findings, from many different angles, supported the conclusion that "from the point of view of reducing prejudice and of creating harmonious intergroup relations, the net gain resulting from the integrated projects is considerable; from the same point of view, the gain created by the segregated bi-racial projects is slight (Deutsch & Collins, 1951, p. 124)."

The study and its findings were widely discussed by public housing officials and by community groups and helped a number of housing authorities to adopt a policy of nonsegregation. The Executive Director of the Housing Authority of the City of Newark, for example, wrote in a postscript to the study:

> In supplying us with an objective picture of race relations in our projects, their study dramatically focused our attention and that of the community at large on matters which, under the press of other business, we had tended to ignore. The study did more than help to focus attention on the basic question of segregation in housing. Perhaps its most important consequence was its usefulness to those community groups concerned with intergroup relations and civil rights. . . . To such groups the study was an invaluable tool in creating the atmosphere which made it possible for the housing authority to adopt and execute a policy of nonsegregation. I don't know how many meetings of such groups I attended, but invariably the Deutsch-Collins study was referred to and quoted. (Deutsch & Collins, 1951, p. 130).

Clearly, then, our study of interracial housing had some immediately useful and significant social consequences. In addition, it served to challenge a widely held opinion that "stateways cannot change folkways," which, not surprisingly, was usually interpreted so as to support the status quo rather than a change in "stateways." Thus, it helped, along with much other research, to provide a supporting rationale for judicial decisions and legislation to bar segregation.

However, I must admit that this research did not contribute significantly to the ideas of social psychology. Intellectually, its merit did not reside in its theoretical innovativeness but rather in its systematic application of existing social-psychological concepts to the important social issues of residential segregation. This is not to say that there is not a need for new ideas and theoretical advances to clarify and develop systematic understanding of intergroup relations. Indeed, some of our current experimental research has this as an objective. But I must confess that as we begin to explore some of the conceptual underpinnings in this area we are pulled in the direction of considering such questions as the relationship between social categories and social coordination. It takes us away from the immediate social urgencies.

Our housing study was not formulated with a theoretical objective and, unfortunately, we were not alert enough to appreciate fully the wider theoretical significance of some of our findings. These findings suggested that behavior change preceded attitudinal change: The white women in the integrated projects often behaved in an unprejudiced manner toward their Negro neighbors before they felt this way. Had we been clever enough to realize the general implications of this finding we might have anticipated the major idea underlying Festinger's theory of cognitive dissonance, which is in essence the converse of the old truism that people tend to act in accord with their beliefs. Namely, people tend to make their beliefs and attitudes accord with their actions. This is a very important idea that has major implications for theoretical and practical work in the area of attitude change. This idea could have emerged from our field study of interracial relations in housing but, alas, it did not.

If now, many years after the completion of each of the two studies (*Interracial Housing* and "An Experimental Study of the Effects of Cooperation and Competition upon Group Process"), I try to assess their social utilities relative to one another, what conclusion seems warranted? Both studies have received considerable recognition within social psychology and both have been honored by being selected for inclusion in *Basic Studies in Social Psychology* (Proshansky & Seidenberg, 1965). However, I clearly have a personal preference that I should confess before attempting to answer the question. My work on cooperation-competition gives me more satisfaction and I have more pride in being its author. The ideas in it are more original and more fundamental to understanding social life irrespective of time or place than the ideas in *Interracial Housing*. Nevertheless, I cannot point to any specific desirable social change that has resulted from my work on cooperation-competition. Whatever social benefits have derived from it have come indirectly through its contribution to the stream of ideas being developed cumulatively by the social sciences that are leading to new perspectives on conflict.

Interracial Housing, on the other hand, has made little new contribution to the ideas of social science, but it has clearly contributed to desirable social change in several instances. However, let me note the obvious. Despite our study and the work of many other social scientists that have demonstrated the social and personal value of racial integration, there is little racial integration in the United States. The available statistics indicate that there is more de facto residential segregation in the United States now than there was 20 years ago. Similarly, as Pettigrew (1969) pointed out: "There is more racial segregation of schools today in the entire United States than there was in 1954 at the time of the Supreme Court decision (p. 4)." With the repeated and continuing frustration of attempts to break down the walls of custom, belief, and institutionalized practice that keep blacks and whites segregated, it is no wonder that the achievement of racial integration is now of less relevance than the enhancement of black power. As far as one can tell, there will be no meaningful racial integration until the economic and political power of black people, and their white allies, is strong enough to shatter the walls of institutionalized indifference and discrimination that perpetuate their isolation and disadvantage. Black pride, cohesive black organization, and effective political alliances are keys to the enhancement of black power; chauvinism and separatism, on the other hand, provide a fragile, illusory, and inherently self-defeating basis for group- or self-esteem. Thus, although in my opinion the findings and recommendations of our study of integrated housing are still valid—integration is still preferable to segregation, history has turned a study that once seemed highly relevant into one that now appears to be somewhat beside the point.

Whatever its changing relevance for immediate social concerns, it was not inevitable that the housing study be lacking in theoretical significance; as I suggested earlier, had I been more keen-witted I might have anticipated the key notion of dissonance theory. Similarly, the study of cooperation-competition need not have been without immediate social consequence. It was conducted in an experimental format that incidentally involved a systematic comparison of two types of classroom grading systems: cooperative and competitive. The results clearly demonstrated some harmful consequences of the competitive grading system and they could have been employed in a campaign to reexamine the prevailing system of grading. Such a campaign was not in existence nor did the thought of fostering one occur to me.

Thus, the potential usefulness of each study was unduly limited by "blinders" I had donned unwittingly. In thinking of the cooperation-competition study as a theoretical inquiry into fundamental issues, I overlooked its immediate social significance. And in conceiving of the interracial housing study in terms of its immediate social relevance, I was insensitive to its broader implications. I am inclined to believe that the "blindness" reflected in both instances is not unique to me but is commonplace in psychology. Psychologists doing research on how to improve the learning of a particular subject matter in the classroom rarely make significant contributions to learning theory, and those seeking to test theoretical notions rarely conduct their research in such a way as to suggest immediate consequences for learning in the school.

Obviously, "blinders" have functions: They reduce distractions and facilitate focused attention. Yet, if worn too long, they limit the scope of vision; a broad perspective is necessary to a socially relevant science. A focus on "science" that excludes "social relevance" as a distraction or on "social relevance" that excludes "science" as irrelevant will in the long run be destructive to both. A society will not long nurture a science that does not nurture society. Nor will there be much to nourish society with unless there is a proliferation of systematic knowledge that is rich and diverse enough to initiate and reliably sustain complex activities in many different settings.

Let me now return to the question of the comparative social utilities of the two studies I have discussed. It should be obvious that there is no simple answer. Both types of studies are needed for a socially relevant science. Moreover, a rigid characterization of the kinds of studies into sharply different categories may be dysfunctional to both. This is not to deny that the primary social value of a theoretical study such as that of cooperation-competition may be manifest only in the long run while the primary utility of an applied study may be in its immediate social consequences. It is evident that in considering what psychologists can contribute to society, we must be concerned with both the future and the present. In many areas of urgent social concern, we do not have enough reliable, systematic psychological knowledge to make any valid social contribution at present. Some of this knowledge can only be acquired by freely ranging investigations that seek to define and formulate the fundamental questions that must be answered before one can identify what knowledge is really relevant to a solution of a problem.

It is a truism that a demand for relevance makes no sense until one can identify what is relevant. History and everyday experience alike testify that the appearance of relevance, the pseudorelevance of surface similarities, can be grossly misleading. It is hard and demanding intellectual work to get beyond the cliches and slogans of the "establishment" or the "antiestablishment" to a fundamental and usable understanding of the important social problems confronting us. It requires the freedom to be irreverent and irrelevant to the current idols and the passing fashions. Nevertheless, a salient concern for social relevance may be a healthy component in the motivation of the work of all psychologists whether they be functioning as researchers, teachers, or practitioners. There may be no long-run future for any of us or for psychology unless some of the urgent social crises facing us are dealt with intelligently. Moreover, whatever little help psychology has to offer now to such situations will be made available largely by the actions of psychologists in attempting to formulate what is relevant in psychology to social action and in psychologists' taking some initiative in helping to get to psychological viewpoints implemented in action. Thus, in my view, psychology needs groups like the Society for the Psychological Study of Social Issues and the Psychologists for Social Action in order to make whatever we know as psychologists play an active educational and political role in relation to present social concerns. We also need psychologists who will make the future contributions of psychology to society more valuable by their willingness to investigate unexplored territory with unorthodox methods even as they lack any assurance that their explorations will have any useful results.

I have gone into this long digression (and it has been longer than I anticipated) as an introduction to some of my experiments on interpersonal conflict because I sense a need to defend the fact that in these experiments the subjects play games. In none do I simulate any particular external reality and, thus, the experiments are not relevant to any given social reality. Yet, I would contend that the unique situations in the laboratory are meaningful, and they permit an economical inquiry into ideas that may be of relevance to many situations in life even though the ideas do not characterize adequately any actual situation of the nonlaboratory world.

EXPERIMENTAL STUDIES

I now turn to a consideration of three experimental studies, one of which is published and two of which are not as yet. I have selected these three studies from many that have been conducted in our laboratory because they all employ the same experimental format and because each started with a concern about ideas relating to foreign policy. All three experiments employ the Acme-Bolt bargaining game, which was demonstrated in one of the APA TV film series, "The Social Animal."

The bargaining game involves two players, each of whom operates a trucking firm ("Acme" or "Bolt"); each gets paid a constant sum of money minus a variable cost for carrying a load of merchandise from his starting point to his destination. The cost is a function of how much time the trip takes. Each player has two routes to his destination: a short main route and a long alternate route (the routes are displayed in Figure 1). Let me note several characteristics of the routes: If a player takes his alternate route, he will lose at least 10¢ on the trip; if both players take the main route they will meet on the one-lane section of this route and will be deadlocked unless one of them backs down. The players are presented with a very simple conflict. It is to each player's interest to go through the one-lane section first, in doing so he earns more; if he backs down or waits, he earns less. It is also to their mutual interest to work out some agreement for using the main route since otherwise they may both end up with a loss.

The game, like most bargaining and conflict situations, contains a mixture of cooperative and competitive features. On the face of it, the bargaining problem is a reasonably simple one. An obvious solution is for the players to agree to "take turns" in going through the one-lane segment of the main route "first." The game took the simple form it did because of the research question I was posing: "What are the factors which affect the ease or difficulty with which bargainers conclude an agreement, when an obviously fair agreement is available?" This question is part of my broader interest in what determines whether a conflict will be resolved cooperatively or competitively.

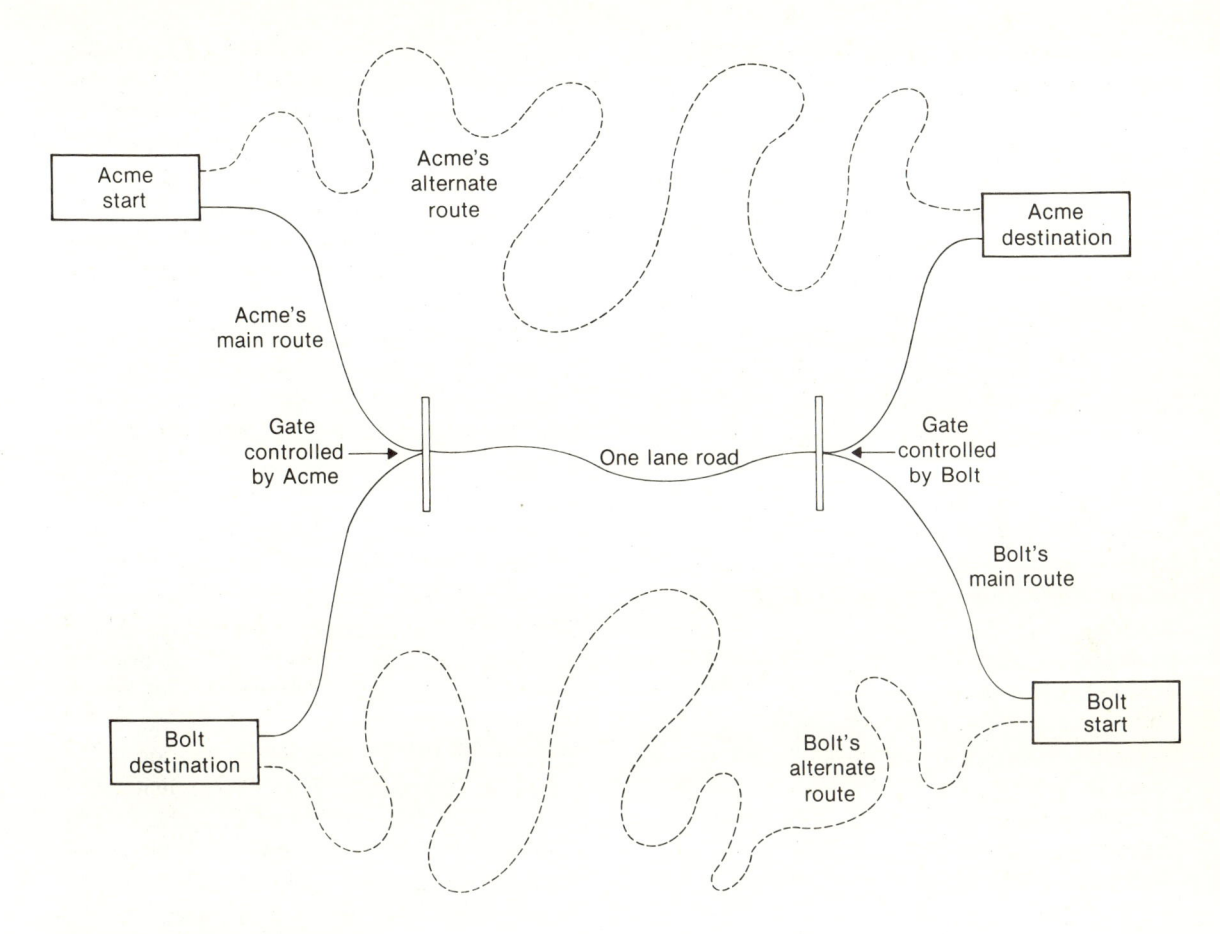

Figure 1. Subject's road map.

The Effect of Threat

Our first bargaining study was concerned with the effect of threat (Deutsch & Krauss, 1960, 1962). The study grew out of my concern with some of the psychological assumptions underlying the concept of "stable deterrence," a notion that was quite fashionable among political scientists and economists connected with the Defense Department in the late 1950s and early 1960s. There are two components to this notion: "stability" and "deterrence." "Stability" is obviously preferable to "instability" in weapon systems. Clearly, it is better not to tempt a surprise attack by possessing arms that are vulnerable to attack nor it is safe to have weapons that can be readily fired as a result of accident, misunderstanding, or insanity. Unfortunately, any critical examination of the arms race or of the systems for controlling weapons and making decisions about their use will reveal that there is considerably less stability in the "stable deterrent" than one needs for reassurance.

While the desirability of "stability" is evident, the merit of an emphasis on "deterrence" as an approach to preventing war did not seem so apparent to me. The reliance on the threat of a severe and inescapable retaliation to deter a potential aggressor seemed less preferable to me, for reasons that I have elaborated elsewhere (Deutsch, 1960, 1962b), than the attempt to establish the kinds of cooperative bonds that might reduce the motivation to aggress. In any case, the reliance on threat seemed dangerous to me because, under a number of circumstances, a threat may provoke the events that it is trying to deter. One such circumstance is when the threatened party sees the threat as an illegitimate attempt to intimidate him, that is, when he perceives the threat to be directed at creating or sustaining an unjust disadvantage for him or an unfair advantage for the threatening party.

With this idea in mind, we formulated an experiment using the Acme-Bolt game. In certain experimental conditions, we introduced "weapons" into the game in the form of gates that a player could close and, by so doing, indicate to the other player that he might be prevented from completing his trip on the main path; by keeping it closed, he would, of course, prevent the other from finishing on the main path. In our first experiment, we ran three basic conditions that varied with regard to the presence or absence of the gates such that both players, only one player, or neither player in a bargaining pair possessed a gate.

Our experiment was guided by two assumptions about threat:

1. If there is a conflict of interest and one person is able to threaten the other, he will tend to use the threat in an attempt to force the other person to yield. This tendency should be stronger, the more irreconcilable (i.e., the more competitive) the conflict is perceived to be. Let me note that I have not suggested that it is inevitable that threat be employed if it is available but rather that the tendency to employ threat will be more likely the stronger the competitive interests and less likely the stronger the cooperative interests of the bargainers in relation to one another. (Let me also note, parenthetically, that I would not be "caught dead" making a noncontingent statement about either the use or effects of threat.)

2. If a person uses threat in an attempt to intimidate another, the threatened person (if he considers himself to be of equal or superior status) will feel hostility toward the threatener and tend to respond with counterthreat and/or increased resistance to yielding. Such a response is more likely the greater the perceived detriment to the other and the lesser the perceived detriment to the self for making such a response. Let me note that this assumption implies that the likelihood of the employment of counterthreat, resistance, or threat is a function of the perceived effectiveness and the perceived costs of doing so. It also implies that the hypothesized negative reaction to threat is based upon the violation of one's normative expectations of how the other should act toward oneself; if the other's threat were perceived as legitimate, a negative response to it would be less likely.

From these assumptions, given the conditions of our experiment, we expected that the subjects would use the gates and, in doing so, would strengthen the competitive interests of the bargainers in relationship to one another by introducing or enhancing the competitive struggle for self-esteem. Strengthening the competitive interests would make it more difficult for the players to come to a cooperative agreement about use of the main route, and the consequence would be that they would have lower joint payoffs. We expected that agreement would be most difficult to arrive at in the "two-gate" situation and least difficult in the "no-gate" situation. The results of the experiment clearly support our assumptions (see Figure 2); the joint outcomes were best in the no-gate and worst in the two-gate condition.

A comparison of the outcomes of the two players in the "one-gate" condition indicated that the player with the gate did better than the one without it in the early periods but that he gradually relinquished his advantage so that at the end both players were cooperating optimally (see Figure 3). Comparisons of the two players with and without a weapon in the one-gate and no-gate conditions, respectively, each of whom faced someone without a weapon, indicated that the player with a weapon in the one-gate situation

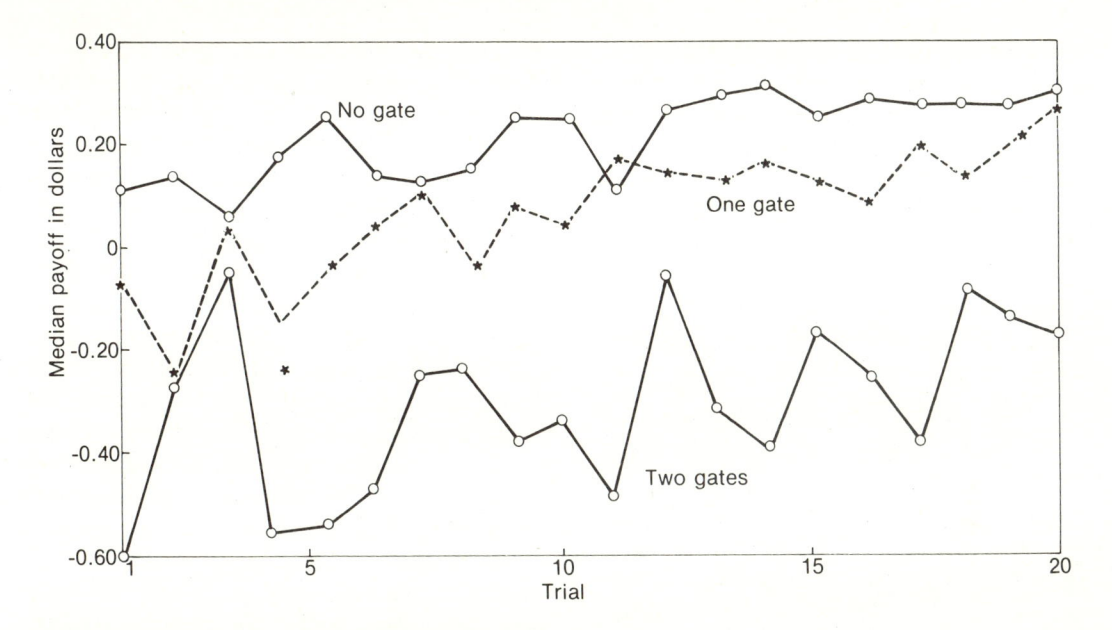

Figure 2. Median joint payoff (Acme + Bolt) over trials.

had poorer outcomes than the player without the weapon in the no-gate condition. Similarly, comparisons of the two players with and without weapons, in the two-gate and one-gate situations, respectively, each of whom faced someone with a weapon, indicated that the player in the two-gate condition had poorer outcomes than the player without a weapon in the one-gate condition. In other words, if one member of a bargaining pair has a weapon, you are better off if you are the one who has it; but you may be even better off if neither of you has a weapon.

The results of this experiment have been replicated many times. It also gave rise to a rash of related experiments. Some were attempts to extend the ideas and methods of the first experiment (Brown, 1968; Gumpert, 1967; Hornstein, 1965; Keiffer, 1968; Krauss, 1966; Krauss & Deutsch, 1966; Nardin, 1967; Smith & Emmons, 1969). Some were based on criticisms of it (Borah, 1963; Gallo, 1966; Kelley, 1965; Shomer, Davis, & Kelley, 1966; Shure, Meeker, & Moore, 1963). Elsewhere (Deutsch, 1966), I have detailed my response to some of the criticisms. Let me recapitulate this briefly by listing the criticism and my response:

1. *The opportunity to threaten is not always used; moreover, threatening devices are sometimes employed for purposes of coordination rather than threat.* These statements are true, but they are not valid criticisms since results such as these would be completely consistent with the theoretical assumptions advanced in the original article, as a careful reading would have revealed. As I have stated earlier, the use of a threat capability is not imevitable and the likelihood of its use for threatening purposes is decreased as the cooperative elements in the situation are increased. Krauss (1966) obtained this result when he varied the degree of cooperativeness in the Acme-Bolt game. Also, a careful examination of Shure's (1963) research strongly suggests that the use of threats as a coordination device occurred in a markedly more cooperative context than was true of our initial experiment. We also have obtained results, in an experiment to be reported later, that suggest that potential weapons can be used for purposes of cooperative coordination if the context is a relatively cooperative one. However, as results by Nardin (1967) demonstrate: When there is no other way of communicating, "threats" may

be viewed as coordination devices, but when it is possible to communicate in some other way threats are likely to be viewed as having a hostile intent and to evoke conflict spirals rather than facilitate cooperation. I believe it is reasonable to assert that although weapons can be used as signaling and coordinating devices under amiable circumstances for cooperative purposes, it is generally safer for bargainers to have signaling devices that cannot be employed as weapons.

2. *The obtained differences result from the fact that the gates force the players to take the alternate route if they are competitive, while if the players are competitive in the no-gate situation they are forced to confront one another and work out an agreement.* This is an interesting criticism, but it is not consistent with the data. It implies that the subjects in the no-gate condition would spend more time in confrontation on the main route than those in the two-gate condition, especially in the early trials. This does not happen. It also would suggest that if the alternate path were eliminated, there would be no initial differences between the two-gate and no-gate conditions. The results of an experiment by Shomer, Davis, and Kelley (1966) show markedly better outcomes in the no-gate condition in initial trials. As one would expect, these differences are eliminated as the game progresses. The existence of the alternate paths permits the continuation of competition without withdrawal from the experiment as the subjects compete to lose least by withdrawing onto their alternate paths; the elimination of the alternate paths means that essentially they are faced with the choice of cooperating or suffering unlimited losses (which is equivalent to withdrawing from the experiment).

3. *The experiment employed trivial incentives, "imaginary money," and the readiness to cooperate would be increased if more important incentives were employed.* Gallo (1966) reports an experiment with a matrix game based on features of the trucking game but differing from it in major respects. Subjects played for real or imaginary money of substantial amounts. His results, under real money incentives, indicated that although the gates reduced the outcomes, the subjects learned to cooperate and achieve positive outcomes despite the gates. Under imaginary incentives, the gates produced a sharp deterioration in outcomes. Gallo's results are not consistent with our results in experiments where we have employed sizable real money incentives. Subjects do end up losing real money in the Acme-Bolt game even when they could each earn up to $6 by cooperating. Moreover, in a recent experiment employing the Prisoner's Dilemma (Gumpert, Deutsch, & Epstein, 1969), we found that subjects were more competitive in their play when they were playing for large amounts of real money than for imaginary money. A careful examination of Gallo's procedures suggests that, unwittingly, in the real money condition he may have led the subjects to believe that the experimenter's criterion for good performance might be earning a sizable amount of money but that this was not the case in the "imaginary money" condition. Rosenthal (1966) has demonstrated how easily this type of experimenter effect can occur.

The Rosenthal effect, more generally, suggests that the notion that points and imaginary money are trivial incentives is much too naive a conception of what motivates a subject in a typical experiment. It is precisely because "doing well" and "being approved and well regarded" by the experimenter may be quite important to the subject that the incentive of earning points is usually not an insignificant one for most subjects. For a similar reason, not allowing oneself to be intimidated in front of the experimenter by illegitimate means (the gate) may also be a strong motivation in the experiment. That is, the insignificant trappings of most laboratory experiments often tap deeply significant motivations because of the symbolic meanings of the behavior in the larger social context

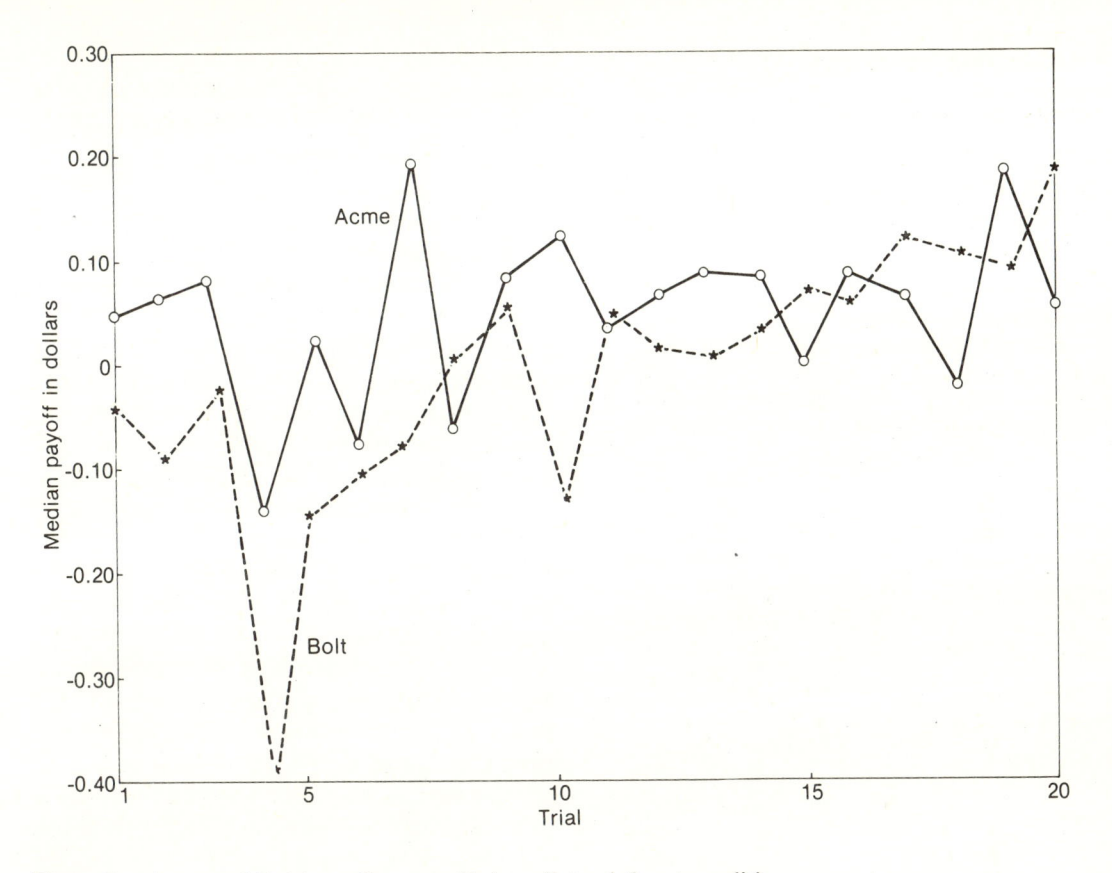

Figure 3. Acme and Bolt's median payoffs in unilateral threat condition.

within which the behavior occurs. (Parenthetically, let me note that in some research we have used the Acme-Bolt game with married couples who were seen by a psychiatrist after they played the game. It was evident from their discussion in the psychiatric interview that their behavior in the game was seen and experienced in terms of its symbolic significance: What happens in the game is deeply significant and of considerable emotional import to them.)

4. *The experiment did not clearly distinguish between the threatening and harmful behavior since the gate could be used for both.* This is a valid point but it is equally valid to say the form of threat made possible by the gate—a behavioral equivalent of "I will interfere with you unless you do what I want"—is not an uncommon type of threat. However, I agree that it is useful to distinguish operationally between "threat" and "punishment" as Hornstein (1965), Gumpert (1967), and Keiffer (1968) have done in our laboratory. There are, of course, many other types of threat than the one we employed. Also, there are many other characteristics of threat that were not, and could not, be investigated in one experiment. I list a few: the magnitude of the threat, its cost to employ, its credibility, its precision, its stability, its clarity, the nature of the values being threatened, the relative threat capabilities of the bargainers, the modes of communication available for expressing the threat, etc. These are worthwhile variables to investigate and some are now being investigated.

Though I do not have space here to summarize the results of these experiments, let me indicate the present status of the ideas that gave rise to this research. At the conclusion of our initial study (Deutsch & Krauss, 1960) we wrote:

> It is, of course, hazardous to generalize from a laboratory experiment to the complex problems of the real world. But our experiment and the theoretical ideas underlying it can perhaps serve to emphasize some notions which, otherwise, have an intrinsic plausibility. In brief, these are that there is more safety in cooperative than in competitive coexistence, that it is dangerous for bargainers to have weapons, and that it is possibly even more dangerous for a bargainer to have the capacity to retaliate in kind than not to have this capacity when the other bargainer has a weapon (p. 189).

These conclusions still seem valid. Now I would add that, in a cooperative context, weapons can be used to facilitate coordination; but, of course, they are rarely used this away except to start horse races. To avoid misinterpretation, I would stress that a credible, appropriate threat *can* induce compliance rather than counterthreat and open resistance if the threatened party perceives itself to have considerably weaker punitive power and/or if the threat is perceived to be a legitimate response to one's own inappropriate behavior. (Again, let me note that I would not be "caught dead" in the noncontingent statement that threat is *never* useful; it should, however, be used with full awareness of its dangers.)

The Effect of Commitment

Such terms as "brinksmanship," "the rationality of irrationality," and "the doctrine of the last clear chance" have been much in vogue among intellectuals who are concerned with formulating a rationale to guide strategic choices in a situation of international conflict. The basic notion underlying these different terms is that a bargainer will gain an advantage if he can commit himself irrevocably so that the last clear chance of avoiding mutual disaster rests with his opponent. A child who works himself up to the point that he will have a temper tantrum if his parents refuse to let him sit where he wants in the restaurant is using this bargaining tactic, as is a driver who cuts in front of you on a highway and appears to be deaf to the insistent blasts of your horn. And so is a nation that says to another nation, as former President Johnson, in effect, told North Vietnam, that our honor as a nation and the sacrifices of our soldiers would not permit a communist take-over in South Vietnam.

It is evident that this type of bargaining maneuver can sometimes be very effective. Yet I wonder, had we not blundered into the atrocities and stupidities of the war in Vietnam partially under the influence of such thinking? Would one expect this type of bargaining tactic to be effective when both sides could resort to it? I also wondered whether it is a ploy that is a suitable for a continuing relationship as it might be for a single, unrepeated encounter? To investigate these questions, Lewicki and I employed a modified version of the Acme-Bolt bargaining game.

Two basic modifications were made. The game was altered so as to resemble more closely the adolescent game of "chicken" by instructing the subjects that if their two trucks met at any point along the one-way section of the main path, the encounter would be defined as a "collision." If there were a collision, the trial would be terminated; both subjects would then be penalized the amount of time taken from the start of the trial to the time of the collision at the cost of 1¢ per second. (A collision would cost each player at least 20¢.) The second modification entailed introducing a commitment device as a replacement for the gates. The commitment device (called "the lock") enabled the subject to lock his truck into forward gear so that his truck had to move forward. Once locked, the position of the gear could not be altered during the trial, and hence, the truck was committed irreversibly to moving forward. When a subject used the lock, the other player was informed of this action by a clear, unambiguous signal.

The subjects in all of the experiments described below were adolescent males attending high schools in New York City. They were recruited by advertisements offering them the opportunity to earn up to $4 per hour. Ten pairs of subjects were used in each of the experimental conditions in each of the experiments.

One-Trial game. In this experiment the subjects were led to believe it was a one-trial game; however, following completion of the initial trial, they played an additional trial. In the second trial, the "no-lock" pairs became the "bilateral lock" pairs and the bilateral lock became the no lock pairs; "Bolt" got the lock from "Acme" in the second "unilateral lock" condition. They played under instructions to make as much money as they could for themselves regardless of how the other player did. The subjects played in one of three experimental conditions: *bilateral lock,* both possessed locks; *unilateral lock,* only Acme possessed the lock; and *no lock,* neither player possessed the lock.

The results (see Table 2) indicated no statistically significant differences among the three experimental conditions on the first trial although there was a tendency for a lower level of joint outcomes as one moved from the no lock to the unilateral lock to the bilateral lock conditions. In the unilateral lock condition, Acme, who possessed the commitment device, had significantly better payoffs than did Bolt, who possessed no such device.

In the second One-Trial game, there was a significant improvement in the joint outcomes of the pairs in the unilateral lock condition with a reduction in the relative advantage for the player possessing the commitment device. The pairs who were in the bilateral lock condition during the first One-Trial game and in the no lock condition during the second game improved their joint outcomes considerably while the pairs who shifted to the bilateral lock from the no lock condition worsened their joint outcomes; there was no effect due to sequence.

These results indicated that a one-sided possession of a commitment device provided a relative advantage to the player, comparing him with the one with whom he was paired. There was no evidence that he had any advantage compared with players in the no lock condition, in which neither player had such a device. There was, however, evidence to indicate that when both players were able to publicly commit themselves irreversibly to "going through first," they did worse than when neither could do so. These were the results for the single encounter for a one-trial game.

Twenty-Trial game. What would happen if the players expect the encounters to be repeated? To investigate this question, we conducted another experiment that completely paralleled the one just described except that the pairs played the game for 20 trials. At the outset they knew that there would be more than 1 trial but they did not know how many until they finished.

If we compare the results for the first trial (see Table 2) of the Twenty-Trial game with those of the first One-Trial game, it is evident that the bargaining pairs did better when they were anticipating a longer game, the difference being most marked for the bilateral lock condition. Again, there was no advantage for Acme, who possessed the lock, in the unilateral lock condition as compared to Acme in the no lock condition; however, he did better than Bolt with whom he was paired in the one-sided condition.

The overall results were not surprising since the One-Trial game is clearly more competitive in structure than the longer game, which permits an equitable solution of alter-

TABLE 2
Mean Payoffs in Cents and Mean Number of Collisions in the One-Trial Games and the First-Trial of the Twenty-Trial Game

Condition	No lock	Unilateral lock	Bilateral lock
First One-Trial game			
Acme payoff	−9.0	−.5	−3.8
Bolt payoff	5.5	−12.1	−12.5
Acme + Bolt	−3.5	−12.6	−16.3
Acme − Bolt	−14.5	11.6	8.7
No. collisions	3	4	5
Second One-Trial game			
Acme payoff	−7.0	2.7	−7.5
Bolt payoff	4.6	8.1	−8.8
Acme + Bolt	−2.4	10.8	−16.3
Acme − Bolt	−11.6	−5.4	−1.3
No. collisions	3	2	6
First trial of Twenty-Trial game			
Acme payoff	6.6	4.8	2.0
Bolt payoff	−1.6	−2.9	9.8
Acme + Bolt	5.0	1.9	11.8
Acme − Bolt	8.2	7.7	−7.8
No. collisions	2	2	1

Note.—N = 10 pairs of subjects on each condition in each game.

nation. Although the differences among conditions in the first trial of the Twenty-Trial game were not statistically significant, I was surprised by the relatively favorable outcomes in the bilateral lock condition.

If we examine the overall results for the 20 trials, we find much the same findings as for the first trial: No significant differences in mean joint payoffs among the conditions, but the bilateral lock condition tended to do best; the possessor of the commitment device did relatively better than the other player with whom he was paired in the one-sided condition but had no advantage over the players in the other conditions; there was some improvement in outcomes from the initial to the final block of trials for all conditions, but it was most marked in the no lock condition. A dominance submission pattern occurred in only 4 of the 10 pairs in the unilateral lock condition (rarely in the other conditions), the other 6 pairs were characterized by frequent collisions before settling down to an alternation pattern that gave them low but essentially equal outcomes.

It was evident that many of the pairs in the bilateral lock condition used their locks as a device for coordination rather than as a means of committing themselves to obtaining a favored outcome. To test our hunch that the use of the locks as coordination devices occurred because of the relatively cooperative context of the experiment, we checked the postexperiment questionnaire data and also ran a further experiment. (Let me note that I believed the context was more cooperative than in our previous experiments with threat because, in our present experiment, the subjects saw each other and waited together in the same room before they took part in the experiment and they could expect that they would leave together after the experiment. In our earlier experiments we had been able to eliminate any prior social contact before the bargaining game.) The questionnaire data indicated that the subjects felt about as much desire to "cooperate with the other player" as to "maximize their own outcome" and very much less desire to "do better than the other person."

"Chicken" versus "problem-solving" instructions. The further experiment involved two additional bilateral lock conditions: a cooperative and competitive one. Our assumption was that the results for the cooperative condition would parallel our prior results with the bilateral lock (i.e., the use of the lock for coordination purposes), but this would not be so for the competitive condition. We created the cooperative condition by using "social problem-solving" instructions and the competitive condition by using "chicken" instructions. The instructions were are follows:

> *"Chicken" instructions.* There are two of you who are going to play a game of "chicken." This experiment has been designed to separate people into two groups: those who give in under pressure, and those who do not. We are interested in observing, when two people are under pressure, who will "chicken out" or back down first. In this game it is possible to win or lose money. It is possible for both of you to profit, or for both of you to lose, or for one of you to profit and the other to lose; this all depends on how you play the game. I want you to feel that it is important for you to earn as much money as you can or to lose as little as possible in this game.
>
> *"Social problem-solving" instructions.* There are two of you who are going to engage in a social problem-solving game. This experiment has been designed to separate people into two groups: those who can arrive at a solution to a problem which will bring maximum benefits to both of the players, and those who cannot work out this solution. We are interested in observing what types of people can arrive at this solution. In this game it is possible to win or lose money. It is possible for both of you to profit, or for both of you to lose, or for one of you to profit and the other to lose; this all depends on how you play the game. I want you to feel that it is important for you to earn as much money as you can or to lose as little as possible in this game.

Table 3 presents the major results. It is obvious that the original bilateral lock condition had effects that were rather similar to the cooperative bilateral lock condition. Our explanation of the findings for the bilateral condition seems reasonably well supported.

Let me summarize the conclusions I have drawn from our initial work on the effect of commitment on bargaining. First, there are many interesting questions that warrant further research in this area; our study is a first-step rather than a concluding or conclusive one. Second, adolescent boys may be more sensible than they are given credit for and possibly less collision prone than American statesmen and some of their social science advisers. They are sufficiently prudent to resist the temptation to "lock themselves in" to positions from which they cannot reverse if they know they are going to have repeated encounters with someone who has a similar capacity. However, when they are prompted to be competitive by the game of chicken or by a single encounter, some of their prudence and also their money are lost. Third, having a commitment device gives the player a relative advantage over the person with whom he is bargaining, but, at least as often, it leads to a preliminary hassle over the attempt to dominate, with neither player ending up in a superior position. In any case, there is no evidence to suggest that the bargainer with a commitment device does better than the bargainer without such a device when each is facing a player who does not have one. Perhaps all of this can be summed up by saying that "locking oneself in" to an irreversible position in order to gain an advantage is rarely more beneficial than cooperating with the other for mutual gain, and it has the prospect of leading to a mutually destructive contest of willpower.

TABLE 3

Mean Payoffs per Trial in Cents and Mean Number of Collisions in the Twenty-Trial Games

Condition	No lock	Unilateral lock	Bilateral lock	Social problem-solving bilateral lock	"Chicken" bilateral lock
Acme payoff	5.06	9.24	6.65	5.47	−14.14
Bolt payoff	3.61	−.37	7.12	8.24	−14.26
Acme + Bolt	8.67	8.87	13.77	13.71	−28.40
Acme − Bolt	1.45	9.61	−.47	−2.77	−.12
No. collisions	5.6	5.8	5.0	4.8	10.7

Note.—N = 10 pairs of subjects in each condition

The Effect of Size of Conflict

Roger Fisher, a professor of international law, in a brilliant paper entitled "Fractionating Conflict" (1964), pointed out that the issues over which nations go to war are big issues that rarely can be adjudicated, whereas little issues can be. In the Cuban missile crisis, neither the United States nor the Soviet Union would have been willing to negotiate about an issue such as "freedom" or "communism" in the Western hemisphere, although they were able to negotiate about the much smaller issue of the location of 72 weapon systems. Fisher's thesis is the familiar one that small conflicts are easier to resolve than large ones. However, he also points out that the participants may have a choice in defining the conflict as a large or small one. Conflict is enlarged by dealing with it as a conflict between large rather than small units (as a conflict between two individuals of different races or as a racial conflict), as a conflict over a large substantive issue rather than a small one (over "being treated fairly" or "being treated unfairly at a particular occasion"), as a conflict over a principle rather than the application of a principle, as a conflict whose solution establishes large rather than small substantive or procedural precedents. Many other determinants of conflict size could be listed. For example, an issue that bears upon self-esteem or change in power or status is likely to be more important than an issue that does not. Illegitimate threat or attempts to coerce are likely to increase the size of the conflict and thus increase the likelihood of a competitive process.

In the Acme-Bolt trucking game there was a very simple method for varying the size of conflict; therefore we decided to conduct an experiment on the effect of size using this game.[1]

Conflict size was manipulated experimentally by varying the length of the one-lane-wide section of road on the main route. In low-conflict conditions this one-lane section was only 4 units in length, while in middle- and high-conflict conditions it was 10 and 18 units long, respectively. The total length of the main route was held constant at 20 units in all conditions. Thus, while in low-conflict conditions only 20% of the main route was one lane wide, in high-conflict conditions it was one lane wide for 90% of the total distance. In order to hold constant the maximum amount of money that subjects in different conflict-size conditions could make the subjects started with different amounts of money in the three conflict conditions. Thus, if players chose the optimally cooperative solution to the bargaining problem and coordinated, they could make the same amount of money in *all* conflict-size conditions. Four-unit pairs began each trip with 48¢ each—so that on any optimally coordinated trip the pair member to go through the one-lane section first (P_1) could make a maximum of 23¢, while the player to go through second (P_2) could made a maximum of 18¢. Similarly, 10-unit pairs began each trip with 52¢ each, such that P_1 and P_2 could make a maximum of 27¢ and 14¢, respectively. Finally, 18-unit pairs began each trip with 57¢ each—with P_1 and P_2 making a maximum of 32¢ and 9¢, respectively. Thus, in all three conflict conditions maximum joint pay on a trip equaled 41¢.

Because we were also interested in studying the effects of the sex of the experimenter, half of the subjects (all of whom were male undergraduates) in each of the size conditions were run be a female experimenter, the other half being run by a male experimenter. All subjects heard the same taped instructions, the voice being that of a male, clearly different from the male experimenter. Both the male and female experimenters employed identical experimental procedures (including the phraseology used in greeting subjects, in leading them through the practice trials, and in reporting scores after each trial of the actual game). Face-to-face contact between experimenter and subjects was brief—involving the greeting and direction of subjects to the experimental room and the administration of two written questionnaires. Subjects knew they were being observed by the experimenter from behind a one-way vision screen, and they knew each other's sex.

Table 4 presents some of the game-playing data. These results can be summarized briefly as follows: As the size of conflict increased, the bargainers experienced significantly greater difficulty in reaching a cooperative agreement about how to use the one-lane path. This increased difficulty was exemplified by a significant deterioration in cooperative behavior (i.e., fewer "cooperative trials," fewer alternations, greater number of —75¢ losses), resulting in significantly poorer bargaining outcomes (lower joint pay).

Male subjects run by a female rather than a male experimenter experienced significantly greater difficulty in reaching a cooperative agreement about the use of the one-lane path. The primary behavioral indicator of this difficulty was the significantly greater number of times that the subjects closed their gates and took the alternate route to their destination—resulting in significantly poorer bargaining outcomes.

TABLE 4
Means for Three Conflict Sizes and for Male and Female Experimenters

Item	Size 4 M	Size 4 F	Size 10 M	Size 10 F	Size 18 M	Size 18 F
Joint payoff per trial in cents	12.68	12.05	18.35	—.55	—1.87	—26.68
No. Cooperative trials per pair	15.20	14.73	14.53	11.20	10.60	6.13
No. trials of maximum losses	1.53	.80	1.27	2.73	4.67	5.20
No. trials in which both subjects used gates	1.40	2.20	1.20	3.00	2.27	5.80

These results suggest that male subjects may experience the situation as a more competitive one when the experimenter is an attractive young woman rather than a member of the same sex. They also support the idea that decreasing the size of the conflict makes it easier for bargainers to come to an agreement that is mutually rewarding. I shall not attempt to spell out the implication of this latter finding beyond what I have stated in my introduction to this experiment. Let me note again that I have described a first experiment dealing with this variable. Clearly, there are many interesting and important steps to be taken beyond this initial experiment if we are to learn how to control the size of the issues in a conflict. It may well be, as Fisher has suggested, that "issue control" is as crucial as "arms control" to the peace of the world.

CONCLUSION

I have been brash enough to claim that the games people play as subjects in laboratory experiments may have some relevance to war and peace. I have implied that the study of interpersonal conflict can provide some insights into international conflict and, let me add, that I believe the reverse is also true: The study of international conflict can give new understanding of interpersonal conflict. It is not only that such terms as "aggression," "deterrence," "threat," "cooperation," "competition," "credibility," and the like seem appropriate in the interpersonal as well as the international context, but also there is, I believe, a real conceptual similarity between the processes at the two levels.

I hope it is clear that I am not saying that the mechanisms or capabilities of acquiring information, making decisions, and acting are similar in individuals, groups, and nations. Nor am I stating that the behavior of individuals and nations will parallel one another if there is no parallel in their relevant properties and external circumstances. Rather, I am asserting that nations as well as individuals acquire information, make decisions, and take actions, and that they will act in similar ways under similar conditions. Thus, each type of unit in a social interaction responds to the other in terms of its information and views of the other; these may or may not correspond to the other's actualities. Moreover, characteristic distortions of the other tend to develop as a function of the type of social interaction, cooperative or competitive, that is occurring between them, whether the interacting units be nations, groups, or individuals.

Of course, it would be enormously convenient if my assumption of a correspondence in processes of social interaction across different types of social units is a valid one. We are in much the same position as the astronomers. It seems unlikely that we shall ever be able to conduct experiments with large-scale events. However, if we are able to identify the conceptual similarities between the large scale and the small, as the astronomers have between the planets and Newton's apple, we may be able to understand, predict, and ultimately control what happens between nations by investigating what happens in interpersonal and intergroup situations with which we can experiment.

My assumption of a correspondence may be wrong. Nature may be more perverse than I believe it to be. The ideas behind the experiments that I and others have been conducting may not have any relevance to conflicts outside the laboratory. Of course, I do not know in advance whether any of this research will have any social usefulness. And, at times, the uncertainty about the significance of the intellectual enterprise that I and my colleagues are engaged in becomes enormously frustrating. It would be reassuring to do something that is obviously useful.

No guarantees can be given to those—from either the right or the left—who are demanding that social science be relevant. We can only guarantee that our efforts will be socially responsible, that our work will seek to be responsive to human concerns, and that we will be continuously concerned with fostering the application of psychological knowledge for the welfare of man. I hope you will agree with me that the phrase "welfare of man" is not limited to one nation, one class, one race, or one discipline.

I have deliberately borrowed the phrase "the welfare of man" from the ethical code of the American Psychological Association. In my view, it is the *ethical* responsibility of *all* psychologists—as individuals and as members of their scientific and professional associations—to see to it that psychology is used for peace rather than war, for reducing the arms race rather than intensifying it, for eliminating ethnocentrism and prejudice rather than fostering them, for removing social and economic injustices and inequalities rather than perpetuating them. Since Hiroshima we can no longer pretend that science or scientists can plead innocence with respect to the social consequences of their scientific activities.

NOTES

[1] This experiment was done with the collaboration of D. Canavan and J. Rubin; L. Rogers helped in the data analysis.

REFERENCES

1. Borah, L. A., Jr. "The effects of threat in bargaining: Critical and experimental analysis," *Journal of Abnormal and Social Psychology,* 1963, Vol. 66, 37-44.

2. Brown, B. "The effect of need to maintain face on interpersonal bargaining," *Journal of Experimental Social Psychology,* 1968, Vol. 4, 107-121.

3. Deutsch, M. "An experimental study of the effects of cooperation and competition upon group process," *Human Relations,* 1949, Vol. 2, 199-231. (a)

4. Deutsch, M. "A theory of cooperation and competition," *Human Relations,* 1949, Vol. 2, 129-151. (b)

5. Deutsch, M. "Some considerations relevant to national policy," *Journal of Social Issues,* 1960, Vol. 17, 57-68.

6. Deutsch, M. "Cooperation and trust: Some theoretical notes," *Nebraska Symposium on Motivation,* 1962, Vol. 10, 275-319. (a)

7. Deutsch, M. "Psychological alternatives to war," *Journal of Social Issues,* 1962, Vol. 18, 97-119. (b)

8. Deutsch, M. "Comments on Kelley's comments," in K. Archibald (Ed.), *Strategic interaction and conflict.* (Berkeley: University of California Press, 1966). (a)

9. Deutsch, M., & Collins, M. E. *Interracial housing: A psychological evaluation of a social experiment.* (Minneapolis: University of Minnesota Press, 1951).

10. Deutsch, M., & Krauss, R. M. "The effect of threat on interpersonal bargaining," *Journal of Abnormal and Social Psychology,* 1960, Vol. 61, 181-189.

11. Deutsch, M., & Krauss, R. M. "Studies of interpersonal bargaining," *Journal of Conflict Resolution,* 1962, Vol. 6, 52-76.

12. Fisher, R. "Fractionating conflict." In R. Fisher (Ed.), *International conflict and behavioral science: The Craigville papers.* (New York: Basic Books, 1964).

13. Gallo, P. S., Jr. "Effects of increased incentives upon the use of threat in bargaining," *Journal of Personality and Social Psychology,* 1966, Vol. 4, 14-21.

14. Gumpert, P. "Some antecedents and consequences of the use of punitive power by bargainers." Unpublished doctoral dissertation, Teachers College, Columbia University, 1967.

15. Gumpert, P., Deutsch, M., & Epstein, Y. "The effect of incentive magnitude on cooperation in the prisoner's dilemma game," *Journal of Personality and Social Psychology,* 1969, Vol. 11, 66-69.

16. Hornstein, H. A. "The effects of different magnitudes of threat upon interpersonal bargaining," *Journal of Experimental Social Psychology,* 1965, Vol. 1, 282-293.

17. Keiffer, M. G. "The effect of availability and precision of threat on bargaining behavior." Unpublished doctoral dissertation, Teachers College, Columbia University, 1968.

18. Kelley, H. H. "Experimental studies of threats in interpersonal negotiations," *Journal of Conflict Resolution,* 1965, Vol. 9, 79-105.

19. Krauss, R. M. "Structural and attitudinal factors in interpersonal bargaining," *Journal of Experimental Social Psychology,* 1966, Vol. 2, 42-55.

20. Krauss, R. M., & Deutsch, M. "Communication in interpersonal bargaining," *Journal of Personality and Social Psychology,* 1966, Vol. 4, 572-577.

21. Nardin, T. "Communication and the effects of threats in strategic interaction," Paper presented at the Fifth North American Peace Research Conference of the Peach Research Society, 1967.

22. Pettigrew, T. "School segregation in current perspective," *Urban Review,* 1969, Vol. 3, 4-9.

23. Proshansky, H., & Seidenberg, B. *"Basic studies in social psychology,"* (New York: Holt, Rinehart & Winston, 1965).

24. Rosenthal, R. *Experimenter effects in behavioral research* (New York: Appleton-Century-Crofts, 1966).

25. Shomer, R. W., Davis, A. H., & Kelley, H. H. "Threat and the development of coordination: Further studies of the Deutsch and Krauss trucking game," *Journal of Personality and Social Psychology,* 1966, Vol. 4, 119-126.

26. Shure, G. H., Meeker, R. J., & Moore, W. M., Jr. "Human bargaining and negotiation behavior: Computerbased empirical studies. I. The effects of threat upon bargaining." (System Development Corporation Document TM-1330/000/00) Santa Monica, California, June 25, 1963.

27. Smith, W. P., & Emmons, T. B. "The influence of outcome information upon competitiveness in interpersonal bargaining," *Journal of Conflict Resolution,* 1969, Vol. 13, 262-270.

THE EFFECTIVENESS OF NOMINAL, DELPHI, AND INTERACTING GROUP DECISION MAKING PROCESSES

Andrew H. Van De Ven
André L. Delbecq

A pervasive concern of contemporary administrators is to find effective methods for making decisions when a number of people from different backgrounds and perspectives need to be involved in the problem-solving process. This research focuses upon this concern by experimentally comparing three alternative methods for group decision making: interacting, nominal, and delphi processes.

The traditional and most widely used approach for group decision making in organizational committee life is the conventional *interacting,* or discussion, group. The typical format followed in interacting group meetings generally begins with the statement of a problem by the group leader. This is followed by an unstructured group discussion for generating information and pooling judgments among participants. The meeting concludes with a majority voting procedure on priorities, or a consensus decision.

The *nominal group technique* (hereafter NGT) is a group meeting in which a structured format is utilized for decision making among individuals seated around a table.[1] This structured format proceeds as follows: (a) Individual members first silently and independently generate their ideas on a problem or task in writing. (b) This period of silent writing is followed by a recorded round-robin procedure in which each group member (one at a time, in turn, around the table) presents one of his ideas to the group without discussion. The ideas are summarized in a terse phrase and written on a blackboard or sheet of paper on the wall. (c) After all individuals have presented their ideas, there is a discussion of the recorded ideas for the purposes of clarification and evaluation. (d) The meeting concludes with a silent independent voting on priorities by individuals through a rank ordering or rating procedure, depending upon the group's decision rule. The "group decision" is the pooled outcome of individual votes.

Unlike the interacting or NGT processes where close physical proximity of group members is required for decision making, participants in the *delphi technique* are physically dispersed and do not meet face-to-face for group decision making.[2] The delphi technique provides for the systematic solicita-

Reprinted by permission of the publisher from *Academy of Management Journal*, Vol. 17 (December, 1974), pp. 605-621. The authors express their appreciation to G. William Walster and David Gustafson for their assistance in the design of this research; to Anne Minahan and John Ross for helpful critical reviews; and to Robert Eberson, Marian Laines, and Dennis O'Brien for their continuous help in conducting the study. The research was supported by the Wisconsin Alumni Research Foundation and released time was given to the principal author by the Center for Business and Economic Research, Graduate School of Business Administration, Kent State University.

tion and collation of judgments on a particular topic through a set of carefully designed sequential questionnaires interspersed with summarized information and feedback of opinions derived from earlier responses (26).

While considerable variance exists in administering the delphi process, the basic approach, and the one used in this research, is as follows: Only two iterations of questionnaires and feedback reports are used. First, a questionnaire designed to obtain infomation on a topic or problem is distributed by mail to a group of respondents who are anonymous to one another. The respondents independently generate their ideas in answering the questionnaire, which is then returned. The responses are then summarized into a feedback report and sent back to the respondent group along with a second questionnaire that is designed to probe more deeply into the ideas generated by respondents in the first questionnaire. On receiving the feedback report, respondents independently evaluate it and respond to the second set of questions. Typically, respondents are requested to vote independently on priority ideas included in the feedback report and to return their second responses, again by mail. Generally, a final summary and feedback report is then developed and mailed to the respondent group.

The present research is a formal experimental comparison of the effectiveness of interacting, nominal, and delphi processes for decision making.

RECENT RESEARCH ON GROUP PROCESSES

In a previous article in the *Journal* (29) the authors reviewed the research literature dealing with alternative processes for group decision making and *theoretically* concluded that structured nominal groups are more effective than conventional interacting group processes for obtaining the ideas of individuals in face-to-face problem solving committees.

With one notable exception, no previous research has experimentally compared NGT and delphi processes. Gustafson et al. (18) tested the comparative effectiveness of independent individuals, interacting, NGT, and delphi processes on a problem of subjective probability estimation. NGT groups were found to be superior to all others in terms of lowest percentage of error and variability of estimations. The variant of the delphi process tested was the worst; interacting groups and individuals working independently emerged second and third best, respectively. A possible explanation for the poor performance of the delphi process may be that invalid experimental manipulations and testing were used. The authors indicate that due to the expensive interrogation and questionnaire format of the delphi technique, a derivative process called Estimate-Feedback-Estimate was used. This derivative process involved groups of four individuals who were asked to independently estimate likelihood ratios, exchange their estimates through written communications, and then re-estimate their likelihood ratios. The Estimate-Feedback-Estimate process permitted social facilitation of people working in the presence of each other. It could be argued that due to the "unnaturalness" of written feedback communications among group members in the presence of one another, the derivative process induced negative social facilitation.

Contrary to the findings of Gustafson and his associates, experiments carried out by Dalkey (5, 6) and Campbell (3) found the delphi process more effective than committee discussions. In these experiments the problem required respondents to estimate the accuracy of a set of facts. The pooled estimates resulting from the delphi technique were found to be more accurate than were the estimates resulting from the committee discussions.

Since this research dealt with relatively objective probability estimation problems, a question arises as to whether the research results would be the same if a more real-life, controversial, and emotionally involving problem were chosen. One may question, too, whether accuracy and variability of estimations are appropriate criteria of the effectiveness of a decision making technique when the nature of the real applied decisions confronting practitioners is subjective, when frequently there is no one correct solution, and when the decision often directly affects the lives and behavior of decision makers. As a result, the affective, emotional, and expressive dimensions of a problem often subordinate the objective, analytical quality of a decision. The practitioner's overriding criterion in the choice of a decision making process may be the perceived satisfaction of participants affected by the decision, at the calculated expense of solution quality. Indeed, since an objective measure of quality may not exist, political acceptability of the decision may become the measure of quality.

EXPERIMENTAL DESIGN

The Experimental Setting and Problem

The present research was conducted in the Division of Student Affairs at a midwestern university. The problem was that of defining the job description of part-time student dormitory counselors who reside in and supervise student living units of university owned or approved housing. A separate survey of students, faculty, administrators, and parents was conducted to validate the premises that this problem was considered (a) to be very difficult, (b) to have no solution that would be equally acceptable to all interest groups involved, and (c) to evoke highly emotional and subjective responses.

Criteria of Effectiveness

The criteria chosen to measure the comparative effectiveness of NGT, delphi, and interacting methods of group decision making were (a) the quantity of unique ideas developed by groups and (b) the perceived satisfaction of groups with the decision making process in which they were involved.

Quantity of Ideas. The greater the quantity of ideas generated through a decision making process, the greater the number of ideas that are considered in making a decision, and the greater the potential for creative decision making (21, 23). The fact that only a few ideas are generated by a problem-solving group does not preclude the possibility that others may exist. However, Maier (22) suggests that "uncreative groups frequently behave as though this were the case."

Since the steps in generating ideas in NGT and delphi procedures are quite similar, it was predicted that the quantity of ideas generated by the two techniques would be about equal. Because participants are encouraged to "hitch-hike" on one another's ideas in NGT, and because of the social facilitation present in a group setting, it was predicted that NGT groups would produce slightly more ideas than comparable delphi groups.

Previous research has found a number of inhibiting influences when interacting groups engage in problem solving. Therefore the authors predicted that NGT and delphi processes would be clearly superior to interacting groups in the quantity of ideas generated.

The quantity of ideas generated was measured by counting the number of unique ideas developed by each NGT, delphi, and interacting group. A panel of four judges reviewed a listing of the raw ideas generated by each group and edited each group's list to eliminate duplications. Discrepancies between judges were discussed among the judges, and group consensus was used to determine whether the idea under discussion was unique or a duplicate of other ideas in the group's list.

Perceived Group Satisfaction. A second criterion often cited in the literature (e.g., 14,

21) and chosen by practitioners to measure the effectiveness of a decision making method is the satisfaction participants perceive with group process and decision outcomes. Even when highly creative decisions are developed, if the decision makers feel dissatisfied with the process or cannot accept the solution, the decision may fail to be adopted (10). The greater the participants' perceived level of satisfaction with a decision making process and outcome, the greater the probability of solution adoption (1, 4, 17, 27).

Participant satisfaction with the process and outcome of NGT, delphi, and interacting groups was measured by having all participants in the three treatments complete a standardized evaluation form immediately following the completion of a treatment. The group evaluation form included the following five items relating to satisfaction:

1. To what extent did you feel free to participate and contribute your ideas?

2. To what extent did you feel your time was well spent in this meeting/completing the delphi questionnaires?

3. How satisfied are you with the quantity (number) of ideas generated by your group?

4. How satisfied are you with the quality of ideas generated by your group?

5. To what extent do you feel the group meetings/series of delphi questionnaires, is an effective way to deal with the problem?

Each item was scored on a five point scale, and the total for all was computed. Thus, perceived satisfaction is a ubiquitous measure that includes the affective and emotional dimensions of participation, as well as the perceived analytical quality of the group's performance.

In the NGT and interacting processes, the subtle dynamics of social interaction can facilitate social cohesion within a group (resulting in high feelings of satisfaction), or facilitate fractionated groups with frustrated members (13, 23, 25). On the other hand, where social interaction is not present, as in the delphi process, the perceived satisfaction of respondents may be solely a function of the perceived objective quantity and quality of ideas generated, and the amount of time saved in not having to attend a meeting (7).

The authors predicted that NGT groups would perceive higher satisfaction than would delphi groups because of the social facilitation provided by face-to-face interactions in NGT groups. Further, it was predicted that participants in NGT groups would perceive greater satisfaction than would participants in interacting groups because of the higher potential for inhibiting influences in the latter, e.g., conformity pressures, dominance of strong personality types, covert personalizing judgments, and status incongruities (30).

It is difficult, however, to predict the difference in perceived satisfaction between participants in delphi and interacting groups. The delphi process provides neutral social satisfaction in the sense that no opportunity is provided for face-to-face interaction. The interacting process provides ample opportunities for social facilitation at the expense of decreased satisfaction due to social inhibitions. A priori, therefore, it was predicted that there would be no difference in perceived satisfaction between delphi and interacting groups.

In summary, two criteria measuring effectiveness were chosen to experimentally compare the NGT, delphi, and interacting processes in regard to (a) quantity of ideas generated and (b) perceived level of satisfaction.

Because of the nature of the problem investigated in this study, it was *believed* that a practitioner would require both high quantity of ideas and high satisfaction by participants to call the outcome of a decision making process effective. Therefore, in constructing a composite measure of effectiveness, equal weights were assigned to the two dependent measures.

Hypotheses

The hypotheses regarding the effects of the three decision making processes on the composite effectiveness measure can be stated as follows:

1. *The NGT process will be more effective than the delphi process.*

2. *The delphi technique will be more effective than the interacting group process.*

The corollary hypothesis is:

The NGT process will be more effective than the interacting group process.

Sample Size and Value of Test Statistic

In order to properly utilize classical hypothesis testing methodology and to enable the use of statistical significance as a quality procedure for measuring magnitudes of effects between the mean effectiveness scores of the three processes, the procedures recently developed by Walster and Cleary (32) and operationalized by Walster and Tretter (33) were utilized. Thus, it was possible to determine simultaneously the appropriate sample size and the critical value of the statistic required to test the foregoing hypothesis in analysis of variance (ANOVA).[3]

This procedure requires that the researcher make two value judgments to determine the appropriate number of observations and the critical value of the variance ratio statistic:

1. Based upon an index of the magnitude of an effect, Δ, what are considered trivial and important differences between the three decision making processes?

2. With what probability does the researcher wish to correctly draw conclusions that there is a trivial or an important effect?

The value judgments made regarding the magnitude of effect between a linear combination of the means of NGT, delphi, and interacting groups were as follows:

1. True values of less than $\Delta_1 = .75\sigma$ will be considered trivial differences between the means of the decision making processes.

2. True values of Δ greater than $\Delta_2 = 1.50\sigma$ will be considered important differences between treatments.

The choices of $\Delta_1 = .75\sigma$ and $\Delta_2 = 1.50$ are illustrated in Figure 1.

The Magnitude of an Effect Considered Trivial = $\Delta_1 = .75\sigma$

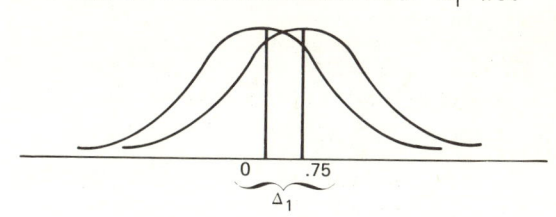

The Magnitude of an Effect Considered Important = $\Delta_2 = 1.50\sigma$

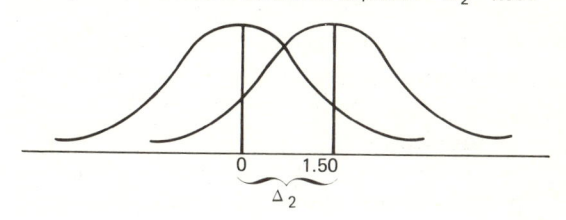

Figure 1

Complete certainty ($p = 1.00$) in drawing correct conclusions about magnitudes of effect would be the ideal. However, because this would require an infinitely large sample size, levels of assurance less than 1.0 are chosen in reaching alternative conclusions regarding trivial and important results. In this case:

1. The level of probability chosen in deciding that a trivial result ($\Delta < \Delta_1 = .75\sigma$) is indeed trivial is at least .85 ($p_1 = .85$), and

2. The level of probability chosen in deciding that an important result ($\Delta < \Delta_2 = 1.50\sigma$) is indeed important is at least .95 ($p_2 = .95$).

These value judgments are illustrated in Figure 1. It is assumed that the practitioner is reluctant to alter his use of conventional group decision making approaches unless convincing evidence indicates that a less conventional method (e.g., the NGT or delphi technique) is more effective than his conventional approach (i.e., use of the interacting group).

The above judgments of the practitioner can be incorporated into the research design by translating the practitioner's concerns into magnitudes of effect regarding the size of observed differences in effectiveness between NGT, delphi, and interacting processes. If it is found that the observed differences between the decision making processes are smaller than $\Delta_1 = .75\sigma$, it is believed that the practitioner will consider this result to be trivial and the effort to alter his customary ways of conducting group meetings to be unwarranted. On the other hand, if observed differences between the decision making techniques are larger than $\Delta_2 = 1.50\sigma$, the practitioner will probably consider this difference important enough for him to alter his decision making process. Finally, should observed differences be greater than $\Delta_1 = .75\sigma$, but smaller than $\Delta_2 = 1.50\sigma$, i.e., $\Delta_1 = .75\sigma < \Delta < \Delta_2 = 1.50\sigma$, the zone of indifference, then it is assumed that the practitioner will suspend judgment in favor of additional data.

On the basis of the value judgments made with regard to magnitudes of effect ($\Delta = .75; \Delta_2 = 1.50$) and probabilities of exercising control over drawing correct conclusions about observed results ($p_1 = .85$; $p_2 = .95$), a "Samfix" computer program developed by Walster and Tretter (33) provides the appropriate number of 20 observations of each decision making process and the critical values of the variance ratio statistic. The F test must be larger than 6.299 to lead to the decision $\Delta < \Delta_2$. Finally, if the F test is greater than 6.280 and smaller than 6.299, judgment is suspended.

Selection and Composition of Groups

Numerous researchers have examined the relationship between group size and heterogeneity of opinions, difficulty in reaching consensus, and patterns of interaction. They have found that as size increases above some limit (perhaps seven), restraints against participation also increase and the most active participant becomes increasingly differentiated (e.g., 2, 8, 16, 19, 20). Yet in most studies comparing alternative decision making processes, the size of groups ranged from two to four members. Since the size of decision making groups and committees encountered in organizational life is considerably larger, one may question whether the research results on two to four members can have a general application. In this research, the size and composition of a group was chosen to be seven participants from heterogeneous backgrounds (e.g., student residents, student housing administrators, faculty, academic administrators).

A stratified random sampling procedure was followed in assigning 420 individuals to 60 heterogeneous groups—20 NGT, 20 delphi, and 20 interacting groups. For each of the NGT and interacting processes, 20 group meetings were conducted with groups of seven persons. In the delphi process the questionnaire responses were collated into the 20 preassigned respondent groups of seven persons, and 20 independent feedback reports were developed. At all times the unit of analysis in each treatment was a group of size seven.

Random Selection of Leaders

The leaders for the NGT and interacting groups were either graduate students or professional planners. The selection of leaders was based upon previous observations in conducting group meetings. The leaders were all about equally qualified in group decision making. From this selected group, leaders were randomly assigned to one of the two processes and then trained to conduct either NGT or interacting group meetings. The leaders conducted meetings only within their assigned treatments.

Experimental Procedures

The delphi process was the only treatment in which subjects did not work in groups but worked independently by responding to two mailed questionnaires. The first questionnaire requested participants to "list the job activities that should be included in a job description of a House Fellow," and to return their responses in a preaddressed mail envelope. Questionnaires were coded and nonrespondents received reminder letters and follow-up telephone calls to insure a high return rate. Questionnaire responses were then collated in terms of the preassigned groups and summarized into 20 independent group feedback reports. On the basis of the feedback reports that included the pooled ideas of other group members, respondents were requested in the second questionnaire to "choose the five most important job activities that should be included in a House Fellow job description." A final feedback report was then constructed for each group. It was mailed back to the respondent groups along with an evaluation form that respondents were asked to complete and again return in a preaddressed mail envelope. Of the 140 respondents who initially agreed to participate in the delphi process, 20 individuals or 14 percent withdrew during the process. This was determined in last-resort follow-up telephone calls to nonrespondents. However, a dropout rate of about equal size occurred among individuals who agreed to participate in NGT and interacting group meetings.

The NGT and interacting groups followed the same respective formats described in the introduction of this paper. Again, as in the delphi process, the same task was assigned to each group. To assure consistency in leadership behavior and in the specific steps followed by groups within each process, NGT and interacting leaders participated in separate briefing sessions prior to each meeting and followed a detailed written format in their meetings. Immediately after the conclusion of each meeting the leader requested participants to complete the evaluation forms. After the NGT and interacting leaders collected the evaluation forms and dismissed their groups, they completed a postmeeting data sheet that included (a) a question to determine if the meeting deviated from the prescribed leader format and (b) a question regarding the leaders' process evaluations of the meetings they had just conducted. Follow-up interviews were held with leaders if the information was not clearly understood by the researchers. Based upon an analysis of these data, the researchers were satisfied that there was consistent performance among the leaders.

Experimental Controls

All decision making processes were conducted independently. To avoid contamination between treatments, NGT leaders were kept separate from interacting leaders at all times. While the leaders knew two types of decision making procedures were being used, no mention was made to leaders of the positive and negative expectations of either process. In addition, group meetings in each treatment were kept physically separated. To avoid grapevine communication problems, all meetings within a particular geographical housing area were conducted simultaneously. All NGT and interacting group meetings were completed in four consecutive evenings.

RESEARCH RESULTS

Table 1 summarized the results of a univariate F test to detect overall differences in effectiveness between NGT, delphi, and interacting group processes. The variance ratio statistic (19.1) is far greater than the critical value of the statistic (6.299). Therefore, with at least a 95 percent probability of being correct, it is concluded that there is an *important difference* (i.e., where $\Delta < \Delta_2 = 1.50$) in effectiveness between the three decision making processes.[4] Since large departures were detected between the treatment means in accordance with Scheffe (24), post-hoc comparisons were made and these also are summarized in Table 1. The differences between the effectiveness of the three decision making processes are as follows: While the difference between NGT and delphi groups is in the predicted direction, it cannot be concluded that it is an important difference. Unlike the overall test, however, it cannot be concluded that this difference is small; only that it is not too large. To *demonstrate* that it is small, a new experiment is required in which this difference is investigated a priori.

However, there are large and important differences between the effectiveness of NGT and interacting groups, and between delphi and interacting groups, as predicted. It can be concluded that the second and third comparisons account for most of the overall significance of the F test.

The hypothesis of large differences in effectiveness between NGT, delphi, and interacting group means is partially supported. On all pair-wise comparisons, differences in effectiveness between the three decision making processes are in the predicted direction. *The degree of differences in effectiveness between NGT and interacting groups and between delphi and interacting groups is important and large. These differences are so convincingly large that if one agrees with the value judgments used regarding what is large and important ($\Delta < \Delta_2 = 1.50$), the practitioner should alter his conventional pattern of using the interacting group meeting in favor of either NGT or delphi techniques on applied problems of the type used in this study.* However, it cannot be concluded with the same degree of confidence that the practitioner should favor the NGT process over the delphi technique since the difference in effectiveness between NGT and delphi is not large.

In order to investigate these differences more deeply, post hoc multiple comparisons were made on the component variables contained within the composite effectiveness source. Ninety-nine percent simultaneous confidence intervals were chosen to test differences between the three decision making processes on the quantity of ideas generated and perceived group satisfaction. They are summarized in Table 1. The differences between NGT, delphi, and interacting groups are as follows:

1. As predicted, there is no significant difference in the quantity of ideas generated by NGT and delphi groups. On the average, however, NGT groups generated 12 percent more unique ideas than did equivalent delphi groups.

2. As predicted, significantly more ideas were developed by delphi than by interacting groups ($p < .01$). The delphi technique generated 1.6 times more ideas than did the interacting group process.

3. As predicted, the greatest difference in terms of the quantity of ideas is between NGT and interacting groups ($p < .01$). On the average, NGT groups generated nearly twice as many ideas as did interacting groups.

4. As predicted, NGT groups expressed significantly greater satisfaction with their process than did delphi respondents ($p < .01$).

TABLE 1
Statistical Findings

Overall UANOVA F-Test on Effectiveness of Decision-Making Processes

Source	SS	d.f.	MS	F
Between groups	3,054.0	2	1,527.0	19.1
Within groups	4,570.9	57	80.2	
Totals	7,624.9	59		

Basic Statistics

Measure	NGT Mean	Delphi Mean	Interact-ing Mean	Standard Error	99% Confidence Interval
Effectiveness	54.1	37.9	26.9	2.8	$10.08 \pm \Psi$
Quantity of ideas	33.0	29.0	18.0	18.5	$4.77 \pm \Psi$
Perceived satisfaction	21.1	19.1	18.8	7.6	$1.97 \pm \Psi$

Post Hoc Comparisons on Composite Effectiveness Measure

Comparison	Contrast	Value of Ψ	Decision
NGT—Delphi	$T_1 = 1\ -1\ \ 0$	$54.1 - 47.9 = 6.2$	Not significant
NGT—Interacting	$T_2 = 1\ \ \ 0\ -1$	$54.1 - 36.9 = 17.2$	Significant
Delphi—Interacting	$T_3 = 1\ \ \ 1\ -1$	$47.9 - 36.9 = 11.0$	Significant

Post Hoc Comparisons on Quantity of Ideas Generated

Comparison	Contrast	Value of Ψ	Decision
NGT—Delphi	$T_1 = 1\ -1\ \ 0$	$33 - 29 = 4$	Not significant
NGT—Interacting	$T_2 = 1\ \ \ 0\ -1$	$33 - 18 = 15$	Significant
Delphi—Interacting	$T_3 = 0\ \ \ 1\ -1$	$29 - 18 = 11$	Significant

Post Hoc Comparisons on Perceived Group Satisfaction

Comparison	Contrast	Value of Ψ	Decision
NGT—Delphi	$T_1 = 1\ -1\ \ 0$	$21.1 - 19.1 = 2.0$	Significant
NGT—Interacting	$T_2 = 1\ \ \ 0\ -1$	$21.1 - 18.8 = 2.3$	Significant
Delphi—Interacting	$T_3 = 0\ \ \ 1\ -1$	$19.1 - 18.8 = 0.3$	Not significant

5. The greatest difference in perceived group satisfaction between the three decision making processes is between NGT and interacting groups, with the former higher than the latter ($p < .01$).

6. As predicted, there is no significant difference in satisfaction between delphi and interacting groups. The satisfaction scores are practically identical for these two decision making techniques.

DISCUSSION

The research results clearly show that important differences exist between NGT, delphi, and interacting processes on an applied problem. However, these quantitative findings do not explain why such differences exist. In order to interpret the results qualitatively and to investigate more deeply the distinguishing process characteristics of NGT, delphi, and interacting groups, open-ended evaluations by participants and leaders were elicited immediately after the conclusion of each decision process.

Included in the evaluation form were two open-ended questions:

1. In general, what did you *like the most* about the meeting/delphi you just participated in?

2. In general, what did you *dislike the most* about the meeting/delphi you just participated in?

For each question, the open-ended responses within each of the 60 groups were content analyzed (15). The 20 group responses in each of the three decision making processes were then tallied and combined under major headings.

A thorough analysis of participants' and leaders' evaluations is available in Van de Ven (28) and provides the bases for profiling the comparative merits of the three decision making techniques. A summary of the qualitative differences that were found between NGT, delphi, and interacting processes is given in Table 2. The qualitative results support present and previous research which finds there are a number of inhibiting influences that reduce the performance of interacting groups in decision making:

1. Because interacting group meetings are unstructured, high variability in member and leader behavior is observed from group to group.

2. Too much effort is directed toward maintaining social-emotional relationships among group members, and too little attention is given to performance of task-instrumental roles.

3. The absence of an opportunity to think through ideas independently results in a tendency for ideas to be expressed as generalizations that are low in quality.

4. Search behavior is reactive and characterized by short periods of focus on the problem, tendencies for task avoidance, tangential discussions, and high efforts in establishing social relationships and generating social knowledge.

5. There is a tendency for group norms to emphasize conforming behavior among members and for discussions to dwell on areas of agreement.

6. There is a tendency to dominance in search, evaluation, and choice of group product by higher status, more expressive, or stronger personality types.

7. There is a tendency for meetings to conclude with high perceived lack of closure, low felt accomplishment, and low interest in future phases of problem solving.

The Delbecq-Van de Ven nominal process, on the other hand, is a structured group meeting that includes a number of facilitative characteristics which act to increase decision making performance of groups. They are:

1. There is consistency in decision making, as low variability in member and leader behavior is observed from group to group.

2. A balanced concern for socio-emotional group maintenance roles and performance of task-instrumental roles offers both social reinforcement and task accomplishment rewards to group members.

3. The opportunity for individuals to think through and write down their ideas results in a tendency for ideas to be problem centered, specific, and of high quality.

4. The structured group norm emphasizes tolerance for nonconforming, incompatible, or conflicting ideas through independent individual expression of ideas without interruptions during the search and choice periods of decision making.

5. The structured process forces equality of participation among members in generating information on the problem. While dominant members are more expressive during the discussion period, their ideas are simply included in the sample of ideas already listed on the chart on the wall. Finally, the silent independent voting on priorities forces equality of participation in choice of the group product.

6. The NGT group meetings tend to conclude with a perceived sense of closure, accomplishment, and interest in future phases of problem solving.

There are both facilitative and inhibitive characteristics in the delphi process which act to increase or decrease decision making performance. The major characteristics of the delphi process that inhibit decision making performance are:

1. There is no opportunity for social-emotional rewards in problem solving. Respondents focus all efforts on task-instrumental role activity, derive little social reinforcement from others, and express a feeling of detachment from the problem solving effort.

2. The absence of verbal clarification or comment on the feedback report of ideas generated by anonymous group respondents creates communication and interpretation difficulties among respondents.

3. Conflicting or incompatible ideas on the feedback report are resolved by simply pooling and adding the votes of group respondents. No opportunity exists for face-to-face problem solving. Thus, while this majority rule procedure identifies group priorities, conflicts are not resolved.

The facilitative characteristics of the delphi process which act to increase decision making performance are:

1. The isolated generation of ideas in writing results in a high quantity of ideas.

2. The process of writing responses to the questions forces respondents to think through the complexity of the problem and to submit specific, high quality ideas.

3. Search behavior is proactive since respondents cannot react to the ideas of others. The period of "problem mindedness" is controlled and separated from the period of "solution mindedness" by the use of different questionnaires for each phase of problem solving.

4. The anonymity and isolation of respondents facilitate a freedom from conformity pressures.

5. The delphi process tends to conclude with a moderate perceived sense of closure and accomplishment, but with detachment.

CONCLUSION

This research made a formal experimental comparison of the effectiveness of alternative group decision making processes on an applied problem that was characterized as very difficult, had no solution that would be equally acceptable to different interest groups, and aroused highly emotional and subjective reactions. Effectiveness was defined as the quantity of unique ideas generated by a group and the perceived level of satisfaction group

TABLE 2
Comparison of Qualitative Differences Between Three Decision Processes
Based upon Evaluations of Leaders and Group Participants

Dimension	Interacting Groups	Delbecq-Van de Ven Nominal Groups	Dalkey Delphi Technique
Overall methodology	Unstructured face-to-face group meeting High flexibility High variability in behavior of groups	Structured face-to-face group meeting Low flexibility Low variability in behavior of groups	Structured series of questionnaires & feedback reports Low variability respondent behavior
Role orientation of groups	Socio-emotional Group maintenance focus	Balanced focus on social maintenance and task role	Task-instrumental focus
Relative quantity of ideas	Low; focused "rut" effect	Higher; independent writing & hitch-hiking round-robin	High; isolated writing of ideas
Search behavior	Reactive search Short problem focus Task-avoidance tendency New social knowledge	Proactive search Extended problem focus High task centeredness New social & task knowledge	Proactive search Controlled problem focus High task centeredness New task knowledge
Normative behavior	Conformity pressures inherent in face-to-face discussions	Tolerance for non-conformity through independent search and choice activity	Freedom not to conform through isolated anonymity
Equality of participation	Member dominance in search, evaluation, & choice phases	Member equality in search & choice phases	Respondent equality in pooling of independent judgments
Method of problem solving	Person-centered Smoothing over and withdrawal	Problem-centered Confrontation and problem solving	Problem-centered Majority rule of pooled independent judgments
Closure decision process	High lack of closure Low felt accomplishment	Lower lack of closure High felt accomplishment	Low lack of closure Medium felt accomplishment
Resources utilized	Low administrative time, and cost High participants time and cost	Medium administrative time, cost, preparation High participant time and cost	High administrative
Time to obtain group ideas	1½ hours	1½ hours	5 calendar months

participants experienced with the decision process. Twenty NGT, 20 delphi, and 20 interacting groups, each composed of seven heterogeneous members, were experimentally compared.

The statistical procedures being developed by Walster, Cleary, and Tretter were incorporated into this experimental design. These procedures provide the researcher with a qualitative method for utilizing classical hypothesis testing methodology in making decisions of interest and relevance to the user of this research—the practitioner.

Utilizing these procedures, it can be said that if one agrees with the stated value judgments regarding what is large and important, the degree of differences in effectiveness between NGT and interacting processes, and between delphi and interacting groups, is important and large. These differences are so convincingly large that the practitioner should change his conventional pattern of using the interacting group meeting process in favor of either NGT or delphi techniques on applied problems of the kind used in this study.

This research suggests that when confronted with a fact finding problem that requires the pooled judgment of a group of people, the practitioner can utilize two alternative procedures: (a) the Delbecq-Van de Ven nominal group technique for situations where people are easily brought together physically, and for problems requiring immediate data, and (b) the Dalkey delphi technique for situations where the cost and inconvenience of bringing people together face-to-face is very high, and for problems that do not require immediate solution. Both the nominal group technique and the delphi method are more effective than the conventional discussion group process.

NOTES

1. NGT was developed by Andre L. Delbecq and Andrew H. Van de Van in 1968 from social-psychological studies of decision conferences, studies of industrial engineering problems of program design in the NASA aerospace field, and social work studies of citizen participation in program planning. Since that time, NGT has gained extensive use and recognition in health, social service, education, industry, and public administration organizations (9, 10, 11, 12, 28, 29, 30, 31).

2. The delphi process was developed by Norman Dalkey and his associates at the RAND Corporation. It has gained considerable recognition and use in public administration agencies for the purpose of achieving a number of possible objectives:

> To determine or develop a range of possible alternatives.
>
> To explore or expose underlying assumptions or information leading to different judgments.
>
> To seek out information which may generate a consensus on the part of the respondent group.
>
> To correlate informed judgments on a topic spanning a wide range of disciplines.

Varied applications of the delphi technique have been demonstrated (3, 5, 6, 7, 26).

3. Space does not permit a detailed discussion of the useful applied statistical tools developed by Webster, Cleary, and Tretter to maintain control over power, and thereby allow statistical significance to be a qualitative decision rule to determine questions of interest in fixed effects ANOVA. For a complete discussion, see the book by Van de Ven (28).

4. It should be noted that the probability of incorrectly deciding that $\Delta < 1.50$ given that $\Delta < .75$ is less than .15. In the terminology of classical hypothesis-testing methodology, the probability of rejecting $H_O: < = 0$ given that the H_O is true is equal to .033 (i.e., a = .003).

REFERENCES

1. Bass, B. M. "When Planning for Others," *Journal of Applied Behavioral Science,* Vol. 6, No. 2 (1970), 151-171.

2. Bouchard, T. J., Jr., and M. Hare. "Size, Performance, and Potential in Brainstorming Groups," *Journal of Applied Psychology*, Vol. 54 (1970), 51-55.

3. Campbell, R. M. *A Methodological Study of the Utilization of Experts in Business Forecasting* (Ph.D. dissertation, University of California, 1966).

4. Clark, T. N. "Institutionalization of Innovations in Higher Education: Four Models," *Administrative Science Quarterly*, Vol. 13 (1970), 1-25.

5. Dalkey, N. C. *Experiment in Group Prediction* (Santa Monica, Calif.: RAND Corp., 1968).

6. Dalkey, N. C. *The Delphi Method: An Experimental Study of Group Opinion* (Santa Monica, Calif.: RAND Corp., 1969).

7. Dalkey, N. C., and O. Helmer. "An Experimental Application of the Delphi Method to the Use of Experts," *Management Sciences*, Vol. 9 (1963).

8. Delbecq, A. L. *Leadership in Business Decision Conferences* (Ph.D. dissertation, Indiana University, Graduate School of Business, 1963).

9. Delbecq, A. L., and A. H. Van de Ven. "Nominal Group Techniques for Involving Clients and Resource Experts in Program Planning," *Academy of Management Proceedings*, 1970, pp. 208-227.

10. Delbecq, A. L., and A. H. Van de Ven. "A Group Process Model for Problem Identification and Program Planning," *Journal of Applied Behavioral Science*, Vol. 7 (1971), 466-492.

11. Delbecq, A. L., and A. H. Van de Ven. "An Approach to the Problem of Formulating Difficult Problems," *American Institute of Decision Scientists Proceedings of the Third Annual Conference*, 1972, pp. 1-15.

12. Delbecq, A. L., A. H. Van de Ven, and D. H. Gustafson. *Group Decision-Making Techniques in Program Planning* (Chicago: Scott, Foresman, 1974).

13. Deutsch, M. "An Experimental Study of the Effects of Cooperation and Competition on Group Process," *Human Relations*, Vol. 2 (1949), 199-231.

14. Filley, A. C. "Utopian Organizations as Alternatives to Present Structures: Organization Invention" (Unpublished paper, University of Wisconsin, Graduate School of Business, 1971).

15. Flanagan, J. F. "The Critical Incident Technique," *Psychological Bulletin*, Vol. 51 (1954), 327-358.

16. Gibb, J. R. "The Effects of Group Size and of Threat Prediction upon Creativity in Problem Solving Situations," *American Psychologist*, Vol. 6 (1951), 324.

17. Greiner, Larry E. "Patterns of Organization Change," in G. W. Dalton, P. R. Lawrence, and L. E. Greiner (eds.), *Organizational Change and Development* (Homewood, Ill.: Irwin, Dorsey, 1970), pp. 213-229.

18. Gustafson, D. H., R. K. Shulka, A. L. Delbecq, and G. W. Walster. "A Comparative Study of Differences in Subjective Likelihood Estimates Made by Individuals, Interacting Groups, Delphi Groups, and Nominal Groups," *Organizational Behavior and Human Performance*, Vol. 9 (1973), 280-291.

19. Hare, A. P. "A Study of Interaction and Consensus in Different Sized Groups," *American Sociological Review*, Vol. 17 (1952), 261-267.

20. Hare, A. P. *Handbook for Small Group Research* (New York: Free Press, 1962).

21. Maier, N. R. F. "Maximizing Personal Creativity Through Better Problem Solving," *Personnel Administration*, Vol. 27, No. 1 (1964), 14-18.

22. Maier, N. R. F., and L. R. Hoffman. "Quality of First and Second Solution in Group Problem Solving," *Journal of Applied Psychology,* Vol. 41 (1964), 310-323.

23. Maier, N. R. F., and A. R. Solem. "The Contribution of the Discussion Leader to the Quality of Group Thinking," *Human Relations,* Vol. 3 (1952), 155-174.

24. Scheffe, H. *The Analysis of Variance* (New York: Wiley, 1958).

25. Torrance, E. P. "Group Decision Making and Disagreement," *Social Forces*, Vol. 35 (1957), 314-318.

26. Turroff, M. "The Design of a Policy Delphi," *Technological Forecasting and Social Change,* Vol. 2 (1970), 149-171.

27. Utterback, James M. "The Process of Technological Innovation within the Firm," *Academy of Management Journal*, Vol. 14 (1971), 75-87.

28. Van de Ven, A. H. *Group Decision Making Effectiveness: An Experimental Study* (Kent, Ohio: Kent State University, CBER Press, College of Business Administration, 1974).

29. Van de Ven, A. H., and A. L. Delbecq. "Nominal Versus Interacting Group Processes for Committee Decision Making Effectiveness," *Academy of Management Journal*, Vol. 14 (1971), 203-212.

30. Van de Ven, A. H., and A. L. Delbecq. "The Nominal Group as a Research Instrument for Exploratory Health Studies," *Journal of the American Public Health Association* (March, 1972), 337-342.

31. Van de Ven, A. H., and A. L. Delbecq. "A Planning Process for Managing Environmental Problem Solving at the Regional Level," *American*

Sociological Association, *Proceedings of the 67th Annual Meeting*, 1972.

32. Walster, G. W., and T. A. Cleary. "The Use of Statistical Significance as a Decision Making Rule," *Sociological Methodology* (1970), 246-254.

33. Walster, G. W., and M. Tretter. "Documentation of a Program Called Samfix" (Unpublished paper, Psychometric Laboratory, University of Wisconsin, 1972).

A STRATEGIC CONTINGENCIES THEORY OF INTRA-ORGANIZATIONAL POWER

D. J. Hickson, C. R. Hinings, C. A. Lee, R. E. Schneck, and J. M. Pennings

Typically, research designs have treated power as the independent variable. Power has been used in community studies to explain decisions on community programs, on resource allocation, and on voting behavior: in small groups it has been used to explain decision making; and it has been used in studies of work organizations to explain morale and alienation. But within work organizations, power itself has not been explained. This paper sets forth a theoretical explanation of power as the dependent variable with the aim of developing empirically testable hypotheses that will explain differential power among subunits in complex work organizations.

The problems of studying power are well known from the cogent reviews by March (1955, 1966) and Wrong (1968). These problems led March (1966: 70) to ask if power was just a term used to mask our ignorance, and to conclude pessimistically that the power of the concept of power "depends on the kind of system we are confronting."

Part of March's (1966) pessimism can be attributed to the problems inherent in community studies. When the unit of analysis is the community, the governmental, political, economic, recreational, and other units which make up the community do not necessarily interact and may even be oriented outside the supposed boundaries of the community. However, the subunits of a work organization are mutually related in the interdependent activities of a single identifiable social system. The perspective of the present paper is due in particular to the encouraging studies of subunits by Lawrence and Lorsch (1967a, 1967b), and begins with their (1967a: 3) definition of an organization as "a system of interrelated behaviors of people who are performing a task that has been differentiated into several distinct subsystems."

Previous studies of power in work organizations have tended to focus on the individual and to neglect subunit or departmental power. This neglect led Perrow (1970: 84) to state: "Part of the problem, I suspect, stems from the persistent attempt to define power in terms of individuals and as a social-psychological phenomenon.... Even sociological studies tend to measure power by asking about an individual.... I am not at all clear about the matter, but I think the term takes on different meanings when the unit, or power-holder, is a *formal group* in an *open system* with *multiple goals*, and the system is assumed to reflect a political-domination model of organization, rather than only a

---

This research was carried out at the Organizational Behavior Research Unit, Faculty of Business Administration and Commerce, University of Alberta, with the support of Canada Council Grants numbers 67-0253 and 69-0714. Reprinted by permission of the publisher from *Administrative Science Quarterly,* Vol. 16 (June, 1971), pp. 216-229.

cooperative model.... The fact that after a cursory search I can find only a single study that asks survey questions regarding the power of functional *groups* strikes me as odd. Have we conceptualized power in such a way as to exclude this well-known phenomenon?"

The concept of power used here follows Emerson (1962) and takes power as a property of the social relationship, not of the actor. Since the context of the relationship is a formal organization, this approach moves away from an overpersonalized conceptualization and operationalization of power toward structural sources. Such an approach has been taken only briefly by Dubin (1963) in his discussion of power, and incidentally by Lawrence and Lorsch (1967b) when reporting power data. Most research has focused on the vertical superior-subordinate relationship, as in a multitude of leadership studies. This approach is exemplified by the extensive work of Tannenbaum (1968) and his colleagues, in which the distribution of perceived power was displayed on control graphs. The focus was on the vertical differentiation of perceived power, that is the exercise of power by managers who by changing their behavior could vary the distribution and the total amount of perceived power.

By contrast, when organizations are conceived as interdepartmental systems, the division of labor becomes the ultimate source of intraorganizational power, and power is explained by variables that are elements of each subunit's task, its functioning, and its links with the activities of other subunits. Insofar as this approach differs from previous studies by treating power as the dependent variable, by taking subunits of work organizations as the subjects of analysis, and by attempting a multivariate explanation, it may avoid some of the previous pitfalls.

ELEMENTS OF A THEORY

Thompson (1967: 13) took from Cyert and March (1963) a viewpoint which he hailed as a newer tradition: "A newer tradition enables us to conceive of the organization as an open system, indeterminate and faced with uncertainty, but subject to criteria of rationality and hence needing certainty ... we suggest that organizations cope with uncertainty by creating certain parts specifically to deal with it, specializing other parts in operating under conditions of certainty, or near certainty."

Thus organizations are conceived of as interdepartmental systems in which a major task element is coping with uncertainty. The task is divided and allotted to the subsystems, the division of labor creating an interdependency among them. Imbalance of this reciprocal interdependence (Thompson, 1967) among the parts gives rise to power relations. The essence of an organization is limitation of the autonomy of all its members or parts, since all are subject to power from the others; for subunits, unlike individuals, are not free to make a decision to participate, as March and Simon (1958) put it, nor to decide whether or not to come together in political relationships. They must. They exist to do so. Crozier (1964: 47) stressed in his discussion of power "the necessity for the members of the different groups to live together; the fact that each group's privileges depend to quite a large extent on the existence of other group's privileges." The groups use differential power to function within the system rather than to destroy it.

If dependency in a social relation is the reverse of power (Emerson, 1962), then the crucial unanswered question in organizations is: what factors function to vary dependency, and so to vary power? Emerson (1962: 32) proposed that "the dependence of actor A upon actor B is (1) directly proportional to A's motivational investment in goals mediated by B, and (2) inversely proportional to the availability of those goals to A outside of the A-B relation." In organizations, subunit B will have more power than other subunits to the extent that (1) B has the capacity to fulfill the requirements of the other subunits and (2) B monopolizes this ability. If a central problem facing modern organizations is uncertainty, then B's power in the organization will be partially determined by the extent to which B copes with uncertainties for other subunits, and by the extent to which B's coping activities are available elsewhere.

Thus, intraorganizational dependency can be associated with two contributing variables: (1) the degree to which a subunit copes with uncertainty for other subunits, and (2) the extent to which a subunit's coping activities are substitutable. But if coping with uncertainty, and substitutability, are to be in some way related to power, there is a necessary assumption of some degree of task interconnection among subunits. By definition, organization requires a minimum link. Therefore, a third variable, centrality, refers to the varying degree above such a minimum with which the activities of a subunit are linked with those of other subunits.

Before these three variables can be combined in a theory of power, it is necessary to examine their definition and possible operationalization, and to define power in this context.

Power

Hinings *et al.* (1967: 62) compared power to concepts such as bureaucracy or alienation or social class, which are difficult to understand because they tend to be treated as "large-scale unitary concepts." Their many meanings need disentangling. With the concept of power, this has not yet been accomplished (Cartwright, 1965), but two conceptualizations are commonly employed: (1) power as coercion, and (2) power as determination of behavior.

Power as coercive force was a comparatively early conceptualization among sociologists (Weber, 1947; Bierstedt, 1950). Later, Blau (1964) emphasized the imposition of will despite resistance.

However, coercion is only one among the several bases of power listed by French and Raven (1959) and applied across organizations by Etzioni (1961); that is, coercion is a means of power, but is not an adequate definition of power. If the direction of dependence in a relationship is determined by an imbalance of power bases, power itself has to be defined separately from these bases. Adopting Dahl's (1957) concept of power, as many others have done (March, 1955; Bennis *et al.*, 1958; Emerson, 1962; Harsanyi, 1962; Van Doorn, 1962; Dahlstrom, 1966; Wrong, 1968; Tannenbaum, 1968; Luhmann, 1969), power is defined as the determination of the behavior of one social unit by another.

If power is the determination of A's behavior by B, irrespective of whether one, any, or all the types of bases are involved, then authority will here be regarded as that part of power which is legitimate or normatively expected by some selection of role definers. Authority may be either more or less than power. For subunits it might be represented by the formally specified range of activities they are officially required to undertake and, therefore, to decide upon.

Discrepancies between authority and power may reflect time lag. Perrow (1970) explored the discrepancy between respondent's perceptions of power and of what power should be. Perhaps views on a preferred power distribution precede changes in the exercise of power, which in turn precede changes in expectations of power, that is in its legitimate authority content. Perhaps today's authority hierarchy is partly a fossilized impression of yesterday's power ranking. However this may be, it is certainly desirable to include in any research not only data on perceived power and on preferred power, but also on positional power, or authority, and on participation, or exercised power (Clark [ed.], 1968).

Kaplan (1964) succinctly described three dimensions of power. The weight of power is defined in terms of the degree to which B affects the probability of A behaving in a certain way, that is, determination of behavior in the sense adopted here. The other dimensions are domain and scope. Domain is the number of A's, persons or collectives, whose behavior is determined; scope is the range of behaviors of each A that are determined. For subunit power within an organization, domain might be the number of other subunits affected by the issues, scope the range of decision issues affected, and weight the degree to which a given subunit affects the decision process on the issues. In published research such distinctions are rarely made. Power consists of the sweeping undifferentiated perceptions of respondents when asked to rank individuals or classes of persons, such as supervisors, on influence. Yet at the same time the complexity of power in organizations is recognized. If it is taken for granted that, say, marketing has most to do with sales matters, that accounting has most to do with finance matters, supervisors with supervisory matters, and so on, then the validity of forcing respondents to generalize single opinions across an unstated range of possibilities is questionable.

To avoid these generalized opinions, data collected over a range of decision topics or issues are desirable. Such issues should in principle include all recognized problem areas in the organization, in each of which more than one subunit is involved. Examples might be marketing strategies, obtaining equipment, personnel training, and capital budgeting.

Some suggested subvariables and indicators of power and of the independent variables are summarized in Table 1. These are intended to include both individual perceptions of power in the form of questionnaire responses and data of a somewhat less subjective kind on participation in decision processes and on formal position in the organization.

It is now possible to examine coping with uncertainty, substitutability and centrality.

Uncertainty and Coping with Uncertainty

Uncertainty may be defined as a lack of information about future events, so that alternatives and their outcomes are unpredictable. Organizations deal with environmentally

TABLE 1.
Variables and operationalizable subvariables

Power (weight, domain, scope)
Positional power (authority)
Participation power
Perceived power
Preferred power

Uncertainty

Variability of organizational inputs
Feedback on subunit performance;
　Speed
　Specificity
Structuring of subunit activities

Coping with uncertainty, classified as:

By prevention (forestalling uncertainty)
By information (forecasting)
By absorption (action after the event)

Substitutability

Availability of alternatives
Replaceability of personnel

Centrality

Pervasiveness of workflows
Immediacy of workflows

derived uncertainties in the sources and composition of inputs, with uncertainties in the processing of throughputs, and again with environmental uncertainties in the disposal of outputs. They must have means to deal with these uncertainties for adequate task performance. Such ability is here called coping.

In his study of the French tobacco manufacturing industry, Crozier (1964: 164) suggested that power is related to "the kind of uncertainty upon which depends the life of the organization." March and Simon (1958) had earlier made the same point, and Perrow (1961) had discussed the shifting domination of different groups in organizations following the shifting uncertainties of resources and the routinization of skills. From studies of industrial firms, Perrow (1970) tentatively thought that power might be due to uncertainty absorption, as March and Simon (1958) call it. Lawrence and Lorsch (1967b) found that marketing had more influence than production in both container-manufacturing and food-processing firms, apparently because of its involvement in (uncertain) innovation and with customers.

Crozier (1964) proposed a strategic model of organizations as systems in which groups strive for power, but his discussion did not clarify how uncertainty could relate positively to power. Uncertainty itself does not give power: coping gives power. If organizations allocate to their various subunits task areas that vary in uncertainty, then those subunits that cope most effectively with the most uncertainty should have most power within the organization, since coping by a subunit reduces the impact of uncertainty on other activities in the organization, a shock absorber function. Coping may be by prevention, for example, a subunit prevents sales fluctuations by securing firm orders; or by information, for example, a subunit forecasts sales fluctuations; or by absorption, for example, a drop in sales is swiftly countered by novel selling methods (Table 1). By coping, the subunit provides pseudo certainty for the other subunits by controlling what are otherwise contingencies for other activities. This coping confers power through the dependencies created.

Thus organizations do not necessarily aim to avoid uncertainty nor to reduce its absolute level, as Cyert and March (1963) appear to have assumed, but to cope with it. If a subunit can cope, the level of uncertainty encountered can be increased by moving into fresh sectors of the environment, attempting fresh outputs, or utilizing fresh technologies.

Operationally, raw uncertainty and coping will be difficult to disentangle, though theoretically the distinctions are clear. For all units, uncertainty is in the raw situation which would exist without the activities of the other relevant subunits, for example, the uncertainty that would face production units if the sales subunit were not there to forecast and/or to obtain a smooth flow of orders. Uncertainty might be indicated by the variability of those inputs to the organization which are taken by the subunit. For instance, a production subunit may face variability in raw materials and engineering may face variability in equipment performance. Lawrence and Lorsch (1967a) attempted categorizations of this kind. In addition, they (1967a: 14) gave a lead with "the time span of definitive feedback from the environment." This time span might be treated as a secondary indicator of uncertainty, making the assumption that the less the feedback to a subunit on the results of what it is doing, and the less specific the feedback, the more likely the subunit is to be working in a vague, unknown, unpredictable task area. Both speed and specificity of feedback are suggested variables in Table 1.

Furthermore, the copious literature on bureaucratic or mechanistic structures versus more organic and less defined structures could be taken to imply that routinized or highly structured subunits, for example, as conceptualized and measured by Pugh et al. (1968), will have stable homogeneous activities and be less likely to face uncertainty. This assumption would require empirical testing before structuring of activities could be used as an indicator of uncertainty, but it is tentatively included in Table 1.

In principle, coping with uncertainty might be directly measured by the difference between the uncertainty of those inputs taken by a subunit and the certainty with which it performs its activities nonetheless. This would indicate the degree of shock absorption.

The relation of coping with uncertainty to power can be expressed by the following hypotheses:

Hypothesis 1. The more a subunit copes with uncertainty, the greater its power within the organization.

The hypothesis is in a form which ignores any effects of centrality and substitutability.

Substitutability

Concepts relating to the availability of alternatives pervade the literature on power. In economics theory the degree of competition is taken as a measure of the extent to which alternatives are available from other organizations, it being implied that the power of an organization over other organizations and customers is a function of the amount of competition present. The same point was the second part of Emerson's (1962) power-dependency scheme in social relations, and the second requirement or determinant in Blau's (1964) model of a power relationship.

Yet only Mechanic (1962) and Dubin (1957, 1963) have discussed such concepts as explanations of organizational power. Mechanic's (1962: 358) hypothesis 4 stated: "Other factors remaining constant, a person difficult to replace will have greater power than a person easily replaceable." Dubin (1957) stressed the very similar notion of exclusiveness, which as developed later (Dubin, 1963: 21), means that: "For any given level of functional importance in an organization, the power residing in a functionary is inversely proportional to the number of other functionaries in the organization capable of performing the function." Supporting this empirically, Lipset *et al.* (1956) suggested that oligarchy may occur in trade unions because of the official's monopoly of political and negotiating skills.

The concept being used is represented here by the term substitutability, which can, for subunits, be defined as the ability of the organization to obtain alternative performance for the activities of a subunit, and can be stated as a hypothesis for predicting the power of a subunit as follows:

Hypothesis 2. The lower the substitutability of the activities of a subunit, the greater its power within the organization.

Thus a purchasing department would have its power reduced if all of its activities could be done by hired materials agents, as would a personnel department if it were partially substituted by selection consultants or by line managers finding their staff themselves. Similarly, a department may hold on to power by retaining information the release of which would enable others to do what it does.

The obvious problem in operationalization is establishing that alternative means of performing activities exist, and if they do, whether they could feasibly be used. Even if agents or consultants exist locally, or if corporation headquarters could provide services, would it really be practicable for the organization to dispense with its own subunit? Much easier to obtain are data on replaceability of subunit personnel such as length of training required for new recruits and ease of hiring, which can be regarded as secondary indicators of the substitutability of a subunit, as indicated in Table 1.

Centrality

Given a view of organizations as systems of interdependent roles and activities, then the centrality of a subunit is the degree to which its activities are interlinked into the system. By definition, no subunit of an organization can score zero centrality. Without a minimum of centrality, coping with uncertainty and substitutability cannot affect power; above the minimum, additional increments of centrality further differentiate subunit power. It is the degree to which the subunit is an interdependent component, as Thompson (1967: 54) put it, distinguishing between pooled, sequential, and reciprocal interdependence patterns. Blau and Scott (1962) made an analogous distinction between parallel and interdependent specialization. Woodward (1965: 126) also introduced a concept of this kind into her discussion of the critical function in each of unit, large batch and mass, and process production: "there seemed to be one function that was central and critical in that it had the greatest effect on success and survival."

Within the overall concept of centrality, there are inconsistencies which indicate that more than one constitutive concept is being used. At the present stage of conceptualization their identification must be very tentative. First, there is the idea that the activities of a subunit are central if they are connected with many other activities in the organization. This workflow pervasiveness may be defined as the degree to which the workflows of a subunit connect with the workflows of other subunits. It describes the extent of task interactions between subunits, and for all subunits in an organization it would be operationalized as the flowchart of a complete systems analysis. For example, the integrative subsystems studied by Lawrence and Lorsh (1967a: 30), "whose members had the function of integrating the sales-research and the production-research subsystems" and which had structural and cultural characteristics intermediate between them, were presumably high on workflow pervasiveness because everything they did connected with the workflows of these several other subsystems. Research subsystems, however, may have been low on this variable if they fed work only to a single integrative, or production, subsystem.

Secondly, the activities of a subunit are central if they are essential in the sense that their cessation would quickly and substantially impede the primary workflow of the organization. This workflow immediacy is defined as the speed and severity with which the workflows of a subunit affect the final outputs of the organization. Zald (1962) and Clark (1956) used a similar idea when they explained differential power among institution staff and education faculty by the close relation of their activities to organization goals.

The pervasiveness and immediacy of the workflows of a subunit are not necessarily closely related, and may empirically show a low correlation. A finance department may well have pervasive connections with all other subunits through the budgeting system, but if its activities ceased it would be some time before the effects were felt in, say, the production output of a factory; a production department controlling a stage midway in the sequence of an automated process, however, could have high workflow immediacy though not high pervasiveness.

The two main centrality hypotheses can therefore be stated as follows:

Hypothesis 3a. The higher the pervasiveness of the workflows of a subunit, the greater its power within the organization.

Hypothesis 3b. The higher the immediacy of the workflows of a subunit, the greater its power within the organization.

CONTROL OF CONTINGENCIES

Hypotheses relating power to coping with uncertainty, substitutability, and the subvariables of centrality have been stated in a simple single-variable form. Yet it follows from the view of subunits as interdependent parts of organizational systems that the hypotheses in this form are misleading. While each hypothesis may be empirically upheld, it is also hypothesized that this cannot be so without some values of both the other main independent variables. For example, when a marketing department copes with a volatile market by forecasting and by switching sales staff around to ensure stable orders, it acquires power only because the forecast and the orders are linked to the workflow of production, which depends on them. But even then power would be limited by the availability of a successful local marketing agency which could be hired by the organization, and the fact that salesmen were low skilled and easily replaceable.

To explain this interrelationship, the concept of control of contingencies is introduced. It represents organizational interdependence; subunits control contingencies for one another's activities and draw power from the dependencies thereby created. As a hypothesis:

Hypothesis 4. The more contingencies are controlled by a subunit, the greater the power within the organization.

A contingency is a requirement of the activities of one subunit which is affected by the activities of another subunit. What makes such a contingency strategic, in the sense that it is related to power, can be deduced from the preceding hypotheses. The independent variables are each necessary but not sufficient conditions for control of strategic contingencies, but together they determine the variation in interdependence between subunits. Thus contingencies controlled by a subunit as a consequence of its coping with uncertainty do not become strategic, that is, affect power, in the organization without some (unknown) values of substitutability and centrality. A strategies contingencies theory of power is therefore proposed and is illustrated by the diagram in Figure 1.

In terms of exchange theory, as developed by Blau (1964), subunits can be seen to be exchanging control of strategic contingencies one for the other under the normative regulation of an encompassing social system, and acquiring power in the system through the exchange. The research task is to elucidate what combinations of values of the independent variables summarized in hypotheses 1-3 allow hypothesis 4 to hold. Ultimately and ideally the aim would be to discover not merely the weightings of each in the total effect upon power, but how these variables should be operationally interrelated to obtain the best predictions. More of one and less of another may leave the resulting power unchanged. Suppose an engineering subunit has power because it quickly absorbs uncertainty by repairing breakdowns which interfere with the different workflows for each of several organizations' outputs. It is moderately central and nonsubstitutable. A change in organization policy bringing in a new technology with a single workflow leading to a single output would raise engineering's centrality, since a single breakdown would immediately stop everything, but simultaneously the uncertainty might be reduced by a maintenance program which all but eliminates the possibility of such an occurrence.

Though three main factors are hypothesized, which must change if power is to change, it is not assumed that all subunits will act in accord with the theory to increase their power. This has to be demonstrated. There is the obvious possibility of a cumulative reaction in which a subunit's power is used to preserve or increase the uncertainty it can cope with, or its centrality, or to prevent substitution, thereby increasing its power, and so on. Nor is it argued that power or authority are intentionally allocated in terms of the theory, although the theory is open to such an inference.

Routinization

Most studies that refer to uncertainty contrast is with routinization, the prior prescription of recurrent task activities. Crozier (1964) held that the power of the maintenance personnel in the tobacco plants was due to all other tasks being routinized. A relative decline in the power of general medical personnel in hospitals during this century is thought to be due to the routinization of some tasks, which previously presented uncertainties which could be coped with only by a physician, and the transfer of these tasks to relatively routinized subunits, such as inoculation programs, mass X-ray facilities, and so on (Perrow, 1965;

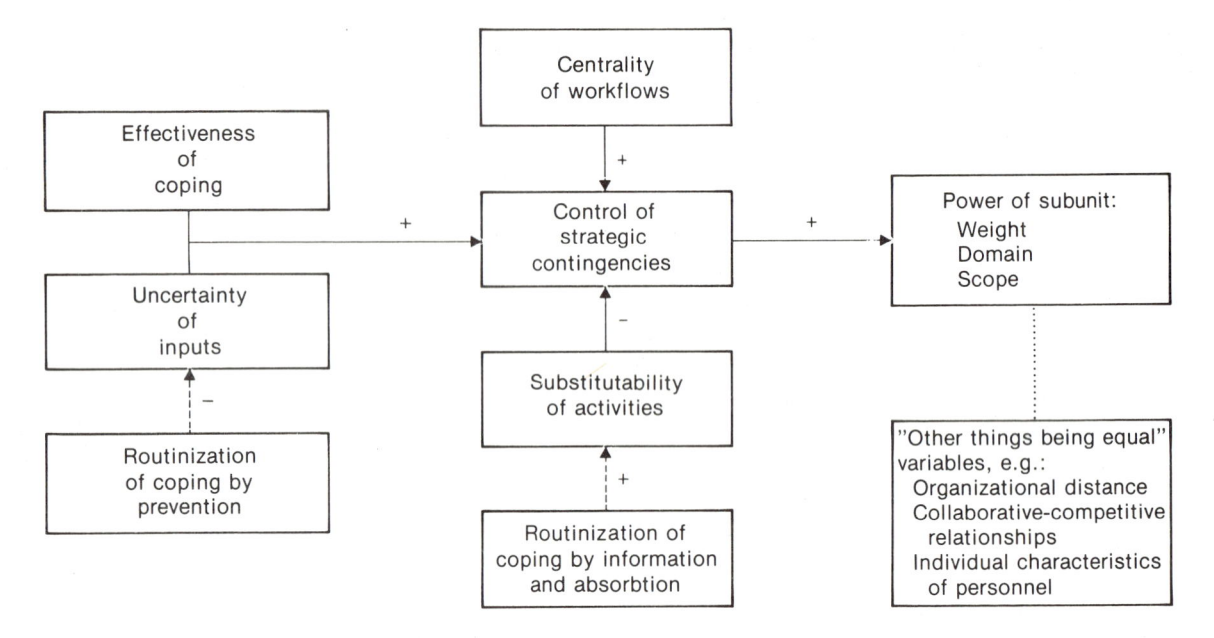

Figure 1. The strategic contingencies theory and routinization

Gordon and Becker, 1964). Crozier (1964: 165) crystallized the presumed effects of routinization; "But the expert's success is constantly self-defeating. The rationalization process gives him power, but the end results of rationalization curtail his power. As soon as a field is well covered, as soon as the first intuitions and innovations can be translated into rules and programs, the expert's power disappears."

The strategic contingencies' theory as developed in Figure 1 clarifies this. It suggests that research has been hampered by a confusion of two kinds of routinization, both of which are negatively related to power but in different ways. Routinization may be (a) of coping by prevention, which prevents the occurrence of uncertainty; and (b) of coping by information or absorption which define how the uncertainty which does occur shall be coped with.

Preventive routinization reduces or removes the uncertainty itself, for example, planned maintenance, which maintenance in Crozier's (1964) tobacco factories would have resisted; inoculation or X-ray programs; and long-term supply contracts, so that the sales staff no longer have to contend with unstable demand. Such routinization removes the opportunity for power, and it is this which is self-defeating (Crozier, 1964: 165) if the expert takes his techniques to a point when they begin not only to cope but to routinely diminish the uncertainty coped with. Thus reducing the uncertainty is not the same as reducing the impact of uncertainty. According to the hypothesis, a sales department which transmits steady orders despite a volatile market has high power; a sales department which reduces the uncertainty itself by long-term tied contracts has low power.

Routinization of coping by information and absorption is embodied in job descriptions and task instructions prescribing how to obtain information and to respond to uncertainty. For maintenance personnel, it lays down how to repair the machine; for physicians, it lays down a standard procedure for examining patients and sequences of remedies for each diagnosis. How does this affect power, since it does not eliminate the uncertainty itself, as preventive routinization does?

What it does is increase substitutability. The means of coping become more visible and possible substitutes more obvious, even if those substitutes are unskilled personnel from another subunit who can follow a standard procedure but could not have acquired the previously unexpressed skills.

There is probably some link between the two kinds of routinization. Once preventive routinization is accomplished, other coping routinization more easily follows, as indeed it follows any reduction of uncertainty.

STUDIES OF SUBUNIT POWER

Testing of Hypotheses on Earlier Work

The utility of the strategic contingencies theory should be tested on published work, but it is difficult to do this adequately, since most studies stress only one possibility. For example, Crozier (1964) and Thompson (1967) stressed uncertainty, Dubin (1963) stressed exclusiveness of function, and Woodward (1965) spoke of the critical function.

The difficulty is also due to the lack of data. For example, among several studies in which inferences about environmental uncertainty are drawn, only Lawrence and Lorsch (1967b) presented data. They combine executive's questionnaire responses on departmental clarity of job requirements, time span of definitive feedback on departmental success in performance, and uncertainty of cause and effect in the department's functional area.

Lawrence and Lorsch (1967b: 127) found that in two food-processing organizations, research was most influential, then marketing, excluding the field selling unit, and then production. However, influence, or perceived power as it is called here, was rated on the single issue of product innovation and not across a range of issues as suggested earlier in this paper; validity therefore rests on the assumption of equal potential involvement of each function in this one issue. Would research still be most influential if the issues included equipment purchase, or capital budgeting, or personnel training? Even so, on influence over product innovation, an uncertainty hypothesis could be said to fit neatly, since the subunits were ordered on perceived uncertainty of subenvironment exactly as they were on influence.

But uncertainty alone would not explain power in the other firms studied. Although in six plastics firms, coordinating sections or integrating units were perceived as having more influence than functional subunits because "integration itself was the most problematic job" (Lawrence and Lorsch 1967b: 62), it was also a central job in terms of workflow pervasiveness.

Furthermore, in two container manufacturing organizations, although the market subenvironment was seen as the least uncertain, the sales subunit was perceived as the most influential (Lawrence and Lorsch 1967b: 111). An explanation must be sought in the contingencies that the sales subunit controls for production and for research. In this industry, outputs must fit varying customer requirements for containers. Scheduling for production departments and design problems for research departments are therefore completely subject to the contingencies of orders brought in by the sales department. Sales has not only the opportunity to cope with such uncertainty as may exist over customer requirements, it is highly central; for its activities connect it directly to both the other departments—workflow pervasiveness—and if it ceased work production of containers would stop—workflow immediacy. The effects of centrality are probably bolstered by nonsubstitutability, since the sales subunit develops a necessary particularized knowledge of customer requirements. Production and research are, therefore, comparatively powerless in face of the strategic contingencies controlled by the sales subunit.

In short, only a sensitive balancing of all three factors can explain the patterns of contingencies from which power strategically flows.

This is plain also in Crozier's (1964) insightful study of small French tobacco-manufacturing plants. Crozier (1964: 109) had the impression that the maintenance engineers were powerful because "machine stoppages are the only major happenings that cannot be predicted"; therefore the engineers had (Crozier, 1964: 154) "control over the last source of uncertainty remaining in a completely routinized organizational system." But this is not enough for power. Had it been possible to contract maintenance work to consulting engineers, for example, then programs of preventive maintenance might have been introduced, and preventive routinization would have removed much of the uncertainty. However, it is likely that union agreements ensured that the plant engineers were nonsubstitutable. In addition, in these small organizations without specialist control and service departments, the maintenance section's work linked it to all production subunits, that is, to almost every other subunit in the plant. So workflow pervasiveness was high, as was workflow immediacy, since cessation of maintenance activities would quickly have stopped tobacco outputs. The control of strategic contingencies which gave power to the engineers has to be explained on all counts and not be uncertainty alone.

Crozier's (1964) study is a warning against the facile inference that a power distribution fitting the strategic contingencies theory is necessarily efficient, or rational, or functional for an organization; for the power of the engineers to thwart the introduction of programmed maintenance was presumably neither efficient, rational, nor functional.

A challenge to the analysis made is presented by Goldner's (1970) description of a case where there was programmed maintenance and yet the maintenance section held power over production. Goldner (1970) attributed the power of the maintenance subunit to knowing how to install and operate such programs, to coping with breakdowns as in the Crozier (1964) cases, and to knowing how to cope with a critical problem of parts supplies. The strategic contingencies theory accords with his interpretation so long as knowing how to install a program takes effect as coping with uncertainty and not yet as preventive routinization which stops breakdowns. This is where an unknown time element enters to allow for changes in the variables specified and in any associated variables not yet defined. For a time, knowing the answer to an uncertainty does confer power, but the analyses of routinization derived from the theory, as shown in Figure 1, suggests that if this becomes successful preventive routinization, it takes a negative effect upon power. The net result for power in Goldner's (1970) case would then be from the interplay of the opposed effects of activities some of which are preventively routinized, thus decreasing power, and some of which continue to be nonroutine, thus increasing power.

On the other hand, Goldner's (1970) description of the powerful industrial relations subunit in the same plant clearly supports the strategic contingencies theory by showing that coping with uncertainty, centrality, and substitutability had the effect predicted here. The industrial relations subunit exploited uncertainty over the supply and cost of personnel, which arose from possible strikes and pay increases, by (Goldner, 1970: 104) "use of the union as an outside threat." It coped effectively by its nonroutinized knowledge of union officials and of contract interpretation; and its activities were centrally linked to those of other subunits by the necessity for uniform practice on wages and employment. Industrial relations staff developed nonsubstitutable interpersonal and bargaining skills.

There are no means of assessing whether the univariate stress on uncertainty in the handful of other relevant studies is justified. Perrow (1970) explained the greater perceived power of sales as against production, finance, and research, in most of 12 industrial firms, by the concept of uncertainty absorption (March and Simon, 1958). Sales was strategic with respect to the environment. Is the one case where it came second to production the only case where it was also substitutable? Or not central?

White (1961) and Landsberger (1961) both suggested that power shifts over periods of time to follow the locus of uncertainty. Both studied engineering factories. From the histories of three firms, Landsberger (1961) deduced that when money was scarce and uncertain, accounting was powerful; when raw materials were short, purchasing was powerful; and, conversely, when demand was insatiable sales were weakened. In the Tennessee Valley Authority, a nonmanufacturing organization, Selznick (1949) attributed the eventual power of the agricultural relations department to its ability to cope with the uncertain environmental threat represented by the Farm Bureau.

Yet while these earlier studies emphasized uncertainty in one way or another, others called attention to substitutability and probably also to centrality. Again the implication is that contingencies are not strategically controlled without some combination of all three basic variables. For example, the engineers described by Strauss (1962, 1964) appeared to have more power than purchasing agents because the latter were substitutable, that is, the engineers can set specifications for what was to be bought even though the purchasing agents considered this their own responsibility. Thompson (1956: 300) attributed variations in perceived power within and between two U.S. Air Force wings to the changing "technical requirements of operations," which may have indicated changing centralities and substitutabilities.

In the absence of data, consideration of further different kinds of organization must remain pure speculation, for example, the power of surgical units in hospitals, the power of buyers in stores, the power of science faculties in universities.

Other Variables Affecting Power

In order that it can be testable, the strategic contingencies theory errs on the side of simplicity. Any theory must start with a finite number of variables and presume continual development by their alteration or deletion, or by the addition of new variables. As stated, the theory uses only those variables hypothesized to affect power by their contribution to the control of contingencies exercised by a subunit. Other possible explanations of power are not considered. This in itself is an assumption of the greater explanatory force of the theory. Blalock (1961: 8) put the problem clearly: "The dilemma of the scientist is to select models that are at the same time simple enough to permit him to think with the aid of the model but also sufficiently realistic that the simplifications required do not lead to predictions that are highly inaccurate."

In recognition of this, Figure 1 includes several "other things being equal" variables as they are called, that may affect power, but are assumed to do so in other ways than by control of contingencies. One such range of possible relevant variables is qualities of interdepartmental relationships, such as competitiveness versus collaborativeness (Dutton and Walton, 1966). Does the power exercised relate to the style of the relationship through which the power runs? Another possibility is pinpointed by Stymne (1968: 88): "A unit's influence has its roots partly in its strategical importance to the company and partly in nonfunctional circumstances such as tradition, or control over someone in top management through, for example, family relationship." The tradition is the status which may accrue to a particular function because chief executives have typically reached the top through it. Many case studies highlight the personal links of subunits with top personnel (Dalton, 1959; Gouldner, 1955). The notion might be entitled the organizational distance of the subunit, a variant of social distance.

Finally, but perhaps most important, individual differences must be accepted, that is, differences in the intelligence, skills, ages, sexes, or personality factors such as dominance, assertiveness, and risk-taking propensity, of personnel in the various subunits.

CONCLUSION

The concept of work organizations as interdepartmental systems leads to a strategic contingencies theory explaining differential subunit power by dependence on contingencies ensuing from varying combinations of coping with uncertainty, substitutability, and centrality. It should be stressed that the theory is not in any sense static. As the goals, outputs, technologies, and markets of organizations change so, for each subunit, the values of the independent variables change, and patterns of power change.

Many problems are unresolved. For example, does the theory implicitly assume perfect knowledge by each subunit of the contingencies inherent for it in the activities of the others? Does a workflow of information affect power differently to a workflow of things? But with the encouragement of the improved analysis given of the few existing studies, data can be collected and analyzed, hopefully in ways which will afford a direct test.

REFERENCES

1. Bennis, Warren G., N. Berkowitz, M. Affinito, and M. Malone. 1958 "Authority, power and the ability to influence." Human Relations, 11: 143-156.

2. Bierstedt, Robert. 1950 "An analysis of social power." American Sociological Review, 15: 730-736.

3. Blalock, Hubert M. 1961 Causal Inferences in Nonexperimental Research. Chapel Hill: University of North Carolina Press.

4. Blau, Peter. 1964 Exchange and Power in Social Life. New York: Wiley.

5. Blau, Peter, and W. Richard Scott. 1962 Formal Organizations: A Comparative Approach. London: Routledge and Kegan Paul.

6. Cartwright, Darwin. 1965 "Influence, leadership, control." In James G. March (ed.), Handbook of Organizations: 1-47. Chicago: Rand McNally.

7. Clark, Burton R. 1956 "Organizational adaptation and precarious values: a case study." American Sociological Review, 21: 327-336.

8. Clark, Terry N. (ed.). 1968 Community Structure and Decision-Making: Comparative Analyses. San Francisco: Chandler.

9. Crozier, Michel. 1964 The Bureaucratic Phenomenon. London: Tavistock.

10. Cyert, Richard M., and James G. March. 1963 A Behavioral Theory of the Firm. Englewood Cliffs, N.J.: Prentice-Hall.

11. Dahl, Robert A. 1957 "The concept of power." Behavioral Science, 2: 201-215.

12. Dahlstrom, E. 1966 "Exchange, influence, and power." Acta Sociologica, 9: 237-284.

13. Dalton, Melville. 1959 Men Who Manage. New York: Wiley.

14. Dubin, Robert. 1957 "Power and union-management relations." Administrative Science Quarterly, 2: 60-81.

15. Dubin, Robert. 1963 "Power, function, and organization." Pacific Sociological Review, 6: 16-24.

16. Dutton, John M., and Richard E. Walton. 1966 "Interdepartmental conflict and cooperation: two contrasting studies." Human Organization, 25: 207-220.

17. Emerson, R. E. 1962 "Power-dependence relations." American Sociological Review, 27: 31-41.

18. Etzioni, Amitai. 1961 A Comparative Analysis of Complex Organizations. New York: Free Press.

19. French, John R. P., and Bertram Raven. 1959 "The bases of social power." In D. Cartwright (ed.), Studies in Social Power: 150-167. Ann Arbor: University of Michigan.

20. Goldner, Fred H. 1970 "The division of labor: process and power." In Mayer N. Zald (ed.), Power in Organizations: 97-143. Nashville: Vanderbilt University Press.

21. Gordon, Gerald, and Selwyn Becker. 1964 "Changes in medical practice bring shifts in the patterns of power." The Modern Hospital (February): 89-91, 154-156.

22. Gouldner, Alvin W. 1955 Wildcat Strike. London: Routledge.

23. Harsanyi, John C. 1962 "Measurement of social power, opportunity costs, and the theory of two-person bargaining games." Behavioral Science, 7: 67-80.

24. Hinings, Christopher R., Derek S. Pugh, David J. Hickson, and Christopher Turner. 1967 "An approach to the study of bureaucracy." Sociology, 1: 61-72.

25. Kaplan, Abraham. 1964 "Power in perspective." In Robert L. Kahn and Elise Boulding (eds.), Power and Conflict in Organizations: 11-32. London: Tavistock.

26. Landsberger, Henry A. 1961 "The horizontal dimension in bureaucracy." Administrative Science Quarterly, 6: 299-332.

27. Lawrence, Paul R., and Jay W. Lorsch. 1967 "Differentiation and integration in complex organizations." Administrative Science Quarterly, 12: 1-47.

28. Lawrence, Paul R., and Jay W. Lorsch. 1967 Organization and Environment. Cambridge: Division of Research, Graduate School of Business Administration, Harvard University.

29. Lipset, Seymour M., Martin A. Trow, and James A. Coleman. 1956 Union Democracy. Glencoe, Ill.: Free Press.

30. Luhmann, Niklaus. 1969 "Klassische theorie der macht." Zeitschrift fur Politik, 16: 149-170.

31. March, James G. 1955 "An introduction to the theory and measurement of influence." American Political Science Review, 49: 431-450.

32. March, James G. 1966 "The power of power." In David Easton (ed.), Varieties of Political Theory: 39-70. Englewood Cliffs. N.J.: Prentice-Hall.

33. March, James G., and Herbert A. Simon. 1958 Organizations. New York: Wiley.

34. Mechanic, David. 1962 "Sources of power of lower participants in complex organizations." Administrative Science Quarterly, 7: 349-364.

35. Perrow, Charles. 1961 "The analysis of goals in complex organizations." American Sociological Review, 26: 854-866.

36. Perrow, Charles. 1965 "Hospitals: technology, structure, and goals." In James G. March (ed.), Handbook of Organizations: 910-971. Chicago: Rand McNally.

37. Perrow, Charles. 1970 "Departmental power and perspectives in industrial firms." In Mayer N. Zald (ed.), Power in Organizations: 59-89. Nashville: Vanderbilt University Press.

38. Pugh, Derek S., David J. Hickson, Christopher R. Hinings, and Christopher Turner. 1968 "Dimensions of organization structure." Administrative Science Quarterly, 13: 65-105.

39. Selznick, Philip. 1949 T.V.A. and the Grass Roots. Berkeley: University of California Press.

40. Strauss, George. 1962 "Tactics of lateral relationship: the purchasing agent." Administrative Science Quarterly, 7: 161-186.

41. Strauss, George. 1964 "Work-flow frictions, interfunctional rivalry, and professionalism." Human Organization, 23: 137-150.

42. Stymne, Bengt. 1968 "Interdepartmental communication and intraorganizational strain." Acta Sociologica, 11: 82-100.

43. Tannenbaum, Arnold S. 1968 Control in Organizations. New York: McGraw-Hill.

44. Thompson, James D. 1956 "Authority and power in 'identical' organizations." American Journal of Sociology, 62: 290-301.

45. Thompson, James D. 1967 Organizations in Action. New York: McGraw-Hill.

46. Van Doorn, Jaques A. A. 1962 "Sociology and the problem of power." Sociologica Neerlandica, 1: 3-47.

47. Weber, Max. 1947 The Theory of Social and Economic Organization. Glencoe, Ill.: Free Press.

48. White, Harrison. 1961 "Management conflict and sociometric structure." American Journal of Sociology, 67: 185-199.

49. Woodward, Joan. 1965 Industrial Organization: Theory and Practice. London: Oxford University Press.

50. Wrong, Dennis H. 1968 "Some problems in defining social power." American Journal of Sociology, 73, 673-681.

51. Zald, Mayer N. 1962 "Organizational control structures in five correctional institutions." American Journal of Sociology, 68: 335-345.

PART FOUR

INDIVIDUAL/ GROUP/ ORGANIZATIONAL INTERFACES

In previous sections various models of group processes and individual behavior were shown to be important and useful in understanding human performance. In this part, we shall attempt to build on these models to show how individual differences interact with group processes to affect job performance. The readings in this part are offered as a starting point for developing greater understanding of the complexity of human behavior. They are divided into three sections, with each section building upon the previous.

The first section is concerned with the effect of various motivational strategies on worker performance and satisfaction. Motivation can be defined as an inner state that activates, energizes, or moves behavior toward goals. When we speak of motivation, we are really asking why a person acts as he or she does. The concept of motivation implies that people choose avenues of behavior to follow. To examine the concept of motivation is to ask what forces make a person select a particular avenue. The second section deals with leadership. Leadership is the process by which an individual influences the behavior of another person or group. When performance problems occur, there is a tendency to feel that they are a result of leadership deficiencies. Yet, failure is often due to the fact that a manager may not administer as well as he should. The third section, on organizational structure and climate, discusses how the structure of an organization can create climates that foster either high or low performance. It is important to understand that various organizational practices, rules, regulations, and physical arrangements can affect the performance and satisfaction of workers.

Motivation

Motivation is a theme pervading all attempts to influence organizational behavior. Managers are always searching for new and more effective means of motivation. Thousands of articles, workshops, and conferences are held each year in an attempt to answer the question "How do I motivate people?" It is too often taken for granted that knowledge of some current theories of motivation and how to apply them are valuable to managers. If we have some knowledge of motivation theory, we may be able to identify what the organization is doing to try to motivate employees.

In the first article, Korman, "Hypothesis of Work Behavior Revisited and an Extension," describes a model relating environmental characteristics to the motivational process. These environmental characteristics interact with the individual's own belief system to affect his or her behavior. The core of the model is that people are motivated to seek a stable world, and hence will attempt to seek outcomes consistent with their belief systems. People's belief systems are a function of environmental experience and learning.

Greene and Craft in their article, "Satisfaction-Performance Controversy—Revisited," examine three assumptions concerning employee satisfaction and performance. The first, and oldest, of these assumptions is that satisfied workers will be motivated to perform effectively. The second is that workers who perform well tend to be satisfied, presumably because they are rewarded for their performance. The last assumption is that both satisfaction and performance are caused by an additional variable or variables. After reviewing research concerning these three assumptions, Greene and Craft conclude that recent evidence is most supportive of the third assumption, that satisfaction and performance are caused by some third, or more, variable(s). More specifically, they suggest the administration of rewards as a prime determinant of both satisfaction and performance. Having reached this conclusion, Greene and Craft provide the manager with a framework, drawing heavily on learning theory, for affecting employee satisfaction and performance. Within this framework Greene and Craft examine the intervening variables and contingencies which are likely to influence the complex relationships between rewards and performance.

Abraham K. Korman

HYPOTHESIS OF WORK BEHAVIOR REVISITED AND AN EXTENSION

The study of work behavior during the past two decades, has been marked by a theory-oriented flavor, but theories are not permanently useful. They need to be looked at periodically and reevaluated as to whether the ideas proposed, and the predictions which stem from them, are still viable. Eventually, all theories come up wanting and a new framework becomes necessary, one better able to handle the accumulating research data. The legitimate goal of all theory is to work itself out of business, and a continuing responsibility of the theorist is to further this process by a continuing examination of his or her own work and an initiation of changes as new data become available.

The first goal of this paper is to review recent research relevant to several hypotheses proposed by the author several years ago (21, 22, 23). A theoretical extension will be proposed to overcome lacks in the original proposals. Evidence relating to this extension will then be reviewed and implications for future research suggested.

THE ORIGINAL HYPOTHESES AND SOME CONSEQUENT EVIDENCE

The original hypotheses (21) constituted a consistency theory of work motivation which could be summarized as follows: All other things being equal, individuals will engage in and find satisfying those behavioral roles which maximize their sense of cognitive balance or consistency.

1. Individuals will be motivated to perform in a manner consistent with their self-images. To the extent that their self-concepts concerning the job or task require effective performance in order to result in "consistent" cognitions, then, to that extent, they will be motivated to engage in effective performance.

2. Individuals will choose and find most satisfying those job and task roles which are consistent with their self-cognitions. To the extent that one perceives the self as competent and need-satisfying, one will choose and find most satisfying those situations which are in balance with these self-perceptions.

Underlying this hypothesis were the following assumptions: One's self-esteem is the extent to which one sees the self as a competent, need-satisfying individual. Differences in such self-evaluation may arise in a number of ways. First a relatively persistent level of self-esteem may be conceived of as a level that occurs relatively consistently across various situations. Second, one's self-perceived com-

Reprinted by permission of the publisher from *Academy of Management Review,* Vol. 1 (January, 1976), pp. 50-63. Earlier versions of some of the ideas discussed here were presented at the 1973 meetings of the Eastern Academy of Management and at a Symposium on Occupational Research and the Navy—Prospectus 1980, which was held in Sand Diego, California in July 1973. I would like to thank my fellow participants in these meetings for their assistance in stimulating the revised formulations discussed here.

petence concerning a particular task or job may vary as a result of differential learning experiences, or the specific characteristics of the moment. Finally, one's self-esteem is also a function of others' expectations at any given time...to the extent that others (a) think that we are competent, need-satisfying and able, and (b) exhibit such thoughts by their behavior toward us, to that extent our self-perceived competence concerning the task is increased. This change takes place because such interpersonal evaluations provide a base of "reality."

Following the development of this framework, the approach was extended to other aspects of work behavior such as "change," "openness to change," and "aggression" (23). First, it was suggested that the same type of social environment which encourages value for the self encourages beliefs in the value of others, and a belief in a variable, changing world. These beliefs then lead to lower value for rules, routinization, hierarchical control systems and those related social phenomena which symbolize lack of belief in the capability of people. This more elaborate framework is presented in Figure 1.

Since these hypotheses were formulated, considerable evidence has accumulated as to their usefulness. The following sections will review this *consequent* research, categorizing the analysis according to several predictions which may be made from the proposed framework. This procedure shows those areas where the hypotheses have been most useful, those where their predictions have been less successful, and those where additional research seems to be necessary.

A. There is a positive correlation between self-esteem and the choice of an occupation which is congruent with one's self-perceived characteristics.

Seven studies provide tests of this prediction. In six, the results are strongly supportive.

Behling and Tolliver (3) had college seniors who were seeking employment rate potential employers on the same semantic differential instrument on which they had rated themselves. Generally, support was found for the prediction that high self-esteem individuals would implement their self-concept in their choice of employers; those with low self-esteem would complement their self-concept, and those medium in self-esteem would do neither consistently. In essentially similar designs, Greenhaus (13), Healy (16), and Leonard, Walsh and Osipow (28) found significant positive relationships between level of self-esteem and congruency between self-perceptions and perceptions of the chosen occupation, with the last study finding the relationship to hold also for second vocational choices.

Assuming that high self-esteem is theoretically coordinate with a high degree of personal stability and integration, then two studies by Walsh and his coworkers are also supportive of the prediction. In the first study, Walsh and Lewis (45) found that individuals of high personal stability and integration were more likely to have made college major choices congruent with their personal characteristics than those with low levels of personal stability and integration. This finding was replicated where the dependent variable was congruence between occupational preferences and self-concept (44).

In the only study testing this prediction which did not find good support, Mansfield (31) found that congruency was fairly similar in both high and low self-esteem respondents. However, trends in the data indicated a better "fit" between self and occupation for high self-esteem than for low self-esteem respondents.

B. There is a negative correlation between lack of trust in the ability of others and the desirability of universal rules for guiding behavior and engaging in work activities which are congruent with one's self-perceived characteristics.

One study relevant to this derivation was supportive. Esposito and Richards (9) found in a

Theoretical Assumptions

People are motivated to seek a stable world, hence will attempt to seek outcomes consistent with belief systems. People's belief systems are a function of environmental experience and learning.

Sequences of Different Environments For Behavior.

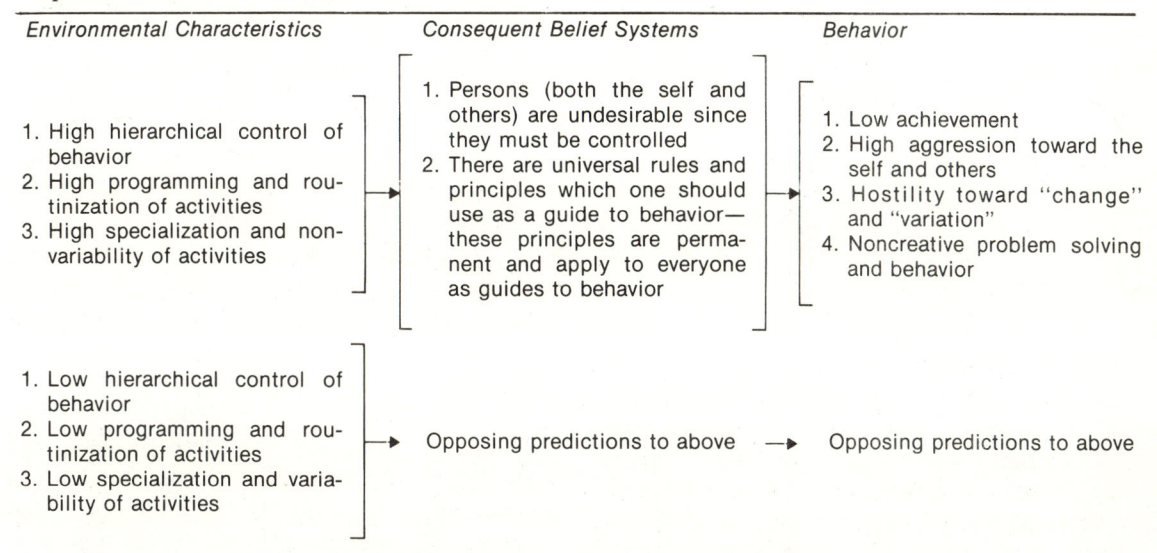

Environmental Characteristics	Consequent Belief Systems	Behavior
1. High hierarchical control of behavior 2. High programming and routinization of activities 3. High specialization and non-variability of activities	1. Persons (both the self and others) are undesirable since they must be controlled 2. There are universal rules and principles which one should use as a guide to behavior—these principles are permanent and apply to everyone as guides to behavior	1. Low achievement 2. High aggression toward the self and others 3. Hostility toward "change" and "variation" 4. Noncreative problem solving and behavior
1. Low hierarchical control of behavior 2. Low programming and routinization of activities 3. Low specialization and variability of activities	Opposing predictions to above	Opposing predictions to above

Source: Korman, A. K. "Organizational Achievement, Aggression and Creativity: Some Suggestions Toward an Integrated Theory," *Organizational Behavior and Human Performance,* Vol. 6 (1971), 593-613.

Figure 1. Summary of model relating environmental antecedents to motivational process.

study of 174 educational supervisors that those who were high in Dogmatism, a measure of these characteristics (22, 23), were less likely to be engaging in tasks that fit their ideal for themselves than those low in Dogmatism.

C. **There is a positive correlation between task success and satisfaction for those high in self-esteem, but no such relationship exists for those low in self-esteem.**

This prediction has been tested often and has been supported in all but one case (5, 14, 35, 42, 46, 48). Clearly, for those high in self-esteem, either measured or experimentally manipulated, task success leads to greater positive affect than does task failure. For those in low self-esteem, the same relationship does not occur.

In the study which does not support this prediction (29), a possible explanation is that the performance criterion used seems to have been ambiguous in that the experimenter did not provide such information. Rather, it was assumed that the Ss, would provide such feedback to themselves, the assumption being that each would utilize similar frameworks for evaluation. This assumption may or may not have been warranted.

D. **There is a positive correlation between self-esteem and the correlation between perceived similarity of others and liking for others.**

The logic of this prediction depends on the assumption that "liking" others is a "favorable" evaluation of others, i.e., if we indicate that we "like" someone similar to ourself, we are favorably evaluating that person. This assumption would indicate a state of imbalance for those expressing this feeling who are also low in self-esteem.

Two studies have tested and supported this derivation. Leonard (27) found in a simulated study of the employment interview that high self-esteem interviewers were more favorably impressed with applicants with similar attitudes than with applicants who were dissimilar. This relationship was reversed for low self-esteem interviewers. In a study of 30 dyads, Senn (41) concluded that positive attraction toward a stranger is positively related toward similarity, as long as the bases for similarity are positively evaluated. The relationship breaks down when the behaviors are negatively evaluated.

E. **Each of the three sources of self-esteem, i.e., chronic self-esteem, task-specific self-esteem and socially-influenced self-esteem, should show positive relationships to performance, all other factors being held equal.**

Up to now the results reported have been quite supportive. Turning to a set of predictions for which the evidence is mixed, an attempt will be made to determine possible reasons for this variance in findings. The relevant research will be reviewed according to the different sources of self-esteem postulated.

In the area of chronic self-esteem, field research tends to be supportive. O'Reilly (37), in a study of white-collar workers in a public organization, found that those who saw themselves as having the abilities necessary for the job performed at a higher level than those who did not see themselves as having the necessary abilities. In similar findings, Mishken (36) reported a significant positive correlation between general self-esteem and overall rated performances for 71 female clerical workers in a large state university. These positive results have not been replicated in an experimental setting. Greenhaus and Badin (14) found that chronic self-esteem did not predict performance on their tasks, while Hechler and Weiner (17) reported that the positive relationship did occur for a quality criterion, but not when productivity was the dependent variable.

In the area of task-specific self-esteem, the author is aware of only one study which made an attempt to examine the effects of this variable, independent of the other two sources of self-esteem proposed. Greenhaus and Badin (14) used an experimental manipulation and the predicted positive relationship with performance was found.

Turning to socially-influenced self-esteem, it becomes necessary to differentiate between field research and experimental studies. In a field study of 85 engineers, Kaufman (18) found results consistent with the prediction that the more one is expected to do by others, the more one thinks of the self, and the higher the level of performance. On the other hand, in a laboratory study in which self-esteem was experimentally manipulated, Weiner (48) found no support. To confuse the matter further, Greenhaus and Badin (14) report support for the prediction only for those subjects who were high authoritarian but not for those who were low. The pattern seems to be similar to that found for chronic self-esteem, i.e., the field investigations support the predictions quite well while the laboratory studies show mixed support.

Why the differences in result? One possible explanation is that the parameters of the experimental paradigm are still not well enough understood to assume that a manipulation designed to achieve "high" or "low" self-esteem actually achieves those results. For example, there has long been controversy in studies testing Adams' (1) equity model as to the appropriate methods for inducing high or low self-esteem. On the other hand, it is conceivable that the manipulations used have been appropriate but that the degree to which the effects of any experimental manipulation will be meaningful enough to affect performance are a function of other parameters about which little is known. Whatever other reasons may also be involved, this inconsistency in the findings from laboratory research should not be allowed to obscure the fact that the results from the field research have been consistently supportive.

F. **Behavior designed to attain personally relevant values is positively related to self-esteem.**

In the one relevant study, a study of insurance company employees, Gavin (10) computed twenty correlations between values and appropriate behavior. Sixteen of these correlations were higher for the high self-esteem group, with five of the differences significant. These results provide some support for the general prediction.

G. **Creative work behavior is negatively related to the degree to which the work environment is marked by hierarchical orientation and high structure concerning rules and work behavior.**

This prediction has been tested and supported in a research study of 72 research biologists by McCarrey and Edwards (33). They found that the role performance of these research scientists was enhanced by the degree to which their work space was *not* marked by a high orientation to management priorities, nor by high structure concerning punctuality and hours of work.

H. **The correlation between measured abilities and job performance is positively related to self-esteem.**

In the one study relevant to this prediction, Mishken (36) computed eight correlations between SET (Short Employment Test) scores and job performance for a group of 71 female clerical employees subgrouped on self-esteem and found the correlations to be higher for the high self-esteem group in 7 of the cases. While this analysis does not statistically qualify as evidence for a moderating effect of self-esteem, the trend is notable. In addition, there is some statistical support for a significant moderating effect in that the correlation between the total SET score and performance was significantly higher for the high self-esteem group than for the low. However, the level of significance was not high ($p < .10$).

I. **For any given population, increasing the level of reward for a specific behavior will have a positive effect on that behavior up to a point. Past that point, the effect on behavior from increasing reward potential will either flatten out or become negative.**

In a series of studies relevant to this prediction, experimental incentives were varied for their effect on (a) interest in a naval career among a random sample of males between 16 and 22 years of age, and (b) reenlistment among those already in the Navy. The results showed that "more is not better" and that increasing incentives beyond a given level resulted in a "boomerang" effect, i.e., the response was less at a higher level of incentive than at a lower (11).

J. **Hierarchical environments which value authority and which legitimatize impersonality, rules and non-concern with people as individuals should be positively correlated with aggression.**

In a review of research relating to societal aggression by Kelman (19), it was concluded that societal aggression is a function of environmental conditions of the type proposed.

K. **The more work experience involves being subject to hierarchical control and**

routinization, the less positive will be attitudes and behavior toward racial and sexual integration in the work and non-work setting.

Three relevant studies are all supportive. Kornhauser (26) found that low-level assembly line workers in the automobile industry had strong negative attitudes toward racial integration, a finding replicated by McWhinney (34) who reported that workers in a plant whose authority structure had moved toward a greater amount of power sharing became more interested in overcoming civil rights problems in their communities. Finally, Greenhaus, Korman and Gavin (15) report a positive correlation between the extent of acceptance of minority-group members and women into the organization and the extent to which the organization was seen as non-authoritarian.

L. Lack of trust in others and respect for rigid, unchanging rules will be negatively related to performance.

In the test of this prediction, support for the proposition was reported by Close (4) based on his finding of a negative correlation between Dogmatism and managerial level.

Summary

The original hypotheses have received considerable support, particularly in field studies. The findings from laboratory studies are frequently but not always supportive. Considering the ambiguity surrounding laboratory experiments and the need for a theory of work behavior to be useful in the field, it seems justified to conclude that the framework has received a considerable degree of support and that continued utilization appears warranted. Thus, while there is no suggestion here that the proposed framework accounts for all work behavior, beliefs as to the value of the self, the value of others and the degree of stability in the world do seem to be significant factors in work behavior and people do tend to choose outcomes consistent with these beliefs.

Changes in the theory are necessary in order to overcome problems in the approach which were not previously recognized.

A THEORETICAL EXTENSION

A reexamination of the framework as a result of this review has pointed to two significant problems not recognized previously. One of these is that the hypotheses predict that high self-esteem people will develop increasingly high self-esteem because of the pattern of their choices, while those who have lower self-esteem will develop lower self-esteem. Similarly, those who exhibit high creativity will become even more creative; those with low aggression will become even less aggressive, and so on. It is clear that there is something wrong with this conception. Not all successful people become increasingly successful and not all failures remain failures. Is it possible to ascertain conditions which lead to changes in behavior over time?

A second weakness of the original hypotheses is their highly individualistic orientation. The focus has been on individual characteristics as the "independent variables." While a role for social influence has been foreseen from the beginning, such processes have been seen up to now as influential on attitudes toward the self and others. Yet, social processes may operate in other ways, such as by providing normative standards for behavior. To illustrate, it is possible that individuals may achieve personal "balance" and consequent satisfaction by some type of behavior and yet also know that they have not met some type of social standard, a cognition that might lead to dissatisfaction along that dimension. For example, the individual with low self-esteem who has chosen and is satisfied with a career where the degree of success is likely to be minimal and where personal needs are not being met, may feel that he/she has not met societal standards for achievement and for attaining personal needs and values. This incongruity should have implications for behavior.

The theoretical extension proposed is that behavior changes over time as a function of the extent to which preexisting personality influences are consistent with contemporary environmental socialization influences. These processes occur, it is proposed, because of the differing attributional and socialization tendencies associated with different personality and environmental influences.

More specifically, individuals who are high in self-esteem and/or who are in non-hierarchical environments are more likely to have favorable self-evaluations and to attribute the results of both their behavioral outcomes and the behaviors of others to individual capability rather than to external forces. For people who are low in self-esteem and/or who are in hierarchical environments, the opposite attributional tendencies are proposed. Support for these theoretical assumptions comes from a number of sources. First, there is Weiner's (47) finding that individuals of high N achievement (who come from non-hierarchical environments) are more likely to attribute success to their own efforts than are those of low N achievement. Second, there is the extensive data cited by Klinger and McNelly (20) and Korman (22, 23) that non-hierarchical environments are associated with high levels of self-esteem and self-value and with higher levels of achieving behavior. Finally, in support of the assumptions as to different attributional processes, there is the research cited by Phares (39):

1. Younger children (who are less in control of their lives than older children) are externally-oriented;

2. Blacks are less likely to believe in internal control of outcomes than whites;

3. Lower social class status is associated with belief in external control of behavior.

As a result of these differing socialization and attribution processes, the following hypotheses are suggested:

Condition A: Contemporary Environmental Influences Are Not Salient.

1. Individuals who are high in self-esteem, value for others and belief in a variable world, as relatively persisting characteristics, will attribute the outcomes of their behavior to themselves, to the extent that situational environmental influences are not salient.

   a) Successful behavior will result in increased self-esteem (since the success is due to the self);

   b) Positive behavior toward others will result in increased value for others (since the positive affect from others as a result of one's own behavior is due to one's utilization of internal control, thus leading to greater value for internal control. The greater the value for internal control, the greater the value for people in general);

   c) Belief that the world can be changed will increase (since change has occurred, and the individual attributes it to the self);

   d) Unsuccessful behavior will lead to redoubled effort for success (because one has violated personal and social norms for success and it is due to the self);

   e) Lack of positive affect from others will lead to redoubled effort for positive affect (because one has not achieved positive affect from others and it is due to the self).

2. Individuals who are low in self-esteem, value for others and receptivity to change are more likely to attribute their behavior to external influences. Mirror images of the above behaviors for these individuals are predicted, with the exception that social standards are more relevant than

TABLE 1.
Summary of Evidence Relating to Extended Model

1. Low self-esteem Ss who denied a social manipulation aimed at inducing low self-esteem did better at a later task than those low self-esteem Ss who did not protest the manipulation.   Pepitone, Faucheaux, Moscovici, Cesa Bianchi, Magistretti, and Iacono (1969)

2. Low self-esteem boys who were held in high esteem by their peers and teachers had greater achievement and self-motivation than those low self-esteem boys who did not have high ratings from their peers and teachers.   Coopersmith (1967)

3. Individuals from backgrounds encouraging belief in control over one's life react more constructively to stress situations than do those coming from backgrounds encouraging powerlessness.   Tiffany and Tiffany (1973)

4. The more hierarchical a society (in terms of economic inequality), the more members of that society will endorse approaches to leadership that involve mistrust of individuals and the need to manipulate them in a political manner.   Bass and Franke (1972)

5. Individuals of high external control are more likely to utilize hierarchical, traditionally authoritarian forms of leadership than those of high internal control.   Goodstadt and Hjelle (1973)

6. Individuals who believe in personal control of behavior outcomes expend more effort on similar tasks subsequent to failure than do those who believe in external control of behavior outcomes.   Weiss and Sherman (1973)

7. Individuals who have performed tasks for money in the past are less likely to perform tasks in the future when money is withdrawn than those who have not performed tasks for money in the past.   Deci (1971, 1972)

personal standards. This will lead to the following:

a) Success will not increase self-esteem (since the success is due to others—e.g. leadership—and not the self);

b) Positive affect from others will not increase value for others (since the interaction has been controlled by others);

c) Successful change will not increase acceptance of variability (since the change has been controlled by others);

d) Unsuccessful behavior will be accepted as appropriate, even though it violates social norms (since external influences are responsible);

e) Behavior involving negative affect with others will be accepted, even though it violates social norms (since external influences are responsible);

f) Behavior involving lack of growth and development will be accepted, even though it violates social norms (since external influences are responsible).

To summarize, it is suggested that in Condition A, behavior remains relatively stable over time as a function of (a) the belief systems proposed, (b) the attributional processes indicated, and (c) the lack of any salient environmental influences.

Condition B: Contemporary Environmental Influences Are Salient and Consistent with Belief Systems. Condition B is an amplification of condition A, in that environmental influences here operate to reinforce the behavior patterns resulting from pre-existing personality characteristics. The effect is to increase the differences over time (e.g. the successful become more successful and the unsuccessful less so) and also the rate at which the changing behaviors occur.

Condition C: Contemporary Environmental Influences Are Salient and Inconsistent with Belief System. It is proposed that behavior will change over time under this condition due to the fact that as a particular environment increases in salience, relative to the influence of an individual's belief system, and its influence is in an opposite direction (e.g. from hierarchical to non-hierarchical), there are changes in both the belief systems of the individual (as a function of the social influence) and the attributional processes used.[1]

To illustrate (using the self-esteem relationship to achievement as illustration):

Case I: When an organization encourages hierarchical control, and achievement success occurs, those who helped in the career success (e.g. supervisors) tend to become valued as a result of the tendency of both the individual and the social influences around him/her, including the leadership, to attribute the causes of successful behavior to external influences and the rewards and punishments they control (e.g. money). This leads to the growth of personal attitudes favoring hierarchical systems of authority (after all, they have been responsible for "success"). This, in turn, leads to achievement failure because there will be increased exposure to hierarchical systems and hierarchical systems lead to low self-esteem. In this way, a high self-esteem person may eventually become a non-achiever.

Case II: When there are social standards for achievement and the environment encourages non-hierarchical thinking and the attribution of behavior to internal causes, it is predicted that achievement failure will lead to higher self-evaluation and success. It is proposed that the positive self-evaluation resulting from the non-hierarchical environment will lead to exploratory behavior that results in greater success than that resulting from the original behavior. This success leads to a higher evaluation of self (because of internal attribution) and, eventually, behaviors more appropriate to achievement success.

Overall, if we consider conditions A, B, and C together, it is hypothesized that sometimes success breeds success and sometimes it breeds failure. Similarly, failure sometimes breeds failure and sometimes breeds success.

Evidence for the Theoretical Extension

Research evidence for these proposals is limited to studies conducted in other contexts by different investigators. The studies summarized in Table 1 are consistent with the general propositions suggested in the areas of achievement and aggression.

Unfortunately, data relevant to other predictions which may be made from the proposals are still not available and must remain as promissory notes for the future. (It should be noted that some data already exist which are inconsistent. Thus, Maracek and Mettee [32] have found in a laboratory study that internal control Ss are more likely to accept failure than those of external control. Reconciliation of these findings with the data presented in Table 1 is clearly necessary.)

Suggested Hypotheses

Perhaps the most important function which a theory provides is to stimulate research in new directions. The approach suggested also makes predictions relevant to other aspects of work behavior. Among these are:

Hypothesis I: Organizational Development programs based on a non-hierarchical model of influence (i.e. which include the active participation of the individuals involved, even if they have not been successful in the past) will be better in the long run than programs which do not solicit participation from the people involved.

Hypothesis II: The introduction of leadership systems designed to match the preferences of individuals may lead to satisfaction in the short run, but will exacerbate differential motivation toward high and low achievement stemming from original personality predispositions. Providing hierarchical leadership for those preferring it will increase their satisfactions on a short-range basis but will minimize their performances in the long run because the hierarchical influence will generate lower self-esteem over time.

Hypothesis III: The more that one has used extrinsic rewards controlled by leadership figures as a mechanism for evaluation of the self and one's behavior, the more likely it is that:

a) One will view the self as being controlled by others; thus, one will see oneself as unworthy, incompetent, and without the confidence to influence one's own fate (i.e., one will develop low self-esteem), with this independent of the actual degree of success in achieving extrinsic values. Hence, phenomena such as middle-age apathy (e.g., "male or female menopause") and lack of work involvement are as likely to occur with materialistic success as with materialistic failure;

b) One will see oneself as unworthy of rewards in general, intrinsic and extrinsic, and will not be motivated to attain them (i.e., one will develop low self-esteem);

c) One will become alienated from one's own feelings, emotions, and values and will not use them as a guide to one's own behavior in determining the choices one makes and one's satisfaction with the outcomes of one's choices (i.e., one will develop low self-esteem).

Other hypotheses are possible. What seems to be most important, though, is that regardless of the hypotheses, it is important to look at longitudinal processes in work behavior. The factors that lead to successful behavior in the short run may not be the same as those that do over the long range, and it is important to begin utilizing such thinking in theorizing.

Comments on the Structural Characteristics of the Proposed Theory

Although the theory proposed involves longitudinal socialization processes, a consistency model of motivation has been held to, in order to account for choice at any point in time. In so doing, several theoretical questions need to be resolved:

1. How can behaviors which are called "ego-enhancing" be accounted for with a consistency model of motivation?

2. What are the boundary conditions of the consistency model? Clearly no motivational theory can account completely for

behavior, whether it is consistency, expectancy-value, anxiety, or any other motivational model.

3. What are the advantages of keeping to a consistency model?

4. What of motivational conflict, e.g. when consistency motivation conflicts with ego-enhancing motivation? Can the conditions under which this will occur be predicted and what will the outcomes be?

From what has been said earlier, there is no necessary contradiction between the adoption of a consistency model and accounting for "growth" behavior (or "decline"). Such behavior does not have to be accounted for by adopting a subjective utility-maximizing model. It may also be accounted for by involving social evaluation processes, as these social evaluations become internalized into the cognitive and attitudinal structure of the individual. As social influence changes (e.g. by making it more or less hierarchical), the individual changes and, consequently, so does the individual's behavior. The more positive the social environment in terms of the favorability of the self-evaluations it encourages, the more positive the behaviors. An examination of longitudinal trends would, therefore, show an increasing "growth" pattern over time.

However, this process leads to "growth" but not "ego-enhancement" if "ego-enhancement" is defined as the seeking of outcomes at any given point in time which are "of greater value" than one sees as equitable with one's self-evaluation. If this definition is adopted, boundary conditions need to be established defining where each theory might be most applicable. First, necessary research designs for testing "ego-enhancing" behavior are:

1. Measurement of self-attitudes and self-perceived equitable outcomes in the given context prior to behavior;

2. Measurement of perceived available outcomes prior to the research along dimensions comparable to those utilized in (a) with some of the available outcomes being greater than those perceived as equitable in (a) and some lower.

Under these conditions, a clear test can be made of the conditions under which the consistency and ego-enhancing models of motivation might be useful. What might these conditions be? Unfortunately, there are few data which meet the necessary methodological guidelines. One hypothesis which can be generated is the following:

1. Assuming that consistency motivation stems in part from the rewards we receive from others—because consistent behavior enables them to predict our behaviors more accurately (24)—the tendency to be consistent would be greatest under the following conditions:

a) When the situation encourages feelings of individuality and nonanonymity (e.g. when the organization is not chaotic or massive in size) so that others know whether one is being consistent or not;

b) When the individuals who are providing the rewards for consistency are valued;

c) When there is need to influence others with one's own desirability and credibility. (In (b) and (c), consistency motivation may operate in the service of some other, more basic motive, such as survival.)

Assuming some boundary conditions to the consistency model, why not have an expectancy-value model for both "ego-enhancing" behavior and "consistent behavior"? This question assumes legitimacy since there are conditions under which similar predictions may be made by both, i.e. when expectancies are low for a given value, the likelihood of behavior **designed to achieve** that value is low. However, the similarities should not mask the differences. The differences do exist and the choice here has been made for a consistency model for the following reasons:

1. Expectancy-value models are unable to account for self-destructive behavior in any meaningful manner. Individuals do engage in suicide (both actual and less dramatic types such as the choice of inadequate careers). Without the distortion of "value" so as to make it philosophically meaningless, the expectancy-value model is able to account for this type of behavior (30).

2. Expectancy-value models have two logical problems which seem difficult to resolve:

    a) If people choose behaviors which lead to the "best possible" outcomes, why are they dissatisfied (30)?

    b) Logically, tests of the theory which do not support predictions may be disputed on the ground that they have not tested and measured all the motivational influences on the person at the time. The only way to deal with this problem is to have all possible values and expectancies measured in all tests of the theory, a philosophical impossibility (24).

3. There is an ambiguity in expectancy-value theory concerning the situation when a person has low expectancies for all possible outcomes. Does he/she behave at all? Does he/she withdraw from behavior? Consistency theory predicts that behavior will take place in a manner designed to achieve low outcomes. It is not clear what the predictions of an expectancy-value framework would be.

4. Expectancy-value theory is a motivational theory which conceptually cannot concern itself with satisfaction as a dependent variable. All other things being equal, a theory which concerns itself with both performance and satisfaction, both relevant to organizational behavior, is to be preferred.

It is for these reasons that the option here has been for a consistency model, an option which may have to be revised should "ego-enhancing" behavior be effectively established with appropriate research methods. Should this occur, it may be necessary to move either toward multiple theories or toward some better over-all integrating framework which brings together the best of both the expectancy-value and consistency models.

NOTES

1. It may be noted that the theoretical extension being proposed involves the same variables being postulated as influencing two types of outcomes. This should not pose a problem for research design since a sequential process is proposed. Thus, at any point in time, motivational processes may be investigated, without concern for post-behavioral attribution. Similarly, attributional processes may be investigated by controlling for the outcome of the individual and then investigating post-outcome behavior.

REFERENCES

1. Adams, J. S. in L. Berkowitz (Ed.), *Advances in Experimental Social Psychology*, Vol. 2 (New York: Academic Press, 1965), 267-299.

2. Bass, B. M. and Richard H. Franke. "Societal Influences on Student Perceptions of How to Succeed in Organizations: A Cross-National Analysis," *Journal of Applied Psychology*, Vol. 56 (1972), 312-318.

3. Behling, O., and J. Tolliver. "Self-Concept Moderated by Self-Esteem as a Predictor of Choice Among Potential Employers," Ohio State University, 1972. Paper presented at Annual Convention, Academy of Management, 1972.

4. Close, M. J. "Dogmatism and Managerial Achievement," *Journal of Applied Psychology*, Vol. 60 (1975), 395-396.

5. Cohen, R. *Effect of Feedback on Test Anxiety and Performance as a Function of Certain*

Personal Characteristics. Unpublished Ph.D. dissertation, New York University, 1971.

6. Coopersmith, S. *The Antecedents of Self-Esteem* (San Francisco: Freeman, 1967).

7. Deci, E. L. "Effects of Externally Mediated Rewards on Intrinsic Motivation," *Journal of Personality and Social Psychology*, Vol. 18 (1971), 105-115.

8. Deci, E. L. "Intrinsic Motivation, Extrinsic Reinforcement, and Inequity," *Journal of Personality and Social Psychology*, Vol. 22 (1972), 113-120.

9. Esposito, J. P., and H. C. Richards. "Dogmatism and the Congruence between Self-Reported Job Preference and Performance among School Supervisors," *Journal of Applied Psychology,* Vol. 59 (1974), 389-391.

10. Gavin, J. F. "Self-Esteem as a Moderator of the Relationship between Expectancies and Job Performance," *Journal of Applied Psychology,* Vol. 58 (1973), 83-88.

11. Glickman, A. S., B. G. Goodstadt, R. G. Frey Jr., A. K. Korman and A. P. Romanczok. *Navy Career Motivation Programs in All-Volunteer Condition.* American Institute for Research, Final Report, Studies in Naval Career Motivation, June 1974.

12. Goodstadt, B. E., and L. A. Hjelle. "Power to the Powerless: Laws of Control and the Use of Power," *Journal of Personality and Social Psychology,* Vol. 27 (1973), 190-196.

13. Greenhaus, J. "Self-Esteem as an Influence on Occupational Choice and Occupational Satisfaction," *Journal of Vocational Behavior,* Vol. 2 (1971), 75-84.

14. Greenhaus, J. H., and I. Badin. "Self-Esteem, Performance and Satisfaction: Some Tests of a Theory," *Journal of Applied Psychology,* in press.

15. Greenhaus, J. H., A. K. Korman, and J. F. Gavin. "Perception of Organizational Climate, Tenure and Job Attitudes." Unpublished paper, 1974.

16. Healy, C. C. "The Relation of Esteem and Social Class to Self-Occupational Congruence," *Journal of Vocational Behavior*, Vol. 3 (1973), 43-51.

17. Hechler, P. D., and Y. Weiner. "Chronic Self-Esteem as a Moderator of Performance Consequences of Expected Pay," *Organizational Behavior and Human Performance,* Vol. 22 (1974), 97-105.

18. Kaufman, H. G. "Relationship of Early Work Challenge to Job Performance, Professional Contributions, and Competence of Engineers," *Journal of Applied Psychology,* Vol. 59 (1974), 377-379.

19. Kelman, H. C. "Violence Without Moral Restraint: Reflections on the Dehumanization of Victims and Victimizers," *Journal of Social Issues,* Vol. 29 (1973) 25-62.

20. Klinger, E., and F. W. McNelly, Jr. "Fantasy Need Achievement and Performance: A Role Analysis," *Psychological Review,* Vol. 76 (1969), 574-591.

21. Korman, A. K. "Toward a Hypothesis of Work Behavior," *Journal of Applied Psychology*, Vol. 54 (1970) 31-41.

22. Korman, A. K. *Industrial and Organizational Psychology* (Englewood Cliffs, N.J., Prentice-Hall, Inc. 1971).

23. Korman, A. K. "Organizational Achievement, Aggression and Creativity: Some Suggestions toward an Integrated Theory," *Organizational Behavior and Human Performance,* Vol. 6 (1971), 593-613.

24. Korman, A. K. *The Psychology of Motivation* (Englewood Cliffs, N.J.: Prentice-Hall, Inc., 1974).

25. Korman, A. K. "Work-Experience, Work-Oriented Intervention, Adult Socialization and Civil Liberties," *Journal of Social Issues*, in press.

26. Kornhauser, A. *Mental Health of the Industrial Worker* (New York: Wiley, 1965).

27. Leonard, R. C. "Self-Concept as a Factor on the Similarity-Attraction Paradigm," *Proceeding of the 81st Annual Convention of the American Psychological Association,* Montreal, Canada, 1973, Vol. 8, 199-200.

28. Leonard, R. C., W. B. Walsh, and S. H. Osipow. "Self-Esteem, Self-Consistency and Second Vocational Choice," *Journal of Counseling Psychology,* Vol. 20 No. 1 (1973), 91-93.

29. Leonard, R. C., and J. Weitz. "Task Enjoyment and Task Perserverance in Relation to Task Success and Self-Esteem," *Journal of Applied Psychology,* Vol. 55 (1971), 414-421.

30. Locke, E. A. "Personal Attitudes and Motivation," *Annual Review of Psychology* (1975), in press.

31. Mansfield, R. "Self-Esteem, Self-Perceived Abilities, and Vocational Choice," *Journal of Vocational Behavior*, Vol. 3 (1973), 433-441.

32. Maracek, J. and D. P. Mettee. "Avoidance of Continued Success as a Function of Self-Esteem

Level of Esteem Certainty and Responsibility for Success," *Journal of Personality and Social Psychology,* Vol. 22 (1972), 98-107.

33. McCarrey, M. W., and S. A. Edwards. "Organizational Climate Conditions for Effective Research Scientist Role Performance," *Organizational Behavior and Human Performance,* Vol. 9 (1973), 439-459.

34. McWhinney, N. (with J. Elden). "Not Industrial Democracy, but a Reticular Society." Paper presented at the Center for Study of Democratic Institutions, Santa Barbara, California, 1971. Not seen—discussed in David Jenkins, *Job Power* (Garden City, N.Y.: Doubleday and Co., 1973), pp. 243-244.

35. Metee, D. R. "Repetition of Unexpected Success as a Function of the Negative Consequences of Accepting Success," *Journal of Psychology and Social Psychology,* Vol. 17 (1971), 332-341.

36. Mishken, M. A. *Self-Esteem as a Moderator of the Relationship between Job Ability and Job Performance.* Ph.D. Dissertation, University of Tennessee, 1973.

37. O'Reilly, A. P. "Perception of Abilities as a Determinant of Performance," *Journal of Applied Psychology,* Vol. 58 (1973), 281-282.

38. Pepitone, A., C. Faucheaux, S. Moscovici, M. Cesa-Bianchi, G. Magistreth, and G. Iacono. *The Role of Self-Esteem in Competitive Behavior.* Unpublished manuscript, University of Pennsylvania, 1969. Not seen—cited in Maracek and Mettee (32).

39. Phares, E. J. *Locus of Control: A Personality Determinant of Behavior* (Morristown, N.J.: General Learning Press, 1973).

40. Raben, C. S. and R. J. Klioski. "The Effects of Expectations upon Task Performance as Moderated by Levels of Self-Esteem," *Journal of Vocational Behavior,* Vol. 3 (1973), 475-483.

41. Senn, D. J. "Attraction as a Function of Similarity-Dissimilarity in Task Performance," *Journal of Personality and Social Psychology,* Vol. 18 (1971), 120-123.

42. Siegel, J., and D. Bowen. "Satisfaction and Performance: Casual Relationships and Moderating Effects," *Journal of Vocational Behavior,* Vol. 2 (1971), 263-269.

43. Tiffany, D. W., and P. G. Tiffany. "Powerlessness and/or Self-Direction?" *American Psychologist,* 1973, pp. 151-161.

44. Walsh, W. B., P. R. Howard, W. F. O'Brien, M. C. Santa-Maria, and C. J. Edmonson. "Consistent Occupational Preferences and Satisfaction, Self-Concept, Self-Acceptance and Vocational Maturity," *Journal of Vocational Behavior,* Vol. 3 (1973), 435-464.

45. Walsh, W. B., and R. O. Lewis. "Consistent, Inconsistent and Undecided Career Preferences, and Personality," *Journal of Vocational Behavior,* Vol. 2 (1972), 309-316.

46. Waters, L. K., and D. Roach. "Self-Esteem as a Moderator of the Relationship Between Task Success and Task Liking," *Psychological Reports,* Vol. 32 (1972), 69-70.

47. Weiner, B. *Theories of Motivation: From Mechanism to Cognition* (Chicago, Ill.: Markham Publishing Co., 1972).

48. Weiner, Y. "Task Ego-Involvement and Self-Esteem as Moderators of Situationally Devalued Self-Esteem," *Journal of Applied Psychology,* Vol. 58 (1973), 225-232.

49. Weiss, H., and J. Sherman. "Internal-External Control as a Predictor of Task Effort and Satisfaction Subsequent to Failure," *Journal of Applied Psychology,* Vol. 57 (1973), 132-136.

THE SATISFACTION-PERFORMANCE CONTROVERSY— REVISITED

Charles N. Greene and Robert E. Craft, Jr.

In a review of literature dealing with the relationship between satisfaction and performance, Brayfield and Crockett (1955) concluded, more than 20 years ago, that "there is little evidence that employee attitudes of the type usually measured in morale surveys bear any simple or, for that matter, appreciable, relationship to performance on the job." In another extensive review of the literature that closely followed that of Brayfield and Crockett (1955), Herzberg, Mausner, Peterson, and Capwell (1957) came to quite a different conclusion: "There is frequent evidence for the often suggested opinion that positive job attitudes are favorable to increased productivity."

Thus, more than two decades after the initial reviews of prior research addressing the satisfaction-performance relationship, and more than four decades after the first investigation of this relationship (Kornhauser and Sharp, 1932), there had developed considerably different viewpoints as to the proper nature of the relationships. Another one and one-half decades passed before Greene (1972a) found the controversy to be quite robust. He identified three essentially distinct positions regarding the relationship between satisfaction and performance: (a) satisfaction causes performance, (b) performance causes satisfaction, and (c) "rewards" as a causal factor. These positions very closely approximate the range of positions on the subject that remain extant, at this writing.

THEORY AND SUPPORT

Satisfaction Causes Performance

A proposition widely held among practitioners, and often identified with the so-called Human Relations Movement, is that a happy worker is a productive worker. According to this proposition, the degree of job satisfaction felt by an employee determines his performance; that is, satisfaction causes performance. This position has had a great deal of intuitive appeal, reflecting the notion that "all good things go together," and the relatively more pleasant approach of increasing an employee's happiness as opposed to dealing directly with his performance. Acceptance of the satisfaction-causes-performance proposition makes sense as a solution, particularly because it represents the path of least resistance in that the manager, by not making rewards contingent on performance, avoids the problems associated with creating dissatisfaction among low performing subordinates. Further, most modern managers view both high satisfaction and high performance as desirable outcomes—both are "good" and, therefore, they *ought* to be related to one another.

Portions of this article are based on and, particularly in the "Implications" section, taken from an earlier article, C. H. Greene, "The Satisfaction-Performance Controversy," *Business Horizons,* Vol. 15, No. 2, pp. 31-41. Used by permission of the publisher.

The strength of this proposition is not relegated solely to the visceral or "gut" reactions of the practicing manager. A number of academicians have found it quite appealing as well. Vroom's valence-force model (Vroom, 1964) is an example of theory-based support for the satisfaction-causes-performance case. In Vroom's (1964) model, job satisfaction reflects the valence (attractiveness) of the job. It then follows from his theory that the force exerted on an employee to remain on the job is an increasing function of the valence of the job. Thus, satisfaction should be negatively related to absenteeism and turnover, and at the empirical level, it is.

Whether or not this valence also leads to higher performance, however, has less empirical support. Vroom's review of twenty-three field studies, which investigated the relationship between satisfaction and performance, revealed an insignificant median static correlation of 0.14; that is, satisfaction explained less than two percent of the variance in performance. The statistically insignificant results and lack of tests of the causality question have not produced strong empirical support for his position.

However, Vroom's report (1964) has not laid this position to rest. Shaw and Blum (1965) reported that group performance is, in part, a function of the group's awareness of member satisfaction. Results of an investigation of direction of causation in the relationship between job satisfaction and work performance (Sheridan and Slocum, 1975) were inconclusive with respect to managers but need satisfaction was found to affect the performance of the operative level employees included in the sample. Thus, there does remain the possibility that satisfaction does lead to performance; for some employees, under some conditions.

Evidence that the satisfaction-causes-performance proposition is alive (if not well) in contemporary academic writing is also attested to by a recent article by Organ (1976). Interpreting previous literature in terms of equity theory and reciprocity in social exchange, Organ asks whether reconstruction of the logic behind the satisfaction-causes-performance hypothesis will call for "a more judicious consideration than we have recently accorded it." Organ further argues that research findings relevant to the hypothesis offer more support than one is usually led to believe, particularly if certain qualifying assumptions are made. Although he presents a cogent and interesting viewpoint, the evidence "reinterpreted" by Organ remains primarily correlational in nature and thus does not overcome the paucity of causal evidence supporting a satisfaction-causes-performance position.

Performance Causes Satisfaction

A second theoretical proposition has been advanced concerning the relationship between satisfaction and performance. This view, represented by the work of Porter and Lawler (1968) posits that satisfaction, rather than being a cause, is an effect of performance; that is, performance *causes* satisfaction. Differential performance determines rewards, that, in turn, produce variation in employees' expressions of job satisfaction. In this view, rewards serve as a moderating variable and satisfaction is considered to be a function of performance related rewards.

At the empirical level, this position has received support from a number of studies. Using cross-lag correlational techniques, Bowen and Siegel (1970) and Greene (1972b) reported finding relatively strong correlations between performance in one period and subsequent expressions of satisfaction (the performance-causes-satisfaction condition). These correlations were significantly higher than the low correlations between satisfaction and performance which followed in a later period (the satisfaction-causes-performance condition). The dynamic correlation coefficients in these two studies were not strong and thus one could not rule out the possibility of a third or additional variables affecting satisfaction and performance and thus the relationship between them. Indeed, in an evaluation of causal models linking the perceived role with job satisfaction, Greene and Organ (1973) offered a revised model in which role perceptions lead to compliance which then lead to performance. Thus performance was mediated by rewards and only then resulted in variations in satisfaction. Thus Porter and Lawler's predictions that differential performance determines rewards and that rewards produce variance in satisfaction has received some support but that support is not unequivocal. Additional support for the Lawler and Porter (1967) model was offered by Slocum (1971). Farris and Lim (1969) and Kavanagh, MacKinney, and Wolins (1970) report performance leading to satisfaction but see the mediating variable as leader behavior. Leader behavior was also seen by Greene (1973b and 1975) and Downey, Sheridan, and Slocum (1976) as moderating the performance-satisfaction relationship. Other variables, such as occupational group (Doll & Gunderson, 1969), self-esteem (Greenhaus & Badin, 1974), job values (Locke, 1973), and ability (Carlson, 1969) have been suggested as variables moderating the relationship between performance and satisfaction.

Rewards as a Causal Factor

Rewards as causal factors are really a subset of a more general proposition that both satisfaction and performance are co-determined by a third (or more) variable(s). Brayfield and Crockett (1955) and Fournet, Distefano, and Pryer (1966) expressed the belief that the relationship between satisfaction and performance is one of concomitant variation rather than cause and effect. Katzell, Barrett, and Parker (1961) saw the correlation between satisfaction and performance as a function of the same situational characteristics; that is, in general mathematical terms, "A" and "B" are a function of "C."

Another form of this covariation proposition is that rewards cause satisfaction, and rewards that are based on current performance cause subsequent performance. According to this proposition, formulated by Cherrington, Reitz, and Scott (1971), there is no inherent relationship between satisfaction and performance. In an experimental investigation of this proposition, they found that "rewarded" subjects expressed significantly greater satisfaction than did "unrewarded" subjects. Further, when rewards (monetary bonuses, in this case) were granted on the basis of performance, the subjects' performances were significantly higher than those of subjects whose rewards were unrelated to their performance. For example, they reported finding that when a low performer was not rewarded, dissatisfaction was expressed but subsequent performance improved. On the other hand, when a low performer was in fact rewarded for low performance, high satisfaction was expressed but performance continued at a low level. A similar pattern of findings was reported in the case of the high performing subjects, except that, the high performing subjects who were not rewarded expressed dissatisfaction as expected, and subsequent performance declined significantly for these subjects. The correlation between satisfaction and subsequent performance, excluding the effects of rewards, was 0.00; that is, satisfaction does *not* cause improved performance.

A subsequent longitudinal field study (Greene, 1973a) investigating the source and direction of causal influence in satisfaction-performance relationships, supports the Cherrington, Reitz, and Scott (1971) findings. Merit pay was identified as a cause of satisfaction and contrary to some current beliefs, was found to be a significantly more frequent source of satisfaction than dissatisfaction. The results of this study further indicated significant relationships between: (a) merit pay and subsequent performance; and (b) current performance and subsequent merit pay. Given the Cherrington, Reitz, and Scott (1971) report that rewards based on current performance caused improvements in subsequent performance, Greene's (1973a) results suggest the possibility of reciprocal causation. In other words, merit pay based on current performance probably caused variations in subsequent performance. The company in this field study evidently was relatively successful in implementing its policy of granting salary increases to an employee based on his performance (as evidenced by the significant relationship found between current performance and subsequent merit pay). The company's use of a fixed annual merit increase schedule may have obscured some of the stronger reinforcing effects of merit pay on performance.

Unlike the Cherrington, Reitz, and Scott (1971) controlled experiment, the fixed merit increase schedule precluded (as it does in many organizations) giving an employee a monetary reward immediately after the successful performance of a major task. This constraint undoubtedly reduced the magnitude of the relationship between merit pay and subsequent performance.

Additional support of the Cherrington, Reitz and Scott position is found by Wanous (1974). In this causal-correlational analysis of the job satisfaction and performance relationship, Wanous concluded that:

> The results indicate that there probably is no single "correct" relationship between satisfaction and performance. Sometimes there appears to be no relationship at all, which is consistent with the view that situations can be created by reward systems that will support any causal model. (page 143)

Reporting elsewhere, Wanous (1973) posits that other variables besides reward systems can contribute to covariation in the satisfaction-performance relationship; i.e., type of satisfaction, work experience of the individual, and type of job situation. In this same vein, Bachman, Smith and Slesinger (1966) report:

> It seems clear that in the present setting that neither variable (satisfaction or performance) is the direct cause of the other. A more likely explanation is that they are both caused in part by the high total control syndrome.

The study investigated the effects of various forms of social control on satisfaction and performance. Similarly, Greene (1972b) reported finding that:

> ... accuracy of the subordinate's perceptions of what his superior expects of him (*role accuracy*) and the extent to which the subordinate complies to these expectations (*compliance*) were significantly related to: (a) job satisfaction expressed by the subordinate and (b) his performance evaluated by his superior.

Downey, Sheridan, and Slocum (1975) also found that variance in task structure significantly influenced satisfaction and performance relationships and, yet, Ivancevich and Donnelly's (1975) findings suggest that organizational structure does not have strong effects on the relationship between these two variables.

Kahn (1960) quite adamantly writes, "I would like to begin by asserting, without qualification, that productivity and job satisfaction do not necessarily go together." He found at International Harvester that intrinsic job satisfaction and satisfaction with the company, supervision, and with reward and mobility opportunities to be either unrelated or moderately negatively related to productivity. Stronger evidence supporting Kahn's position was provided by Turcotte (1974), who found high satisfaction to be associated with low performance and even cases of high performing groups in which overall satisfaction was quite low.

IMPLICATIONS FOR MANAGEMENT

Although it is clear that both employee satisfaction and performance are the result of complex processes that have not yet been completely articulated, it is equally apparent that there are steps that management can take to significantly influence the relationship between these. It is now fairly well established that rewards can produce variance in satisfaction. For the manager who is desirous of enhancing the satisfaction of employees, whether for philosophical motives or to reduce absenteeism and turnover, this may be an end-state that is valued for its own merits. However, if the manager's goal is to increase employee performance, it is equally clear that increasing subordinate's satisfaction will have no effect, *pro forma*, on their performance.

Fortunately, for manager and subordinate alike, the evidence to date clearly supports the conclusion that performance and satisfaction are covariants of a third variable (or variables). Particularly promising is the finding that rewards based on current performance significantly affect subsequent performance. In other words, while the manager cannot hope that performance will inevitably follow satisfaction, he can be consoled by the fact that there is evidently no theoretical or empirical reason to settle for only satisfaction or for only performance. Indeed, there seems to be a great deal that the contemporary manager can do to influence concomitant increase in both employee satisfaction and employee performance. The route to this achievement is not, however, the path of least resistance for the manager. In addition to constraints arising from organizational patterns, resource limitations and collective bargaining agreements, it would seem that increasing numbers of today's employees subscribe to the egalitarian philosophy articulated by John Rawls (1975) and other disciples of the non-performance contingent view of man's rights to the fruits of industrial society. According to the egalitarian argument, the fruits of modern society are the accomplishment of society at large. Therefore, all members of society are entitled to enjoy these fruits without contingencies, or constraints, beyond their membership in society.

Granting differential rewards on the basis of differences in subordinate performance will cause subordinates to express varying degrees of satisfaction or dissatisfaction. And, even if the manager is successful in overcoming obstacles to the implementation of performance-contingent reward systems, an uncomfortable position will follow—particularly with respect to his relationship with the low performer. The manager will be forced, and repeatedly, to defend his performance evaluations until the low performer responds to the new contingencies or gives up and leaves the organization. Even so, substantial benefits should offset these short-run costs. Equity theory posits that performance-contingent rewards will result in equity since the most satisfied employees are the rewarded high performers and the organization will be more successful in retaining its most productive employees.

However, as one is often reminded, "There is, indeed, no such thing as a free lunch." Faced with constraints, limited resources for rewards and limited expertise in performance appraisal techniques, it is all too apparent that the manager's task here will not be easy. The relationship between rewards and performance is often not as simple or direct an one would think, for at least two reasons. *First*, there are other causes of performance that may have a more direct bearing on a particular problem. Wanous (1973) has suggested type of satisfaction (intrinsic job satisfaction, satisfaction with company, etc.), work experience, and the job environment might be significant causal variables. *Second* is the question of the appropriateness of the reward itself, that is, what is rewarding for one person may not be rewarding for another. In short, the manager will need to consider other potential causes of performance and a range of rewards in addressing any particular performance problem.

Non-motivational Factors

The element of performance that relates most directly to the discussion thus far is effort. Effort is that element which can produce the performance to which the rewards are to be linked. If the worker believes that the magnitude of the rewards forthcoming is contingent on performance and that this performance is a function of effort expended, then the motivational force developed in the job will be expressed in performance-related effort. Even so, however, there remain other non-motivational considerations that might best be considered prior to an analysis of means by which the manager can effectuate the desired motivation.

Direction. Suppose, for example, that an employee works hard at the job, yet performance is inadequate. What can the manager do to alleviate the problem? The manager's first action should be to identify the cause. One likely possibility is what can be referred to as a "direction problem."

Several years ago, the Minnesota Vikings' defensive end, Jim Marshall, very alertly gathered up the opponent's fumble and then, with obvious effort and delight, proceeded to carry the ball some fifty yards into the wrong end zone. This is a direction problem in its purest sense. For the employee working under more usual circumstances, a direction problem generally stems from lack of understanding of what is expected or what a job well done looks like. The action indicated to alleviate this problem is to clarify or define in detail for the employee the requirements of the job. The manager's own leadership style may also be a factor. In dealing with an employee with a direction problem, the manager needs to exercise closer supervision and to initiate structure or focus on the task, as opposed to emphasizing consideration or relations with the employee (House, 1971).

In cases where this style of behavior is repugnant or inconsistent with the manager's own leadership inclinations, an alternative approach is to engage in mutual goal setting or management-by-objectives techniques with the employee. Here, the necessary structure can be established, but at the subordinate's own initiative, thus creating a more participative atmosphere. This approach, however, is not free of potential problems. The employee is more likely to make additional undetected errors before performance improves, and the approach is more time-consuming than the more direct route.

Ability. What can the manager do if the actions taken to resolve the direction problem fail to result in significant improvements in performance? The subordinate still exerts a high level of effort and understands what is expected—yet continues to perform poorly. At this point, the manager may begin, justifiably so, to doubt the subordinate's ability to perform the job. When this doubt does arise, there are three useful questions, suggested by Mager and Pipe (1970), to which the manager should find answers before treating the problem as an ability deficiency: Could the subordinate do it if really necessary? What if the subordinate's life depended on it? Are his present abilities adequate for the desired performance?

If the answers to the first two questions are negative, then the answer to the last question also will be negative. The obvious conclusion is that an ability deficiency does, in fact, exist. Most managers, upon reaching this conclusion, begin to develop some type of formal training experience for the subordinate. This is unfortunate and frequently wasteful. There is probably a simpler, less expensive solution, as will be noted shortly. Formal training is usually required only when the individual has never done the particular job in question or when there is no way in which the ability requirement in question can be eliminated from the job.

If the individual formerly used the skill but now uses it only rarely, systematic practice will usually overcome the deficiency without formal training. Alternatively, the job can be changed or simplified so that the impaired ability is no longer crucial to successful performance. If, on the other hand, the individual once had the skill and still rather frequently is able to practice it, the manager should consider providing greater feedback concerning the outcome of efforts. The subordinate may not be aware of the deficiency and its effect on performance, or may no longer know how to perform the job. For example, elements of the job or the relationship between the job and other jobs may have changed, and the subordinate simply is not aware of the change.

Where formal training efforts are indicated, systematic analysis of the job is useful for identifying the specific behaviors and skills that are closely related with successful task performance and that, therefore, need to be learned. Alternatively, if the time and expense associated with job analysis are considered excessive, the critical incidents approach, as Folley (1969) suggests, can be employed toward the same end.[1] Once training needs have been identified and the appropriate training technique employed, the manager can profit by asking one last question: "Why did the ability deficiency develop in the first place?"

Ultimately, the answer rests with the selection and placement process. Had a congruent person-job match been attained at the outset, the ability deficiency would have never presented itself as a performance problem.[2]

Performance Obstacles. When inadequate performance is not the result of a lack of effort, direction, or ability, there is still another potential cause that needs attention. Custer's 7th Cavalry undoubtedly expended a great deal of effort at the Little Big Horn. Unambiguous direction of subordinates may well have been "Old Yellow Hair's" long suit and surely the veterans of the Plains Wars had developed some minimal ability to fight. Yet, the results of this apparently highly motivated effort (Custer is reported to have urged his men to "give no quarter" as they attacked the seemingly unprepared Indian camp), were probably not quite what our "manager"-hero desired. Obstacles beyond the control of the subordinates can arise to interfere with performance. Three thousand Sioux and Northern Cheyenne warriors presented such an obstacle. Though this is admittedly a dramatic example, the 103 odd years since have not led to the removal of all the potential obstacles to performance. Indeed, performance obstacles can take many forms to the extent that their number, independent of a given situation, is almost unlimited.

However, the contemporary manager might survey the scene with less dismay than did Custer's superior, General Crook. More common potential obstacles may include lack of time or conflicting demands on the subordinate's time, inadequate work facilities, restrictive policies or "right ways of doing it" that inhibit performance, lack of authority, insufficient information about other activities that affect the job, and lack of cooperation from others with whom he must work.

An additional obstacle, often not apparent to the manager in face-to-face interaction with a subordinate, is the operation of group goals and norms that run counter to organizational objectives. Where the work group adheres to norms of restricting productivity, for example, the subordinate will similarly restrict performance to the extent that identification is closer with the group than with management.

Many performance obstacles can be overcome either by removing the obstacle or by changing the subordinate's job so that the obstacle no longer impinges on his performance. When the obstacle stems from group norms, however, a very different set of actions is required. Here, the actions that should be taken are the same, essentially, as those that will be considered shortly in coping with lack of effort on the part of the individual. In other words, the potential causes of the group's lack of effort are identical to those that apply to the individual.

The Motivational Problem

Thus far, performance problems have been considered in which effort was not the source of the performance discrepancy. While reward practices constitute the most frequent and direct cause of effort, there are, however, other less direct causes. Direction, ability, and performance obstacles may indirectly affect effort through their direct effects on performance. For example, an individual may perform poorly because of an ability deficiency and, as a result, exert little effort on the job. Here, the ability deficiency produces low performance, and the lack of effort on the individual's part results from his expectations of failure. Thus, actions taken to alleviate the ability deficiency should result in improved performance and, subsequently, in higher effort.

Effort is that element of performance which links rewards to performance. The relationship between rewards and effort is, unfortunately, not a simple one. As indicated in the figure, effort is considered not only as a function of the (a) value and (b) magnitude of reward, but also as a function of the (c) individual's perceptions of the extent to which greater effort on his part will lead to higher performance, and (d) that his high performance, in turn, will lead to rewards. Therefore, a manager who is confronted with a subordinate who exerts little effort must consider these four attributes of reward practices in addition to the more indirect, potential causes of the lack of effort. The key issues in coping with a subordinate's lack of effort—the motivation problem—or in preventing such a problem from arising, involve all four of the attributes of rewards just identified (Porter & Lawler, 1968).[3]

Appropriateness of the Reward. Regardless of the extent to which the individual believes that hard work determines his own performance and subsequent rewards, little effort will expended unless these rewards are valued— that is, the rewards must have value in terms of the individual's own need state. An accountant, for example, may value recognition from the boss, an opportunity to increase the scope of the job, or a salary increase; however, it is unlikely that the same value would be ascribed to a ten-year supply of budget forms.

In other words, there must be consistency between reward and what the individual needs or wants and recognition that there are often significant differences among individuals in what they consider rewarding. Similarly, individuals differ in terms of the *magnitude* of that valued reward that is positively reinforcing. A seven or eight percent salary increase may motivate one person but have little or no positive effect on another person at the same salary level. Furthermore, a sizable reward in one situation might be considered small by the same individual in a different set of circumstances.

These individual differences, particularly those concerning what rewards are valued, raise considerable question about the adequacy of current organization reward systems, virtually none of which make any formal recognition of individual differences. Lawler, for example, has suggested that organizations could profit greatly by introducing "cafeteria-style" wage plans (Lawler, 1971). These plans allow an employee to select any combination of cash and fringe benefits desired. An employee would be assigned "X" amount in compensation, which may then be divided up

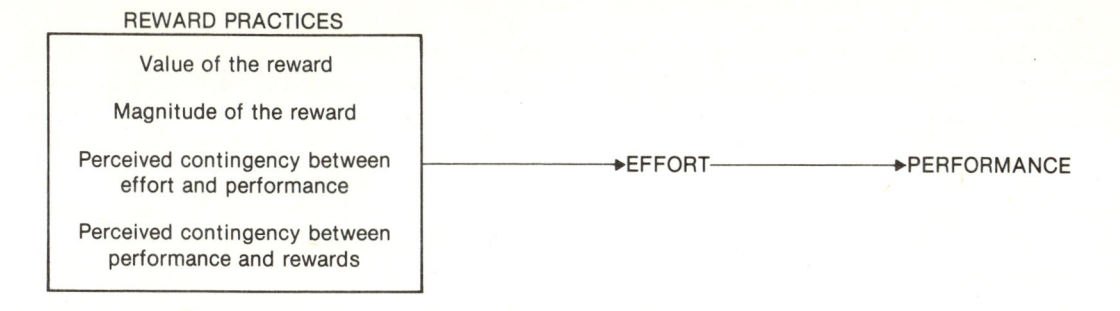

```
┌─────────────────────────────┐
│      REWARD PRACTICES       │
│                             │
│    Value of the reward      │
│                             │
│   Magnitude of the reward   │
│                             │
│  Perceived contingency between│───────▶ EFFORT ────────▶ PERFORMANCE
│    effort and performance   │
│                             │
│  Perceived contingency between│
│    performance and rewards  │
└─────────────────────────────┘
```

Figure 1. Rewards and effort

among a number of fringe benefits and cash. This practice would ensure that employees receive only those fringe benefits they value; from the organization's point of view, it would reduce the waste in funds allocated by the organization to fringe benefits not valued by its members. As a personal strategy, however, the manager could profit even more by extending Lawler's plan to include the entire range of non-monetary rewards.

Rewards can be classified into two broad categories, extrinsic and intrinsic. Extrinsic rewards are those external to the job, but in the context of the job, such as job security, improved working facilities, praise from one's boss, status symbols, and, of course, pay, including fringe benefits. Intrinsic rewards, on the other hand, are rewards that can be associated directly with the "doing of the job," such as a sense of accomplishment after successful performance, opportunities for advancement, increased responsibility, and work itself.

Thus, intrinsic rewards flow immediately and directly from the individual's performance on the job and, as such, may be considered as a form of self-reward. For example, one essentially must decide for one's self whether the level of performance is worthy of a feeling of personal achievement. Extrinsic rewards, to the contrary, are administered by the organization; the organization first must identify good performance and then provide the appropriate reward.

Generally speaking, extrinsic rewards have their greatest value when the individual is most strongly motivated to satisfy what Maslow has referred to as lower level needs—basic physiological needs and needs for safety or security, and those higher level ego needs that can be linked directly to status. Pay, for example, may be valued by an individual because of a belief that it is a determinant of social position within the community or because it constitutes a means for acquiring status symbols.

Jorgenson, Dunnette, and Pritchard (1973) have reported that there was a general trend for subjects in their study to perceive money as more important over time relative to other outcomes. This is consistent with the reinforcement theory position that money is a powerful generalized, conditioned reinforcer in our society. That is, by its association with other desirable outcomes such as status, promotion, recognition, as well as what it can buy, money has acquired the effect of a powerful secondary reinforcer. Furthermore, at least one investigator, Schwab (1973), reported finding that "... males did not value pay more than females, older employees did not value pay less than younger employees and lower paid employees did not value pay more than higher paid employees as has been found previously." Indeed, it may well be the case that inappropriate appreciation for the subtleties of reinforcement contingencies has contributed to an apparently widespread tendency to disdain the effectiveness of monetary rewards.

The potency of pay as a reinforcer notwithstanding, there are other rewards potentially susceptible to the control of the manager. Intrinsic rewards are more likely to be valued by the individual after lower level needs have been satisfied. This is not, however, a "sufficient" condition for using intrinsic rewards since individuals vary significantly with respect to the extent to which higher order needs are motivating (e.g., Hackman and Lawler, 1971). In other words, for most people, there must be an adequate level of satisfaction with the extrinsic rewards before intrinsic rewards can be utilized effectively. For these employees, the manager needs to provide meaningful work assignments; that is, work with which the subordinate can identify and become personally involved. Challenging yet attainable goals can be established or, in some cases, it may be more advantageous to create conditions that greatly enhance the likelihood that the subordinate will succeed, thus increasing the potential for attaining feelings of achievement, advancement and recognition. The manager may also consider such means as increased delegation or other forms of job enlargement for extending the scope and depth of the jobs of subordinates shown to be motivated by higher level needs—thereby increasing these subordinates' sense of responsibility and providing greater opportunity to make the job into something more compatible with the higher level needs.

In short, managers should as closely as possible match the rewards at their disposal, both extrinsic and intrinsic rewards, with what the subordinate indicates a need or desire for. This must be done with a full appreciation for individual differences in response to various reinforcers. Second, the manager should, by varying the magnitude and timing of the rewards granted, establish clearly in the subordinate's mind the desired effort-performance-reward contingencies.

Establishing the Contingencies. The contingency between effort and performance (that is, the extent to which the individual believes that working harder will improve performance) is largely a function of confidence in one's own ability and of perceptions of the difficulty of the task and absence of obstacles standing in the way of successful task performance. When the effort-performance contingency is not clear for these reasons, the manager should consider several actions. Perhaps work can be reassigned or the task made more consistent with individual perceptions of own ability; or the problem treated as a "real" ability deficiency; or the apparent performance obstacles removed; or the individual simply reassured.

The second contingency, the individual's belief that the rewards received reflect accomplishments, is usually more difficult to establish. Here, two rather vexing predicaments are frequently encountered, both of which stem primarily from administration of extrinsic rewards. First, the instrument (usually a merit evaluation or performance appraisal device) may inaccurately measure the individual's contribution and thus performance is rewarded in error. Reward schedules constitute the source of the second problem. Given fixed reward schedules (that is, the ubiquitous annual salary increase) adopted by the great majority of organizations, there is more frequently than not a considerable delay between task accomplishment and bestowal of the reward. As a result, the individual may not only fail to perceive the intended contingency but may incorrectly associate the reward with behavior just prior to being rewarded. In other words, the individual may perceive a nonexistent contingency, and subsequent behavior will reflect that contingency and, this time, go unrewarded. As operant theory suggests, an important component of the performance-reward contingency is the time interval between performance and reward (Kesselman, Wood, & Hagen, 1974).

Reward Schedules. The manner in which a given reward, or reinforcer, is scheduled is as strong a determinant of the effectiveness of that reward as is the value of the reward itself; or, for that matter, any other attribute of the reward. In organizations, the only plausible forms of reward schedules are intermittent as opposed to the continuous reward schedule in which the reward or punishment is administered after every behavioral sequence to be conditioned. In the case of the intermittent schedules, the behavior to be conditioned is reinforced only occasionally. There are four schedules of interest to the manager, each with varying degrees of effect on performance as a number of investigations in the field of experimental psychology have revealed.

1. *Fixed-interval schedule.* Rewards bestowed after a fixed period, usually since the last time the reward was administered. This type of schedule is reflected in schedules where pay is earned on an hourly basis, generally paid on a weekly or monthly fixed schedule. Annual salary increases are also examples of this type of schedule. Typically, the individual will exhibit a "scalloped" performance pattern, with performance rising just prior to the time of reinforcement and then returning to a lower level until just before the next administration of reinforcement.

2. *Variable-interval schedule.* Rewards are administered at designated time periods, but the intervals between the periods vary. For example, a reward may be given one day after the last rewarded behavior sequence, then three days later, then one week later, and so on, but only if the behavior to be conditioned actually occurs. This schedule results in fairly consistent rates of performance over long periods of time. Praise or other forms of social reinforcement from one's peers and superior, as an example, usually occur according to a variable-interval schedule, not by intention but simply because they are too involved with their own affairs to provide systematic reinforcement.

3. *Fixed-ratio schedule.* Reinforcement is provided after a fixed number of responses or performances by the individual. Incentive wage plans so frequently utilized in organizations constitute the prime example of this type of schedule. It is characterized by higher rates of effort than the interval schedules unless the ratio is large. When significant delays do occur between rewards, performance, much like in the fixed schedule, declines immediately after the reward is bestowed and improves again as the time for the next reward approaches. In fact, it is more commonly the case that rewards (in this case wages) are "earned" and/or recorded on a fixed-ratio schedule but actually delivered on a fixed-interval schedule; i.e., paid once a week or once a month. This undoubtedly "dampens" the effect of the ratio schedule.

4. *Variable-ratio schedule.* The reward is administered after a series of responses or performances, the number of which varies from the granting of one reward to the next.

For example, an individual on a 15:1 variable-ratio schedule might be reinforced after ten responses, then fifteen responses, then twenty responses, then ten responses, and so on, an average of one reinforcement for every fifteen responses. This schedule tends to result in performance that is higher than that of a comparable fixed-ratio schedule, and the variation in performance both before and after the occurrence of a reward or reinforcement is considerably less.

Virtually all managers must function within the constraints imposed by a fixed interval schedule (weekly or monthly payday) or fixed-ratio schedule (wage incentives). It is unlikely that in a society where the security and physiological survival of the worker and dependents is tied to a predictable stream of income, that workers can live with the uneven timing of a basic wage delivered on a variable time or variable ratio schedule.

However, this fact should not preclude consideration of mixed or multiple schedules; that is, concomitant use of variable and fixed schedules. A basic wage, sufficient to provide the employee with a reliable, predictable ability to meet physiological and contractual needs such as food purchases, auto and home payments, etc., might well be used in conjunction with a bonus that is *delivered* on a variable interval or variable-ratio schedule. Even the "basic" wage can be made performance-contingent to the extent that its magnitude is determined by piece rate or level of performance. Further, other reinforcers may be even more susceptible to the use of variable schedules; such as praise, salary increases, time-off, feedback, and so forth. The entire range of non-monetary rewards could be more effectively scheduled on a variable-interval (in some cases, variable-ratio) basis, assuming such scheduling is done in a systematic fashion.

CONCLUSIONS

This article has reviewed recent research concerning the relationship between satisfaction and performance and attempted to update an appraisal of its implications for the practicing manager. Three basic propositions were identified: (a) Satisfaction-causes-performance, (b) Performance-causes-satisfaction, and (c) Both satisfaction and performance are caused by an additional variable(s), primarily rewards.

The oldest of these propositions, that satisfaction-causes-performance, is still widespread, continuing to appeal to both practitioners and academicians. A more recent proposal is that performance-causes-satisfaction. This position has gained considerable following, especially in academic circles. However, empirical support for neither of these first two propositions is convincing, though more promising for the second than for the first.

Instead, recent evidence is more indicative of the third proposition, that satisfaction and performance are covariants of a third (or more) variable(s). The most significant co-determinant identified to date is the administration of rewards. Though complex, the relationship is essentially this: (a) rewards constitute a more direct cause of satisfaction than does performance and (b) not satisfaction, but rewards based on current performance, cause subsequent performance.

For the manager concerned with the well-being of subordinates, the implication of the finding that rewards cause satisfaction is quite clear. In order to achieve this end, the manager must provide rewards that have value in terms of the subordinate's own need state and provide them in sufficient magnitude and on an appropriate schedule as to be positively reinforcing.

The manager whose goal is to increase a subordinate's performance, on the other hand, is faced with a more difficult task for two reasons. First, the relationship between rewards and performance is not a simple one. Second, there are other causes of performance —direction, the subordinate's ability, and existence of performance obstacles standing in the way of successful task performance— which the manager must deal with, also.

The relationship between rewards and performance is complex because in reality there is at least one intervening variable and more than one contingency that need to be established. An employee exerts high level effort usually because of the valued rewards associated with high performance. Effort, the intervening variable, may be considered a function of the value and magnitude of the reward and the extent to which the individual believes that high effort will lead to high performance and that high performance, in turn, will lead to rewards.

Therefore, the manager in addition to providing appropriate rewards, must establish contingencies between effort and performance and between performance and rewards. The first contingency, the extent to which the individual believes that hard work determines performance, is perhaps the more readily established. This contingency is a function, at least in part, of the individual's confidence in his own abilities, perceptions of the difficulty of the task, and the presence of performance obstacles. When a problem does arise here, the manager can take those actions indicated earlier in this article to overcome an apparent ability deficiency or performance obstacle. The performance-reward contingency requires the manager, by means of accurate performance appraisals and appropriate reward practices, to clearly establish in the subordinate's mind the belief that performance determines the magnitude of the rewards received.

The establishment of this particular contingency, unfortunately, is becoming increasingly difficult as organizations continue to rely more heavily on fixed salary schedules and nonperformance-related factors (for example, seniority) as determinants of salary progression. However, the manager can, as a supplement to organizationally determined rewards, place more emphasis on non-monetary rewards and both the cafeteria-style reward plans and variable-interval schedules for their administration.

It is apparent that the manager whose objective is to significantly improve subordinates' performance has assumed a difficult by by no means impossible task. The path of least resistance—that is, increasing subordinates' satisfaction—*simply will not work.*

However, the actions suggested concerning reward practices and, particularly, establishment of appropriate performance-reward contingencies, will result in improved performance, assuming that such improvement is not restricted by ability or direction problems or by performance obstacles. The use of differential rewards may require courage on the part of the manager, but failure to use them will have far more negative consequences. A subordinate will repeat that behavior which was rewarded, regardless of whether it resulted in high or low performance. A rewarded low performer, for example, will continue to perform poorly. With knowledge of this inequity, the high performer, in turn, will eventually reduce performance or seek employment elsewhere.

NOTES

1. See, for example, J. D. Folley, Jr., "Determining Training Needs of Department Store Personnel," *Training Development Journal,* 1969, Vol. 23, 24-27, for a discussion of how the critical incidents approach can be employed to identify job skills to be learned in a formal training situation.

2. For a useful discussion of how ability levels can be upgraded by means of training and selection procedures, the reader can refer to Larry L. Cummings and Donald P. Schwab, *Performance in Organizations: Determinants and Appraisal* (Glenview, Ill.: Scott, Foresman & Co.) 1972.

3. Portions of the discussion in this section are based in part on Cummings and Schwab, *Performance in Organizations,* and Lyman W. Porter and Edward E. Lawler, III, "What Job Attitudes Tell About Motivation," *Harvard Business Review,* LXVI (January-February, 1968), pp. 118-126.

REFERENCES

Bachman, J. G., C. Smith, and J. A. Slesinger, "Control, performance and satisfaction: An analysis of structural and individual effects," *Journal of Personality and Social Psychology*, 1966, Vol. 4, 127-136.

Bowen, D. and J. P. Siegel, "The relationship between satisfaction and performance: The question of causality," *Proceedings of the Annual Convention of the American Psychological Association,* 1970.

Brayfield, A. H., and W. H. Crockett, "Employee attitudes and employee performance," *Psychological Bulletin*, 1955, Vol. 52, 396-424.

Carlson, R. E., "Degree of job satisfaction as a moderator of the relationship between job performance and job satisfaction," *Personnel Psychology*, 1969, Vol. 22, 159-170.

Cherrington, D. L., H. J. Reitz, and W. E. Scott, Jr., "Effects of contingent and noncontingent reward on the relationship between satisfaction and task performance," *Journal of Applied Psychology,* 1971, Vol. 55, 531-537.

Cummings, L. L. and D. P. Schwab, *Performance in Organizations: Determinants and Appraisal* (Glenview, Ill.: Scott, Foresman & Co.) 1972.

Doll, R. E., and E. K. E. Gunderson, "Occupational group as a moderator of the job satisfaction-job performance relationship," *Journal of Applied Psychology*, 1969, Vol. 53, 359-361.

Downey, H. K., J. E. Sheridan, and J. W. Slocum, "Analysis of relationships between leader behavior and subordinate job," *Academy of Management Journal*, 1975, Vol. 18, 253-262.

Downey, H. K., J. E. Sheridan, and J. W. Slocum, Jr., "The path-goal theory of leadership: A longitudinal analysis," *Organizational Behavior and Human Performance*, 1976 (in press).

"Egalitarianism: Mechanisms for redistributing income," *Business Week,* December 8, 1975, pp. 86-90.

"Egalitarianism: Threat to a free market," *Business Week*, December 1, 1975, pp. 62-65.

"Egalitarianism: The corporation as villain," *Business Week*, December 15, 1975, pp. 86-88.

Farris, G. F., and F. G. Lim, Jr., "Effects of performance on leadership, cohesiveness, influence, satisfaction and subsequent performance," *Journal of Applied Psychology*, 1969, Vol. 53, 490-497.

Fournet, G. P., M. K. J. Distefano, and M. W. Pryer, "Job satisfaction: Issues and problems," *Personnel Psychology,* 1966, Vol. 19, 165-183.

Folley, J. D., Jr., "Determining training needs of department store personnel," *Training Development Journal*, 1969, Vol. 23, 24-27.

Greene, C. N., "The satisfaction-performance controversy," *Business Horizons,* 1972a, Vol. 15(5), 31-41.

Greene, C. N., "A causal interpretation of relationship among pay, performance, and satisfaction." Paper presented at *Annual Meeting of the Midwest Psychological Association*, 1972b, Cleveland, Ohio.

Greene, C. N., "Relationships among role accuracy, compliance, performance evaluation and satisfaction," *Academy of Management Journal,* 1972c, Vol. 15, 205-215.

Greene, C. N., "Causal connections among managers pay, job satisfaction and performance," *Journal of Applied Psychology*, 1973a, Vol. 58, 95-100.

Greene, C. N., "A longitudinal analysis of relationships among leader behavior and subordinate performance and satisfaction," *Proceedings of the 33rd Annual Meeting of the Academy of Management*, 1973b.

Greene, C. N., and D. W. Organ, "An evaluation of causal models linking the perceived role with job satisfaction," *Administrative Science Quarterly,* 1973, Vol. 18, 95-103.

Greene, C. N., "The reciprocal nature of influence between leader and subordinate," *Journal of Applied Psychology*, 1975, Vol. 60, 187-193.

Greenhaus, J. H., and I. J. Badin, "Self-esteem, performance and satisfaction: Some tests of a theory," *Journal of Applied Psychology,* 1974, Vol. 59, 722-726.

Hackman, J. R., and E. E. Lawler, III, "Employee reactions to job characteristics," *Journal of Applied Psychology*, 1971, Vol. 55, 259-286.

Herzberg, F., B. Mausner, R. O. Peterson, and D. F. Capwell, "Job attitudes: A review of research and Opinion," (Pittsburgh, Pa.: Psychological Service of Pittsburgh) 1957.

House, R. J., "A path goal theory of leader effectiveness," *Administrative Science Quarterly,* 1971, Vol. 16, 321-339.

Ivancevich, J. M., and J. H. Donnelly, Jr., "Relation of organizational structure to job satisfaction, anxiety-stress and performance," *Administrative Science Quarterly,* 1975, Vol. 20, 272-280.

Jorgenson, D. O., M. D. Dunnette, and R. D. Pritchard, "Effects of the manipulation of a performance-reward contingency on behavior in a simulated work setting," *Journal of Applied Psychology,* 1973, Vol. 57, 271-280.

Kahn, R. L., "Productivity and job satisfaction," *Personnel Psychology,* 1960, Vol. 13, 275.

Katzell, R. A., R. S. Barrett, and T. C. Parker, "Job satisfaction, job performance and situational characteristics," *Journal of Applied Psychology,* 1961, Vol. 45, 65-72.

Kavanagh, M. J., A. C. MacKinney, and L. Wolins, "Satisfaction and morale of foremen as a function of middle manager's performance," *Journal of Applied Psychology*, 1970, Vol. 54, 145-156.

Kesselman, G. A., M. T. Wood, and E. L. Hagen, "Relationships between performance and satisfaction under contingent and noncontingent reward systems," *Journal of Applied Psychology,* 1974, Vol. 59, 374-376.

Lawler, E. E., III, *Pay and Organizational Effectiveness: A Psychological View* (New York: McGraw-Hill Book Company) 1971.

Lawler, E. E., III, and L. W. Porter, "The effect of performance on job satisfaction," *Industrial Relations*, 1967, Vol. 7, 20-28.

Locke, E. A., "Job satisfaction and job performance: A theoretical analysis," *Organizational Behavior and Human Performance,* 1970, Vol. 5, 484-500.

Mager, R. F., and P. Pipe, *Analyzing Performance Problems* (Belmont, Cal.: Lear Siegler, Inc.) 1970.

Organ, D. W., "A reappraisal and reinterpretation of the satisfaction-causes-performance hypothesis," *Academy of Management Journal,* 1976.

Porter, L. W., and E. E. Lawler, III, *Management Attitudes and Performance* (Homewood, Ill,: Richard D. Irwin, Inc.) 1968.

Porter, L. W., and E. E. Lawler, III, "What job attitudes tell about motivation," *Harvard Business Review,* 1968, Vol. 66, 118-126.

Schwab, D. P., "Impact of alternative compensation systems on pay valence and instrumentality perceptions," *Journal of Applied Psychology,* 1973, Vol. 58, 308-312.

Shaw, M. E., and J. M. Blum, "Group performance as a function of task difficulty and the group's awareness of member satisfaction," *Journal of Applied Psychology,* 1965, Vol. 49, 151-154.

Sheridan, J. E., and J. W. Slocum, Jr., "The direction of the causal relationship between job satisfaction and work performance," *Organizational Behavior and Human Performance,* 1975, Vol. 14.

Slocum, J. W., Jr., "Motivation in managerial levels: Relationship of need satisfaction to job performance," *Journal of Applied Psychology,* 1971, Vol. 55, 312-316.

Turcotte, W. E., "Control systems, performance and satisfaction in two state agencies," *Administrative Science Quarterly,* 1974, Vol. 19, 60-73.

Vroom, V. H. *Work and Motivation* (New York: John Wiley & Sons) 1964.

Wanous, J. P., "A causal-correlational analysis of the job satisfaction and performance relationship," *Proceedings of the 33rd Annual Meeting of the Academy of Management,* 1973.

Wanous, J. P., "A causal-correlational analysis of the job satisfaction and performance relationship," *Journal of Applied Psychology,* 1974, Vol. 59, 139-144.

Leadership Process

Leadership is a vital process in organizations. Leadership has been defined as an influence process. The leader's influence aids him/her in achieving and maintaining a high level of subordinate task motivation and willingness to implement decisions. In addition to motivating subordinates, leaders in organizations usually perform a number of other important functions (see readings by Mintzberg, in Part Two). The article by Vroom and Yetton, "A Normative Model of Leadership Styles," provides a framework for understanding the interrelationship between leader behavior and decision making. Vroom and Yetton propose a normative model of appropriate managerial decision making styles for different contingencies. The core of their model is the distinction between decision quality and subordinate acceptance of the decision. The situation is analyzed in terms of quality and acceptance for a particular decision and the factors moderating the effect of various decision making styles on decision quality and acceptance.

A model that has been derived from the expectancy theory of motivation is the path-goal theory of leadership. The core of the path-goal theory of leadership is the effect of leader behavior on subordinate motivation. The motivation functions of the leader consist of increasing personal payoffs to subordinates for work-goal attainment, and making the paths to these payoffs easier to travel by clarifying means to reach valued outcomes, reducing roadblocks, and increasing opportunities for subordinates' personal satisfactions. Leader behavior which results in the subordinate expectation that effort will lead to valued outcomes will increase subordinate motivation, which in turn will usually lead to higher group performance. The effects of leader behavior on subordinate expectations varies with the situation. When the job is highly structured, directive leader behavior may have negative effects on employees. When the job is less clear or involves a good deal of managerial discretion, a directive style may clarify the relationship between individual activity and the objectives of the job. House and Mitchell, "Path-Goal Theory of Leadership," reviews different contingencies affecting leader behavior.

In the last article in this section, Miles and Ritchie, "Participative Management: Quality vs. Quantity," adds new depth to the concept of participative management. The authors distinguish between participation used by a leader because he wishes to gain cooperation from his subordinates and participation used by a leader because he respects the abilities of subordinates and wishes to utilize their expertise. Miles and Ritchie see the former type of participation as stemming from the Human Relations model and the latter from the Human Resources model. In essence, the authors explore the differences between the quantity and the quality of participation used by a leader. In the article, data is presented which indicates that subordinate satisfaction is highest when the leader seeks both quantity and quality of participation from his subordinates. Finally, the authors discuss how the concept of quality of participation can be used to answer some of the more common criticism of participative management theory. Namely, that participative management is sometimes not possible because of time constraints, technological barriers, and the leader's temperament.

A NORMATIVE MODEL OF LEADERSHIP STYLES

*Victor H. Vroom
and Philip W. Yetton*

One of the most persistent and controversial issues in the study of management is that of participation in decision-making by subordinates. Traditional models of the managerial process have been autocratic in nature. The manager makes decisions on matters within his area of freedom, issues orders or directives to his subordinates, and monitors their performance to ensure conformity with these directives. Scientific management, from its early developments in time and motion study to its contemporary manifestations in mathematical programming, has contributed to this centralization of decision-making in organizations by focusing on the development of methods by which managers can make more rational decisions, substituting objective measurements and empirically validated methods for casual judgments.

In contrast, social psychologists and other behavioral scientists who have turned their attention toward the implications of psychological and social processes for the practice of management have called for greater participation by subordinates in the problem-solving and decision-making processes. The empirical evidence provides some, but not overwhelming, support for beliefs in the efficacy of participative management. Field experiments on rank-and-file workers by Coch and French (1948), Bavelas (reported in French, 1950), and Strauss (reported in Whyte, 1955) indicate that impressive increases in productivity can be brought about by giving workers an opportunity to participate in decision-making and goal-setting. In addition, several correlational field studies (Katz, Maccoby, and Morse, 1950; Vroom, 1960) indicate positive relationships between the amount of influence supervisors afford their subordinates in decisions that affect them and individual or group performance.

On the other hand, in an experiment conducted in a Norwegian factory, French, Israel, and Ås (1960) found no significant differences in production between workers who did and those who did not participate in decisions regarding the introduction of changes in work methods. To complicate the picture further, Morse and Reimer (1956) compared the effects of two programs of change, each of which was introduced in two divisions of the clerical operations of a large insurance company. One of the programs involved increased participation in decision-making by rank-and-file workers, while the other involved increased hierarchical control. The results show a significant increase in productivity under both programs, with the hierarchically controlled program producing the greater increase.

The investigations cited constitute only a small portion of those which are relevant to the effects of participation. The reader interested in a more comprehensive review of that evidence should consult Lowin (1968), Vroom (1970), and Wood (1974). We conclude, as

Reprinted from *Leadership and Decision-Making*, by Victor H. Vroom and Philip W. Yetton, by permission of University of Pittsburgh Press. © 1973 by the University of Pittsburgh Press.

have other scholars who have examined the evidence, that participation in decision making has consequences that vary from one situation to another. Given the potential importance of this conclusion for the study of leadership and its significance to the process of management, social scientists should begin to develop some definitions of the circumstances under which participation in decision making may contribute to or hinder organizational effectiveness. These could then be translated into guidelines to help leaders choose leadership styles to fit the demands of the situations they encounter.

In this [article] one approach to dealing with this important problem will be described. A normative model is developed which is consistent with existing empirical evidence concerning the consequences of participation and which purports to specify a set of rules that *should* be used in determining the form and amount of participation in decision-making by subordinates in different classes of situations. This chapter presents the basic assumptions that have guided the development of the normative model and the situational attributes that are contained within it.

BASIC ASSUMPTIONS

1. *The normative model should be constructed in such a way as to be of potential value to managers or leaders in determining which leadership methods they should use in each of the various situations that they encounter in carrying out their formal leadership roles. Consequently, it should be operational in that the behaviors required of the leader should be specified unambiguously.*

To be operational, a prescriptive statement must permit the person to determine whether or not he is acting in accordance with the statement. The statement "In case of headache, take one aspirin tablet at intervals of four hours" is quite operational in this sense. It specifies the activities to be performed and the conditions under which they are to be performed. On the other hand, the statement "To maintain one's health, one should lead a clean life" is not operational. The activities subsumed by "leading a clean life" are subject to many differences in interpretation, and there is no clear indication in the statement of the conditions under which the activities are to be carried out.

Many of the prescriptions of behavioral scientists are far closer in operationality to the second statement than to the first. Leaders are told to exhibit maximum concern for people and for production or to develop relationships with subordinates that are supportive. Such prescriptions have some informational value but fall short of the degree of operationality that we believe could be achieved.

2. *There are a number of discrete social processes by which organizational problems can be translated into solutions, and these processes vary in terms of the potential amount of participation by subordinates in the problem-solving process.*

The term "participation" has been used in a number of different ways. Perhaps the most influential definitions have been those of French, Israel, and Ås (1960) and Vroom (1960), who define participation as a process of joint decision-making by two or more parties. The amount of participation of any individual is the amount of influence he has on the decisions and plans agreed upon. Given the existence of a property such as participation that varies from high to low, it should be possible to define leader behaviors representing clear alternative processes for making decisions that can be related to the amount of participation each process affords the managers' subordinates.

A taxonomy of decision processes created for normative purposes should distinguish among methods that are likely to have different outcomes but should not be so elaborate that leaders are unable to determine which method they are employing in any

TABLE 1. Decision Methods for Group and Individual Problems

Group Problems	Individual Problems
AI. You solve the problem or make the decision yourself, using information available to you at the time.	AI. You solve the problem or make the decision by yourself, using information available to you at the time.
AII. You obtain the necessary information from your subordinates, then decide the solution to the problem yourself. You may or may not tell your subordinates what the problem is in getting the information from them. The role played by your subordinates in making the decision is clearly one of providing the necessary information to you, rather than generating or evaluating alternative solutions.	AII. You obtain the necessary information from your subordinate, then decide on the solution to the problem yourself. You may or may not tell the subordinate what the problem is in getting the information from him. His role in making the decision is clearly one of providing the necessary information to you, rather than generating or evaluating alternative solutions.
CI. You share the problem with the relevant subordinates individually, getting their ideas and suggestions without bringing them together as a group. Then *you* make the decision, which may or may not reflect your subordinates' influence.	CI. You share the problem with your subordinate, getting his ideas and suggestions. Then you make a decision, which may or may not reflect his influence.
CII. You share the problem with your subordinates as a group, obtaining their collective ideas and suggestions. Then you make the decision, which may or may not reflect your subordinates' influence.	GI. You share the problem with your subordinate, and together you analyze the problem and arrive at a mutually agreeable solution.
GII. You share the problem with your subordinates as a group. Together you generate and evaluate alternatives and attempt to reach agreement (consensus) on a solution. Your role is much like that of chairman. You do not try to influence the group to adopt "your" solution, and you are willing to accept and implement any solution which has the support of the entire group.	DI. You delegate the problem to your subordinate, providing him with any relevant information that you possess, but giving him responsibility for solving the problem by himself. You may or may not request him to tell you what solution he has reached.

given instance. The taxonomy to be used in the normative model is shown in Table 1.

The table contains a detailed specification of several alternative processes by which problems can be solved or decisions made. Each process is represented by a symbol (AI, CI, GII, DI) which will be used throughout this book as a convenient method of referring to each process. The letters in this code signify the basic properties of the process (*A* stands for autocratic; *C*, for consultative; *G*, for group; and *D*, for delegated). The roman numerals that follow the letters constitute variants on that process. Thus AI represents the first variant on an autocratic process; AII, the second variant; and so on.

It should be noted that the methods are arranged in two columns corresponding to their applicability to problems which involve the entire group or some subset of it (hereafter called group problems) or a single subordinate (hereafter called individual problems). If a problem or decision clearly affects only one subordinate, the leader would choose among the methods shown in the right-hand column; if it has potential effects on the entire group (or subset of it) he would choose among the methods shown in the left-hand column. Those in both columns are arranged from top to bottom in terms of the opportunity for subordinates to influence the solution to the problem. The distinction between group and individual problems can be illustrated with the following examples.

Group Problems

A. Sharply decreasing profits for the firm has resulted in a directive from top management that makes it impossible to take on any new personnel even to replace those who leave. Shortly after this directive is issued, one of your five subordinates resigns to take a job with another firm. Your problem is how to rearrange the work assignments among the remaining four subordinates without reducing the total productivity of the group.

B. You have been chosen by your firm to attend a nine-week senior executive program at a famous university. Your problem is to choose one of your subordinates to take your place during your absence.

C. You have two main projects under your direction with three subordinates assigned to each. One of these projects is three months behind schedule with only six months remaining before the work *must* be completed. Your problem is to get the project back on schedule to meet the completion date.

Individual Problems

D. As principal of an elementary school, you often handle disciplinary cases. Over the last six months, one of your fifteen teachers has referred an inordinately large number of cases to your attention. This fact, combined with other information you have received, leads you to believe that there is a serious breakdown of discipline within that teacher's classroom.

E. The cost figures for section *B* have risen faster than those of the other three similar sections under your direction. The manager of section *B* is your immediate subordinate.

F. You have the opportunity to bid on a multi-million-dollar government contract. While the decision will be made by top management, you have to formulate a recommendation that has a high probability of being accepted. You have only one subordinate who is a specialist in the area in which the contract is to be granted, and you will have to rely heavily on him to present and defend the recommendation to top management. As you see it, there are at least three options: to bid as prime contractor; to bid as subcontractor for another firm planning to bid as prime contractor; or to do nothing.

The person in the leadership position could presumably employ any one of the alternatives on the left-hand side of Table 1 (AI, AII, CI, CII, GII) for problems *A, B,* and *C* and could employ any one of the alternatives on the right-hand side of Table 1 (AI, AII, CI, GI, DI) for problems *D, E,* and *F*. Since the two sets of alternatives have three common decision processes (AI, AII, CI), this categorization effectively eliminates from consideration GI and DI as relevant decision processes for group problems (like *A, B,* and *C*) and eliminates CII and GII for individual problems (like *D, E,* and *F*). The reader can verify for himself the appropriateness of these exclusions.

Table 2 shows the relationship between the methods shown in Table 2 and those described in prior taxonomies. Our methods appear as row headings, and the names of other authors or researchers appear as column headings. If there seems to be correspondence between the definition of one of our methods and that used by a given author, his term appears in the intersection of row and column. A vacant cell, defined by the intersection of a column and row, indicates that the investigator whose name heads the column does not recognize any style corresponding to that in the row heading. If a

TABLE 2. Correspondence Between Decision Processes Employed in the Model and Those of Previous Investigators.

	Lewin, Lippitt, and White (1939)	Maier (1955)	Tannenbaum and Schmidt (1958)				Heller (1971)			Likert (1967)	
AI	Autocratic leadership	Autocratic management	Manager makes decision and announces it					Own decision with detailed explanation	Own decision without detailed explanation	Exploitive authoritative (system 1)	Benevolent authoritative (system 2)
AII											
CI		Consultative management	Manager presents tentative decision, subject to change	Manager sells decision	Manager presents problem, gets suggestions, makes decision	Manager presents ideas and invites questions	Prior consultation with subordinate(s)			Consultative (system 3)	
CII											
GI							Joint decision-making with subordinate(s)				
GII	Democratic leadership	Group decision	Manager defines limits, asks group to make decision			Manager permits group to make decisions within prescribed limits				Participative group (system 4)	
DI	Laissez-faire leadership						Delegation of decision to subordinate(s)				

column is partitioned within a row, it means that the investigator uses a finer breakdown than that employed in the model. Similarly, if a column entry cuts across two or more rows, it indicates that the model employs a finer breakdown than that made by the investigator. The relationships presented in Table 2 are matters of judgment and are merely intended to suggest the correspondence or lack of correspondence existing between the taxonomy that is used here and those which were previously employed.

3. *No one leadership method is applicable to all situations; the function of a normative model should be to provide a framework for the analysis of situational requirements that can be translated into prescriptions of leadership styles.*

The fact that the most effective leadership method or style is dependent on the situation is becoming widely recognized by behavioral scientists interested in problems of leadership and administration. A decision-making process that is optimal for a quarterback on a football team making decisions under severe time constraints is likely to be far from optimal when used by a dean introducing a new curriculum to be implemented by his faculty. Even the advocates of participative management have noted this "situational relativity" of leadership styles. Thus, Argyris (1962) writes:

> No one leadership style is the most effective. Each is probably effective under a given set of conditions. Consequently, I suggest that effective leaders are those who are capable of behaving in many different leadership styles, depending on the requirements of reality as they and others perceive it. I call this "reality-centered" leadership. (p. 81)

We must go beyond noting the importance of situational factors and begin to move toward a road map or normative models that attempt to prescribe the most appropriate leadership style for different kinds of situations. The most comprehensive treatment of situational factors as determinants of the effectiveness and efficiency of participation in decision-making is found in the work of Tannenbaum and Schmidt (1958). They discuss a large number of variables, including attributes of the manager, his subordinates, and the situation, which ought to enter into the manager's decision about the degree to which he should share his power with his subordinates. But they stop at this inventory of variables, and do not show how these might be combined and translated into different forms of action.

4. *The most appropriate unit for the analysis of the situation is the particular problem to be solved and the context in which the problem occurs.*

While it is becoming widely recognized that different situations require different leadership methods, there is less agreement concerning the appropriate units for the analysis of the situation. One approach is to assume that the situations that determine the effectiveness of different leadership styles correspond to the environment of the system. Thus, Bennis (1966) argues that egalitarian leadership styles work better when the environment of the organization is rapidly changing and the problems with which it has to deal are continually being altered. If this position were extended to provide the basis for a comprehensive normative model, one would prescribe different leadership styles for different systems but make identical prescriptions for all leadership roles within a system.

Alternatively, one might assume that the critical features of the situation concern the role of the leader, including his relations with his subordinates. Examples would include Fiedler's (1967) three dimensions of task structure, leadership position power, and leader-member relations. Implicit is the assumption that all problems or decisions made within a single role require a similar leadership style. Normatively, one might prescribe different amounts or forms of participation for two different leaders but prescribe identical amounts or forms of participation for all problems or decisions made by a single leader within a single role.

The approach taken here is to select the properties of the problem to be solved as the critical situational dimensions for determining the appropriate form or amount of participation. Different prescriptions would be made for a given leader for different problems within a given role. It should be noted that constructing a normative model with the problem rather than the role or any organizational differences as the unit of analysis does not rule out the possibility that different roles and organizations may involve different distributions of problem types that, in aggregate, may require different modal styles or levels of participation.

5. *The leadership method used in response to one situation should not constrain the method or style used in other situations.*

Implicit in the use of the attributes of the particular problem to be solved or decision to be made as the unit of analysis is the assumption that problems can be classified such that the relative usefulness of each alternative decision process is identical for all problems in a particular classification. A corollary to this assumption is that the process or method used on problems of one type does not constrain that used on problems of a different type. It is only in this way that prescriptions could be made for a given problem without knowing the other problems encountered by a leader or his methods for dealing with them.

This assumption is necessary to the construction of a normative model founded on problem differences. It may seem inconsistent with the view, first proposed by McGregor (1944), that consistency in leadership style is desirable because it enables subordinates to predict their superiors' behavior and to adapt to it. However, predictability does not preclude variability. There are many variable phenomena which can be predicted quite well because the rules or processes that govern them are understood. The antithesis of predictability is randomness, and, if McGregor is correct, a normative model to regulate choices among alternative leadership styles should be deterministic rather than stochastic. The model to be developed here is deterministic; the normatively prescribed method for a given problem type is a constant.

CONCEPTUAL AND EMPIRICAL BASIS OF THE MODEL

A model designed to regulate, in some rational way, choices among the decision methods shown in Table 1 should be based on sound empirical evidence concerning their likely consequences. The more complete the empirical base of knowledge, the greater the certainty with which one can develop the model and the greater will be its usefulness. In this section we will restrict ourselves to the development of a model concerned only with group problems and, hence, will use only the methods shown in the left-hand column of Table 1.

We will now consider the empirical evidence that can at present be brought to bear on such a normative model. You will note that much of the evidence is incomplete, and future research should prove helpful in providing a firmer foundation for a model. In this analysis it is important to distinguish three classes of outcomes that influence the ultimate effectiveness of decisions. These are:

1. the quality or rationality of the decision;
2. the acceptance of the decision by subordinates and their commitment to execute it effectively;
3. the amount of time required to make the decision.

The evidence regarding the effects of participation on each of these outcomes or consequences has been reviewed elsewhere (Vroom 1970). He concluded that:

> the results suggest that allocating problem solving and decision-making tasks to entire groups as compared with the leader or manager in charge of the groups, requires a greater investment of man hours but produces higher acceptance of decisions and a higher probability that the decisions will be executed efficiently. Differences between these two methods in quality of decisions and in elapsed time are inconclusive and probably highly variable.... It would be naive to think that group decision-making is always more "effective" than autocratic decision-making, or vice versa; the relative effectiveness of these two extreme methods depends both on the weights attached to quality, acceptance and time variables and on differences in amounts of these outcomes resulting from these methods, neither of which is invariant from one situation to another. The critics and proponents of participative management would do well to direct their efforts toward identifying the properties of situations in which different decision-making approaches are effective rather than wholesale condemnation or deification of one approach. (Vroom, pp. 239-40)

Stemming from this review, an attempt has been made to identify these properties of the situation, which will be the basic elements in the model. These problem attributes are of two types: (1) those which specify the importance for a particular problem of quality and acceptance (see A and E below), and (2) those which, on the basis of available evidence, have a high probability of moderating the effects of participation on each of these outcomes (see B, C, D, G, and H below). The following are the problem attributes used in the present form of the model.

A. *The importance of the quality of the decision.* According to Maier (1955, 1963), decision quality refers to the "objective or impersonal" aspects of the decision. For groups embedded within formal organizations with specifiable goals, the relative quality of a set of alternative decisions can be expressed in terms of their effects, if implemented with equal expenditure of energy, on the attainment of those goals.

The first attribute refers to what Maier (1963) has termed the quality requirement for the decision. There are some problems for which the nature of the solution reached within identifiable constraints is not at all critical. The leader is (or should be) indifferent among the possible solutions since their expected value is equal, provided that those who have to carry them out are committed to them. Typically, the number of solutions that meet the constraints is finite, and the alternatives are obvious or do not require substantial search. In such instances, there is no technical, rational, or analytic method of choosing among the alternatives.

In Maier's new-truck problem (Maier, 1955), the issue of which of the five truck drivers should get the new truck has no quality requirement. The foreman is (or should be) indifferent among the various possible alternatives provided they are accepted by the men. On the other hand, the problem of which truck should be discarded to make way for the new one does have a quality requirement. The five present trucks vary in age and condition, and a decision to discard other than the poorest truck in the set would be irrational.

While on a consulting assignment, the senior author encountered another problem which may help to illustrate the meaning of the term "quality requirement." A plant manager and his staff were about to move into a new plant. On inspecting the plans, he discovered that there were insufficient reserved parking places (directly in front of the building) to accommodate all six of his department heads. The design of the building permitted only four such parking places with all other cars having to park across the street in a large parking lot. There was no possible way to increase the number of parking spaces without modifying the design of the structure, and the costs would be prohibitive. Any solution to the parking-space allocation problem would have satisfied the plant manager provided it had the support of his department heads, each of whom, incidentally, expected to receive a reserved parking place. The problem had no quality requirement since he was indifferent among all possible solutions which met the constraints.

In both of the examples given, the constraints were imposed on the leader by forces outside him. The foreman had only one new truck to allocate among his drivers, and the plant manager could do nothing to increase the size of the reserved parking lot. In other instances, the quality requirement can be eliminated from the problem if the leader *imposes* constraints on the possible solutions. By attaching suitable constraints, quality requirements can be eliminated from such problems as the choice of personnel to be assigned to work on each shift, the design of a vacation schedule showing when each person should take his vacation, and the selection of a time at which to hold a meeting.

At the other end of the dimension specified by this attribute are so-called strategic decisions (Ansoff, 1965), which involve the allocation of scarce resources and are not easily reversible. At what level should we price our products? What new businesses should we acquire? Where should we locate our plants? What is the most effective advertising policy? These are just a few of the problems and decisions which have marked consequences for the effectiveness of the organization. No leader should be indifferent among possible alternative courses of action. Even though the relative consequences of the alternatives may not be known at any given point in time, the specific course chosen is going to make a difference in the degree to which the system attains its goals. In such instances, the variance in contribution to organizational objectives of alternative courses of action is large, and the rational quality of the decision is of central importance.

The function of this attribute in the model is to determine the relevance to the choice of decision process of such considerations as the nature and location of information or expertise necessary to generate and evaluate alternatives. If the quality of the decision is unimportant, then attributes B, C, D, and G below can be shown to be irrelevant to the prescription of that process.

B. The extent to which the leader possesses sufficient information/expertise to make a high-quality decision by himself. The quality of the decisions reached by any decision-making process is dependent on the resources the leader is able to utilize. One of the most critical of these resources is information. If a rational solution to the problem is to be obtained, alternatives must be generated and evaluated in terms of their organizational consequences. Any such activities require the use of the relevant information and expertise by participants in the decision process.

It is possible to distinguish two different kinds of information that are potentially relevant to problem-solving in an organizational setting. One is information necessary to the task of evaluating the relative quality or rationality of different alternatives. The other is information concerning the preferences of subordinates and their feelings about the alternatives.

These two kinds of information and associated expertise need not be correlated. One leader may be extremely knowledgeable about the terrain to be traversed and its possible pitfalls, and he may have worked out an elegant means of attaining the external objective. However, he may be completely unaware of the preferences of his men. Another may be uninformed about the external environment but highly sensitive to the attitudes and feelings of his subordinates. A low correlation between these two components of information is suggested by research on role differentiation in problem-solving groups. Task facilitative leadership tends to be carried out by different persons than socio-emotional leadership (Bales and Slater, 1955).

The information referred to in attribute B deals with the external goals and the consequences of actions on the part of the system for their attainment. In other words, we are interested only in the degree to which the leader possesses facts and skills relevant to the quality of the decision. Thus in evaluating the level of this attribute in the case of a head dietitian in a hospital faced with the task of preparing the week's menus, one would be concerned with such things as her knowledge of the components of a balanced diet, the availability and cost of different food products, and the existence of special dietary requirements among the patient load. One would not be concerned with the kinds of foods that her staff liked to consume, prepare, or deliver. Similarly, in evaluating the information possessed by a university department chairman faced with the problem of selecting a text to be used by members of his department in teaching the introductory course, the relevant questions would concern his knowledge of the alternatives as they relate to the goal of education and not his information regarding the preferences of those assigned to teach the course.

In defining this attribute solely in terms of information or expertise in matters relating to the quality of the decision, we intend not to render unimportant the task of having decisions accepted by subordinates, but rather to recognize the conceptual and empirical independence of the two kinds of information. As will be seen later in the description of other problem attributes, acceptance requirements are an integral part of the framework being developed.

The decision-making processes shown in Table 1 differ in terms of the amount of information and expertise that can be brought to bear on the problem. For example, in AI, only information available to the leader may be utilized in problem-solving, whereas in GII the information base extends to all group members including the leader.

There has been little research on the determinants of whether the leader's information is adequate to deal with the problems he encounters. Since he has been selected by somewhat different criteria, may have received special training, and has access to different information, there is strong *a priori* reason to believe that his information base will be different from (and in most cases superior to) that of the average group member. However, its absolute level must be assumed to be variable with the nature of the problem. There are undoubtedly some situations in which the leader possesses all of the necessary information and others for which his information is critically deficient. In the model, this attribute determines the importance of choosing a decision-making process that augments the information base of the decision.

Kelley and Thibaut (1969) have reviewed the literature on group and individual problem solving and have advanced a set of hypotheses concerning the conditions in which a group solution is likely to be higher than, equal to, or lower in quality than that of the best member of the group. The studies were conducted principally on ad hoc leaderless groups in laboratory settings, so it is not clear that the best member would always have been a formal leader. However, their hypotheses may ultimately prove fruitful in relating variation on the attribute defined above to problem differences.

Kelley and Thibaut suggest that: (1) group decisions are likely to be above the level of the most proficient member when the problem has multiple parts and when group members have uncorrelated (complementary) deficiencies and talents; (2) groups are likely to perform at the level of the most proficient member when the problem is simple (very few steps are required for its solution) and the solution is highly verifiable by all persons in possession of the original facts; and (3) groups are likely to do less well than the best member when the solution requires thinking through a series of interrelated steps or stages, applying a number of rules at each point, and always keeping in mind conclusions reached at earlier points.

C. The extent to which subordinates, taken collectively, have the necessary information to generate a high-quality decision. This attribute is similar to *B* above except that it deals with the resources of subordinates rather than the leader. There are some situations in which these resources may in fact be very small. For example, the problem may be a highly technical one, and the subordinates may lack any knowledge needed to deal with it. On the other hand, in problems with multiple parts and where the level of information needed to deal with these parts is uncorrelated, the potential contribution of subordinates may be very high. This attribute is relevant to the choice of a decision process only when the information available to the leader is deficient. It determines whether the information search activities can be conducted within the group as part of the decision-making activity or whether, in order to obtain a high-quality decision, it will be necessary to go outside the group for the necessary information.

D. The extent to which the problem is structured. A distinction is frequently made between problems or decisions that are structured or programmed, and those which are unstructured or nonprogrammed (Simon, 1960). Structured problems are those for which the alternative solutions or methods for generating them and the parameters for their evaluation are known. There are typically specific procedures within the organization for handling them. Under these circumstances, the decision is made once all the necessary information has reached a central source, in this case the leader. The process is essentially that of the "wheel" in communication net experiments, which has been found to be more efficient for the solution of simple problems than less centralized networks (Shaw, 1964).

However, if the problem is unstructured and the relevant information widely dispersed among persons, the organizational task is somewhat different. Under these circumstances it is less clear what information is relevant, and empirical evidence appears to favor a less centralized network which permits those with potentially relevant information to interact with one another in the course of solving the problem. This process is more akin to that in the circle networks, which have been found to be more effective in solving complex problems (Shaw, 1964). Within the model, this attribute bears on the relative efficiency of information collection activities that involve interaction among subordinates (that is, CII and GII) and those which do not involve such interaction (AII and CI).

E. The extent to which acceptance or commitment on the part of subordinates is critical to the effective implementation of the decision. In most situations, the effectiveness of an organizational decision is influenced both by its quality or rationality and by the extent to which it is accepted by subordinates. A decision can be ineffective because it did not utilize all of the available information concerning the external environment or because it was resisted and opposed by those who had to implement it.

The distinction between quality and acceptance is reminiscent of Bales's (1949) distinction between problems of the group involving goal achievement and adaptation to external demands and problems involving internal integration and expression of emotional tensions. Bales divides problems into two groups, adaptive-instrumental problems and integrative-expressive problems. In the framework being developed, quality and acceptance requirements are seen not as discrete types or even as opposite ends of a single continuum but rather as two separable dimensions. Just as the quality of the decision varies in importance from one problem to another, so also does the acceptance of the decision by subordinates, and there is no necessary correlation between these two dimensions.

There are two classes of situations in which acceptance of the decision by subordinates may be regarded as irrelevant to its effective implementation. One of these is what Maier (1970) has termed "outsider problems." In an "outsider problem," the subordinates are not involved in the execution of the decision. One may still desire their participation in order to enhance the quality of the solution, but the decision will be implemented by the leader or some other group. Acceptance by this particular set of persons is not critical to the ultimate success or failure of the decision.

The second type of situation in which acceptance or commitment to the decision by subordinates is not critical is that in which subordinates will be required to execute the decision but its nature is such that compliance on their part, rather than acceptance or commitment, is sufficient. Typically in such situations, subordinates' actions necessary for implementation of the decision are specific; the leader is able to monitor or observe these actions, and he controls rewards and punishments, which he is able to mete out accordingly. Both in the larger society and in organizations, people carry out directives to which they feel no personal commitment and, in fact, may be strongly opposed. The forces operating on them are "induced" forces rather than "own" forces (Lewin, 1935), and the conditions necessary for the successful induction of a force must be present. The actions must be observable by others who wish to see the directive carried out, and these others must control rewards and/or penalties, which are meted out in accordance with the degree of compliance observed.

Acceptance becomes more critical as the effective execution of the decision requires initiative, judgment, or creativity on the part of subordinates or when one or more of the conditions necessary for obtaining compliance breaks down; for example, the leader is unable to monitor subordinates' behavior and reward or punish deviations. Within the model, the interaction of this attribute with the following one determines the importance of attempting to develop subordinates' commitment to the final solution by employing a participative decision-making process.

F. The prior probability that the leader's autocratic decision will receive acceptance by subordinates. The relationship between participation in decision-making and the acceptance of decisions be subordinates is marked but probably not invariant with the nature of the problem and the context within which it occurs. Thus, Vroom (1960) found that the effects of participation varied with the subordinate's need for independence and authoritarianism. Similarly, in a field experiment in a Norwegian factory, French, Israel, and Ås (1960) discovered that the effects varied with subordinates' perceptions of the legitimacy of their participation, and Marrow (1964) has provided a brief account of some of the problems that occurred when the Harwood Manufacturing Company attempted to increase participation in decision-making, which had proved highly successful in their plants in the United States, in their newly acquired subsidiary in Puerto Rico.

It appears that participation is not a necessary condition for the acceptance of decisions. There are some circumstances in which the leader's decision has high prior probability of being accepted by subordinates. These circumstances are predictable from a knowledge of the relationship between the leader and his subordinates. French and Raven (1959) distinguish among five bases of power all of which are defined in terms of the relationship between the source and object of influence. Three of these bases (legitimate power, expert power, and referent power) are hypothesized to produce "own" forces on the object of influence to engage in the indicated action, thereby conforming to our definition of acceptance. Thus, the subordinates may accept the leader's decision because they believe that it is his legitimate right to make that decision by virtue of the position he occupies (legitimate power), because he is the acknowledged expert and the only one capable of taking all the necessary factors into consideration (expert power), or because he is strongly admired by them (referent power). In such situations, it is not at all difficult for the leader to "sell" his decision to his subordinates, thereby gaining the necessary acceptance.

There are many situations in which the prior probability of acceptance of a decision by subordinates will vary with the nature of the solution adopted. Some alternatives may be acceptable to subordinates and some may not. In effect, the prior probability of acceptance becomes a property of a solution rather than a property of the problem. To deal with the potential complexities introduced by this state of affairs, the following guidelines are suggested. For problems with a quality requirement (attribute A), the relevant prior probability of acceptance is that of the highest quality alternative known to the leader. Thus, if the leader has worked out a solution to a complex production-scheduling problem using critical path analysis and were convinced that it would work and would be superior to the present method and other alternatives known to him, one would be interested in the prior probability that this new method would be accepted by his subordinates.

For problems without a quality requirement, the relevant prior probability of acceptance is the highest value for any of the solutions meeting the constraints specified. In a case described earlier in this chapter—that of the plant manager assigning four reserved parking places among his six department heads—the level specified for prior probability would be that of the most palatable alternative to his subordinates.

This attribute is relevant to the choice of method only where acceptance is required in order for the decision to be effectively implemented (attribute E). It, in turn, determines whether participation in decision-making is necessary in order to attain that acceptance.

G. The extent to which subordinates are motivated to attain the organizational goals as represented in the objectives explicit in the statement of the problem. In all problems, there are one or more goals to be achieved. Ultimately, it is the attainment of those goals that determines whether the problem is actually solved. In effect, the general goal of organizational effectiveness is replaced by surrogate and more operational goals such as improving the safety record, reducing costs by 30 percent, or reorganizing to adapt to a cut in manpower while maintaining volume.

It is assumed that the quality of the decision reached is dependent not only on the information or expertise of those participating in it, but also on their disposition to use their information in the service of the goals stated in the problem. This phenomenon has seldom been examined in laboratory experiments on group problem-solving, where participants are motivated to solve the problem as accurately and as quickly as possible. But in formal organizations, there are many situations in which the goals of the group members may be in conflict with those stated in the problem. For example, decisions concerning the wage levels or the work loads of the participants may be among those which personal rather than organizational goals might dominate the search for and the evaluation of alternatives.

This problem attribute is similar to what Maier (1963) terms "mutual interest," and to the potential amount of trust that the leader can place in his subordinates to solve the

TABLE 3. Problem Attributes

A. If decision were accepted, would it make a difference which course of action were adopted?
B. Do I have sufficient information to make a high-quality decision?
C. Do subordinates have sufficient additional information to result in a high-quality decision?
D. Do I know exactly what information is needed, who possesses it, and how to collect it?
E. Is acceptance of decision by subordinates critical to effective implementation?
F. If I were to make the decision by myself, is it certain that it would be accepted by my subordinates?
G. Can subordinates be trusted to base solutions on organizational considerations?
H. Is conflict among subordinates likely in preferred solutions?

problem in the best interest of the organization. It determines the potential risk to the quality of the decision of methods like GII in which the leader relinquishes his final control over the decision.

H. The extent to which subordinates are likely to be in disagreement over preferred solutions. Conflicts or disagreements among group members over the appropriate solution are quite common features of decision-making in organizations. It is possible for group members to agree on a common goal but disagree over the best means of attaining it. Such disagreements can result from access to different information or from the fact that personal gains or losses from different solutions are negatively correlated.

There is substantial evidence from the literature in social psychology (see Brown, 1965) to indicate that interaction among people tends to increase their similarity in attitudes and opinions. Members of a group with initially wide variance in individual judgments will tend to converge on a common position. This process seems to be enhanced when the issue is relevant to their interaction and when the problem is of mutual interest. Thus, Kelley and Thibaut (1969) note in their review of the literature on group problem-solving that "group problem discussion generates pressures toward uniformity" (p. 71). This attribute determines the importance of choosing a decision-making process (CII and GII) in which subordinates interact in the process of solving the problem, as opposed to those (AII and CI) in which no such interaction takes place.

Table 3 shows the same eight problem attributes expressed in the form of questions which might be used by a leader in diagnosing a particular problem before choosing his leadership method. In phrasing the questions, technical language has been held to a minimum. Furthermore, the questions have been phrased in yes-no form, translating the continuous variables defined above into dichotomous variables. For example, instead of attempting to determine how important the decision quality is to the effectiveness of the decision (attribute *A*), the leader is asked in the first question to judge whether there is any quality component to the problem. Similarly, the difficult task of specifying exactly how much information the leader possesses that is relevant to the decision (attribute *B*) is reduced to a simple judgment by the leader concerning whether he has sufficient information to make a high quality decision.

Expressing what are obviously continuous variables in dichotomous form greatly simplifies the problem of incorporating these attributes into a model that can be used by leaders. It sidesteps the problem of scaling each problem attribute and reduces the complexity of the judgments required of leaders.

It has been found that managers can diagnose a situation quickly and accurately by answering a set of eight questions. But how can such responses generate a prescription for the most effective leadership method or decision process? What kind of normative model of participation in decision-making can be built from this set of problem attributes. These questions and our mode of resolving them will be taken up next.

A NORMATIVE MODEL

Let us assume that you are a manager faced with a concrete problem to be solved. We will also assume that you have judged that this problem could potentially affect more than one of your subordinates. Hence, it is what we have defined as a group problem, and you have to choose among the five decision processes (AI, AII, CI, CII, GII) shown at the left side of Table 1.

On *a priori* grounds any of these five decision processes could be called for. The judgments you have made concerning the status of each problem's attributes can be used to define a set of feasible alternatives. This occurs through a set of rules that eliminate decision processes from the feasible set under certain specifiable conditions.

The rules are intended to protect both the quality and the acceptance of the decision. In the present form of the model, there are three rules that protect decision quality and four that protect acceptance. The seven rules are presented here both as verbal statements and in the more formal language of set theory. In the set theoretic formulation, the letters refer to the problem attributes as stated in question form in Table 3. The letter A signifies that the answer to question A for a particular problem is *yes*; $\bar{A}$ signifies that the answer to that question is *no*; $\cap$ signifies intersection; $\Rightarrow$ signifies "implies"; and $\overline{AI}$ signifies not AI. Thus $A \cap B \Rightarrow \overline{AI}$ may be read as follows: when both the answer to question A is yes and the answer to question B is no, AI is eliminated from the feasible set.

1. *The information rule*. If the quality of the decision is important and if the leader does not possess enough information or expertise to solve the problem by himself, AI is eliminated from the feasible set. (Its use risks a low-quality decision.)

$$(A \cap \bar{B} \Rightarrow \overline{AI})$$

2. *The trust rule*. If the quality of the decision is important and if the subordinates cannot be trusted to base their efforts to solve the problem on organizational goals, GII is eliminated from the feasible set. (Alternatives that eliminate the leader's final control over the decision may jeopardize its quality.)

$$(A \cap \bar{G} \Rightarrow \overline{GII})$$

3. *The unstructured problem rule*. When the quality of the decision is important, if the leader lacks the necessary information or expertise to solve the problem by himself, and if the problem is unstructured, that is, he does not know exactly what information is needed and where it is located, the method used must provide not only for him to collect the information but to do so in an efficient manner. Methods which involve interaction among all subordinates with full knowledge of the problem are likely to be both more efficient and more likely to generate a high-quality solution to the problem. Under these conditions, AI, AII, and CI are eliminated from the feasible set. (AI does not provide for him to collect the necessary information, and AII and CI represent more cumbersome, less effective, and less efficient means of bringing the necessary information to bear on the solution of the problem than methods that do permit those with the necessary information to interact.)

$$(A \cap \bar{B} \cap \bar{D} \Rightarrow \overline{AI}, \overline{AII}, \overline{CI})$$

4. *The acceptance rule*. If the acceptance of the decision by subordinates is critical to effective implementation, and if it is not certain that an autocratic decision made by the leader would receive that acceptance, AI

and AII are eliminated from the feasible set. (Neither provides an opportunity for subordinates to participate in the decision, and both risk the necessary acceptance.)

$$(\bar{E} \cap \bar{F} \Rightarrow \overline{AI}, \overline{AII})$$

5. *The conflict rule.* If the acceptance of the decision is critical, an autocratic decision is not certain to be accepted, and subordinates are likely to be in conflict or disagreement over the appropriate solution, AI, AII, and CI are eliminated from the feasible set. (The method used in solving the problem should enable those in disagreement to resolve their differences with full knowledge of the problem. Accordingly, under these conditions, AI, AII, and CI, which involve no interaction or only "one-to-one" relationships and therefore provide no opportunity for those in conflict to resolve their differences, are eliminated from the feasible set. Their use runs the risk of leaving some of the subordinates with less than the necessary commitment to the final decision.)

$$(E \cap \bar{F} \cap H \Rightarrow \overline{AI}, \overline{AII}, \overline{CI})$$

6. *The fairness rule.* If the quality of decision is unimportant, and if acceptance is critical and not certain to result from an autocratic decision, AI, AII, CI, and CII are eliminated from the feasible set. (The method used should maximize the probability of acceptance as this is the only relevant consideration in determining the effectiveness of the decision. Under these circumstances AI, AII, CI, and CII, which create less acceptance or commitment than GII, are eliminated from the feasible set. To use them will run the risk of getting less than the required acceptance of the decision.)

$$(\bar{A} \cap E \cap \bar{F} \Rightarrow \overline{AI}, \overline{AII}, \overline{CI}, \overline{CII})$$

7. *The acceptance priority rule.* If acceptance is critical, not assured by an autocratic decision, and if subordinates can be trusted, AI, AII, CI, and CII are eliminated from the feasible set. (Methods which provide equal partnership in the decision-making process can provide greater acceptance without risking decision quality. Use of any method other than GII results in an unnecessary risk that the decision will not be fully accepted or receive the necessary commitment on the part of subordinates.)

$$(E \cap \bar{F} \cap G \Rightarrow \overline{AI}, \overline{AII}, \overline{CI}, \overline{CII})$$

It should be noted that some rules are nested within other rules such that violating one rule is a special case of violating another. Consider an unstructured problem in which the leader does not have sufficient information on which to make a high quality decision. Rule 1 excludes the use of AI (no opportunity to collect data), and rule 3 excludes AI, AII, and CI (no opportunity for group problem-solving). If rule 1 is violated in a problem for which rule 3 is applicable, then rule 3 is also violated. Since the applicability of rule 1 to the problem is a necessary but not sufficient condition for the applicability of rule 3, one can view rule 3 as "nested within" rule 1. Similarly, rules 5, 6, and 7 are nested within rule 4. Rule 4 is the basic acceptance rule which excludes AI and AII when acceptance is necessary and unlikely to exist for an autocratic decision. Rules 5, 6, and 7 further limit the feasible set as a function of additional properties of the problem. Thus, in the same way as the applicability of rule 1 is a necessary but not sufficient condition for the applicability of rule 3, rule 4 is necessary but not sufficient for rules 5, 6, and 7.

In applying these rules to a problem, you will find that it helps to represent them pictorially in the form of a decision tree. Figure 1 shows a simple decision tree that serves this purpose. The problem attributes are arranged along the top of the figure. To apply the rules to a particular problem, one starts at the left-hand side and works toward the right, asking oneself the question immediately above any box that is encountered. When a terminal node is reached, the number designates the problem type which in turn designates a set of methods that remain

A. If decision were accepted, would it make a difference which course of action were adopted?
B. Do I have sufficient information to make a high-quality decision?
C. Do subordinates have sufficient additional information to result in high-quality decision?
D. Do I know exactly what information is needed, who possesses it, and how to collect it?
E. Is acceptance of decision by subordinates critical to effective implementation?
F. If I were to make the decision by myself, is it certain that it would be accepted by my subordinates?
G. Can subordinates be trusted to base solutions on organizational considerations?
H. Is conflict among subordinates likely in preferred solutions?

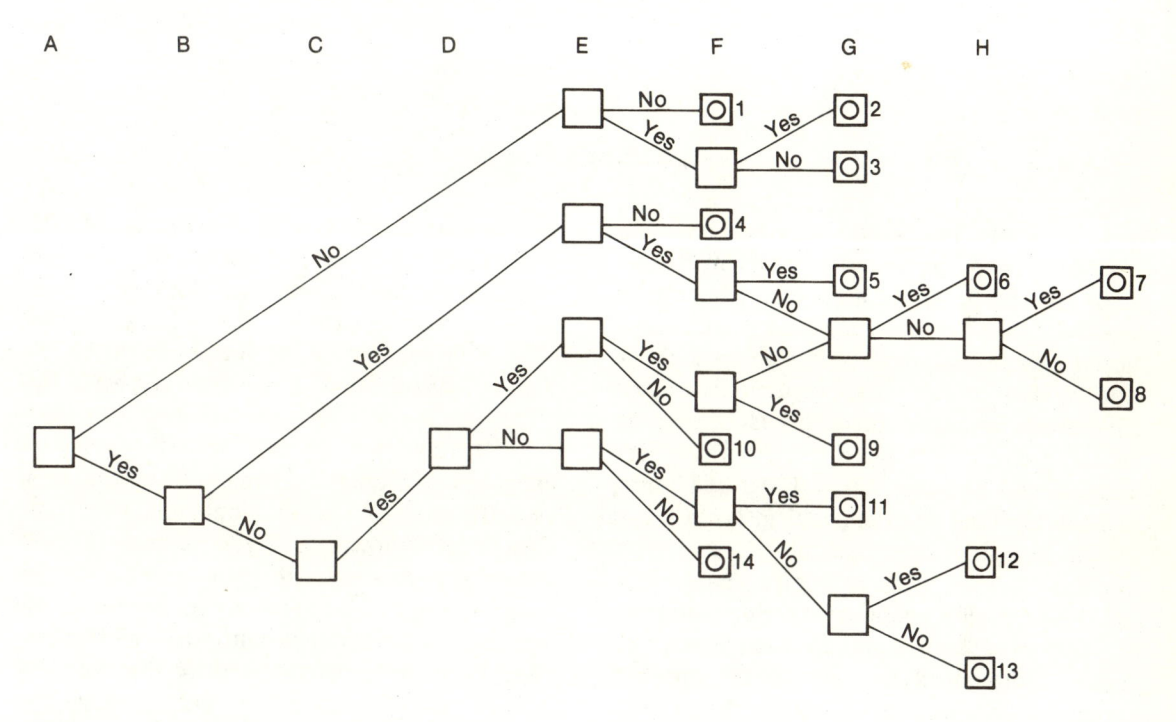

Figure 1. Problem types.

feasible after the rules have been applied.[1] It can be seen that this method of representing the decision tree generates fourteen problem types. Problem type is a nominal variable designating classes of problems generated by the paths that lead to the terminal nodes. Thus, all problems that have no quality requirement and in which acceptance is not critical are defined as type 1; all problems that have no quality requirement, in which acceptance is critical, but the prior probability of acceptance of the leader's decision is high, are defined as type 2, and so on.[2]

The feasible set for each of the fourteen problem types is shown in Table 4. It can be seen that there are some problem types for which only one method remains in the feasible set, others for which two methods remain feasible, and still others for which five methods remain feasible. It should be recalled that the feasible set is defined as the methods that remain after all those which violate rules designated to protect the quality and acceptance of the decision have been excluded.

Choosing Among Alternatives in the Feasible Set

When more than one method remains in the feasible set, there are a number of alternative decision rules which might dictate the choice among them. One, which will be examined in

TABLE 4. Problem Types and the Feasible Set of Decision Methods

Problem Type	Acceptable Methods
1	AI, AII, CI, CII, GII
2	AI, AII, CI, CII, GII
3	GII
4	AI, AII, CI, CII, GII*
5	AI, AII, CI, CII, GII*
6	GII
7	CII
8	CI, CII
9	AII, CI, CII, GII*
10	AII, CI, CII, GII*

*Within the feasible set only when the answer to question G is yes

greater depth, utilizes the number of man-hours required to solve the problem as the basis for choice. Given a set of methods with equal likelihood of meeting both quality and acceptance requirements for the decision, it selects the method that requires the least investment in man-hours. This is deemed to be the method furthest to the left within the feasible set. Thus, if AI, AII, CI, CII, and GII are all feasible, as in problem types 1 and 2, AI would be the method chosen. This decision rule acts to minimize man-hours, subject to quality and acceptance constraints.

Figure 2 shows the decision tree with methods prescribed for each of the problem types. In addition, two other attributes have been added to cover cases in which the group does not have sufficient information to make a decision. The attributes regulate predecisional activities such as problem identification and prior information collection. They do not affect choice of method except insofar as the net result of these activities is to affect the status of the situational attributes for that problem.

This decision rule for choosing among alternatives in the feasible set results in the prescription of each of the five decision processes in some situations. Method AI is prescribed for four problem types (1, 2, 4, and 5); AII is prescribed for two problem types (9 and 10); CI is prescribed for only one problem type (8); CII is prescribed for four problem types (7, 11, 13, and 14); and GII is prescribed for three problem types (3, 6, and 12). The relative frequency with which the five decision processes would be prescribed for any leader would, of course, be dependent on the distribution of problem types in his role.

It should be noted that the order of problem attributes is irrelevant to the final specification of the decision-making process. The order shown in Figure 2 was selected because it minimizes the number of branches and terminal nodes necessary to determine the process in accordance with the rules given. Any other order would increase the complexity of the decision tree and increase the number of terminal nodes. For example, if conflict were switched from position H to position A and each other attribute advanced by one position, the number of terminal nodes would be increased from fourteen to twenty-six.

The Composition of the Group

In phrasing the attributes in the model for group problems, the term subordinates has been used frequently. Attribute C deals with the information possessed by subordinates, attribute F with the prior probability of acceptance of the leader's decision by subordinates, and so on. The choice of the term subordinate to refer to other potential par-

A. If decision were accepted, would it make a difference which course of action were adopted?
B. Do I have sufficient information to make a high-quality decision?
C. Do subordinates have sufficient additional information to result in high-quality decision?
D. Do I know exactly what information is needed, who possesses it, and how to collect it?
* Is necessary additional information to be found within my entire set of subordinates?
† Is it feasible to collect additional information outside group prior to making decisions?
E. Is acceptance of decision by subordinates critical to effective implementation?
F. If I were to make the decision by myself, is it certain that it would be accepted by my subordinates?
G. Can subordinates be trusted to base solutions on organizational considerations?
H. Is conflict among subordinates likely in preferred solutions?

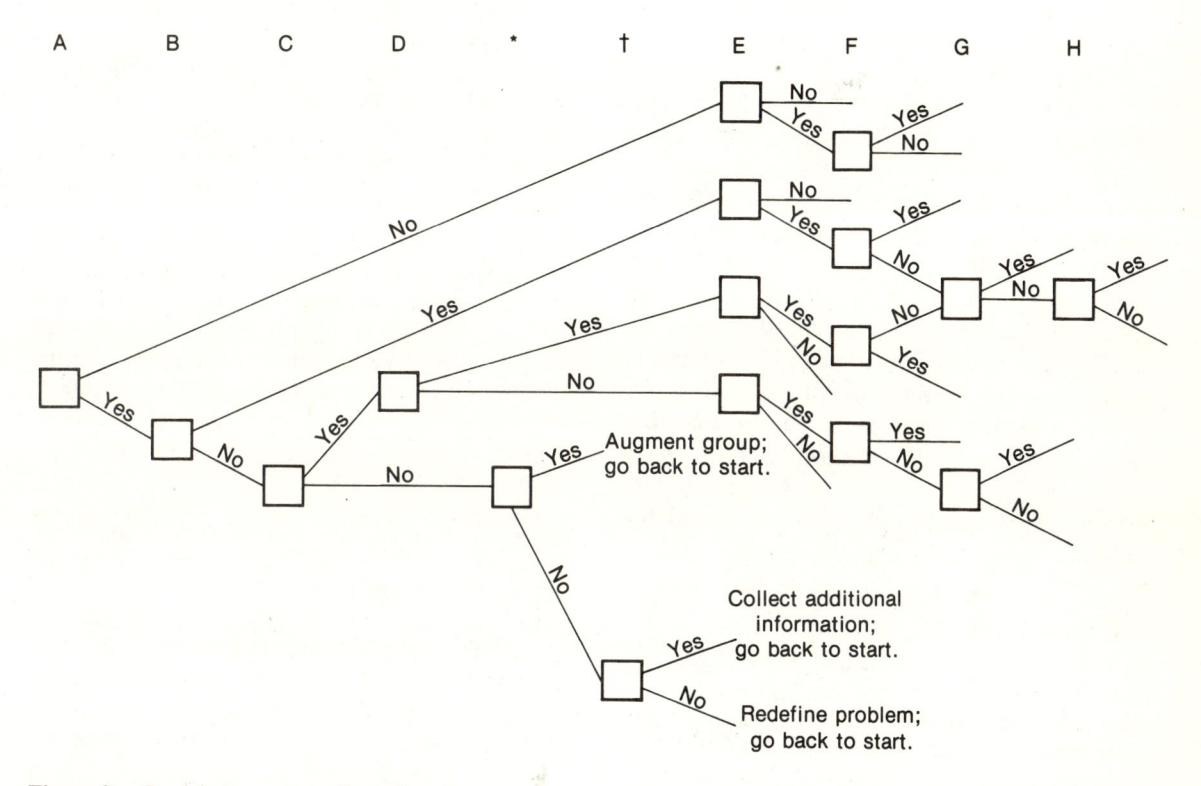

Figure 2. Decision—process flow chart.

ticipants in the decision-making process should not be taken to mean that the members of the group are necessarily those defined by the organization chart as reporting to the leader. Many problems cut across organizational boundaries, and the groups, task forces, or committees set up to solve them are made up of persons from many different parts of the organization. Such problem-solving units typically have a leader, chairman, or head, and we consider the attributes as being equally relevant for this leader's choice of decision-making process as in the more traditional case of a formal organization unit. Thus, the subordinates referred to in the problem attributes can be taken more broadly to mean members of the group formally established to deal with that problem.

But what of the case in which the group of potential participants is ambiguous and not defined by any existing organizational unit, even one with temporary membership? Does the model have any implications for the composition of the group where none has existed in the past? These questions are potentially separable from the model, which deals primarily with the choice of decision-making process given a specified leader, problem, and group. The following mechanisms are, however, consistent with the basic framework and may be useful as a point of departure for future thinking and research on the subject. Let us begin by defining as the group that set of persons or their representatives who are potentially affected by the decision. This set of persons may be the entire set of subordinates reporting to the leader; they may be a subset of those subordinates; or they may be persons from different parts of the formal organization. In the event that this group, including the leader, does not have the necessary information and expertise, the model shown in Figure 2 provides a means of augmenting the size of the group (see pre-decisional mechanism) until such time as the necessary information is represented within the group. It is only at that time when the decision-making process can be determined through the use of the model.

NOTES

1. Rule 2 has not been applied to problem types 4, 9, 10, 11, and 14. This rule eliminates GII from the feasible set when the answer to question *G* is no. Thus, we can distinguish two variants of each of these types.

2. An inspection of the structure of the flow diagram reveals that three problem types (6, 7, and 8) can be further subdivided. To each of these three terminal nodes, there are two alternative paths, which diverge at attribute *B* (leader's information). Thus, one could broaden the classification of problem types, differentiating those of types 6, 7, and 8 into subcategories.

REFERENCES

Ansoff, H. I., *Corporate strategy* (New York: McGraw-Hill) 1965.

Argyris, C., *Interpersonal competence and organizational effectiveness* (Homewood, Ill.: Irwin) 1962.

Bales, R. F., and P. E. Slater, "Role differentiation in small groups," in *Family, socialization and interaction process,* by T. Parsons, R. F. Bales, *et al.* (Glencoe, Ill.: Free Press) 1955.

Bennis, W. G. *Changing organizations* (New York: McGraw-Hill) 1966.

Brown, R. *Social psychology* (New York: Free Press) 1965.

Coch, L., and J. R. P. French, Jr. "Overcoming resistance to change," *Human Relations,* 1948, Vol. 1, 512-32.

Fiedler, F. E. *A theory of leadership effectiveness* (New York: McGraw-Hill) 1967.

French, J. R. P., Jr., "Field experiments: changing group productivity," in *Experiments in social process: a symposium on social psychology,* ed. J. G. Miller (New York: McGraw-Hill) 1950.

French, J. R. P., Jr., J. Israel, and D. As, "An experiment on participation in a Norwegian factory," *Human Relations,* 1960, Vol. 13, 3-19.

French, J. R. P., Jr., and B. Raven, "The bases of social power," in *Studies in social power,* ed. D. Cartwright (Ann Arbor, Mich.: Institute for Social Research) 1959.

Heller, F. A. *Managerial decision making* (London: Tavistock) 1971.

Katz, D., N. Maccoby, and N. C. Morse, "Productivity, supervision, and morale in an office situation" (Ann Arbor: University of Michigan, Institute for Social Research) 1950.

Kelley, H., and J. Thibaut, "Group problem solving," in *Handbook of social psychology,* edited by G. Lindzey and E. Aronson, Vol. 4, pp. 1-101 (Reading, Mass.: Addison-Wesley) 1969.

Lewin, K. *A dynamic theory of personality* (New York: McGraw-Hill) 1935.

Lewin, K., R. Lippitt, and R. K. White, "Patterns of aggressive behavior in experimentally created social climates," *Journal of Social Psychology,* 1939, Vol. 10, 271-99.

Likert, R. *The human organization* (New York: McGraw-Hill) 1967.

Lowin, A., "Participative decision making: a model, literature critique, and prescriptions for research," *Organizational Behavior and Human Performance,* 1968, Vol. 3, 68-106.

McGregor, D., "Getting effective leadership in the industrial organization," *Advanced Management,* 1944, Vol. 9, 148-53.

Maier, N. R. F. *Psychology in industry*. 2nd ed. (Boston: Houghton Mifflin) 1955.

Maier, N. R. F. *Problem-solving discussions and conferences: leadership methods and skills* (New York: McGraw-Hill) 1963.

Maier, N. R. F. *Problem solving and creativity in individuals and groups* (Belmont, Calif.: Brooks-Cole) 1970.

Marrow, A. J., "Risk and uncertainties in action research," *Journal of Social Issues,* 1964, Vol. 20, 5-20.

Shaw, M. E., "Communication networks" in *Advances in experimental psychology,* edited by L. Berkowitz, Vol. 1, pp. 111-147 (New York: Academic Press) 1964.

Simon, H. A. *The new science of management decision* (New York: Harper) 1960.

Tannenbaum, R., and Schmidt, W., "How to choose a leadership pattern," *Harvard Business Review,* 1958, Vol. 36, 95-101.

Vroom, V. H. *Some personality determinants of the effects of participation* (Englewood Cliffs, N.J.: Prentice-Hall) 1960.

Vroom, V. H., "Industrial social psychology," in *Handbook of social psychology,* edited by G. Lindzey and E. Aronson, Vol. 5, pp. 196-268 (Reading, Mass.: Addison-Wesley) 1970.

Whyte, W. F. *Money and motivation: an analysis of incentives in industry* (New York: Harper) 1955.

Wood, M. J. "Power relationships and group decision making in organizations, *Psychological Bulletin,* 1974 (in press).

Robert J. House
Terence R. Mitchell

PATH-GOAL THEORY OF LEADERSHIP

An integrated body of conjecture by students of leadership, referred to as the "Path-Goal Theory of Leadership," is currently emerging. According to this theory, leaders are effective because of their impact on subordinates' motivation, ability to perform effectively and satisfactions. The theory is called *path-goal* because its major concern is how the leader influences the subordinates' perceptions of their work goals, personal goals and paths to goal attainment. The theory suggests that a leader's behavior is motivating or satisfying to the degree that the behavior increases subordinate goal attainment and clarifies the paths to these goals.

HISTORICAL FOUNDATIONS

The path-goal approach has its roots in a more general motivational theory called expectancy theory.[1] Briefly, expectancy theory states that an individual's attitudes (e.g., satisfaction with supervision or job satisfaction) or behavior (e.g., leader behavior or job effort) can be predicted from: (1) the degree to which the job, or behavior, is seen as leading to various outcomes (expectancy) and (2) the evaluation of these outcomes (valences). Thus, people are satisfied with their job if they think it leads to things that are highly valued, and they work hard if they believe that effort leads to things that are highly valued. This type of theoretical rationale can be used to predict a variety of phenomena related to leadership, such as why leaders behave the way they do, or how leader behavior influences subordinate motivation.[2]

This latter approach is the primary concern of this article. The implication for leadership is that subordinates are motivated by leader behavior to the extent that this behavior influences expectancies, e.g., goal paths and valences (e.g., goal attractiveness).

Several writers have advanced specific hypotheses concerning how the leader affects the paths and goals of subordinates.[3] These writers focused on two issues: (1) how the leader affects subordinates' expectations that effort will lead to effective performance and valued rewards, and (2) how this expectation affects motivation to work hard and perform well.

While the state of theorizing about leadership in terms of subordinates' paths and goals is in its infancy, we believe it is promising for two reasons. First, it suggests effects of leader behavior that have not yet been investigated but which appear to be fruitful areas of inquiry. And, second, it

---

Reprinted by permission of the publisher from *Journal of Contemporary Business,* Autumn, 1974, pp. 81-98. This article is also reprinted in *Readings in Organizational and Industrial Psychology* by G. A. Yukl and K. N. Wexley, 2nd edition (1975). The research by House and his associates was partially supported by a grant from the Shell Oil Company of Canada. The research by Mitchell and his associates was partially supported by the Office of Naval Research Contract NR 170-761, N00014-67-A-0103-0032 (Terence R. Mitchell, Principal Investigator).

suggests with some precision the situational factors on which the effects of leader behavior are contingent.

The initial theoretical work by Evans asserts that leaders will be effective by making rewards available to subordinates and by making these rewards contingent on the subordinate's accomplishment of specific goals.[4] Evans argued that one of the strategic functions of the leader is to clarify for subordinates the kind of behavior that leads to goal accomplishment and valued rewards. This function might be referred to as path clarification. Evans also argued that the leader increases the rewards available to subordinates by being supportive toward subordinates, i.e., by being concerned about their status, welfare and comfort. Leader supportiveness is in itself a reward that the leader has at his or her disposal, and the judicious use of this reward increases the motivation of subordinates.

Evans studied the relationship between the behavior of leaders and the subordinates' expectations that effort leads to rewards and also studied the resulting impact on ratings of the subordinates' performance. He found that when subordinates viewed leaders as being supportive (considerate of their needs) and when these superiors provided directions and guidance to the subordinates, there was a positive relationship between leader behavior and subordinates' performance ratings.

However, leader behavior was only related to subordinates' performance when the leader's behavior also was related to the subordinates' expectations that their effort would result in desired rewards. Thus, Evans' findings suggest that the major impact of a leader on the performance of subordinates is clarifying the path to desired rewards and making such rewards contingent on effective performance.

Stimulated by this line of reasoning, House, and House and Dessler advanced a more complex theory of the effects of leader behavior on the motivation of subordinates.[5]

The theory intends to explain the effects of four specific kinds of leader behavior on the following three subordinate attitudes or expectations: (1) the satisfaction of subordinates, (2) the subordinates' acceptance of the leader and (3) the expectations of subordinates that effort will result in effective performance and that effective performance is the path to rewards. The four kinds of leader behavior included in the theory are: (1) directive leadership, (2) supportive leadership, (3) participative leadership and (4) achievement-oriented leadership. Directive leadership is characterized by a leader who lets subordinates know what is expected of them, gives specific guidance as to what should be done and how it should be done, makes his or her part in the group understood, schedules work to be done, maintains definite standards of performance, and asks that group members follow standard rules and regulations. Supportive leadership is characterized by a friendly and approachable leader who shows concern for the status, well-being and needs of subordinates. Such a leader does little things to make the work more pleasant, treats members as equals and is friendly and approachable. Participative leadership is characterized by a leader who consults with subordinates, solicits their suggestions and takes these suggestions seriously into consideration before making a decision. An achievement-oriented leader sets challenging goals, expects subordinates to perform at their highest level, continuously seeks improvement in performance *and* shows a high degree of confidence that the subordinates will assume responsibility, put forth effort and accomplish challenging goals. This kind of leader constantly emphasizes excellence in performance and simultaneously displays confidence that subordinates will meet high standards of excellence.

A number of studies suggest that these different leadership styles can be shown by the same leader in various situations.[6] For example, a leader may show directiveness toward subordinates in some instances and be participative or supportive in other instances.[7] Thus, the traditional method of characterizing a leader as either highly participative and supportive *or* highly directive is invalid; rather, it can be concluded that leaders vary in the particular fashion employed for supervising their subordinates. Also, the theory, in its present stage, is a tentative explanation of the effects of leader behavior—it is incomplete because it does not explain other kinds of leader behavior and does not explain the effects of the leader on factors other than subordinate acceptance, satisfaction and expectations. However, the theory is stated so that additional variables may be included in it as new knowledge is made available.

PATH-GOAL THEORY

General Propositions

The first proposition of path-goal theory is that leader behavior is acceptable and satisfying to subordinates to the extent that the subordinates see such behavior as either an immediate source of satisfaction or as instrumental to future satisfaction.

The second proposition of this theory is that the leader's behavior will be motivational, i.e., increase effort, to the extent that (1) such behavior makes satisfaction of subordinate's needs contingent on effective performance and (2) such behavior complements the environment of subordinates by providing the coaching, guidance, support and rewards necesary for effective performance.

These two propositions suggest that the leader's strategic functions are to enhance subordinates' motivation to perform, satisfaction with the job and acceptance of the leader. From previous research on expectancy theory of motivation, it can be inferred that the strategic functions of the leader consist of: (1) recognizing and/or arousing subordinates' needs for outcomes over which the leader has some control, (2) increasing personal pay-offs to subordinates for work-goal attainment, (3) making the path to those payoffs easier to travel by coaching and direction, (4) helping subordinates clarify expectancies, (5) reducing frustrating barriers and (6) increasing the opportunities for personal satisfaction contingent on effective performance.

Stated less formally, the motivational functions of the leader consist of increasing the number and kinds of personal payoffs to subordinates for work-goal attainment and making paths to these payoffs easier to travel by clarifying the paths, reducing road blocks and pitfalls and increasing the opportunities for personal satisfaction en route.

Contingency Factors

Two classes of situational variables are asserted to be contingency factors. A contingency factor is a variable which moderates the relationship between two other variables such as leader behavior and subordinate satisfaction. For example, we might suggest that the degree of structure in the task moderates the relationship between leaders' directive behavior and subordinates' job satisfaction. Figure 1 shows how such a relationship might look. Thus, subordinates are satisfied with directive behavior in an unstructured task and are satisfied with nondirective behavior in a structured task. Therefore, we say that the relationship between leader directiveness and subordinate satisfaction is contingent upon the structure of the task.

The two contingency variables are (a) personal characteristics of the subordinates and (b) the environmental pressures and demands with which subordinates must cope in order to accomplish the work goals and to satisfy their needs. While other situational factors also may operate to determine the effects of leader behavior, they are not presently known.

With respect to the first class of contingency factors, the characteristics of subordinates, path-goal theory asserts that leader behavior will be acceptable to subordinates to the extent that the subordinates see such behavior as either an immediate source of satisfaction or as instrumental to future satisfaction. Subordinates' characteristics are hypothesized to partially determine this perception. For example, Runyon [8] and Mitchell [9] show that the subordinate's score on a measure called *Locus of Control* moderates the relationship between participative leadership style and subordinate satisfaction. The Locus-of-Control measure reflects the degree to which an individual sees the environment as systematically responding to his or her behavior. People who believe that what happens to them occurs because of their behavior are called internals; people who believe that what happens to them occurs because of luck or chance are called externals. Mitchell's findings suggest that inernals are more satisfied with a participative leadership style and externals are more satisfied with a directive style.

A second characteristic of subordinates on which the effects of leader behavior are contingent is subordinates' perception of their own ability with respect to their assigned tasks. The higher the degree of perceived ability relative to task demands, the less the subordinate will view leader directiveness and coaching behavior as acceptable. Where the subordinate's perceived ability is high, such behavior is likely to have little positive effect on the motivation of the subordinate and to be perceived as excessively close control. Thus, the acceptability of the leader's behavior is determined in part by the characteristics of the subordinates.

The second aspect of the situation, the environment of the subordinate, consists of those factors that are not within the control of the subordinate but which are important to need satisfaction or to ability to perform effectively. The theory asserts that effects of the leader's behavior on the psychological states of subordinates are contingent on other parts of the subordinates' environment that are relevant to subordinate motivation. Three broad classifications of contingency factors in the environment are:

The subordinates' tasks.

The formal authority system of the organization.

The primary work group.

Assessment of the environmental conditions makes it possible to predict the kind and amount of influence that specific leader behaviors will have on the motivation of subordinates. Any of the three environmental factors could act upon the subordinate in any of three ways: first, to serve as stimuli that motivate and direct the subordinate to perform necessary task operations; second, to constrain variability in behavior. Constraints may help the subordinate by clarifying expectancies that effort leads to rewards or by preventing the subordinate from experiencing conflict and confusion. Constraints also may be counterproductive to the extent that they restrict initiative or prevent increases in effort from being associated positively with rewards. Third, environmental factors may serve as rewards for achieving desired performance, e.g., it is possible for the subordinate to

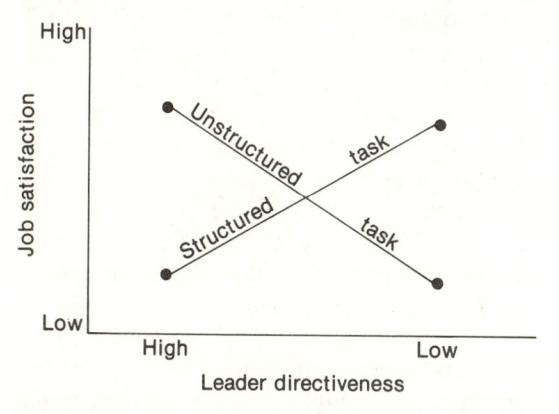

Figure 1. Hypothetical relationship between directive leadership and subordinate satisfaction with task structure as a contingency factor.

receive the necessary cues to do the job and the needed rewards for satisfaction from sources other than the leader, e.g., co-workers in the primary work group. Thus, the effect of the leader on subordinates' motivation will be a function of how deficient the environment is with respect to motivational stimuli, constraints or rewards.

With respect to the environment, path-goal theory asserts that when goals and paths to desired goals are apparent because of the routine nature of the task, clear group norms or objective controls of the formal authority systems, attempts by the leader to clarify paths and goals will be both redundant and seen by subordinates as imposing unnecessary, close control. Although such control may increase performance by preventing soldiering or malingering, it also will result in decreased satisfaction (see Figure 1). Also with respect to the work environment, the theory asserts that the more dissatisfying the task, the more the subordinates will resent leader behavior directed at increasing productivity or enforcing compliance to organizational rules and procedures.

Finally, with respect to environmental variables the theory states that leader behavior will be motivational to the extent that it helps subordinates cope with environmental uncertainties, threats from others or sources of frustration. Such leader behavior is predicted to increase subordinates' satisfaction with the job context and to be motivational to the extent that it increases the subordinates' expectations that their effort will lead to valued rewards.

These propositions and specification of situational contingencies provide a heuristic framework on which to base future research. Hopefully, this will lead to a more fully developed, explicitly formal theory of leadership.

Figure 2 presents a summary of the theory. It is hoped that these propositions, while admittedly tentative, will provide managers with some insights concerning the effects of their own leader behavior and that of others.

EMPIRICAL SUPPORT

The theory has been tested in a limited number of studies which have generated considerable empirical support for our ideas and also suggest areas in which the theory requires revision. A brief review of these studies follows.

Leader Directiveness

Leader directiveness has a positive correlation with satisfaction and expectancies of subordinates who are engaged in ambiguous tasks and has a negative correlation with satisfaction and expectancies of subordinates engaged in clear tasks. These findings were predicted by the theory and have been replicated in seven organizations. They suggest that when task demands are ambiguous or when the organization procedures, rules and policies are not clear, a leader behaving in a directive manner complements the tasks and the organization by providing the necessary guidance and psychological structure for subordinates.[10] However, when task demands are clear to subordinates, leader directiveness is seen more as a hindrance.

However, other studies have failed to confirm these findings.[11] A study by Dessler[12] suggests a resolution to these conflicting findings—he found that for subordinates at the lower organizational levels of a manufacturing firm who were doing routine, repetitive, unambiguous tasks, directive leadership was preferred by closed-minded, dogmatic, authoritarian subordinates and nondirective leadership was preferred by non-authoritarian, open-minded subordinates. However, for subordinates at higher organizational levels doing nonroutine, ambiguous tasks, directive leadership was preferred for both authoritar-

Leader behavior	and	contingency factors	cause	subordinate attitudes and behavior
1 Directive		1 Subordinate characteristics Authoritarianism Locus of control Ability	Influence → Personal perceptions	1 Job satisfaction Job → rewards
2 Supportive				2 Acceptance of leader Leader → rewards
3 Achievement-oriented		2 Environmental factors The task Formal authority system Primary work group	Influence → Motivational stimuli Constraints Rewards	3 Motivational behavior Effort → performance Performance → rewards
4 Participative				

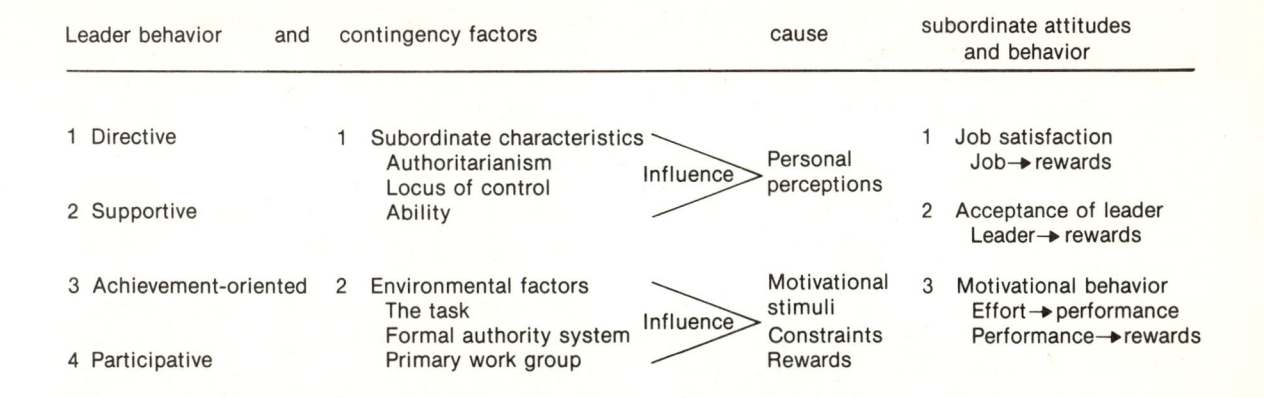

Figure 2. Summary of Path-Goal Relationships

ian and nonauthoritarian subordinates. Thus, Dessler found that two contingency factors appear to operate simultaneously: subordinate task ambiguity and degree of subordinate authoritarianism. When measured in combination, the findings are as predicted by the theory; however, when the subordinate's personality is not taken into account, task ambiguity does not always operate as a contingency variable as predicted by the theory. House, Burill, and Dessler recently found a similar interaction between subordinate authoritarianism and task ambiguity in a second manufacturing firm, thus adding confidence in Dessler's original findings.[13]

Supportive Leadership

The theory hypothesizes that supportive leadership will have its most positive effect on subordinate satisfaction for subordinates who work on stressful, frustrating or dissatisfying tasks. This hypothesis has been tested in 10 samples of employees,[14] and in only one of these studies was the hypothesis disconfirmed.[15] Despite some inconsistency in research on supportive leadership, the evidence is sufficiently positive to suggest that managers should be alert to the critical need for supportive leadership under conditions where tasks are dissatisfying, frustrating or stressful to subordinates.

Achievement-Oriented Leadership

The theory hypothesizes that achievement-oriented leadership will cause subordinates to strive for higher standards of performance and to have more confidence in the ability to meet challenging goals. A recent study by House, Valency and Van der Krabben provides a partial test of this hypothesis among white collar employees in service organizations.[16] For subordinates performing ambiguous, nonrepetitive tasks, they found a positive relationship between the amount of achievement orientation of the leader and subordinates' expectancy that their effort would result in effective performance. Stated less technically, for subordinates performing ambiguous, nonrepetitive tasks, the higher the achievement orientation of the leader, the more the subordinates were confident that their efforts would pay off in effective performance. For subordinates performing moderately unambiguous, repetitive tasks, there was no significant relationship between achievement-oriented leadership and subordinate expectancies that their effort would lead to effective performance. This finding held in four separate organizations.

Two plausible interpretations may be used to explain these data. First, people who select ambiguous, nonrepetitive tasks may be different in personality from those who select a repetitive job and may, therefore, be more responsive to an achievement-oriented leader. A second explanation is that achievement orientation only affects expectancies in ambiguous situations because there is more flexibility and automony in such tasks. Therefore, subordinates in such tasks are more likely to be able to change in response to such leadership style Neither of the above interpretations have been tested to date; however, additional research is currently under way to investigate these relationships.

Participative Leadership

In theorizing about the effects of participative leadership it is necessary to ask about the specific characteristics of both the subordinates and their situation that would cause participative leadership to be viewed as satisfying and instrumental to effective performance.

Mitchell recently described at least four ways in which a participative leadership style would impact on subordinate attitudes and behavior as predicted by expectancy theory.[17] First, a participative climate should increase the clarity of organizational contingencies. Through participation in decision making, subordinates should learn what leads to what. From a path-goal viewpoint participation would lead to greater clarity of the paths to various goals. A second impact of participation would be that subordinates, hopefully, should select goals they highly value. If one participates in decisions about various goals, it makes sense that this individual would select goals he or she wants. Thus, participation would increase the correspondence between organization and subordinate goals. Third, we can see how participation would increase the control the individual has over what happens on the job. If our motivation is higher (based on the preceding two points), then having greater autonomy and ability to carry out our intentions should lead to increased effort and performance. Finally, under a participative system, pressure towards high performance should come from sources other than the leader or the organization. More specifically, when people participate in the decision process they become more ego-involved; the decisions made are in some part their own. Also, their peers know what is expected and the social pressure has a greater impact. Thus, motivation to perform well stems from internal and social factors as well as formal external ones.

A number of investigations prior to the above formulation supported the idea that participation appears to be helpful,[18] and Mitchell presents a number of recent studies that support the above four points.[19] However, it is also true that we would expect the relationship between a participative style and subordinate behavior to be moderated by both the personality characteristics of the subordinate and the situational demands. Studies by Tannenbaum and Alport and Vroom have shown that subordinates who prefer autonomy and self-control respond more positively to participative leadership in terms of both satisfaction and performance than subordinates who do not have such preferences.[20] Also, the studies mentioned by Runyon[21] and Mitchell[22] showed that subordinates who were external in orientation were less satisfied with a participative style of leadership than were internal subordinates.

House also has reviewed these studies in an attempt to explain the ways in whch the situation or environment moderates the relationship between participation and subordinate attitudes and behavior.[23] His analysis suggests that where participative leadership is positively related to satisfaction, regardless of the predispositions of the subordinates, the tasks of the subjects appear to be ambiguous and ego-involving. In the studies in which the subjects' personalities or predispositions moderate the effect of participative leadership, the tasks of the subjects are inferred to be highly routine and/or nonego-involving.

House reasoned from this analysis that the task may have an overriding effect on the relationship between leader participation and subordinate responses, and that individual predispositions or personality characteristics of subordinates may have an effect only under some tasks. It was assumed that when task demands are ambiguous, subordinates will have a need to reduce the ambiguity. Further, it was assumed that when task demands are ambiguous, participative problem solving between the leader and the subordinate will result in more effective decisions than when the task demands are unambiguous. Finally, it was assumed that when the subordinates are ego-involved in their tasks they are more likely to want to have a say in the decisions that affect them. Given these assumptions, the following hypotheses were formulated to account for the conflicting findings reviewed above:

- When subjects are highly ego-involved in a decision or a task and the decision or task demands are ambiguous, participative leadership will have a positive effect on the satisfaction and motivation of the subordinate, *regardless* of the subordinate's predisposition toward self-control, authoritarianism or need for independence.

- When subordinates are not ego-involved in their tasks and when task demands are clear, subordinates who are not authoritarian and who have high needs for independence and self-control will respond favorably to leader participation and their opposite personality types will respond less favorably.

These hypotheses were derived on the basis of path-goal theorizing; i.e., the rationale guiding the analysis of prior studies was that both task characteristics and characteristics of subordinates interact to determine the effect of a specific kind of leader behavior on the satisfaction, expectancies and performance of subordinates. To date, one major investigation has supported some of these predictions [24] in which personality variables, amount of participative leadership, task ambiguity and job satisfaction were assessed for 324 employees of an industrial manufacturing organization. As expected, in nonrepetitive, ego-involving tasks, employees (regardless of their personality) were more satisfied under a participative style than a nonparticipative style. However, in repetitive tasks which were less ego-involving the amount of authoritarianism of subordinates moderated the relationship between leadership style and satisfaction. Specifically, low authoritarian subordinates were *more satisfied* under a participative style. These findings are exactly as the theory would predict, thus, it has promise in reconciling a set of confusing and contradictory findings with respect to participative leadership.

SUMMARY AND CONCLUSIONS

We have attempted to describe what we believe is a useful theoretical framework for understanding the effect of leadership behavior on subordinate satisfaction and motivation. Most theorists today have moved away from the simplistic notions that all effective leaders have a certain set of personality traits or that the situation completely determines performance. Some researchers have presented rather complex attempts at matching certain types of leaders with certain types of situations, e.g., the articles written by Vroom and Fiedler in this issue. But, we believe that a path-goal approach goes one step further. It not only suggests what type of style may be most effective in a given situation—it also attempts to explain *why* it is most effective.

We are optimistic about the future outlook of leadership research. With the guidance of path-goal theorizing, future research is expected to unravel many confusing puzzles about the reasons for and effects of leader behavior that have, heretofore, not been solved. However, we add a word of caution: the theory, and the research on it, are relatively new to the literature of organizational behavior. Consequently, path-goal theory is offered more as a tool for directing research and stimulating insight than as a proven guide for managerial action.

NOTES

1. T. R. Mitchell, "Expectancy Model of Job Satisfaction, Occupational Preference and Effort: A Theoretical, Methodological and Empirical Appraisal," *Psychological Bulletin* (1974).

2. D. M. Nebeker and T. R. Mitchell, "Leader Behavior: An Expectancy Theory Approach," *Organization Behavior and Human Performance,* Vol. 11 (1974), pp. 355-367.

3. M. G. Evans, "The Effects of Supervisory Behavior on the Path-Goal Relationship," *Organization Behavior and Human Performance,* Vol. 55 (1970), pp. 277-298; T. H. Hammer and H. T. Dachler, "The Process of Supervision in the Context of Motivation Theory," Research Report No. 3 (University of Maryland, 1973); F. Dansereau, Jr., J. Cashman and G. Graen, "Instrumentality Theory and Equity Theory As Complementary Approaches in Predicting the Relationship of Leadership and Turnover Among Managers," *Organization Behavior and Human Performance,* Vol. 10 (1973), pp. 184-200; R. J. House, "A Path-Goal Theory of Leader Effectiveness," *Administrative Science Quarterly,* Vol. 16, 3 (September 1971), pp. 321-338; T. R. Mitchell, "Motivation and Participation: An Integration," *Academy of Management Journal,* Vol. 16, 4(1973), pp. 160-179; G. Graen, F. Dansereau, Jr. and T. Minami, "Dysfunctional Leadership Styles," *Organization Behavior and Human Performance,* Vol. 7 (1972), pp. 216-236; "An Empirical Test of the Man-in-the-Middle Hypothesis Among Executives in a Hierarchical Organization Employing a Unit Analysis," *Organization Behavior and Human Performance,* Vol. 8 (1972), pp. 262-285; R. J. House and G. Dessler, "The Path-Goal Theory of Leadership: Some *Post Hoc* and *A Priori* Tests," in J. G. Hunt, ed., *Contingency Approaches to Leadership* (Carbondale, Ill.: Southern Illinois University Press), 1974.

4. M. G. Evans, "Effects of Supervisory Behavior"; "Extensions of a Path-Goal Theory of Motivation," *Journal of Applied Psychology,* Vol. 59 (1974), pp. 172-178.

5. R. J. House, "A Path-Goal Theory;" R. J. House and G. Dessler, "Path-Goal Theory of Leadership."

6. R. J. House and G. Dessler, "Path-Goal Theory of Leadership;" R. M. Stogdill, *Managers, Employees, Organization* (Columbus, O.: Ohio State University, Bureau of Business Research, 1965); R. J. House, A. Valency and R. Van der Krabben, "Some Tests and Extensions of the Path-Goal Theory of Leadership."

7. W. A. Hill and D. Hughes, "Variations in Leader Behavior As a Function of Task Type," *Organization Behavior and Human Performance* (1974).

8. K. E. Runyon, "Some Interactions Between Personality Variables and Management Styles," *Journal of Applied Psychology,* Vol. 57 3 (1973), pp. 288-294; T. R. Mitchell, C. R. Smyser and S. E. Weed, "Locus of Control: Supervision and Work Satisfaction," *Academy of Management Journal.*

9. T. R. Mitchell, "Locus of Control."

10. R. J. House, "A Path-Goal Theory; R. J. House and G. Dessler, "Path-Goal Theory of Leadership;" A. D. Szalagyi and H. P. Sims, "An Exploration of the Path-Goal Theory of Leadership in a Health Care Environment," *Academy of Management Journal* (in press); J. D. Dermer, "Supervisory Behavior and Budget Motivation" (Cambridge, Mass.: unpublished, MIT, Sloan School of Management, 1974); R. W. Smetana, "The Relationship Between Managerial Behavior and Subordinate Attitudes and Motivation: A Contribution to a Behavioral Theory of Leadership" (Ph.D. diss., Wayne State University) 1974.

11. S. E. Weed, T. R. Mitchell and C. R. Smyser, "A Test of House's Path-Goal Theory of Leadership in an Organizational Setting" (paper presented at Western Psychological Assoc., 1974); J. D. Dermer and J. P. Siegel, "A Test of Path-Goal Theory: Disconfirming Evidence and a Critique" (unpublished, University of Toronto, Faculty of Management Studies) 1973; R. S. Schuler, "A Path-Goal Theory of Leadership: An Empirical Investigation" (Ph.D. diss., Michigan State University, 1973); H. K. Downey, J. E. Sheridan and J. W. Slocum, Jr., "Analysis of Relationships Among Leader Behavior, Subordinate Job Performance and Satisfaction: A Path-Goal Approach" (unpublished mimeograph, 1974); J. E.

Stinson and T. W. Johnson, "The Path-Goal Theory of Leadership: A Partial Test and Suggested Refinement," *Proceedings* (Kent, Ohio: 7th Annual Conference of the Midwest Academy of Management, April 1974), pp. 18-36.

12. G. Dessler, "An Investigation of the Path-Goal Theory of Leadership" (Ph.D. diss., City University of New York, Bernard M. Baruch College) 1973.

13. R. J. House, D. Burrill and G. Dessler, "Tests and Extensions of Path-Goal Theory of Leadership, I" (unpublished, in process).

14. R. J. House, "A Path-Goal Theory"; R. J. House and G. Dessler, "Path-Goal Theory of Leadership;" A. D. Szalagyi and H. P. Sims, "Exploration of Path-Goal;" J. E. Stinson and T. W. Johnson, "The Path Goal Theory of Leadership: A Partial Test and Suggested Refinement," *Proceedings* (Midwest Academy of Management, 1974); R. S. Schuler, "Path-Goal: Investigation;" H. K. Downey, J. E. Sheridan and J. W. Slocum, Jr., "Analysis of Relationships;" S. E. Weed, T. R. Mitchell and C. R. Smyser, "Test of House's Path-Goal."

15. A. D. Szalagyi and H. P. Sims, "Exploration of Path-Goal."

16. R. J. House, A. Valency and R. Van der Krabben, "Tests and Extensions of Path-Goal Theory of Leadership, II" (unpublished, in process).

17. T. R. Mitchell, "Motivation and Participation."

18. H. Tosi, "A Reexamination of Personality As a Determinant of the Effects of Participation," *Personnel Psychology,* Vol. 23 (1970), pp. 91-99; J. Sadler, "Leadership Style, Confidence in Management and Job Satisfaction," *Journal of Applied Behavioral Sciences,* Vol. 6 (1970), p. 3-19; K. N. Wexley, J. P. Singh and J. A. Yukl, "Subordinate Personality As a Moderator of the Effects of Participation in Three Types of Appraisal Interviews," *Journal of Applied Psychology,* Vol. 83 1(1973), pp. 54-59.

19. T. R. Mitchell, "Motivation and Participation."

20. A. S. Tannenbaum and F. H. Allport, "Personality Structure and Group Structure: An Interpretive Study of Their Relationship Through an Event-Structure Hypothesis," *Journal of Abnormal and Social Psychology,* Vol. 53 (1956), pp. 272-280; V. H. Vroom, "Some Personality Determinants of the Effects of Participation," *Journal of Abnormal and Social Psychology,* Vol. 59 (1959), pp. 322-327.

21. K. E. Runyon, "Some Interactions Between Personality Variables and Management Styles," *Journal of Applied Psychology,* Vol. 57, 3 (1973), pp. 288-294.

22. T. R. Mitchell, C. R. Smyser and S. E. Weed, "Locus of Control."

23. R. J. House, "Notes on the Path-Goal Theory of Leadership" (Toronto: University of Toronto, Faculty of Management Studies, May 1974).

24. R. S. Schuler, "Leader Participation, Task Structure and Subordinate Authoritarianism" (unpublished mimeograph, Cleveland State University, 1974).

PARTICIPATIVE MANAGEMENT: QUALITY VS. QUANTITY

Raymond E. Miles
J. B. Ritchie

Just as other vintage theoretical vehicles have demonstrated amazing durability on the academic stage, the theory of participative management has shown a remarkable facility for holding the spotlight of debate in the management literature. For this and other theories, however, it should be noted that it is often clever direction and staging, rather than substance, which sustains audience interest.

Having signaled this caveat, we must admit to some feeling of trepidation as we suggest another inquiry into this now middle-aged set of concepts. We do so, however, because we believe some of the recent findings from our continuing research on the process and effects of participation justify further examination of this theory. We should add that our research and its implications are unlikely to do much to resolve the polemics between those who view participation as the solution to all organizational ailments and those who consider it a humanistic palliative which threatens the moral fiber of managerial prerogatives. Nevertheless, we feel our findings may prove valuable to the much larger group for whom the concept of participation is neither panacea nor plague, but simply confusing.

In our view, a prime source of confusion surrounding the concept of participation is its *purpose*. We noted this confusion a few years ago,[1] drawing from our research the conclusion that most managers appeared to hold at least two different "theories" of participation. One of these, which we labeled the *Human Relations* model, viewed participation primarily as a means of obtaining cooperation—a technique which the manager could use to improve morale and reduce subordinate resistance to his policies and decisions. The second, which we labeled the *Human Resources* model, recognized the untapped potential of most organizational members and advocated participation as a means of achieving direct improvement in individual and organizational performance. Predictably, managers viewed the *Human Relations* model as appropriate for their subordinates while wanting their superior to follow the *Human Resources* logic.

Our recent research draws attention to a closely related, and probably equally important, source of confusion involving the *process* of participation. Our earlier descriptions of the purpose of participation under the Human Relations and Human Resources models implied that it is not only the degree of participation which is important, but also the nature of the superior-subordinate interaction. Upon reflection, the notion that both the quality and quantity of participation must be considered seems patently obvious. Rather surprisingly, however, the quality variable in

© 1971 by the Regents of the University of California. Reprinted from *California Management Review,* Volume XIII, number 4, pp. 48-56, by permission of the Regents.

the participative process has been infrequently specified in management theory, and even more rarely researched.

The lack of specific focus in theory or research on the quality aspect of the participative process has led, in our view, to the promulgation of a simple "quantity theory of participation," a theory which implies only that some participation is better than none and that more is better than a little. Clearly, a concept which, whether intended or not, appears to lump all participative acts together in a common category ignores individual and situational differences and is therefore open to a variety of justified criticisms. It is just such a simplified view that allows its more vitriolic critics to draw caricatures extending the participative process to include a chairman of the board consulting with a janitor concerning issues of capital budgeting—the sort of criticism which brings humor to journal pages but contributes little to our understanding of participation.

Recognizing these key sources of confusion, our current studies have been aimed at increasing our understanding of the process of participation under the Human Relations and Human Resources models. Specifically, we have attempted, within a large sample of management teams, to identify and measure the amount of superior-subordinate consultation and a dimension of the quality of this interaction—the superior's attitude which reflects the degree to which he has confidence in his subordinates' capabilities. (Our research approach and findings are described in a later section.) As indicated, in our theoretical framework both the quantity and quality of participation are important determinants of subordinate satisfaction and performance. For these analyses, we have focused on the impact of these variables, both separately and jointly, on the subordinate's satisfaction with his immediate superior. Our findings, we believe, clarify the role which quality plays in the participative process and add substance to the Human Relations-Human Resources differentiation.

In the following sections we explore further the concepts of quantity and quality of participation, integrate these into existing theories of participative management, and examine the implications of our research for these theories and for management practice.

THE QUALITY CONCEPT AND MANAGEMENT THEORY

A simple, and we believe familiar, example should assist us in firmly integrating the quantity-quality variables into the major theories of participative management and perhaps demonstrate, in part at least, why we are concerned with this dimension. Most of us have had the following experience:

> An invitation is received to attend an important meeting (we know it is important because it is carefully specified as such in the call). A crucial policy decision is to be made and our views and those of our colleagues are, according to the invitation, vital to the decision.
>
> Having done our homework, we arrive at the meeting and begin serious and perhaps even heated discussion. Before too long, however, a light begins to dawn, and illuminated in that dawning light is the fact that the crucial decision we had been called together to decide . . .

With a cynical, knowing smile, the typical organization member completes the sentence by saying "had already been made." It is helpful, however, to push aside the well-remembered frustration of such situations and examine the logic of the executive who called the meeting and the nature of the participative process flowing from his logic.

We can easily imagine (perhaps because we have frequently employed the same logic) the executive in our example saying to himself, "I've got this matter pretty well firmed, but it may require a bit of selling—

I'd better call the troops in and at least let them express their views." He may even be willing to allow some minor revisions in the policy to overcome resistance and generate among his subordinates a feeling of being a part of the decision.

PURPOSES OF PARTICIPATION

Clearly defined in our example and discussion is the tight bond between the purpose of participation and the quality of ensuing involvement. And, underlying the purpose of participation is the executive's set of assumptions about people—particularly his attitudes concerning the capabilities of his subordinates.

Three theoretical frameworks describe this linkage between the manager's basic attitudes toward people and the amount and kind of consultation in which he is likely to engage with his subordinates. It is worth a few lines to compare these theory systems and to apply them to our example. Listed chronologically, these frameworks are:

- The Theory X-Theory Y dichotomy described by the late Douglas McGregor,[2]
- The System I, II, III, IV continuum defined by Rensis Liker,[3]
- Our own Traditional, Human Relations, Human Resources classification.[4]

TERMINOLOGY

We have been criticized for referring to an essentially autocratic (nonparticipatory) style of management as traditional. Such a style is no longer traditional in the sense that it is prescribed, taught, or openly advocated by a majority of modern managers. Our research suggests that most managers consider such a style to be socially undesirable and few will admit adherence to it in concept or practice.

Nevertheless, we would argue that many if not most of our institutions and organizations are still so structured and operated that this style is alive and well today in our society. Many schools, hospitals, labor unions, political parties, and a substantial number of business enterprises frequently behave, particularly at the lower levels, in a manner which can only be described as autocratic. Thus even though their policy statements have been revised and some participative trappings have been hung about, the main thrust of their activity is not greatly changed from what it was twenty, thirty, perhaps even fifty years ago—they behave in a traditional manner toward the structure and direction of work. Further, the assumptions of the Traditional model are, in our view, still widely held and espoused in our society—the rhetoric has improved, but the intent is the same. These assumptions seem to us still to be part of our "traditional" approach to life. If our views are accurate, Traditional model is therefore still an appropriate tag.

McGregor's Theory X, Likert's System I, and our Traditional model describe autocratic leadership behavior coupled with tight, unilateral control, and little or no subordinate participation in the decision process. Theory X and the Traditional model explicitly delineate the superior's assumptions that most people, including subordinates, are basically indolent, self-centered, gullible, and resistant to change and thus have little to contribute to the decision-making or control process. Focusing more on descriptive characteristics and less on an explicit set of assumptions, Likert's System I manager is pictured only as having no confidence or trust in his subordinates. At the other extreme, Theory Y, System IV, and our Human Resources model define a style of behavior which involves subordinates deeply in the decision process and emphasizes high levels of self-direction and self-control. Again, both Theory Y and the Human Resources model make the logic underlying such behavior explicit—that most organization members are capable of contributing more than demanded by their present jobs and thus represent untapped potential for the organization, potential which the capable manager develops and invests in improved performance. A System IV superior is described simply as one having complete confidence and trust in subordinates in all matters. In between these extremes fall Likert's Systems II and III and our Human Relations model. Systems II and III describe increasing amounts of subordinate participation and self-control, as their superior's attitudes toward them move from "condescending" to "substantial, but not complete" confidence and trust. Our Human Relations model views the superior as recognizing his subordinates' desire for involvement but doubting their ability to make meaningful contributions.

THEORY AND MANAGEMENT PRACTICE

Comparing these frameworks with our example, it is clear that the executive calling the meeting was not operating at the Theory X, System I, Traditional end of the participative continuum. Had he followed the assumptions of these models, he would simply have announced his decision, and if a meeting were called, use it openly to explain his views. Similarly, it seems doubtful that our executive was following the Theory Y, System IV, or Human Resources models. Had he been, he would have called the meeting in the belief that his subordinates might make important contributions to the decision process and that their participation would possibly result in constructing a better overall policy. He would have had confidence and trust in their ability and willingness to generate and examine alternatives and take action in the best interest of the organization.

Instead, the meeting in the example and those from our own experience seem to be defined almost to the letter by our Human Relations logic and the behavior described in Likert's Systems II and III. The casual observer, and perhaps even the more naive participant, unaware of the reasoning of the executive calling the meeting, might well record a high level of involvement during the session—participation high both in quantity and quality. Most of the participants, however, would be much less charitable, particularly about the meaningfulness of the exercise. They would sense, although the guidance was subtle, that at least the depth of their participation was carefully controlled, just as they would be equally alert to the logic underlying the meeting strategy.

ALTERNATIVE THEORIES

Having described varying degrees of quantity and quality participation flowing from alternative theories of management, and having attempted to link to a common experience through our meeting example, it is not difficult to conjecture about the relationships between these variables and subordinate satisfaction. We would expect subordinate satisfaction to move up and down with both the quantity and the quality of participation, and there is already some evidence, with regard to the amount of participation, at least, that it does. Thus we would expect, particularly within the managerial hierarchy, that their satisfaction would be lowest when both quantity and quality of participation were lowest—as the Traditional model is approached—and highest when both quantity and quality are high—when participation moves toward the type described in the Human Resources model.

Predicting satisfaction under the Human Relations model is less easy. If the superior's behavior is blatantly manipulative, we might expect satisfaction to be quite low despite high participation. But, if the superior's logic were less obvious, even to himself, we might expect his subordinates to be somewhat pleased to be involved in the decision process, even if their involvement is frequently peripheral.

We cannot precisely test the impact of these models on subordinate satisfaction, but our recent research does provide some evidence with regard to these conjectures, and it is therefore appropriate that we briefly describe the method of our investigation and look at some of our findings.

RESEARCH APPROACH

The findings reported here were drawn from a broader research project conducted among management teams (a superior and his immediate subordinates) from five levels in six geographically separated operating divisions of a West Coast firm.[5] The 381 managers involved in the study ranged from the chief executive of each of the six divisions down through department supervisors.

From extensive questionnaire responses we were able to develop measures of the three variables important to these analyses: *quantity of participation, quality of participation, and satisfaction with immediate superiors*. Our measure of quantity of participation was drawn from managers' responses to questions concerning how frequently they felt they were consulted by their superior on a number of typical department issues and decisions.[6] This information allowed us to classify managers as high or low in terms of the amount of participation they felt they were allowed. For a measure of the quality of this participation, we turned to the responses given by each manager's superior. The superior's attitudes toward his subordinates—his evaluation of their capabilities with regard to such traits as judgment, creativity, responsibility, perspective, and the like—were analyzed and categorized as high or low compared to the attitudes of other managers at the same level. Finally, our satisfaction measure was taken from a question on which managers indicated, on a scale from very satisfied to very dissatisfied, their reactions to their own immediate superiors.

FINDINGS

The first thing apparent in our findings, as shown in each of the accompanying figures, is that virtually all the subjects in our study appear reasonably well satisfied with their immediate superiors. This is not surprising, particularly since all subjects, both superiors and subordinates, are in managerial positions. Managers generally respond positive (compared to other organization members) on satisfaction scales. Moreover, supporting the organization's reputation for being forward looking and well managed, most participants reported generally high levels of consultation, and superiors' scores on confidence in their subordinates were typically higher than the average scores in our broader research.

Nevertheless, differences do exist, differences which, given the restricted range of scores, are in most instances highly significant in statistical terms. Moreover, they demonstrate that both the quantity and the quality of participation are related to managers' feelings of satisfaction with their immediate superiors.

As shown in Figure 1, the quantity of participation achieved is apparently related to managers' feelings of satisfaction with their superiors. (The taller the figure—and the smaller the numerical score—the more satisfied is that group of managers.) Managers classified as low (relative to the scores of their peers) in terms of the extent to which they are consulted by their superiors are less well satisfied than those classified as high on this dimension. The difference in the average satisfaction score for these groups is statistically significant. The average satisfaction score for the low consultation group (2.13) falls between the satisfied and the so-so (somewhat satisfied-somewhat dissatisfied) categories. For the high consultation group, the score (1.79) falls between the satisfied and the highly satisfied categories.

A slightly stronger pattern of results is apparent when managers are regrouped in terms of the amount of confidence which their superiors have in them (Figure 2). Managers whose superiors have relatively high trust and confidence scores are significantly more satisfied (1.72) than are their colleagues

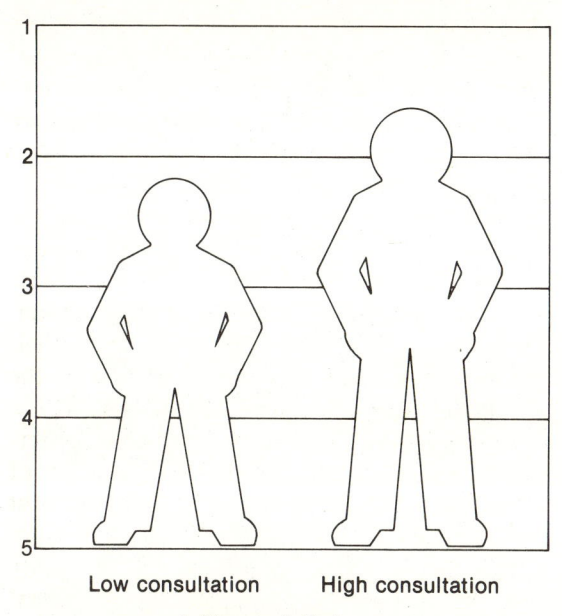

Figure 1. Amount of superior consultation and subordinate satisfaction

1 Very satisfied
2 Satisfied
3 Somewhat satisfied
  Somewhat dissatisfied
4 Dissatisfied
5 Very dissatisfied

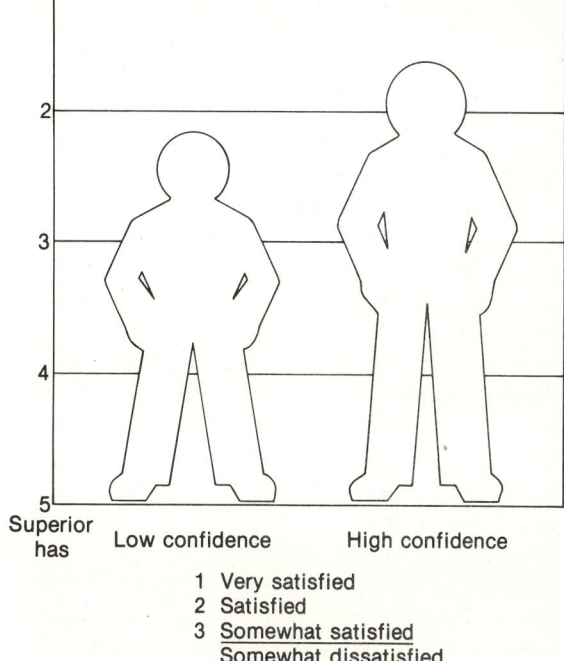

Figure 2. Superior's confidence in subordinates and subordinate satisfaction

1 Very satisfied
2 Satisfied
3 Somewhat satisfied
  Somewhat dissatisfied
4 Dissatisfied
5 Very dissatisfied

(2.16) whose superiors have relatively lower scores on this dimension.

Finally, our results take on their most interesting form when managers are cross-classified on both the quantity and quality dimensions of participation. As shown in Figure 3, the progression in satisfaction is consistent with our theoretical formulation. Especially obvious is the comparison between managers classified as low both in amount of consultation received and the extent to which their superior has confidence in them (2.26) and managers who are rated high on both variables (1.55). Of interest, and relevant to our later discussion, managers whose superiors have high confidence in them but who are low in amount of participation appear slightly more satisfied (1.95) than their counterparts who are high in amount of participation but whose superiors are low in terms of confidence in their subordinates (2.05).

LINKING FINDINGS TO THEORY

The bulk of our findings, particularly as illustrated in Figure 3, thus appears to support our conjectures. Managers who least value their subordinates' capabilities and who least often seek their contributions on department issues have the least well satisfied subordinates in our study. It would probably be incorrect to place the Traditional (Theory X, System I) label on any of the managers in our sample, yet those who, relative to their peers, lean closest to these views do so with predictable results in terms of subordinate satisfaction.

Similarly, managers who, relative to their peers, are both high in their respect for their

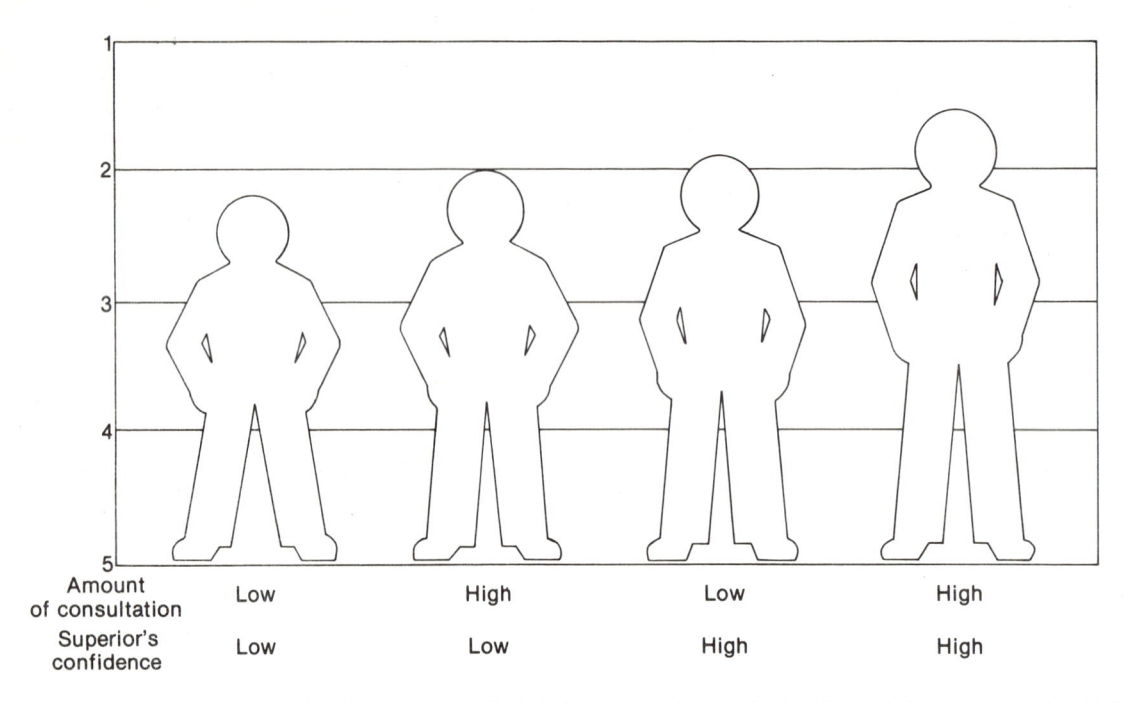

240   INDIVIDUAL/GROUP/ORGANIZATIONAL INTERFACES

Amount of consultation	Low	High	Low	High
Superior's confidence	Low	Low	High	High

1 Very satisfied   2 Satisfied   3 Somewhat satisfied/Somewhat dissatisfied   4 Dissatisfied   5 Very dissatisfied

Figure 3. Effects of amount of consultation and superior's confidence in subordinates on subordinate satisfaction.

subordinates' capabilities and who consult them regularly on departmental issues also achieve the expected results. Precise labeling is again probably inappropriate, yet managers whose attitudes and behavior are closest to the Human Resources (Theory Y, System IV) model do in fact have the most satisfied subordinates.

Further, those managers who consult their subordinates frequently but who have little confidence in their ability to make a positive contribution to department decision-making, and who thus fall nearest to our Human Relations model, have subordinates who are more satisfied than those under the more Traditional managers but are significantly less satisfied than the subordinates of Human Resources managers.

The majority of our findings support the major formulations of participative management theory, but they also suggest the need for elaboration and clarification. This need is brought to attention by the total pattern of our findings, and particularly by the results for one of our categories of managers—those high in superiors' confidence but relatively low in participation. Recall that, while the differences were not large, this group had the second highest average satisfaction score in our sample—the score falling between that of the Human Relations (high participation, low superior confidence) group and that of the Human Resources (high on each) group. Moreover, for the two groups characterized by high participation, there is substantially higher satisfaction for those whose superior reflects high confidence in his subordinates. Clearly, any theory which focused on the amount of participation would not predict these results. Rather, for these managers at least, the quality of their relationship with their superiors as indicated by their superiors' attitude of trust and confidence in them appears to modify the effects of the amount of participation.

IMPLICATIONS FOR THEORY

The quality dimension of the theory of participative management has not been fully developed, but its outlines are suggested in our own Human Resources model and in McGregor's Theory Y framework. McGregor stressed heavily the importance of managers' basic attitudes and assumptions about their subordinates. In expanding on this point,[7] he suggested that a manager's assumptions about his subordinates' traits and abilities do not bind him to a single course of action. Rather, he argued that a range of possible behaviors is appropriate under Theory Y or Human Resources assumptions—a manager with high trust and confidence in his subordinates could and should take into account a variety of situational and personality factors in deciding, among other things, when and how to consult with them. Extending this reasoning, one can even imagine a Theory Y or Human Resources manager actually consulting with his subordinates less often than some of his colleagues. Nevertheless, the nature and quality of participation employed by such a manager, when it occurs, would presumably be deeper and more meaningful, which would be reflected in high levels of subordinate satisfaction and performance.

This view of the superior-subordinate interaction process, emphasizing as it does the quality of the interaction rather than only the amount, can be employed to answer three of the more pervasive criticisms of participative management. These criticisms—each of which is probably most accurately aimed at the simple quantity theory of participation—focus on the inappropriateness of extensive consultation when the superior is constrained by time, technology, and his own or his subordinates' temperament.

THE TIME CONSTRAINT

"In a crisis, you simply do not have time to run around consulting people." This familiar explication is difficult to debate, and in fact, would receive no challenge from a sophisticated theory of participation. In a real building-burning crisis, consultation is inappropriate, and unnecessary. A crisis of this nature is recognized as such by any well-informed subordinate and his self-controlled cooperation is willingly supplied. The behavior of both superior and subordinate in such a situation is guided by the situation and each may turn freely and without question to the other or to any available source of expertise for direction or assistance in solving the problem at hand.

Many crises, however, do not fit the building-burning category, and may be much more real to one person, or to one level of management, than to those below him. Our experience suggests that managers may not be nearly as bound by their constraints as they frequently claim to be, or if they are constrained, these limits are either known in advance or are open to modification if circumstances demand. Rather, in many instances it appears that managers employ the "time won't permit" argument primarily to justify autocratic, and at least partially risk-free, behavior. If he succeeds, the credit is his, if he fails, he can defend his actions by pointing out that he had no time to explore alternatives.

Such self-defined, or at least self-sustaining, crises are most frequently employed by the manager with a Human Relations concept of participation—one who views participation primarily as a means of obtaining subordinate cooperation and who focuses mainly on the amount of formal involvement required. The crisis itself can be employed in place of participation as the lever to obtain cooperation and there is clearly no time for the sort of routine, frequently peripheral consultation in which he most often indulges.

Conversely, the manager with high trust and confidence in his subordinates' capabilities, the Human Resources manager, is less likely to employ time constraints as a managerial tactic. In real crises he moves as rapidly as the situation demands. He is, however, more likely, because of his normal practices of sharing information with his subordinates, to have a group which is prepared to join him in a rapid review of alternatives. He is unconcerned with involvement for the sake of involvement and thus his consultation activities are penetrating and to the point. His subordinates share his trust and feel free to challenge his views, just as he feels free to question their advice and suggestions openly.

THE TECHNOLOGY BARRIER

"Look, I've got fifteen subordinates scattered all over the building. What do you expect me to do—shut down the plant and call a meeting every time something happens?" This argument is obviously closely linked to the time constraint argument—technology is a major factor in determining the flow and timing of decisions. Similarly, it too flows from a Human Relations-quantity oriented view of participation.

A good manager obviously does not regularly "stop the presses" and call a conference. He has confidence in his subordinates' abilities to handle problems as they appear and to call him in when the problem demands his attention. This confidence is, however, reinforced by joint planning, both one-to-one and across his group of subordinates, before the operation gets under way. Having agreed in advance on objectives, schedules, priorities, and procedures, involvement on a day-to-day basis may be minimal. The manager in this instance does not seek participation to obtain cooperation with his views. Both the manager and his subordinates view the regularly scheduled work-planning and review sessions as important because they result in well-considered solutions to real problems.

THE TEMPERAMENT BARRIER

"I'm simply not the sort who can run around to his subordinates asking them how things are going—it's just not my style." The manager who made this statement did so somewhat apologetically, but there was little for him to be apologetic about. He had a high-performing group of subordinates, in whom he placed high trust and confidence, who were in turn highly satisfied with their boss. Further, while he did not seek their views on a variety of routine departmental matters, and his subordinates did not drop in to his office to chat, he freely shared all departmental information with them and on a regular basis worked with his subordinates in coordinating department plans and schedules. In addition, he practiced a somewhat formal but effective form of management by objectives with each of his subordinates.

This manager and, unfortunately, many of the more outspoken critics of participative management, tend to feel that consultation must be carried out in a gregarious, back-slapping manner. Joint planning is a decision-making technique, and not a personality attribute. Extreme shyness or reserve may be an inhibiting factor, but is not an absolute barrier. Trust and confidence in subordinates can be demonstrated as effectively, if not more effectively, by action as by words.

Similarly, as suggested earlier, the manager who holds a Human Resources view of participation acknowledges personality and capability differences among his subordinates. He feels a responsibility to the organization and to his subordinates to assist *each* to develop continuously his potential for making important contributions to department performance. He recognizes that individuals move toward the free interchange of ideas, suggestions, and criticisms at different paces. However, by demonstrating his own confidence in his subordinates' capabilities and in their potential, he tends to encourage more rapid growth than other managers.

CONCLUDING COMMENTS

Our continuing research on the purpose and process of participative management has, in our view, contributed additional support for the Human Resources theory of participation. It has emphasized that when the impact on subordinates is considered, the superior's attitude toward the traits and abilities of his subordinates is equally as important as the amount of consultation in which he engages.

This not-so-startling finding allows expansions and interpretation of modern theories of participation to counter criticisms which may be properly leveled at a simple quantity theory of participation. However, although our findings have obvious implications for both theory and management behavior, they too are open to possible misinterpretation. It is possible to read into our findings, as some surely will, that subordinate consultation may be neglected, that all that matters is that the superior respect his subordinates.

Such a philosophy—tried, found wanting, and not supported by our findings—is embodied in the frequent statement that "all you need to do to be a good manager is hire a good subordinate and turn him loose to do the job as he sees fit." Such a philosophy, in our view, abdicates the superior's responsibility to guide, develop, and support his subordinates. The most satisfied managers in our sample were those who received high levels of consultation from superiors who valued their capabilities. It is our view that effective participation involves neither "selling" the superior's ideas nor blanket approval of all subordinate suggestions. Rather, it is most clearly embodied in the notion of joint planning where the skills of both superior and subordinate are used to their fullest.

Our findings emphasize the importance of attitudes of trust and confidence in subordinates, but they do not indicate their source. It is possible, but unlikely, that those superiors in our sample who reported the highest levels of trust and confidence in their subordinates did so because their subordinates were in fact of higher caliber than those of their colleagues. Within our large sample of managers, several indicators—education, age, experience, for example—suggest that managers' capabilities are roughly evenly distributed across levels and divisions within the organization.

Another possible reason for differences in superiors' attitudes on this dimension is that they are caused by interaction with subordinates, rather than being a determinant of the nature of this interaction. That is, the manager who attempts consultation which is highly successful increases his confidence in his subordinates and thus develops broader involvement. This seems to be a highly plausible explanation which has implications for management development. In fact, there is growing evidence that managers who experiment with participative techniques over lengthy periods do develop both a commitment to such practices and additional trust in their subordinates.

NOTES

1. See Raymond E. Miles, "Human Relations or Human Resources?" *Harvard Business Review* (July-August 1965), p. 149.

2. See Douglas McGregor, *The Human Side of Enterprise* (New York: McGraw-Hill) 1960; and *The Professional Manager* (New York: McGraw-Hill) 1967.

3. See Rensis Likert, *New Patterns of Management* (New York: McGraw-Hill) 1961; and *The Human Organization* (New York: McGraw-Hill) 1967.

4. See Raymond E. Miles, "The Affluent Organization," *Harvard Business Review* (May-June 1966), p. 106; and Raymond E. Miles, Lyman W. Porter, and James A. Craft, "Leadership Attitudes Among Public Health Officials," *American Journal of Public Health* (December 1966), p. 1990.

5. Other findings from this research are reported in L. V. Blankenship and Raymond E. Miles, "Organization Structure and Management Decision Behavior," *Administrative Science Quarterly* (June 1968), p. 106 and in Karlene Roberts, L. V. Blankenship, and R. E. Miles, "Organizational Leadership, Satisfaction, and Productivity: A Comparative Analysis," *Academy of Management Journal* (December 1968), p. 401.

6. For more detailed analysis of these data see J. B. Ritchie and Raymond E. Miles, "An Analysis of Quantity and Quality of Participation as Mediating Variables in the Participative Decision Making Process," *Personnel Psychology*.

7. Douglas McGregor, *The Professional Manager* (New York: McGraw-Hill) 1967, p. 79.

Organizational Structure and Climate

The structure of an organization consists of relatively fixed relationships among jobs and groups of jobs. The formal structure is created by managerial decisions that (1) define jobs, (2) group jobs into departments, (3) determine the size of groups reporting to a single manager, and (4) delegate authority to the manager.

The decisions that managers must make in designing the structure of an organization are related to these four steps. The bureaucratic theory of organizational design argues that effective organization structures tend to have specialized jobs, groups of individuals doing the same job in the same department, narrow spans of control, and centralized authority and responsibility systems. The article by Emery, "Bureaucracy and Beyond," critically examines the bureaucratic model in today's society. The core of Emery's article concerns our present position in the evolution of organizations. Emery believes that Fayol, Taylor, and Weber observed four major managerial trends: (1) we have increased the gap between top management and workers, thus making organizational change dependent on bureaucratic coercion; (2) we have created an environment such that 300 or so large corporations could control and/or account for most of the goods and services produced; (3) we have developed a bureaucracy that separates management from owners, and (4) we have created organizations that are likely to follow their own lines of action regardless of the individuals in the organization. Emery argues against the bureaucratic form of organization as the ideal structure because of its inherent inability to adapt to environmental change. Changes are essential if an organization is to survive the future. These changes, according to Emery, will permit workers to organize into semi autonomous groups that will control and coordinate the members' efforts and assume responsibility for the group's performance.

Schneider, "Organizational Climates: An Essay," concludes this section by illustrating how various organizational structures, leadership styles, and motivational strategies affect the employee's perception of the organization's climate. Climate refers to molar perceptions people have of their work settings. Each work organization probably creates a number of climates. These climate perceptions result in people behaving similarly or differently. When a system's practices and procedures support and reward individual differences, individual behavior in the organization will differ. Schneider points out a number of problems in conducting research in the climate area and also the potential benefits that can be derived from research in this area.

BUREAUCRACY AND BEYOND

Fred E. Emery

From Max Weber to Jacques Ellul, we have heard that our vast bureaucratic organizations are an inevitable outgrowth of the technical revolution in industry. By the same token, it is implied that only further technical advances in automation can free men of the need to serve in such organizations.

On the contrary, I do not think that any sort of "technical determinism" can explain the organizational developments we have seen in the twentieth century. Certainly, if we try to see the present in historical perspective, we find that our ability to harness energy for productive purposes began to have massive effects in the period 1880-1900. However, the subsequent expansion was premised on the development of ways of efficiently organizing large numbers of people about complex tasks. It is in these developments that organizational choice existed. Furthermore, I think that the choices that were made at that time currently constitute the major obstacles to further organizational development.

The significance of the period around 1900 for the emergence of our present form of industrial society can best be shown by referring to the United States. Growth in scale in the decades immediately preceding 1880 was impressive in percentage terms, so much so that after 1880 the organizational problem was unavoidable. On the one hand, the legal problems arising from the divorce of ownership and managerial responsibility were finding a solution in the device of the corporation. On the other hand, the fundamental task of creating stable productive organizations of people performing tasks was undertaken by men like Taylor and Gilbreth. It was they who focused on the interface where human efforts interact with materials and inanimate energy sources to produce a product.

Most attention has been given to the emergence of the great, overarching corporations like United States Steel, ICI, and I. G. Farben, partly as a result of the liberal and Marxist critique of monopolies. The work of Taylor and Gilbreth appeared to be of limited historical interest at the stage of imposing industrial discipline on migrant peasants, and subsequently just a narrow discipline concerned with the details of work organization in certain industries.

As we look back I think it is easier to see now that it was Taylor, Gilbreth, and then Ford—with his first car assembly line in 1912—who shaped the industrial society of today. The economies of scale that were made possible by the large steam engine could not have been achieved by the traditional forms of work organization, either craft-centered or a loosely organized gang system. In both cases a boss conveyed what he wanted done and the workers decided how they would go about the job, the tools they would use, and the pace at which they would work. This was

---

Reprinted by permission of the publisher from Organizational Dynamics, Vol. 2, no. 3 (Winter, 1974), © 1974 by AMACOM, a division of American Management Associations.

a viable way of operating in small establishments where working conditions could be established by face-to-face negotiations between boss and worker. In the large establishments, however, there was no such social mechanism to control the exchange of labor for wages and typically no time-honored local standards of what constituted "a fair day's work," since each new technological change created new kinds of work. In these establishments systematic soldiering on the job was the order of the day. As Taylor put it, "It is well within the mark that in 19 out of 20 industrial establishments the workmen . . . deliberately work as slowly as they dare." The self-reliant craftsman and the multiskilled semi autonomous group that were the source of efficiency in small-scale industry were the bane of large-scale enterprises.

WHAT IS SCIENTIFIC MANAGEMENT?

There is widespread understanding of the general contribution of Taylor and Gilbreth to the founding of industrial engineering and its parallel in the office O & M (organization and methods). We need to pay more attention, however, to Taylor's insistence that he was advancing a new philosophy for organizational design, not just a set of mechanisms or techniques. If we look more closely at what Taylor means by scientific management, the essential components, or steps, can be summarized as follows:

1. Determine as objectively as possible the quantity and skill level of the work that has to be done to achieve the designated task goal.

2. Break this total work load down into one-man shift units so that:

   a) All control and coordination functions are concentrated in staff and supervisory roles (for example, work planning, task allocation, records, allocation of rewards and punishments).

   b) Skilled operations are concentrated in specialized roles from which nonskilled tasks have as far as possible been removed (as, for example, in Gilbreth's classic redesign of the bricklayer's job). That way, one pays skill rates only for skilled work.

   c) The remaining semiskilled and unskilled work roles are specialized in order to minimize the training required for efficient performance.

3. Ensure that for each work role—staff, supervisor, or operator—there are:

   a) Unambiguous job specifications for each individual.

   b) Clear and measurable standards of individual performance (group or gang working being forbidden).

   c) Continuous records of individual performance, with a mechanism for regular feedback from supervisor to the individual.

4. Select the appropriate people to fit the roles that have thus been designed—for example, you choose donkeys for donkey jobs.

I agree with Taylor that there was a design philosophy in these prescriptions, but I do not believe that it was a *new* philosophy. Elsewhere I have argued that there are only two basic design principles for adaptive systems. Redundancy is essential for adaptiveness. This redundancy may be obtained either by designing in redundant, easily replaceable parts or from designing potentially redundant functions into the parts. Put more simply, an organization can be designed to be adaptive by strengthening and elaborating special social mechanisms of control or by increasing the adaptiveness of its individual members. The former design philosophy has some advantages when the cost of individual parts is low, when skills are scarce and relatively expensive, and when shared values about the organization's goals are weak. But it does not have the learning capabilities or range of adaptiveness provided by the latter design philosophy.

Taylor made it very clear that he was espousing the design philosophy based on redundant parts, and he seemed to be relatively unmoved by what this choice implied: "The workmen frequently say when they first come under this system, 'Why, I am not allowed to think or move without someone interfering or doing it for me!' The same criticism and objection, however, can be raised against all other modern subdivisions of labor." Taylor operated, of course, against a societal background in the United States around 1890 that favored industrial designs based on the concept of redundant parts and offered real prospects of greater wealth for all.

PRECURSORS OF SCIENTIFIC MANAGEMENT

The next step in my argument is that Taylor's scientific management was an adaptation of the basic bureaucratic model developed by earlier Asian civilizations for their great engineering works, widespread administrative systems, and large military operations. In his book *The Myth of the Machine*, Mumford quotes from Petrie:

> We know from mummy records how minutely work was subdivided. Every detail was allotted to the responsibility of an individual; one man prospected, another tested the rock, a third took charge of the products. There are over 50 different qualities and grades of officials named in the mining expeditions.

While the measurable man-shift unit was the brick from which these bureaucratic organizations arose, the basic design module was the section that contained few enough workers so that they could be directly overseen by a section boss whose own performance, in turn, could be overseen, measured, and recorded by the next level of supervision. Behind all this overseeing, measuring, and recording was, of course, a system of coercive measures imposed from above, as was also true of the systems evolved by Taylor, Gilbreth, and Ford. To quote Mumford further: "The Egyptian magistrate, Erman observes, cannot think of these people otherwise than collectively: the individual workman exists for him no more than the individual soldier exists for our higher army officers." Precisely. "This was the original pattern of the archetypal megamachine and has never been radically altered," asserts Mumford.

Weber makes the connection more explicit:

> To this day there has never existed a bureaucracy which could compare with that of Egypt.... It is equally apparent that today we are proceeding toward an evolution which resembles that system in every detail, except that it is built on other foundations (than slavery), on technically more perfect, more rationalized, and therefore much more mechanized foundations.

Taylor and company introduced this ancient Asiatic model into the mainstream of Western society by showing how even the newest kind of work resulting from technological change could be standardized into average man-units of effort, with coordination centralized in management hands. Particularly, Taylor and others showed that when "scientific" methods of measurement and selection were adopted, controls over individual effort could be so finely tuned that the gross methods of coercion used by the ancient "megamachines" (and Hitler's slave labor factories) were unnecessary.

The apogee of scientific management was the mass assembly line that Ford introduced in 1912. By relating inanimate energy sources to the transport of materials and parts as well as to their physical transformation, Ford did to industrial and machine production what Gilbreth had done to bricklaying—practically every skilled task was broken down into a number of unskilled components, including supervisory skills. The speed of the line standardized individual efforts and coordinated their individual contributions. Special inspectorial control systems controlled the quality of individual efforts.

The particular significance of the assembly line is that it epitomized the logic of design based on redundant parts. It is ironic, perhaps, that it was a Western innovation, but then we had the surplus energy to replace what is probably the most natural contribution of man to production—simply moving himself.

From World War I onward, Taylorism received a major impetus from the military. The so-called new science of organizations was replete with concepts of line-staff relations, chain of command, and span of control. After World War II the emphasis shifted to coordination problems and the weapon-system-related techniques of PERT, PPBS, network analysis, and so forth—still largely derived from experience in military operations.

I have said enough about this point. In the period 1880-1900 we were faced with a dilemma about how to effectively organize the large productive organizations that had become possible with our new capabilities for energy generation. The brutal coercion of ancient bureaucracies and early British industrialization were not feasible choices. Scientific management was a realistic alternative. This path was taken and the decision was heavily reinforced by the experience that civilians had with wartime mobilization during the first half of this century.

WHERE WE STAND NOW

In 1974, at what point are we in the evolution of organizations? My own view is that four major consequences have flowed from the success of the contributions of Taylor, Gilbreth, and Ford and the militarization of our organizational thinking:

- We had cauterized the connection between the workers, office or industrial, and those at the bottom of the executive structure. Or, as Wilfred Brown would put it, we had increased the gap-at-the-bottom of the executive chain. As a result, organizational change was becoming ever more dependent on bureaucratic coercion.

- An organizational form for control and coordination had emerged that seemed to make it entirely feasible that 300 or so corporations could in the near future account for most of the production of goods and services in the Western, noncommunist world—an Orwellian prospect for the individual.

- Bureaucratization had proceeded to the stage where even top management echelons were divorced in critical ways from ownership. Their performance was judged against decision rules that concerned the narrowly defined, and preferably quantitatively defined, interests of their particular bureaucracy. This in no way reduced the impact each giant had on the other. On the contrary, it increased "relevant uncertainty" for all, as each giant sought to move on its own narrowly defined terms.

- The growth of the large corporations had qualitatively changed the character of the social environments within which they act and plan to act. Quite simply, they are now "turbulent environments" that are likely to follow their own lines of action regardless of the size, shape, or direction of the input of the individual organization. There are many ways of spelling this out, but essentially there is no way that any individual organization can find an adaptive solution on its own. The computer-based arts of corporate and strategic planning of which we are so proud are premised on a world of large, competing, but independent sources of social and economic power—the world of yesterday. That kind of planning can no more help us than it helped the late President Johnson's much-vaunted moves toward the Great Society. As the actions and successes of Nader, Carson, and the conservationists have shown, in this "richly connected," deeply interdependent environment only an identification of shared social values provides a basis for concerted and conscious social change. On this basis it is possible for new and, one hopes, temporary organizational forms to emerge that relate old organizations in a matrix fashion that can transcend their old introversions. On the basis of shared values and the emergence of matrix organizations, it is possible for effective adaptive planning to emerge.

THE CASE AGAINST BUREAUCRACY

This brings me to the nub of my argument that the bureaucratic solution to economically harnessing the exploitation of inanimate energy has not only brought us to this pretty pass, the turbulent social field, but has also sapped and undermined our ability to reduce the turbulence and to map and determine our own futures.

Let me explain what I mean by that last charge against the bureaucratic model. I do not think a foreign technique of organization can be introduced into a culture without creating pervasive and potentially shattering effects. Many years ago Ralph Linton gave us a detailed study of the Madagascan tribe that went from dry rice cultivation to wet rice cultivation, with all of its greater productive potential. They moved back to dry cultivation because they were not prepared to sacrifice their values and way of life for this foreign technology. We do not seem to have widely appreciated this message, although Chaplin's "Modern Times" has continued to haunt us for more than 30 years with a sense that something was wrong with the emerging picture of industrialized society. Perhaps we have been overimpressed by the great changes that have taken place in the external conditions of work. Very few now work in the back breaking, exposed, and dangerous conditions that were the lot of the majority before World War I and of great numbers up until the late 1940s.

This overlooks the more vital question of the clash in values inherent in the choice between the two basic design models outlined earlier. Asian cultures have typically favored the design based on redundant parts. Even with Mao's revolutionary doctrine and emphasis on group-working in agriculture and industry the emphasis is on the fact that the individual should be related to the group, as the tool is to the user. Western cultures and the traditional forms of work organization that Taylor set out to destroy have typically favored the design based on multiskilled individuals, some of whose skills are at any one time redundant to the task in hand. Their work groups are the means, or the tool, for achieving jointly agreed-upon ends. Forbes, in his *Conquest of Nature,* replying to Ellul's argument for technological determinism, puts his finger on this value clash:

> Roman agronomists regarded animals and slaves as interchangeable "pieces of machinery." Their concept was tacitly rejected by the idea of the inherent dignity of man that came with an introduction of Christianity.

I think the break was at Thermopylae, but that is of little moment here. What is of moment is that the bureaucratic model in its day-to-day operation conveys a value message to all who work in such organizations or have significant dealings with them—and that means practically all of us—that *you* do not count, *you* can be rubbished, *you* are replaceable. All of which is counter to Western culture. The contradiction has only been exacerbated by the bureaucratization of educational institutions to allow for economic processing of masses of students. (This makes one wonder which is the "counter culture" in our present society.)

Just how bureaucratic structures convey the value message can be much more closely pinpointed; it is not simply through the threat of unemployment if the individual fails to meet the expectations of the organization. We have firmly based scientific knowledge of what a job needs to provide if a person is to develop greater self-reliance and self-respect and achieve a sense of dignity. The job must provide optimal variety, opportunity to learn on the job and go on learning, adequate scope for decision making, mutual support and respect from co-workers, a meaningful task, and the opportunity for a desirable future. It is precisely these things that are negated by a bureaucratic organization of work. Optimal variety is knocked on the head by standardization of effort; continued learning is defeated by job simplification; elbow room on the job is restricted by shifting all possible controls to supervisors and staff planners; mutual support and respect are replaced not by the impersonality with which bureaucracies are usually charged but by invidious interpersonal comparisons as individuals seek to ease or improve their personal lot and by self-serving cliques that form to improve their lot vis-a-vis their co-workers; meaningfulness of the individual's task tends to disappear in the interest of job simplification and the centralization of responsibility for "whole tasks" in supervisory hands; the desirable future of job security and promotion that the industrial and administrative bureaucracies hold out to middle-level and lower-level employees becomes in fact something of a Pilgrim's Progress—a life of endless vicissitudes on the way to Heaven.

When people spend their lives in these kinds of jobs they are very likely to respond to the challenges of our current turbulent environment in maladaptive ways. If they are ordinary cogs, they will favor passive maladaptive responses. One might dismiss this as the "TV and beer can" response, but I am afraid that this misses the social significance of what we can see about us. The ground movement of masses of people, similarly disposed by their lot in work life, whether blue- or white-collared, is shaking the basis of our society and rendering precarious even our most ancient religious institutions. Briefly, these people will be sorely tempted to simplify the world about them by adopting a more superficial stance—that of Marcuse's "one-dimensional man"—denying concern for all but their own kind and adopting an attitude of "I'm all right, Jack." These attitudes, or social orientations, are of temporary protective value to the individual but reduce the chances of people's becoming involved in jointly shaping their futures.

From the leadership, the big wheels in the bureaucratic organizations, we are probably faced with an active but no less maladaptive response to our present circumstances. The selection of leadership in a bureaucratic structure suffers from an inherent fault. At any point in the executive structure the would-be successors are specialists in their function and are neither learned nor tested in the other functions that, together with theirs, define the managerial responsibility of their superior. In practice it means, for instance, that in selecting a new chief executive one has to decide whether the organization, in its next phase, needs to be strong on production, marketing, financial controls, capital raising, or some other specific area. The only general criteria that can override the qualifications of specialist skills are those that mark the good bureaucrat—getting standard effort out of his subordinates under varying circumstances without rocking the boat. This implies that the chief executive has a lot of loyalty and commitment to the larger system. He must be prepared to manage the system so that his subordinates make sacrifices even when he knows it would be in their own interests to do otherwise. This ability to get work out of others will, on average, tend to override the argument of special skills. Specialist skills may often be advanced for a particular appointment, but the pervasive and underlying question is, "Is he a good executive?" If a person's track record is good in this respect he may be considered capable of mobilizing in others the special skills he lacks.

This is why I think that, in general, the leaders in bureaucratic organizations will seek to find answers in their past, where they made no detected mistakes. These active maladaptive responses are of basically three kinds, corresponding to the same system dimensions on which passive maladaptive responses were classified: First is synoptic idealism, the belief that if we can cram everything into a computerized model of reality the experts will come up with our future—for example, Jay Forrester and Meadows' exercise at M I T. Second is authoritarianism. If the whole society is bureaucratized, we will put an end to this counter culture nonsense. Third is evangelicism. (We can dismiss the Billy Graham version.) The most relevant form of this response is the belief that if we keep the G N P growing everything else will fall into place—which is remarkably close to Taylor's justification for bureaucratizing work.

I have delineated the passive and active maladaptive responses that bureaucratic employment tends to generate, but I think we should also briefly examine the effects on those who are not directly employed in bureaucratic organizations. First, we have considerable areas of employment where traditional Western workshop practices prevail. However, when one looks closer at operations such as gasoline stations, engineering subcontracting, and farms, the overwhelming impression is that they are sorely pressed by the large bureaucratic organizations that control their critical inputs and their output markets. Their economic viability is increasingly dependent on a "spare parts" attitude by the bureaucratic sector toward their staffs and themselves.

I have already mentioned what I think has happened in our educational institutions.

For the Western type of nuclear family structure the situation has been potentially even more disastrous. It is hard to separate the basic notion of individual dignity from the socialization that is possible only in the nuclear family. However, crucifying this family on the demands brought home by bureaucratized breadwinners and bureaucratized students leaves us not surprisingly with a high casualty rate. Rising divorce rates, "suburban neurosis," and schizophrenia reflect this imposition. It would be difficult to argue that these phenomena reflect inherent defects of this family system. The same may not hold true of our traditional back-up systems of religious beliefs—but it may.

THE WAY OUT

This may seem a dismal prospect, and one that inevitably lands us in the world of *Clockwork Orange, 1984, Karp's Number 1,* and all that. However, I do not think there is any real chance of this. The unacceptable nature of total bureaucratization has been adequately spelled out in practice by Nazi Germany, Stalinism, and, in miniature, by Lordstown. The unanimous agreement among Norwegian leaders, trade union, management, and government in 1961-62 that industry had to be democratized at the work-face convinced me, personally, that Western societies were not about to sacrifice their long cultural heritage for "cream on their strawberries." Developments since then, culminating in the O'Toole report, *Work in America,* sponsored by the Department of Health, Education, and Welfare, have only confirmed this belief.

Admittedly, it will be hard to de-bureaucratize the industrial corporations and administrative structures of societies that are very heterogeneous in their national origins and hence their values, such as that of the United States, or deeply rooted in a feudal past, such as those of France and Germany. Despite these difficulties, I think Western societies will successfully re-integrate their productive and administrative structures with their traditional cultural values. My optimism is based not only on what has happened in the sixties—at Volvo, for example—but on the fact that a willingness to look at the technological requirements of a productive system as closely as Taylor did has, in my experience, always yielded a "democratic" design solution at least as productive as a design based on the bureaucratic concept of redundant parts.

It might seem that men could meet part of their present needs by simply debureaucratizing their organizations. That this is not a viable solution is well demonstrated by the anemic failure to change the nature of industrial life of movements such as the human relations movement of the 1940s and '50s and the job enrichment movement of the sixties. The efficiency of an organization can only be *reduced* if its various parts or aspects are designed according to contradictory design principles. There must be interfaces between such aspects or parts, and at these interfaces the conflict in principles would undermine coordination. In discussing how the U.S. aerospace industry was forced by environmental pressures toward the second design principle in R & D work but were, overall, hung up on the first principle, Kingdon observes in his study *Matrix Organization:*

> Of course, these two principles, or organizational purposes, may not always be in accord with each other. In fact, it is more nearly the case that the two are in conflict with one another and that conflict resolution is a necessary part of the matrix organizational form.

The target that men will increasingly set for themselves is not just de-bureaucratization but the positive target of redesigning their work organizations on the second principle, that is, of democratizing work. The movement to do just that can be clearly traced from the first experiment in the Bolsover coal mine in 1952 to the publication of *Work in America.*

The details of this change need not concern us in this context. However, the broader aspects deserve comment. First, the essential change in the design of work organizations is that the basic organizational module is changed from the unit of one-man, one-job under direct supervisory control to the semi-autonomous group of people carrying responsibility for a unitary task. In this latter type of organization the interface between the individual and the organization, no matter how large it is, is the face-to-face group.

This goes beyond what is usually called job enrichment. Job enrichment efforts share the same aim of humanizing work but concentrate on the building brick of the individual-task relationship. Typically, these efforts leave untouched the bureaucratic design module, with responsibility for control and coordination firmly in the hands of the supervisor. By contrast, when semi-autonomous groups replace this module, control and coordination of members' efforts become the responsibility of the group. Within the limits of their autonomy and their agreed-upon objectives it is up to the groups how they enrich the individual jobs, how far they go with multi-skilling. The supervisory functions that remain entail not the exercise of power over individuals but the coordination of the group's legitimate requirements to do its job with the resources and objectives of the organization. That is, the supervisor ceases to be "a man of two faces" and becomes a manager in the full sense.

The success that has been achieved by reorganizing work around small, relatively autonomous groups would seem to follow from the shift in instrumentality. When the small social system becomes an instrument for its members there is a tendency for it to become *variety increasing:* They are able to pursue not only production goals but also purposes and even ideals that pertain to themselves, the ideals of homonomy, nurturance, humanity, and beauty.

Second, the starting points of this movement give some explanation of why I think this will become the dominant trend in Western industry. The first moves were in the science-based industries, particularly the process industries. The very nature of their technologies challenged the rationality of bureaucratic organization. Only in the seventies did the assembly line become a key focus. This time it came as a revulsion against the toollike use of human beings. This general revulsion has already spread to challenge most forms of bureaucratized work, mental as well as manual, professional as well as nonprofessional. The other aspect is that first and deepest commitments to change came from Scandinavia. I believe that it was easier to start there not only because of the socially advanced nature of Norwegian and Swedish society, but also because they were smallish, culturally homogeneous societies. Their industrialization had started late and had neither created deep divisive class hatreds nor widely divided them from their pre-industrial culture. Multinationals like I C I, Philips, and Shell and larger countries like France and Germany have started to grasp the nettle. Perhaps it will be their example, rather than any number of O'Toole reports, that will induce a more coherent response in the U.S.A.

ORGANIZATION CLIMATES: AN ESSAY

Benjamin Schneider

The purposes of this essay are to (a) present some evidence about the importance of the climate concept as an aid in understanding employee behavior in work organizations, and (b) provide a framework for guiding future climate research. An exhaustive review of the climate literature will not be presented since this has been accomplished by others (Hellriegel and Slocum, 1974; James and Jones, 1974; Payne and Pugh, 1975). Rather the focus will be on the conceptualization/operationalization issues in assessing climate and the differentiation of climate from job satisfaction.

The general nature and function of organizational climate perceptions has been explored elsewhere.[1] It has been shown that people in work settings form climate perceptions because apprehending order in the world is a basic human chore and that these climate perceptions function as frames of reference against which the appropriateness of behavior may be judged for the balance or homeostasis it will achieve with the setting. In addition, some implications of climate for understanding individual differences in worker behavior, and the prediction of such behavior, have been identified. It may be concluded, as Tagiuri noted, that

> it is clear that the term [climate] is used in widely disparate contexts. Yet each time it refers to some feature or characteristic of the environment that has consequences for the behavior of an individual or group, and to which the person is somehow sensitive... When everything else is held constant but climate, behavior differs. The term appears to meet the need for a synthetic, molar concept of the environment (Tagiuri, 1968, p. 18).

An important issue is the assessment of climate. It should be noted, for example, that in many so-called climate studies, no assessments of climate through the eyes of the people behaving in the situation were collected (Andrews, 1967; Dunnette, 1973; Frederiksen, et al., 1972). Some evidence, however, does exist to suggest that *experimental manipulations* hypothetically leading to the creation of different kinds of climates are reflected in people's perceptions (Dieterly and Schneider, 1974; Litwin and Stringer, 1968) and that climate perceptions of people in ongoing organizations are correlated with the

---

Reprinted by permission of the publisher from *Personnel Psychology,* Vol. 28 (1975) pp. 447-479. As printed here this is a heavily abstracted version of the original paper. The writing of this paper was supported in part by the Personnel and Training Research Programs, Psychological Sciences Division, Office of Naval Reseach under Contract No. N00014-67-A-0239-0025, Contract Authority Identification Number NR151-350, Benjamin Schneider and H. Peter Dachler, Principal Investigators. The author has received valuable comments from H. Dachler, D. Eden, M. Eran, I. Goldstein, D. Hall, R. Payne, J. Schneider, and P. Weissenberg on earlier versions of the paper. Much of the writing of the essay was accomplished on leave as a Fulbright scholar, Bar Ilan University, Ramat-Gan. Israel, 1973-74.

perceptions of external observers (Pritchard and Karasick, 1973).

However, these few studies do not tell us *how* to measure climate, *what* to measure, nor how climate measures are different from other measures of people's attitudes, particularly job satisfaction. It is these important problems to which we turn.

STRUCTURE, CLIMATE, AND SATISFACTION

Some preliminary conceptual distinctions between structure, climate and satisfaction are necessary.

Structure

Structure has referred to properties and processes of organizations that exist without regard to the human component of the system. Such organizational features as size, product, manufacturing process, hierarchical structure, and number of levels (Porter and Lawler, 1965) describe the structural characteristics of organizations. Structural features of organizations may *determine* some of the behavior that occurs in an organization, but it is not necessary to examine human behavior in order to describe an organization's structure.

Climate

Climate research has been concerned with a description of the forms or styles of behavior in organizations. In nearly all instances research from a number of vantage points has assumed that, on the basis of perceptions of organizational practices and procedures, individuals develop a global or summary perception of their organization (James and Jones, 1974; Schneider, 1973; Sells, 1968; Tagiuri, 1968).

The "number of different vantage points" referred to above concerns the way the climate construct is conceptualized by different researchers. Some have conceptualized climate as a dependent variable where the focus has been an understanding of the causes of climate perceptions (e.g., Dieterly and Schneider, 1972; Litwin and Stringer, 1968). Others (e.g., Frederiksen, et al., 1972; Pritchard and Karasick, 1973) conceptualized climate as an independent variable, a cause of attitudes or behavior. Still others (e.g., Hall and Schneider, 1973; Likert, 1967) conceptualize climate as a mediating variable, a variable whose existence is thought to serve as a cognition mediating organizational behavior and individual behavior.

Satisfaction

Satisfaction has also been conceptualized as an independent, mediating, and dependent variable. However, while climate research nearly always refers to some direct perception of the work or organizational situation, the concept of job satisfaction implies an evaluation of the work or organization. Job satisfaction research, then, concentrates on the individual's affective state: evaluation of organizational structure, practices and procedures and/or evaluation of the outcomes derived from organizational participation.

The idea that job satisfaction should be an assessment of the affective state of the person is precisely the logic underlying the largest proportion of attitude research. Affect served as the guiding theme for the development of techniques for the assessment of attitudes.

The prepotence of the evaluative component in research on attitudes in work organizations has resulted in the tendency to equate such research with satisfaction research. The very word "satisfaction" equates such research with affect.

Summary

An organization's structural characteristics may be viewed as one of the causes of both climate and satisfaction. For example, structural characteristics may determine some of the forms of behavior organizations display and thus determine some of the enduring patterns of behavior which employees will encounter in the organization (Payne, Pheysey, and Pugh, 1971). The studies of Lawler, Hall, and Oldham (1974) and Payne and Mansfield (1973), using climate as a dependent variable and structure as an independent variable, represent this orientation. It should be noted that these research efforts have yielded few strong patterns of relationships between structure and climate.

Job satisfaction may concern the same structural work world involved in climate research but job satisfaction implies an evaluation of structure in terms of some personal system of needs or values. For climate, perceptions of practices and procedures may be organized into a theme characterizing the organization; the organization's order is apprehended. For satisfaction, the same perceptions may be organized into a theme representing the affective state of the *individual*. By referencing structural conditions to some internal system of values, the result is a summary of the person rather than a way of characterizing the organization.

Consideration of three research and conceptualization issues serves to clarify the distinctions just made, especially the distinctions between satisfaction and climate: (1) level of *abstraction* (micro vs. macro perceptions); (2) level of *affect* (description vs. evaluation in perception); and (3) level of *analysis* (individual vs. organization as unit of analysis). A fourth issue, choosing *what* climate to study, rounds out these important research considerations.

LEVEL OF ABSTRACTION

Level of abstraction refers to how much of an inference or abstraction is required by a person in responding to questions. For example, questions asked to indicate how many co-workers they have or how often they get paid, i.e., questions of absolute frequency or amount, requires little inference or abstraction by organizational members. Asked, however, to report the extent to which their co-workers are well-informed about current events or the extent to which the organization's pay policy is one which ties pay to performance, may require considerable information processing and abstracting of informational cues.

Micro features of an organization, then, are those that are relatively easy to define. These features of organizations are analogous to the atmospheric features (temperature, precipitation, winds) meteorologists assess in their studies of atmospheric climate. Macro features, in the extreme, require abstractions about, or summaries of, micro features; they are abstractions of organizational practices and procedures. Labeling a set of atmospheric features to be a particular kind of meteorological climate (blizzard, storm), is the same as an organizational climate label attached to a particular set of organizational practices and procedures.

Climate has been variously treated as an independent, dependent, and intervening variable. As a dependent variable, climate has been assessed most typically by having people in the situation describe existing or inferred situational practices and procedures. In Dieterly and Schneider's (1974) research, for example, three features of a situation were experimentally manipulated and the descriptions of the practices and procedures (four kinds of practices and procedures) resulting from the manipulations were collected by questionnaire. However, Dieterly and Schneider failed to label the various sets of practices and procedures with climate labels. George and Bishop (1971), Lawler, Hall, and Oldham (1974), Payne and Mansfield (1973), and Payne, Pheysey, and Pugh (1971), all using climate as a dependent variable measured through questionnaires, similarly failed to name different sets of practices and procedures with climate labels. These studies suggest that climate, conceptualized as a dependent variable, has not been thought to be a macro construct.

However, when Litwin and Stringer (1968) treated climate as an independent variable and manipulated organizational practices and procedures, they labeled the different manipulations as representing different kinds of climate and found, for the different climates, different kinds of behaviors. Andrews (1967), Argyris (1957), Frederiksen, et al. (1972), Lewin, et al. (1939) and Pritchard and Karasick (1973) have also treated climate as an independent variable and also labeled different sets of practices and procedures as representing different climates. As independent variable, then, climate has clearly been a macro construct; if you will, an atmospheric presence.

Researchers who use climate in an intervening variable sense also label various sets of practices and procedures with climate names. Hall and Schneider (1973) speak of a "climate for psychological success," McGregor (1960) of a "Theory X" or "Theory Y" climate, Likert (1967) of a "System (1, 2, 3, 4) Climate." These researchers, then, generally use climate in a *pre-defined* or *a priori* way, specifying the kinds of practices and procedures they hypothesize lead people to think of their organization's climate in a particular way.

Note that regardless of the way climate is used, the emphasis has always been on practices and procedures and/or a composite label, that is, on various levels of abstraction but trying to stay at the descriptive end of a level of affect continuum. Researchers who have treated climate as a dependent variable have tended not to go so far as to label sets of practices and procedures. This makes their research less molar and less climate-like.

It is quite important to note that as one moves closer to molar perceptions each person's way of processing and abstracting information may result in the climate perceptions being more affectively tinged than more micro perceptions will be. Examples are a "friendly" climate, or a "confusing" climate. Thus, with climate perceptions, because they are abstractions or even inferences, affect can become an important issue.

LEVEL OF AFFECT

Satisfaction is on the evaluative side of the level of affect continuum and refers to evaluations of organizational practices and procedures or the outcomes attained from organizational participation. These are the satisfied/not satisfied, good/bad, just/unjust kinds of reactions to (as compared to abstractions of) structures, practices and procedures and, perhaps, even climate. Returning again to the meteorological analogy, each of the atmospheric features existing in a particular region of the earth may be assessed and the resultant set of measures may be labeled "Arctic Climate." Each of the features making up an "Arctic Climate" may be responded to on a scale of affect and the composite may similarly be evaluated. Since how one labels the composite is more of a personal matter than how one describes the atmospheric features, there is more of the person in the composite than in the features.

This suggests, of course, that climate perceptions and job satisfaction indices will be correlated and raises the problem of distinguishing between perceptions of organizational practices and procedures vs. reactions to those same practices and procedures. However, while climate researchers have been fairly consistent in their descriptive orientation, in job satisfaction research there has been considerable confusion about how affectively loaded measures of satisfaction should be. Some job satisfaction measures contain only statements of practices and procedures, i.e., items of different levels of *abstraction;* when micro in level of abstraction, satisfaction of people is inferred from the practices and procedures people report exist

(Schneider and Alderfer, 1973). The JDI (Job Descriptive Index) measure of satisfaction (Smith, Kendall, and Hulin, 1969) is one in which a conscious mixing of relatively micro descriptive and evaluative items was accomplished (it is intriguing to note that this measure of job satisfaction is called the Job *Descriptive* Index). Scale scores obtained from the JDI are used to make inferences about satisfaction. For the JDI, such an inference is legitimate because items were retained in the scale's development if they were valid discriminators between satisfied and dissatisfied workers. Other scales for assessing job satisfaction have not been as careful in the selection of items.

Payne (1973), however, has taken the Work Itself scale from the JDI and sorted the items into clearly evaluative items ("satisfying, better than other jobs I've had, worthwhile, boring, wrong sort of job for me") and clearly descriptive items ("needs a lot of skill, same day after day, needs a lot of experience, takes it out of you, simple, routine") and shown that: (1) the evaluative items correlate well with each other (mean inter-item r = .50) while the descriptive items do not (mean inter-item r = .12); and (2) when correlated with Hoppock's (1935) global measure of job satisfaction the average evaluative item correlated .56 while the average descriptive item correlated .13. Indeed, Smith, Smith, and Rollo (1974) have recently factor-analyzed the JDI and found two Work scales—a descriptive one and an evaluative one.

Johanesson (1973) has examined evidence which he suggests supports the idea that climate is a reinvention of the satisfaction wheel. Through a series of cluster analyses of "climate" and "satisfaction" items he found five clusters. Three of the five clusters showed some overlap in "satisfaction" and "climate" items. This was the basis for his conclusions that the two constructs were the same! Payne (1973), and Hellriegel and Slocum (1974) among others (Downey, Hellriegel, Phelps, and Slocum (1975), Lafollette and Sims (1975), and Schneider and Snyder (1975), however, have all shown how climate and satisfaction relate differently to other indices of organizational effectiveness.

An example of inadvertently combining evaluative with descriptive procedures for assessing satisfaction is Porter's (1961) Need Satisfaction Questionnaire (NSQ). Porter (1961) developed the idea that assessment of need satisfaction among managers was relatively unresearched. He adapted the theory of Maslow (1954) and the writings of McGregor (1960) to the development of a measure of need satisfaction. Porter conceptualized satisfaction as the discrepancy between what people describe as existing in their work environment and what they think should exist. A series of 13 items was prepared to which each respondent indicated "how much of the characteristic there is now" and "how much should there be." While this procedure has been used in hundreds of studies (Lawler, 1973), a close examination of the NSQ indicates that some of the items fail to assess conditions on the job. For example: "How much of a feeling of security exists in your job?" or "How much is a feeling of accomplishment characteristic of your job?" Since jobs do not feel, what is being assessed is an evaluation of outcomes rather than a description of practices and procedures. To then subtract the "should be" from the "is now" means that one affective response is being subtracted from another.

Perhaps the best example of a clearly evaluative macro measure of job satisfaction is the Faces Scale (Kunin, 1955). In this measure the respondent is asked to choose, from among a set of faces, the one which best represents his/her general satisfaction. The faces range from a frown to a smile. Without getting involved in the arguments surrounding Herzberg's (cf. 1966) theory, Herzberg's idea of asking people about "good" and "bad" days or " . . . what made you particularly satisfied" is also a molar evaluative methodology. Unfortunately, as noted earlier, most job satisfaction research has not asked for employee evaluations alone; satisfaction is inferred from employee descriptions of their work world (Schneider and Alderfer, 1973).

In the sense that some climate researchers infer rather than assess climate, job satisfaction and climate research have been similar. However as noted above both kinds of research may employ a common or highly similar set of descriptions of organizational practices and procedures and make inferences about organizational climate or about employee job satisfaction. I would maintain that the inference about climate is more defensible than the inference about satisfaction. That is, if satisfaction indeed implies a good-bad or like-dislike kind of evaluation, to infer satisfaction based on organizational practices and procedures is similar, although not as extreme as making the inferential leap that a particular set of meteorological features will be liked or disliked by all.

Thus, when meteorologists assess atmospheric features and label a particular set as connoting a particular climate, this label of the composite set of features is closer to the data than is an evaluation of the set of features. For meteorological climate, the data are combined and labeled in a nonevaluative way. In order to determine satisfaction from a set of features, it is necessary to have the set of features as well as an evaluation of each of the features. Following attitude theory, inferring a person's satisfaction from perceptions of organizational practices and procedures is similar to an inference about affect based on a person's beliefs. Yet numerous researchers (e.g., Porter and Hackman, 1968) have shown that the belief and evaluative components are not the same in the understanding they yield regarding employee behavior.

This argument makes most sense when we recall that climate should represent what is "out there" while satisfaction should connote some internal state. If climate should be a description of what is out there, and if climate is to be assessed through (or on the basis of) descriptions of organizational practices and procedures, the reliability of the descriptions of what is "out there" becomes a crucial concern. This is a concern because our measurement procedures are not as reliable as those employed in meteorology.

LEVEL OF ANALYSIS

Early climate research was based on the belief that the topic of interest was something beyond the individual. Lewin, et al. (1939) set up sets of practices and procedures, labeled those sets with different climate names (authoritarian, democratic, laissez-faire) and examined differences in the behavior of boys in the different climates. Argyris (1957) carefully described the practices and procedures in a bank, labeled that set ("Right-type") and predicted how members in the bank would behave given the set of practices and procedures he observed. In Gestalt psychological terms, these researchers took a number of environmental cues and, on this basis, formed a composite descriptor. The composite descriptor was a label and the label represented or stood for a particular network of practices and procedures.

More recently a number of researchers have collected individuals' descriptions of organizational practices and procedures and treated those individual level data *as if* those data represented what the *organization* was like. For example, Pritchard and Karasick (1973), as part of a larger study, asked managers to describe their organization's practices and procedures, then correlated individual descriptions with individual performance ($\bar{r}$ = n.s.) and satisfaction ($\bar{r}$ = .50) and proceeded to speak about the effects of organizational climate on satisfaction. One conclusion drawn on the basis of these data was that climate and satisfaction were essentially equivalent (Guion, 1973; Johanesson, 1973).

However, in another part of the same paper Pritchard and Karasick reported correlations between *work unit* climate and work group satisfaction, finding only one significant correlation. There is a discrepancy in results obtained at the work unit level and those obtained at the individual level. One possibility for this discrepancy is that the descriptions of organizational practices and procedures by different people reveal no inter-rater agreement. When climate and satisfaction scores are averaged *within* a work group and then correlated *across* work groups, a high correlation cannot be established because the averages have little or no reliability. But Pritchard and Karasick report that 80% of the correlations between work group climate (practices and procedures) and work group *effectiveness* were significant; apparently averaged descriptions of practices and procedures are reliable or they would not correlate with effectiveness. Perhaps, then, it is the lack of agreement on people's reported satisfaction that results in the lack of relationship between work group practices and procedures and work group satisfaction.

Some data exist to support this hypothesis. Schneider and Snyder (1975) showed that for between-position (5 positions) agreement on descriptions of organizational practices and procedures (6 kinds), the ratio of positive to negative significant correlations was 4 to 1, but for satisfaction measures in which people were directed to indicate their feelings (8 kinds), the ratio of positive to negative significant correlations was 3:2.

Even if one accepts the hypothesis that employee satisfaction with organizational participation is more contaminated by personal variables than are descriptions of organizational practices and procedures, it is still possible that correlations between people's descriptions and their satisfaction do exist. However, unless the individuals in a work setting *evaluate* things similarly (i.e., they have similar systems of needs and values), the correlations between satisfaction and descriptions at the work-group or organizational level will not necessarily be high. Schneider and Snyder (1975) showed this to also be true.

Aggregate reports of practices and procedures can be reliable. An individual's report will not be a very reliable report of what is happening in the situation. On the other hand, it is clear that such individual perceptions (what James and Jones [1974] call "psychological climate") may be quite useful in making predictions about individual behavior or in understanding the process by which individuals form climate perceptions. The choice of a unit for analysis is then not an either-or problem but one of carefully defining the problem and then making the choice (Schneider, 1973).

Prior to leaving this topic it is necessary to speak to the issue of the unit of analysis problem in *developing* climate surveys. When the decision has been made to use climate as an index of each person's "psychology of the organization" then it is appropriate to develop measures in which individuals are the unit of analysis. For example, a common strategy is to write a set of somewhat molar descriptors, administer them to people in an organization and factor analyze the resultant item-item correlation matrix. It is clear that the resultant factors will reflect the individual differences in the way people report the system's practices and procedures. These factors, because they represent *individual* differences should not be used in research when the chosen unit of analysis is other than the individual.

If a measure is desired that will reveal work group, functional, or organizational differences in climate then the measure must be developed on such a non-individual unit of analysis. Here the reliability across participants in a common work setting can be built on by pooling item responses in *a* setting and factor-analyzing the item intercorrelations obtained *across* settings. The resultant factors will represent differences between settings; the factors can be used to reveal system, not individual, differences.

But what if one wishes to assess the climate of *an* organization (work unit, position) and no existing measure seems relevant? In this situation, a potential strategy is to administer a survey to the employees and then, rather than factor- or otherwise item-analyzing responses, simply calculate means and sigmas *and keep items with low sigmas.* These are the items on which people in the system agree. How to decide the *content* of the items is an issue discussed below.

WHAT KIND OF CLIMATE SHOULD BE STUDIED?

In a number of ways this question is similar to the one a personnel selection researcher must ask in deciding upon the choice of selection procedures. The researcher knows that a number of different procedures have been shown to yield reliable predictions. He/she also has some idea about which kinds of procedures tend to be effective for particular kinds of criteria. Some procedures are useful for a number of different criteria, others are more narrow in their usefulness. The choice of procedures comes down to some "hunch" (Guion, 1965) or, better, some hypothesis about the most relevant procedures for a particular criterion.

The same kind of logic may apply to choosing what to study in climate research: it depends upon the purpose(s) of the study. The Pritchard and Karasick (1973) study described earlier is a good example of this kind of thinking. In one part of their study they were interested in comparing a consultant's composite description of two organizations (achievement-oriented, dynamic vs. conservative, static) with dimensions of practices and procedures as described by the members of the two organizations. Although they had an 11-dimension measure at their disposal they determined that only 7 of them were relevant for examining this relationship. Five of the seven chosen dimensions behaved as hypothesized. These are the kinds of decisions that must be made by climate researchers as well as selection researchers; what is relevant for the problem at hand.

A second question addressed by Pritchard and Karasick was whether the practices and procedures in work-groups were correlated with work-group effectiveness. Here the appropriate unit of analysis is the work group; the question determined the unit of analysis. However, since the work groups in the company tended to agree on six of the eleven dimensions, only the five dimensions on which there was variability could be expected to be related to differences in effectiveness. Four of the five were so related. Again, the researchers chose the variables to be included based on selection research-type considerations.

Unfortunately, we have not reached the stage of sophistication required to be able to specify which kinds (dimensions) of practices and procedures are relevant for understanding particular criteria in specific collectivities (work groups, positions, functions, etc.). What does seem to be clear is that dimensions of practices and procedures will probably be differentially relevant depending upon the purpose of the study. This suggests that omnibus climate measures should not be indiscriminately used in hopes of "finding something." Campbell's (Pritchard and Karasick, 1973) measure has 22 dimensions and House and Rizzo's (1972) has 19 but so many dimensions will probably not be relevant for a particular study.

Collections of people, like individuals, behave. They behave toward various aspects of their internal and external environments and they behave differently depending upon the nature of the routine and nonroutine problems that confront them. The climates in which people function are composed of the many practices and procedures that occur in their situation. Thus work settings develop practices and procedures with regard to pay policies ("reward orientation"), supervisory style ("consideration—initiating structure"), obsolescence, turnover, leadership, or any one of a thousand different potential foci. People, just as they conceptualize themselves along many dimensions (husband or wife, father or mother, Church or Country Club member, and so forth; see Hall [1971]), also conceptualize their work setting along a number of dimensions. The question of dimension salience, however, becomes relevant in the context of a particular criterion.

A review of the literature reveals that many climate researchers have indeed assessed the specific climate in which they were interested rather than attempting to develop some omnibus measure. For example, Fleishman's (1953) work on leadership climate was an attempt to specifically isolate the management practices and conditions when those undergoing human relations training failed to implement what they learned; thus, a climate for leadership. Litwin and Stringer's (1968) provocative research examined the practices and procedures under which such motives as nAch, nAff and nPow would be most likely to become manifest; a climate for motivation. Schneider and Bartlett's (1968, 1970) research in life insurance agencies has explored climates for new employees, while Taylor (1972) examined climates for creativity and Renwick (1975) speaks about a climate for conflict resolution.

The point is that these researchers were attempting to assess the pattern of formal and informal practices and procedures which resulted in some criterion behavior of interest in that specific situation. All of the researchers could have investigated the same set of organizations because each of those climates may exist, to some extent, in every organization. What to look at and which level to look at depends upon the criterion of interest. It is necessary to note, however, that the indiscriminate use of the term "organizational climate" should be supplanted by use of the word "climate" to refer to a climate for something. Thus, "organizational climate" should refer to an area of research rather than a specific unit of analysis or a particular set of dimensions. Within the general research area, there may be any number of kinds of climates identified depending upon the criterion of interest. The use of the plural term "climates" in the title of this paper should now be clear.

SUMMARY

In this part of the paper I have stressed some logical and conceptual distinctions between job satisfaction and organizational climate. It was argued that confusion over three problems has led some authors to suggest that climate may be a redundancy. First, it was noted that the word satisfaction implies an affective internal state while the word climate refers to a molar description of a situation. Second, the point was made that these molar descriptions are composites of practices and procedures people encounter in their work worlds; that climate is an abstraction of or a labeling of a specific set of practices and procedures. Third, literature was reviewed suggesting that the basic satisfaction research orientation, coming from early attitude theory research, has been affectively and individually oriented while climate research has been more descriptively and organizationally oriented. Research confusing the affective/descriptive and individual/organizational issues was cited.

Also discussed were issues regarding the uncertainty over the appropriate unit of analysis in climate research and some of the issues concerning conceptualization of climate as an independent, dependent, or mediating variable. It was noted that choice of the unit of analysis and conceptualization of climate for a particular study depended upon the problem to be researched in a given study. The problem with using the individual as the unit of analysis in the development of climate measures when the goal is to reveal systems differences was noted. It was argued that organizations have many climates and the researcher's chore is to identify which climate to study intensively; this decision is an important one for it determines units of analysis and the conceptualization of the role climate plays in the research. Some research was reported which suggests that when the responses of a number of people to a questionnaire descriptive of organizational practices and procedures are pooled or averaged, the resultant average is a measure with acceptable reliability.

CONCLUSIONS

The ideas that have been presented may be summarized as follows:

1. Climate refers to molar perceptions people have of their work settings.

2. These molar perceptions have a psychological unity being based on actual or inferred events, practices and procedures that occur in the daily life of a system.

3. People have no choice about developing these psychologically meaningful molar perceptions because they are necessary as a frame of reference for gauging the appropriateness of behavior.

4. Each work organization probably creates a number of different types of climates. One way of thinking about these different climates is to consider the kind of outcome behavior(s) the climates would lead to (e.g., leadership, creativity, the display of individual differences). Another way is to think of the unit of analysis (work group, position, function, organization) of interest.

5. Climate perceptions may result in people behaving similarly or differently. When a system's practices and procedures support and reward individual differences then individual behavior in an organization will differ. These differences in behavior, however, will follow from shared perceptions regarding a climate for the display of those individual differences.

6. People in a work setting tend to share their perceptions of the work setting's climates, although the degree of sharing is not very great with current measures.

7. Measures of climate have not been sufficiently descriptive nor frequently-enough analyzed at an organizational level of analysis for definitive statements to be made about the validity of climate perceptions. What does seem clear is the "objective" measures of structural characteristics are generally not strongly related to the more psychologically based climate measures. This suggests that process, not structure, is at the root of climate perceptions.

8. In the best of cases climate researchers have concentrated on the development of measures that are descriptive of organizational practices and procedures. However, generally speaking those researchers who have treated climate as a dependent variable have not explicitly made a connection between a set of practices and procedures and the climate(s) those practices and procedures may produce. More careful labeling of climates is necessary for all uses of the climate construct and conceptualization and assessment of precisely how practices and procedures become climate perceptions is required.

9. Climate, as a perception of the external world, is conceptually, and in some cases empirically, different from job satisfaction which should be the study of man's internal affective state. Both clearly fall in the domain of research called "attitude research" but clear distinctions should be maintained between affect and description and units of analysis.

10. This essay suggests the importance of climate for understanding how organizational

practices and procedures are reflected in human behavior. The concept, as I have presented it, clearly falls in the domain of cognitive theory wherein man is conceptualized as a thinking creature who organizes his world meaningfully and behaves on the basis of the order he perceives and creates.

In conclusion, the following definition of climate is proposed:

> Climate perceptions are psychologically meaningful molar descriptions that people can agree characterize a system's practices and procedures. By its practices and procedures a system may create many climates. People perceive climates because the molar perceptions function as frames of reference for the attainment of some congruity between behavior and the system's practices and procedures. However, if the climate is one which rewards and supports the display of individual differences, people in the same system will not behave similarly. Further, because satisfaction is a personal evaluation of a system's practices and procedures, people in the system will tend to agree less on their satisfaction than on their descriptions of the system's climate.

NOTE

1. In the original of this paper, the first section dealt with the function of climate perceptions in detail.

REFERENCES

Andrews, J. D. W., "The achievement motive and advancement in two types of organizations," *Journal of Personality and Social Psychology,* 1967, Vol. 6, 163-168.

Argyris, C., "Some problems in conceptualizing organizational climate: A case study of a bank," *Administrative Science Quarterly,* 1957, Vol. 2, 501-520. (a)

Dieterly, D. and B. Schneider, "The effect of organizational environment on perceived power and climate: A laboratory study," *Organizational Behavior and Human Performance,* 1974, Vol. 11, 316-337.

Downey, H. K., D. Hellriegel, M. A. Phelps, and J. W. Slocum, "Organizational climate and job satisfaction: A comparative analysis," *Journal of Business Research,* 1974, Vol. 2, 233-248.

Dunnette, M. D., "Performance equals ability and what?" (Unpublished manuscript, University of Minnesota, Department of Psychology, Tech. Report No. 4009, 1973). [1]

Fleishman, E. A., "Leadership climate, human relations training, and supervisory behavior," *Personnel Psychology,* 1953, Vol. 6, 205-222.

Frederiksen, N., "Factors in In-Basket performance," *Psychological Monographs,* 1962, Vol. 76 (22, Whole no. 541).

George, J. R. and L. K. Bishop, "Relationship of organizational structure and teacher personality characteristics to organizational climate," *Administrative Science Quarterly,* 1971, Vol. 16, 467-475.

Guion, R. M. *Personnel testing* (New York: McGraw-Hill) 1965.

Guion, R. M., "A note on organizational climate," *Organizational Behavior and Human Performance,* 1973, Vol. 9, 120-125.

Hall, D. T., "A theoretical model of career subidentity development in organizational settings," *Organizational Behavior and Human Performance,* 1971, Vol. 6, 50-76.

Hall, D. T. and B. Schneider, *Organizational climates and careers: The work lives of priests* (New York: Seminar Press) 1973.

Hellriegel, D. and J. W. Slocum, Jr., "Organizational climate: Measures, research and contingencies," *Academy of Management Journal,* 1974, Vol. 17, 255-280.

Herzberg, F., *Work and nature of man* (Cleveland: World Publishing) 1966.

Hoppock, R. *Job-satisfaction* (New York: Harper & Row) 1935.

House, R. J., and J. R. Rizzo, "Toward the measurement of organizational practices: Scale development and validation," *Journal of Applied Psychology,* 1972, Vol. 56, 388-396.

James, L. R. and A. P. Jones, "Organizational climate: A review of theory and research," *Psychological Bulletin,* 1974, Vol. 81, 1096-1112.

Johanesson, R. E., "Some problems in the measurement of organizational climate," *Organizational Behavior and Human Performance,* 1973, Vol. 10, 118-144.

Kunin, T., "The construction of a new type of attitude measure," *Personnel Psychology,* 1955, Vol. 8, 65-78.

LaFollette, W. R. and H. P. Sims, Jr., "Is satisfaction redundant with climate? *Organizational Behavior and Human Performance,* 1975, Vol. 13, 257-278.

Lawler, E. E., III, *Motivation in work organizations* (Belmont, Calif.: Wadsworth) 1973.

Lawler, E. E., III, D. T. Hall, and G. R. Oldham, "Organizational climate: Relationship to organizational structure, process and performance," *Organizational Behavior and Human Performance,* 1974, Vol. 11, 139-155.

Lewin, K., R. Lippitt, and R. K. White, "Patterns of aggressive behavior in experimentally created 'social climates,'" *Journal of Social Psychology,* 1939, Vol. 10, 271-299.

Likert, R. A. *The human organization* (New York: McGraw-Hill) 1967.

Litwin, G. H. and R. A. Stringer, Jr. *Motivation and organizational climate* (Boston: Division of Research, Harvard Business School) 1968.

Maslow, A. H. *Motivation and personality* (New York: Harper & Row) 1954.

McGregor, D. M. *The human side of enterprise* (New York: McGraw-Hill) 1960.

Payne, R. L., "Prospects for research on organizational climates," unpublished manuscript, Department of Psychology, The University, Sheffield, 1973.

Payne, R. L. and Mansfield, R. M., "Relationships of perceptions of organizational climate to organizational structure, context and hierarchical position," *Administrative Science Quarterly,* 1973, Vol. 18, 515-526.

Payne, R. L., D. C. Pheysey, and D. S. Pugh, "Organization structure, organizational climate, and group structure: An exploratory study of their relationships in two British manufacturing companies," *Occupational Psychology,* 1971, Vol. 45, 45-56.

Payne, R. L. and D. S. Pugh, "Organization structure and organization climate," in M. D. Dunnette (Ed.), *Handbook of industrial-organizational psychology* (Chicago: Rand McNally) 1975, pp. 1125-1174.

Porter, L. W., "A study of perceived need satisfaction in bottom and middle management jobs," *Journal of Applied Psychology,* 1961, Vol. 45, 1-10.

Porter, L. W. and J. R. Hackman, "Expectancy theory predictions of work effectiveness," *Organizational Behavior and Human Performance,* 1968, Vol. 3, 417-426.

Porter, L. W. and E. E. Lawler, III, "Properties of organization structure in relation to job attitudes and job behavior," *Psychological Bulletin,* 1965, Vol. 64, 23-51.

Pritchard, R. K. and B. W. Karasick, "The effects of organizational climate on managerial job performance and job satisfaction," *Organizational Behavior and Human Performance,* 1973, Vol. 9, 126-146.

Renwick, P. A., "Perception and management of superior-subordinate conflict," *Organizational Behavior and Human Performance,* 1975, Vol. 13, 444-456.

Schneider, B., "The perception of organizational climate: The customer's view," *Journal of Applied Psychology,* 1973, Vol. 57, 248-256.

Schneider, B. and C. P. Alderfer, "Three studies of need satisfaction in organizations," *Administrative Science Quarterly,* 1973, Vol. 18, 489-505.

Schneider, B. and C. J. Bartlett, "Individual differences and organizational climate, I: The research plan and questionnaire development," *Personnel Psychology,* 1968, Vol. 21, 323-333.

Schneider, B. and C. J. Bartlett, "Individual differences and organizational climate, II: Measurement of organizational climate by the multi-trait-multirater matrix," *Personnel Psychology,* 1970, Vol. 23, 493-512.

Schneider, B. and R. A. Snyder, "Some relationships between job satisfaction and organizational climate," *Journal of Applied Psychology,* 1975, Vol. 60, 318-328.

Sells, S. B. "An approach to the nature of organizational climate," in R. Tagiuri and G. Litwin (Eds.), *Organizational climate: Explorations of a concept* (Boston: Division of Research, Harvard Business School) 1968.

Smith, P. C., L. W. Kendall, and C. L. Hulin, *The measurement of satisfaction in work and retirement: A strategy for the study of attitudes* (Chicago: Rand McNally) 1969.

Smith, P. C., O. W. Smith, and J. Rollo, "Factor structure for blacks and whites of the Job Descriptive Index and its discrimination of job satisfaction," *Journal of Applied Psychology,* 1974, Vol. 59, 99-100.

Tagiuri, R., "The concepts of organizational climate," in R. Tagiuri and G. Litwin (Eds.), *Organizational climate: Explorations of a concept* (Boston: Division of Research, Harvard Business School) 1968.

Taylor, C. W. (Ed.). *Climate for creativity* (Elmsford, N.Y.: Pergamon) 1972.

PART FIVE

CHANGE PROCESSES

This last major part of the reader concentrates both on the nature of planned changes and on several of the more common approaches managers utilize to bring about changes in their organizations. No assumption is made regarding only one right set of values and attitudes for undertaking change or for bringing about the desired changes. This part does focus on deliberate, "voluntary," and planned changes that are designed to enhance the effectiveness of the organization. Thus changes that are imposed on the organization by stronger forces, such as a powerful union or requirements by the federal government's anti-pollution standards, are not considered.

Nature of Planned Change

Planned changes within an organization are undertaken to better achieve the established objectives or to attain new objectives. Because of rapid changes in an organization's external environment, the availability of new and more efficient technologies, and changes in the expectations and abilities of their own employees, today's organizations are continuously faced with the need to plan for and implement changes. The purpose of this section is to only consider several of the more basic issues involved in examining the nature of planned change within organizations.

The first paper in this section, Hellriegel and Slocum's "Towards A Typology of Organizational Change Models," provides a contingency framework for analyzing and comparing some twelve organizational change approaches. These twelve approaches are considered in terms of their impact on major system variables in organizations, the type of change agent most likely to utilize each approach, and the relatively affective, cognitive, and trusting behaviors required for the successful utilization of each approach. This paper serves to: (1) provide a partial means for gaining an overall perspective on a number of the change approaches in the organizational behavior and management literature that are often discussed in isolation; (2) provide a systematic means for readily understanding the contingencies under which each approach is likely to be effective or ineffective; and (3) develop the position that management often needs to use several approaches over the span of a major organizational change program. The overriding theme of this paper is that there is no single "best" approach for changing an organization.

The second article in this section, "OD Reaches Adolescence: An Exploration of Its Underlying Values," takes quite a different twist. Friedlander explores different values and philosophies which can underlie organizational change and development. Each of three basic values and the interplay between them are discussed in relation to organizational development—one of the main stems of organizational change. However, these basic values are likely to be more or less important as philosophical underpinnings to any type of change approach. The three basic values are identified as *rationalism, pragmatism,* and *existentialism*. *Rationalism* stresses the importance of logic, consistency, and determinism. *Pragmatism* emphasizes the importance of usefulness, effectiveness, and the inherent value of anything that works. Pragmatism continually addresses questions of "how" to change something whereas rationalism asks "why" something does or does not change. Finally, *existentialism* addresses issues of one's own inner experiences and subjective view of personal or external changes. The choice of change approaches, their means of implementation, and the significance assigned to different types of changes are likely to vary according to the relative emphasis placed on these three basic values.

TOWARD A COMPARATIVE TYPOLOGY FOR ASSESSING ORGANIZATIONAL CHANGE MODELS

Don Hellriegel
John W. Slocum, Jr.

INTRODUCTION

The primary objective of this paper is to present a comparative framework for analyzing 12 models of organizational change by examining the way each model deals with system variables, the type of change agent most likely to use the approach, and the relative degree of affective, cognitive, and trusting orientations needed by the client system and change agent to be effective. That is, we are concerned with the different system variables that change agents and managers engage in with respect to the generation of organizational change and the system variables most likely to be affected by the change.

We do not mean to imply that our analysis is exhaustive. First, there exist other change models (10) that could have been included. The twelve models chosen for inclusion are, however, in our view, quite significant with respect to both the theory and application of approaches to change. Second, the analysis is oversimplified in several respects: (1) each change model is based on extensive theory-research and there is no attempt to review this literature because it would require a treatment of far greater length and depth than can reasonably be attempted here; (2) in focusing on system variables, we are neglecting other possible dimensions of organizational change models along which comparative frameworks could be drawn (5, 21). These systems variables may, however, prove to be the most critical factors in a theory of organization and change.

In the following sections, we first provide a brief description of the four system variables as well as a brief comparison of the change models in terms of their relative emphasis on these variables. Following this, there is an analysis of the type of change agent most likely to use each model, and the client system's relative need to respond in affective/emotional, cognitive, and trusting modes. Finally, some inferences are drawn for the application of the comparative frameworks for managers and change agents.

TOWARD A COMPARATIVE TYPOLOGY

The concept of systems is an old one, but is steadily growing in popularity with the increasing realization that organizations are complex social systems and that changes occurring in one part of a system frequently have larger effects across the entire organization (or subsystem). According to Leavitt (15), organizations can be viewed as complex systems containing at least four interacting variables: task, structure, technology, and people. The successes and failures of change

---

This paper was first presented at the 36th Annual National Meeting of the Academy of Management, August 11-14, 1976.

interventions may be rooted in whether or not the organization is perceived as a total system or just an aggregation of independent parts. From our review of the literature on the change models included here and following a modified version of Leavitt's typology, we have been able to categorize the approaches to organizational change with respect to these four variables. Let's briefly define each of these variables.

The *task* variable refers to whether the job is simple or complex, novel or repetitive, standardized or unique (26). Some tasks, such as the placement of a bumper on an automobile, are highly standardized, repetitive, require little cognitive skill, and are simple, whereas the design of a new jet liner is unique, novel, and requires a high degree of complex cognitive skills. The task's domain can also create independent, interdependent, or dependent relations between individuals and/or groups in an organization. The *structure* variable refers to the systems of roles, communication, authority, responsibility, rules, decision-making, reward structures, and the like (20). Each organization and/or subsystem has its own structure that specifies power relations among roles. The *people* variable refers to those individuals working within the organization. This includes their attitudes, values, norms, personal styles, and motivations (1). Finally, the *technological* variable refers to problem-solving methods or techniques including computers, computer languages, drill presses, and so forth, that the organization uses to transform its inputs into outputs (18).

Beer (8) contends that it is inappropriate to label any one approach to change more effective than others. One of the key contingencies influencing the choice of which system variable to change or to begin the process of change is the nature of the problem encountered by the client system. However, there is a growing body of literature that suggests the initial definition of the problem to be solved is strongly influenced by the individual's problem-solving style, particularly those in strategic positions. Problem-solving can be viewed in terms of processes through which individuals organize information from the environment and evaluate it. Using the psychological functions of Carl Jung, managerial problem-solving can be classified along two dimensions: perceptual (information gathering) and decision-making (information evaluation). For example, those managers who are sensation-thinkers tend to be risk avoiders and are concerned with getting into the specifics of a problem and solving it, whereas intuitive-thinkers tend to be risk-takers and are concerned with global aspects and ignore details of the situation. While managers can have other types of problem-solving styles, it is interesting to note that people with different styles tend to interpret and resolve their problems according to how they perceive the environment and evaluate information (9, 12). In sum, the individual's problem-solving style and the exigencies facing the organization (or subsystem) probably interact to determine which system variables will be manipulated in change efforts. In any event, the caveat that the change approach chosen should be a function of the identified change problem may not be nearly as straightforward a prescription as it appears to be on the surface.

A change approach that emphasizes the development of group problem solving for production workers who are basically dissatisfied and frustrated with highly controlled, boring, and routine jobs could easily accentuate the problem. The opportunity for these workers openly to discuss the nature of their work without the opportunity to make changes in the ways the tasks are being performed may well increase their feelings of meaninglessness, hopelessness, and boredom. In this instance, it may be better to focus on the task itself and provide opportunities for workers to enrich their jobs (8). A structural change toward decentralization of decision-making could alter who (people) performs certain organizational tasks. But, decentralization of decision-making might also change the technology for performing the tasks as well as the attitudes and values of employees performing them. A technological change, for example, the introduction of electronic data-processing systems in insurance companies in the mid-50's, caused changes in the organization's structure (i.e., communicational channels, number of hierarchical levels, locus of decision making), changes in people (their numbers, skills, motivations), and changes in the performance of tasks (the ability to use complex operations research models to solve problems) (27).

Organizational change can be introduced through alternation of any one of these major system variables used singly or in combination. However, each change approach is likely to focus more intensively on one or another variable. People-focused approaches try to change organizations by modifying the attitudes, values, problem-solving styles, and interpersonal processes or organizational members. It is assumed that people represent the major force either pressing for or resisting the change. A common thread in these approaches is the redistribution and sharing of power between organizational members. The redistribution or sharing of power can be accomplished by encouraging independent decision-making by the target individuals, open communication channels, and participation in the decision-making process. The major people-focused approaches included in this typology are survey feedback (4), grid organization development (3), transactional analysis (11), and sensitivity training (2).

Task-focused approaches emphasize increasing or decreasing the task difficulty and/or task variability in a position or work unit (26). Thus the targets for change are the activities performed by each person or work group—when, where, with whom, how long, how often, and how much. Task-focused approaches included in the typology are behavior modification (17), job enrichment (7), autonomous groups (19), and management by objectives (6). Although there is a certain amount of overlap between the task and structure approaches, the continuum generally ranges from events within the individual's work group to those that occur external to it.

The structural-focused approaches emphasize: role prescriptions, proscriptions, and relationships; adding or eliminating roles and units; coordinative mechanisms; rules; spans of control; hierarchical levels; reward structures; and authority distribution. The only structural-focused approaches included in the typology are role relations (25), decentralization (16), and matrix organization (13).

While recognizing technology is not the only source or approach to change, Toffler characterizes it as "... that great, growling engine of change" (24, p. 277). Conceptualizations of technology have ranged from a narrow perspective of including only machines to the extremely broad definition of equating it with any means-end chain that produces a product or service reliably. For our purposes, the technological approach to change focuses on "... tools in a general sense, including machines, but also including such intellectual tools as computer languages and contemporary and mathematical techniques" (18, p. 277). The only technology-focused approach to organizational change included here is computer systems.

Comparison of Approaches

Figure 1 provides an overview of the change approaches in terms of their focus and relative direct impact on the four major system variables (people, task, structure, and technology). In Figure 1, each approach is characterized in terms of whether it usually has a very high, high, moderate, or low direct impact on each of the four systems variables.

Change approaches	Relative direct impact on major system variables			
	People	Task	Technology	Structure
People focus:				
Survey Feedback	High	Low to Moderate	Low	Low to Moderate
Grid organization development	High	Moderate	Low	Low to High
Transactional analysis	Very High	Low to Moderate	Low	Low
Sensitivity training	Very High	Low	Low	Low
Task focus:				
Behavior modification	Moderate	High	Low	Moderate to High
Autonomous groups	Moderate to High	Very High	Low to Moderate	Low to High
Job enrichment	Moderate to High	Very High	Low to Moderate	Low to High
Management by objectives	Moderate to High	High	Low	Low to Moderate
Structure focus:				
Role relations	Low to Moderate	Moderate to High	Low	Very High
Matrix organization	Low	Moderate to High	Low	Very High
Decentralization	Low	Moderate to High	Low to Moderate	Very High
Technology focus:				
Computer systems	Low to Moderate	Moderate to High	Very High	Low to High

Figure 1. Comparisons in relative direct impact of selected change approaches

For those approaches which often vary in their degree of impact on a particular system variable, we indicate a range. For example, the management by objectives change approach frequently varies between a moderate to high direct impact on the people variable but low to moderate on structural dimensions. In reviewing the matrix in Figure 1, a word of caution is in order. It is possible that any one of the change approaches could ultimately and substantially impact all four of the major system variables. Our interpretation is based on the typical nature, focus, and orientation of each change approach in the literature, rather than its unanticipated, indirect, or ultimate consequences. It is also evident that the very rudimentary natures of some of these approaches have certain common, overlapping attributes. For example, job-enrichment and autonomous-groups approaches have several elements in common—both provide individuals decision-making automony, feedback, task significance, and task identification.

Extended Comparative Typology

The previous system's typology can be extended by considering four additional variables that appear to be useful in differentiating change models. These variables are type of change agent, cognitive emphasis, affective/emotional emphasis, and the need for trusting behaviors. These additional comparative dimensions and their relationships to the previously identified change models are indicated in Figure 2.

Whatever a change agent's orientation to social intervention, he/she employs a number of diagnostic dimensions for assessing the client system. Tichy (22, 23) points out that

Change approaches	Types change agents*	Cognitive emphasis	Affective/ emotional emphasis	Need for trusting behaviors
People focus:				
Survey feedback	OD	Moderate	Low to Moderate	Moderate
Grid organization development	OD	High	Moderate	High
Transactional analysis	OD	Moderate to High	Moderate to High	High
Sensitivity training	OD	Low to Moderate	High to Very High	Very High
Task focus:				
Behavior modification	PCT	High	Low	Low
Autonomous groups	PCT, OD	High	Low to Moderate	High
Job enrichment	PCT	Moderate to High	Low to Moderate	High
Management by objectives	PCT, OD	High	Low	Moderate
Structural focus:				
Role relations	AFT, PCT, OD	High	Low	Low to Moderate
Matrix organizations	AFT, PCT	High	Low	Moderate
Decentralization	AFT, PCT, OD	High	Low	Low to Moderate
Technology focus:				
Computer systems	AFT, PCT	Very High	Low	Low

* OD = Organizational development type
PCT = People-change type
AFT = Analysis-from-the-top type

Figure 2. Comparisons along four dimensions of selected change approaches

the change approaches used by change agents are directly related to their predispositions. Tichy's research suggests that three types of change agents are usually employed by organizations to facilitate or bring about change. These are: People Change Technology (PCT); Analysis from the Top (AFT); and Organization Development (OD). The characteristics of each type are dealt with extensively by Tichy and will only be summarized here.

The *people-change-technology* type often works to achieve change in the functioning of individuals. These agents are usually concerned with improving motivation, job satisfaction, and productivity. The focus is on individual and organizational self-development through job enrichment, management by objectives, role clarification, individual styles, and the like. The basic assumption of these change agents is that if individuals change their behavior the organization will also change, especially if enough or the right individuals in the organization change. PCTs work most directly on integrating the informal, "natural" system with the formal system and individual/psychological variables. The *organization-development* change agent works to improve the organization's problem-solving capabilities by helping the members learn to help themselves. This involves assisting organization members to work out their interpersonal problems, communications, conflicts of interest, career plans, and other interpersonal issues. They use approaches such as team building, survey feedback, transactional analysis, and sensitivity training to reach their goals. On of the basic assumptions is that efficiency will improve by increasing the participation in decision-making and changing the organization's "climate." The *analysis-from-the-top* change agent, which is most in contrast to the other two types, relies primarily on structural and technological change approaches. Methods used by these agents include changing the decision-making structure of the organization, technological innovations, job training in areas such as computerized information systems, and new reward systems. The underlying assumption of these agents is that if the organization relies more on impersonal technical criteria and structural changes, its efficiency will increase.

These three types of change agents can be directly integrated into our systems typology. The OD change agent is more likely to examine people as forces either pressing upward or downward to change; the PCT agent is more likely to examine both people and structure, and the AFT change agent is more likely to examine the technological forces. The change agent's selection of forces is likely to be influenced by his/her own goals, background, values, cognitions, and those of the situation facing the client system. While several change models are cross-listed for various change agents, there appears to be a relationship between diagnostic categories of relevant system variables and subsequent interventions. The most important factors change agents examine during diagnosis may also tend to be the things which are typically worked on to create change in the client's system. For example, for PCTs, individual and psychological factors are most often looked at during diagnosis and the change process, whereas the OD change agents are more likely to work directly on the client's organizational climate. Thus, are we to conclude that change agents are like the blind men who tried to describe the elephant after each touched different parts of the elephant? Probably yes and no. The relationships indicated in Figure 2 suggest that various change agents may use the same change models—for example, management by objectives, but that the change agents will employ them from his/her perspective. Thus, the OD's use of MBO might stress the participation in the objective setting aspect of the approach, whereas the PCT change agent might emphasize the structure of the client's system and how it interacts with the formal objectives and subobjectives.

In attempting to conceptualize the change process, Figure 2 specifies three additional dimensions of change models—cognitive, affective, and trusting behaviors.

The *cognitive dimension* refers to the extent to which an approach focuses on technical knowledge and skills. AFT, and to a moderate degree PCT, change agents are particularly likely to emphasize these aspects in their change technologies. The *affective/emotional dimension* refers to the extent to which the approach focuses on attitudes, individual problem-solving styles, and other interpersonal processes (14). OD change agents often work most effectively when the client system also perceives that the system's problems are more important in this area than the cognitive area. The *need for trusting behaviors dimension* refers to the extent to which the change approach requires action that increases one's vulnerability to another whose behavior is not under one's control. In situations like these, the penalty one suffers if the other abuses that vulnerability is greater than the benefit one gains if the other does not abuse that vulnerability (28). Our ranking of an approach as requiring low trusting behavior by those directly affected by the change should not be interpreted as distrust. It simply means that the change approach, to be successful, is not heavily dependent on establishing a high-trust relationship between the change agent and the organization or between various members of the organiztion. For example, if the client system does not want to establish a high-trust relationship, a sensitivity-training change agent's technology will probably be of limited value to the client system, whereas a change approach that focuses on technology might be more congruent with the client's value system.

While it is dangerous to generalize about the cognitive, affective, and need for trusting behaviors dimensions, it is useful to note some possible parallels between the change models in the change agent's "repertoire" and the responses needed by the client system to facilitate the change agent's intervention. These relative emphases are probably reciprocal relationships that are established between the client and change agent. All too often the change agent and client system may get bogged down in a fruitless debate about whether it is better to employ primarily cognitive focused approaches or education-affective focused approaches. This debate is further intensified by attempting to answer the question of whether attitude changes precede or follow changes in behavior. For example, a desire by the change agent to alter customary interaction patterns in an organization or values may require that the organization's climate be diagnosed. Unless the client system is receptive to an analysis that assesses the system's affective and trusting behavior, the client system is likely to stall the efforts by the change agent.

In sum, Figure 2 characterizes each change approach as very high, high, moderate, or low in relation to the cognitive, affective, and need for trusting behaviors dimensions. If a change model may often vary in terms of these dimensions as a result of different forms of application, we have indicated our judgment as to the typical range.

IMPLICATIONS

The processes and findings derived from systematically comparing the twelve change approaches in terms of the eight dimensions in this paper should have implications for practitioners and researchers alike. While not intending to discount the potential importance of differences in means, it appears that some of these approaches can be clustered in terms of similarity of goals, variables intended to be influenced, and even means. These similarities do not appear to be commonly recognized. In part, this may be due to the tendency for some approaches to be viewed as mutually exclusive rather than quite overlapping. Of course, this tendency may be reinforced through the use of argot unique in some of these approaches. It may be that we too infrequently expend the energies to identify common threads of meaning between approaches to change.

In contrast, this analysis also suggests some of the systematic ways by which various change approaches seem to differ in very substantive ways. One possible consequence of clearly identifying these differences may be to reduce the all too common tendency to label one approach as good, right, or desirable and another as bad, wrong, or undesirable. This analysis suggests that some approaches are more likely to be more effective in impacting and exerting direct leverage on some system variables than others as well as possessing different foci in terms of change agents, cognitive emphasis, affective/emotional emphasis and need for trusting behaviors.

Finally, it is hoped that this paper has served to add an analytical underpinning to the often heard statement that there is no single "best" approach for changing an organization. This is because there is not, in our judgment, a single point or variable (i.e., people, task, technology, or structure) for gaining leverage to begin and/or carry out the process of planned change. Moreover, the widespread and manifest recognition of organizations or subunits as systems means there are interrelationships between the people, task, technology, and structure variables. Accordingly, major organizational change programs are likely to need to incorporate a combination of approaches to maximize the positive and minimize the adverse and unanticipated consequences so often forthcoming when more limited change approaches are utilized. The typology presented may be somewhat useful in making assessments about some of the more commonly employed change approaches and the possible need to use them in combination with one another. In sum, it is hoped this paper has provided an overall and comparative perspective on the numerous change approaches being discussed in the management literature, but often in isolation of each other.

REFERENCES

1. Argyris, Chris, *Integrating the Individual and the Organization* (New York: John Wiley) 1964.

2. Back, K., *Beyond Words: The Story of Sensitivity Training and the Encounter Movement* (New York: Russell Sage Foundation) 1972.

3. Blake, R., and J. Mouton, *The Managerial Grid* (Houston: Gulf Publishing Co.) 1964.

4. Bowers, D. D., "OD Techniques and Their Results in 23 Organizations: The Michigan IC Study," *Journal of Applied Behavioral Science*, vol. 9, no. 1, (Jan./Feb., 1973), pp. 21-43.

5. Bowers, David G., Jerome Franklin, and Patricia A. Pecorella, "Matching Problems, Precursors, and Intervention in OD: A Systemic Approach," *Journal of Applied Behavioral Science*, vol. 11, no. 4 (Oct., Nov., Dec., 1975), pp. 341-409.

6. Carroll, S. J., and H. L. Tosi, *Management by Objectives: Applications and Research* (New York: MacMillan) 1973.

7. Davis, L. E. and J. C. Taylor (eds.), *Design of Jobs* (Middlesex, Eng.: Penguin) 1972.

8. Dowling, William F., "To Move An Organization: The Corning Approach To Organization Development," *Organizational Dynamics*, vol. 3, 1975, pp. 16-34.

9. Hellriegel, Don, and John Slocum, "Managerial Problem Solving Styles: A Contingency View," *Business Horizons*, vol. 19, no. 6 (Dec., 1975), pp. 29-37.

10. Huse, Edgar H., *Organization Development and Change* (St. Paul: West Publishing Co.) 1975.

11. Jongeward, D. and contributors, *Everybody Wins: Transactional Analysis Applied to Organizations* (Reading: Addison-Wesley) 1973.

12. Kilmann, Ralph H. and Ian I. Mitroff, *Defining Real World Problems: A Social Science Approach* (St. Paul: West Publishing Co.) in press.

13. Kingdon, Donald Ralph, *Matrix Organization: Managing Information Technologies* (London: Tavistock) 1973.

14. Lawrence, P. and J. Lorsch, *Developing Organization: Diagnosis and Actions* (Reading: Addison-Wesley) 1969.

15. Leavitt, H., "Applied Organizational Change in Industry: Structural, Technological, and Humanistic Approaches" in *Handbook of Organizations*, J. March, ed. (Chicago: Rand McNally & Co.) 1965, p. 1144.

16. Luke, Robert A., Peter Block, Jack M. Davey, and Vernon R. Averch, "A Structural Approach to Organizational Change," *Journal of Applied Behavioral Science*, vol. 9, no. 5 (Sept.-Oct., 1973) pp. 611-635.

17. Luthans, Fred and Robert Kreitner, *Organizational Behavior Modification* (Glenview: Scott, Foresman) 1975.

18. Mesthene, Emmanuel G., *Technological Change: Its Impact on Man and Society* (Cambridge: Harvard University Press) 1970.

19. Miller, E. J. and A. K. Rice, *Systems of Organization: The Control of Task and Sentient Boundaries* (London: Tavistock Publications) 1967.

20. Perrow, Charles, *Complex Organizations* (Glenview: Scott, Foresman) 1972.

21. Sashkin, M., W. Morris, and L. Horst, "A Comparison of Social and Organizational Change Models," *Psychological Review*, vol. 80, (1973), pp. 510-526.

22. Tichy, N., "Agents of Planned Social Change: Congruence of Values, Cognitions and Actions," *Administrative Science Quarterly*, vol. 19, no. 2 (June, 1974) pp. 164-182.

23. Tichy, N., "How Different Types of Change Agents Diagnose Organizations," *Human Relations*, vol. 28, (1975), pp. 771-799.

24. Toffler, D., *Future Shock* (New York, Bantam Books) 1970.

25. Tushman, Michael, *Organizational Change: An Exploratory Study and Case History*, IGR Paperback No. 15 (Ithaca: New York State School of Industrial and Labor Relations, Cornell University) 1974.

26. Van de Ven, Andy and Andre Delbecq, "A

Task Contingent Model of Work-Unit Structure," *Administrative Science Quarterly,* vol. 19, no. 2, (June, 1974), pp. 183-197.

27. Whisler, Thomas L., *Information Technology and Organizational Change* (Belmont, Calif.: Wadsworth) 1970.

28. Zand, Dale E., "Trust and Managerial Problem Solving," *Administrative Science Quarterly,* vol. 17, no. 2 (June, 1972), pp. 229-239.

OD REACHES ADOLESCENCE: AN EXPLORATION OF ITS UNDERLYING VALUES

Frank Friedlander

OD has reached adolescence. Some may use this occasion to celebrate and acclaim its bright future, others may lament its shortcomings and claim that it will never amount to anything, and still others may be concerned with its growth and development—the values, disciplines, and activities from which it has emerged and from which it can gain further nurturance and identity. It is the latter with which I am concerned—particularly the underlying and emerging set of values which have not only given to OD its current identity but also its potentialities and its dilemmas.

I am particularly interested in OD because (1) it is an important part of my own professional identity and (2) because OD seems to be a unique blend of rationalism, pragmatism, and existentialism—quite different, for example, from some of its ancestral disciplines such as psychology, sociology, and anthropology. It is far younger, less polarized into representative factions, less known and accepted by the general public, more interdisciplinary, less represented by academicians than by practitioners. Perhaps many fields began this way. But perhaps also by understanding the adolescent as an adolescent we can encounter and relate to him with greater care and acceptance—as well as confront him with increased options for development. That caring, that confrontation, that understanding is not only by us—but also of us. *We* are the adolescent.

Most of us are aware of two of the major components of OD's heritage: the development of T Groups or laboratory learning, and the establishment of action-research feedback methodologies, both of which began in the late 1940s. By the late 1950s, both components had made sufficient and integrated progress in application to organizational issues to mark these years, perhaps, as encompassing the "birth of OD." Most of us (over 40) can also recall OD's infancy and puberty—its continued focus on the T Group as the mode of action and learning, its need for legitimization and respect, its finding an early home in NTL and later in variously named academic and organizational departments, its struggle to become a profession relevant to organizations, its creation of the OD Network to fulfill needs for collegial support and recognition, and its striving to become a research-based behavioral science. It is, of course, still struggling with these issues. But the underlying struggle for OD is less with these specific manifestations than with the underlying values upon which it has grown and currently stands.

By values I simply mean an underlying philosophy and perspective, a preference and judgment of what is worthwhile and worthy.

Reproduced by special permission from *The Journal of Applied Behavioral Science,* "OD Reaches Adolescence: An Exploration of its Underlying Values," by Frank Friedlander. Volume 12, #1, pp. 7-21. Copyright NTL Institute, 1976.

It is by understanding these diverse grandparental values that we can understand the contemporary adolescent.

THE FAMILY BACKGROUND

The grandparents of OD can be thought of as three basic value stances (and philosophies which engender these values): rationalism, pragmatism, and existentialism (Hainer, 1968). In one sense these are immortal grandparents. They have spawned numerous endeavors, disciplines, and professions, and will continue to be a major influence on these fields and on those yet to come.

The rationalist grandparent of OD (whom we'll call Rati) stressed upon her children the importance of logic, consistency, and determinism. Rati was a cool and somewhat distant and disengaged grandparent. Often she lectured her children with such proclamations as, "There is a cause for everything; there is only one meaning to every message; anyone competent reaches the same answer; all events are reproducible and determined; they are separated from time, place, and ambient conditions; propositions should mean what they say and say what they mean."

The pragmatist grandparent (whom we'll call Prag) made sure his children saw the paramount importance of usefulness, effectiveness, and the inherent worth of something or anything that works. Prag was a kind but stern parent. He would often sit his children down in comfortable surroundings and impart such wisdom as, "Start with what you know—that which is accepted for the time being; there are several meanings to what people say, and what is important is that we test those meanings to arrive at a common understanding; meaning for each of us emerges from practice, not from definition; meaning is what the consensus of the people involved say it is; we need to keep reformulating until we know the requirements of reality; anything or anybody is acceptable if it is useful, if it is proven by exploration to be relevant or necessary for a given task, and if it works."

The learning or knowledge-getting model proposed by Prag was essentially practice ⟶ experiment ⟶ testing reality ⟶ better practice. His method was that of recurrent formulation, deduction, testing reality, detection of differences between expectations and findings, feeding back the error into the formulation until the difference between expectation and the latest look at reality became small. Prag was often willing to announce his discoveries when he had simply established a correlation between his expectations and his results: for example, the cigarette-health problem. He placed great interest on the validity of the experiment, the statistical statements that represent a measure of likelihood of the same results happening by chance. Human behavior, then, is limited to observables, to stimuli or responses, and to their correlations—what we can detect and validate. The learning model for Rati was somewhat different. She started with a generalized concept, defined her terms, stated her assumptions, applied a logic, and drew conclusions or made predictions. Thus information led to understanding, the areas not understood, and the search for knowledge. Reason, data, and logical consistency were the essential ingredients in the search for truth. Prag, on the other hand, was most motivated by the immediate situation and the pressures for improvement and effectiveness.

Thus, Rati and Prag, two of OD's major ancestors, each confronted life quite differently. Rati's search was for the "ultimate truth," the plan, the nature of things. Her mission was to describe the universe as it is, no matter how tasteful or distasteful her findings. Prag's mission, on the other hand, was to fashion the universe according to a desired set of characteristics. Examples of occupations which manifest high doses of rationalism are the purer philosophical, political, and scientific theorists, and logicians.

Prag is represented in a general way by what goes on in most organizations today—the common-sense mode of decision making, communication, conflict, policy formulation, and negotiation. More specifically, we find heavy doses of Prag in personnel work, industrial and labor relations, public relations, production, training, and quality control.

The courtship of these two reflected their similarities and differences. Prag had been restless for some time; he had tried out a number of female partners and experimented with a variety of techniques to improve his performance—all of which had worked or not worked. But experimentation becomes tedious at some point—even sexual experimentation. Prag had some vague notion that there must be some higher-order rationale that would suddenly give him vast insight and prowess to attain far higher levels of everyday life. In short, he was ready for a new love affair—or at least to improve his self and life ways.

Rati, on the other hand, was finding herself vaguely unsatisfied and increasingly frustrated in the isolation of her ivory tower: she had the uneasy feeling that life must offer more than purity, unknown potential, righteousness, and truth. She needed an arena in which her vast potential could be given freely and in which her mission of truth and reason could be reinforced. She wanted to be seen as worthwhile.

In one sense, Prag was saying, "Show me who I am and help me improve," while Rati was saying, "I want to show you who I am, how beautiful I can be with (for) you. Perhaps through you I can understand and fit together nature's larger plan." Prag would continually ask "how," while Rati would ask "why." This is not exactly the "perfect" match, but it clearly held forth promises of mutual enrichment, exploitation, and turmoil.

The courtship of these two was respectable and seductive. On their dates, Rati would expound on truth and its systematic discovery and Prag would sense all sorts of solid possibilities in himself and in her. Rati would enjoy her feeling of being attractive to and wanted and needed by Prag. They seldom discussed their differences, and generally guided their relationship away from disagreements, of which they had many. When things got too warm, close, or intense (which could lead either to fight or to genuine contact), Rati would pronounce, "Let's not get emotional," and Prag would be tentatively satisfied with this state of affairs. These pleasurable games continued until they both felt bored, at which time they decided they might liven up their relationship by getting married. Having each come from respectable families, their marriage was blessed by both sets of parents.

Their wedding night was a reiteration and extension of their courtship, as well as a prophecy of what was to come. Prag made all sorts of efforts to extend himself, but never quite succeeded. He was determined to prove and improve himself, but his sole focus on high performance forced him to lose touch with the broader enjoyments of interchange. Rati, in turn, tried to expose many of her talents and resources to him, but more in ways that enhanced her charm than in ways Prag could actually use for his own success.

Although it was a bit frustrating, both saw it as a beginning to better things. Prag had long since learned that every effort was only an approximation to improvement, that their first night implied a need for feedback of error into improved reformulation and model building. Rati, meanwhile, saw their first night (like their courtship) as a brief statement of the larger plan. It was but one moment's revelation of this plan. The future would offer more. Thus neither Prag nor Rati were terribly involved in the here-and-now meaning of their existence: both relied more on their vision of the future.

And so went their relationship for the first few years—each becoming mildly disillusioned with the other, but not giving up. It was never clear whether the marriage contract included both the improvement of Prag's way of life and performance and the enhancement of Rati's identity as the giver of rationality. It was obvious that each one wanted something from the relationship, but neither could extend sufficiently to enter the other's world. Rati certainly took the more aggressive role as time went on—imposing, seducing, selling, in order to help Prag—with the latter increasingly feeling misunderstood, manipulated, and imposed upon. And gradually Prag found himself with less need to be helped than to be understood, with less need for an aggressive and tempting partner than for a congenial and accepting friend, and with less desire to improve his performance than to learn to live with his normal inadequacies.

The relationship, however, was a respectable, legitimate, and fairly stable one. Infighting, disagreements and frustration, and occasional references to separation were aired only in the confines of the household. It was a reasonable, if not exciting, marriage. To augment their respectability, and to carry on their separate if not blended traditions, Rati and Prag did what many couples do. They bore a number of offspring. They bickered a good deal about a name for their first child—each one wanted it to symbolize his or her dream—and finally Rati suggested a compromise. They called their first child Scientific Management, or Sam for short.

Sam promised a reasonable blend of his parent's genes: the application of science to the enhancement of the management of organizations. As it turned out, Sam, like many offspring, did not (and perhaps could not) live up to the dreams of his parents. Sam's applications to management were restricted to observable, quantifiable standards for simple, low-level job operations.

After Scientific Management came a second child—with a second compromise name—Management Science (nicknamed Mas). Mas had various aliases used later in life, such as Organizational Science and Operations Research, and talked a jargon few could fathom—which added to his charm. Prag, on the other hand, favored some of the later offspring, notably Survey Research; Personnel Appraisal, Testing, and Selection; Personnel and Organizational Research; MBO; Open Systems Planning; Instrumented Forms of Individual and Group Interaction; and Manpower Planning and Development. All of these children, of course, resembled or borrowed in some degree from both parents. They tried to apply their rationalistic heritage pragmatically to real-life situations, and to build these experiences back into better rationales and revised models. So went the marriage of Prag and Rati; and their offspring did partially achieve what the two parents were not able to accomplish as partners. Today they live in the same household, accept each other's shortcomings, but devote much of their energy and attention to separate worlds.

Time passed. Then, one fateful day, after some years of marriage, Prag met a stranger. It was at a time when he was into the depths of his practice—mildly frustrated with his lack of progress and development. Existentialism—Exi as he was later to call her—came over him like a wave. She was an aesthetic, sensuous experience he had never before encountered. For Exi, everything began with her *own* experience, her *own* subjective sense of phenomena as she personally perceived and experienced them. It was fruitless and meaningless to define concepts, said Exi. She was content to describe these using crude symbols (sentences, gestures, words), and she was well aware that these symbols were simplified versions of experience.

Exi felt that experience itself was nonverbal, uncommunicable, almost autistic. She accepted her own continual rediscovery that communication of the complete depth and wealth of her experience was not possible. When she found another person whose experience was similar to hers, then she became aware that a sort of resonance took place between whoever spoke and whoever listened. It was feelingful, even though partial, communication, which she called "good vibes." When she was asked by "strangers" to describe an experience, she would frequently reply simply that she could not do so. "I guess you have to experience it to understand it," she would say.

Only her here-and-now existence had primary meaning for Exi; the "past" was over and the "future" was not here yet. Temporal prediction was not only irrelevant but was impossible.

Exi, unlike Rati, became easily bored with analytic discussions, particularly about people. When someone would encourage her to analyze her own behavior, her personality characteristics, her life-style, she would pause, smile, and respond, "My existence precedes my essence." Experience precedes concepts about the experience.

Propositions, for Exi, could have *many* meanings, and different people would derive different conclusions, perhaps even self-contradictory ones. Her concepts arose out of her unique human processes of perceiving, of pattern forming, of symbolizing, of conceptualizing. But none of these was necessarily a conscious process.

Exi's mode of exploration was phenomenological. What she experienced formed the basis for meaningful concepts. For Exi, to experience was broader than to experiment. The latter implied boundaries, controls, rules of evidence, initial purpose. To experience implied openness to uncertainty, no a priori relevance, and ambiguity about ordering or magnitude. Exi's learning process was experience⟶ awareness⟶ choice⟶ commitment ⟶ becoming.

Exi was represented in such fields and movements as humanistic and transpersonal psychology, encounter groups as they occurred in a variety of personal growth centers, body therapies such as structural integration (Rolfing), sensory awareness, massage, dance, yoga, *t'ai chi chuan,* fantasy and drug experimentation, experience in states of subjective reality (Castaeda), spiritualism, and the Oriental meditations and philosophies.

Of course, this set of respective values clearly contrasted with those of Prag, as well as with those of Rati. (See the comparison of all three in Figure 1.) Perhaps part of the attraction of Exi to Prag was that she represented so much that was foreign to him—the very concept of a personalized human experience, the focus on one's here-and-now experience, the immodest but freeing stance of non-logic, of non-definition, of non-prediction. Exi represented to Prag a legitimized humanness (it *felt* almost like immorality)—a freer, more lifelike, more subjective reality that touched him to his pragmatic depths.

Exi's attraction to Prag was strong but less clear. She sensed their relationship as one in which she could experience herself in ways different from before. She had known several previous lovers, but Prag represented a new and different way of extending her personal experience into the interpersonal domain—for changing her mode from being with herself in the presence of another to being *with* another. With Prag, particularly, this implied the chance to implement herself and her experiential mode of existence within the realm of the practical, the applied. When she verbalized her experience of him, she saw him use this as a source of feedback, learning, and development. Prior to this she had not seen relationships as opportunities for learning or changing as much as for mere experiencing. But Prag would frequently ask her for comments and suggestions on his own behavior; and she found him listening to these, trying new behaviors, and asking her for her reactions to these.

Prag and Exi, of course, had many differences. Although these were attractive differences, they did cause difficulties. One underlying difference, for example, was

	RATIONALISM	PRAGMATISM	EXISTENTIALISM
Purpose	to discover truth	to improve practice	to experience, choose, commit
Basic activity	think (knowledge-building)	do (acting)	exist (being)
Learning paradigm	conceptualize → define → manipulate ideas	practice → experiment → valid feedback → improvement	experience → choose → commit
Terms are	precisely defined	tentatively defined	need not be defined
Meaning emerges from	definition (concepts)	practice (results)	experience (perception)
Ingredients for learning	concepts, assumptions, logic	practice, experiment, feedback	awareness and confrontation of one's existence
Locus of knowledge	the conceptual model	the organizational practice	the individual experience
Reality is	objectivity and truth	workability and practice (validity)	subjective perception
Causes of good communication	semantic precision	consensual listening and understanding	shared feeling and resonance

Figure 1. Some components of three value sets relevant to organization development

Prag's emphasis on achievement and success, which he defined in terms of performance, versus Exi's focus on sheer existence, with all its euphoria, terror, and underlying absurdity. Perhaps she had Prag in mind when she once said (or was it Camus?) that, "The absurd is man's longing for reason in the universe, and the universe's lack of it." Prag was quite insistent that he knew why he was here—that he knew the meaning of success in this world. Frequently he defined it in terms of external criteria: recognition, power, status, and money and what it brings. Exi would reply (borrowing undoubtedly from her school days) that "underachievers have more fun." At other times, Prag would impatiently complain to Exi, "Don't just stand there—do something!" Exi would draw upon her experiences and dalliance with the Eastern philosophies and reply calmly, "Prag, *don't* just do something, stand there."

The only way to end such hassles was to go to bed. But even here their experiences were different—Prag seeing intercourse as a sequential and programmatic series of activities leading up to and including orgasm. The criteria of good intercourse were high performance and release. This contrasted with Exi, who sensed lovemaking as an ultimately spontaneous, carefree, and aesthetic experience. Both Exi's lovemaking and, indeed, her entire life are characterized by T. S. Eliot's lines:

> We shall not cease from exploration,
> And the end of all our exploring,
> Will be to arrive where we started,
> And know the place for the first time.

For Prag, ending where you started meant starting from square one. Progress, not a personal or sensual experience, was his most important product.

Both Prag and Exi understood and experienced their relationship as an intense and temporary one. It wasn't that either planned that it should be short-lived; but each saw it as a committed, here-and-now experience, rather than long-term.

Prag and Exi had several offspring, but it was never quite clear whether some of these were perhaps the result of Exi's other encounters even while the relationship with Prag took place. Many of these offspring were practical applications of existentialism and humanism to everyday organizational life: T Groups, Encounter Groups, Gestalt Therapy—all within organizational settings. They turned out to be a close-knit sibling group, who learned much from one another.

At one time, several of these offspring moved into a commune that also housed some of their half-brothers and sisters: Survey Research and Feedback, various Systems Perspectives, Organization Theory and Research. It is not quite clear who was rooming with whom or making love with whom. In this commune all children were the collective responsibility of all adults—whether or not these were the actual parents. It was in the commune that OD was born and brought up.

Who were OD's mother and father? The evidence from traditional sources is skimpy. Perhaps we can rely on genealogists like French and Bell (1973) who make the case that OD's parents are (1) Laboratory Training methods and (2) Survey Research and Feedback. This sounds quite plausible and acceptable. Others (Friedlander & Brown, 1974) add that OD emerged not only as a result of advances in behavioral theory and practice but also from the demands of a changing environment, which provided the fertility for it to be born and nurtured. These demands included an increasing need for more flexible and responsive organizational structures, changes in life styles and values of our working force, increases in levels of mobility and education, a decreased level of organizational loyalty and dependence, a gradual shift from organizational relevance to personal relevance, an increased effort to challenge authority, and a preference trend toward collaborative rather than hierarchical roles.

Certainly these were all hotly debated topics in the commune where OD grew up.

Given this changing cultural milieu and the active presence of at least two able-bodied adults, let's look at what happened in the late 1940s as OD's parents (the organizational application of laboratory training and the development of action-research-feedback methods) made their alliance fruitful. In 1946, a workshop held in Connecticut and staffed by Lewin, Benne, Bradford, and Lippitt was important in the emergence of laboratory training and the formation of NTL. Laboratory training was clearly an insightful and highly personal experience for participants while they were on that cultural island. But as they returned to their more permanent organizations, much of their enthusiasm and plans for actualization of learnings and self quickly dissipated, or were overcome by the alien "real world" culture. One important conflict between Exi and Prag was soon labeled (probably by a rationalist) as the "transfer-of-training" problem. It set in motion efforts to bridge personal and group learning with organizational settings and issues.

Over the next decade, Douglas McGregor and John Paul Jones, working at Union Carbide; and Herb Shepard, Paul Buchanan, Bob Blake, and Murray Horowitz, working in various parts of Esso, were attempting to bridge the gap between laboratory training and complex organizational settings. They were strong supporters of the union between Exi and Prag. Meanwhile, at about the same time, the Research Center for Group Dynamics was founded by Kurt Lewin. During the next ten years efforts were made to develop action-research methods that would apply the objectivity and concepts of behavioral research to pragmatic organizational issues. Key figures in this movement were Festinger, Lippitt, French, Cartwright, Deutsch, Mann, and Likert. The two themes of application of Laboratory Training (linking Pragmatism and Existentialism) and Action-Research-Feedback methods (linking Pragmatism and Rationalism) developed conjointly during this ten-year period, spawning the field of Organization Development in the late 1950s. And so the marriage of Rationalism and Pragmatism, and the latter's affair with Existentialism, seemed to influence the colleagues and parents of Organization Development—and Organization Development became a clear reflection of its heritage.

THE ADOLESCENT: THINKING, DOING, BEING AWARE

Today, OD is a strapping youth—eager, energetic, confused, looking for an identity, looking to prove himself, wondering what he will be and do when he grows up, wondering if he ever will. He is proud but insecure, strong but clumsy, boastful but shy, interested in meeting many but often preferring solitude, wanting to get with others but not knowing how, sowing his wild oats but hoping he hasn't wasted his talents, amazed and excited by his obvious potency but a bit frightened by it also. Indeed, OD has reached adolescence.

Like many adolescents, OD is the product of both his current sociocultural environment and his heritage. Many of the current dilemmas, conflicts, issues, and imbalances within him are the representations of dilemmas and struggles between his ancestors: rationalism, pragmatism, and existentialism.

To understand the tensions with OD, let's trace these ancestral themes as they are enacted today. Rationalism pushes contemporary OD toward becoming more scientific, more theoretical and conceptual, more logical, more mathematical; toward abstract models; toward building theories; toward understanding the determinants of our organizational, social and personal worlds. Pragmatism pushes OD in the direction of becoming more useful—how does OD increase effectiveness, performance, productivity; how can OD determine expected or alternative organizational processes and structures; and how can it feed back information into the organization to reduce the gap between the way it is now and the way it would be better? Existentialism within OD pushes the organization to become more humanistic, more aware, more emerging, more person-growth oriented. The rationalist learns by thinking; the pragmatist by doing; and the existentialist by becoming aware.

The rationalistic force within OD stems largely from its disciplinary forebears. These are principally psychology (personality and social psychology), sociology (organizational and systems), and anthropology (cultural and social). Within these disciplines, theories of personality, small group, organization, and systems have stretched toward their developmental directions—toward personal growth, group dynamics, organizational change, and systems development. More recent integrations include theories of learning, information, organization, and systems—several of which have found a safer, more fruitful home in the newer interdisciplinary departments in universities. Within the confines of most universities and publication systems, rationalistic perspectives of OD are encouraged, taught, and rewarded. The rationalistic roots of OD, then, are clearly embedded within its basic underlying disciplines. The pure rationalist brings a high value of conceptualizing and understanding to OD, and of building models of organization and development. In doing these, he draws heavily on his disciplinary background.

The pragmatic force in OD is clearly in applications toward organizational improvement. The pragmatist draws upon his practical knowledge of the organization rather than upon disciplinary knowledge. The emphasis is upon "know-how" rather than "know-about." He listens carefully, plans, and acts. Since he derives his wisdom from events within the organization, he places a high value on the "data" that are emerging and upon evaluation of action outcomes. The pragmatist brings to the organization his value of planning, of doing, of improving.

He, therefore, typically emphasizes diagnosis, strategy planning, clear interventions and action steps, and a thorough evaluation. This sequence provides him with a situation-specific organizational knowledge and evaluations for improvement. He will thus tend to replace the rationalist's conceptual models of organizations with first hand action research.

The existential force within OD focuses primarily upon the experience of the individual, his personal choices and commitments within the organizational field. The OD existentialist is less interested in diagnosis than in understanding the experiential flow of the individual, less interested in strategizing and planning for change than in offering clarification of individual choices, less interested in changing the individual than in accepting him, and less interested in evaluating change than in the individual's commitment to his own choices. The rationalist's value of building increasingly precise models of organization and development and the pragmatist's value of improvement in organizational practice are replaced for the existentialist by a high value placed on individual experience and acceptance of the person within the organizational setting.

These descriptions suggest a number of divergent perspectives and conflicting values among OD's three main ancestors. They frequently squabble among themselves in terms of what's important. For example, the rationalist's high value of building precise models of organization and OD conflict with the pragmatist prime value of improving organization effectiveness; and both of these conflict with the existentialist value of personal (not organizational) acceptance (not improvement) based upon subjective awareness and experience (not on objectively and externally constructed models).

The rationalist's entry into the organization is with "prebuilt" concepts and models, and his interest in taking away knowledge to build better models makes him seem abstract as well as irrelevant and unconcerned about the organization, its problems, and its people. The focus of the rationalist on things and ideas to the exclusion of human experience runs the risk for the existentialist of dehumanizing the organization, and for the pragmatist of leaving out the practical necessity of "the people factor."

The pragmatist's entry into the organization—with designs, exercises, planned interventions, training programs, and evaluation instruments—frequently seems like an irrelevant intrusion. His stance that "if it works, it's good" jars the rationalist's need for an overarching rationale or framework, and is an intrusion on the existentialist, who feels put upon. The rationalist fears that the pragmatist will become the victim of "whatever works" —a technique, a fad, a method that has always been used—with little interest or knowledge of how these fit into a larger organizational schema. And the existentialist is sorely suspicious that "whatever works" may turn out to be a mechanistic *manipulation of the person*—e.g., that the pragmatist may see laboratory training as improvement of public relations rather than interpersonal relations, or survey research as a catharsis for the organization rather than as a diagnosis for purposes of development and change.

In contrast, the existentialist mode of "getting with" people, their issues, and their experiences is seen by the pragmatist and rationalist as slow, irrelevant to the organization, overly loose, unproductive, and sometimes simply mystique or therapy. The existentialist as an organization developer runs the risk of pushing experience, intuition, subjectivity, and an idealized humanistic vision beyond the realms of organizational life. The practical issues of the organization as producer may be irrelevant to her, and she may create vulnerability among her existential organizational converts.

A basic dilemma for the OD professional is whether to foster the individual client's self-acceptance and help him clarify his experience and choices (existentialist); whether to become the (subtle) protagonist by suggesting or designing new experiences for the individual so he will improve (pragmatist); or whether to portray and gather knowledge for building more valid models (rationalist). This dilemma presents three distinct roles for OD professionals: "the accepter of experience," "the change agent," or "the conceptual teacher-learner." The focus is on subjective awareness, designing for and development of others, or objective knowledge. Is OD experience, change, or theory?

A second dilemma for the OD professional concerns his perspective of time. The OD existentialist places a high value on the here-and-now experience of the individual—the ever-present present, which may reflect history and prophecy but which focuses on the current moment. The rationalist perspective is based on the flow of time; the present is merely the moment's reflection of a plan already determined in the past and to be extended in the future. While the rationalist is content with discovering the plan, the pragmatist wants to do something about it—to foster it—to actually do the planning. The rationalist's concern for discovering the plan together with the pragmatist value to act on it frequently combine to meet the organization's needs for mapping out its continuity and future. OD, then, focuses on five-year plans, production schedules, MBO, career planning, and management succession schedules. These are all to the dismay of the existentialist, who never quite acknowledges the future—and frequently sees it as an avoidance of the present.

Rati, Prag, and Exi obviously represent ideal or pure types in this discussion. I have drawn them as such because each set of values is thereby epitomized and clarified. In actuality, I think OD draws upon all three value sets. It is a blend of knowledge-theory, of practice-change, and of an experiential-humanistic venture. The nature of this blend, of course, depends on the particular OD person and upon the particular organizational situation.

If the rationalist parts of us do not listen and speak, we become alienated from our disciplinary basis and our knowledge-building process; if the pragmatic parts of us are mute, we become distant and irrelevant to our organizational bases and our change orientation; and if we deny our existential values, we depersonalize our own subjective experience and become alienated from ourselves and our important others. The adolescent OD can grow by appreciating and making the most of his inheritance—by drawing fully upon *all* of his qualities.

OD not only feels the potentials and the strains from his ancestors but is frequently denounced for failures due to improper blends of these traits. Sometimes he takes after one side of the family to such a degree that his actions seem unbalanced and irresponsible. Censure follows. But perhaps that is the way of the teen-ager. We expect so much from an adolescent, and it would really be great if he would only follow our sage advice. But he doesn't. And in this sense, perhaps adolescent OD is just a chip off the old block(s).

REFERENCES

French, W. L., & C. H. Bell, *Organization development* (Englewood Cliffs, N.J.: Prentice-Hall) 1973.

Friedlander, F., & L. D. Brown, "Organization development," *Annual Review of Psychology,* 1974, Vol. 25, 313-341.

Hainer, R. M., "Rationalism, pragmatism, and existentialism: Perceived but undiscovered multicultural problems," in E. Glatt and M. W. Shelly (Eds.), *The research society* (New York: Gordon & Breach) 1968.

Some Approaches to Planned Change

The four readings in this section were chosen because each one portrays a different, but important, approach for changing an organization or one of its units. These approaches include management by objectives, survey feedback, job enrichment, and structural change. You may find it useful to refer back to Figures 1 and 2 (pages 273 and 274) in the reading by Hellriegel and Slocum. These figures can provide, at a quick glance, a basic understanding of the nature and focus of each of the approaches. Moreover, a review of these figures suggests a number of other approaches not covered here because of space limitations that might have been included.

The first reading in this section by French and Hollmann, "Management by Objectives: The Team Approach," describes two forms of the management by objectives approach. One form involves superior and subordinate interactions, whereas the other involves a team-centered approach. The team-centered approach is thought to be more effective when there is: (1) a high degree of interdependency between jobs, and (2) a need to assure optimal coordination of objectives between jobs. The processes recommended for implementing the team approach to management by objectives are presented as well as the contingencies that are likely to influence successful implementation.

Bowers and Franklin, "Survey-Guided Development: Using Human Resources Measurement in Organizational Change," provide guidance as to how organizational members might be helped to help themselves change their organization. The primary objective of the survey-feedback approach is to improve the relationships among the members of each organizational unit and between organizational units through the discussion of their common concerns. Typically, a standardized questionnaire is completed anonymously by members of the whole organization or by members of a particular department, division, or plant. The questionnaire usually taps members' perceptions and attitudes on a wide range of issues important to the organization and its members. After tabulating these questionnaires, the results become the basis for problem-solving discussions within the organization. Bowers and Franklin explain this process in detail and illustrate how it can effectively facilitate organizational change.

The nature of the tasks performed by individuals is the focus of attention in the job-enrichment approach discussed by Hackman, et al., in "A New Strategy for Job Enrichment." They indicate how jobs can be enriched, the characteristics of enriched jobs, the potential benefits of enrichment, and the contingencies under which job enrichment is likely to be effective. Rather than seeking to improve the relationships between people or jobs, job enrichment zeroes in on the nature of the tasks being performed by individuals. This approach often attempts to increase the responsibilities and individual autonomy in a job. Thus, unlike the team model of the management by objectives approach, there is often an attempt to reduce the interdependencies between jobs. This reading also provides a useful framework for diagnosing when job enrichment is likely to be effective.

The final reading, by Luke, et al., "A Structural Approach to Organizational Change," reports on a broad ranging change program in an analytical case study and explains the processes by which the organizational structure as well as the employees' behaviors and attitudes were changed. This study challenges the common management assumption that close control of individuals is always necessary to accomplish the organization's objectives. Through a number of structural changes, the retail food organization went from close control of employees to a form of training and consultation of employees by higher management. The change program was evaluated in terms of profit and productivity measures as well as employee attitudes. This case study illustrates the general types of processes, issues, and assessments that need to be considered in any type of change program. Thus you should not get bogged down in the details of the specific changes made in this retail food organization. Finally, this reading provides a concrete example of organization development that makes use of external consultants to bring about change.

Wendell L. French
Robert W. Hollmann

MANAGEMENT BY OBJECTIVES: THE TEAM APPROACH

Study of the many books, articles, case studies, speeches, and discussions about management by objectives (MBO) indicates that most forms of this approach tend to reinforce a one-to-one leadership style. It is also apparent that MBO efforts vary from being highly autocratic to highly participative among organizations and even within some organizations. In this article we present a case and strategy for *collaborative* management by objectives (CMBO), a participative, team-centered approach. This approach has a number of unique features that will minimize some of the deficiencies in more traditional versions, but as we shall see, the skills involved and the organizational climate required for its optimal effectiveness may not come easily.

ONE-TO-ONE MBO

Let us first compare the autocratic and participative characteristics of one-to-one versions of MBO. Examples 1a through 1d in Table 1 illustrate how this form can differ along the autocratic-participative continuum. In one contemporary version of MBO, the superior prepares a list of objectives and simply passes them down to the subordinate. In a second version, the superior prepares the subordinate's list of objectives and allows him or her ample opportunity for questions and clarification. In a third version, the subordinate prepares his own list of objectives and submits this list to his superior for discussion and subsequent editing and modification by the superior. And in a fourth version, the superior and subordinate independently prepare lists of the subordinate's objectives and then meet to agree upon the final list. Similar degrees of subordinate participation also can occur at other steps in the MBO process (in determination of objective measures of performance and in the end-of-the-period evaluation, for example). Obviously many variations are possible, but the point is that the different versions of one-to-one MBO can fall anywhere along the traditional autocratic-participative continuum.

DEFICIENCIES IN ONE-TO-ONE MBO

Disregarding the likely long-range inadequacies of any autocratic form of MBO, we believe that the one-to-one mode has a number of critical deficiencies. First, one-to-one MBO does not adequately account for the interdependent nature of most jobs, particularly at the managerial and supervisory levels. Second, it does not assure optimal coordination of objectives. And third, it does not always improve superior-subordinate relationships, as is widely claimed by MBO proponents (we do not know whether a team approach always will improve relations either, but we are much more optimistic about the

© 1975 by the Regents of the University of California. Reprinted from *California Management Review,* Volume XVII, number 3, pp. 13-22, by permission of the Regents.

TABLE 1. Objective Setting in Different Versions of MBO

Degree of Subordinate Influence on Objectives	Very Little	Some	Moderate	Considerable
Individual Orientation	1a. Superior prepares list of subordinate's objectives and gives it to subordinate.	1b. Superior prepares list of subordinate's objectives; allows opportunity for clarification and suggestions.	1c. Subordinate prepares list of his objectives; superior-subordinate discussion of tentative list is followed by editing, modification, and finalization by superior.	1d. Superior and subordinate independently prepare list of subordinate's objectives; mutual agreement reached after extensive dialogue.
Team Orientation	2a. Superior prepares individual lists of various subordinates' objectives; hands out lists in group meeting and explains objectives.	2b. Superior prepares unit and individual objectives; allows opportunity for questions and suggestions in group meeting.	2c. Superior prepares list of unit objectives which are discussed in group meeting; superior decides. Subordinates than prepare lists of their objectives, discuss with superior; individuals' objectives discussed in team meeting with modifications made by superior after extensive dialogue.	2d. Unit objectives, including team effectiveness goals, are developed among superior, subordinates, and peers in a group meeting, usually by consensus; superior and subordinates later independently prepare lists of subordinates' objectives, reach temporary agreement; subordinates' objectives finalized after extensive discussion in team meeting.

latter). These deficiencies pertain to all versions of one-to-one MBO, regardless of how autocratic or participative, although we believe that the deficiencies would be more salient under autocratic supervisory behavior. Let us examine these limitations more closely.

Managerial Interdependence

A number of writers have pointed out that one-to-one, superior-subordinate MBO does not recognize the interdependent or complementary nature of managerial jobs.[1] We concur with this criticism and believe that effective implementation of MBO requires a "systems view" of the organization. Each manager functions in a complex network of vertical, horizontal, and diagonal relationships, and his success in achieving his objectives is often (if not always) dependent upon the communication, cooperation, and support of other managers in this network.

The relevance of managerial interdependence is particularly evident when MBO is used with staff managers. A number of authors have described the difficulties in applying MBO to staff positions.[2] We need not reiterate their ideas here, except to stress the point that the advisory and supportive nature of staff work dictates that a staff manager's objectives be highly interrelated with the activities and objectives of other managers, both line and staff. Furthermore, staff objectives are often more qualitative than quantitative, and therefore more difficult to set and measure. Asking the staff manager to set either qualitative or quantitative objectives in isolation from those upon whom his attainment of these objectives is largely dependent does not make good sense.

An indication of the lack of attention to the interdependent nature of managerial jobs can be found in two recent works, one including descriptions of MBO programs in four British firms,[3] the other including five American companies.[4] Eight of the nine companies require that forms be filled out in the MBO programs, but in only one company's form is there any space for the manager to specify the extent to which his objectives require involvement of other managers.

Coordination of Objectives

Another deficiency is associated with this interdependency. One of the highly touted advantages of MBO is that it results in effective coordination of objectives; that is, there is better integration (including minimization of gaps and duplication) of the objectives of all managers in the work unit. While this is certainly a desirable benefit, it must be recognized that one-to-one MBO places the responsibility for such coordination entirely upon the superior, since he is the only person in the MBO process to have formal contact with all subordinate managers. In effect, the superior is required to function as a "central processing center of objectives."

We believe that one-to-one MBO simply does not provide the opportunity for maximum coordination of objectives. The superior may be able to marginally, or even adequately, coordinate the objectives of his immediate subordinates on a one-to-one basis, but this procedure does not really do justice to the subtleties of interdependent relationships. Under such circumstances, except for information transmitted informally and sporadically between peers in on-the-job interaction, subordinate managers have little knowledge or understanding of each other's objectives. On the other hand, if these subordinates were provided with the opportunity for dynamic interactive processes in which their objectives are systematically communicated and adjusted, final objectives probably would be more effectively coordinated.

The deficiency in the coordination of objectives is magnified in cases of managers performing highly interrelated tasks but working in different departments. For example, a sales manager in a marketing division organized along product lines needs to coordinate his objectives with those of the appropriate production manager responsible for manufacturing the product. The sales manager may meet his objective of a 5 percent increase in the sales of product X, but the organization is likely to suffer a loss of future sales and customers if the manufacturing output of product X, which is based upon the production manager's objectives, is inadequate to meet these sales commitments. One-to-one MBO between the sales and production managers and their respective superiors provides no systematic method for integrating their objectives, and accordingly, these two managers must rely entirely upon their own initiative for the development of integrating mechanisms. Quite frankly, we doubt that this haphazard approach results in optimal coordination.

Improved Superior-Subordinate Relationships

The participative, or mutual involvement, form of one-to-one MBO is extolled largely for the improvement in superior-subordinate relationships it is expected to bring about. Not all research supports this claim, however. For example, Tosi and Carroll found that even after an intensive and carefully planned MBO program that stressed subordinate participation, subordinate managers did not feel that the superior-subordinate relationship had improved significantly in terms of helpfulness on the part of the superior.[5] While the researchers offered no specific empirical reasons for this finding, other authors have suggested factors that might provide some explanation.

Kerr believes that the typical organization hierarchy creates a superior-subordinate status differential that acts as a deterrent to the expected improvement in relationships.[6] For instance, when MBO is conducted in a somewhat autocratic manner the status differential inhibits the subordinate from challenging the decisions of his boss or the objectives he has established. Even in cases of greater subordinate involvement, status differences may hinder attainment of the desired ideal mutuality in the MBO process. A similar note is struck by Levinson, who believes that rivalry between a boss and his subordinate can easily impede the creation or maintenance of a positive relationship.[7] It is important to point out that Tosi and Carroll also found that the same MBO program stressing increased subordinate participation resulted in no significant increase in subordinates' perceived influence in the goal-setting process.[8] Perhaps superior-subordinate status differentials or rivalry were operating in this organization.

Incompatibility between the superior's role as a coach and his role as a judge may also hamper the superior-subordinate relationship. Researchers at The General Electric Company concluded that the two primary purposes of performance appraisal (performance improvement and salary adjustment) are in conflict.[9] They suggested that these two purposes could be better accomplished in two separate interviews—a proposal with which we agree. Yet even in this approach, it is easy to see the difficult position in which the superior is placed: prior to and during one interview he is expected to *constructively* evaluate the subordinate's performance and help him formulate plans for improvement, while in the second interview he is expected to *judiciously* evaluate the subordinate's performance in order to make crucial salary recommendations and to inform the subordinate of his decision. Only an exceptionally talented person could shift adroitly between these two roles (especially with the same subordinate), and it is our opinion that most managers have great difficulty doing so. Thus, an MBO program that requires the superior to have complete responsibility in performing these incompatible roles, even in separate interviews, could easily strain rather than improve superior-subordinate relationships.

TEAM COLLABORATION IN MBO

We believe that MBO could be strengthened considerably by increasing the opportunities for systematic collaboration among managers. Furthermore, MBO programs based on cooperative teamwork and group problem solving would represent a positive step toward rectifying some of the deficiencies found in one-to-one MBO. Ironically, in his original description of MBO, Drucker said, "Right from the start . . . emphasis should be on team-work and team results," [10] but it doesn't look to us as if the MBO movement has gone this way. A number of other authors have called for group or peer goal setting and evaluation in MBO,[11] but with few exceptions [12] suggestions for a group approach to MBO generally have not been augmented with systematic guidelines or frameworks for implementation.

MBO programs described in the literature and in operation that *do* acknowledge the collaborative dimension can be classified in three categories. First, there are programs that superficially refer to the need for some sort of collaborative effort during the MBO process. For example, the MBO instruction manual may include a statement such as: "Each manager should exert maximum effort to ensure that his objectives are effectively coordinated with those of other managers in his work group." Under this unsystematic approach, then, collaboration is left entirely to each manager's own initiative.

Second, there are programs that provide some formal means for collaboration (see examples 2b and 2c in Table 1). For instance, Wikstrom describes one company program that includes "cross-checking meetings" in which managers present their tentative goals, check the impact of these goals on one another, and make adjustments before finalizing the goals.[13] In a similar vein, Raia suggests team reviews between the superior and his subordinates.[14] Based upon a joint problem-solving approach, these regular review sessions are intended to measure the team's progress toward its goals and to improve team relationships. Raia also encourages the use of a "responsibility matrix" to identify the degree to which various other management positions are related to the major activities a manager performs to accomplish his specific objectives.[15] In essence, then, programs in this second category include collaboration as a tangential aspect of an essentially one-to-one approach.

Third, there are MBO programs that include systematic collaboration as an integral part of the entire process (see example 2d in Table 1). The three-day team objectives meeting described by Reddin illustrates this approach.[16] In this program each team (superior and his immediate subordinates) concentrates on such matters as team-effectiveness areas, team-improvement objectives, team decision making, optimal team organization, team meeting improvements, team-effectiveness evaluation, and team-member effectiveness. Such collaborative approaches appear to have many features congruent with contemporary organization development (OD) and are qualitatively quite different from one-to-one approaches.

MBO AND OD CONTRASTED

One way to describe how CMBO differs qualitatively from a one-to-one approach is to contrast the one-to-one version with the emerging field of OD, which has a strong emphasis on team collaboration. Organization development, in the behavioral-science meaning of the term,[17] is a broader strategy for organizational improvement than is MBO, but it can include the collaborative version as we shall describe it. For instance, Blake and Mouton's six-phase grid OD program includes teamwork development (phase 2) and intergroup development (phase 3), both of which include collaborative goal setting.[18] In fact, they suggest that MBO can be "introduced as the culminating action of Teamwork Development." [19]

Some of the differences, as we see them, between the traditional one-to-one MBO and OD are shown in Table 2. Traditional MBO concentrates on the individual, on goal setting for the individual, on rationality, and on end results. In contrast, OD focuses on how individuals see the functioning of their teams and the organization, on nonrationality as well as rationality, and on means as well as ends. In addition, OD has a recurring component of system diagnosis that seems to be minimal or absent from the traditional forms of MBO. Further, OD efforts usually move toward legitimizing open discussion of individual career and life goals, which most MBO programs largely ignore.

A STRATEGY FOR COLLABORATIVE MBO

Contemporary organization-development efforts can provide insights and some of the technology for more widespread emergence of collaborative forms of MBO. We would like to propose a nine-phase strategy for Collaborative MBO. Basically, the essential process is one of overlapping work units interacting with "higher" and "lower" units on overall organizational goals and objectives, unit goals and objectives, and individuals interacting with peers and superiors on role definition and individual goals and objectives.

Phase I: Diagnosis of Organizational Problems

A collaborative organizational diagnosis, by discussions or questionnaires involving a cross-section of organization members, suggests the usefulness of a CMBO effort in solving *identified problems*. It appears to us that MBO, as frequently practiced, is a solution in search of a problem. For a variety of reasons, including the existence of a strong goal emphasis under some other name, overwork of many key people in the organization, or problems requiring other solutions, MBO may not be timely or appropriate.

Phase II: Information and Dialogue

Workshops on the basic purposes and techniques of CMBO are held with top management personnel, followed by workshops at the middle- and lower-management levels. These workshops can be conducted by qualified members of the personnel or training departments, by line managers trained in the approach, or if the organization prefers, by a qualified consultant. Having top-level managers conduct the workshops with middle and lower managers may speed up the process of shifting toward the more supportive climate necessary for CMBO.

Phase III: Diagnosis of Organizational Readiness

This diagnosis, based upon interviews and group meetings, must indicate an interest in and a willingness to use the process on the part of several organizational units, especially those at the top of the organization. Ideally, a number of overlapping units should express a desire to implement CMBO; for example, in addition to the president of a manufacturing firm and his immediate subordinates expressing interest, the manufacturing director and his immediate subordinates may want to be involved, and two of these subordinate managers may wish to start the process with their subordinate teams, and so forth. Favorable interest in CMBO from a few units randomly scattered throughout the organization would probably be inadequate to create enough interaction and momentum to give the approach a fair try. A good deal of diagnosis of organizational readiness will have already occurred in the information-and-dialogue phase. Similarly, diagnosis of organizational readiness may reveal the need for supplemental CMBO workshops for some units or for suspending the CMBO effort.

Phase IV: Goal Setting—Overall Organization Level

Overall organization goals and specific objectives to be achieved within a given time period are defined in team meetings among top executives, largely on the basis of consensus. It is important that this phase be an interactive process with middle and lower levels of the organization; inputs about organization

TABLE 2. Traditional MBO Compared with OD

What Traditional (One-to-One) MBO Seems to Do	What OD Seems to Do
1. Assumes there is a need for more goal emphasis and/or control.	1. Assumes there may be a variety of problems; a need for more goal emphasis and/or control may or may not be a central problem.
2. Has no broad diagnostic strategy.	2. Uses an "action-research" model in which system diagnosis and rediagnosis are major features.
3. Central target of change is the individual.	3. Central target of change is team functioning.
4. Asks organization members to develop objectives for key aspects of their jobs in terms of quantitative and qualitative statements that can be measured.	4. Asks organization members to provide data regarding their perceptions of functional/dysfunctional aspects of their units and/or the total organization.
5. Emphasizes avoidance of overlap and incongruity of goals. Assumes things will be better if people understand who has what territory.	5. Emphasizes mutual support and help. Assumes that some problems can stem from confusion about who has what responsibilities, but also looks at opportunities for mutual help in the many interdependent components across jobs.
6. Focuses on the "formal" aspects of the organization (goals, planning, control, appraisal).	6. Initially taps into "informal" aspects of the organization (attitudes, feelings, perceptions about both the formal and informal aspects—the total climate of the unit or organization).
7. Focuses on individual performance and emphasizes individual accountability.	7. Focuses on system dynamics that are facilitating or handicapping individual, team, and organizational performance; emphasizes joint accountability.
8. Legitimizes for discussion nonrational aspects (feelings, attitudes, group phenomena) of organization life as well as rationality; frequently legitimizes open exploration of career and life goals.	8. Stresses rationality ("logical" problem solving, man's economic motives).
9. Focuses on both ends and means of the human-social system (leadership style, peer relationships, and decision processes, as well as goals and "hard data").	9. Focuses on organizational end results of the human-social system (particularly as measured by "hard data") such as sales figures, maintenance costs, and so forth.
10. Has extensive interpersonal relations, group dynamics, and intergroup "technology" for decision making, communications, and group task and maintenance processes.	10. Has little interpersonal-relations "technology" to assist superior and subordinate in the goal-setting and review processes.

goals and objectives from subordinate managerial and supervisory levels must be obtained during (or before) this phase.

Phase V:
Goal Setting—Unit Level

Unit goals and objectives essential to achieving overall organization goals and objectives are defined in team situations, largely by consensus. Again, this is an interactive process between higher units and their respective subordinate units.

Phase VI:
Goal Setting—Individual Level

This phase begins with individual managers developing their specific objectives in terms of results to be achieved and appropriate time periods. Personal career and development goals are part of this "package." If desired, the manager's superior may simultaneously develop a list of objectives for the subordinate. The superior and subordinate discuss, modify, and tentatively agree on the subordinate's objectives. These discussions are followed by group meetings in which team members discuss each other's objectives, make suggestions for modification, and agree upon each manager's final list of objectives.

Phase VI assumes that there is agreement on the major responsibilities and parameters of the team members' roles. If major responsibilities need to be reviewed or redefined, the following sequence is used as the preliminary stage of phase VI: (1) individual team members list their major responsibilities; (2) individual team members meet with their superior to discuss, modify, and tentatively agree upon their major responsibilities; and (3) team members discuss and work toward consensus on their major responsibilities in group meetings.

Phase VII:
Performance Review

On a continuing basis, either the subordinate or the superior initiates discussion whenever progress toward objectives should be reviewed; matters of team concern are discussed in regularly scheduled team meetings. Particularly relevant at this stage are occasions when internal or external factors suggest the need for revision in the original set of goals and objectives; if appropriate, these revisions should be made in collaborative team meetings.

At the end of the agreed-upon time period, each manager prepares a report on the extent to which his objectives have been achieved and discusses this report in a preliminary meeting with his superior. These reports then are presented by each individual in a group meeting, with the discussion including an analysis of the forces helping and hindering attainment of objectives. This review process occurs at all levels (organization, unit, and individual) and ordinarily would start at the lower levels as a convenient way to collate information.

Phase VIII:
Rediagnosis

Diagnosis needs to reoccur, but at this phase it is the CMBO process itself that needs examining, as well as the readiness of additional units to use CMBO. Is the CMBO process helping? hindering? in what way? What is the process doing to the relationships between superiors and subordinates and within teams? Something has gone awry if goal setting and performance review are perfunctory or avoided, if the process seems unattached to the basic processes of getting the work of the organization done, or if relationships are becoming strained. On the other hand, if superiors and subordinates and teams find that the process is challenging and stretches and develops their capabilities, and if they feel good about it, the CMBO process is probably on the right track toward increased organizational effectiveness. Ideally such diagnosis should be ongoing as the CMBO process evolves.

Phase IX:
Recycle

Assuming that rediagnosis has resulted in the decision to continue the CMBO effort, the cycle of phases IV through VIII is repeated, probably once a year at the overall organization level. Ongoing individual and team progress reviews may result in modification of unit- or individual-level goals more often than once a year. Through periodic problem sensing and rediagnosis, the details of the process will undoubtedly be modified to more adequately meet the needs of teams and individuals. The nine-phase strategy for implementing CMBO is presented in Figure 1.

SOME CONTINGENCIES

CMBO is not likely to be an easy process for many organizations. Initial successes depend upon a strong desire on the part of the top-management team to cooperate with and help each other. In addition, the process requires some modicum of skill in interpersonal relations and group dynamics. Training in these skills can accompany the CMBO effort, or if an OD effort is under way, such skills will be emerging as part of this broader process.

Proper timing in the introduction of CMBO is also very important. CMBO is by no means a managerial panacea; it should be introduced only when diagnosis suggests its applicability and usefulness as well as organizational readiness. A CMBO effort can be time-consuming, and strong resistance can occur if the process is thoughtlessly superimposed at the wrong time—for example, during a period when people are preoccupied and harried with the annual budgeting process or faced with a major external threat to the organization. It is equally important to recognize that the utility of diagnosing organizational readiness is contingent upon the adequacy of information presented to managers in the CMBO workshops (phase II).

Successful expansion of the process to lower levels of the organization requires commitment to and skills in participative management, as well as a willingness and ability to diagnose the impact of the goal-setting and

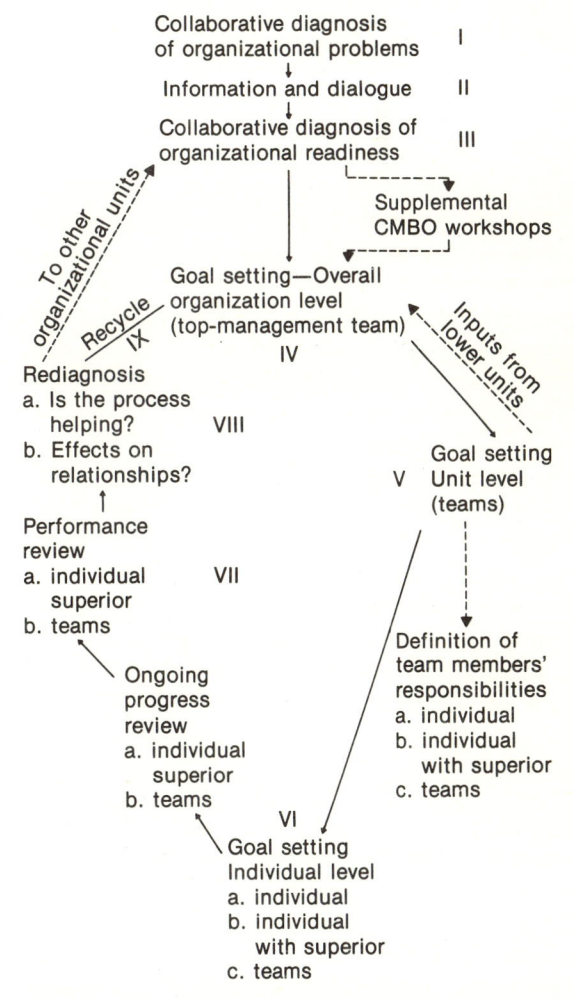

Figure 1. A strategy for implementing collaborative management by objectives

review processes on organization members and organizational functioning. Such a diagnosis of how things are going might result, for instance, in temporarily postponing phase VI. Successful completion of phases I through V and the appropriate team aspects of phases VII through IX might in itself be a major achievement and a move forward in organizational effectiveness. Developing effective group dynamics takes time and an organization should proceed with caution in this area. A major shift to a collaborative mode cannot be made overnight.

THE MERITS OF CMBO: RESEARCH AND PRACTICE CLUES

There are a number of clues to the merits of a Collaborative MBO approach (that is, the kind that has a team emphasis, is truly collaborative, and exists in a climate of mutual support and help) in research reports and in practice. Likert cites a study of a sales organization in which salesmen held group meetings at regular intervals to set goals, discuss procedures, and identify results to be achieved before the next group meeting.[20] During these meetings the superior acted as a chairman; he stressed a constructive, problem-solving approach, encouraged high performance, and provided technical advice when necessary. The results of the study showed that salesmen using group meetings had more positive attitudes toward their jobs and sold more on the average than salesmen not using group meetings. According to Likert:

> Appreciably poorer results are achieved whenever the manager, himself, analyzes each man's performance and results and sets goals for him. Such man-to-man interactions in the meetings, dominated by the manager, do not create group loyalty and have far less favorable impact upon the salesmen's motivation than do group interaction and decision meetings. Moreover, in the man-to-man interaction little use is made of the sales knowledge and skills of the group.[21]

Another recent study found that managers' perceptions of the supportiveness of the organizational climate and their attitudes toward MBO were significantly related.[22] A supportive climate was viewed in terms of such features as high levels of trust and confidence between superiors and subordinates, multidirectional communication aimed at achieving objectives, cooperative teamwork, subordinate participation in decision making and goal setting, and control conducted close to the point of performance (self-control). Essentially, this climate was seen as comparable to Likert's Participative Group (System 4) management system.[23] The results of the study showed significant ($p < 0.01$) positive correlations between the supportiveness of the climate and how effective managers believed the MBO process to be. Managers' evaluations of MBO effectiveness were assessed in six areas: (1) planning and organizing work, (2) objective evaluation of performance, (3) motivation of the best job performance, (4) coordination of individual and work-group objectives, (5) superior-subordinate communication, and (6) superior-subordinate cooperation. Even more important was the significant ($p < 0.01$) positive correlation between supportiveness of the climate and managers' overall satisfaction with MBO as it related to their jobs.[24]

Holder describes how consensus decision making has been used at Yellow Freight System, Inc. since the early 1950s.[25] Work groups in the firm are organized according to the "linking-pin concept"[26] and decisions, including those dealing with managers' objectives, are made on a consensus basis within each work group. The writer's account is unclear as to whether consensus MBO operates throughout the management hierarchy; however, his description indicates that it extends to at least the regional-manager level. Although Holder provides no objective measure of effectiveness, he suggests that the length of time for which the program has been used attests to its success.

Finally, in explaining a job-enrichment program in a European chemical company, Myers reports: "In 1970, more than 40,000 additional employees conferred in work teams and functional groups to define criteria against which their performance could be measured and to set tangible goals."[27] According to Myers, the program has (a) moved decision making down to the levels where the work is performed, (b) resulted in better integration of individual and organizational goals, (c) required managers to rely upon interpersonal competence rather than official authority to get results, and (d) reduced the traditional barrier between management and nonmanagement. We think this experience is particularly significant; if operative work groups can effectively set objectives in a collaborative environment, it seems reasonable to expect that managers would also be able to do so.

CONCLUSIONS

The findings of these studies and organizational programs help confirm our belief that Collaborative Management by Objectives can work. We feel that CMBO, as we have described it, is congruent with a participative, team-leadership style and can avoid many of the dysfunctional spin-offs of the prevailing one-to-one versions of MBO. We do not wish to imply, however, that CMBO will work in all organizations and under any circumstances. Care must be taken to ensure that appropriate conditions are present before and that necessary skills emerge during the implementation of CMBO.

Successful application of CMBO requires that managers be motivated to shift the climate of the organization, or at least the climate of those units using CMBO, in the direction of more teamwork, more cooperation, more joint problem solving, and more support. While a team approach per se would tend to diminish the dysfunctional consequences of status differentials and could shift the locus of commitments among people away from the one-to-one arena toward the lateral or interdependent team arena, a team approach void of mutual support and group skills could create more problems than it would solve. Training of work teams in skills of communication, group processes, and joint problem solving is vital to this shift toward a more supportive climate.

Equally vital to the success of CMBO are skills in diagnosis—both the original diagnosis that identifies the need and readiness for CMBO and the subsequent diagnoses that tune into managers' perceptions of the functional and dysfunctional aspects of the CMBO process and their assessment of the emerging climate. Such continuous "tracking" will be hard work, but the resulting opportunities for modification and other corrective action should make the CMBO process that much more relevant to the needs of the organization and its members.

The nine-phase strategy we have proposed is one way of introducing more systematic collaboration into the MBO process. While it will undoubtedly take considerable effort and attention to make the CMBO strategy work well, this approach can help people, teams, and units become more goal-directed without undermining efforts to maintain or create a participative, responsive team climate in the organization.

NOTES

1. See, for example, Gerard F. Carvalho, "Installing Management by Objectives: A New Perspective on Organization Change," *Human Resource Management* (Spring 1972), pp. 23-30; Robert A. Howell, "A Fresh Look at Management by Objectives," *Business Horizons* (Fall 1967), pp. 51-58; Charles L. Hughes, "Assessing the Performance of Key Managers," *Personnel* (January-February 1968), pp. 38-43; Bruce D. Jamieson, "Behavioral Problems with Management by Objectives," *Academy of Management Journal* (September 1973), pp. 496-505; Harold Koontz, "Making Managerial Appraisal Effective," *California Management Review* (Winter 1972), pp. 46-55; and Harry Levinson, "Management by Whose Objectives?" *Harvard Business Review* (July-August 1970), pp. 125-134.

2. See, for example, Thomas P. Kleber, "The Six Hardest Areas to Manage by Objectives," *Person-*

nel Journal (August 1972), pp. 571-575; Dale D. McConkey, "Staff Objectives Are Different," *Personnel Journal* (July 1972), p. 477ff.; and Burt K. Scanlan, "Quantifying the Qualifiable, or Can Results Management Be Applied to the Staff Man's Job?" *Personnel Journal* (March 1968), p. 162ff.

3. John W. Humble, ed., *Management by Objectives in Action* (New York: McGraw-Hill) 1970.

4. Walter S. Wikstrom, *Managing by- and with-Objectives* (New York: National Industrial Conference Board, 1968).

5. Henry Tosi and Stephen J. Carroll, Jr., "Improving Management by Objectives: A Diagnostic Change Program," *California Management Review* (Fall 1973), pp. 57-66.

6. Steven Kerr, "Some Modifications in MBO as an OD Strategy," *Proceedings, 1972 Annual Meeting,* Academy of Management, 1973, pp. 39-42.

7. Harry Levinson, "Management by Objectives: A Critique," *Training and Development Journal* (April 1972), pp. 3-8; see also Levinson, op. cit.

8. Tosi and Carroll, op. cit.

9. Herbert H. Meyer, Emanual Kay, and John R. P. French, Jr., "Split Roles in Performance Appraisal," *Harvard Business Review* (January-February 1965), pp. 123-129.

10. Peter F. Drucker, *The Practice of Management* (New York: Harper & Bros.) 1954, p. 126.

11. See, for example, Carvalho, op. cit.; Wendell French, *The Personnel Management Process: Human Resources Administration,* 3d ed. (Boston: Houghton Mifflin) 1974; Howell, op. cit.; Charles L. Hughes, *Goal Setting* (New York: American Management Association) 1965, p. 123; Jamieson, op. cit.; Kerr, op. cit.; and Levinson, "Management by Whose Objectives?" op. cit.

12. A notable exception is W. J. Reddin, *Effective Management by Objectives: The 3-D Method of MBO* (New York: McGraw-Hill) 1971, chapter 14. Also see Wendell French and Cecil H. Bell, Jr., *Organization Development: Behavioral Science Interventions for Organization Improvement* (Englewood Cliffs, N.J.: Prentice-Hall) 1973, pp. 167-168; and Anthony P. Raia, *Managing by Objectives* (Glenview, Ill.: Scott, Foresman) 1974.

13. Wikstrom, op. cit., pp. 22-23.

14. Raia, op. cit., p. 110.

15. Ibid., pp. 75-78.

16. Reddin, op. cit.

17. French and Bell, op. cit., p. 15.

18. Robert R. Blake and Jane S. Mouton, *Corporate Excellence Through Grid Organization Development* (Houston: Gulf Publishing, 1968); and Robert R. Blake and Jane S. Mouton, *Building a Dynamic Corporation Through Grid Organization Development* (Reading, Mass.: Addison-Wesley) 1969.

19. Blake and Mouton, *Corporate Excellence,* p. 110.

20. Rensis Likert, *The Human Organization* (New York: McGraw-Hill) 1967, pp. 55-59.

21. Ibid., p. 57.

22. Robert W. Hollmann, "A Study of the Relationships Between Organizational Climate and Managerial Assessment of Management by Objectives," unpublished Ph.D. dissertation, University of Washington, 1973.

23. Likert, op. cit.; and Rensis Likert, *New Patterns of Management* (New York: McGraw-Hill) 1961.

24. Hollmann, op. cit.

25. Jack J. Holder, Jr., "Decision Making by Consensus," *Business Horizons* (April 1972), pp. 47-54.

26. Likert, *New Patterns of Management* and *The Human Organization* (New York: McGraw-Hill) 1961 and 1967.

27. M. Scott Myers, "Overcoming Union Opposition to Job Enrichment," *Harvard Business Review* (May-June, 1971), pp. 37-49.

SURVEY-GUIDED DEVELOPMENT: USING HUMAN RESOURCES MEASUREMENT IN ORGANIZATIONAL CHANGE

David G. Bowers
Jerome L. Franklin

As it exists today, organizational development (OD) in various forms and practices includes many common values and goals. However, there is also a considerable degree of difference in the various concepts, procedures, and assumptions that are identified within this field. The common elements reflect to some extent the fact that those engaged in the field share some aspects of their backgrounds. The differences reflect different evolutionary streams from which the practice of OD has emerged. Much of what is currently considered within the realm of OD can be traced to the fields of adult education, personnel training, industrial consultation, and clinical psychology. Organizational development now represents a crystallization of the experiences of practitioners from these fields. Examples of the techniques and procedures that have evolved in this way include sensitivity training, human relations training, team development training, process consultation, and role-playing.

Some portion of what presently may be considered organizational development came into existence through a different route, which is perhaps best described as a concern for the utilization of scientific knowledge. This data-based type of development and, specifically, the survey feedback technique, originated not from the search by practitioners for more effective helping tools, but from the concern of organizational management researchers for better ways of moving new scientific findings from the producers (researchers) to the consumers (organizational managers).

This view is clearly spelled out in the prospectus which launched the organizational behavior research program at the Institute for Social Research over 25 years ago:

> The general objective of this research program will be to discover the underlying principles applicable to the problems of organizing and managing human activity. *A second important objective of the project will be to discover how to train persons to understand and skillfully use these principles* (9, p. 2).

> The major emphasis during the last 4 years of the project will be on the experimental verification of the results and *especially on learning how to make effective use of them in everyday situations*. . . . Each experiment will be analyzed in terms of measures made before and after the experiment, and often a series of measures will be made during the experiment (9, p. 10).

> The entire progress of our society depends upon our skill in organizing our activity. Insofar as we can achieve efficiently through systematic research new understandings and skills instead of relying on trial and error behavior, we can speed the development of a society capable of using constructively the resources of an atomic age. Unless we achieve this understanding rapidly and intelligently, we may destroy ourselves in trial and error

Reprinted by permission of the publisher from *Journal of Contemporary Business,* Vol. 1, No. 3 (Summer, 1972), pp. 43-55.

bungling. Understanding individual behavior is not enough, nor is an understanding of the principles governing the behavior of men in small groups. We need generalizations and principles which will point the way to organizing human activity on the scale now required (9, p. 12).

This same prospectus also stated that the basic measurement tool to be used in the proposed studies would be the sample survey, employing procedures that the proposers had developed during their years with the Program Surveys Division of the Department of Agriculture. It was also stated that the study design would be generally like that employed by Rensis Likert in the Agency Management Study (7).

Thus the stage was set for an organizational development emphasis that first engaged in scientific search for principles of organizational management, and then, once such principles were established, set forth to identify effective implementation strategies for them. This plan was provided impetus by real-life circumstances. Researchers rapidly discovered that the generation of sound findings regarding organizational management was one thing and their implementation quite another. Two factors seriously diminished the effective use of early findings. First, although survey items referred to work-world events, there was often no readily accepted "map" tying what was measured to operating realities in ways that were readily understood. Second, because there was a lack of implementation procedures geared to the data, presentation of findings normally involved a narrative report. As a result of both of these factors, there was a great propensity either to file the report away, to pass it along to lower levels accompanied by vague directives to "use it," or simply to seize selectively upon bits which reinforced managers' existing biases (3).

THE NATURE OF SURVEY FEEDBACK

In an effort to solve this problem, Floyd Mann and his colleagues at the Institute for Social Research developed the *survey-feedback* procedure as an implementation tool. No authoritative volume has as yet been written about this development tool. Partially as a result of this absence of detailed description, many persons mistakenly believe that survey feedback consists of a rather superficial handing back of tabulated numbers and percentages, but little else. On the contrary, where the survey feedback is employed with skill and experience, it becomes a sophisticated tool for using the data as a springboard to development. Data are typically tabulated for each and every work group in an organization, as well as for each combination of groups that represents an area of responsibility, including the total organization.

Each supervisor and manager receives a tabulation of this sort, containing data based on the responses of *his own* immediate subordinates, together with documents describing their interpretation and use. A resource person, sometimes from an outside (consulting) agency and at other times from the client system's own staff, usually counsels privately with the supervisor-recipient about the contents of the package and then arranges a suitable time when the supervisor can meet with his subordinates to discuss the findings and their implications. The resource person attends that meeting to provide help to the participants, both in the technical aspects of the tabulations and in the process aspects of the discussion.

Procedures by which the feedback process progresses through an organization may vary from site to site. In certain instances a "waterfall" pattern is adhered to, in which the process substantially is completed at high-level groups before moving down to subordinate groups. In other instances, feedback is more or less simultaneous to all groups and echelons.

By whichever route it takes, an effective survey-feedback operation depicts the organization's groups as moving, by a discussion process, from the tabulated perceptions, through a cataloging of their implications, to commitment for solutions to the problems that the discussion has identified and defined.

THE NECESSITY OF DIFFERENTIAL DIAGNOSIS

From these general and specific concerns there has emerged a viewpoint, largely identified with persons associated with the Institute for Social Research, that constructive change is measurement-centered, beginning with a quantitative reading of the state of the organization and direction of movement. Even more than this, change is, throughout, a rational process that makes use of information, pilot demonstrations, and the persuasive power of evidence and hard fact.

A successful change effort begins with rigorous measurement of the way in which the organization presently is functioning. These measurements provide the material for a diagnosis, and the diagnosis forms the basis for the design of a program of change activities. Likert has stated this quite pointedly in an early publication:

> One approach that can be used to apply the findings of human relations research to your own operation can be described briefly. Your medical departments did not order all of your supervisors nor all of your employees to take penicillin when it became available, even though it is a very effective antibiotic. They have, however, administered it to many of your employees. But not the process of deciding when it should be administered. The individual was given certain tests and measurements obtained—temperature, blood analyses, etc. The results of these measurements were compared with known facts about diseases, infections, etc., and the penicillin was prescribed when the condition was one that was known or believed to be one that would respond to this antibiotic.
>
> We believe the same approach should be used in dealing with the human problems of any organization. This suggests that human relations supervisory training programs should not automatically be prescribed for all supervisory and management personnel. Nor should other good remedies or methods for improvement be applied on a blanket basis to an entire organization hoping it will yield improved results (5, p. 35).

One of the reasons for the importance of the diagnostic step early in the life of a change program is stated explicitly in the preceding quotation: it will increase the probability of focusing upon the right, not the wrong, problems, and it will add to the likelihood of the right, not the wrong, course of treatments being prescribed. A clear statement of the problems, courses of action, and change objectives, based upon sound measurements allied to the best possible conceptualization from research and theory, will maximize the likelihood that true causal conditions, rather than mere symptoms, will be dealt with (2).

THE RATIONALE FOR SURVEY-GUIDED DEVELOPMENT

The preceding sections have pointed to the existence of two somewhat different approaches to organization development. One, growing out of applied practice, is identified more obviously with the laboratory approach to education. It uses the *immediate* behavior (verbal and nonverbal) of the participants as the source material around which development forms. It focuses much more upon the "here-and-now" than upon the "there-and-then" and emphasizes experience-based learnings. It focuses more sharply on issues related to interpersonal processes than those less observable issues of role and structure.

The other approach, which we propose to elaborate on in greater detail, is related more obviously to an information-systems approach to adaptation. This approach uses participants' summarized perceptions of behavior and situation as the source material around which development is focused. It focuses on the "there-and-then" at least as much as upon the "here-and-now," attaches considerably more importance to cognitive understanding than does the other approach, and is concerned with such issues as role and structure, at least as much as with those of interpersonal process.

These brief identifications are more descriptive than explanatory. A true understanding of the survey-guided approach requires that we look more closely at the assumptions which it appears to make and the operating propositions which it derives from those assumptions.

Like most organization development techniques, survey feedback is only one aspect of a measurement-guided approach to change. As a tool or procedure, it emerged as a response to a practical need to see research findings implemented. It did not emerge as the logical conclusion of a formal body of scientific thought, and it remains for us presently to search, after the fact, for a rationale about how and why it works.

In this vein, two bodies of scientific thought seem relevant. One comes from the research done in the area of perception and involves the fundamental concept that a difference between perceptions is motivating —an idea originally and most clearly stated by Peak (8). This is perhaps illustrated by the following example: if I perceive, on the one hand, that I cannot complete a particular piece of work by the end of the normal work day and perceive, on the other hand, that that work must be complete by the start of office hours in the morning, I am motivated to work late or to take home a work-loaded briefcase.

According to this view, the perceptions must be associated, i.e., they must be seen as belonging to the same "domain." I may perceive that I do not play the piano as well as Arthur Rubenstein, but this discrepancy is hardly motivating, because I do not consider myself to be a professional concert pianist. Although associated, the perceptions must be different, yet not so different as to destroy their association. The perceptions may be related to emotion-laden or "feelings" issues, or they may consist of different perceptions of conditions in the external world. Peak illustrates the process by drawing an analogy:

> Think of a thermostat. Here there are two events. One is the temperature setting (an expected state if you will). The other event or term in the system is the height of the mercury in the tube, representing the present state of affairs (room temperature). These are analogous then to the two events in our motive construct, and disparity exists between them when there is a difference in the setting and in the temperature reading. Now, the second feature of our motive construct, which is called contact or association, is provided by the structure of the thermostat and is not modifiable in this system as it is in the motive system. In other words, the two terms (or events) remain in association. Only disparity can vary, and when there is disparity there is "motivation" and action; i.e., the furnace starts to run. The results of this action are fed back to produce change in one of the terms of the disparity relation (the mercury level). When the disparity disappears through rise in temperature or resetting of the thermostat, action ceases . . . But since the thermostat lacks the capacity to stop action through isolation, and in the simple design we have described, cannot select different actions, the model must be regarded merely as illustrative. . . . (8, pp. 172-173).

Another closely related set of ideas comes from engineering psychology and begins with the observation that human behavior is goal-seeking or goal-oriented. As such, behavior is characterized by a search for processes by which the human being controls his environment, i.e., means by which he reshapes it toward more constructive or productive ends.

Oversimplifying the control process greatly, at least four elements are involved: (1) a model, (2) a goal, (3) an activity, and (4) feedback. The *model* is a mental picture of the surrounding world, including not only structural properties, but cause-and-effect relations. It is built by the person(s) from past accumulations of information, stored in memory. From the workings of the model and from the modeling process which he employs, alternative possible future states are generated, of which one is selected as a *goal*. At this point what is called the "goal selection system" ends and what is known as the "control system" *per se* begins. *Activities* are initiated to attain the goal, and *feedback,* which comes by some route from the person's environment, is used to compare, confirm, adjust, and correct responses by signaling departures from what was expected.

The process as just described is beguilingly simple. However, in actual life it is often extremely complex. The thermostat example, although embodied in a marvelous and valuable piece of equipment, is basically a simple instance of an adaptive system. Others are much more complicated, such as that contained in the role of a Mississippi riverboat pilot. The shifting character of currents and channels make this adaptive task quite complex. Therefore the difficulty in this as in other complex systems stems from not having learned how to predict system performance under various conditions. As one of the foremost human factors writers has described it, "The ability to predict system performance is in major respects the same as the ability to control the system" (4, p. 42).

The human organization reflects the same type of a complex, difficult control system, in part for these same reasons. Activity is only as good as the model which leads to it, yet human organizations are often managed according to grossly imperfect models (models which ignore much of what is known from research about organizational structure and functioning).[1] Predictability is enhanced, in human systems as elsewhere, by quantification, yet many of the relationships are often not quantified, if, indeed, they are recognized at all.

In the absence of a sound model, what is expected varies with immediate experience. It is for this reason that objective feedback on organizational functioning is absolutely essential in organizational development. In its absence, true deviations are unknown because expectations constantly adjust to incurred performance.

From this very condensed discussion, it is apparent that when organizational change is viewed as a problem in optimal control or adaptation (which it inherently is) several things are required:

- An adequate model—one which is a valid representation of that external reality known as "the organization," including both structural properties, knowledge of cause-effect relations, and predictive capability;

- A goal—a preferred potential future state, generated by the model;

- An activity—selected as instrumental to attaining that goal;

- Objective feedback—about deviations from what the model would lead us to expect.

These two sets of concepts—the one drawn from basic work in the area of perception, the other taken from the human factors work of engineering psychology—provide jointly a plausible rationale for survey-guided development. As in the human factors area, feedback of information about the actual state of functioning provides key input to selecting development goals and making midcourse corrections. It tells the developing system what needs to be done. The power source, which in human factors descriptions is shown as an external input, is in survey-guided development provided by the sort of discrepancy described by Peak. Survey feedback, by pointing to the existence of differences between what is actually going on and what the model indicates one wants and needs, provides the energy (motivation) to undertake change activities.

In detail, as in general, organizational development (as the survey-guided approach envisions) may be seen as an analogue of adaptation as described by human factors theorists. What they have termed the "goal selection system" is, in survey-based development, the *diagnostic* process. What they have referred to as the "control system" is the *therapeutic* process.

To serve its function within the diagnostic process, the work group draws inputs from the same sorts of areas drawn upon by all adaptive systems:

- From high-level systems: from the larger organization, its top management, and from society in general in the form of performance trends, top management evaluations, labor relations trends, changes in laws or regulations, etc.

- From its own information about the model which they have thus far accepted, as well as information concerning past experiences and results.

- From a reading of how things actually are: from the survey; through what we have described as survey feedback, which deals largely with intragroup behavior, attitudes, and relationships; and from a more formal *diagnosis* (an analytic report prepared by persons skilled in the survey data area) which deals with intergroup and systemic properties.

- From the environment: in many forms, but particularly from the "change agent," the organizational development scientist-consultant who helps to catalyze the overall change process.

Each of these input sources has potential impact by virtue of its presence or comparative absence, its kind, and its quality. For example, the higher-level system inputs ordinarily create some degree of felt urgency. Often, discrepancy generated by this input motivates the initial search and culminates in serious consideration of organizational development as a possible course of action. The extent to which these inputs encourage the development efforts of the client entity is also critical. Many of the development failures occur in instances in which higher-level system inputs are either lacking, which indicates acquiescence, or instead, are signaling outright disapproval of organizational development. A general example of such an instance might involve a supervisor who verbally acquiesces to an organizational development effort for his subordinates but behaves and rewards his subordinates for behaving in ways which are incongruent with the values, assumptions, and goals that are emphasized in organizational development. Efforts that proceed in the face of such higher-level system inputs run a great risk of death by neglect.

From the group's own information storage comes the model of organizational functioning already held by group members. This includes information regarding past organizational practices (behaviors, interaction patterns, managerial styles) as well as outcomes at various levels of finality (absenteeism, turnover, profit, production efficiency, growth, etc.).

The survey provides a means by which multiple perceptions of behaviors and organizational conditions related to effectiveness can be gathered, compiled, and compared. As has been indicated above, one must consider not one, but two, separate input streams from the survey. One of these input streams consists of the survey-feedback process itself, in which tabulations of the group's *own data*, especially concerning its internal functioning, is used as a springboard to the identification, understanding, and solving of problems. The other consists of a more formal diagnosis, prepared by persons skilled in multivariate analysis, and focuses on those problem streams which occur in the system as a whole and which can be seen only by careful comparison of the tabulated data of many groups.

THE CHANGE AGENT'S ROLE

The change agent, as an adjunct person, seems to have no exact counterpart in *manual* control problems. The reason for his presence in organizational development is that a model of organizational functioning and human behavior is not as simple or programmable as that involved in manual control. Reading and digesting survey data are not the same as reading a gauge. Accomplishing an organizational "correction" is much more complicated than pushing a button or turning a wheel a certain number of degrees. In most instances the controller in organizational change—the client group—must be shown what the "gauge" says and how to read it, and must be guided through the operations of making the desired changes. The survey discrepancy, properly digested with the aid of the change agent, both builds the *motivation* to make the change and indicates *what* changes in functioning must occur. However, the change agent helps the client group learn *how* to make the necessary changes.

The primary role of the change agent in survey-guided development is that of a transducer (i.e., an energy link between scientific knowledge regarding principles of organizational functioning and the particular organization or group with which he is working). As such, the change agent enters into both the diagnostic and therapeutic phases of the development effort. During the diagnostic phase, the model that the change agent presents must be reasonably complete, predictive, and adequate to provide the client with useful information. If the model lacks any of these characteristics, the change agent will be supplying the system with little more than noise.

In addition to having these characteristics, the model must be presented to the members of the group or organization accurately and adequately. The issue of acceptance is critical: the best model loses its value unless it is understood in useful ways by members of the system. The model and evidence in its support must be presented in such a manner that acceptance is based upon rational evaluation of the evidence as well as the experiences and insights of those involved in the organization. During this activity, the change agent must have the model clearly in mind, must be able to present the model and its evidence clearly, and must also be able to call upon his group process and related skills to facilitate understanding and acceptance.

As in any other situation in which the talents and knowledge of one man are to be made available to assist another, the manner in which that occurs is, of course, important. In the area of human organizational development, of all places, it is important that the knowledge be made available in a supportive, not a demeaning, fashion; it is not to be "laid on," ordered into place, or delivered as some form of speech from a pretentious throne. Skill in patient explanation, in aiding understanding, and in helping the client entities themselves to come to grips with reality—in short, the whole array of interpersonal skills —is extremely important. But the change agent must have the knowledge of what must be explained, the grasp of what must be understood, and the comprehension of what that reality is.

In this vein, the change agent facilitates the understanding and digesting of diagnostically useful information. In the survey-guided approach, this role involves helping members of the system to understand better the survey-feedback information. It also may involve a range of activities, from a detailed explanation of the meaning and relevance of certain content areas to helping group members understand information from the survey in terms of the here-and-now of the feedback meeting process. In addition, he aids the client group members in setting goals and formulating action plans for the development effort. In this activity, as in the others, the change agent may serve both as a source of information (e.g., suggesting potential actions to be undertaken or considered) and as a facilitator who focuses upon the group's processes.

The change agent also serves as a transducer in the therapeutic phase of survey-guided organizational development. Once a diagnosis has pointed to problem areas in organizational functioning, the change agent provides a link between scientific knowledge regarding effective methods of correcting specific problems and the problems exhibited in the immediate situation. A variety of activities may be undertaken during this phase. Each has, as its ultimate goal, movement toward the model of organizational functioning held (after its initial establishment) by both change agent and clients.

In part, the specific type of activity undertaken depends upon the stage in the therapeutic phase. In the early stages, the change agent is likely to be involved largely with supplying informational inputs regarding specific possible activities, helping organizational members cope with attitudinal shifts, and handling defensive reactions. The motivation to change created by a discrepancy between the ideal model and the actual state of the organization is alone not sufficient to produce change. Methods of actually accomplishing the change must also be evident to organizational members. In this respect, the change agent in part fulfills his transducer role by informing members of the client system of the available alternatives.

In later stages the change agent is often involved with skill acquisition and perfection by group members. The range and variety of potentially necessary skills is large. Problem-solving, giving and receiving personal feedback, listening, general leadership, goal-setting, resolving conflict, and diagnosing group processes are but a few of those which might be cited. The change agent must not only know which skills are needed, but also must be competent in guiding their acquisition. It is as a result of this acquisition and perfection of skill that organizational members come to rely less on the change agent and more on themselves in movement toward the goal.

In addition to the emphasis on skills, the change agent provides and facilitates informal intermediate-phase feedback during the therapeutic phase. For example, he may provide the group with feedback in the form of process comments inserted during or after key intragroup interactions. He may also facilitate attempts by the members themselves to gather and understand information regarding their progress toward accepted goals.

A RECAPITULATION

As the preceding pages have indicated, the survey-guided approach suggests several general propositions regarding: (1) certain basic assumptions of organizational development, (2) change processes, and (3) the change agent's role.

Basic Assumptions of OD

• There are systemic properties; i.e., characteristics of the organization as a total system, not definable by the simple sum of individual and/or group behaviors.

• A *model* of organizational functioning which includes these systemic properties, reflecting available evidence and testable by quantifiable and scientific means, should be used as a basis for development efforts.

• Systemic properties in particular can improve only as a result of *carefully sequenced planned interventions.*

• *Valid information* about the state of group and organizational functioning (objective and useful reflections of reality) is best obtained from summarized, quantified longitudinal perceptions. (There-and-then data are at least as useful as here-and-now data.)

• A *diagnosis* based upon a quantitative comparison with the model and prepared by competent professionals should be used to evaluate the organization on both intragroup and systemic levels.

• *Prescription* of intervention activities should be *diagnostically based.*

Change Processes

• *Motivation* is created by the realization that the actual state differs from the accepted model (i.e., a discrepancy exists between that which is desired and that which exists).

• The discrepancies exist in terms of both *intragroup* and *systemic* processes and properties.

• Change involves a *sequence of events* including informational inputs; formation of a model; selection of a goal; assessment of the situation; formation of a diagnosis; feedback; adjustment; and reevaluation.

Change Agent's Role and Activities

• The change agent acts as a *transducer* between scientific knowledge regarding organizational functioning and change processes, on the one hand, and the particular situation, on the other.

• He has a *model* of organizational functioning and *works toward* its realization.

• Except in those rare instances which require a nondirective stance, the change agent is an *active advocate of goal-oriented behavior*. He evaluates and helps the client group to *evaluate progress toward the goal*, but he is not punitive.

• He must have a *wide range of knowledge and skills* and not be bound to one or two particular techniques.

These general propositions of survey-guided development are illustrated as a flow of events in Figure 1.

PERSPECTIVE AND PROLOGUE

We conclude by offering an apology to the reader who anticipated a less labored description. What has been written has been, in many ways, a rather technical document. It reflects our strong belief that organizational development rightfully is becoming more a science than an art. This view was expressed several years ago by one of the authors:

> By science I mean discernable in replicatable terms—objective, understandable (rather than "mystique"), verifiable, and predictive. Should these conditions for organizational development fail to be met, it will go the way of the Great Auk and the "Group Talking Technique." In short, organizational development will die, having been remembered as one more fad.
>
> Organizational development cannot survive on the good will of top management persons who are already sold on its potential and effectiveness. It can survive only if it proves its method and its contribution beyond reasonable doubt to the hard-headed skeptics. Organizational development must prove with hard, rigorous evidence that it can beneficially affect: (a) the volume of work done by the organization, (b) the cost per unit of doing the organization's work, and (c) the quality of work done (1, p. 62).

The same article described barriers which, up to that time, had impeded the progress of organizational development as a science:

• The lack of a "critical mass" of knowledge in the field.

• The tendency for organizational development to take the form of a single general practitioner, operating on an isolated island.

• The absence of an adequate measuring instrument, geared to an adequate model of organizational functioning, for use in organizational development efforts.

Within the last decade, considerable progress has been made on each of these fronts. Books and articles, describing and integrating findings in this field, have appeared in increasing numbers and richness. This present journal issue is a case in point.

To the extent that our own experience is typical, opportunities for researchers and change agents to collaborate in multifaceted, large system development efforts have emerged.

Efforts have similarly been undertaken by a number of persons to develop procedures and instruments for rigorous description of

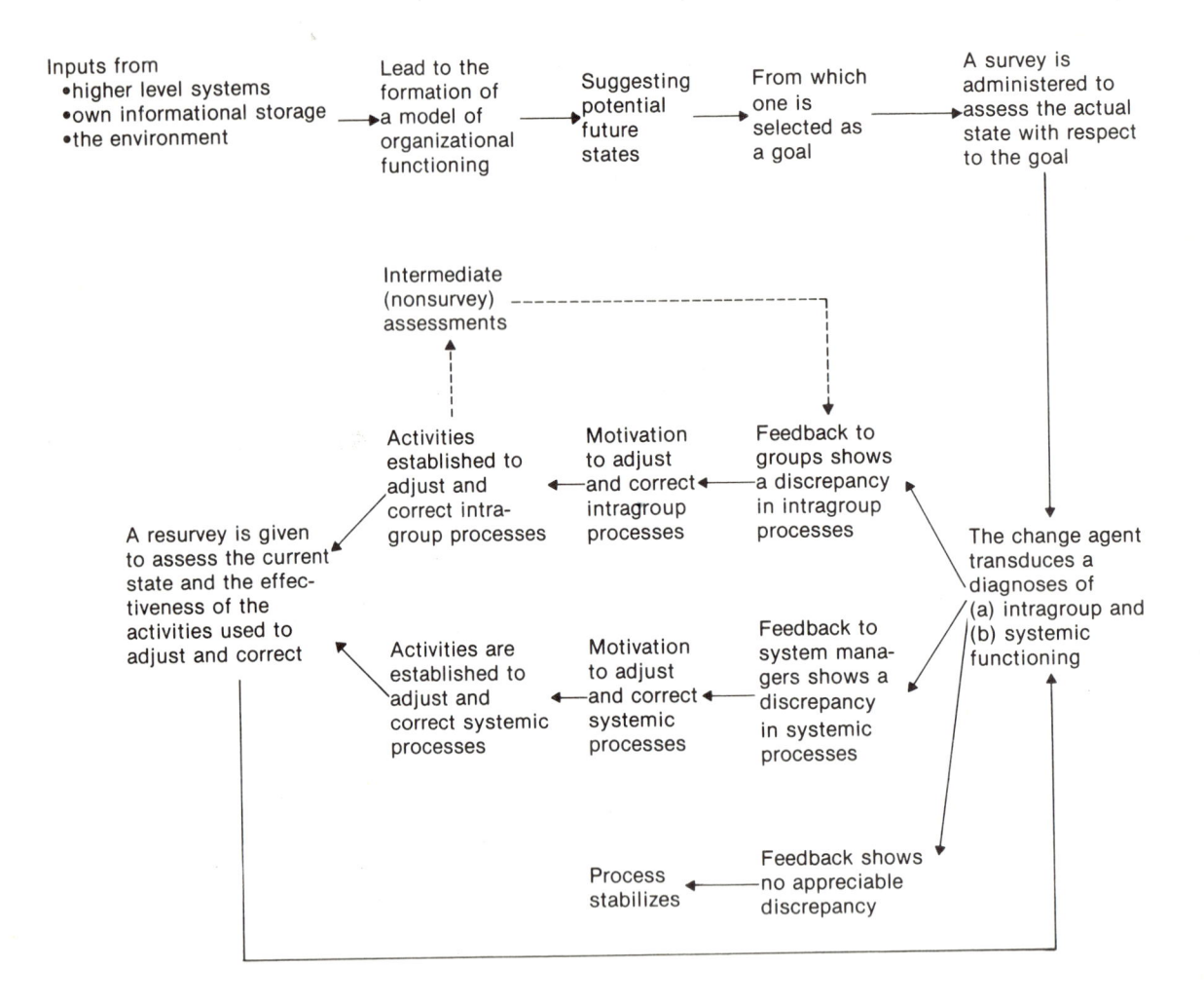

Figure 1. Survey-guided development

change agent interventions and their immediate effects.

Finally, we feel that survey-guided development has pressed, from its own necessity, the construction of reliable, valid, standardized instruments for assessing organizational functioning.

The availability of such instruments, together with the accumulating critical mass of knowledge, leads us to considerable optimism concerning the future of organizational development in general and concerning the survey-guided approach in particular.

NOTE

1. It should be recognized that the term "model" may refer to any of a wide range of alternatives, from very simple predictive notions (e.g., "a democratic supervisor gets results") to quite complex theories, such as Likert's System Four.

REFERENCES

1. Bowers, D. G., The Scientific Data-Based Approach to Organization Development, Part 2, in A. L. Hite, ed., *Organizational Development: The State of the Art* (Ann Arbor, Michigan: Foundation for Research on Human Behavior) 1971.

2. Bowers, D. G., *System 4: The Ideas of Rensis Likert* (New York: Basic Books) 1972.

3. Katz, Daniel, and Robert L. Kahn, *The Social Psychology of Organizations* (New York: John Wiley & Sons) 1966.

4. Kelley, C. R., *Manual and Automatic Control* (New York: John Wiley & Sons) 1968.

5. Likert, R., Findings of Research on Management and Leadership. *Proceedings, Vol. 43,* Pacific Coast Gas Assn., 1952.

6. Likert, R., *The Human Organization* (New York: McGraw-Hill) 1967.

7. Likert, R. and J. M. Willets, *Morale and Agency Management* (Hartford, Conn.: Life Insurance Agency Management Association) 1940. 4 vols.

8. Peak, H., Attitude and Motivation, in M. R. Jones, ed., *Nebraska Symposium on Motivation* (Lincoln, Nebraska: University of Nebraska Press) 1955.

9. Survey Research Center, *A Program of Research on the Fundamental Problems of Organizing Human Behavior* (Ann Arbor, Michigan: University of Michigan) 1947.

10. Taylor, J. C. and D. G. Bowers. *The Survey of Organizations: A Machine-Scored, Standardized Questionnaire Instrument* (Ann Arbor, Michigan: Institute for Social Research) 1972.

J. Richard Hackman, Greg Oldham, Robert Janson, and Kenneth Purdy

A NEW STRATEGY FOR JOB ENRICHMENT

Practitioners of job enrichment have been living through a time of excitement, even euphoria. Their craft has moved from the psychology and management journals to the front page and the Sunday supplement. Job enrichment, which began with the pioneering work of Herzberg and his associates, originally was intended as a means to increase the motivation and satisfaction of people at work—and to improve productivity in the bargain.[1,2,3,4,5] Now it is being acclaimed in the popular press as a cure for problems ranging from inflation to drug abuse.

Much current writing about job enrichment is enthusiastic, sometimes even messianic, about what it can accomplish. But the hard questions of exactly what should be done to improve jobs, and how, tend to be glossed over. Lately, because the harder questions have not been dealt with adequately, critical winds have begun to blow. Job enrichment has been described as yet another "management fad," as "nothing new," even as a fraud. And reports of job-enrichment failures are beginning to appear in management and psychology journals.

This article attempts to redress the excesses that have characterized some of the recent writings about job enrichment. As the technique increases in popularity as a management tool, top managers inevitably will find themselves making decisions about its use. The intent of this paper is to help both managers and behavioral scientists become better able to make those decisions on a solid basis of fact and data.

Succinctly stated, we present here a new strategy for going about the redesign of work. The strategy is based on three years of collaborative work and cross-fertilization among the authors—two of whom are academic researchers and two of whom are active practitioners in job enrichment. Our approach is new, but it has been tested in many organizations. It draws on the contributions of both management practice and psychological theory, but it is firmly in the middle ground between them. It builds on and complements previous work by Herzberg and others, but provides for the first time a set of tools for *diagnosing* existing jobs—and a map for translating the diagnostic results into specific action steps for change.

What we have, then, is the following:

1. A theory that specifies when people will get personally "turned on" to their work. The theory shows what kinds of jobs are most

© 1975 by the Regents of the University of California. Reprinted from *California Management Review,* Volume XVII, number 4, pp. 57 to 71, by permission of the Regents. The research activities reported were supported in part by the Organizational Effectiveness Research Program of the Office of Naval Research, and the Manpower Administration of the U.S. Department of Labor, both through contracts to Yale University.

likely to generate excitement and commitment about work, and what kinds of employees it works best for.

2. A set of action steps for job enrichment based on the theory, which prescribe in concrete terms what to do to make jobs more motivating for the people who do them.

3. Evidence that the theory holds water and that it can be used to bring about measurable —and sometimes dramatic—improvements in employee work behavior, in job satisfaction, and in the financial performance of the organizational unit involved.

THE THEORY BEHIND THE STRATEGY

What Makes People Get Turned on to Their Work?

For workers who are really prospering in their jobs, work is likely to be a lot like play. Consider, for example, a golfer at a driving range, practicing to get rid of a hook. His activity is *meaningful* to him; he has chosen to do it because he gets a "kick" from testing his skills by playing the game. He knows that he alone is *responsible* for what happens when he hits the ball. And he has *knowledge of the results* within a few seconds.

Behavioral scientists have found that the three "psychological states" experienced by the golfer in the above example also are critical in determining a person's motivation and satisfaction on the job.

- *Experienced meaningfulness:* The individual must perceive his work as worthwhile or important by some system of values he accepts.
- *Experienced responsibility:* He must believe that he personally is accountable for the outcomes of his efforts.
- *Knowledge of results:* He must be able to determine, on some fairly regular basis, whether or not the outcomes of his work are satisfactory.

When these three conditions are present, a person tends to feel very good about himself when he performs well. And those good feelings will prompt him to try to continue to do well—so he can continue to earn the positive feelings in the future. That is what is meant by "internal motivation"—being turned on to one's work because of the positive internal feelings that are generated by doing well, rather than being dependent on external factors (such as incentive pay or compliments from the boss) for the motivation to work effectively.

What if one of the three psychological states is missing? Motivation drops markedly. Suppose, for example, that our golfer has settled in at the driving range to practice for a couple of hours. Suddenly a fog drifts in over the range. He can no longer see if the ball starts to tail off to the left a hundred yards out. The satisfaction he got from hitting straight down the middle—and the motivation to try to correct something whenever he didn't—are both gone. If the fog stays, it's likely that he soon will be packing up his clubs.

The relationship between the three psychological states and on-the-job outcomes is illustrated in Figure 1. When all three are high, then internal work motivation, job satisfaction, and work quality are high, and absenteeism and turnover are low.

What Job Characteristics Make It Happen?

Recent research has identified five "core" characteristics of jobs that elicit the psychological states described above.[6,7,8] These five core job dimensions provide the key to objectively measuring jobs and to changing them so that they have high potential for motivating people who do them.

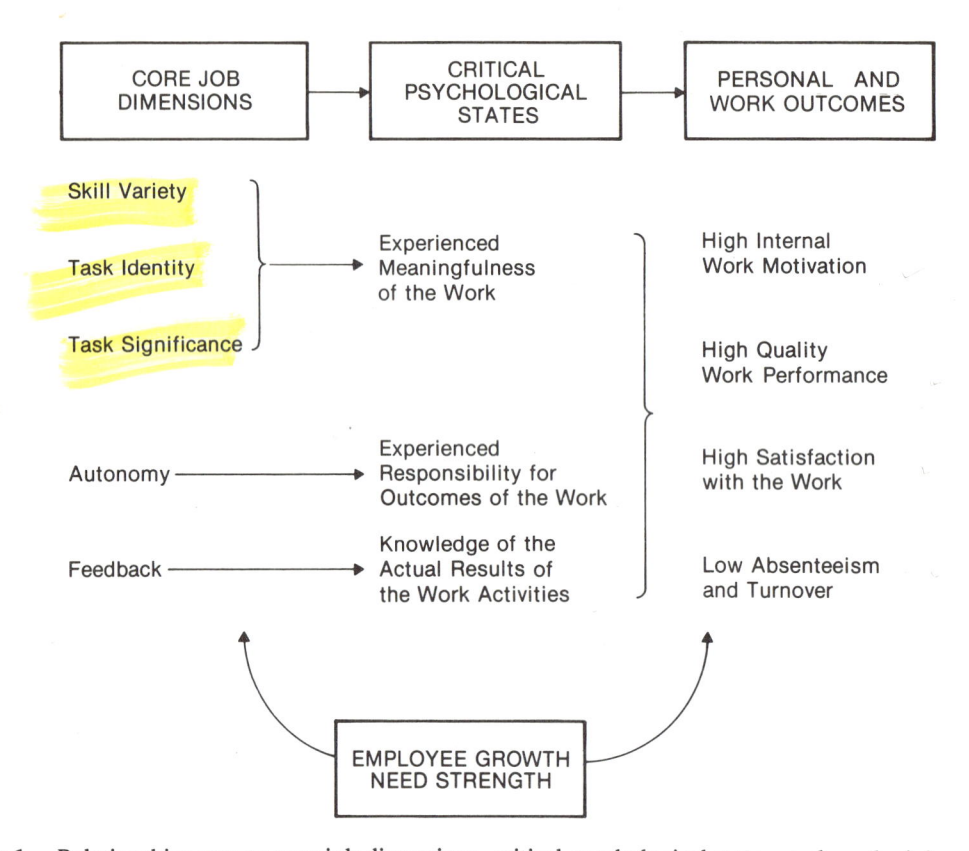

Figure 1. Relationships among core job dimensions, critical psychological states, and on-the-job outcomes

Toward Meaningful Work. Three of the five core dimensions contribute to a job's meaningfulness for the worker:

1. Skill Variety—the degree to which a job requires the worker to perform activities that challenge his skills and abilities. When even a single skill is involved, there is at least a seed of potential meaningfulness. When several are involved, the job has the potential of appealing to more of the whole person, and also of avoiding the monotony of performing the same task repeatedly, no matter how much skill it may require.

2. Task Identity—the degree to which the job requires completion of a "whole" and identifiable piece of work—doing a job from beginning to end with a visible outcome. For example, it is clearly more meaningful to an employee to build complete toasters than to attach electrical cord after electrical cord, especially if he never sees a completed toaster. (Note that the whole job, in this example, probably would involve greater skill variety as well as task identity.)

3. Task Significance—the degree to which the job has a substantial and perceivable impact on the lives of other people, whether in the immediate organization or the world at large. The worker who tightens nuts on aircraft brake assemblies is more likely to perceive his work as significant than the worker who fills small boxes with paper clips—even though the skill levels involved may be comparable.

Each of these three job dimensions represents an important route to experienced meaningfulness. If the job is high in all three, the worker is quite likely to experience his job as very meaningful. It is not necessary, however, for a job to be very high in all three dimensions. If the job is low in any one of them, there will be a drop in overall experienced meaningfulness. But even when two dimensions are low the worker may find the job meaningful if the third is high enough.

Toward Personal Responsibility. A fourth core dimension leads a worker to experience increased responsibility in his job. This is *autonomy,* the degree to which the job gives the worker freedom, independence, and discretion in scheduling work and determining how he will carry it out. People in highly autonomous jobs know that they are personally responsible for successes and failures. To the extent that their autonomy is high, then, how the work goes will be felt to depend more on the individual's own efforts and initiatives—rather than on detailed instructions from the boss or from a manual of job procedures.

Toward Knowledge of Results. The fifth and last core dimension is *feedback*. This is the degree to which a worker, in carrying out the work activities required by the job, gets information about the effectiveness of his efforts. Feedback is most powerful when it comes directly from the work itself—for example, when a worker has the responsibility for gauging and otherwise checking a component he has just finished, and learns in the process that he has lowered his reject rate by meeting specifications more consistently.

The Overall "Motivating Potential" of a Job. Figure 1 shows how the five core dimensions combine to affect the psychological states that are critical in determining whether or not an employee will be internally motivated to work effectively. Indeed, when using an instrument to be described later, it is possible to compute a "motivating potential score" (MPS) for any job. The MPS provides a single summary index of the degree to which the objective characteristics of the job will prompt high internal work motivation. Following the theory outlined above, a job high in motivating potential must be high in at least one (and hopefully more) of the three dimensions that lead to experienced meaningfulness and high in both autonomy and feedback as well. The MPS provides a quantitative index of the degree to which this is in fact the case (see Appendix for detailed formula). As will be seen later, the MPS can be very useful in diagnosing jobs and in assessing the effectiveness of job-enrichment activities.

Does the Theory Work for Everybody?

Unfortunately not. Not everyone is able to become internally motivated in his work, even when the motivating potential of a job is very high indeed.

Research has shown that the *psychological needs* of people are very important in determining who can (and who cannot) become internally motivated at work. Some people have strong needs for personal accomplishment, for learning and developing themselves beyond where they are now, for being stimulated and challenged, and so on. These people are high in "growth-need strength."

Figure 2 shows diagrammatically the proposition that individual growth needs have the power to moderate the relationship between the characteristics of jobs and work outcomes. Many workers with high growth needs will turn on eagerly when they have jobs that are high in the core dimensions. Workers whose growth needs are not so strong may respond less eagerly—or, at first, even balk at being "pushed" or "stretched" too far.

Psychologists who emphasize human potential argue that everyone has within him at least a spark of the need to grow and develop personally. Steadily accumulating evidence shows, however, that unless that spark is pretty strong, chances are it will get snuffed out by one's experiences in typical

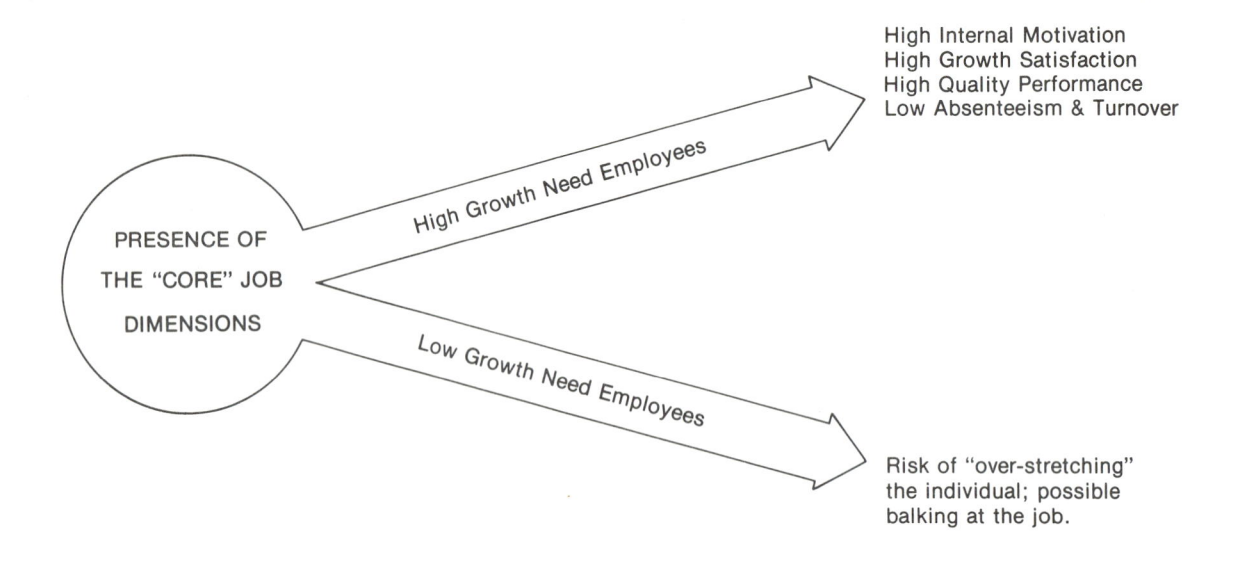

```
                                              High Internal Motivation
                                              High Growth Satisfaction
                                              High Quality Performance
                                              Low Absenteeism & Turnover
                        High Growth Need Employees ↗
   PRESENCE OF
   THE "CORE" JOB
   DIMENSIONS
                        Low Growth Need Employees ↘
                                              Risk of "over-stretching"
                                              the individual; possible
                                              balking at the job.
```

Figure 2. The moderating effect of employee growth-need strength

organizations. So, a person who has worked for twenty years in stultifying jobs may find it difficult or impossible to become internally motivated overnight when given the opportunity.

We should be cautious, however, about creating rigid categories of people based on their measured growth-need strength at any particular time. It is true that we can predict from these measures who is likely to become internally motivated on a job and who will be less willing or able to do so. But what we do not know yet is whether or not the growth-need "spark" can be rekindled for those individuals who have had their growth needs dampened by years of growth-depressing experience in their organizations.

Since it is often the organization that is responsible for currently low levels of growth desires, we believe that the organization also should provide the individual with the chance to reverse that trend whenever possible, even if that means putting a person in a job where he may be "stretched" more than he wants to be. He can always move back later to the old job—and in the meantime the embers of his growth needs just might burst back into flame, to his surprise and pleasure, and for the good of the organization.

FROM THEORY TO PRACTICE: A TECHNOLOGY FOR JOB ENRICHMENT

When job enrichment fails, it often fails because of inadequate *diagnosis* of the target job and employees' reactions to it. Often, for example, job enrichment is assumed by management to be a solution to "people problems" on the job and is implemented even though there has been no diagnostic activity to indicate that the root of the problem is in fact how the work is designed. At other times, some diagnosis is made—but it provides no concrete guidance about what specific aspects of the job require change. In either case, the success of job enrichment may wind up depending more on the quality of the intuition of the change agent—or his luck—than on a solid base of data about the people and the work.

In the paragraphs to follow, we outline a new technology for use in job enrichment which explicitly addresses the diagnostic as well as the action components of the change process. The technology has two parts: (1) a set of diagnostic tools that are useful in evaluating jobs and people's reactions to them prior to change—and in pinpointing exactly what aspects of specific jobs are most critical to a successful change attempt, and (2) a set of "implementing concepts" that provide concrete guidance for action steps in job enrichment. The implementing concepts are tied directly to the diagnostic tools; the output of the diagnostic activity specifies which action steps are likely to have the most impact in a particular situation.

The Diagnostic Tools

Central to the diagnostic procedure we propose is a package of instruments to be used by employees, supervisors, and outside observers in assessing the target job and employees' reactions to it.[9] These instruments gauge the following:

1. The objective characteristics of the jobs themselves, including both an overall indication of the "motivating potential" of the job as it exists (that is, the MPS score) and the score of the job on each of the five core dimensions described previously. Because knowing the strengths and weaknesses of the job is critical to any work-redesign effort, assessments of the job are made by supervisors and outside observers as well as the employees themselves—and the final assessment of a job uses data from all three sources.

2. The current levels of motivation, satisfaction, and work performance of employees on the job. In addition to satisfaction with the work itself, measures are taken of how people feel about other aspects of the work setting, such as pay, supervision, and relationships with co-workers.

3. The level of growth-need strength of the employees. As indicated earlier, employees who have strong growth needs are more likely to be more responsive to job enrichment than employees with weak growth needs. Therefore, it is important to know at the outset just what kinds of satisfactions the people who do the job are (and are not) motivated to obtain from their work. This will make it possible to identify which persons are best to start changes with, and which may need help in adapting to the newly enriched job.

What, then, might be the actual steps one would take in carrying out a job diagnosis using these tools? Although the approach to any particular diagnosis depends upon the specifics of the particular work situation involved, the sequence of questions listed below is fairly typical.

Step 1. Are motivation and satisfaction central to the problem? Sometimes organizations undertake job enrichment to improve work motivation and satisfaction of employees when in fact the real problem with work performance lies elsewhere—for example, in a poorly designed production system, in an error-prone computer, and so on. The first step is to examine the scores of employees on the motivation and satisfaction portions of the diagnostic instrument. (The questionnaire taken by employees is called the Job Diagnostic Survey and will be referred to hereafter as the JDS.) If motivation and satisfaction are problematic, the change agent would continue to Step 2; if not, he would look to other aspects of the work situation to identify the real problem.

Step 2. Is the job low in motivating potential? To answer this question, one would examine the motivating potential score of the target job and compare it to the MPSs of other jobs to determine whether or not *the job itself* is a probable cause of the motivational problems documented in Step 1. If the job turns out to be low on the MPS, one would continue to Step 3; if it scores high, attention should be given to other possible reasons for the motivational difficulties (such as the pay system, the nature of supervision, and so on).

Step 3. What specific aspects of the job are causing the difficulty? This step involves examining the job on each of the five core dimensions to pinpoint the specific strengths and weaknesses of the job as it is currently structured. It is useful at this stage to construct a "profile" of the target job, to make visually apparent where improvements need to be made. An illustrative profile for two jobs (one "good" job and one job needing improvement) is shown in Figure 3.

Job A is an engineering maintenance job and is high on all of the core dimensions; the MPS of this job is a very high 260. (MPS scores can range from 1 to about 350; an "average" score would be about 125.) Job enrichment would not be recommended for this job; if employees working on the job were unproductive and unhappy, the reasons are likely to have little to do with the nature or design of the work itself.

Job B, on the other hand, has many problems. This job involves the routine and repetitive processing of checks in the "back room" of a bank. The MPS is 30, which is quite low—and indeed, would be even lower if it were not for the moderately high task significance of the job. (Task significance is moderately high because the people are handling large amounts of other people's money, and therefore the quality of their efforts potentially has important consequences for their unseen clients.) The job provides the individuals with very little direct feedback about how effectively they are doing it; the employees have little autonomy in how they go about doing the job; and the job is moderately low in both skill variety and task identity.

For Job B, then, there is plenty of room for improvement—and many avenues to examine in planning job changes. For still other jobs, the avenues for change often turn out to be considerably more specific: for example, feedback and autonomy may be reasonably high, but one or more of the core dimensions that contribute to the experienced meaningfulness of the job (skill variety, task identity, and task significance) may be low. In such a case, attention would turn to ways to increase the standing of the job on these latter three dimensions.

Step 4. How "ready" are the employees for change? Once it has been documented that there is need for improvement in the job—and the particularly troublesome aspects of the job have been identified—then it is time to begin to think about the specific action steps which will be taken to enrich the job. An important factor in such planning is the level of growth needs of the employees, since employees high on growth needs usually respond more readily to job enrichment than do employees with little need for growth. The JDS provides a direct measure of the growth-need strength of the employees. This measure can be very helpful in planning how to introduce the changes to the people (for instance, cautiously versus dramatically), and in deciding who should be among the first group of employees to have their jobs changed.

In actual use of the diagnostic package, additional information is generated which supplements and expands the basic diagnostic questions outlined above. The point of the above discussion is merely to indicate the kinds of questions which we believe to be most important in diagnosing a job prior to changing it. We now turn to how the diagnostic conclusions are translated into specific job changes.

The Implementing Concepts

Five "implementing concepts" for job enrichment are identified and discussed below.[10] Each one is a specific action step aimed at improving both the quality of the working experience for the individual and his work productivity. They are: (1) forming natural work units; (2) combining tasks; (3) establishing client relationships; (4) vertical loading; (5) opening feedback channels.

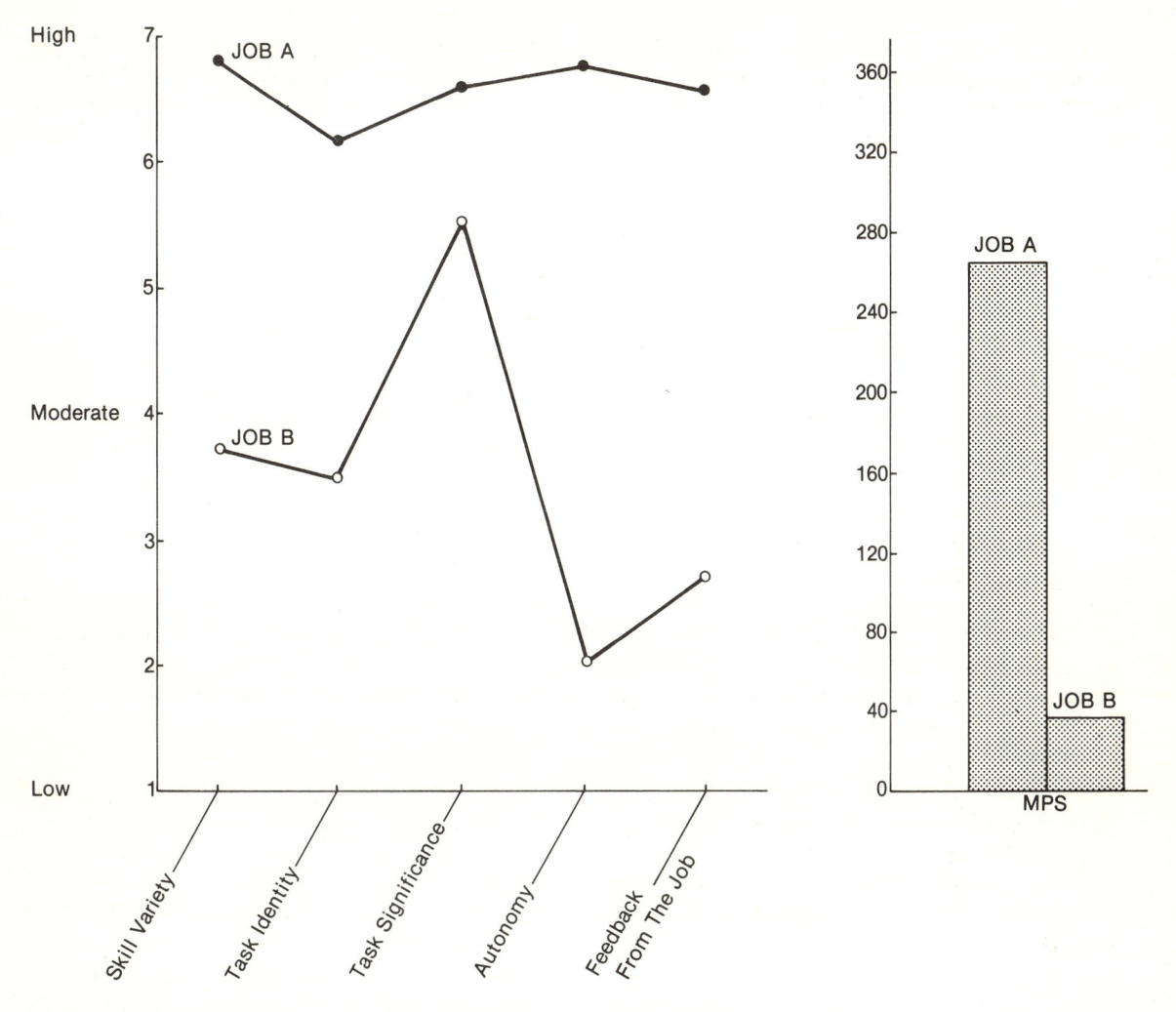

Figure 3. The JDS diagnostic profile for a "good" and a "bad" job

The links between the implementing concepts and the core dimensions are shown in Figure 4—which illustrates our theory of job enrichment, ranging from the concrete action steps through the core dimensions and the psychological states to the actual personal and work outcomes.

After completing the diagnosis of a job, a change agent would know which of the core dimensions were most in need of remedial attention. He could then turn to Figure 4 and select those implementing concepts that specifically deal with the most troublesome parts of the existing job. How this would take place in practice will be seen below.

Forming Natural Work Units. The notion of distributing work in some logical way may seem to be an obvious part of the design of any job. In many cases, however, the logic is one imposed by just about any consideration except job-holder satisfaction and motivation. Such considerations include technological dictates, level of worker training or experience, "efficiency" as defined by industrial engi-

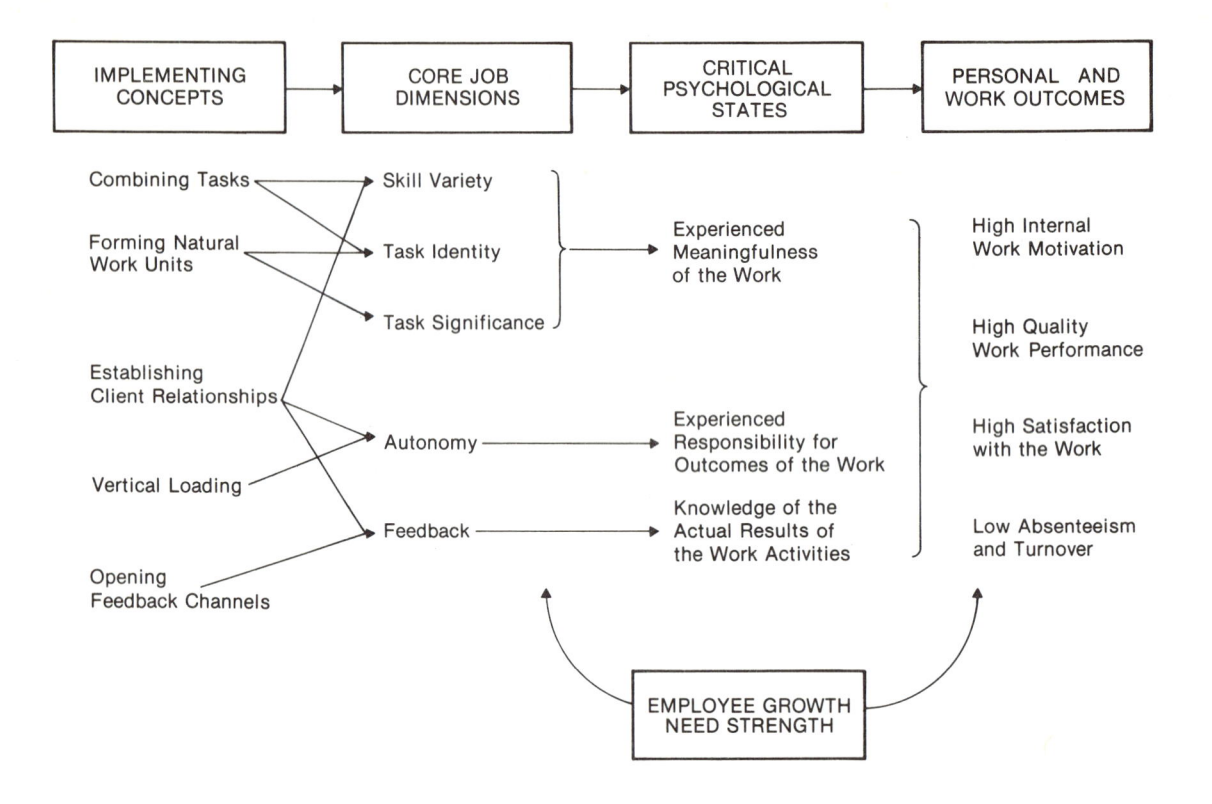

Figure 4. The full model: how use of the implementing concepts can lead to positive outcomes

neering, and current work load. In many cases the cluster of tasks a worker faces during a typical day or week is natural to anyone *but* the worker.

For example, suppose that a typing pool (consisting of one supervisor and ten typists) handles all work for one division of a company. Jobs are delivered in rough draft or dictated form to the supervisor, who distributes them as evenly as possible among the typists. In such circumstances the individual letters, reports, and other tasks performed by a given typist in one day or week are randomly assigned. There is no basis for identifying with the work or the person or department for whom it is performed, or for placing any personal value upon it.

The principle underlying natural units of work, by contrast, is "ownership"—a worker's sense of continuing responsibility for an identifiable body of work. Two steps are involved in creating natural work units. The first is to identify the basic work items. In the typing pool, for example, the items might be "pages to be typed." The second step is to group the items in natural categories. For example, each typist might be assigned continuing responsibility for all jobs requested by one or several specific departments. The assignments should be made, of course, in such a way that work loads are about equal in the long run. (For example, one typist might end up with all the work from one busy department, while another handles jobs from several smaller units.)

At this point we can begin to see specifically how the job-design principles relate to the core dimensions (cf. Figure 4). The ownership fostered by natural units of work can make the difference between a feeling that work is meaningful and rewarding and the feeling that it is irrelevant and boring. As the diagram shows, natural units of work are directly related to two of the core dimensions: task identity and task significance.

A typist whose work is assigned naturally rather than randomly—say, by departments—has a much greater chance of performing a whole job to completion. Instead of typing one section of a large report, the individual is likely to type the whole thing, with knowledge of exactly what the product of the work is (task identity). Furthermore, over time the typist will develop a growing sense of how the work affects co-workers in the department serviced (task significance).

Combining Tasks. The very existence of a pool made up entirely of persons whose sole function is typing reflects a fractionalization of jobs that has been a basic precept of "scientific management." Most obvious in assembly-line work, fractionalization has been applied to nonmanufacturing jobs as well. It is typically justified by efficiency, which is usually defined in terms of either low costs or some time-and-motion type of criteria.

It is hard to find fault with measuring efficiency ultimately in terms of cost-effectiveness. In doing so, however, a manager should be sure to consider *all* the costs involved. It is possible, for example, for highly fractionalized jobs to meet all the time-and-motion criteria of efficiency, but if the resulting job is so unrewarding that performing it day after day leads to high turnover, absenteeism, drugs and alcohol, and strikes, then productivity is really lower (and costs higher) than data on efficiency might indicate.

The principle of combining tasks, then, suggests that whenever possible existing and fractionalized tasks should be put together to form new and larger modules of work. At the Medfield, Massachusetts, plant of Corning Glass Works the assembly of a laboratory hot plate has been redesigned along the lines suggested here. Each hot plate now is assembled from start to finish by one operator, instead of going through several separate operations that are performed by different people.

Some tasks, if combined into a meaningfully large module of work, would be more than an individual could do by himself. In such cases, it is often useful to consider assigning the new, larger task to a small *team* of workers—who are given great autonomy for its completion. At the Racine, Wisconsin, plant of Emerson Electric, the assembly process for trash disposal appliances was restructured this way. Instead of a sequence of moving the appliance from station to station, the assembly now is done from start to finish by one team. Such teams include both men and women to permit switching off the heavier and more delicate aspects of the work. The team responsible is identified on the appliance. In case of customer complaints, the team often drafts the reply.

As a job-design principle, task combination, like natural units of work, expands the task identity of the job. For example, the hot-plate assembler can see and identify with a finished product ready for shipment, rather than a nearly invisible junction of solder. Moreover, the more tasks that are combined into a single worker's job, the greater the variety of skills he must call on in performing the job. So task combination also leads directly to greater skill variety—the third core dimension that contributes to the overall experienced meaningfulness of the work.

Establishing Client Relationships. One consequence of fractionalization is that the typical worker has little or no contact with (or even awareness of) the ultimate user of his product or service. By encouraging and enabling employees to establish direct relationships with the clients of their work, improvements often can be realized simultaneously on three of the core dimensions. Feedback increases, because of additional opportunities for the individual to receive praise or criticism of his work outputs directly. Skill variety often increases, because of the necessity to develop and exercise one's interpersonal skills in maintaining the client relationship. And autonomy can increase because the individual often is given personal responsibility for deciding how to manage his relationships with the clients of his work.

Creating client relationships is a three-step process. First, the client must be identified. Second, the most direct contact possible between the worker and the client must be established. Third, criteria must be set up by which the client can judge the quality of the product or service he receives. And whenever possible, the client should have a means of relaying his judgments directly back to the worker.

The contact between worker and client should be as great as possible and as frequent as necessary. Face-to-face contact is highly desirable, at least occasionally. Where that is impossible or impractical, telephone and mail can suffice. In any case, it is important that the performance criteria by which the worker will be rated by the client must be mutually understood and agreed upon.

Vertical Loading. Typically the split between the "doing" of a job and the "planning" and "controlling" of the work has evolved along with horizontal fractionalization. Its rationale, once again, has been "efficiency through specialization." And once again, the excess of specialization that has emerged has resulted in unexpected but significant costs in motivation, morale, and work quality. In vertical loading, the intent is to partially close the gap between the doing and the controlling parts of the job—and thereby reap some important motivational advantages.

Of all the job-design principles, vertical loading may be the single most crucial one. In some cases, where it has been impossible to implement any other changes, vertical loading alone has had significant motivational effects. When a job is vertically loaded, responsibilities and controls that formerly were reserved for higher levels of management are added to the job. There are many ways to accomplish this:

• Return to the job holder greater discretion in setting schedules, deciding on work methods, checking on quality, and advising or helping to train less experienced workers.

• Grant additional authority. The objective should be to advance workers from a position of no authority or highly restricted authority to positions of reviewed, and eventually, near-total authority for his own work.

• Time management. The job holder should have the greatest possible freedom to decide when to start and stop work, when to break, and how to assign priorities.

• Troubleshooting and crisis decisions. Workers should be encouraged to seek problem solutions on their own, rather than calling immediately for the supervisor.

• Financial controls. Some degree of knowledge and control over budgets and other financial aspects of a job can often be highly motivating. However, access to this information frequently tends to be restricted. Workers can benefit from knowing something about the costs of their jobs, the potential effect upon profit, and various financial and budgetary alternatives.

When a job is vertically loaded it will inevitably increase in *autonomy*. And as shown in Figure 4, this increase in objective personal control over the work will also lead to an increased feeling of personal responsibility for the work, and ultimately to higher internal work motivation.

Opening Feedback Channels. In virtually all jobs there are ways to open channels of feedback to individuals or teams to help them learn whether their performance is improving, deteriorating, or remaining at a constant level. While there are numerous channels through which information about performance can be provided, it generally is better for a worker to learn about his performance *directly as he does his job*—rather than from management on an occasional basis.

Job-provided feedback usually is more immediate and private than supervisor-supplied feedback, and it increases the worker's feelings of personal control over his work in the bargain. Moreover, it avoids many of the potentially disruptive interpersonal problems that can develop when the only way a worker has to find out how he is doing is through direct messages or subtle cues from the boss.

Exactly what should be done to open channels for job-provided feedback will vary from job to job and organization to organization. Yet in many cases the changes involve simply removing existing blocks that isolate the worker from naturally occurring data about performance—rather than generating entirely new feedback mechanisms. For example:

• Establishing direct client relationships often removes blocks between the worker and natural external sources of data about his work.

• Quality-control efforts in many organizations often eliminate a natural source of feedback. The quality check on a product or service is done by persons other than those responsible for the work. Feedback to the workers—if there is any—is belated and diluted. It often fosters a tendency to think of quality as "someone else's concern." By placing quality control close to the worker (perhaps even in his own hands), the quantity and quality of data about performance available to him can dramatically increase.

• Tradition and established procedure in many organizations dictate that records about performance be kept by a supervisor and transmitted up (not down) in the organizational hierarchy. Sometimes supervisors even check the work and correct any errors themselves. The worker who made the error never knows it occurred—and is denied the very information that could enhance both his internal work motivation and the technical adequacy of his performance. In many cases it is possible to provide standard summaries of performance records directly to the worker (as well as to his superior), thereby giving him personally and regularly the data he needs to improve his performance.

• Computers and other automated operations sometimes can be used to provide the individual with data now blocked from him. Many clerical operations, for example, are now performed on computer consoles. These consoles often can be programmed to provide the clerk with immediate feedback in the form of a CRT display or a printout indicating that an error has been made. Some systems even have been programmed to provide the operator with a positive feedback message when a period of error-free performance has been sustained.

Many organizations simply have not recognized the importance of feedback as a motivator. Data on quality and other aspects of performance are viewed as being of interest only to management. Worse still, the *standards* for acceptable performance often are kept from workers as well. As a result, workers who would be interested in following the daily or weekly ups and downs of their performance, and in trying accordingly to improve, are deprived of the very guidelines they need to do so. They are like the golfer we mentioned earlier, whose efforts to correct his hook are stopped dead by fog over the driving range.

THE STRATEGY IN ACTION: HOW WELL DOES IT WORK?

So far we have examined a basic theory of how people get turned on to their work; a set of core dimensions of jobs that create the

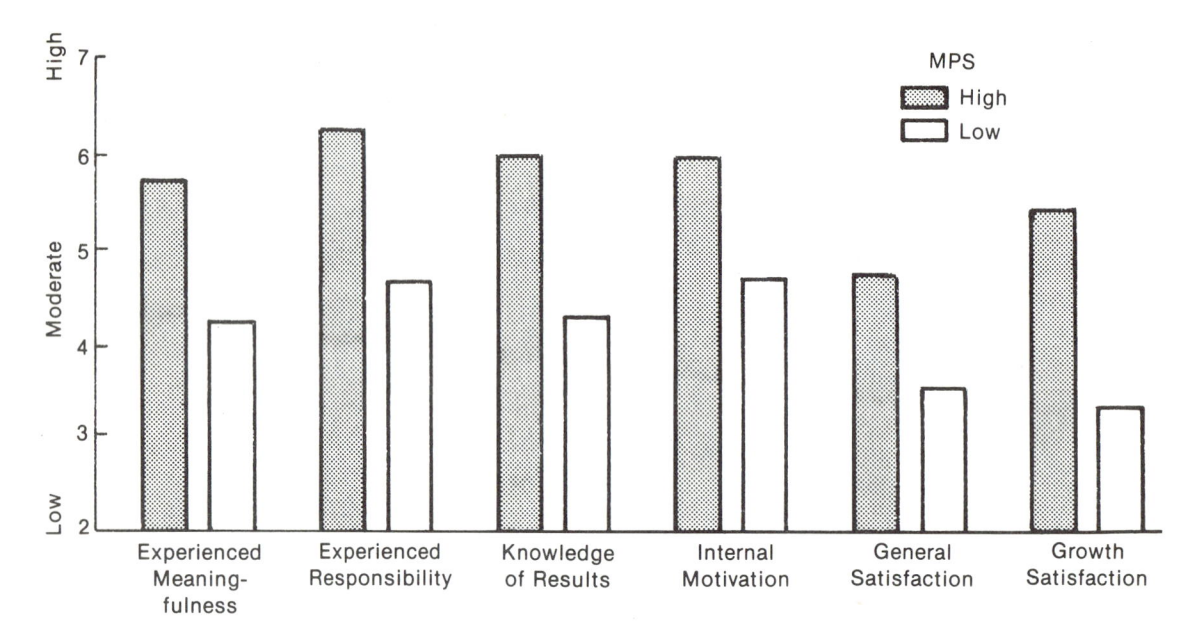

Figure 5. Employee reactions to jobs high and low in motivating potential for two banks and a steel firm.

conditions for such internal work motivation to develop on the job; and a set of five implementing concepts that are the action steps recommended to boost a job on the core dimensions and thereby increase employee motivation, satisfaction, and productivity.

The remaining question is straightforward and important: *Does it work?* In reality, that question is twofold. First, does the theory itself hold water, or are we barking up the wrong conceptual tree? And second, does the change strategy really lead to measurable differences when it is applied in an actual organizational setting?

This section summarizes the findings we have generated to date on these questions.

Is the Job-Enrichment Theory Correct?

In general, the answer seems to be yes. The JDS instrument has been taken by more than 1,000 employees working on about 100 diverse jobs in more than a dozen organizations over the last two years. These data have been analyzed to test the basic motivational theory—and especially the impact of the core job dimensions on worker motivation, satisfaction, and behavior on the job. An illustrative overview of some of the findings is given below.[8]

1. People who work on jobs high on the core dimensions are more motivated and satisfied than are people who work on jobs that score low on the dimensions. Employees with jobs high on the core dimensions (MPS scores greater than 240) were compared to those who held unmotivating jobs (MPS scores less than 40). As shown in Figure 5, employees with high MPS jobs were higher on (a) the three psychological states, (b) internal work motivation, (c) general satisfaction, and (d) "growth" satisfaction.

2. Figure 6 shows that the same is true for measures of actual behavior at work—absenteeism and performance effectiveness—although less strongly so for the performance measure.

3. Responses to jobs high in motivating potential are more positive for people who have strong growth needs than for people

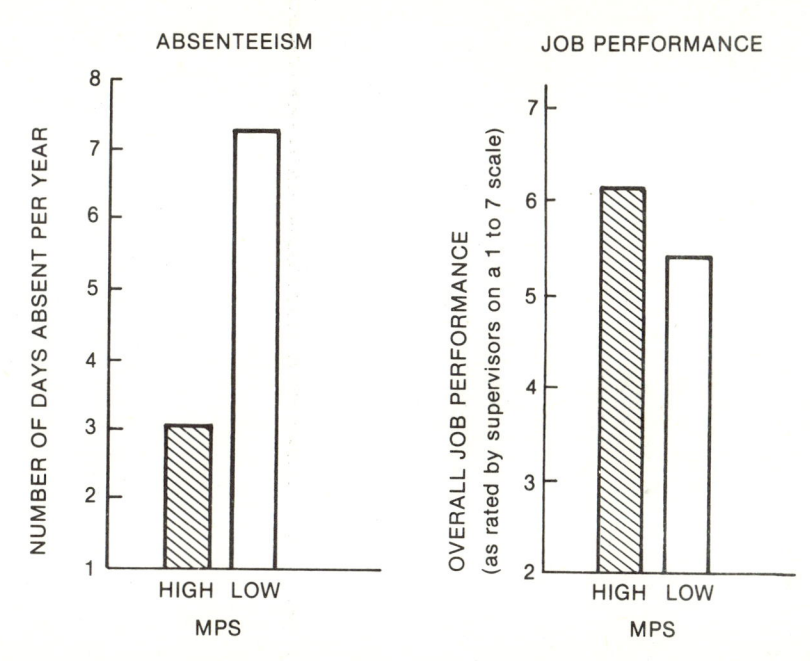

Figure 6. Absenteeism and job performance for employees with jobs high and low in motivating potential

with weak needs for growth. In Figure 7 the linear relationship between the motivating potential of a job and employees' level of internal work motivation is shown, separately for people with high versus low growth needs as measured by the JDS. While both groups of employees show increases in internal motivation as MPS increases, the *rate* of increase is significantly greater for the group of employees who have strong needs for growth.

How Does the Change Strategy Work in Practice?

The results summarized above suggest that both the theory and the diagnostic instrument work when used with real people in real organizations. In this section, we summarize a job-enrichment project conducted at The Travelers Insurance Companies, which illustrates how the change procedures themselves work in practice.

The Travelers project was designed with two purposes in mind. One was to achieve improvements in morale, productivity, and other indicators of employee well-being. The other was to test the general effectiveness of the strategy for job enrichment we have summarized in this article.

The work group chosen was a keypunching operation. The group's function was to transfer information from printed or written documents onto punched cards for computer input. The work group consisted of ninety-eight keypunch operators and verifiers (both in the same job classification), plus seven assignment clerks. All reported to a supervisor who, in turn, reported to the assistant manager and manager of the data-input division.

The size of individual punching orders varied considerably, from a few cards to as many as 2,500. Some work came to the work group with a specified delivery date, while other orders were to be given routine service on a predetermined schedule.

Assignment clerks received the jobs from the user departments. After reviewing the work for obvious errors, omissions, and legibility problems, the assignment clerk parceled out the work in batches expected to take about one hour. If the clerk found the work not suitable for punching it went to the supervisor, who either returned the work to the user department or cleared up problems by phone. When work went to operators for punching, it was with the instruction "Punch only what you see. Don't correct errors, no matter how obvious they look."

Because of the high cost of computer time, keypunched work was 100 percent verified—a task that consumed nearly as many man-hours as the punching itself. Then the cards went to the supervisor, who screened the jobs for due dates before sending them to the computer. Errors detected in verification were assigned to various operators at random to be corrected.

The computer output from the cards was sent to the originating department, accompanied by a printout of errors. Eventually the printout went back to the supervisor for final correction.

A great many phenomena indicated that the problems being experienced in the work group might be the result of poor motivation. As the only person performing supervisory functions of any kind, the supervisor spent most of his time responding to crisis situa-

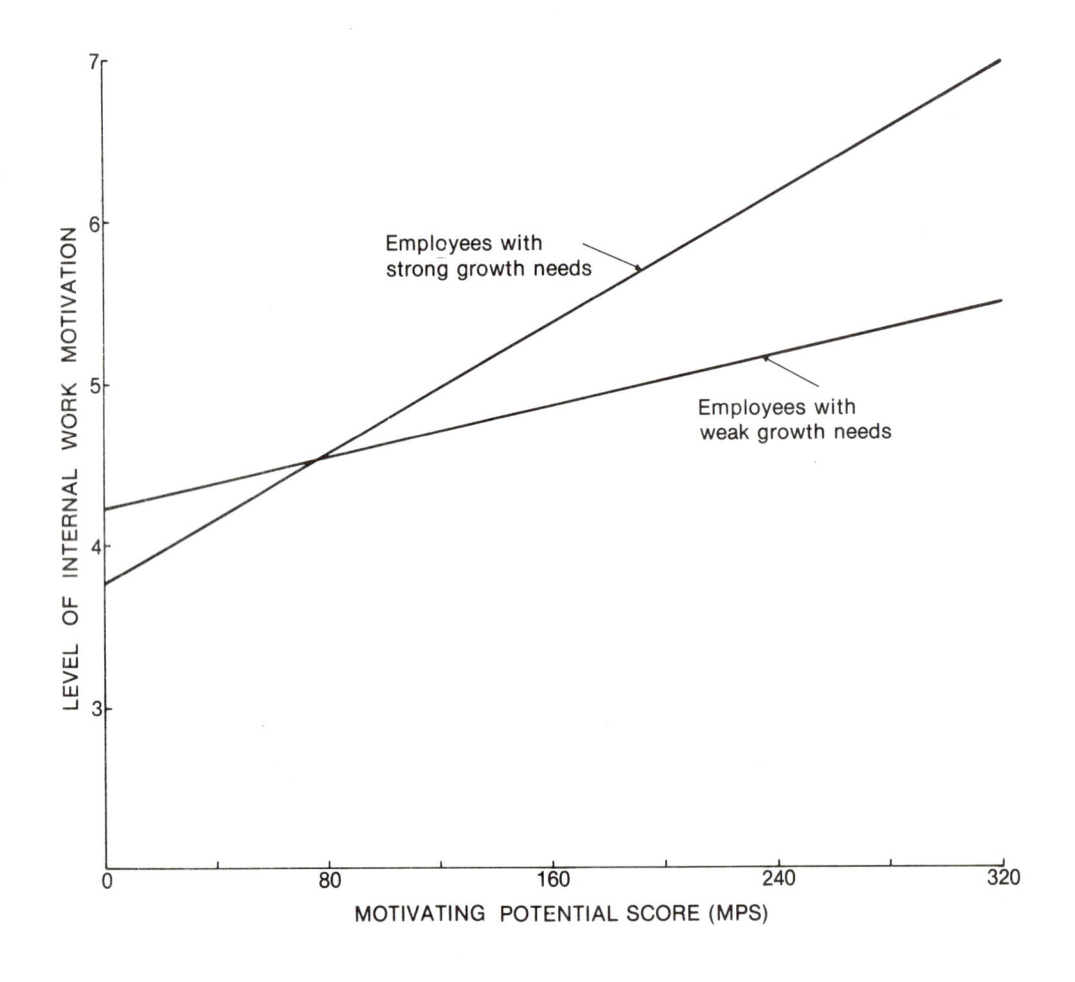

Figure 7. Relationship between the motivating potential of a job and the internal work motivation of employees. (Shown separately for employees with strong versus weak growth-need strength.)

tions, which recurred continually. He also had to deal almost daily with employees' salary grievances or other complaints. Employees frequently showed apathy or outright hostility toward their jobs.

Rates of work output, by accepted work-measurement standards, were inadequate. Error rates were high. Due dates and schedules frequently were missed. Absenteeism was higher than average, especially before and after weekends and holidays.

The single, rather unusual exception was turnover. It was lower than the companywide average for similar jobs. The company has attributed this fact to a poor job market in the base period just before the project began, and to an older, relatively more settled work force—made up, incidentally, entirely of women.

The Diagnosis

Using some of the tools and techniques we have outlined, a consulting team from the Management Services Department and from Roy W. Walters & Associates concluded that the keypunch-operator's job exhibited the following serious weaknesses in terms of the core dimensions.

Skill Variety: there was none. Only a single skill was involved—the ability to punch adequately the data on the batch of documents.

Task Identity: virtually nonexistent. Batches were assembled to provide an even work load, but not whole identifiable jobs.

Task Significance: not apparent. The keypunching operation was a necessary step in providing service to the company's customers. The individual operator was isolated by an assignment clerk and a supervisor from any knowledge of what the operation meant to the using department, let alone its meaning to the ultimate customer.

Autonomy: none. The operators had no freedom to arrange their daily tasks to meet schedules, to resolve problems with the using department, or even to correct, in punching, information that was obviously wrong.

Feedback: none. Once a batch was out of the operator's hands, she had no assured chance of seeing evidence of its quality or inadequacy.

Design of the Experimental Trial

Since the diagnosis indicated that the motivating potential of the job was extremely low, it was decided to attempt to improve the motivation and productivity of the work group through job enrichment. Moreover, it was possible to design an experimental test of the effects of the changes to be introduced: the results of changes made in the target work group were to be compared with trends in a control work group of similar size and demographic makeup. Since the control group was located more than a mile away, there appeared to be little risk of communication between members of the two groups.

A base period was defined before the start of the experimental trial period, and appropriate data were gathered on the productivity, absenteeism, and work attitudes of members of both groups. Data also were available on turnover; but since turnover was already below average in the target group, prospective changes in this measure were deemed insignificant.

An educational session was conducted with supervisors, at which they were given the theory and implementing concepts and actually helped to design the job changes themselves. Out of this session came an active plan consisting of about twenty-five change items that would significantly affect the design of the target jobs.

The Implementing Concepts and the Changes

Because the job as it existed was rather uniformly low on the core job dimensions, all five of the implementing concepts were used in enriching it.

Natural Units of Work. The random batch assignment of work was replaced by assigning to each operator continuing responsibility for certain accounts—either particular departments or particular recurring jobs. Any work for those accounts now always goes to the same operator.

Task Combination. Some planning and controlling functions were combined with the central task of keypunching. In this case, however, these additions can be more suitably discussed under the remaining three implementing concepts.

Client Relationships. Each operator was given several channels of direct contact with clients. The operators, not their assignment clerks, now inspect their documents for correctness and legibility. When problems arise, the operator, not the supervisor, takes them up with the client.

Feedback. In addition to feedback from client contact, the operators were provided with a number of additional sources of data about their performance. The computer department now returns incorrect cards to the operators who punched them, and operators correct their own errors. Each operator also keeps her own file of copies of her errors. These can be reviewed to determine trends in error frequency and types of errors. Each operator receives weekly a computer printout of her errors and productivity, which is sent to her directly, rather than given to her by the supervisor.

Vertical Loading. Besides consulting directly with clients about work questions, operators now have the authority to correct obvious coding errors on their own. Operators may set their own schedules and plan their daily work, as long as they meet schedules. Some competent operators have been given the option of not verifying their work and making their own program changes.

Results of the Trial

The results were dramatic. The number of operators declined from ninety-eight to sixty. This occurred partly through attrition and partly through transfer to other departments. Some of the operators were promoted to higher-paying jobs in departments whose cards they had been handling—something that had never occurred before. Some details of the results are given below.

Quantity of Work. The control group, with no job changes made, showed an increase in productivity of 8.1 percent during the trial period. The experimental group showed an increase of 39.6 percent.

Error Rates. To assess work quality, error rates were recorded for about forty operators in the experimental group. All were experienced, and all had been in their jobs before the job-enrichment program began. For two months before the study, these operators had a collective error rate of 1.53 percent. For two months toward the end of the study, the collective error rate was 0.99 percent. By the end of the study the number of operators with poor performance had dropped from 11.1 percent to 5.5 percent.

Absenteeism. The experimental group registered a 24.1 percent decline in absences. The control group, by contrast, showed a 29 percent *increase.*

Attitudes toward the Job. An attitude survey given at the start of the project showed that the two groups scored about average, and nearly identically, in nine different areas of work satisfaction. At the end of the project the survey was repeated. The control group showed an insignificant 0.5 percent improvement, while the experimental group's overall satisfaction score rose 16.5 percent.

Selective Elimination of Controls. Demonstrated improvements in operator proficiency permitted them to work with fewer controls. Travelers estimates that the reduction of controls had the same effect as adding seven operators—a saving even beyond the effects of improved productivity and lowered absenteeism.

Role of the Supervisor. One of the most significant findings in the Travelers experiment was the effect of the changes on the supervisor's job, and thus on the rest of the organization. The operators took on many responsibilities that had been reserved at least to the unit leaders and sometimes to the supervisor. The unit leaders, in turn, assumed some of the day-to-day supervisory functions that had plagued the supervisor. Instead of spending his days supervising the behavior of subordinates and dealing with crises, he was able to devote time to developing feedback systems, setting up work modules, and spearheading the enrichment effort—in other words, managing. It should be noted, however, that helping supervisors change their own work activities when their subordinates' jobs have been enriched is itself a challenging task. And if appropriate attention and help are not given to supervisors in such cases, they rapidly can be come disaffected—and a job-enrichment "backlash" can result.[11]

Summary

By applying work-measurement standards to the changes wrought by job enrichment—attitude and quality, absenteeism, and selective administration of controls—Travelers was able to estimate the total dollar impact of the project. Actual savings in salaries and machine rental charges during the first year totaled $64,305. Potential savings by further application of the changes were put at $91,937 annually. Thus, by almost any measure used—from the work attitudes of individual employees to dollar savings for the company as a whole—the Travelers test of the job-enrichment strategy proved a success.

CONCLUSIONS

In this article we have presented a new strategy for the redesign of work in general and for job enrichment in particular. The approach has four main characteristics:

1. It is grounded in a basic psychological theory of what motivates people in their work.

2. It emphasizes that planning for job changes should be done on the basis of *data* about the jobs and the people who do them—and a set of diagnostic instruments is provided to collect such data.

3. It provides a set of specific implementing concepts to guide actual job changes, as well as a set of theory-based rules for selecting *which* action steps are likely to be most beneficial in a given situation.

4. The strategy is buttressed by a set of findings showing that the theory holds water, that the diagnostic procedures are practical and informative, and that the implementing concepts can lead to changes that are beneficial both to organizations and to the people who work in them.

We believe that job enrichment is moving beyond the stage where it can be considered "yet another management fad." Instead, it represents a potentially powerful strategy for change that can help organizations achieve their goals for higher quality work—and at the same time further the equally legitimate needs of contemporary employees for a more meaningful work experience. Yet there are pressing questions about job enrichment and its use that remain to be answered.

Prominent among these is the question of employee participation in planning and implementing work redesign. The diagnostic tools and implementing concepts we have presented are neither designed nor intended for use only by management. Rather, our belief is that the effectiveness of job enrichment is likely to be enhanced when the tasks of diagnosing and changing jobs are undertaken *collaboratively* by management and by the employees whose work will be affected.

Moreover, the effects of work redesign on the broader organization remain generally uncharted. Evidence now is accumulating that when jobs are changed, turbulence can appear in the surrounding organization—for example, in supervisory-subordinate relationships, in pay and benefit plans, and so on. Such turbulence can be viewed by management either as a problem with job enrichment or as an opportunity for further and broader organization development by teams of managers and employees. To the degree that management takes the latter view, we believe, the oft-espoused goal of achieving basic organizational change through the redesign of work may come increasingly within reach.

The diagnostic tools and implementing concepts we have presented are useful in deciding on and designing basic changes in the jobs themselves. They do not address the broader issues of who plans the changes, how they are carried out, and how they are followed up. The way these broader questions are dealt with, we believe, may determine whether job enrichment will grow up—or whether it will die an early and unfortunate death, like so many other fledgling behavioral science approaches to organizational change.

APPENDIX

For the algebraically inclined, the Motivating Potential Score is computed as follows

$$MPS = \left[\frac{\text{Skill Variety} + \text{Task Identity} + \text{Task Significance}}{3}\right] \times \text{Autonomy} \times \text{Feedback}$$

It should be noted that in some cases the MPS score can be *too* high for positive job satisfaction and effective performance—in effect overstimulating the person who holds the job. This paper focuses on jobs which are toward the low end of the scale—and which potentially can be improved through job enrichment.

REFERENCES

1. F. Herzberg, B. Mausner and B. Snyderman, *The Motivation to Work* (New York: John Wiley & Sons) 1959.

2. F. Herzberg, *Work and the Nature of Man* (Cleveland: World) 1966.

3. F. Herzberg, "One More Time: How Do You Motivate Employees?" *Harvard Business Review* (1968), pp. 53-62.

4. W. J. Paul, Jr.; K. B. Robertson and F. Herzberg, "Job Enrichment Pays Off," *Harvard Business Review* (1969), pp. 61-78.

5. R. N. Ford, *Motivation Through the Work Itself* (New York: American Management Association) 1969.

6. A. N. Turner and P. R. Lawrence, *Industrial Jobs and the Worker* (Cambridge, Mass.: Harvard Graduate School of Business Administration) 1965.

7. J. R. Hackman and E. E. Lawler, "Employee Reactions to Job Characteristics," *Journal of Applied Psychology Monograph* (1971), pp. 259-286.

8. J. R. Hackman and G. R. Oldham, *Motivation Through the Design of Work: Test of a Theory,* Technical Report No. 6, Department of Administrative Sciences, Yale University, 1974.

9. J. R. Hackman and G. R. Oldham, "Development of the Job Diagnostic Survey," *Journal of Applied Psychology* (1975), pp. 159-170.

10. R. W. Walters and Associates, *Job Enrichment for Results* (Reading, Mass.: Addison-Wesley) 1975.

11. E. E. Lawler III; J. R. Hackman, and S. Kaufman, "Effects of Job Redesign: A Field Experiment," *Journal of Applied Social Psychology* (1973), pp. 49-62.

A STRUCTURAL APPROACH TO ORGANIZATIONAL CHANGE

Robert A. Luke, Jr., Peter Block, Jack M. Davey, and Vernon R. Averch

This is a report of an OD program which resulted in significant delegation of authority and changed the attitudes of several key executives from a belief in close, continuous supervision to the view that most lower management will work productively without close supervision if given the opportunity and training. The innovative features of this case are twofold: First, the change was accomplished by structural alterations; and, secondly, the consultants were more architects than trainer-interveners. The real change agents in this case were line executives. The consultants worked closely with these executives to shape and mold a new structure, but it was the latter who were actually responsible for the changes.

OD consultants often define their role as conducting events, training programs, and personal consultation in order to change a client's attitude about people and his relationships with them:

> Organization Development is a response to change, a complex educational strategy intended to change the beliefs, attitudes, values and structures of organizations so they can better adapt to the dizzying rate of change. Whatever the strategy, organization development almost always concentrates on the values, attitudes, relations and organizational climate—the "people" variables—as the point of entry rather than on the goals, structure and technologies of the organization (Bennis, 1969, p. 2).

By way of contrast, the OD effort reported here focused on changing the structure of the organization, i.e., the role responsibilities and relationships of organizational members and their centers of accountability, from which behavioral changes and, finally, attitudinal changes flowed. The program significantly altered the chain of command by creating new roles, modifying existing roles, and changing the managerial style of middle and top management. The project proved an effective means of developing managerial personnel and enabling personnel at several levels of management to gain more control over their jobs and environments.

Lawrence (1958) and Dalton, Barnes, and Zaleznik (1968) report on similar structural change programs, which were completely designed and carried out by top management of the organizations under study. Their reports are a researcher's description and analysis of structural change efforts and, as such, provided useful guidelines to the consultants involved in this case. Beer, Pieters, Marcus, and Hundert (1971) report on a program initiated at Corning Glass Works, which resulted in a new organizational role—

Reproduced by special permission from *The Journal of Applied Behavioral Science*, "A Structural Approach to Organizational Change," by Robert A. Luke, Jr., Peter Block, Jack M. Davey, and Vernon R. Averch, Vol. 9, No. 5, pp. 611-635, NTL Institute, 1973. The authors would like to acknowledge the effort and contribution made to the program by Charles Johnson, Alan Steiger, and Edward Weiss, the Management Development Team.

an integrator—that greatly facilitated the problem-solving capabilities of multifunctional task forces. Beer and Huse (1972) demonstrate that structural and interpersonal changes can support and reinforce each other in a systems approach to organizational change.

BACKGROUND

The client organization is a large retail food chain with annual sales of $800 million and a work force of about 18,000. In 1969, a new top management team initiated an OD program to improve employee training. For two years, the program emphasized training events designed to effect attitudinal and behavioral changes (Averch & Luke, 1971). This effort aroused the interest of several top executives, who believed OD would make a contribution to the company. These executives allowed the OD staff to attend, as members, key meetings.

The senior author's participation in one of these meetings, the Store Operations Meeting, led to the development of the project described here. A monthly Store Operations Meeting is chaired by the Corporate Vice President of Store Operations, his staff, and the person (Store Operations Manager) charged with overall store performance and second in authority to the Divisional Vice Presidents. These meetings, attended by the four Divisional Store Operations Managers, test ideas for new work systems and design methods for implementing them in the stores.

During the September 1970 meeting, concern was expressed about the slowness with which a grocery management system for ordering and stocking merchandise was being implemented in the stores. In an earlier field test it had proved to be an efficient management system. Training Store Managers to use this system was delegated to the District Manager (DM), the direct supervisor of 10-15 stores. A lengthy discussion of his role revealed that though he was supposed to be a trainer and resource person, as well as supervisor of the Store Manager, a DM actually devoted his time to inspecting stores and personnel to make sure that company standards were met. DMs did not view training as a priority. They merely outlined the new system and told Store Managers to implement it. Results were therefore sporadic.

During the October meeting, the group considered ways of helping the DM implement the grocery system. Three alternatives were proposed. One was to create a new job, that of a grocery specialist who would work for the DM and put in the system. This was a typical method of introducing new procedures: create a specialist in that area and charge him with implementation. The second suggestion was to assign a current store manager to spend half his time training other managers in the system. The third alternative, suggested by the OD staff, was to change the role of the DM from a line executive to a consultant without line authority, and make him available to managers in all areas of store operations, including system implementation. The rationale for this suggestion was that the close, inspection-like supervision of Store Managers by the DM and Specialists resulted in an overload for the Store Manager, who was often in a position of trying to please his many bosses. He therefore had minimal control over his store and little time for training or implementing new work methods. With less direct supervision and more training available from a consultant, it was hypothesized that Store Managers could more effectively manage their stores.

Historically, the company had relied on close supervision at all levels. The idea that Store Managers could manage their units effectively without direct supervision seemed absurd to several members. However, the chairman and one Store Operations Manager (the third author), who volunteered a district of 15 stores, felt the consultant concept might be a way of developing more competent Store Managers. The OD staff was asked to develop a proposal for a consultant structure, which is outlined in Figure 2. Figure 1 depicts the traditional DM-Specialist structure.

The basic functions in running a store are twofold. Merchandising consists of developing sales programs that yield an acceptable profit, attract customers, and ensure product variety. Store Operations, as the name implies, is concerned with the mechanics of getting work done—scheduling employees, stocking shelves, ringing registers—in a way that is economical but still attractive to customers. Under the traditional structure, three lines of authority reach the store. Merchandisers develop the sales program, which is passed by their assistant, the Coordinator, to Specialists, and then to department heads. Operational responsibilities are initiated by the Store Operations Manager and transmitted to the Store Managers by the District Manager, who is also responsible for overseeing the grocery merchandising program. The Store Manager therefore left the perishable department of his store to his department heads and their Specialists, and restricted his activities primarily to the grocery and front-end departments. This limited his ability to manage the entire store. In addition, his boss, the District Manager, when visiting the store, would inspect for problems—dirty floors, poor appearance of personnel, inadequate checkout service, incorrect prices, and so on. With the traditional structure and DM role, a Store Manager was primarily concerned with maintaining standards and overseeing the grocery department; he had little time or sense of priority for training, management, and new systems in the organization.

In the consultant structure, the roles of District Manager and Specialists were changed from supervisory to consultant to the Store Manager. Department heads were to report to

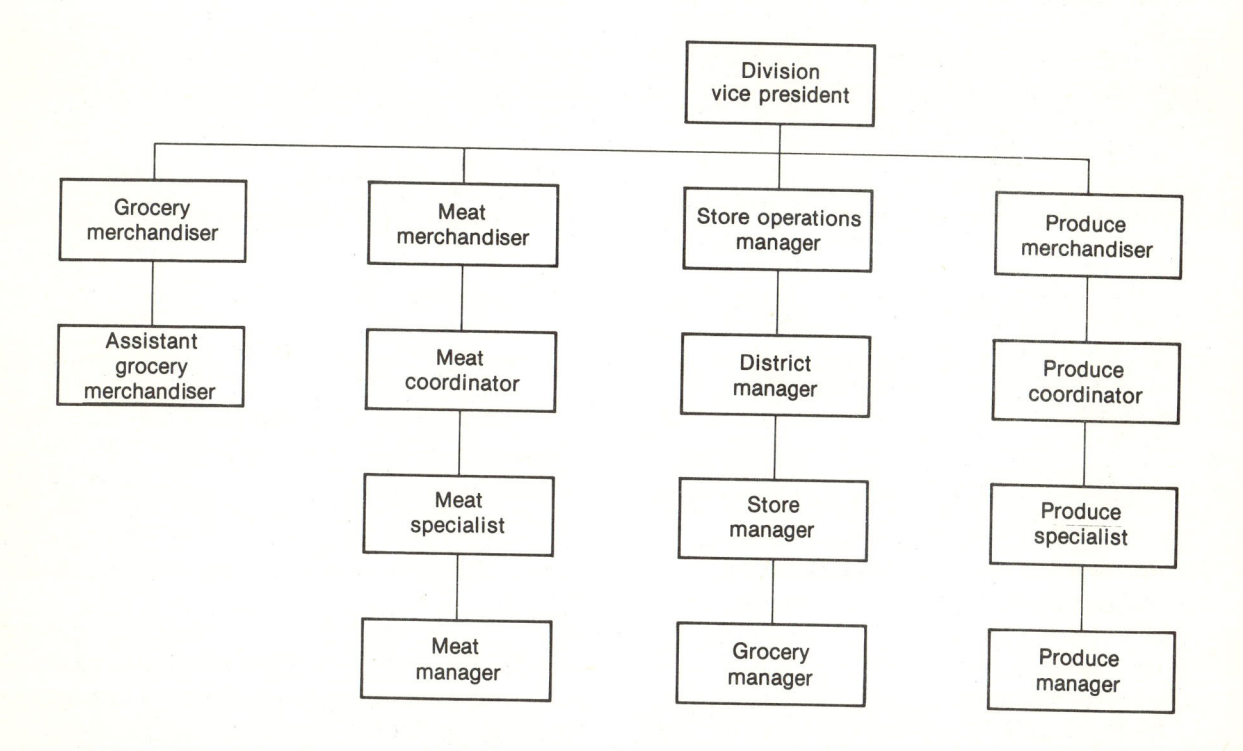

Figure 1. Traditional district manager—specialist structure

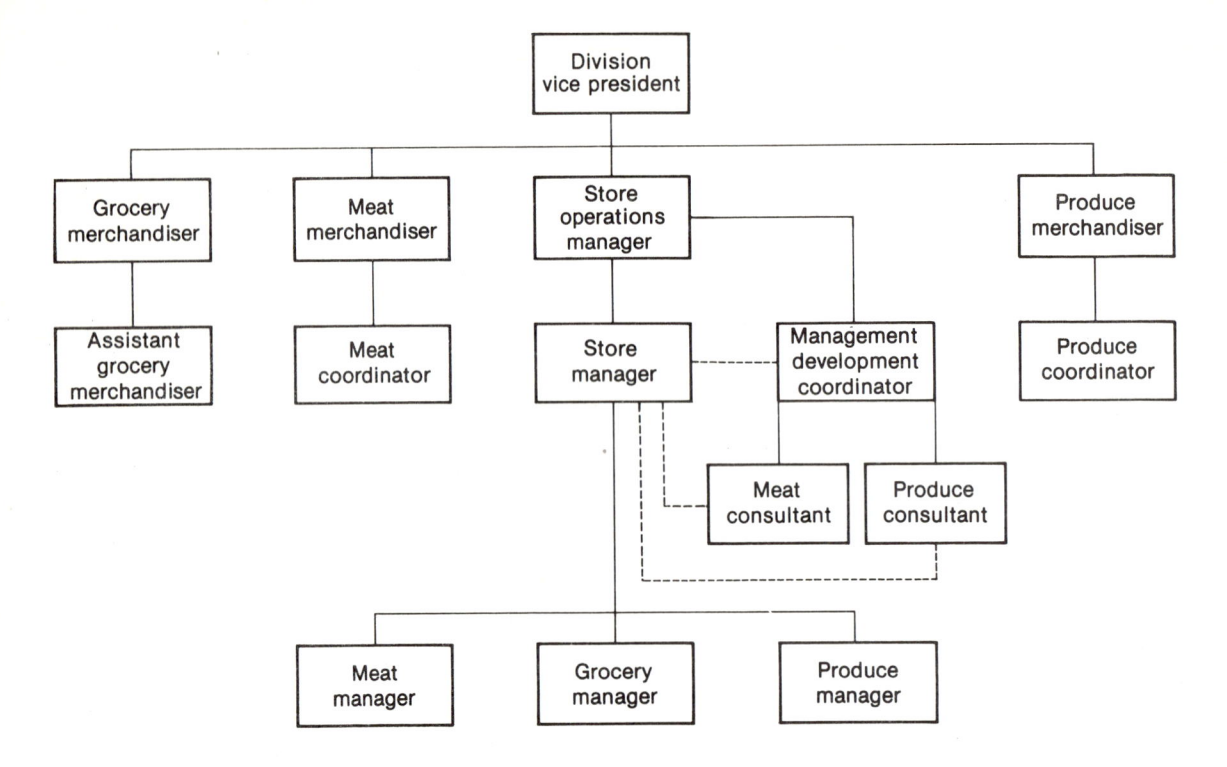

Figure 2. Proposed consultant structure for store management development

the Store Manager, while the managers reported directly to the Store Operations Manager. The Management Development Coordinator (MDC)—the title dreamed up for the ex-DM—and the meat and produce specialists, now called consultants, were to function as a team, under the leadership of the MDC, to consult with and train managers in all areas of store management. Within the limits of overall company policy, the manager now had the final say about in-store priorities. The consultants had no line authority; the Store Operations Manager now supervised and evaluated in-store performance.

METHOD

This structural change is similar in type and intent to that described by Lawrence (1958). In that case, top management designed the change without behavioral science consultation. In this case, however, the first, second, and fourth authors served as OD consultants to the project. The third author was the major client and change agent. He frequently referred to "our view from the cat bird seat," and that is an accurate description of our relationship to the project. Our primary roles were as consultants to him, the MDC team, and Merchandisers.

Following the November 1970 Operations Meetings, the four authors developed the consultant model and a method of implementation, which was presented for approval at the January 1971 Division Managers' Meeting—a monthly meeting of the top 25 executives. The Division Vice President and the President agreed to try it on an experimental basis and to review the results in six months.

To test the new structure's effectiveness in developing a range of managers, we selected an average district composed of managers with varying competencies. To have chosen only the best managers obviously would have stacked the deck. We also selected a current DM for the MDC role, to see if a DM could in fact operate effectively as a consultant. The Operations Manager and senior author jointly interviewed four DMs (selected by the Operations Manager as most promising) and independently selected the same man. The new consultant was the youngest DM, with the least amount of time "on the road," but was the only one of the four who asked some hard questions about the merit of the whole idea. He had been with the company for 12 years, having worked his way up to DM from clerk.

We felt that the selection of the MDC was critical to the project. Lawrence (1958), in describing the management-initiated program at Food World, concluded that the ability of DMs to adapt their managerial style to the new rules was largely responsible for the success of the program in several districts.

Training Needs

The next step was to select meat and produce specialists to serve on the MDC team as consultants for perishables. This selection was left to the MDC because it was important that he have confidence in his assistants.

All three new consultants were highly competent in store operating methods, but we felt they needed training in human relations and consultation skills to perform their new roles effectively. Their training in management had been solely a function of their experience: When a person is promoted to District Manager, he is simply given the keys to a company car and told to supervise his stores.

In February 1971, the new consultants attended a week-long sensitivity training program to accelerate their team building and to increase their awareness of the impact of their behavior on others. In their new roles, they would have no line authority for influencing managers and would therefore be more dependent on their own interpersonal competencies. In addition, the new structure would facilitate their use of interpersonal skills and awarenesses gained at the program. By definition the consultant role meant that the MDC members would not be as subject to hierarchical constraints of organizations, which typically discourage the use of interpersonal skills learned at T Groups.

The consultant skill training for the MDC members was done on the job, following their return from the T Group, while they were still a District Manager and Specialists with line authority. The OD staff rode with each man on his visits to a store, observing his style and method of working with store personnel. Between stores, at lunch, and over end-of-the-day cocktails, we analyzed with them why they handled situations as they did, what their objectives were in particular stores and whether or not they were accomplished, and what impact they had on the people with whom they worked. We would occasionally suggest different forms of behavior for them to try out the next day and we would then analyze the results. At the end of this month-long process, all three knew, in terms of their own behavior and recent experience in the stores, what it meant to be a consultant rather than a boss.

While the consultant training was taking place, the OD staff, under the leadership of the Operations Manager, held meetings with divisional executives to map guidelines and establish evaluation measures (to be reported later). A week before implementation of the experimental consultant structure, the OD staff conducted a two-day team development workshop for the MDC team, the managers in their new district (we felt the MDC team should work with a new group of managers rather than having to undo relationships with the current managers), and the division management. The purpose of the workshop was to establish the MDC's credibility and accelerate the relationship building between MDC team members and their new store managers, who did not believe the company was actually committed to allowing them to manage their stores with the consultant resources of the MDC team. The workshop included typical relationship-building activities and role plays designed to demonstrate how the MDC team and division management would respond to problems in the experimental district. Figure 3 shows the ground rules for the consultant district and those for traditional districts. The differences were major and called for new behavior at all levels of the division.

One change not explicitly reflected in Figure 3 is the Divisional Perishable Merchandisers' loss of control over the specialists (see Figures 1 and 2). Formerly, the merchandiser or coordinator closely directed the activity of specialists; under the consultant structure, the consultants on perishables reported to the MDC. Much of the resistance to the consultant structure came from Divisional and Corporate Merchandisers, and one reason was a loss of staff from their organization.

THE CONSULTANT STRUCTURE

Start-Up

The consultant structure, thoroughly planned and written out, went into effect in April 1971, the beginning of the June quarter. It was immediately beset with major problems.

Two weeks later, the Division decided on a major sales promotion for these stores and felt the managers were not capable of handling the promotion without supervision. It sent teams of people from the office into the stores for three weeks to oversee the promotion. The MDC team was taken off the road and put to work in a store being remodeled. In the Division's eyes, the business needs were more critical than the experiment, though they did protect the status of the MDC team by avoiding asking them to play a supervisory role during the promotion. Nevertheless, this reintroduction of supervision of the stores was a clear message to all that the Division felt uncomfortable about the managerial competencies of the store managers. Although that was probably an accurate judgment, the promotion plan considerably heightened the managers' skepticism about company commitment to the consultant structure. The first and third authors had their first real confrontation over the issue of the company's commitment to developing managers. This episode marked the beginning of a productive discussion about how managers can be developed on the job without causing serious damage to the business. Following the promotional effort, which lasted four weeks, the MDC team really began its consultant role.

The team members had to establish their credibility with the managers all over again, and it is to their credit that they were able to do so. At this point, the success or failure of the project was very much in their hands. Rather than ignoring or pooh-poohing the managers' feelings, as would be typical, the MDC team dealt directly with them while beginning to develop working contracts.

Problems began to occur in the meat and produce departments and store-wide payroll, a predicted consequence of the learning curve experienced by the managers as they take over management of their stores. Store Operations responded by holding weekly group meetings in which the managers were told of the problems and exhorted to improve. Store Operations described them as "hammer and tong" meetings. After several such meetings, little improvement was noted, and Store Operations was becoming increasingly frustrated in not being able to get the managers to improve. The OD staff suggested that Store Operations instead perform their control and management role through individual performance appraisal sessions with the managers. The Operations Manager agreed to try this approach. He discontinued the weekly meetings and conducted an hour-long review with each manager at the manager's store. (He felt he would get better results by going to the store instead of calling the managers

Ground Rules for Consultant District

1. Consultants will make appointments for store visits and develop a quarterly contract with each manager.

2. Store managers' performance will be evaluated by the Store Operations Manager. MDC team will have no evaluation responsibilities for managers.

3. Store Managers are responsible for total store results.

4. Consultants' performance would be evaluated by Store Operations Manager on the basis of their ability to perform as consultants and on the basis of managers' opinion of their helpfulness.

Ground Rules for DM District

DM visits stores unannounced to inspect for adherence to company standards.

DM evaluates a manager's performance and conveys his evaluation to the Store Operations Manager.

Store Manager responsible for results in grocery and front-end departments only. Perishable specialists responsible for results in meat and produce departments.

District Manager and Specialists' performance evaluated by Store Operations on the basis of results in the stores.

Figure 3. Differences in ground rules for consultant vs. traditional district store management

into the office.) During the first half of each review, the Operations Manager went over the figures, identifying areas that needed improvement and complimenting managers on areas that were doing well. The second half of the review was the manager's time to talk about his problems. These reviews represented the first time an Operations Manager had ever spent an hour with each manager in a district on his performance, and the experience was highly satisfactory for both. The managers were ecstatic at being able to talk nose-to-nose with their Operations Manager, and the Operations Manager reported he developed a much better understanding of the managers and conditions in their stores. The performance reviews remain as the primary control vehicle for Operations and represent one example of management's loosening up its supervisory control patterns.

The district received an inordinate number of visits from corporate executives, many of whom came "not to praise Caesar but to bury him." The consultant approach was viewed very skeptically by many, who would report problems and apparent examples of the structure's failings to the Divisional Vice President and the company's Executive Vice President. The OD staff's response was to ask these people to chart the results—sales, gross profits, payroll percent, and so on—in the consultant district and in the control district rather than relying on periodic "eyeballing" to evaluate the effectiveness of the consultant district. With the exception of the meat department, which everyone, including the managers, acknowledged would take the longest to learn to manage, there were no differences in financial and performance results between the two districts. As the second author was fond of saying, "At least we're up to the level of no difference." This was considered a success of sorts, in view of the fact that the betting around parts of the company was that the consultant stores would simply go under.

At this time the MDC members were encountering two major problems. The managers were not asking for help. In the early stages, the opportunity to manage their own stores went to their heads, and they would call the consultants only on minor problems or to bail them out of serious situations that usually could have been prevented by earlier planning with their consultants. In addition, the Merchandisers continued to see the produce and meat consultants as their staff and would ask them to go to stores to resolve particular problems. This put pressure on the consultants: to be consultants rather than bosses, they could not carry out the orders of the Merchandisers. Merchandisers and Coordinators were supposed to communicate directly with the Store Managers within the new structure, but this was inconvenient for the Merchandisers—and old habits die hard.

A major review meeting, involving the Division Management, Corporate Merchandisers, the MDC team, and the OD staff, was held in July. All the above problems were thoroughly discussed and the following modifications made:

1. The MDC members, still acting as consultants and not supervisors, could take more initiative in pointing out problems and suggesting solutions, but it was still the manager's decision to act on the consultant's recommendations. A consultant was given the option of not working with a manager if he felt a particular manager was avoiding him.

2. The Corporate Meat Merchandiser agreed to design a management training program for the managers. This represented the first such training program for Store Managers by a Merchandising office.

3. The ground rule was established that when a representative of Divisional and/or Corporate management visits a store, he will inform the manager of his observations and can suggest that the manager call his consultant. Previously, top-echelon visitors would order the manager to make changes on the spot or inform Store Operations but not the manager.

The meeting also cleared the air, and the consultant structure operated more according to plan for the remainder of the six-month period, with one major problem still unresolved. Division management, and particularly Store Operations, continued to feel uneasy about the managers' developing competencies. They therefore retained many of the former functions of the DM, such as calling stores weekly to adjust their labor budget or sales projections and inspecting the stores for appearance and adherence to standards. During the transition period, while the managers were developing, Store Operations still had to meet their responsibilities; as a result, the Operations Manager became a "high-priced DM" for about six months. This put an enormous work load on Operations, for they still had five other districts to manage; and they had to be convinced, through the efforts of the Store Managers, that the latter could adequately manage their stores. The managers' positive response to the performance reviews was the first indication Operations had that this might be possible; and toward the end of the six months, Operations saw more and more improvement in the stores. Hence, at the end of the six months, Operations people were on the verge of becoming believers.

SIX MONTHS LATER

At the end of the six-month trial period, the consultant structure was operating according to plan. Operations continued to retain the controls the DM previously exercised and there continued to be no difference in the performance between the two structures. The consultant structure was designed to replace close supervision with training, on the hypothesis that this would develop the capabilities of Store Managers. As we have seen, the "hard" measures demonstrated no difference between consulted managers and supervised managers, though it is important to remember that the Divisional office still maintained a high degree of control over the managers' budgets. Hence, at this point, the performance data are inconclusive.

To assess the impact of the experiment on the Store Managers, the OD staff administered a nine-item questionnaire to managers in the experimental and control districts. The questions were intended to assess the managers' feeling of support from management, the degree to which their abilities were being used, and the degree to which they felt involved in decisions. The baseline data were collected in April 1971, two weeks before the start of the experiment (Table 1). The postmeasure was taken in October 1972 (Table 2).

Table 1 shows that, prior to the experiment, the supervised managers gave higher than average responses to six of the nine items. In comparison to the soon-to-be consulted managers, supervised managers felt their boss (DM) complimented them more on a good job, they were more knowledgeable about DM standards for evaluation, received more help in problem solving and support with higher management from this DM, felt problems were being more confronted, and that their skills and abilities were being used better. Consulted managers felt they were slightly more consulted on decisions, received slightly more encouragement from their DM to exercise judgment and initiative, and saw a career with the company as somewhat more attractive.

Table 2 shows the amount of change in the two groups' average responses to the same items six months later. At T_2, "boss" was interpreted to mean MDC team by the consulted managers. Table 2 shows rather clearly that, from the managers' perspective, the consultant structure had accomplished its primary developmental goal of increasing the utilization of managers' skills. The consulted managers show a noticeable positive increase on all but one item while the supervised managers show a decrease on six items and slight gains on three.

It is important to mention that during these six months, the Division encountered a

TABLE 1.

Average of Consulted and Supervised Managers' Responses to Project Evaluation Questions at T_1

Items	Consulted Managers ($N=15$)	Supervised Managers ($N=15$)	Difference
1. How often does your immediate boss encourage you to show initiative and exercise judgment? (never/always)	4.57	4.44	+.13
2. To what extent does your boss compliment you when you have done a good job? (never/always)	3.57	4.11	−.54
3. To what extent do you know the standards your immediate boss uses to evaluate your performance? (never know/always know)	3.72	4.00	−.28
4. How would you rate the help your immediate boss provides you in solving problems? (never helpful/always helpful)	3.86	4.34	−.48
5. To what extent do you feel your immediate boss backs you up with higher management? (never/always)	4.29	4.44	−.15
6. To what extent do you feel problems are being faced rather than ignored? (never faced/always faced)	3.72	4.22	−.50
7. How well do you feel your skills and abilities are being used? (not used/used very well)	3.57	4.23	−.66
8. How would you rate the extent to which you are consulted when decisions are made which affect your work? (never/always)	4.28	4.00	+.28
9. How attractive does a career with the company appear? (unattractive/quite attractive)	4.43	4.22	+.21

TABLE 2.
Amount of Change in Consulted and Supervised Managers' Average Responses to Project Evaluation Questions—T_1 to T_2

Items	Consulted Managers ($N=15$)	Supervised Managers ($N=15$)	Difference
1. How often does your immediate boss encourage you to show initiative and exercise judgment?	+.18	+.37	−.19
2. To what extent does your boss compliment you when you have done a good job?	+.76	−.08	+.84
3. To what extent do you know the standards your immediate boss uses to evaluate your performance.	+.61	+.01	+.60
4. How would you rate the help your immediate boss provides you in solving problems?	+.97	−.14	+1.14
5. To what extent do you feel your immediate boss backs you up with higher management?	+.21	−.64	+.85
6. To what extent do you feel problems are being faced rather than ignored?	+.63	+.08	+.55
7. How well do you feel your skills and abilities are being used?	+.55	−.03	+.58
8. How would you rate the extent to which you are consulted when decisions are made that affect your work?	+.14	−.20	+.34
9. How attractive does a career with the company appear?	+.01	−.22	+.23

severe decline in sales, experienced a large union wage settlement, and underwent a rather traditional cost-cutting program. In all districts except the consultant district, this meant that supervisors were exercising much closer control over managers. Managers in the consultant district were given guidelines for reducing costs but had more leeway in their execution than did the supervised managers. The closer supervision of the supervised managers may well explain the decreases on those items measuring support from management, career attractiveness, and the degree to which they were consulted on decisions.

The OD staff also conducted open-ended interviews with the MDC team and consulted managers, which demonstrated that the managers neither wanted nor appreciated the traditional DM function. In response to the question, "What do you miss under this style of working that you had when you had a District Manager?" 13 said they missed "nothing"—and that's their word. Many volunteered that they did not *miss* "the aggravation of do-it-my-way," "being treated like a child," "getting my ass kicked," "never knowing what he [the DM] is going to do when he comes around," "bone-crushing meetings," and more. Many consulted managers talked about a newfound sense of pride in their work and a new feeling of wanting to advance in the company. To a man, they expressed a great deal of respect and affection for the Operations Manager, whom many had previously spoken of in less glowing terms, and they felt that his performance appraisals were helpful in their development as store managers. In short, the consulted managers were "turned on."

CONSEQUENCES

Reactions of the Consultants

All three continue to miss the authority and control they had as members of a DM team and some of the traditional prestige and status associated with authority. Nevertheless, they also feel they have gained in-depth experience in dealing with people and in effective problem solving. Members of a DM team have formal line authority—or a club, as it is more popularly known. Whether or not the club is used, its mere existence does make managers listen more carefully and respond more quickly. Without the club, the consultants have had to rely on their interpersonal skills to accomplish work. Evidence of their effectiveness is shown in Table 2, question 4. Consulted Store Managers perceive the consultants as more helpful on solving problems than control managers perceive their DM team to be, which suggests that the consultant structure has developed capabilities for interpersonal competence and problem-solving training through the new role and behavior of the MDC team.

The report itself was submitted to the Division management and to the President. This, and the fact that the consulted stores were at least holding their own in terms of performance, enabled management to agree to continue and expand the experiment. Within six months, two additional consultant structures were implemented.

Personnel Changes

One consequence of the initial consultant structure, which continued from October 1971 to February 1972, was that each manager's performance was much more visible to Operations since it was far more intimately involved in the stores and with the managers. It became apparent that two managers, who had the most years of service with the company, were unable to manage a store effectively without direct supervision. They made the least use of the consultants and found it most difficult to make decisions on their own. They were transferred out of the district and replaced by men who Operations felt could manage their stores independently of close supervision. Operations put two other managers who were having difficulty into each other's store. One went from a high to a low volume store, usually considered a demotion, and, with fewer responsibilities, performed quite well. The manager who went from a lower to a higher volume store, usually considered a promotion, surprised Operations by doing an outstanding job. Hence, 13 of the original 15 managers were still in the district a year later and were doing at least an adequate job.

Cutting the Umbilical Cord

By March 1, 1972, the Division management felt confident that this group of managers could manage their own stores. At their initiative, Operations decided to go the whole route. For the first time in the company's history, a group of managers were given sole responsibility for meeting their quarterly sales and labor budget. Usually, Operations, through the DM, would call managers weekly, asking them to increase or decrease hours or sales projections. Until now, Operations had used this approach with the consulted managers. For this quarter, however, the managers were to receive no instructions but would review their budgets with the Operations Manager at the end of the 4th, 8th and 13th week. Sometime in the future, as managers acquire more competence—and Operations more confidence in their competence—managers may be able to run their budgets for a quarter or even a year.

Performance Results

A district's quarterly performance is measured by the percentage of increase or decrease in sales, its increase or decrease in sales per man hour (number of labor hours divided into sales), and its increase or decrease in labor percent (labor dollars expended expressed as a percentage of sales), when compared to the same quarter in the previous year. Improvement, or lack thereof, is a major indicator for measurement of the value of new programs.

TABLE 3
Rate of Change in Sales, Sales Per Man Hour, and Labor Percent in the Consulted District and Supervised Districts During the June 1972 Quarter Compared Against the June 1971 Quarter

District	Sales	Sales Per Man Hour	Labor Percent
1.	−19.7%	−$3.26	+ 1.5%
2.	− 4.3	−$1.19	+ 1.0
3.	−12.8	+$1.20	+ 1.2
4.	− 6.0	−$2.13	+ 1.1
5. [Consulted]	− 5.4	+$1.38	+ .4
6.	−11.6	−$ .20	+ 1.0
Division Average	−11.7	−$ .58	+ .9

Applying these measures to the June 1972 quarter, we find the consultant district had the smallest decrease in sales (sales throughout the division declined 1971-1972), the smallest increase in labor percent (all labor percents increased), and was one of two showing an increase in sales per man hour (Table 3). As a district, the consultant district had the best showing for the June 1972 quarter. Table 3a shows the performance of the districts on the same measures for the June 1971 quarter. Table 3b compares the rank-order improvement position of each district for the two quarters. As a total district, it is interesting to note the consultant district was in fifth position in 1971 (clearly in the bottom half) but had attained the number one position by 1972. At the end of the first year of the experiment, the consultant district had outperformed the other five from 1971 to 1972.

Table 4 compares districts' performances against their June quarter, 1972, budget. The consultant district is the only district to meet or exceed its budget in all three categories. This suggests that the consulted managers were better able to manage their budgets than were their supervised colleagues.

On the basic of these results, Operations believes managers can assume major responsibility for profit goals, and it has taken the necessary steps to implement that view. (Gross profit responsibility is usually tightly controlled by the Merchandisers.)

CONCLUSIONS

Attitude Change

Perhaps the most significant change associated with the consultant structure is not the change in behavior and performance of the managers, but the *change in attitudes about supervision.* Not all executives are convinced, but the Operations Manager, the Divisional Vice President, the Corporate Vice President of Store Operations, and the President now believe that 75-80 percent of current managers can contribute more to the company if they are supported and trained rather than merely closely supervised. The possible consequences of this attitude shift for the management philosophy and structure of the company are obvious. *It is also important to underscore that this change in attitude occurred as a function of these executives' direct experience with a situation intimately familiar to them. It is unlikely they would have occurred as the result of a specific OD attitude-training intervention in this company.*

Behavioral Changes

Changes in behavior took place at the level of Store Manager, who made more decisions, become more involved in perishable departments, and made regular request for help; at the level of District Manager and Specialist, *who identified problems, suggested solutions,*

TABLE 3a.
Rate of Change in Sales, Sales Per Man Hour, and Labor Percent in the Consulted District and Supervised Districts During the June 1971 Quarter Compared Against the June 1970 Quarter

District	Sales	Sales Per Man Hour	Labor Percent
1.	+10.0%	+$1.32	+.9%
2.	− 8.6	+$4.12	+.4
3.	+ 7.9	+$2.94	+.3
4.	+25.0	+$2.28	+.4
5. [Consulted]	+ 9.8	+$ .49	+.9
6.	− 7.3	+$ .38	+.7

TABLE 3b.
Comparison of the Districts' Improvement Rank-Order Positions in June 1971 (Table 3a) and June 1972 Quarter (Table 3)

District	Sales 1971	Sales 1972	Sales Per Man Hour 1971	Sales Per Man Hour 1972	Labor Percent 1971	Labor Percent 1972	District Rankings* 1971	District Rankings* 1972	1971-1972 Difference
1.	2	6	4	6	5.5	6	4	6	−2
2.	6	1	1	4	2.5	2.5	3	2	+1
3.	4	5	2	2	1	5	2	4.5	−2.5
4.	1	3	3	5	2.5	4	1	4.5	−3.5
5. [Consulted]	3	2	5	1	5.5	1	5	1	+4.0
6.	5	4	6	3	4	2.5	6	3	+3.0

*Determined by ranking of sum of ranks for each year.

and *trained managers instead of simply inspecting their performance;* at the level of Store Operations Manager, *who now meets with his managers on a regular and individual basis to plan with them and discuss their performance instead of relying on a District Manager to convey his orders and giving managers no performance feedback;* and at the level of Divisional Vice-President, *who took an obvious risk in allowing the project to start in the first place and supporting and developing it throughout the first year again, these behavioral changes did not occur solely out of a belief that individuals should gain more control over their lives or that training and feedback are inherently good things. They were required to support the change in structure, which was deemed necessary because the old structure was not helping the company move as fast as it wanted, in developing managers and implementing system.* One moral, therefore, for OD practitioners might be that form follows function, not vice versa.

Resistance, Risk, and Ethics

The executives most opposed to the consultant structure also tended to be those executives who (1) were the firmest believers that "everyone needs a boot in the ass," or (2) lost staff and therefore power under the consultant structure—the Merchandisers, or (3) both. Most executives had worked their way up from stock boy level under a management structure of close supervision. For many, the consultant approach disconfirmed the merit of a management style which they had skillfully learned and mastered over the years and on which a large measure of their positive self-concept undoubtedly rested. Similar discomfort was noticeable among other District

TABLE 4.

Performances in Terms of Sales, Sales Per Man Hour and Labor Per Cent, in Relation to June 1972 Quarterly Budgets of Consulted District and Supervised Districts

District	Sales	Sales Per Man Hour	Labor Per Cent
1.	−5.0%	−$1.45	+.3%
2.	−6.5	−$ .52	+.3
3.	−3.7	−$ .13	+.1
4.	−2.9	−$ .69	+.1
5. [Consulted]	+ .1	+$ .49	−.2*
6.	−4.8	+$ .59	−.1

*A savings against the plan in labor dollars of $15,534.

Managers, who, seeing the amount of company interest in and support of the MDC team, began to wonder about the security of their positions. It was also evident among most Merchandisers, who, actively or passively, resisted the consultant project.

Although the Store Managers responded enthusiastically, the consultant structure meant new evaluation criteria for them. Just doing well what their bosses asked of them no longer sufficed. The two managers who could not manage without close supervision were demoted as a result. Hence, there was an element of risk in the project for managers, and the project was imposed on them; they really did not have the option to say no.

The risk was high for the MDC team as well. They too had risen through the ranks to their current positions of District Manager and Specialist, and one reward for their efforts was the authority and prestige of line positions. The consultant structure removed their line authority, a fact which we have seen they continued to lament, and thereby removed some prestige from them in the eyes of many. Had the project failed, the MDC members stood to lose the most. Though they were given the formal opportunity to decline, all three would have found it difficult to decline a new position for which they had been hand-picked. So, in reality, their freedom of choice was also limited. In their case, and in the case of the managers, the success of the project has enhanced their individual standing in the eyes of company executives. By virtue of their pioneering, visible positions, the MDC team and managers received far greater attention and positive evaluation by management than have their colleagues in other districts. In their case, the risk paid off. Nevertheless, the consultant project raises important ethical questions for both executives and the OD staff. For example, how much should others be asked to risk for the sake of change that executives and OD staff feel will benefit the company and contribute to people's development and autonomy? To spare the reader a long discourse on ethical dilemmas for which there are no definitive solutions, suffice it to say that the planning, design, experience, and evaluation were conducted in an open atmosphere which allowed all the opportunity to voice their views and exert influence. Of course, we did not realize a totally democratic situation: strands of vested interest and political pressures were evident (e.g., let's not speak out publicly about a program the President, Division Vice

President, or Operations Manager—depending on what level one is in—endorses). We did fully share intentions and plans, and we asked critics to support their views with data and applied the same criteria to our enthusiasm. As a result, we like to think the project was conducted ethically, though we are fully aware that some coercion and imposition occurred.

IMPLICATIONS FOR THE OD CONSULTANT

Unlike many OD programs which use training interventions—T Groups, team building, workshops focusing on management by objectives, and others—the OD staff saw its role as that of an architect, i.e., one who makes himself familiar with the client's problems and needs and works with the client to design a structure to meet the need, but leaves the final acceptance decision to the client. We proposed a new structure, offered some training experiences (the off-site T Group and 2-day team building laboratory), recommended new behavior (that the MDC be a consultant, that the Operations Manager conduct performance appraisals), and continually evaluated results. In each case, the client made the final decision, and, as a result, our influence on the system was determined by the client's perceptions of how well our designs or recommendations met his needs.[2] This is not a model of subservience, for our recommendations and urgings are consistent with our beliefs in the value of training and of increased autonomy as well as authentic confrontation and evaluation; and they are clearly different from recommendations that most executives would have made to speed up the implementation of the grocery system. The architect style did seem to enable the client to own the changes rather than merely to rely on our expertise and recommendations.

The use of any OD strategy is a design question, and we present for the reader's consideration the model of architect to be included with other models of training and consultation for system change.

FUTURE DIRECTIONS

As this report is being written, June 1972, the Corporate Human Resources and Store Operations staff is preparing a proposal that will create a management division task force for each of the four divisions. The task forces will be composed of a vertical slice of current management and will plan the management structure and needed training supports—both interpersonal and technical skill development training—required in each division. If accepted, the task forces will represent the company's first commitment to involving in management planning those who will be affected. It will also represent its first commitment to using the Human Resources staff in management planning. Prior to this proposal, all such planning and decision making were done by a select few executives who met in private. Under the terms of the proposal, the task forces will be coordinated by members of the Human Resources and Store Operations departments.

Hence, though the initial consultant project proved successful, its contribution to the company does not rest only in its demonstration of the structure's effectiveness as a management development program. More importantly, the structure has had an impact on the attitudes of many organization members who now accept McGregor's (1960) theory that people in organizations seek challenge and responsibility to the benefit of themselves and the organization. If the consultant structure experience will also change the *process* of management, it will have been successful beyond our wildest expectations of October 1970.

POSTSCRIPT [3]

The division management task forces met through the summer of 1972 and developed the following management structure: The role of Store Operations Manager would be deleted and two new *staff* roles created for each division—Sales Manager, charged with coordinating the division's sales program, and an Administrative Service Manager, charged with coordinating the quarterly budget-setting process. Each role reports to the Division Manager. In place of District Managers, a new role was created, that of a Zone Manager, who reports directly to the Division Manager and has line responsibility for sales, budget, profit, and personnel functions throughout 18 to 20 stores. The Zone Manager's role is clearly that of a line manager and as such can introduce the needs of his particular area into the Division's planning in the areas mentioned above. Working for the Zone Manager is a produce trainer, meat trainer, and grocery trainer, each of whom serves as consultant staff to the 18-20 Store Managers in the same way as did the Management Development Team in the consultant structure. In addition, face-to-face quarterly performance appraisals are now in effect between each two levels from Corporate Senior Vice President to Store Clerk; and an incentive bonus plan, based on performance and store conditions, has been introduced for Store Managers.

The changes made by the task forces have resulted in a more direct line relationship between stores and the division office, considerably reduced the number of people exercising line authority over the Store Manager, and retained the practice of training and development as a management strategy. Full implementation of the structure is one to two years away. A recent study indicates a 15 percent improvement in productivity for those stores now operating under the structure and a generally high level of acceptance of the structure by those participating in it. The consultant structure, as described in this case study, has been eliminated as the new structure takes effect.

NOTES

1. The division vice president identified a control district which he felt was most similar to the consultant district among the other five districts.

2. Not all our recommendations were accepted. Training the MDC team and manager to conduct in-store meetings, performance appraisals with employees, and a team development workshop for the division management are examples of recommendations that were not accepted.

3. This article was completed in June 1972. The authors are pleased to report that during the intervening year the company has continued to make major changes in its management structure, building on the consultant experiment.

REFERENCES

Averch, V. & R. Luke, "Organization development: The view from within," *Training and Development Journal,* 1971, Vol. 25 (9), 38-42.

Beer, M. & E. Huse, "A systems approach to organization development," *Journal of Applied Behavioral Science,* 1972, Vol. 8 (1), 79-101.

Beer, M., G. R. Pieters, S. H. Marcus, & A. T. Hundert, "Improving integration between functional groups: A case in organization change and implications for theory and practice," Symposium presented at American Psychological Association Convention, Washington, D. C., September 1971.

Bennis, W., *Organization development* (Reading, Mass.: Addison-Wesley) 1969.

Dalton, G., L. Barnes, & A. Zaleznik, *The distribution of authority in formal organizations* (Boston: Division of Research, Harvard Business School) 1968.

Lawrence, P., *The changing of organizational behavior patterns* (Boston: Division of Research, Harvard Business School) 1958.

McGregor, D., *The human side of enterprise* (New York: McGraw-Hill) 1960.

CROSS REFERENCE TABLE

For relating the articles in this reader to the authors' *Organizational Behavior: Contingency Views* and other similar textbooks

Parts in *Readings in Organizational Behavior: Contingency Views*

Selected Textbooks Covering Organizational Topics	PART I Foundations	PART II Individual Processes	PART III Group Processes	PART IV Individual/Group/ Organizational Interfaces	PART V Organizational Change
Behling, O. and Schriesheim, C. *Organizational Behavior.* (Boston: Allyn & Bacon, 1976)	Chaps. 14 & 15	Chaps. 3, 4 & 5	Chaps. 6 & 7	Chaps. 8, 9, 10 & 12	Chaps. 11 & 13
Coffey, R., Athos, A., and Reynolds, P. *Behavior in Organizations: A Multidimensional View.* (Englewood Cliffs: Prentice-Hall, Inc., 1975)	Chaps. 1 & 2	Chaps. 6, 7 & 13	Chaps. 3, 4 & 5	Chaps. 8, 9 & 11	Chap. 12
Cohen, A., Fink, S., Gadon, H. and Willits, R. *Effective Behavior in Organizations.* (Homewood: Richard D. Irwin, 1976)	Chap. 1	Chap. 8	Chaps. 3, 4, 5, 9 & 12	Chaps. 2, 7 & 11	Chap. 13
Davis, K. *Human Behavior at Work.* (New York: McGraw-Hill, 1972)	Chaps. 1 & 17	Chaps. 13, 14, 20, 24 & 25	Chaps. 14, 15, & 23	Chaps. 2, 3, 4, 5, 6, 7, 8 & 18	Chaps. 9 & 10
Filley, A., House, R. and Kerr, S. *Managerial Process and Organizational Behavior.* (Chicago: Scott, Foresman and Co., 1976)	Chaps. 2 & 3	Chaps. 4, 5, 7 & 9	Chaps. 8 & 16	Chaps. 10, 11, 12 & 13	Chaps. 15, 20 & 21
Gibson, J., Ivancevich, J., and Donnelly, J. *Organizations: Behavior, Structure and Process.* (Dallas: Business Publications, Inc. 1976)	Chap. 2	Chaps. 3, 5 & 13	Chaps. 7 & 13	Chaps. 6, 8, 9, 10, 11 & 12	Chaps. 15 & 16

CROSS REFERENCE TABLE [Cont.]

Selected Textbooks Covering Organizational Topics	PART I Foundations	PART II Individual Processes	PART III Group Processes	PART IV Individual/Group/ Organizational Interfaces	PART V Organizational Change
Hellriegel, D. and Slocum, J. *Organizational Behavior: Contingency Views.* (St. Paul, Minn.: West Publishing Co., 1976)	Chaps. 1, 2 & 3	Chaps. 4, 5 & 6	Chaps. 7 & 8	Chaps. 9, 10 & 11	Chaps. 12 & 13
Herbert, T. *Dimensions of Organizational Behavior.* (New York: Macmillan, 1976)	Chap. 1	Chaps. 8, 9, 10 & 11	Chaps. 14, 15, 16 & 19	Chaps. 5, 6, 7, 11, 12, 13, 18 & 20	Chaps. 17, 22 & 23
Huse, E. and Bowditch, J. *Behavior in Organizations.* (Reading: Addison-Wesley Publishing Co., 1977)	Chaps. 1, 2, & 9	Chaps. 3, 4, & 8	Chaps. 4, 5, & 6	Chaps. 3, 7, & 9	Chaps. 10, 11, 12, 13 & 14
Luthans, F. *Organizational Behavior.* (New York: McGraw-Hill Book Co., 1973)	Chaps. 4 & 5	Chaps. 11, 14, 15, 16 & 18	Chap. 19	Chaps. 6, 17 & 21	Chaps. 20 & 22
Porter, L., Lawler, E., and Hackman, R. *Behavior in Organizations.* (New York: McGraw-Hill Book Co., 1975)	Chaps. 8, 9 & 10	Chaps. 2, 5, 6, 7 & 12	Chaps. 13 & 14	Chaps. 3 & 4	Chaps. 15, 16 & 17
Wieland, G. and Ullrich, R. *Organizations: Behavior, Design and Change.* (Homewood: Dorsey Press, 1976)	Chaps. 8 & 13	Chaps. 6 & 9	Chaps. 3, 7 & 10	Chaps. 1, 2, 4 & 12	Chaps. 15, 16, 17, 18 & 19